How ... .rite the
History of the New World

Epistemology ? Philosophy of Knowledge

CULTURAL SITINGS

Elazar Barkan, Editor

CULTURAL SITINGS presents focused discussions of major contemporary and historical cultural issues by prominent and promising scholars, with a special emphasis on multidisciplinary and transnational perspectives. By bridging historical and theoretical concerns, CULTURAL SITINGS develops and examines narratives that probe the spectrum of experiences that continuously reconfigure contemporary cultures. By rethinking chronology, agency, and especially the siting of historical transformation, the books in this series go beyond disciplinary boundaries and notions of what is marginal and what is central to knowledge. By juxtaposing the analytical, the historical, and the visual, this challenging series provides a venue for the development of cultural studies and for the rewriting of the canon.

How to Write the History of the New World

Histories, Epistemologies, and Identities in the Eighteenth-Century Atlantic World

Jorge Cañizares-Esguerra

STANFORD
UNIVERSITY
PRESS

Stanford,
California

Published with the support of the Leon E. Seltzer Memorial
Book Fund and of the State University of New York at Buffalo

Stanford University Press
Stanford, California
© 2001 by the Board of Trustees of the
Leland Stanford Junior University

Printed in the United States of America
on acid-free, archival-quality paper

Library of Congress Cataloging-in-Publication Data

Cañizares-Esguerra, Jorge.
  How to write the history of the New World : histories,
epistemologies, and identities in the eighteenth-century
Atlantic world / Jorge Cañizares-Esguerra.
      p.   cm.
  Includes bibliographical references and index.
  ISBN 0-8047-4084-4 (alk. paper) ISBN 0-8047-4693-1 (pbk.: alk. paper)
  1. Latin America — History — 18th century — Historiography.
  2. Historians — Europe — Attitudes.   3. Historians — Latin
America — Attitudes.   I. Title.
F1412.C25 2001
980 — dc21   00-050486

Typeset by BookMatters in 10/13 Electra

Original printing 2001
Last figure below indicates year of this printing:
10   09   08   07   07   06   05   04   03   02

To Sandra, who has sheltered me through the fiercest storms.
To Sebastián and Andrea, whose eyes caress my soul.
To Claudio and Consuelo, who gave birth to me twice.

Acknowledgments

I have contracted a formidable number of debts over the course of many years. I should first thank the many friends and teachers at the University of Wisconsin at Madison who generously shared their time and ideas with me, particularly the members of the History of Science Department. Thomas Broman, Harold Cook, Victor Hilts, and Louise Robbins diligently read the whole or parts of the original dissertation and gave thoughtful advice. Frank Salomon and Steve Stern offered their critical perspective as the Latin Americanists in my committee. My second greatest collective debt is to my former colleagues at Illinois State University, in particular to Mohamad Tavakoli Targi, who enhanced my horizons, and John Freed, who made me feel important.

I should also extend my gratitude to numerous individuals who read the whole or parts of this book at different stages. Anthony Grafton repeatedly gave careful and erudite advice. Anthony Pagden plowed through both the dissertation and the book and twice tendered pointed and timely suggestions. Felipe Fernández-Armesto submitted the final draft to the rigor of his wide-angled scholarship, picking up errors and strengthening interpretations. Richard Kagan and Karen Ordhal Kupperman caught mistakes and helped me rectify them. William Taylor offered learned and astute commentary that allowed me to tighten the argument in the last two chapters. Antonio Lafuente, Charles Ronan, and Chuck Walker read different chapters, contributing to making them better.

This book could have not been written without the intellectual, logistical, or emotional support of many individuals in many countries. A cadre of historians and friends at the Consejo Superior de Investigaciones Científicas invariably made my trips to Madrid fun and intellectually stimulating: Antonio Lafuente, Leoncio López Ocón, José Luis Peset, Juan Pimentel, Fermín del Pino, Miguel Angel Puig-Samper, and Jaime Vilchis. José Alcina-Franch invited me one afternoon to his home to answer my queries. In Valencia, Antonio Mestre and Mariano Peset went out of their way to facilitate my access to the Archivo Histórico Mayasiano at the College of Corpus Christi. In

Alcalá de Henares, Father José Torres García, the curator of the provincial archive of the Jesuits, made my visits pleasant and fruitful. In Mexico City, Leonor Esguerra, Cecilia Moreno, and Germán Gutiérrez generously opened their home to me and showered me with endless intellectual and emotional stimuli. Pili Alonso let me rent a room in her home and on more than one occasion allowed me to taste the products of her legendary cooking skills. The late Roberto Moreno de los Arcos offered scholarly advice and let me peek into the holdings of his large library. Juan José Saldaña was instrumental in facilitating access to an e-mail account at the Universidad Nacional Autónoma de México. In Paris, my sister Mariana helped obtain microfilms and copyright permits from the Bibliothèque Nationale and dealt with its labyrinthine bureaucracy. David Brading treated me to pizza in Cambridge (England) and helped me to rethink my work. In Washington, D.C., Jeffrey Speicher instructed me in the cultural complexities of a world that is not yet my own and helped me correct the infelicities of my writing in English.

Many individuals have also indirectly supported this book. Marcos Cueto in Lima was always thoughtful and helpful. Paul Gootenberg, Lance Grahn, Jaime E. Rodríguez, Frank Salomon, Francisco Scarano, and Eric Van Young generously offered professional support writing letters of recommendation on my behalf.

Several fellowships and awards permitted me to complete the book. Funds obtained while in graduate school from the University of Wisconsin at Madison and from the Joint Committee on Latin America and Caribbean Studies of the Social Science Research Council and the American Council of Learned Societies allowed visits to archives and libraries in France, Mexico, and Spain for a year. Three University Research Grants at Illinois State University paid my way to archives in London and Spain. I was able to devote one year exclusively to writing largely thanks to a National Endowment for the Humanities Fellowship spent at the John Carter Brown Library and a membership at the Institute for Advanced Study in Princeton. The staff, faculty, and directors of these two institutions should be praised for creating extraordinarily stimulating environments. At Princeton, I benefited from the readings and discussions of the seminar on historical thought in the early modern Hispanic and Andean worlds conducted by Sabine MacCormack. I obtained from the Julian Park Publication Fund at SUNY–Buffalo a small stipend to pay for the copyright permissions for some of the illustrations. Finally, generous financial aid from the College of Arts and Science and the History Department at SUNY–Buffalo made possible the publication of color illustrations.

I also owe a debt of gratitude to the personnel of the various archives and libraries whose services I have used: the Memorial Library at the University of Wisconsin; the Milner Library at Illinois State University; the library of the University of Illinois at Urbana-Champaign; the Firestone Library at Princeton University; the New York Public Library; the Tozzer and Widener Libraries at Harvard University; the Latin American Library at Tulane University; the St. Louis University Vatican Film Library in St. Louis; the Newberry Library in Chicago; the Bibliothèque Nationale in Paris; the British Library in London; the Biblioteca Nacional, the Centro de Estudios de Historia de México (CONDUMEX), the library of the Colegio de México, the Archivo General de la Nación, and the archive of the Museo Nacional de Antropología in Mexico City; the libraries of the Palacio Real, the Consejo de Investigaciones Científicas, and the Fundación Universitaria Española, and the Biblioteca Nacional and the archives of the Museo Naval, the Jardín Botánico, and the Royal Academy of History in Madrid; the Archivo Provincial de los Jesuitas in Alcalá de Henares; the Archivo Hispánico Mayaniense in Valencia; and the Archivo de Indias in Seville.

I profited from the queries and suggestions of audiences at the University of Wisconsin, the University of Minnesota, the Institute for Advanced Studies, Barnard College at Columbia University, Illinois State University, the University of California–Irvine, and the Consejo Superior de Investigaciones Científicas in Madrid. A small section of Chapter 1 appeared before in the *Journal of Early Modern History*; my thanks to the Dutch publisher Brill for allowing me to reproduce this material.

At Stanford University Press, Muriel Bell, Kate Washington, and Anna Eberhard Friedlander diligently and professionally guided me through the long process of bringing a manuscript to print. Peter Dreyer, my copy editor, was a learned, rigorous, and astute reader who saved me from committing errors of all kinds.

My life would have taken a radically different path had I not been touched by the words, vision, and laughter of Ecuadorian and Colombian friends, many of whom are now dead. Their smiles still haunt my imagination; this book is a tribute to them. Without the support of my symbolic and actual families, this project would have foundered. Fernando Montenegro Torres never allowed me to slip into facile, comfortable stereotypes, nor did he let me forget the past. My siblings, Claudio, Mariana, and Bernardo, their families, and my parents, Claudio and Consuelo, freely gave affection and support. Finally, Sandra, Sebastián, and Andrea have left their imprints on the pages of this book; they know where to find the watermarks.

Contents

Contents

Contents

Illustrations

Illustrations

PLATES

Plates follow page 252.

How to Write the
History of the New World

NOTE ON ACCENTS

Written accents in Nahuatl words tend to reflect Spanish pronunciations, and have not been marked. Accents in Spanish and French have been modernized in all references, names, and titles.

Introduction

During the eighteenth century, far-reaching debates took place about how to write the history of the New World and its peoples. Today, we treat the testimony of past historical actors with skepticism, because we assume that individuals are unaware of the "deeper" historical forces ordering their lives and perceptions. It is a tenet of the historical profession that only time affords observers the distance to discern the linguistic, economic, political, and cultural structures that configure our lives. Rather than separating "primary" from "secondary" sources as the first, most basic methodological step, historians in practice first draw a distinction between published and archival documents. To historians, published sources are the conscious narratives of individuals and communities and therefore document forms of self-delusion or artful rhetorical manipulation. Archival documents, on the other hand, catch historical actors off guard. Historians treat published and archival accounts as "unwitting witnesses," forcing from them evidence that these witnesses did not originally intend to yield. Historians are trained to read sources "against the grain," refusing to take the testimony of the past at face value. This book seeks to show that these modern (and postmodern) historiographical sensibilities originated in the eighteenth century in seemingly obscure epistemological disputes.

As new critical techniques for creating and validating knowledge came of age in Europe, some scholars began to call into question the authority and reliability of the sources that historians and chroniclers had traditionally used. Authors set out to read sixteenth-century Spanish accounts of the Indies in the light of contemporary social science, and the testimony of the first European witnesses to the New World suddenly lost credibility. These accounts, authors argued, contradicted many of the laws of social development. This approach was pioneered by editors of travel compilations, who were confronted with scores of old, new, and forged accounts of exotic lands. The new art of reading also coincided with the rise of the "philosophical traveler," who, unlike his counterparts in the past, was not satisfied with collecting tales of wonder. Philosophical travelers consciously sought to avoid the perceptual distortions that besieged untrained witnesses, while drawing significant lessons about the human societies and nature of the places they visited. These new forms of weighing and assessing the value of sources and witnesses were, in turn, closely related to the rapid development in the eighteenth century of the "bourgeois public sphere." In it, the male critic sought to assert his authority and credibility in the marketplace of ideas unsoiled by feminine emotions and unswayed by powerful patrons.

But the accounts left by conquistadors, pirates, merchants, and missionaries were not the only sources European historians had used to reconstruct the past of the New World. They had long relied on indigenous writings produced by the highland societies of Mesoamerica and the Andes. Over the course of the eighteenth century, however, these sources lost most of their previous appeal in Europe and began to be collected rather for what they had to say about the development of the human mental faculties. Whereas, in the past, chroniclers had relied on information stored in Inca quipus and Aztec and Mayan codices to reconstruct Amerindian dynastic genealogies and migrations in European historiographical idioms, eighteenth-century European scholars now became interested in sources in nonalphabetic scripts as evidence from which to piece together the history of progress of the mind. Spaniards had long regarded New World quipus, logograms, and pictograms as primitive scripts. Yet sources written using these scripts were the backbone of most sixteenth-century accounts of the American past. In the new European histories of writing of the eighteenth century, however, scripts became tightly linked with the worth and credibility of the information they stored. By and large, it was conservatives seeking to bolster the credibility of the Bible who penned the new evolutionary histories of writing. As they cast doubt on the alternative chronologies stored in Egyptian hieroglyphs and Chinese ideograms, these European writers invented evolutionary and teleological histories of writing, along with evolutionary scales of trust, that profoundly affected the historiography of the American continent.

The call to scrap both sixteenth-century European accounts of the New World and indigenous narratives stored in nonalphabetical scripts was complemented by a search for new historiographical techniques and new types of evidence. Systems of writing, for one thing, became material evidence that could help conjecturally reconstruct past migrations and developments. Grammars, fossils, mountains, animal behavior, and the distribution of fauna and flora were used as well. The deployment of such new techniques and evidence led to bold new hypotheses about the history of the Americas. The humidity of tropical America, its distinct animal species, and the alleged primitive and degenerate character of the Indians and Creole settlers (particularly Spanish American ones) was held to confirm that the continent had either witnessed catastrophic geological convulsions or recently emerged from the waters. Although casting Indians and Spanish American Creoles (people of European descent born in America) as effeminate degenerates was hardly novel, the scope and reach of the new historical narratives were impressive.

Such negative portrayals of the nature and peoples of the Americas forced authors to reevaluate antiquated humanist depictions of Amerindian societies. In the early seventeenth century, authors such as the Inca Garcilaso de la Vega (1539–1616) had depicted Inca society as resembling that of ancient Rome, but the new accounts of the eighteenth century began with sustained critiques of the errors of perception to which facile classical analogies led. It was only in the early nineteenth century, however, that Alexander von Humboldt (1769–1859) and other writers came not merely to reject the use of classical analogies but also to offer new ones. A new more positive, less skeptical, European historiography of the New World was inaugurated with von Humboldt, largely because ancient Amerindian societies now appeared as Asian, "oriental" polities.

The reaction in Spain to these new historiographical developments was one of ambivalence. On the one hand, the lure of "modernity" moved many authors to reject traditional Spanish historiography on the land and peoples of the New World. On the other hand, Spaniards understood that questioning of the credibility of Iberian sources could not be dissociated from the Protestant assault on Spanish colonialism that had begun in the late sixteenth century in the wake of the Dutch revolt. In this context, eighteenth-century Spanish historiography on the New World became first and foremost a reconstruction of self-identity. To be sure, patriotism had long exercised the imagination of Iberian scholars, but in the eighteenth century, patriotism was balanced by calls to renovate the economy and culture of Spain, which allegedly had fallen behind the rest of western Europe.

Spanish historiography on the New World proved aggressively critical much earlier than that of the rest of Europe. From the 1740s on, writing a new history of America became the central preoccupation of one of the new institutions for cultural renewal created by the Spanish Bourbons, the Royal Academy of History. But for all the consensus about the need to do away with outdated chronicles and unreliable accounts, and for all the anger against misleading northern European characterizations of the "Spanish mind," authors could not agree on much else. At least three different paradigms for writing a new history emerged in Spain over the course of the century. Paradoxically, non-Castilian scholars led all these schools, demonstrating perhaps that the provinces were more interested in crafting a "Spanish" identity than the Castilian core. Valencians, Aragonese, Asturians, and Catalans were at the forefront of the movement to write new, patriotic, yet critical, histories of America. Of these schools, the one led by the Valencians Gregorio Mayans and Juan Bautista Muñoz left behind the most lasting imprint by bringing about the consolidation of all Spanish colonial historical records under a single roof in the Archive of the Indies.

In the Spanish American colonies, the call to write a new history was equally aggressive. Yet the new histories in Spanish America were significantly different from those that appeared in Europe, including Spain. Spanish Americans, to be sure, were intent on offering alternative narratives to those developed in Europe, ones in which Amerindians and Creoles did not appear as degenerate and effete. In doing so, however, Spanish American writers also articulated a powerful and creative critique of Eurocentric epistemologies. A product of the Spanish American Enlightenment as well as of baroque culture, patriotic epistemology exposed the shortcoming and limitations of Europeans who sought to write natural histories of the New World and its peoples. If eighteenth-century northwestern Europeans invented the persona of the philosophical traveler, contemporary Spanish American authors took this construct apart. Creole-clerical authors — native-born religious and secular priests — proved to be creative and daring in this respect.

Patriotic epistemology reflected the longings of the Creole upper classes in Spanish America to have "kingdoms" of their own. It was a clerical, aristocratic discourse that created and validated historical knowledge along a sliding scale of credibility, which, in turn, was linked to racial estates and nested social hierarchies. Surprisingly, the heroes of Spanish American authors were ancient or sixteenth-century Amerindian historians. The historiographical shortcomings of the past stemmed from the inadequate use made of good Amerindian sources, the patriotic epistemologists argued: earlier histories had either relied on the misleading testimony of colonial Amerindian plebes or misinterpreted reliable accounts by precolonial or early colonial Amerindian nobles. Distinguishing between the testimony of upper-class Amerindian informants and that of commoners was central to the new Spanish American historiography. Mestizos — those of mixed Amerindian,

African, and European ancestry — were perceived as a threatening presence that blurred boundaries, and their testimony was seen as worthless.

By and large, the story I am about to tell has remained untold. Moreover, although this book is about debates on how to write the history of the New World, it omits the historiography produced in the British American colonies. Compared to the vast amounts of scholarship put forth by Spanish American Creoles, British colonial historiography appears negligible and derivative. That this has not been recognized before is unsurprising. In northern European and Anglo-American consciousness, Spain and Spanish America have been cast as "backward" ever since the seventeenth century.

This book has taken more years to write than I care to admit. Most of its sources lie in manuscripts scattered on the two sides of the Atlantic. To study them, I visited scores of archives and libraries in England, France, the United States, Spain, and Mexico. I carry away many pleasant memories of my travels, but the intellectual journey of discovery has also been challenging and heart-wrenching.

The book began as an effort to locate the "dispute over the New World" in the context of more recent literature on the history of science. The "dispute," discussed by Antonello Gerbi (1955), was the celebrated debate between, among others, the French naturalist Georges-Louis Leclerc, comte de Buffon (1707–1788), and the British American Creole Thomas Jefferson (1743–1826). In the process of studying the dispute, however, I came across the writings of Spanish Americans who, like Jefferson, replied to the negative views of the Americas advanced by Buffon and his followers.

At the time, I was seeking to escape the gravitational pull of my past. I had migrated from Ecuador to the United States, not by choice but forced by geopolitical developments in Central America and the northern Andes that among other things wiped out a generation of my peers, many of them friends and deeply original thinkers. Seeking to escape my own ghosts, I left a career in medicine and a passionate commitment to social justice in Latin America. In the United States, I embarked on a new path, one characterized by solitary research on the esoteric and unashamedly Euro- and Anglocentric field of the history of science. It took some years of healing and learning for me to be ready to face Latin America again. Unexpectedly, my research on Buffon brought me back to the region, for I found soul mates in the Spanish American Creoles who sought to respond to the French naturalist, particularly those Jesuits who after careers of youthful religious zeal at home had turned to a life of scholarship in exile in Italy.

As I sought to expand Gerbi's account, I became interested in studying the contradictions and tensions of Creole consciousness, poised between an external world characterized by European arrogance and a world within riven by the tensions of secular social injustice and racism. How could the Spanish American clerical elite embrace indigenous history as their own? Were their ideas simply a passive reworking and manipulation of European ones, as I had long been taught? What was colonialism all about?

After spending a year abroad in Spain and Mexico and collecting reams of what then seemed indigestible and useless information about natural history, the social sciences, and historiography in the eighteenth century, I discovered that, for all its insights, Gerbi's account of the "dispute over the New World" did not address a fundamental aspect of the debate: upon whose sources and authority to write the history of the Americas? Ever since then, I have been working out the details of this fundamental question. And a study that was initially intended to be in the history of science became a history of New World historiography.

In Chapter 1, I identify and describe a new art of reading that appeared in northern Europe sometime in the mid eighteenth century and that was used to dismiss sources and testimonies that had long been used to write the history of the New World and its peoples. Unlike Renaissance arts of reading, this new art did not privilege eyewitnesses. As part of larger scholarly debates about the probability of miracles, some authors began to argue that testimonies needed to be judged by their internal consistency, not by the social standing or learning of the witnesses. The link between these complex epistemological debates and the historiography of the New World, I contend, should be found in two closely related yet distinct places: the philosophical traveler and a peculiar new genre of compilations of travel accounts that I have called philosophical. I also argue that this critique of traditional sources led to the search for new forms of evidence, and ultimately to the writing of conjectural, "philosophical" histories of the land and peoples of America in which evidence from linguistics, natural history, ethology, and geology took precedence. The new historiography challenged traditional European historiographical assumptions about the histories of the peoples of the New World, particularly the Inca and Aztec empires, which had long been depicted as polities resembling ancient Rome.

Chapter 1 contributes, therefore, to what Lorraine Daston has called "historical epistemology," a new field that traces the social and cultural roots of such new early modern categories as "facts," "experiments," and "objectivity."

It suggests that our modern (and postmodern) historiographical sensibilities might have originated in seemingly peripheral debates in the eighteenth century. In this light, the New World was as significant in eliciting the fundamental tenets of contemporary historians as it was in shaping the economies of the Atlantic world.

Chapter 2 continues some of the themes of Chapter 1, particularly those related to the history of credibility and authority, but from the perspective of debates over literacy and writing. I argue that Amerindian sources also lost credibility over the course of the eighteenth century in Europe. This was a radical new departure, for in the past Europeans had accepted indigenous sources written in nonalphabetic scripts at face value. To be sure, this chapter takes issue with current scholarship, such as that of Walter Mignolo (1995), that maintains that Europeans in the Renaissance, particularly Spaniards, looked down upon indigenous scripts and writings as worthless and primitive. Notwithstanding Spanish views of Mesoamerican codices and Inca quipus as primitive, sixteenth-century chroniclers and historians went out of their way to retrieve the information stored in Amerindian sources. Moreover, these authors did so despite their awareness that indigenous historical narratives were biased, contradictory, and written for the purpose of legitimating local rulers and bolstering ethnic pride. As scholars in the seventeenth and eighteenth centuries began to churn out evolutionary theories of writing, however, this Renaissance take on Amerindian sources and scripts unraveled. My narrative confirms many of the views of Stephen Toulmin (1990), who has argued that the so-called Enlightenment reversed the more generous and tolerant views on diversity held by Renaissance humanists.

The new histories of writing were intimately linked to emerging evolutionary scales of credibility. When conservative scholars such as Giambattista Vico (1668–1744) invented histories of writing, they discredited sources written in nonalphabetic scripts, because ancient Egyptian and Chinese sources and chronologies challenged the authority of the Bible. In the process, nonalphabetic scripts such as those of the highland Mesoamerican and Andean peoples became firmly linked in the European imagination with primitive, unreliable observers. In the eighteenth century, European scholars collected and studied Mesoamerican codices and Inca quipus to demonstrate the evolution of mental faculties in conjectural and philosophical histories of progress.

Chapter 3 deals with the reception in Spain of many of these historiographical developments and is based largely on archival material. I argue that Spain took the lead in the effort to do away with old sources and narratives on the American past and in the process created many new institutions. One of the main preoccupations of the Royal Academy of History, founded in the early eighteenth century, was the writing of new, critical natural and civil histories of the New World. Many of the developments in historiography attributed to Leopold von Ranke (1795–1886) were first elaborated in Spain during passionate historiographical debates on how to write a new history of America. Spanish authors privileged primary sources (which they called "public") over printed sources, which they thought biased and written to support specific agendas. Such emphasis on the study of public documents led to the creation in the 1780s of the Archivo de Indias, one of the largest archives of Spanish colonial documents ever assembled.

I also argue that the Spanish Enlightenment was a patriotic movement. Resistance to the cartoonish representation of the "Spanish mind" by other Europeans and the realization that colonial empires were lost or won by those who controlled the description of lands and peoples moved authors to call urgently for the renewal of Spanish historiography, cartography, and botanical studies. Intellectuals became adamant about the need to produce new histories of colonization and discovery, and to control the naming of American plants and places, if the empire of Spain was to survive. But despite all the effort and resources invested in the eighteenth century in writing new histories of America, the record of publication in Spain was dismal. Rivalries among different corporations and groups of courtiers, usually representing different geographical regions, condemned most such writings to the obscurity of private and public archives, where many of them are still patiently awaiting publication.

In Chapter 4, I move to the New World, particularly to the viceroyalty of New Spain, where most antiquarian debates took place. I argue that Spanish American historiography on the New World was anything but conservative. Every bit as much as the Europeans, Spanish American authors sought aggressively sweeping historiographical renewal. Moreover, they showed themselves exquisitely aware of the epistemological underpinnings of the new northern European historiography, and by the mid eighteenth century, they had began to produce forceful epistemological critiques of this literature. A form of patriotic epistemology emerged that highlighted the limited ability of outsiders ever to comprehend the history of America and its peoples.

Patriotic epistemology was not only aimed against outsiders, however, but also against commoners. Spanish American authors, by and large, were Creole clerics who came to regard the precolonial and early colonial Amerindian upper classes as their own ancestors, but concomitantly despised plebeian mestizos and Amerindians. Patriotic epistemology was the discourse of a patrician class that evaluated sources according to the social standing of witnesses. Creole clerics argued that the history of America had been misinterpreted because early European authors lacked the linguistic tools and the practical knowledge of Native Americans to understand the sources and to evaluate and weigh their credibility.

Chapter 5 continues the analysis of the vast new scholarship on the history of America and its peoples that appeared in Spanish America during the second half of the eighteenth century. Through an analysis of three separate antiquarian controversies, I maintain that the Spanish American Enlightenment was a deeply original and creative movement, and was not limited simply to mirroring or contesting European ideas. Moreover, I seek to characterize the Baroque in the Spanish colonies by its emblematic view of nature. In the Baroque understanding, religious images and Mesoamerican scripts held arcane symbolic meanings and were used as Neoplatonic seals. This characterization of the Baroque departs from earlier ones, including that of José Antonio Maravall, who depicts the Baroque as the product of an exuberant, hybrid, yet deeply conservative imagination that flourished in the seventeenth century.[1] In my interpretation, however, the Baroque was both an aggressively modern movement, always in search of radical renewal (in that it was willing to cast textual authorities aside), and a Neoplatonic discourse that sought to read and deploy images to control the sacred powers of nature, which in Spanish America lasted well into the early nineteenth century.

Methodologically, this book follows key insights of postcolonial scholarship. I assume that all sorts of submerged voices dwell in the body and margins of texts, which can nevertheless be recovered through techniques of rhetorical analysis pioneered by postmodern literary critics. I also assume that the emphasis in traditional historiography on identities as oppositional binaries (i.e., colonized-colonizers; Amerindian-European) misses many of the actual interactions ("hybridities") that characterize colonial situations. Third, inasmuch as I take individual as well as national "identities" to be contingent (socially constructed) and contested, I indulge in painstaking reconstructions of historical contexts. Fourth, I believe that asymmetrical power relations, colonial or otherwise, are usually imagined in gendered terms. Fifth, I assume that colonies and metropolises cannot be studied in isolation, and that their historical trajectories are informed by their mutual interactions. Finally, I seek to break loose from the North Atlantic paradigms of progress and modernization underlying *all* national historiographies.[2]

There is, however, another element to add to this list. In an age of globalization, in which universities encourage students to take courses on Latin America to gain exposure to "Non-Western" peoples, I assume that the tradition that locates the "West" somewhere adjacent to the North Atlantic is amusingly pompous. It is not my intention here to offer alternatives to traditional definitions of the "West," although I believe that by encapsulating its essential dimensions in concepts as abstract and quaint as "rationality," "democracy," and "individual freedom," these definitions are rendered useless. Nor is it my intention simply to claim closer cultural proximity to "continental" Europe for Latin America than for the United States.[3] My intention is rather to challenge stereotypes and superficial characterizations.

The reader of this book has most likely been socialized into constructs that assign non-Western attributes to both Latin America and Spain, where the Inquisition purportedly stifled all novelty and people have ever since been condemned to derivative and second-rate intellectual pursuits. It is my contention that the term "West" in "America" (another pompous term in the inventory of the same cultural geography that has the West bordering the North Atlantic) works its magic through negation, policing the boundaries of what is appropriate for others to study. In the case of the subjects discussed in this book, these boundaries have made it difficult for historians even to consider the possibility that voluminous and even pioneering scholarship (by Western standards) on epistemology could have been produced in Spain and Spanish America in the eighteenth century. These boundaries have also, so to speak, rendered many academics in the United States intellectually "color-blind": just as the physically color-blind substitute gray for the color absent from their visual palettes, these academics dismiss those pursuits that blur our sharp mental cultural geographies as either improperly Latin Americanist or not sufficiently Europeanist. The unspoken assumption is that Latin Americanists should not be writing the intellectual history of the West, on the one hand, and Europeanists should not be meddling with the "Third World," on the other, where only stories of strife and exploitation are worth chronicling. After a few years of teaching Latin American history in universities in the United States, I have learned that the public expects from historians of the region cautionary tales of revolutionary violence and, if socially conscious, stories of cunning peasants resisting treacherous oligarchs. I am a storyteller of a different kind, who believes that there ought to be other tales for the public to consume.

Toward a New Art of Reading and
New Historical Interpretations

In 1776, in *The Wealth of Nations*, Adam Smith (1723–1790) suggested that six-teenth-century Spanish witnesses reporting on Amerindian societies were ei-ther purposefully or unconsciously lying. Smith highlighted contradictions in those early accounts that affirmed the high population density of the indige-nous communities. Yet everything suggested, according to Smith, that Native American societies had had a lower agricultural carrying capacity than that of the contemporary Tartars of the Ukraine. Moreover, the accounts described how the Spaniards' armies, although hardly more than five hundred strong, often went hungry and, when fed, consumed so much of the small available food supply that the natives starved to death. The reports also indicated that the Amerindians had transacted their affairs without metal currency, limiting themselves to barter, which in turn suggested that "there was accordingly scarce any division of labour" among the Mexica (Aztecs) and the Incas.

Clearly, something was amiss. Societies at such low levels of economic development, he argued, could not have sustained large populations or been as culturally and politically advanced as the early Spanish reports main-tained. "The story of this populousness and high cultivation," Smith con-cluded, was in "great measure fabulous."[1] That same year, in Amsterdam, a few hundred miles away, an article by the geographer Samuel Engel (1702-1784) on advances in New World geography appeared as part of a supplement to the *Encyclopédie*. Engel, a typical erudite mapmaker, did not take to sea with telescopes and pendulums; instead, he was trained to identify place lo-cations by collating and contrasting reports by pilots and travelers. In his ar-ticle, Engel offered criteria for evaluating the trustworthiness of travel reports. In so doing, he argued that the credibility of early Spanish accounts of the New World was seriously in doubt. These reports had in the past been held to be *indubitable par tout le monde*, Engel noted, but now they were deemed utterly unreliable, largely because no other European witnesses had been al-lowed to enter the Spanish domains to either confirm or rebut the accounts.[2]

Indeed, at the time of Smith and Engel, something was radically changing in Europe regarding the credit given to sixteenth-century accounts of the New World. Witnesses whose testimonies had never been doubted were now considered untrustworthy. In 1774, in the second edition of his *Histoire philosophique des deux Indes*, a bestseller on Europe's early modern commercial expansion, the abbé Guillaume-Thomas-François Raynal (1713–1796) argued that had Locke, Buffon, and Montesquieu visited America in the sixteenth century, they would have had the chance to study humanity arrested at its earliest stage of development. "However," Raynal complained, "this brutal and savage state of nature has been disfigured after having met the greedy and ferocious Christians."[3] The argument was simple: ignorant soldiers and clerics had been the first to explore America. Had philosophers such as Buffon and Montesquieu visited the New World while it was still in its pristine, unspoiled state, knowledge of its lands and peoples would have survived. Unfortunately, however, the first Europeans ashore were ignorant religious fanatics, who not only failed to understand the peoples they encountered but bludgeoned them to death. The unreliability of the early European reports lay in the nature of the witnesses. In the third edition of his *Histoire* in 1781, Raynal maintained that "the indifference of the [Spanish] conquerors to all things that did not satisfy their insatiable greed" blinded them to everything else. All that could therefore be said with certainty of, say, Mexico was that Moctezuma Xocoyoltzin had ruled there when the Spaniards arrived. Everything else was "confusing, contradictory and full of the most absurd fables to which human credulity could ever be exposed." Clearly, without more French and English "philosophical" observers being allowed to enter Spanish America and study its ruins, Raynal argued, the past of the indigenous civilizations would be irretrievably lost.[4]

Smith and Raynal belonged to a group of scholars who in the last quarter of the eighteenth century began to call into question the credibility of reports not written by trained "philosophical travelers." According to these skeptics, early European witnesses of America had seen things that were simply not there. Moreover, Spaniards, in particular, being ignorant, patriotic, and credulous, had lacked sufficient curiosity to pose important philosophical questions about the peoples and lands they encountered.

Although skepticism about travelers and traditional sources had deep roots in the seventeenth century, if not earlier, Smith's and Raynal's observations were new and revealed a qualitatively different form of being skeptical, a new form of reading sources. A new "art of reading" appeared in "northern" Europe sometime in the mid eighteenth century. Unlike Renaissance arts of reading, this new art did not privilege eyewitnesses. Authors argued that testimonies needed to be judged by their internal consistency, not by the social standing or learning of the witnesses. The link between these complex epistemological debates and the historiography of the New World can be found in two closely related yet distinct places: the philosophical traveler and the genre of compilations of travel accounts. The persona of the philosophical traveler emerged as an ideal in Europe in the mid seventeenth century when scholars began to call into question the reliability and training of travelers to exotic lands, and as the new experimental philosophy matured in salons and academies all over Europe. New "philosophical" compilations of travel narratives also called into question the credibility of the conquistadors, missionaries, and bureaucrats who had described the grandeur of the Aztecs and Incas. Editors and travelers began to read all earlier eyewitness accounts of the New World through the lens of contemporary social theory.

The *Recherches philosophiques sur les américains* of Cornelius de Pauw (1734–1799) was perhaps the philosophical compilation that had the greatest impact. Histories and travel compilations written thereafter, including those by the abbé Raynal, Adam Smith, William Robertson (1721–1793), and Alexander von Humboldt followed many of de Pauw's leads. De Pauw was instrumental in making the connection between a critique of sources and the search for new forms of evidence and methodologies. Working in a lively new genre that sought to connect the past of the earth to that of humankind, de Pauw created a conjectural portrait of the history of the New World in which evidence from linguistics, natural history, ethology, and geology took precedence. Like the French naturalist Buffon before him, he depicted Amerindians and Creoles alike as degenerate and effete, and such reconstructions of the American past flourished thereafter.

The new historiography also challenged traditional European assumptions about the histories of the Inca and Aztec polities, long portrayed as having resembled the ancient Roman empire. With Alexander von Humboldt, however, the "Orient," not Rome, became the preferred model for interpreting the past of the highland polities of Mesoamerica and the Andes. This oriental analogy set off a new, less skeptical, more positive, historiographical wave, that of the romantic period, which, however, lies outside the purview of this study.

Philosophical Travelers and the Humanist Art of Reading

Sixteenth- and seventeenth-century reports of the New World began to lose credibility when they began to be compared with the writings of the new philosophical travelers. To understand the rise of the skeptical attitude toward the early reports on America and its peoples, we therefore need first to understand the epistemological debates surrounding the persona of the philosophical traveler. From these debates came new standards for validating knowledge and experience while visiting foreign lands.

By the first decades of the eighteenth century, travel literature had become firmly associated with lying and deception. "[Travel accounts] are in our present Days, what Books of Chivalry were in those of our Forefathers," Lord Shaftesbury complained bitterly in 1711.[5] In 1758, L. Davis and C. Reymers, the English translators of *Relación historica de un viaje a América meridional* by Antonio de Ulloa (1716–1795) and Jorge Juan y Santacilia (1713–1773), two Spanish naval officers who had escorted the expedition led by the French academicians Charles-Marie de La Condamine (1701–1774), Pierre Bouguer (1698–1758), and Louis Godin des Odònais (1704–1760) to the Andes, insightfully captured the changing mood of their age. Throughout the seventeenth century, Davis and Reymers noted, travel accounts had enjoyed great popularity, so much so that John Locke read them avidly in order to write his *Essay Concerning Human Understanding*. Travel accounts ignited the imagination and sparked the curiosity of several generations, introducing them to a life of learning and scholarship. But by the eighteenth century, travel accounts had "quickly lost that credit which novelty only gave them, and being once exploded by sensible judges have gradually sunk, first into contempt and then into the oblivion they deserve."[6] Travel literature was becoming firmly associated with the taste of a populace enamored of marvels and false curiosities.

The first line of defense of the learned against deception was to summon their own to do the reporting. The eighteenth century was a century obsessed with what Shaftesbury called the "Study of Human Affections."[7] Psychology, as Frank Manuel (1959) has shown, came of age grappling with the alleged pathological manifestations of the minds of most people, namely, superstition and "enthusiasm." But, from its inception, psychology was also an effort to describe the workings of the minds of "reasonable" men. As Lorraine Daston has argued, entire branches of mathematics, such as classical probability theory, developed in an attempt to describe numerically how the enlightened few made reasonable decisions.[8] A discourse emerged that divided the world sharply in two: on one hand, the fear-stricken, perceptually deluded majority, and, on the other, the reasonable few, whose minds had been trained to understand the world accurately.[9]

Focusing on the perceptual limitations of those who had traditionally written travel narratives — missionaries, traders, soldiers, and sailors — critics proposed that the enlightened visit foreign lands themselves to discover the truth. In 1755, for example, Rousseau called on men like Buffon, Montesquieu, D'Alembert, Charles Pinot Duclos (1704–1772), and Etienne Bonnot de Condillac (1714–1780) to go out and explore the world. Rousseau complained that travelers had been describing societies for centuries but to no avail. Sailors, merchants, and soldiers were "classes [who could not be expected] to provide good observers." The fourth group, the missionaries, although learned, also had "prejudices of [lowly] status." Clearly, a new category of traveler was needed, consisting of those whose "eyes [are] made to see the true features that distinguish nations."[10]

Calls for trained observers to visit exotic lands did not begin with Rousseau. They first surfaced as early as the mid seventeenth century in the methodological disputes of experts sent out by academies and courts. Amédée François Frézier (1682–1773) and Louis Feuillée (1660–1732) , for example, visited the New World in the early eighteenth century on separate expeditions supported by the French crown to spy on Spain in the South Seas. Each belonged to different traditions of observation and training. Frézier was a daring, hands-on entrepreneur, whereas Feuillée was a scholar-astronomer and natural historian. Their debate over the merit of each other's observations is most illuminating, showing that the new philosophical traveler appeared amid disputes about the use of instrumentation and reason to control and discipline human perception, and in debates about the value of new techniques of visual representation.

Louis Feuillée, a Minim friar and mathematician at the court of Louis XIV, was sent to the New World in the first decade of the eighteenth century to draw accurate maps and to report on medicinal and natural resources in the Spanish colonies.[11] Amédée Frézier, a military engineer sent by the French to spy on the strength of Spanish fortifications and ports in the South Seas, greeted Feuillée's original 1714 report with contempt. Frézier maintained that Feuillée had overlooked practical information that pilots and merchants needed for navigation and business. Feuillée, he argued, had substituted astronomical observation done from the security of his cabin offshore for hands-on practical reporting. Worst, the bookworm Feuillée had showed an exaggerated interest in irrelevant natural curiosities.[12]

Feuillée responded to this tirade in 1725 by arguing that Frézier was an ignorant pilot who knew nothing about the tricks of human perception. Frézier, he maintained, drew inaccurate maps largely because he did not know how to use instruments such as pendulums and telescopes. Mapmakers needed to perform accurate observations of the satellites of Jupiter in order to identify longitudes, and it was therefore no surprise that Frézier, an ignorant sailor, drew inaccurate maps. Instruments and reason were needed to correct grossly inaccurate human perceptions. Making fun of Frézier, who from afar had described penguins as having fur, not feathers, Feuillée insisted that "we should not believe that all judgments that follow our observations are equally exact; [our perception] often errs when we lack the help of reason [and instruments]."[13]

Feuillée also suggested that more than reason and instruments were needed to correct human perception. Evidence that the right observational procedures had been followed was also required. Feuillée cast his report as a journal, with painstaking descriptions of measurements and calculations, as well as visual representations of instruments, so that readers, not only his academician peers, could bear witness, and thus assent, to the making of new "facts." Feuillée thus deployed rhetorical and visual techniques that Steven Shapin and Simon Schaffer have traced back to the appearance of the new social and epistemological category of "matter of fact" in early modern Europe. Shapin and Schaffer have argued that in a period characterized by social, economic, and religious doubt, old conceptions of science that led to certainty through deduction lost their appeal. Matters of fact became the only solid, uncontested foundation of knowledge. But the road to the identification of facts was plagued by epistemological doubts. Natural philosophers thought that instruments and experimental apparatus were required to coerce facts from nature. Moreover, natural philosophers identified matters of fact through consensus in polite conversation and through collective witnessing of experimental displays, both carried out in semi-public settings such academies and salons. These new forms of academic sociability sought to widen consensus by bringing in readers as "virtual witnesses" in the collective construction of matters of fact. Through new rhetorical and visual techniques, authors reenacted experimental displays for those readers who had been left out.[14] Feuillée was well aware of these new forms of vicarious witnessing and sociability when he introduced illustrations of instruments and detailed descriptions of the settings in which his astronomical observations and calculations had taken place.

Feuillée was also aware, it seems, of developments in the use of illustrations in travel accounts. The appearance of illustrations in travel accounts, as Bernard Smith has argued, was closely connected to the general critique of the accuracy of human perception and the rise of the philosophical traveler. As scholars became aware of the ambiguity associated with reading, a new preoccupation developed with ascertaining facts through illustrations. Scholars thought that facts delivered in writing might be polysemic if read by culturally diverse audiences. To avoid this danger, philosophical travelers made a point of painting or drawing their subjects, or of bringing along artists in the hope of capturing an unambiguous, undistorted reality.[15] Feuillée included numerous depictions of fauna, flora, and peoples in his report.

In a long rebuttal, Frézier sought to distance himself from the criticisms leveled by Feuillée. He was no ignorant observer, he said, but a learned engineer, and he had also used instruments to correct his observations. He also included numerous illustrations of his trips to the viceroyalty of Peru (Fig. 1.1).[16] This short account of the methodological debates between Feuillée and Frézier shows that the philosophical traveler emerged as part of a larger controversy over the limitations of human perception. Not surprisingly, philosophical travelers themselves were the first to voice criticism of earlier reports by ignorant witnesses. Of all people, Frézier saw fit to criticize the authority of early Spanish accounts of the Incas. Historians like the Inca Garcilaso de la Vega who had portrayed the Incas as an ancient classical and virtuous polity, Frézier suggested, were contradicted by the scarcity of extant material remains. Inca ruins were puny, not worthy of the serious attention of European travelers.[17] Moreover, Frézier argued, Garcilaso's dynastic genealogy of the Incas was contradicted by other evidence found in Cuzco.[18]

The French mathematician Charles-Marie de La Condamine, perhaps the most respected eighteenth-century European philosophical traveler to visit the Andes, also found it impossible to reconcile what he saw as the manifest stupidity of contemporary Peruvian Amerindians with Garcilaso's portrait of a glorious Inca past (Fig. 1.2). La Condamine, who spent between 1735 and 1745 in the viceroyalty of Peru doing astronomical measurements in an attempt to settle a learned dispute between Cartesians and Newtonians over the shape of the earth, considered that the destructive effect of Spanish colonialism on the human spirit was not enough to explain the dramatic decline of the natives from their alleged former grandeur to their present wretchedness. He thus suggested that Garcilaso had been lying.[19] In a memoir on Inca ruins delivered to the Berlin Academy of Sciences in 1746, La Condamine contrasted Garcilaso's descriptions of Inca provincial palaces with his own study of Inca antiquities and voiced skepticism as to the credibility of some of Garcilaso's observations. Finally, La Condamine claimed that he could not vouch for the reliability of Garcilaso's descriptions of Cuzco, the capital of the Incas.[20]

Eighteenth-century learned audiences preferred the new accounts of the

FIGURE 1.1. Ancient and eighteenth-century Andean technologies, including Inca royal paraphernalia. From Amédée François Frézier, *Relation du voyage de la Mer du Sud* (Paris, 1732). Courtesy of the John Carter Brown Library, Brown University, Providence, R.I.

philosophical travelers and began to grow suspicious of the value of earlier Spanish reports. Yet for all their suspicion, readers were not about to dismiss Spanish accounts of the New World's past, in part because they complied with traditional historiographical standards. Audiences who had been educated in the ideas of Cicero knew that history was about persuading audiences to behave virtuously, but without lying. Since the time of Lucian of

FIGURE 1.2. Classical tropes organized not only narratives of the Incas but also their portrayals, as seen in this illustration for the 1737 French edition of Garcilaso's *Comentarios reales,* entitled *Histoire des Incas* (Amsterdam, 1737). Note especially the classical statuary in the niches of the Inca's throne room. Courtesy of the John Carter Brown Library, Brown University, Providence, R.I.

Samosata (C.E. 125–200), historians had been called on to avoid taking partisan stances, to shun hearsay, and not to surrender to the demands of patrons.[21] Lucian's criteria of independence, moderation, and use of unmediated eyewitness accounts remained essential for historians through the ages, even for early European reporters on the New World.

Well aware of the Renaissance emphasis on the historiographical value of firsthand reporting, Spaniards in the New World committed their own experiences to writing. Moreover, unlike humanists in Europe, they did not have a corpus of classical texts regarding America, which could have been used to validate their assertions. Spaniards therefore relied even more on the rhetoric of the "I-witness." As Anthony Pagden has shown, Spanish observers of the New World, who had widely different political agendas and widely different interpretations of Native American societies, developed a complex rhetoric of trust in an effort to compensate for the lack of a tradition of authoritative written sources.[22] Confronted with conflicting reports and interpretations, observers of each party asserted the accuracy of their perceptions compared with those of their rivals and exaggerated their accuracy.

It is plausible to argue that the culture of humanism encouraged audiences to believe earlier European accounts of America. Humanists were at the forefront of the revival of skepticism in the early modern period and privileged the study of rhetoric and persuasion precisely because they understood that absolute truths could never be attained; the "arts of reading" developed by humanists aimed at spotting forged documents.[23] By and large, however, humanist reading did not seek to identify inconsistencies in the testimony of untrained eyewitnesses. Humanist philology may, in fact, have helped reinforce the emphasis put on the testimony of eyewitnesses. As an art of reading that sought to spot linguistic inconsistencies between the words used in a document and the age in which the document had allegedly been penned, philology was on the face of it a collective editorial effort to get rid of reports that had demonstrably not been written by witnesses.[24] Although Julian Franklin has argued that Renaissance humanists developed an art of reading whose central concern was the evaluation of the testimony of witnesses, this art of reading was preoccupied with apportioning credit according to the social standing and motivation of witnesses. This is not surprising, because Renaissance societies were organized on the principle of corporate privileges, and scholarship depended on the favor and patronage of social superiors.[25]

In the Renaissance art of reading, audiences and editors treated the character and social standing of the witnesses as paramount when doubts about the reliability of an account surfaced. Take, for example, the case of the 1633 French translation of Garcilaso's history of the Incas by Jean Baudoin (1590?–1650). Baudoin attacked those who argued that Garcilaso's history was an entertaining fable as narrow-minded bigots who thought that nothing of importance ever occurred outside Paris. Blinded by their provincial view of the world, Baudoin maintained, the skeptics overlooked Garcilaso's *naissance et vertu*: his credibility ultimately rested on his high social standing in Inca society as the son of an Inca princess.[26] In 1737, Jean-Frédéric Bernard (d. 1752) observed that as an admitted patriot, Garcilaso had had motive enough to exaggerate the real accomplishments of the Incas, pointing out that his history was full of incidents that defied everyday European life experience. Yet drawing perhaps on the late-seventeenth-century critical principles sketched by the Dutch scholar Jacobus Perizonius (1651–1715), who held that scholars should not be so narrow and provincial as to reject accounts of foreign traditions that appeared strange, Bernard maintained that Garcilaso was a credible author. There were reasons to believe Garcilaso, Bernard contended. Had he lied, his Spanish and Amerindian rivals would have denounced him immediately. According to Bernard, too, however, Garcilaso's high social standing in Inca society was his most important asset. Being of Inca royal blood, Garcilaso was privy to secrets that no other observer could have known.[27]

The issue of the character of witnesses likewise led Davis and Reymers, its English translators, to defend the accuracy and reliability of the *Relación histórica* by La Condamine's Spanish escorts Ulloa and Juan y Santacilia, in which they published observations of their own. "It is of great consequence to know the characters of the authors we peruse," Davis and Reymers argued, "that we may judge of the credit that is due to their reports, as this [*sic*] as well in point of abilities, as of veracity, for many writers impose on the world, not through an evil intention of deceiving others, but because they have been deceived themselves. They relate falsehoods but they believe them."[28] Davis and Reymers did not make much of the fact that Ulloa and Juan were trained observers familiar with the latest European findings and had used state-of-the-art equipment. Their authority ultimately derived from their character and lack of obvious motives to deceive.

Early modern European editors necessarily relied on Spanish accounts of Spanish America — "a vast land about which we need to know much but that [is] almost unknown," the Minim friar Louis Feuillée observed — because it was largely closed to other Europeans.[29] John Green (fl. 1730–1753), editor of the Astley collection of voyages and travels, argued that he had no choice but to rely on Spanish sources. To detect errors in and reconcile differences among travelers' accounts, large numbers of reports on the same land were needed. The scarcity of reports on places such as Spanish America, where only one or two were available, forced editors to rely on "writers of the country to which the fact relates."[30]

The epistemological critiques of philosophical travelers did not devalue Spanish sources on the New World, which continued to be regarded as trustworthy, partly because they had been written by witnesses and partly because, even when their reliability was called into question, the humanist art of reading, which emphasized evaluating the social position of witnesses, confirmed their value. Why, then, did Spanish sources on the New World lose credibility? The answer lies in the emergence in the second half of the eighteenth century of a very different art of reading.

Compilations of Travel Narratives

In eighteenth-century debates about the probability of miracles, new forms of "internal" criticism superseded traditional "external" techniques of judging the value of testimony, Lorraine Daston argues: whereas external criticism had focused on evaluating the character of witnesses (social standing, education, motives), internal criteria stressed the coherence of reports.[31] It is plausible to argue that the epistemological debates over miracles spilled over into the literature on the New World and its peoples. These new internal techniques of criticism eroded the credibility of early European accounts of the Americas.

Voltaire, who thought that "not even eyewitnesses should be believed when they go against common sense," advocated the use of internal criteria to weigh the credibility of historical testimony. Sources should be read in an *esprit philosophique*.[32] Voltaire's method consisted in refusing "to believe every historian, ancient or modern who reported things that went against nature and the beat of the human heart." Faithful to this principle, Voltaire argued in 1748 that Spanish witnesses who described the New World as inhabited by cannibals who "ate humans as frequently as we eat goats" were lying. Such accounts were untrustworthy, for eating human flesh was unnatural, a practice only appealing to small bands of hungry savages.[33] A year later, in 1749, Buffon also applied internal forms of criticism. The apparent lack of any extant architectural monuments, the "wild" and uncultivated aspect of the landscape found by the Europeans upon their arrival, the very traditions of the Aztec and Inca states as young monarchies, and the ease with which the Spaniards had conquered the New World all indicated that Spanish reports alleging high original population densities in the Americas were wrong. How could societies that had left no great material remains behind and that had failed to transform the landscape have developed the agricultural carrying capacity to sustain large populations? According to Buffon, everything indicated that all Native Americans were recent arrivals living in sparsely inhabited communities.[34]

Voltaire's and Buffon's logical deconstruction of Spanish reports was limited to reports on cannibals and demography. They did not offer sweeping generalizations about the reliability of the entire corpus of early European accounts. Thoroughgoing critiques of early European testimonies had to wait for the appearance of a new genre in the literature of travel accounts, namely, "philosophical" compilations of travel narratives. I use the term "philosophical" to refer to one specific type in a vast corpus of compilations of travel narratives.

Travel compilations are a genre as old as the Renaissance. Early modern European overseas expansion led to the rise of this new genre that sought to systematize accounts of exotic lands by conquistadors, sailors, pilots, merchants, missionaries, and bureaucrats and make them available to wide audiences at home. Sixteenth- and seventeenth-century compilations such as those edited by Giovanni Ramusio (1485–1557), Richard Eden (1521?–1576), Richard Hakluyt (1552?–1616), Samuel Purchas (1577?–1626), and Melchisédec Thévenot (1620–1692) sought to quench the thirst of audiences increasingly given to scrutinizing long-held beliefs in light of the widely different customs, creeds, and societies of distant peoples.

By the late seventeenth century, the study of travel accounts was presented as an alternative to formal scholarly pursuits. Locke recommended reading of travel reports as the best way to approach the study of human understanding. John Harris (1667?–1719), a Fellow of the Royal Society and editor of an important early-eighteenth-century compilation, contrasted learning gained through "sever" studies and learning gained through the reading of travel accounts. Travel accounts, he argued, exposed the source of "ignorance and mistakes" of the ancients, "[for they] reason[ed] themselves into notions which experience shows us to be false." Travel accounts called attention to curiosities and extraordinary phenomena, which in turn led to new knowledge that showed the vacuity of the learning of the ancients. Travel accounts, in short, were a cure for pedantry. Pedants, Harris argued, "ingulphed [themselves] in some studies that swallow [them] up so that [they] have no longer attention to anything else." By exposing the reader to a "perpetual variety of subjects," travel accounts, showed pedants the "folly of pursuing a single scheme of science."[35] Travel accounts thus seemed to have contributed to the creation of the category of "matters of facts," namely, uncontested evidence whose function in Baconian natural histories was to falsify hypotheses and show the folly of all system builders.

The popularity of travel reports led in turn to an explosion of publications of new and old unpublished accounts and to the appearance of fake and fictional ones. Faced with hundreds of reports, editors of travel compilations now had to make hard choices. Editorial criteria varied, however, according to the nature and purpose of the compilation.

Three different forms of travel compilations appeared in the course of the eighteenth century. First, there were those who, following in the footsteps of Hakluyt, Purchas, and Ramusio, presented the most authoritative sources in some kind of chronological and regional order. The 1705 edition of Harris's *Navigantium (or Compleat collection of voyages)* and the 1708 *Histoire universelle des voyages* attributed to the abbé de Bellegarde (Jean-Baptiste Morvan [1648–1734]) best represent this tradition. For all the seeming simplicity of this strategy, determining what counted as an authoritative source implied a process of selection. Harris, for example, developed a methodology to separate the chaff from the wheat. Travelers who spent many years in a foreign land were more credible than those who passed through it quickly, as were those who had written their reports immediately after their trips, because, according to Harris, fading memories tended to play tricks on the imagination. Credibility was also related to learning, social standing, and the national or personal interests motivating the author's report.[36] There was nothing extraordinary about Harris's strategy; it was simply an extension of traditional Renaissance source criticism to compilations of travel accounts.

Things got slightly more complicated when editors went beyond mere compilations to write narratives that were altogether new texts, syntheses of many accounts. In these new syntheses, the creation of a separate narrative out of accounts that were often mutually contradictory not only avoided repetition but also identified contradictions among reports of travelers who had visited the same land. Borrowing their techniques from Renaissance philologists, editors acquired and collated original manuscripts, identified contradictory accounts in all available printed reports, apportioned credit to opposing testimonies, and constructed a single authoritative synthesis, a reconstruction by a traveler endowed, as it were, with many eyes. "By having the remarks of several authors before him in one view," John Green argued, seeking to justify the new editorial strategy, "a collector is best able to see their errors and defects, and consequently, to adjust, correct, and supply them." Both editor and reader gained from this method. Comparing reports allowed editors to identify an original source from derivative accounts, as well as authors who had committed plagiarism. Reading, on the other hand, became easier, inasmuch as the narrative was unencumbered by repetition. "Instead of a great many imperfect accounts, which the authors separately afford," Green maintained, "[the reader] will be furnished with one complete description, compiled from them all."[37] It was this synthesis that allowed Green to claim that his compilation should in fact be considered a new system of modern geography and history.

The most popular of the new syntheses were those of John Green, the abbé Antoine-François Prévost (1697–1763), and the abbé Joseph de La Porte (1713–1779). Each editor saw his own as superseding all previous compilations and fought protracted methodological battles with the others. After having translated Green's compilation into French with only slight corrections to avoid repetitions, Prévost, for example, decided that Green had failed to deliver his promised new system and set out to improve on Green by publishing scores of new volumes of synthesis. Prévost's changes were merely cosmetic, however, and, like Green, he continued to synthesize all available accounts into a single narrative.[38] Prévost's compilation omitted the Middle East and Europe, however, and La Porte thought that it focused too much on nautical (not overland) voyages. To improve on it, La Porte organized his own collection around hundreds of fictional letters by a philosophical traveler to a *salonnière*. Moreover, he eliminated all references to personal adventures in the letters of his fictional philosophical traveler, on the grounds that they did not contribute anything to learning and had clogged Prévost's narrative. But for all the alleged methodological improvements over Prévost's compilation, La Porte's remained a synthesis of all available authoritative, albeit conflicting, reports about different parts of the world.

A third, more systematic strategy appeared, too, beginning with Harris's second edition of 1744, in which travel accounts were entirely subordinated to larger "philosophical" purposes. Countering critics who argued that travel accounts and travel itself were dangerous, because they perverted youth and "kindl[ed] a wild and ungovernable humour in the minds of young people," Harris argued that travelers and readers needed tutors to truly take advantage of their trips. In the same way that travelers had tutors to "correct their extravagancies and restrain their impetuosity and oblige them to make observations as would otherwise escape them," readers needed smart editors to prevent them from drowning in a sea of entertaining but disjointed facts.[39] The thread that would help orient young minds, Harris believed, was the history of commerce. According to Harris, travel accounts could be used to show the history of global commercial interactions, of the civilizing and unifying power of commerce.[40] However, he could not deliver a philosophical history of commerce and limited himself to writing synthetic accounts of places in which descriptions of ports, volume of trade, and natural resources became paramount.

Charles de Brosses (1709–1777), known as the président de Brosses, succeeded where Harris failed. Although his compendium was a rather traditional compilation of accounts of voyages to the South Seas, organized in strict chronological order, he used them to identify the best place to create a new type of colony, entirely based on trade and commercial exchange and committed to the scientific study of exotic places, rather than their destruction. This forerunner of the ideology of nineteenth-century European colonialism concluded from the collected reports that France should establish his new commercial utopia in Polynesia.[41]

In the 1770s, the abbé Pierre-Joseph-André Roubaud (1730–1791) produced a history of the world based mostly on travelers' accounts. Roubaud argued in his *Histoire générale* that Asians, Africans, and Americans lacked writing, or that their sources were either inaccurate or unavailable, and that therefore only a critical reading of travelers' reports could provide the material upon which indirectly to reconstruct their histories.[42]

Philosophical compilations of travel accounts thus began to emphasize the internal over the external; that is, to apportion credit to reports based on the merits of the story itself and not on an evaluation of the character of the reporter. Two late-eighteenth-century philosophical compilations, written by Cornelius de Pauw and the abbé Raynal, will help clarify this transition and show why Spanish writings on the New World suddenly lost all credibility.

Cornelius de Pauw's New Art of Reading

Cornelius de Pauw was a prolific and very influential author. His various books on ancient Americans, Egyptians, Chinese, and Greeks went through numerous editions and were the subject of endless debates in salons and academies on both sides of the Atlantic. Yet today he has been nearly forgotten. De Pauw's *Recherches philosophiques sur les américaines*, which appeared in Berlin in 1768–69, while its author was at the court of Frederick the Great, lured there briefly as a private reader to the Prussian monarch, was conceived as a new approach to the study of travel accounts. Dismissing those who merely compiled travel reports, de Pauw used travelers' accounts as sources for the study of pressing philosophical questions.[43]

At the time when de Pauw set out to complete his *Recherches*, Europe was awash in reports about the New World and debates sparked by those reports. Sailors, merchants, pilots, missionaries, and bureaucrats confirmed the existence of Amazons and Patagonian giants. Reports of communities of hermaphrodites in Florida, albinos in Darien, and black Amerindians in Guyana were gaining importance in Europe as scholars grappled with new theories of heredity to explain the origins of racial variations. Revived accounts of American cannibalism provided ammunition for many parties engaged in furious ideological struggles over alternate visions of human nature. Descriptions of America's singular fauna and flora, and of the seemingly uniform bodily complexions of Amerindians, were introduced in argument either to defend Adam or to toss him out of world history.

De Pauw's analysis of these wondrous phenomena was initially based on traditional forms of criticism. Consider, for example, his analysis of reports of Patagonian giants. First, he identified all accounts in chronological order, including those that had failed to report any giants. He then described the professions and social standing of the witnesses (e.g., missionary, merchant, pilot, philosophical traveler). Finally, he pitted accounts against one another to highlight their contradictions, particularly as regards the alleged height of the giants (Fig. 1.3). Operating on the assumption that merchants, sailors, and missionaries were credulous witnesses, de Pauw argued that all such accounts were unreliable, because not a single living giant had ever been captured and displayed, even though all known human types, including pygmies, had been exhibited in Europe. The New World bones in cabinets of curiosities that were adduced in support of the reports of giants were those of animals, collected by ignoramuses untrained in comparative anatomy. Given the contradictions in the sources and the absence of any material evidence, de Pauw therefore confidently dismissed the reports of giants as figments.[44]

For all his skill at deploying traditional forms of criticism, de Pauw privileged internal analysis. He subjected reports to an excruciating philosophical examination in which the coherence of the testimony took precedence over the character of the witness as the organizing critical principle. Consider, for example, his analysis of reports of Amazons, republican communities of warrior women who kidnapped neighboring males to mate and let only their daughters live. Debates over their existence flared up in the wake of La Condamine's 1745 publication of his *Relation abrégée d'un voyage fait dans l'intérieur de l'Amérique méridionale*. La Condamine who had sailed to Peru with a team of French academicians led by the mathematician Bouguer and the naturalist Godin to settle a learned dispute between Cartesians and Newtonians over the shape of the earth, returned to France empty-handed, eight years too late to have any impact on the resolution of the debate and with a dismal record to show, including the death of a member of his expedition killed by a mob in the city of Cuenca in today's Ecuador.[45]

138 DEFENSE

droit où il ne débarqua point (*). Mais qu'impor-
te-t-il à l'existence de ces prétendus Géants qu'on
les ait vus dans la terre Del Fuego, ou fur le bord
septentrional du Détroit? puisque l'Auteur convient,
que Biron dit avoir vu des hommes hauts de neuf
pieds; mais je nie que Biron dise qu'il les a me-
surés.

Quand un Géant est trouvé, la chose du monde
la plus facile est de le mesurer.

I I.

Qui croiroit que les différents Voyageurs, qui
parlent des Patagons, varient entr'eux de quatre-
vingt-quatre pouces, fur leur taille? Cependant cela
est aussi vrai que cela est inouï.

(**) Selon la Giraudais, ils sont hauts d'environ — — 6 pieds.
Selon Pigafetta, — — 8 —

(*) L'Auteur des *Recherches Philosophiques* dit expressé-
ment dans une note à la page 306. T. I. qu'il n'a pas connu
la latitude de l'endroit où Biron a cru voir des Géants.
S'il avoit connu exactement la latitude & la longitude de
cet endroit, il l'eût indiqué par le moyen de ses cartes, à
une minute près. Or le critique n'indique pas lui-même la
position de cet endroit, parcequ'il ne l'a pas sue. On a publié jusqu'à trois relations du voyage de Biron, qui ont
toutes été inconnues à Dom Pernety, & parcequ'elles lui
ont été inconnues, il dit qu'on les a falsifiées. Il y a plus de
cent &cinquante Auteurs qu'il étoit absolument nécessaire
de consulter fur l'Amérique, qui lui ont été inconnus,
& après cela il n'est pas étonnant qu'il ait eu recours à
l'Atlas historique du compilateur Gueudeville.
(**) Le 31. Mai 1766, *ayant relâché dans la baye Boucaut
avec trois hommes de son équipage, Mr. de la Giraudais vit un
grand nombre de Sauvages, il y en avoit jusqu'à 28 cents, y
compris les femmes & les enfants, tous d'une très-grande taille,
plusieurs d'environ six pieds. Relat. de la Giraudais.*

DES RECHERCHES PHILOSOPH. &c. 189

Selon Biron, — — 9 pieds.
Selon Aris, — — 10 —
Selon Jantzon, — — 11 —
(*) Selon Dom Pernety, ils sont au
moins hauts de 12 à 13 pieds, ce
qui donne pour la hauteur moyenne 12½ —
Selon Argenfola, — — 13 —

Il résulte de ce calcul qu'à 12 pouces par pied,
ces Voyageurs varient entr'eux de 84 pouces, ce qui
fait déja beaucoup plus que la taille d'un homme
ordinaire. Or, pour trouver lequel de tous ces Voyageurs mérite le plus de croyance, il faut bien sup-
poser, que c'est ou la Giraudais, ou Argenfola
III.

De tous ceux qui doivent avoir vu des Géants
en Amérique, aucun n'a su dire s'ils ont de la barbe,
ou si à l'instar des autres Américains; ils ont le men-
ton naturellement ras. Au reste je ne suis pas étonné
que, personne n'ayant pensé à mesurer ces prétendus
Monstres, personne n'ait aussi pensé à les observer.

(*) Je fixe ici la hauteur des Géants de Dom Pernety d'a-
près le squelette dont il parle à la page 72 de sa Dissertation.
Car s'il s'est imaginé, qu'on a réellement trouvé en Amérique un homme mort dont la taille étoit haute au moins
de 12 à 13 pieds, il s'est sans doute aussi imaginé, qu'on ren-
contre en Amérique des hommes vivants de cette hauteur-là.
Tout ceci est fort conséquent : là où les corps morts ont la
stature gigantesque, il faut bien qu'il y ait des Géants; mais
si malheureusement ce squelette avoit appartenu à un Che-
val, alors tout ceci se feroit plus si conséquent. Je dirai dans
la suite, qu'en ne supposant ce squelette que de douze pieds
& demi de haut, il se trouveroit qu'il avoit appartenu à un
individu qui étoit plus que Géant. Ainsi il y a dans la narration de Dom Pernety un double merveilleux, & il n'a
laissé après lui qu'Argenfola, comme on le voit par mon
calcul.

FIGURE 1.3. This page typifies De Pauw's critical method. He first gathered most available reports on Patagonian giants. He then brought together different testimonies on the giants' height to highlight contradictions and dismiss all accounts. From Cornelius de Pauw, *Recherches philosophiques sur les américains* (Berlin, 1770). Courtesy of the John Carter Brown Library, Brown University, Providence, R.I.

To save his reputation and to attract large Parisian audiences, La Condamine organized his journal around highly contentious and fashionable issues. Did El Dorado, the mythical city of gold in the Amazon basin, and Amazons, really exist? Could the Amerindian poison curare retain its potent paralyzing power long enough to be transported and used in European wars? Was there a connection between the Amazon and Orinoco rivers, and was transcontinental navigation possible?

La Condamine cast his journal as an attack on the conclusions reached by the Spaniard Joseph Gumilla (d. 1750), a Jesuit charged with the missions of the Orinoco, who had published a natural and civil history of the region in Madrid in 1741. Gumilla denied that there was a connection between the Amazon and the Orinoco, but said that El Dorado did, indeed, exist.[46] La Condamine dismissed Gumilla's views as those of a traveler who was both too skeptical and too credulous. The Spanish Jesuit had, on the one hand, chosen to dismiss substantial evidence by reputable eyewitnesses proving the connection of the two rivers. On the other hand, he had given too much credit to the testimony of a handful of Amerindians about the existence of El Dorado. La Condamine refused, moreover, to believe Gumilla's account of a snake that could attract large animals with its breath and then eat them, commenting, "I would still be doubtful even if I thought I had seen it."[47]

La Condamine typified the philosophical traveler who was aware of the inadequacies of human perception and hence doubted the bare testimony of the senses. To illustrate this, the opening page of the *Relation abrégée* shows a map of the Amazon basin drawn in dotted lines by the reputable Jesuit Samuel Fritz (1654–1724?), without the help of telescopes and pendulums, overlapped by an accurate and reliable map drawn by La Condamine himself (Fig. 1.4).

Despite his criticisms of Gumilla, La Condamine willingly embraced the reports of Amerindians when it came to the Amazons. Inasmuch as the natives who claimed to have seen these female warriors spoke mutually unintelligible languages, and thus could have not have communicated to collude in the deception of European travelers, La Condamine chose to believe reports of them. He thought that the ultimate test for the existence of Amazons was not the deceptive testimony of the senses but logic. Amerindians treated their wives so badly, he argued, that communities of runaway women made perfect sense. If runaway slaves could form maroon societies, indigenous women, who were even more exploited than African slaves, might well have created female communities.[48]

De Pauw, who regarded La Condamine as one of the few reliable witnesses to have penetrated the Spanish American empire, derived his dismal view of native Americans largely from the French academician's journal, in which La Condamine claimed that all Amerindians were insensitive and stupid by nature.[49] Yet de Pauw proved merciless when it came to La Condamine's belief in Amazons. According to de Pauw, communities of females living in aristocratic republics, hijacking males once a year to inseminate them, and killing their male children did not make much sense. It was true, de Pauw conceded, that there were females capable of practicing infanticide, but these were isolated cases. Communities of mothers killing their offspring went against human nature, for nature had made mothers nurturing. The alleged Amazons could not be both mothers and warriors. Finally, to clinch his critique of La Condamine, de Pauw argued that females could be monarchs but were incapable of ruling republics, where power was administered by many.[50] De Pauw also chastised La Condamine for believing Amerindian oral testimonies. After all people liked to believe in things that were clearly unreal, such as vampires and demons. "Peoples all over the world," de Pauw reminded La Condamine, "are the same; they are infants incapable of seeing and reporting." "A philosopher," he concluded, "should [therefore] not stop to consider their testimonies any more than he believes the deposition of an imbecile."[51]

This elaborate philosophical analysis of sources led de Pauw to deconstruct early Spanish accounts of the Amerindian empires. According to him, the only source on the history of the Incas worth addressing was Garcilaso's. Garcilaso had maintained that the Incas kept their records in quipus, knotted strings, not alphabetical writing. He had also argued that the great legislator Manco Capac had turned the savages of Cuzco into civilized agriculturists, and that the eleven rulers who followed Manco Capac had all been sage and prudent, spreading civilization and a humane solar religion all over the Tawantinsuyu as the empire expanded through gentle conquest. Garcilaso, finally, had argued that the Incas had palaces, cities, universities, and astronomical observatories, as well as pious and prudent laws. De Pauw read Garcilaso carefully and attacked most of the latter's premises. Although he regarded Garcilaso as an ignorant chauvinist, he focused on Garcilaso's arguments, not his motivations.[52]

Authors had long subjected Garcilaso's account to the test of internal logical consistency. The anonymous editor of the 1744 French edition of Garcilaso's history of the Incas, for example, found fault with his method and rearranged the entire structure of the text, turning Garcilaso's narrative into an encyclopedia, with entries on the dynastic genealogies, astronomy, agriculture, and religion of the Incas. As the editor reorganized the text, he spotted contradictions. According to Garcilaso, astronomy had matured in Peru under the third Inca ruler. The editor considered this statement ludicrous, because more than three generations were clearly needed for a nation to develop a science as complex as astronomy. The editor could not tell whether Garcilaso was lying or whether the Incas were in fact older than had traditionally been assumed.[53] Antonio de Ulloa also spotted contradictions in Garcilaso's narrative. Garcilaso's account of the transition of the Incas from savagery to civilization under Manco Capac was suspect, Ulloa thought, because no one could have transformed a society so swiftly. Instead of dismissing Garcilaso's history of the Incas entirely, however, Ulloa concluded that the pre-Inca polities could not have been the bands of savages that Garcilaso had led readers to believe they were.[54] Rather than merely pointing out contradictions in isolated passages, however, de Pauw dismissed Garcilaso entirely.

Laws existed only when they were written down and codified, de Pauw ar-

FIGURE 1.4. Map highlighting the need for instrumentation, from Charles-Marie de La Condamine, *Relation abregée d'un voyage fait dans l'interieur de l'Amérique méridionale* (Paris, 1745). The Jesuit Samuel Fritz drew the map in dotted lines, said to be inaccurate, without the help of telescopes and time-keeping devices. La Condamine's version is in solid lines and allegedly more accurate. Courtesy of the John Carter Brown Library, Brown University, Providence, R.I.

gued, so it was inherently contradictory to contend that the Incas had enjoyed wise laws when they lacked writing. Unwritten rules were not laws, because they changed according to the whim of the times and the imagination of tyrants. There were other serious logical flaws in Garcilaso's narrative too. The claim that one man, Manco Capac, had single-handedly transformed highland savages into civilized creatures in one generation was patently absurd. The Jesuit missions in Paraguay, which had most recently succeeded in transforming savages into settled, civilized agriculturists, had taken no less than fifty years to do so; moreover, they had used harsh policies to prevent the natives from escaping. Societies did not evolve by leaps, but, like nature, were organized on the principle of plenitude, moving in a sequence of stages — evenly, harmoniously, and slowly. Garcilaso's chronology of the Incas was absurd. He claimed that forty years after the death of Manco Capac, the new ruler had built astronomical observatories in Cuzco to determine solstices and equinoxes, but to evolve from a state of savagery to sophisticated astronomical knowledge required more than forty years. Finally, based on his principle of the harmoniously integrated evolution of social institutions, de Pauw insisted that the Incas could not have been an advanced agricultural society without at the same time having iron, money, and writing — all technologies they had lacked.

De Pauw zeroed in on other inconsistencies of Garcilaso's account as well. For example, Garcilaso had presented Inca rulers as patriarchal yet prudent, preoccupied with the welfare of the majority. But how could rulers have been prudent and gentle when the Incas had never developed institutions to balance and check the power of their monarchs? A fair, gentle patriarch was a contradiction in terms. So, too, was the idea that the Incas had fought just wars of conquest. Moreover, even if one conceded that the Incas had in fact been fair, prudent, and gentle, what were the chances, de Pauw ironically asked, of getting twelve such rulers in a row? De Pauw applied the same unrelenting critical techniques to tear apart all Spanish versions of the history of Mexico. Curiously enough, however, these very techniques led de Pauw to conclude that the indigenous Mexican societies were older than Spanish historians had led their readers to believe.[55]

De Pauw's *Recherches* triggered a groundswell of opposition by scholars operating under more traditional critical paradigms. The Benedictine Antoine-Joseph Pernety (1716–1801), who like de Pauw was a courtier of Frederick the Great's, responded first in 1770. Pernety assembled evidence by reliable eighteenth-century philosophical travelers who demonstrated that the climate of the Americas was temperate and benign, not cold and wet as de Pauw maintained. Pernety included the testimony of Feuillée, Frézier, and La Condamine, as well as that of British travelers, on the grounds that unlike Spaniards, they came from nations "that were not used to exaggerating [*flatter*] and lying in their reports."[56] De Pauw responded immediately, insisting that his book was not about the present state of the New World, but about its condition when the first Europeans arrived. Particularly in North America, colonists had cleared forests, drained swamps, and cultivated the land, so the territories philosophical travelers visited were no longer the places the first Europeans had described.[57] Pernety responded with a two-volume compilation of excerpts by sixteenth-century witnesses, most of whom were Spaniards. He thus simply fell back on Renaissance critical principles that privileged the authority of witnesses.[58]

In *De l'Amérique et des américains, ou Observations curieuses de philosophe La Douceur, qui a parcouru cet hemisphere pendant la derniere guerre, en faisant le noble metier de tuer des hommes sans les manger* (1771), Zacharie de Pazzi de Bonneville (ca. 1710–ca. 1780) (or Pierre Poivre, Pernety, or some other writer) challenged a key element of de Pauw's theory — namely, the idea that societies did not make leaps in their progress but evolved, predictably, slowly, and harmoniously. Quite the contrary, the "philosophe La Douceur" asserted, progress was not the result of slow transformation but of chance, serendipitous technological innovation and cross-cultural encounters. Past accounts of indigenous New World societies might well therefore be reliable.[59] Personal experience, not authority, was the ultimate basis for belief, and as one who had spent nine years traveling in the New World, the writer dismissed de Pauw as an armchair philosopher, unqualified to speak on American matters. Unlike the writer, La Condamine, whose testimony de Pauw had used to characterize the Amerindians as inherently stupid, had visited only a tiny area of the Spanish American empire, and his generalizations were untrustworthy. "As for the rest," the writer argued in a passage intended to ridicule de Pauw's reliance on the testimony of philosophical travelers over that of sailors and merchants, "if all the geometricians and academicians of Europe say black when I see white, I just do not believe them."[60]

In insisting that the credibility of testimony depended solely on its being that of a witness, "La Douceur" misunderstood de Pauw's new art of reading. De Pauw was in any case not someone to be easily discouraged by criticism, and in 1774 he published *Recherches philosophiques sur les Egyptiens et les Chinois*, in which he sharpened his critical techniques of internal reading, this time deploying them against classical Greek sources on ancient Egypt and Jesuit and Chinese testimonies on China. Again, de Pauw worked on the assumption that the reports of these witnesses "had never been examined with the care they merited," and that most witnesses were unreliable because they had "spirits easily given to the marvelous."[61]

The result of de Pauw's new exercise of internal criticism was very damaging to the image of the virtuous Chinese so widely accepted in Europe. De Pauw's treatise originated in an attempt to discredit the great eighteenth-century orientalist Joseph de Guignes (1721–1800), who had argued in 1759 that China was a colony of ancient Egypt. For proof, Guignes showed that Chinese ideograms were remarkably similar to Phoenician script (which in turn, he thought, derived from Egyptian hieroglyphs).[62] Unimpressed by Guignes's philological expertise, de Pauw set out to demonstrate the distinct and separate histories of the Egyptians and the Chinese. Describing the differences in diet, styles of painting, architecture, sciences, and political and religious institutions between the two nations, he contrasted the medical wisdom, religious piety, political balance, and good taste of the ancient Egyptians with the poor diet, despotism, lack of astronomical knowledge, absurd moral philosophy, and shallow aesthetics of the Chinese. China was a nation where eunuchs ruled, infanticide and torture were endemic, and famines and plagues occurred frequently. Not only was China a desert, de Pauw contended, because the population had abandoned the countryside to live in coastal cities (giving foreigners the false impression of populousness), but slavery, polygamy, and female servitude were encouraged there. Finally, China was a land of ignorant, intolerant monks and of courtiers utterly dependent on Europe for astronomical and calendrical expertise.[63]

This drew a wave of angry responses from French Sinophiles. Jesuits, Physiocrats (who thought of China as an ideal agricultural state led by enlightened absolute monarchs), and Voltaire (who found in Chinese moral philosophy an ally in his battle to institute a secular moral philosophy) all lashed out angrily at de Pauw.[64] One author in particular sought to challenge de Pauw's dismissal of Greek, European, and Chinese sources. Jean-Benoît Schérer (1741–1824), a German diplomat at the court of Saint Petersburg, called de Pauw to task for being unwilling to consider "at least the faint traces of truth [vraisemblance] found dispersed in the writings of antiquity," particularly those of Philostratus, Strabo, Pliny, Plutarch, and Herodotus. More problematic was the fact that de Pauw had dismissed as fiction reports on China by such Jesuit luminaries as Antoine Gaubil (1689–1759) and as fabulous the testimony of prestigious authors of the likes of the abbé Noël-Antoine Pluche (1688–1761), Etienne Fourmont (1683–1745), and Thomas Shaw (1694–1751).[65] Falling back on the humanist privileging of witnesses,

Schérer argued that it was impossible that "all these savants could have col-luded to give the public only fables on China" and even more unlikely that they "could have been so prejudiced and lacking in judgment not to distin-guish the truth from the false."[66]

It is not clear who was the victor in the court of enlightened opinion, but de Pauw's *Recherches* on the Chinese and Egyptians came to enjoy great pop-ularity, particularly in Germany.[67] In 1776, de Pauw was invited to write the article "America" for the supplement to the *Encyclopédie*, in which he found space, once again, to vent his passionate critique of the power of the untrained and undomesticated senses ever to comprehend the world.[68] This is not the place to examine the impact of de Pauw's critical techniques on the Enlightenment. Suffice it to say that they carried the day, at least in north-western Europe. I have already mentioned Adam Smith's critique of Spanish sources following de Pauw's publication, and an even more relevant example for the purposes of this chapter is the abbé Raynal's compendium of travelers' stories, *Histoire philosophique des deux Indes*, a bestseller in late-eighteenth-century France, which played a significant role in articulating political dis-content on the eve of the Revolution.

Scholars have correctly read Raynal's *Histoire philosophique* (particularly the last two editions) as having been written collectively by a *société de gens de lettres* that counted Diderot among its most significant members. It has like-wise correctly been argued that this collective *Histoire philosophique* sought to offer a new colonial ideology and a powerful republican critique of the ancien régime.[69] It is, however, a modest, derivative work. From the beginning of his career as a provincial youth finding his bearings in Paris, Raynal had become closely acquainted with the genre of travelers' tales. Paradoxically, he replaced the abbé La Porte as the parish priest of Saint-Sulpice when the latter left to become one of the leading editors of travel compilations in Europe. More-over, from 1747 to 1752, as a literary correspondent of Duchess Luise Dorothea of Saxe-Gotha, Raynal penned numerous critical reviews of contemporary travel compendiums.[70] He finally resolved his dissatisfaction with all available compilations by writing his own *Histoire philosophique*. In it, Raynal drew on travel reports to chronicle the European expansion to the East and West Indies and to describe the transformation of Europe and its colonial societies into a global commercial community.[71] Raynal's *Histoire philosophique* has clear precedents in Harris's *Navigantium* and Brosses's *Histoire des navigations*, however, both texts that had already set out to prove the civilizing and inte-grative role of commerce and trade.

What is of interest here it that Raynal's *Histoire philosophique* changed substantially as it went through three different editions. It is clear that many of the changes were owed largely to the assimilation of de Pauw's critical insights. In the first edition of 1770, Raynal assumed a critical tone that would have delighted de Pauw. "Facts like plants," Raynal argued, "suffer alterations as they get farther from their original source. Truth mutates into error as the distance of time and place help hide the causes [of events]. As lies are popularized, they begin to enjoy an unprescribed right, based on the credulity of the ignorant and the silence of the savants, for the former don't dare to doubt, whereas the latter don't dare to dispute."[72] Not only did Raynal share de Pauw's vague dissatisfaction with "false opinions," but he also thought that of all places on earth, the New World was the least known. Echoing ideas that appear to have been widely shared by savants of the time, Raynal maintained that the public should not expect to find in the writings of "barbarous soldiers, greedy merchants, and missionaries" an accurate description of America. According to Raynal, these travelers had clearly proven unable "to grasp accurately and philosophically this [new] half of the universe." It was the task of the philosophical compiler to glean the seeds of truth buried in the reports of travelers in order "to see America at last as nature made it."[73] But for all these claims, in the first 1770 edition, Raynal did not call into question the authority of Spanish sources.

In books 6 and 7 of the 1770 edition, Raynal tackled Mexico and Peru. In book 6, he expressed high esteem for the Mexica, precisely because he chose to believe the Spanish accounts, but he identified a tension in the Spanish sources. According to the sources, the Mexica had lacked technologies such as writing, iron tools, and beasts of burden; however, these same sources claimed that the Aztecs had been able to build majestic cities, palaces, and temples. De Pauw would have immediately tossed out these reports as self-contradictory and unreliable. Raynal, however, thought differently and concluded that the Mexica were a nation of unparalleled genius, capable of amazing architectural feats with very limited resources.[74]

Raynal maintained the same exaggerated admiration for Amerindian civilizations in book 7, devoted to Peru and to the Incas. Manco Capac, the Inca ruler who had civilized the Peruvians, was one of the greatest legislators in human history, Raynal argued, surpassed only by Confucius, who had made the Chinese virtuous without recourse to superstitious religious cults.[75] Swallowing Garcilaso whole, Raynal portrayed Inca society as one of the most humane polities in the historical record.[76]

In 1774, however, this view of the Aztecs and Incas was drastically modified in the second edition of Raynal's *Histoire philosophique*, in which he embraced de Pauw's dismissal of Spanish sources. The inconsistencies in Spanish sources that had led Raynal to hail the unexampled creativity of the Mexica in 1770 now became the basis for his skepticism. Reports of majestic temples and cities in the absence of iron tools, writing, and domesticated beasts of burden, Raynal argued, echoing de Pauw, could only be the product of the unphilosophical, undisciplined perceptions of Spanish authors.[77]

In his treatment of the Incas in the second edition, Raynal introduced a curious division between Spanish accounts of the Inca polity and descriptions of Inca material culture. Spanish descriptions of Inca roads, aqueducts, fortifications, palaces, temples, and cities were clearly the products of a feverish imagination. They contradicted contemporary evidence by learned witnesses such as La Condamine, Frézier, Ulloa, and others who had not found sufficient extant material evidence.[78] Curiously enough, however, Raynal maintained that Spanish sources were reliable when it came to descriptions of the Inca polity. According to Spanish accounts, the Incas had had no concept of private property; land was assigned to individual families to tend, but never to sell, transfer, or dispose of at will; and under this system, Inca agriculture had prospered. The absence of private property, Raynal thought, as a typical political economist, was a recipe for poverty and arrested development, not agrarian prosperity. There was another inconsistency in the Spanish sources as well. The sources, particularly Garcilaso, painted the Inca rulers as prudent, gentle patriarchs, always caring for the welfare of the majority. Yet they failed to describe any institutions designed to check and balance the power of these absolute monarchs. De Pauw had already identified this incoherence and had dismissed the Spanish accounts altogether. Raynal read more deeply in the sources, however, and found in them a solution to the contradictions. Inca agricultural prosperity in the absence of private property and Inca gentle patriarchalism in the absence of balancing institutions were possible because state revenues had come from lands allotted to the Inca, not from personal tribute. In the Inca polity as sketched by Spanish sources, the monarch was forced to treat laborers well so that they would work his land. Labor tribute also meant that revenue was not elastic, putting a limit on the "orientalization" and corruption of the court, and thus on Inca tyranny.[79] Having used Spanish sources to reconstruct this complicated system of indirect balances, Raynal concluded that the sources were trustworthy because the Spaniards were simply too ignorant to have invented such a complex system. "According to several philosophers," Raynal maintained, "these descriptions [of the Incas] are the product of the naturally exalted imagination of a few Spaniards; however, how many brigands among the destroyers of the bright area of the New World (*cette partie brillante du nouveau monde*) were enlightened enough to have invented a fable so well designed?" Imaginations like those of the Spaniards could not have invented so philosophical a political utopia.[80] The trope that the very ignorance of Spanish observers ensured the limited reliability of Spanish sources lingered on. It became a key critical principle in William Robertson's *History of America*.

The Critique of Classical Analogies in the Historiography of the New World

In 1777, William Robertson, rector of the University of Edinburgh and head of the Scottish Presbyterian Church, published his *History of America*. Robertson had long been preoccupied with explaining the causes of European commercial expansion and to that end wrote histories of Scotland (1759) and of Charles V (1769). In his *History of America*, working in the shadow of de Pauw and Raynal, he sought to explore Europe's expansion to the New World. As a humanist historian, Robertson was an heir of Cicero and aimed at moving his audience to act by masterful rhetoric. His *History of America* included lengthy accounts of Columbus's voyages of discovery and of the conquests of Mexico and Peru by Cortés and Pizarro that were lifted, David Brading has argued, from the writings of the Spanish royal chronicler of the Indies, Antonio de Herrera y Tordesillas (d. 1625).[81]

Robertson was also an antiquarian who enjoyed collecting and studying manuscripts and rare books and weighing the credibility of sources. Unlike de Pauw and Raynal, however, he did not seek to offer a thoroughgoing analysis of travelers' accounts of the New World. Rather, Robertson's history seems concerned with rejecting the promiscuous use of classical analogies that in the past had characterized the study of precolonial Amerindian polities. The guiding critical principle behind his work was, therefore, to prove that witnesses who did not understand the rules of social evolution drew false analogies that led to profound distortions of the past.

The use of classical analogies to interpret ancient Amerindian polities pervaded all Spanish sixteenth- and seventeenth-century historiography. Bartolomé de las Casas (1474–1566) in *Apologética historia sumaria* (before 1559) wrote a defense of Amerindian rights by casting Amerindian polities as classical societies in religion, economics, and politics. By the same token, in *Comentarios reales de los Incas* (1609), Garcilaso presented the Inca empire as the New World's much-improved version of imperial Rome: Rome and the

Incas had paved the way for the spread of Christianity. Finally, in 1684, in his influential *Historia de la conquista de Mexico*, Antonio de Solís (1610–1686) introduced Cortés as a modern Alexander, with the Aztecs as virtuous Persians.

As interest grew in classical religious phenomena as a manifestation of a primitive mentality, the use of classical analogies to interpret Amerindian societies became even more entrenched. Frank Manuel has shown that, since the mid seventeenth century, European scholars had begun to read ancient Greek and Roman myths, not as sophisticated moral, political, or philosophical allegories, but as the garbled products of fear and ignorance. In the process, scholars and antiquarians became deeply interested in studying contemporary savages as forms of frozen classical polities.[82] Authors assumed that the Amerindians had been mysteriously arrested in stages of progress comparable to those of ancient Mediterranean societies.[83] *La vie et les moeurs des sauvages américains comparée aux moeurs des premier tems* (1724–32) by Joseph François Lafitau (1670?–1740?), a Jesuit who spent many years as a missionary in French North America, typifies this tradition. Combining classics and American ethnography in fruitful cross-fertilization, Lafitau sought to prove that, like the ancient Romans and Greeks, contemporary Hurons and Iroquois thought symbolically, and that they had similar creeds and rituals.[84]

Over the course of the eighteenth century, however, some authors became hostile to the use of such comparisons. De Pauw was one of these. Arguing that Garcilaso had misleadingly portrayed Inca society as being of the Roman type, he dismissed the Peruvian's claims, and he was unimpressed by Lafitau's scholarship too.[85] Among those who most forcefully rejected the use of classical analogies was William Robertson, who attributed the origins of the perceptual distortions of European reporters of the New World to the promiscuous use of classical similes. Like de Pauw and Raynal, Robertson started from the assumption that even witnesses "to whose testimony great respect is due" should not be believed if they described things that went against common sense. After subjecting them to the forms of internal criticism that de Pauw had pioneered, Robertson dismissed Spanish accounts of the populousness of precolonial America.[86] He assumed that the testimonies of "vulgar travelers, of sailors, traders, buccaneers, and missionaries," offered, by and large, only "superficial remarks." It was the duty of the critic, Robertson argued, "[to] pause, and, comparing detached facts, endeavor to discover" what witnesses really would have seen had their senses and minds been duly trained.[87] To see objects "as they really are," it was not enough to overcome "vulgar prejudices" and be "possessed of no less impartiality than discernment." Even more important, the observer should not be "carried away" by appearances.[88]

Ever since Sir Francis Bacon had argued that names, the idols of the marketplace, shaped the way people perceived reality, scholars began to pay attention to how misnomers were responsible for creating individual or collective self-delusion.[89] Seeking to offer a new ideological blueprint for French colonial expansion, Brosses called attention in *Du culte des dieux fétiches* (1760) to the power that names had in determining scholars' perceptions of both "savages" and the Egyptian past: "Among savages the names of 'God or Spirit' do not signify what they mean among us. In reasoning about their [primitive] manner of thinking, we must . . . be careful not to attribute to them our ideas because they are at present attached to the same words which the savages used, and not to impute to them our principles and our reasoning."[90] Neither Egyptian hieroglyphs nor Guinea fetishes, Brosses argued, represented sophisticated knowledge stored in arcane animal symbols. Rather, they were manifestations of primitive animal worship. By using the name "God" to describe primitive creeds, scholars had distorted the true nature of the contemporary African and ancient Egyptian religions. In 1767, Adam Ferguson (1723–1816), who along with Robertson was a leading member of the Scottish Enlightenment, criticized historians who used words such as "royal" and "noble" to describe medieval rulers. Modern audiences read into such terms their own experience, namely, one in which commoners and nobles did not mingle. But in the Middle Ages, rulers helped out their maids and did not shy away from manual labor. Employing contemporary social categories to describe past rulers only served to confuse, rather than illuminate, the past.[91]

Inspired by the Baconian critique of the perceptual delusion caused by the idols of the marketplace, Robertson claimed that traditional reporters had used "names and phrases appropriated to the institutions and refinements of polished life" to refer to what in fact were American savages.[92] On the basis of classical analogies, unphilosophical observers in America had called petty rulers "emperors"; hamlets, "palaces"; and a few hangers-on, "courts." According to Roberston, of all witnesses, Spaniards, in particular, who were "far from possessing the qualities requisite for observing the striking spectacle presented to their view," had applied misleading "standards of excellence" to judge other societies.[93] "[E]ngrossed by the doctrines of their own religion, and habituated to its institutions," Catholic friars had set out to discover sublime mysteries and complex religious institutions that "resembled those objects of their veneration" among primitives. "In such unintelligent and credulous guides," Robertson concluded, "we can place little confidence."[94]

To understand Robertson's rejection of the usage of classical and Christian analogies to interpret Amerindian societies, we need to turn briefly to the theoretical principles that organized his historiography. Like Raynal, Robertson was, in J. G. A. Pocock's words, a "commercial humanist," that is, a scholar who sought to prove that the rise of commerce did not threaten civic virtues.[95] In the introductory volume to his *History of the Reign of the Emperor Charles V* (1769), Robertson offered an extraordinary sociological analysis of the decline of Rome and the rise of the modern European states. Unlike traditional civic humanists, who interpreted the decline of Rome as the result of the triumph of effeminate oriental luxury over virile republican virtues, Robertson argued that Rome collapsed for lack of appropriate political checks and balances. Lack of parliaments, not excessive commerce, caused nations to decline. Progress, according to Robertson, resulted from the taming of the violent passions and the growth of needs and desires among self-interested individuals. The Crusades, new discoveries, the rise of cities, and the growth of courts of law had caused the new European nations unintentionally to develop commerce and internal and external balances of power. With the development of modes of production from hunting to herding to agriculture to commerce, individual needs and desires multiplied, and, with them, sociability. As the division of labor increased, so too did mutual dependency, which in turn caused people to refine their social skills and to put their reason to work in the pursuit of their own self-interest. In the course of creating commercial societies, violent passions gave way to politeness and prudence.[96]

This view of history encouraged Robertson to see the world as a living museum in which different peoples occupied different levels in a great tableau of emotional and economic development. It became a truism at Robertson's time that the European expansion of the previous two centuries had made possible access to types of human experience never before catalogued. According to Edmund Burke, Robertson's friend, the earth was "[a] great map of mankind unrolled at once [in which] no state of gradation of barbarism, and no mode of refinement is [missing]."[97] In Burke's eyes, Robertson's genius lay in his creative use of this vast new museum to go beyond the history of progress of the ancients. Robertson thought that America held the keys to understanding the earliest stages of the mind, stages with which ancient writers had never been familiar. America was a place where "man appears under the rudest form in which we can conceive him to subsist," and therefore a place where one could "examine the sentiments and actions of human beings in the infancy of social life."[98] Unphilosophical observers had failed to realize that the crucial distinction between America and the ancient world was that they belonged to different stages of social development and therefore could not be compared. Misleading perceptions originated in the effort to comprehend Amerindians through the eyes of those trained to see the classical world.

Such criticism of naïve observers, particularly Spaniards, did not cause Robertson to dismiss all early European reports of the New World. Like Raynal, Robertson sought to read deeper into the accounts to identify some kernel of truth. Conversant with a long historiographical critical tradition that maintained that even ancient fables should not be dismissed, but rather interpreted as veiled references to past historical realities, Robertson thought that the responsibility of the scholar consisted in stripping fables of their credulous accretions to reconstruct the history of ancient peoples and migrations.[99] He was, to be sure, unwilling to give "a hasty assent, on the slightest evidence, to whatever has the appearance of being strange and marvelous." Yet he was also cautious about dismissing anything. It would presumptuous, he maintained, "to set bounds to [nature's] fertility and reject indiscriminately every relation that does not perfectly accord with our limited observations and experience."[100] This ambivalence led him to argue that writers like de Pauw had taken the criticism of Spanish sources too far. "The warm imagination of the Spanish writers [to be sure] had added some embellishment to their descriptions," he maintained, "[but this cannot] justify the decisive and peremptory tone with which several authors pronounce all [their] accounts to be the fictions of men who wished to deceive, or who were delighted in the marvelous."[101]

Like Raynal, Robertson contended that some Spanish descriptions of Amerindian societies must be accurate because they depicted institutions the reporters did not know from experience in Europe and could not have invented. Spanish witnesses, for example, had offered descriptions of Aztec institutions such as postal service, city regulations, and some forms of administration of justice that were unknown to sixteenth-century Europeans. "Who among the destroyers of this great empire," Robertson asked rhetorically, "was so enlightened by science, or so attentive to the progress and operations of men in social life, as to frame a fictitious system of policy, so well combined and so consistent, as that which they delineate in their accounts of the Mexican government?" It was hard to believe "that the illiterate conquerors of the New World should have formed, in any one instance, a conception of customs and laws beyond the standard of improvement of their own age and country."[102] The emphasis on Spanish ignorance forced Robertson, as it had Raynal before him, to acknowledge that some of these sources might in fact be telling the truth.

The Italian political economist Gian Rinaldo Carli (1720–1795) also employed the trope of Spanish ignorance to validate some early European accounts of the New World. In 1780, in his *Lettere americane*, Carli set out to demonstrate that the long-submerged continent of Atlantis had once connected the New and Old Worlds. This land bridge had apparently allowed for earlier migrations, but Atlantis had sunk before ironworking, metal currency, and writing ever developed in the Old World, explaining why the Amerindians did not have these. Although his history of America was written in the same conjectural and philosophical key as those of Buffon, de Pauw, Raynal, and Robertson, Carli reached very different conclusions regarding the Incas. Although too much of a modern not to be critical of early European accounts of the New World, he struggled to follow Garcilaso in depicting Inca society as a virtuous polity of the classical type. Like Robertson and Raynal before him, he thus accorded credibility to Spanish sources to support his view of the Incas, partly on the grounds that Spanish observers were too ignorant to have invented political utopias on their own. Some of these sources were trustworthy because they were "public," Carli argued — that is, they had been written for powerful patrons who could have punished the writers had they known they were being lied to.[103] Other sources were reliable because they contained descriptions of indigenous polities that were too complex to be fraudulent. None of the early Spanish observers, including the Jesuit José de Acosta (1539–ca. 1600), whom Robertson praised as a philosopher, had sought to understand the causes of the phenomena they observed, Carli thought. Since these observers described social institutions they could not have invented, their reports were of necessity trustworthy.[104]

The ambivalence of Robertson and Carli about the value of Spanish sources was typical of the new historiography on the New World that emerged in the wake of de Pauw's *Recherches* and Raynal's *Histoire philosophique*. A new art of reading, which in order to apportion credit privileged the logical consistency of testimonies, demonstrated the contradictions in most Spanish histories of America and its peoples. Unphilosophical Spaniards had been easily deceived by superficial resemblances between the new societies they encountered and their own. For example, they had drawn promiscuously on classical analogies, representing the societies of the Inca and Mexica as virtuous polities of the Roman type. Superstitious friars had added additional layers of confusion when they read the primitive religions of "savages" as diabolically distorted versions of Christianity. Amid such confusion, however, Spaniards had caught glimpses of reality. The very ignorance of the observers guaranteed the credibility of portions of their testimonies.

Conjectural and Philosophical Histories of America

But once all traditional sources had been questioned, how should one write the history of America and its peoples? Those authors who questioned the credibility of early European accounts of the New World drew on new types of evidence and articulated bold new historical narratives.

The search for alternative forms of historical evidence to substitute for untrustworthy literary sources began in earnest in the second half of the seventeenth century. Biblical criticism and the revival of skepticism cast doubt on the value of *all* ancient literary sources. In 1674, in his *Histoire critique du Vieux Testament*, Richard Simon (1638–1712) made it painfully clear that the Pentateuch, traditionally attributed to Moses, had in fact been the work of many ages and scribes. François La Mothe le Vayer's *De peu de certitude qu'il y a dans l'histoire* (1668), Charles de Saint-Evremond's *Réflexions sur les divers génies du peuple romain* (1684), and Pierre Bayle's *Dictionnaire historique et critique* (1697) showed that the ideal of truth was unattainable in history that used literary sources. Not only were ancient sources biased, contradictory, and often self-consciously deceiving, these authors argued, but biased, partisan, and misleading writers also wrote contemporary accounts. Reaction in the scholarly community to the new criticism of literary sources was forthcoming. Jean Le Clerc's *Ars critica* (1697) and Jacobus Perizonius's *Oratio de fide historiarium contra Pyrrhonismum historicum* (1702) offered new critical arts of reading that encouraged scholars to check and compare sources to ascertain the reliability of reports and to reject reports that were not intrinsically credible.

There were also those who set out to look for forms of evidence distinct from traditional literary sources. Scholars such Jacob Spon (1647–1685), Luc d'Achery (1609–1685), Jean Mabillon (1632–1707), and Bernard de Montfaucon (1655–1741) developed new disciplines and arts of reading evidence from ruins, coins, public documents (charters), and inscriptions.[105] Led by Nicolas Fréret (1688–1749), euhemerists of a new type at the Académie des inscriptions et belles-lettres in Paris argued that myths could be stripped of their fabulous accretions to yield important and reliable information about the obscure past. Some scholars even began to call on "nature." In

1755, for example, Rousseau suggested that his history of the origins of civil society, which conflicted with that in the Bible, was more credible. Although rhetorically he conceded that his account should "not to be taken for historical truths," Rousseau worked on the assumption that "the Books of your Fellow-men" lied consistently about the past, whereas "nature never lied."[106] Accordingly, Rousseau drew most of the evidence for his interpretation of the past from natural history, namely, animal behavior and ethnography. This kind of appeal to "nature" proved central for those who having called the value of Spanish accounts into question had to rewrite the history of the New World from scratch.

In exchange for the unreliable, "hallucinated" reports of Spaniards, de Pauw offered an interpretation of the history of America and its peoples that drew on facts he gleaned from the natural history of the continent upon the European arrival.[107] After scouring the literature, de Pauw found evidence that confirmed that America had suffered a traumatic geological catastrophe. Fossil bones of gigantic animals (which he thought were the first to die in deluges); large bodies of water, both lakes and rivers; earthquakes and active volcanoes still rocking the earth; seashells strewn over all the low valleys; ores of heavy metals protruding in the surface of the land (which the earth's primitive sedimentation should have buried deep inside it) were some of the evidence.[108] The damp, putrid environment of the New World also clearly accounted for the smaller number and size and monstrous appearance of American quadrupeds (e.g., animals with extra ribs, no tails, or unequal number of toes in the anterior and posterior claws); the degeneration of foreign animals (only pigs had prospered in America, because they lived off refuse and thrived in moist environments); the successful development of "watery" plants from the Old World, such as rice, melons, citrus, and sugarcane; the proliferation of insects and reptiles; the abundance of poisonous plants, whose virtues only the savages knew (botany being *l'unique étude du sauvage*); and the American origin of syphilis (humanity's scourge, for which not even the mineral riches of Brazil and Potosí could begin to compensate Europe).[109] De Pauw concluded that a flood had suddenly transformed a continent of big animals and millenarian civilizations into a land enveloped by miasmas. America's coldness and humidity had in turn emasculated its fauna and peoples. De Pauw presented all natives as *insensible*, or insensitive, yet also effete.

Drawing on an ancient medical tradition that assumed that males were "drier" than females, de Pauw argued that Native American males lacked beards as much as courage, had long hair, were never bald, lived longer

45

(aging was associated with "dryness"), and often even had milk in their breasts.[110] Their humid temperament caused their "genius to be limited, without elevation, without audacity; [they were] of inferior character, naturally inclined to carelessness and inactivity. Their feebleness made them vindictive like females."[111] Female natives, on the other hand, were monsters. Their extra humidity lubricated their uterine muscles, and they thus had painless deliveries. With more milk than any "woman in the universe," female natives nursed their children into adulthood.[112] In a period when the discourse of nervous "sensibility" sought to explain gender differences — portraying women as naturally "excitable" — de Pauw cast Amerindians as lacking in sensibility, that is, as the exact opposite of European females.[113] He apparently saw no contradiction between this claim and his portrayal of the natives as "humid" and thus effete.

This image of the natives as "insensitive" allowed de Pauw to explain why upon their arrival Europeans had found a sparsely populated continent. Buffon and others had argued that thin demographic patterns of settlement indicated that the Amerindians had recently arrived, with no time to become populous. De Pauw, however, thought that the Amerindians were ancient arrivals, millenarian inhabitants of the continent who, as a consequence of the flood that had destroyed the New World, had become incapable of feeling passion and sexual urges.[114] To mate, the females had to use insect bites and rubber rings to swell the penises of their partners.[115] Most of the males were homosexual.[116] When Europeans arrived, the native females became their concubines and allies. "Among the reasons that accelerated the servitude of the New World," de Pauw contended, was that one invariably found native women "more interested in the cause of the Europeans than the Europeans themselves."[117]

According to Antonello Gerbi, de Pauw's bold new conjectural history of America drew its key elements from Buffon.[118] As keeper of the Jardin du Roi and of the king's natural history collections, and a dabbler in experimental philosophy, Buffon became acquainted with fauna, flora, and fossils from all over the world. Beginning in 1749, he began to offer one of several conjectural histories of the earth, which, he said, was gradually becoming colder. Originally, the poles had been like the tropics, with large herbivores, but gradually, as the land became colder and uninhabitable, the animals and flora had migrated toward the equator. If fossils were the evidence that Buffon used to reconstruct the migration of fauna and flora, it was variations of skin color that he used to reconstruct the history of humankind: humans who moved away from the heat became whiter, and those who moved toward warmer areas became darker.[119]

This model worked well for the Old World but failed miserably to explain phenomena in America. Despite the New World's many climates, skin color variations were almost imperceptible. Worse, no blacks seemed to have ever appeared in the American tropics. Buffon solved the problem by claiming that America was a new continent that had recently emerged from the waters. By postulating that the natives were newcomers, he was able to argue that the environment had not yet created racial variations in America. He also maintained that special meteorological mechanisms rendered the American tropics much cooler than those of Africa.[120]

For his conjectural history of the earth to work, Buffon had to solve additional challenges posed by the American continent. To explain why there were no large herbivores in the New World tropics, Buffon drew on an age-old tradition that linked geological catastrophes with organic flaws perpetuated over generations. The humidity of the New World, particularly in South America, had weakened all organic matter and had rendered all quadrupeds small, more homogeneous, insensitive, and effete. Mountain ranges in Central America had kept Old World species (especially large animals, which had constantly migrated and rejuvenated North America) from reaching South America, where animals remained different both from those of the Old World and those of the north.[121] Although Buffon at times played with the idea that the continent's humidity had affected the Amerindians as well, making some of them effete and beardless, by and large, his model excluded humans.[122] De Pauw, however, applied the model of organic degeneration to all American natives.

Buffon's and de Pauw's conjectural reconstructions were part of the larger eighteenth-century trend of explaining the origins of human institutions in light of geological history. In 1766, for example, Nicolas-Antoine Boulanger offered a model to account for the birth of all world religions as the consequence of great primeval geological catastrophes. In a secular version of St. Augustine's account of the biological roots of original sin, Boulanger argued that superstition was the product of a quasi-inherent biological fear produced by the great earthly convulsions of the past.[123] Raynal drew on these views. Beginning in the first edition of his *Histoire philosophique*, Raynal repeated de Pauw's thesis of a separate American deluge followed by universal organic degeneration.[124] He also embraced Boulanger's argument and claimed that since America was still going through frequent earthly convulsions,

Amerindians were more fearful and thus more superstitious than any other people on earth.[125] In the second edition of the *Histoire philosophique*, Raynal deployed de Pauw's attribution of the Amerindians' arrested development to their supposed lack of sexual energy.[126] Robertson was somewhat more cautious and refused to embrace these large systems; however, he agreed that there was something exceptional about the New World: it was colder and wetter than the Old World.[127]

For all his caution, Robertson also sought to reconstruct the history of the New World conjecturally. Like many of his contemporaries, he thought that to recreate the past of the Americas, evidence other than the Spanish literary sources was needed. Robertson, however, did not draw from natural history or medical discourses as did Buffon and de Pauw. He drew from the discipline of political economy for inspiration. As has been noted, he belonged to a larger Scottish movement that attributed the evolution of social and legal institutions to the development of human desires and saw reason as a byproduct of the need to manage selfish interests in an increasingly complex world, where survival demanded growing mutual and collective interdependence. In this connection, Robertson became particularly interested in the lives of Amerindians, whose development he placed at two slightly different stages of socialization: hunter-gatherers and primitive agriculturists.

What is particularly fascinating about the reconstructions of the Amerindians' past put forth by Robertson and other Scottish conjectural historians is that they had trouble fitting the Amerindians into a model that envisaged the slow taming of the passions through four evolutionary stages, hunting, herding, agriculture, and commerce. The evolution of the passions in America seemed not follow this model. The Mexica, for example, "had made the greatest progress in the arts of policy . . . [yet] they were, in several respects, the most ferocious, and the barbarity of some of their customs exceeded even those of the savage state."[128] Robertson's model of the evolution of the passions carried the implicit expectation that a society engaged in trade and commerce, like that of the Aztecs, would not indulge in barbarous customs such as ritual cannibalism. The behavior of the Incas also posed a challenge. As shepherds and primitive agriculturists, the Peruvians might have been expected to be aggressive warriors, but the Incas had not put up much of a fight in face of the Spanish onslaught: a "people so little advanced in refinement, [should not have been] so totally destitute of military enterprise."[129]

Another Scottish conjectural historian, Henry Home, Lord Kames (1696–1782), reflected at length on the social curiosities of the New World. In 1778 in the second edition of his *Sketches of the History of Man*, Kames expressed bewilderment over the peculiar nature of the New World. "America is full of wonders," he concluded. Why, "instead of advancing, like other nations toward maturity of society and government," had most Amerindians continued "to this hour in their original state of hunting and fishing"? Why had America remained scarcely populated, the land for all practical purposes "empty"? Kames noted many other curious social phenomena that also challenged the Scottish model of developmental stages. North Americans were hunter-gatherers but nevertheless "had advanced to some degree of agriculture without passing through the shepherd-state." The more civilized Mexicans and Peruvians had been surrounded by hunters, revealing a gap in the sequence of developmental stages and the incomprehensible rise of two civilizations in almost complete isolation. The Aztecs, who had shown "such a proficiency in the art of war and in the art of peace, [were] with respect to religion . . . no better than savages," challenging the widely held beliefs that economic progress made peoples gentle and that social institutions developed simultaneously. Finally, the hereditary and absolute government of the Incas had been far milder than the elective government of the Aztecs, "in contradiction to political principles."[130] Other human and social phenomena also puzzled Kames, such as why the tropics of America and the Old World had witnessed such distinct evolutionary social developments. Unlike in torrid Africa, where only peoples "little better than savages" lived, the tropics of the New World had produced "highly polished [peoples] in the arts of society and government."[131] One problem in particular exercised Kames's imagination and led him to postulate a theory of racial polygenism. America was a continent of many climates, yet Amerindians were by and large racially homogeneous. It followed, therefore, that separate origins, not climate, were the cause of racial variations.[132] These kinds of philosophical questions were precisely the type that the Spaniards had allegedly failed to pose and that spurred authors of the likes of Buffon, de Pauw, Raynal, and Robertson to write new histories of America and its peoples.

Amerindians as Evidence

Paradoxically, the search for alternatives to traditional literary sources of information led European scholars to assume that Amerindians were "peoples without history." As Europeans grew increasingly skeptical of the Bible and of their own oral and written traditions, they began to look for firmer foundations upon which to build new national and continental historical accounts. As ethnography gradually replaced literary sources as evidence for reconstructing Europe's "obscure" ages, Amerindians came to be perceived as early humans, literally frozen in time.

To respond to the late-seventeenth-century skeptical critique of the credibility of literary sources, many historians abandoned the study of the "obscure" ages altogether, dismissing it as the province of old-fashioned pedants. In *Letters on the Study and Use of History*, Henry St. John, Viscount Bolingbroke (1678–1751), argued in the 1730s that all literary sources, classical texts as well the Bible, were unreliable, full of contradictions, and even absurd. Although Bolingbroke thought that a high degree of probability about events of the past could ultimately be ascertained by collecting and collating sources, he also thought that it did not make sense to seek to reconstruct the "obscure" past, which pedantic etymologists had long sought to describe. "[All] ancient history," he concluded, "never will gain any credit with any reasonable man."[133] In 1741, Charles Mackie, holder of the first chair of history at the University of Edinburgh and Robertson's teacher, also derided the "fondness for high antiquities."[134] Finally, in 1761, David Hume declared that the history of the obscure ages was altogether useless, unless it was limited to the polite reading of Greek and Roman mythology.[135]

Not all scholars heeded the admonitions of Bolingbroke, Mackie, and Hume, however, and new ways of studying European prehistory soon made themselves manifest, drawing on the evidence afforded by the contemporary peoples of the New World. Like Rousseau, the Scottish historian Adam Ferguson urged that the "domestic antiquities of every nation . . . be received with caution," being "for the most part, mere conjectures or the fictions of subsequent ages."[136] Alternative sources were needed, including the study of oral popular traditions, although in Ferguson's opinion these were only capable of revealing the mental spirit of an age, not its history. As for the use of evidence drawn from animals (including the "wild" children found roaming in the forests of Europe throughout the eighteenth century), Ferguson dismissed it as inappropriate and misleading, for unlike the primates that Rousseau privileged, humans had always lived in "troops." Moreover, humans had souls. Facing this dearth of alternative evidence to reconstruct the obscure ages, Ferguson argued that the only reliable evidence left was ethnography. Reports by reliable philosophical travelers on contemporary non-European societies, which had been arrested at older stages of development, were the literary sources scholars had long been looking for to write the history of the obscure ages of Europe. "It is in their present condition [in the customs of the American tribes]," Ferguson argued, "that we are to behold as in a mirror, the features of our own progenitors."[137]

Conjectural historians such as Ferguson regarded the world as a living museum where the evidence needed to reconstruct the obscure history of Europe was displayed. As Brosses put it in a memoir addressed to the Académie des inscriptions in 1766: "The best way to understand what once happened in little known ages is to observe what occurs in modern times in parallel circumstances."[138] The Scott Sir James Mackintosh (1765–1832) argued in 1798 that in the century of the Enlightenment, "many dark periods of history have been explored," precisely because "many hitherto unknown regions of the globe have been visited and described by travelers and navigators not less intelligent than intrepid." For Mackintosh, the relationship between European history and overseas expansion lay in the character of the evidence being unveiled by philosophical travelers: "We can [now] examine almost every variety of character, manners, opinions and feelings and prejudices of mankind into which they can be thrown either by rudeness of barbarism or by the capricious corruption of refinement." This was the material historians could use to reconstruct the past, obscure ages of Europe: "History is now a museum, in which specimens of every variety of human nature may be studied."[139] Amerindians occupied the first "dioramas" in the museum of the living. In the four-stage version of development rigidly espoused by Robertson and Kames, hunting was the primeval stage in a process tending toward increasing division of labor and sociability. Amerindians were either hunter-gatherers (all except the Aztecs and Incas) or very primitive agriculturists (Incas and Aztecs).[140] Only the latter, therefore, had "history," but it was history too recent to bother about. Paradoxically, however, these "peoples without history" constituted reliable grounds upon which to reconstruct the history of Europe's own obscure ages.[141]

The Pursuit of Objectivity

De Pauw always sought to be objective. "I have not paid attention to either my prejudices or conjectures," he says in his *Recherches* on the Americans. "I have relied on facts as my only witnesses; I have deduced causes and principles from nature itself, not from my ideas."[142] Throughout his life, he remained committed to this objectivity. "It should be known," he explains in the opening pages of his *Recherches* on the Egyptians, "that our object is to cite facts alone."[143] In 1787, in *Recherches philosophiques sur les Grecs*, in which he argues that the Athenians single-handedly created classical Greece against the will of bloodthirsty barbarians and unenlightened shepherds such as the Lacedaemonians, Aetolians, Arcadians, and Thessalians, he insists that his work is "coherent and philosophical. [In it] the marvelous has no place and the facts are evaluated rigorously before they are admitted in the order of historical truths."[144] Raynal also made objectivity one of his central methodological concerns. In 1781, in the third and final edition of his *Histoire philosophique*, Raynal claims to have consecrated his life to "consulting the most educated men of all nations. I have interrogated the living and the dead . . . I have weighed their authority; I have contrasted their testimonies; I have clarified the facts." He aspired to an invisible authorial presence: "If my work still finds a few readers in the centuries to come and faced with my aloofness to passions and prejudices, I want them not to know what country I am from, under what government I have lived, what employment I have had, and what religion I have professed."[145]

De Pauw's rhetoric of rigor and restraint and Raynal's rhetoric of angelic detachment were part the same discourse that led many European authors to dismiss the entire corpus of Spanish historiography and rewrite the history of the New World based on alternative forms of evidence. Lorraine Daston and Peter Galison have argued that ideals of objectivity in the eighteenth century were somewhat different from those that characterized the nineteenth century. Whereas in the nineteenth century, authors strove to erase all human traces from the observation and recording of data by mechanizing these procedures, eighteenth-century scholars linked objectivity to the idiosyncratic, quasi-artisanal personal skills of the observers.[146] Be that as it may, the search for objectivity in both centuries was related to efforts to rein in the body, demanding ascetic behavior and forms of self-restraint from observers. Simon Schaffer has shown that in the course of the eighteenth century, the search for objectivity led to protracted debates on the body as an "apparatus." Most authors agreed that the information acquired by the body was untrustworthy. Moreover, the enthusiasm for Mesmerism among the upper classes in Paris in the late eighteenth century, with its attendant episodes of hypnosis and individual and collective psychosomatic cures, made it painfully clear to scholars that not even upper-class testimony could be trusted. They argued that the imagination had complete command, not only over the mechanisms of perception, but over the entire body, and that only those members of the republic of letters able to rationalize away any perceptual evidence and bodily behavior that went against the laws of nature were trustworthy.[147]

The rhetoric of objectivity was also related to broader social and cultural changes in the republic of letters. Cultural historians of the Enlightenment such as Dena Goodman and Dorinda Outram have argued that changes in salon culture and the rise of the "bourgeois public sphere" stimulated developments in the rhetoric of objectivity. As new markets for periodicals and books emerged, the male "critic" appeared, claiming independence from the distorting effect of courtly patronage. Women had long wielded power in and set the agendas of salons, but these same market forces provoked critics to sever ties with salons and *salonnières*, which contributed to linking objectivity with masculinity. The newly liberated critic could thus claim to be sheltered, not only from the pressures of patronage, but from feminine emotions as well.[148]

The various strands of the eighteenth-century rhetoric of objectivity come together in the life and scholarship of William Robertson. Like de Pauw and Raynal, Robertson also aspired to forms of angelic detachment. In a letter to the historian Edward Gibbon, he declared that it was his duty to "deliver his evidence as if upon oath."[149] According to Alex Stewart, his early biographer, Robertson guarded "against the influence of feelings . . . which might in any degree mislead his judgment" and did not "admit facts without due evidence, in all the false colouring, in which passion or prejudice might have disguised them."[150] Robertson was committed to forms of epistemological moderation in historiography because he supported religious toleration.

According to Richard Sher, the Scottish Presbyterian Church, which had long been known for espousing a militant form of Calvinism, underwent a significant reorientation under the aegis of William Robertson between 1750 and 1780. Traditionally closer to the concerns and "enthusiasm" (i.e., intolerance) of the populace than to the goals of university-based professional elites, the Presbyterian clergy were forced to change after a group of "moderates" led by Robertson took control of the Church away from the Popular Party. The Moderates set in motion a series of reforms that encouraged "politeness" and high intellectual standards. Through a tolerant yet conservative environment, the Moderates took control of the University of Edinburgh and promoted a remarkable intellectual awakening among the Scottish clergy.[151] Jeffrey Smitten has argued that central to this transformation was Arminianism, a theology that advocated moderate skepticism and contended that inasmuch as the causes of natural phenomena were ultimately unknown, all metaphysical disputations were superfluous. Toleration was the necessary consequence of such an epistemological stance.[152]

In *The History of Scotland* (1759), Robertson set very high standards of scholarship, digging, collecting, and reading hundreds of manuscripts and primary sources, and always paying attention to the interests behind the sources. "[Scotland has] produced historians of considerable merit," he explained in the preface to the book, "[but] truth was not the sole object of these authors. Blinded by prejudices, and heated by the part they themselves had acted in the scenes they describe, they wrote an apology for a faction, rather than the history of their country."[153] Robertson departed from polemical historiography by deliberately seeking to avoid partisan interpretations of the past. His account of Mary, Queen of Scots, who had traditionally been the subject of heated partisan debates (Puritans representing her as an evil Catholic woman and Jacobites and Tories as a victim of zealot religious reformers), steered clear of controversy. Robertson's history was immediately hailed as an example of impartial, prudent, and moderate scholarship.[154] Horace Walpole (1717–1797) commended him for his objectivity: "On a subject which we are foolish enough to make *party*, you preserve your judgment unbiased."[155] In 1769, in *The History of Charles V*, Robertson again strove to be objective. His moderate evaluation of the Reformation became exemplary. Robertson was "never betrayed into fiery zeal, or intemperate invective," his editor and biographer Alex Stewart wrote. "He estimates, with the most scrupulous regard to justice, the motives of the great actors in those eventful scenes; and adverts, with equal fidelity, to the errors and faults of those who were chiefly instrumental in promoting the Reformation, and those who were most interested in opposing progress."[156] In *The History of America* (1777), Robertson's moderation caused him some trouble. Critics complained that in his effort to please the Spaniards, he had concealed the "enormities" committed by Spain in America.[157] Spaniards, on the other hand, praised his impartiality, and he was elected a member of the Spanish Royal Academy of History.

Clearly, the populace of Edinburgh did not appreciate Robertson's moderation. After he spearheaded an effort to end legal discrimination against Catholics in Scotland, he received numerous death threats, and his house came close to being ransacked and burnt by the mob. The "No-Popery" riots of 1779 marked the end of Robertson's "moderate regime" in the Scottish Presbyterian Church, and in 1780, he retired from ecclesiastical politics and saw control of the Church slip back to the Popular Party.[158] In such a hostile political environment, Robertson could nevertheless afford to be "tolerant" and objective in his historiography, because by and large, his income did not depend on patronage, but on the anonymous forces of the marketplace. As the public bought Robertson's works avidly and as publishers competed for his manuscripts, Robertson became wealthy enough to be the first clergyman in Scotland to afford his own carriage.[159] Robertson's rhetoric of epistemological moderation cannot be severed from the parallel development in Scotland and England of a dynamic public sphere operating through the anonymous market that sheltered authors from the whims of patrons and the contempt of the populace.

New Similes, Same Historiography

In 1810, Alexander von Humboldt published his *Vues des cordillères et monuments de peuples de l'Amérique*. Reviewers of the 1814 English edition greeted the book with harsh criticisms. Humboldt, reviewers agreed, was repetitive and lacked rigor. By the time his *Personal Narrative of Travels to the Equinoctial Regions* appeared in an English translation in 1818, his entire work was judged by a reviewer to be so "jumbled and broken that [it] resembles [like the picture of the New Continent that Humboldt has presented to our notice] truly the elements of the poetic chaos."[160] *Vues* was a treatise organized around learned commentaries on a series of sixty-nine plates of picturesque views of Mexican and Andean scenery and of Amerindian antiquities. Most of the Amerindian plates included material objects and pages of diverse Mesoamerican codices in collections in Mexico and Europe. The reviewers of the *Quarterly Review* and *Monthly Review* assailed Humboldt for failing to understand the principles of internal criticism. According to one, based on erroneous Spanish glosses to Mexica calendrical documents, Humboldt had concluded that the Aztec developed very sophisticated astronomical systems, including knowledge of the causes of eclipses and the ability to determine the true length of the year (365.243 days). The reviewer expressed bewilderment that Humboldt had failed to realize that this astronomical knowledge was not in the documents themselves but in the Spanish glosses. Humboldt had failed to realize, the reviewer maintained, that both the primitive aesthetic conventions in the calendars and the natives' primitive systems of writing directly contradicted their alleged astronomical sophistication. How could readers believe that peoples whose "picture language or such rude representations of the objects of sense . . . the first and rudest efforts to record ideas" were the same peoples whose astronomical systems Humboldt had described?[161] Humboldt's problem, reviewers thought, was that he had relied on Spanish interpretations and sources.[162] A reviewer in the *Monthly Review* refused even to address those sections of Humboldt's work devoted to the study of Amerindian antiquities, saying that they were interesting only to those "who are converts to the notion that the inhabitants of America had made, at the time of the Spanish invasion, such a progress in civilization as entitled their history to the study of a philosophical inquirer."[163] Reviewers were quick to pardon Humboldt for the repetitive and undigested nature of his narrative, however, because "the countries which he explores [are] so little known to Europeans, that a traveler cannot possibly lose himself without finding something to entertain or instruct us."[164] Humboldt had been intoxicated by the sight of land that in the hands of ignorant Spaniards had remained without description. Having penetrated an "entirely new world" that had barely "been examined and described [before] by men of science," he was somewhat justified in offering a narrative in which his attention wandered in undisciplined fashion from one curious new physical or moral phenomenon to the next.[165]

Humboldt's new history of America and its early reception, particularly in England, are evidence that a new European historiographical paradigm, less critical of early Spanish sources on the New World, was emerging. The transition from de Pauw to Humboldt was, to be sure, related to the many new cultural and political developments in Europe brought about by the French Revolution. Humboldt's history was also the product of someone acquainted with an impressive amount of scholarship produced by Spanish American authors unknown to previous European authors. The change, however, was ultimately linked to the articulation of new analogies that allowed Humboldt to break away from the paralyzing skepticism engendered by the critique of the use of classical similes to study the past of the New World and its peoples.

In *Vues*, Humboldt set out to address critics like de Pauw and Robertson, who had denounced flawed and unreliable histories of the New World based on false classical analogies. Humboldt moved the debate forward by offering a solution to the impasse. Like Robertson and de Pauw, Humboldt was convinced that the Incas and Aztecs were no Romans. Instead, he depicted Amerindian societies as oriental in type. There was nothing novel about this. De Pauw had, in fact, written his *Recherches* on the Chinese and Egyptians to ridicule the great French orientalist Joseph de Guignes, who had claimed that the Chinese were a colony of Egypt, and that the civilizations of Mesoamerica had begun as Chinese colonial outposts.[166] However, whereas learned Europeans had grown used to the notions, first introduced by the Jesuits, of Chinese society as a virtuous classical polity and Chinese cosmologies as enlightened prefigurations of Christian doctrine, Humboldt denied any *racial* or cultural connection between Asiatic (and Amerindian) societies and those of classical Greece and Rome.

According to Humboldt, Amerindian and Asian societies were of a monastic type that had effaced individual expression and personal freedom.

Echoing ideas, first developed by the German classicist J. J. Winkelmann (1717–1768), that enjoyed wide circulation in learned neoclassical circles, Humboldt found in architecture a reflection of the inner character of peoples and a window to the understanding of essential distinctions between the West and Asia. Asiatic and Amerindian ruins and artifacts, he said, were the work of peoples who had failed to develop art because they had stamped out all forms of individualistic expression. In their mimetic accuracy and inner sensibilities, however, the monuments of Greeks, Romans, and, later, Europeans, gave evidence of societies that encouraged experimentation, innovation, and technical change.[167]

Asians and Amerindians were unchanging orientals, linked both racially and historically, whose myths, calendars, and religious institutions seemed to have stemmed from common originals, Humboldt contended. Inspired by the linguistic discoveries of Sir William Jones (1746–1794) and other British and French orientalists in India, he even posited that the seemingly unrelated and widely diverse linguistic structures of Amerindian languages could eventually be traced back to a central Asian ur-language.[168] Moreover, Humboldt argued that Asians and Amerindians had originated in a common racial type. Although present-day Mongoloid and Amerindian skulls belonged to two different races, there were enough resemblances for them to have originated from the same Central Asian ur-race.[169]

By drawing on recently coined neoclassical and romantic theories of aesthetics and skull typologies, Humboldt showed a way out of the paralyzing skepticism that had been engendered some forty years earlier by de Pauw's and Robertson's criticism of the promiscuous use of classical analogies to interpret Amerindian societies. Humboldt could now confidently maintain that "my own recent investigations on the natives of America appear at an epocha in which we no longer deem unworthy of attention whatever is not conformable to that style, of which the Greeks have left such inimitable models."[170]

Humboldt started from more positive premises than de Pauw and Robertson and was therefore prepared to be more generous to the embattled Spanish sources. His *Vues* began with a forceful defense of the quantity and quality of Spanish reports on the New World. Sixteenth-century Spanish descriptions of America, he said, were as numerous and accurate as the ones his contemporaries enjoyed of the peoples and lands of the South Pacific, with perhaps the only difference being that the latter contained illustrations, whereas those by the Spaniards did not. Amerindian monuments having been destroyed, Humboldt regretted that early travelers had not included illustrations, rendering researchers dependent on ambivalent written descriptions. He also regretted that having uncovered contradictions in the reports of Spanish witnesses, scholars had decided to dismiss all Spanish reports out of hand. Humboldt complained that eighteenth-century philosophes had uncritically lumped together reports by witnesses and those by armchair authors, and that philosophes had fashionably paraded their modernity by making a point of dismissing everything written by missionaries.[171]

Humboldt culminated his writings on the Spanish American empire with five volumes entitled *Examen critique de l'histoire de la géographie du noveau continent* (1836–39), a work that could easily be construed as a defense of the credibility of Spanish testimonies. Interested in reconstructing the history of science in order to prove that societies went through slow and sustained progress, and that "the grand European discoveries were not the result of a happy coincidence," Humboldt set out to demonstrate that the age of exploration (and the Renaissance) occurred only because of intellectual (and technological) forces that had long been unfolding during the Middle Ages.[172] Humboldt turned his capacious mind to the study of cosmography, navigation, and geography in the fifteenth and sixteenth centuries, paying particularly attention to developments in the Iberian peninsula and therefore reading widely in Spanish and Portuguese sources. He argued that his close knowledge of some of the same places visited by fifteenth- and sixteenth-century Spaniards made him better able to judge their true worth and credibility. These sources had barely been mined, he concluded; they contained much useful information that had escaped the attention of modern geographers and historians of the New World; and "progressively and for a long time to come, [their study] will yield precious results regarding events that transpired both in ancient America and in the years following the [European] discovery [of the New World]."[173]

According to Humboldt, part of the problem with the early Spanish sources lay in the fact that many reports had remained unavailable to European historians. After expressing regret that the efforts of the Royal Chronicler of the Indies, Juan Bautista Muñoz (1745–1799), to publish documents in eighteenth-century Spain had failed, Humboldt hailed as a scholarly landmark the appearance in 1825–37 of a collection of Spanish primary sources on the fifteenth-century Spanish Atlantic expeditions edited by Martín Fernández de Navarrete. Humboldt argued that in the early Spanish sources lay the "seeds of the most important physical verities," and that authors such as José de Acosta, Gonzalo Fernández de Oviedo (1478–1557), and the Franciscan Gregorio García (d. 1627) offered important philosophical insights.[174] Reversing views dominant since de Pauw, Raynal, and Robertson, Humboldt claimed that sixteenth-century Spanish authors had tackled complex issues such as the origins of racial variations; the causes of biogeographical distribution of fauna and flora; the study of human migrations through linguistic filiation; and the study of the causes of oceanic currents, winds, volcanic activity, and earthquakes, all formidable puzzles still besetting scholars.

With Humboldt, European historiography on the New World seemed to have come almost full circle. If Humboldt restored the value of sixteenth-century European witnesses, particularly of the maligned Spaniards, he also continued the tradition of scholarship, inaugurated by Buffon and de Pauw, that relied primarily on extraliterary evidence. Moreover, Humboldt strengthened, rather than weakened, the new genre of philosophical histories of the Americas. Chapter 2 will show how scholars dealt with sources produced not by European observers but by Amerindians.

CHAPTER 2

Changing European Interpretations of the Reliability of Indigenous Sources

Forced to choose between contradictory Spanish and indigenous accounts of the death of Moctezuma Xocoyoltzin (r. 1502–20 in the Codex Mendoza), the sixteenth-century Spanish Dominican friar Diego Durán (d. 1588), who between 1576 and 1581 wrote a history of the Mexica and treatises on their divinatory calendars and monthly religious festivities, chose the latter. Spaniards had traditionally argued that his own people had stoned Moctezuma to death. The indigenous sources that Durán had before his eyes told a slightly different story. After routing Cortés's army and recapturing Tenochtitlan, the capital of the Mexica, the natives found Moctezuma lying in a pool of blood, stabbed five times in the chest, surrounded by the corpses of several nobles, who had also been murdered. Although this account was an obvious challenge to official Spanish historiography, Durán saw himself with no choice but to follow it, for the story was recounted in native documents that used Mesoamerican script. "Had their history not said it, had the paintings that I have seen not certified it," Durán argued, "it would have been difficult for me to believe [the account of Moctezuma's death]. However I am obliged to put what the [indigenous] authors I have followed in this history tell me, in writing and painting."[1] In the historical sections of his works, Durán limited himself to translating Mexica manuscripts, often uncritically.[2] Durán's choice when confronted with two contradictory accounts of the death of Moctezuma, one left by Spanish witnesses and the other in documents recorded in Mexica script, typifies the great authority that European scholars accorded Amerindian historical sources in the sixteenth and early seventeenth centuries.

Durán's methods contrast sharply with those followed by eighteenth-century European scholars. While in exile in Italy, the Spanish American Jesuit Francisco Xavier Clavijero (1731–1787) had written a history of ancient Mexico, *Storia antica del Messico* (1780–81), to denounce skeptics such as De Pauw, Robertson, and Raynal and to reconstruct the many cycles of civilizations in Mesoamerica that had culminated with the Aztecs. When a translation of Clavijero's book appeared in London in 1787, the translator, Charles Cullen, expressed high hopes for its reception in English. Convinced that "partiality, prejudice, ignorance, and credulity have occasioned [sixteenth- and seventeenth-century Spanish historians] to blend so many absurdities and improbabilities with their accounts that it has not been merely difficult but altogether impossible to ascertain the truth," Cullen argued that not even the efforts of Robertson to find what "was naturally curious or politically interesting" in the history of the New World had been enough to bring order to the subject.[3] Although Robertson had struggled mightily to "extricate facts from the confusion of different [Spanish] authors [in whose works] what is true does not always appear possible and what appears probable is not always true," the Scot had ultimately been constrained by distance, both geographical and cultural, which had kept him away from "essential documents which are preserved in archives of the New World." Clavijero, however, had been born in Mexico, where he had spent forty years and studied those "essential documents" that others had failed to consult, namely, the "historical paintings [of the Amerindians] and other monuments of antiquity."[4]

English critics, who denounced the translation for the precise reasons that had moved Cullen to publish it in the first place, soon dashed Cullen's high hopes. The year Cullen's translation appeared, an anonymous reviewer in the *London Review* declared Clavijero's history worthless. Taking his cues from Bolingbroke and Hume, the reviewer first argued that writing the "earliest part of the history" of even those nations that had once "lorded over the universe" was in itself a waste of time, an activity for pedants like Milton, whose "mighty genius and immense learning [had] sunk under the weight of the annals of the Heptarchy." Good history, the reviewer maintained, was European modern history, capable of teaching moral lessons to the present. The history of the Aztecs involved barbarians and had no moral to teach. The reviewer's second criticism went to the heart of Clavijero's historiography, for the Jesuit had presented his work as the product of many years of study and meditation on Amerindian documents housed in the Mexican libraries of the Jesuit order. "The Abbé," the reviewer maintained, had built on no better foundation than "records [of] pictures either painted or wrought with party-coloured feathers." Built on such flimsy foundations, Clavijero's work was "an enormous structure of two solid quartos [in the English translation] stuffed with impossible facts, absurd exaggerations, and such a barbarous jargon of uncouth names, as to be within one degree of absolute unintelligibility."[5]

For the reviewer, the problem with Clavijero's work lay in its historiographical assumptions. Clavijero had presented the dynastic genealogies, wars, conquests and even royal speeches of the peoples of central Mexico, allegedly going all the way back to the year 596 C.E. The history of England during the same years, the reviewer claimed, was not remotely as tidy as that recounted by Clavijero for Mexico. Yet England, unlike Mexico, had written historical records. Clavijero, the reviewer maintained, had been moved by patriotic enthusiasm and had projected onto Amerindian "paintings" his own unbridled imagination. Mexican indigenous records were primitive paintings, not writings, and therefore utterly unreliable. "All the history, therefore, anterior to the Conquest by Cortés, the Abbé must forgive us if we receive with very great distrust."[6]

One might argue that having thrown out Spanish records, late-eighteenth-century critics could have used indigenous sources as an alternative, more ancient, and, thus, more reliable form of evidence. The most elementary principle of historical criticism put forth by Renaissance philologists held that historians should always look for primary sources. If it was clear that Spaniards like Durán had derived their facts about the history of the peoples of the New World from indigenous records, why did eighteenth-century conjectural historians not follow the advice of Renaissance philologists? Why not turn to the original sources to do away with the previous layers of Spanish interpretations in the same way that Renaissance humanists had cleared away the accretions added by medieval commentators from classical sources?

The English review of Clavijero's work suggests that the reason for this refusal can be found in changing perceptions of the value of indigenous systems of writing. The various Mesoamerican scripts (Nahua, Zapotec, Mixtec, and Maya) refused neat classifications: each included combinations of pictograms, ideograms, logograms, and even phonograms (the latter appeared more prominently in Maya writing systems and in sixteenth-century Mexica manuscripts [Figs. 5.8 and 5.9]).[7] Inca quipus were even more puzzling: knots woven along strings of different colors, which in turn ramified themselves endlessly (Fig. 2.7).[8] It could be argued, therefore, that the shift from Durán's willingness to believe Amerindian sources to the refusal of the reviewer of Clavijero's history to give them credit was the result of some major change in European perception of the reliability of nonalphabetical scripts in keeping historical records. However, the most significant reason lies somewhere else, as seen in another review in an English journal, this time of one of Alexander von Humboldt's works.

In an 1816 article in the *Quarterly Review* devoted to an analysis of the English edition of Humboldt's *Vues des cordillères*, the anonymous reviewer treated the book harshly. Humboldt was presented as a disorganized and credulous thinker who had embraced Spanish interpretations of Mexican indigenous sources and had therefore drawn unwarranted conclusions about ancient connections between Asia and Mexico. Mexican history had been lost forever, the reviewer suggested, owing partly to the ignorance of early Spanish observers and partly to the impossibility of understanding the meaning of extant indigenous documents. Spaniards had failed as cultural translators, and no reliable interpretations of the scripts could now be offered. Yet the reviewer was not about to summon scholars to condemn indigenous writings to historiographical oblivion. In fact, he applauded Humboldt for his efforts at collecting indigenous Mexican sources. "We do not mean to deny," the reviewer said, "that the first attempts, however rude, of an unenlightened people to register events, communicate ideas, and render visible the operations of the mind, are void of interest; on the contrary we consider them as so many landmarks by which we trace, in the most interesting manner, the progress of the intellectual faculties of man."[9]

For the reviewer, the value of collecting and studying Mexican writings lay not in the information that they stored, but in what they revealed about the development of the mental faculties. Humboldt's efforts to collect Mexican codices were therefore commendable. According to this new form of understanding indigenous documents, in burning Amerindian sources, the Spanish conquistadors had robbed the scholarly world not of accurate historical records, but of tools for studying the ways in which the mind had developed its powers of abstraction over time. Renaissance scholars thought that indigenous scripts, however limited, registered historical events. Enlightenment literati thought that scripts were material evidence upon which to reconstruct conjectural histories of the development of the mind. In this chapter, I study this crucial transformation of European consciousness.

Primitive Scripts, Reliable Historical Documents

When Francisco Hernández (1514–1587) was sent to the New World by Philip II in the 1570s to collect information on new species of plants for the royal pharmacy, he had no idea that he would have to put together a massive natural history of the flora of central Mexico against the will of indigenous informants, who constantly misled him and lied about the properties of plants. In a poem dedicated to the great Spanish humanist Arias Montano, Hernández complained that local shamans lied about the names and properties of plants, and that he had to depend on his own arts and on God's divine providence to cure the sick.[10] Despite this frustrating experience, Hernández not only completed his natural history of plants and animals but also wrote a treatise on Mexican antiquities, largely based on the information collected by Franciscan friars from Nahua scribes.[11] Read from our modern perspective, one is startled by the historiographical assumptions of sixteenth-century Spanish historians of the New World. Against a background of generalized doubt about the reliability of Amerindian informants, Spaniards by and large believed that indigenous documents in nonalphabetical scripts kept trustworthy historical records.[12] Sixteenth-century Spanish historians like Hernández and Durán not only studied, collected, and translated native sources but, more important, thought that those sources contained reliable historical narratives.

This interpretation runs contrary to that recently offered by Walter Mignolo, who has argued that unlike the Greeks, who grounded wisdom on orally transmitted forms of knowledge, sixteenth-century Spaniards grounded knowledge on alphabetical writing and the book. Since God had transmitted his dispensation through the written word, societies that lacked "writing" were considered not only outside the pale of civilization but of humanity as well. Mignolo has argued that in the sixteenth century, Spaniards looked down upon Aztec and Inca systems of writing as primitive. Alphabetic writing was the only script thought capable of recording the voice accurately and therefore of engraving society's memories and laws. By giving room to the loose oral interpretation of scribes, all other forms of writing led to ambiguity in the transmission of historical records. Amerindian nonalphabetic scripts were, therefore, considered incapable of accumulating knowledge, which was the foundation of civilization.[13] Moreover, not having found alphabetic records of the Roman type constituting an orderly chronological narrative in the New World, the Spaniards thought that the Amerindians had no history. Spanish scholars accorded Inca and Aztec documents the same level of epistemological validity that they accorded coins or medals.[14]

Mignolo has also argued that when Inca and Aztec records were seen as actual "books," they were either dismissed or burned because they recorded knowledge believed to have been dictated by the devil. Alphabetic script was perceived to be the only medium "in which truth finds its warranty."[15] Since sixteenth-century Spanish scholars already operated under an evolutionary view of writing, such views led in turn to an evolutionary view of the book in which medieval meanings of "reading," to discern in a oral context, as in the process involved in reading Mesoamerican scripts and Inca quipus, and of "book" and "text," to "make," or "to weave," as in the case of the Inca quipus, were ignored.[16] Renaissance Spanish scholars had forgotten the context in which writing took place in their recent medieval past, a context dominated by orally transmitted information. Sixteenth-century Spanish authors thus misunderstood not only Amerindian systems of writing but also the history of their own cultural tradition. They classified Inca quipus and Mesoamerican "paintings" as objects, not books.

According to Mignolo, only a few challenges emerged to these views. In his *Della historia dieci dialoghi* (1560), for example, the Italian scholar Francesco Patrizi (1529–1597) called for the creation of a new historiography that privileged images and other nonwritten sources over written ones. Patrizi's views, to be sure, went unattended.[17] The Amerindians themselves, particularly those trained by Spanish humanist friars, voiced another challenge to the Spanish Christian paradigm of literacy. Two Nahua chroniclers, Francisco de San Antón Muñón Chimalpain Cuauhtlehuanitzin (1579–1660) and Fernando de Alva Ixtlilxochitl (1578–1650), strove to show that Mesoamerican and European historical records were equivalent. They collected Mexican codices and translated them verbatim into the Roman alphabet, both in Nahuatl and Spanish. Moreover, Alva Ixtlilxochitl insisted that ancient Nahua historians and systems of keeping historical records (codices, songs, and rhetorical speeches) were among the most reliable and accurate in the world.[18]

For all his value at calling scholarly attention to the role that the ideology of literacy has played in colonial and postcolonial societies as a tool of "Western" domination, Mignolo, however, is somewhat misleading.[19] Take, for example, the case of Alva Ixtlilxochitl. Mignolo presents him as an isolated challenge to Spanish views of literacy, yet Alva Ixtlilxochitl was himself a product of the very ideology Mignolo purports to describe. The Franciscans trained Alva Ixtlilxochitl, a member of the Nahua nobility. Although his political interests were admittedly different from those of his teachers (to advance the claims of his Amerindian lineage in the cramped and contested space of indigenous politics in colonial Mexico), his techniques and sensibility with respect to collecting and glossing Nahua sources were no different. Among Alva Ixtlilxochitl's friends was Juan de Torquemada (1557–1664), a Spanish friar who set out to rewrite available interpretations of Mesoamerican history upon a detailed reading of dozens of Mesoamerican codices. Torquemada and Alva Ixtlilxochitl not only shared the same historiographical views but also admired each other's scholarship.[20]

There are numerous other examples offered by Mignolo himself that appear to undermine certain of his views. The work of the Franciscan friar

Bernardino de Sahagún (d. 1590), whose efforts at collating and translating Nahua documents written in local scripts culminated in the creation of an extremely thorough encyclopedia of Nahua lore, the Florentine Codex, in Mignolo's own words, showed that "alphabetic and picture writing systems were part of [a] dialogue."[21] Sahagún organized into a European encyclopedic format the information he obtained in many cycles of interviewing local scribes. The very passages of the Florentine Codex quoted by Mignolo in which Sahagún describes his methodology reveal that the Franciscan friar took Nahua sources very seriously, and that Sahagún understood his task to be that of a humanist philologist working with classical and patristic sources, namely, the culturally and historically informed exegesis of and commentary on words and texts.[22]

There are also passages by Toribio de Benavente, Motolinía (d. 1568), one of the first Franciscans to arrive in Mexico and a leading figure in the initial stages of the "spiritual conquest" of Mexico, characterized by large-scale Amerindian conversion. As Mignolo demonstrates, Motolinía's *Memoriales* (1536–43) classified the books of the Aztecs into five different categories — ritual calendars; books of dreams; auguries; "horoscopes" used to determine the names of children; and historical annals — only to call on friars to destroy them. Such passages appear to confirm all and every one of Mignolo's assertions. Yet Mignolo is also aware that in those passages, Motolinía spares from destruction one of the five categories of Aztec books, namely, historical annals. Mexican historical books, according to Motolinía, were not inspired by the devil; they were reliable historical narratives and told the truth about the past.[23]

Motolinía's distinction between two types of documents was typical of Spanish views of Mesoamerican sources. On the one hand, there were "painted" indigenous documents that recorded religious ceremonies, divinatory rituals, and cosmogonies, which were to be destroyed and burned — paradoxically, out of fear, not contempt. On the other hand, there were historical annals, assumed to be accurate and associated with indigenous writing. The case of Diego de Landa (1524–1579), also studied by Mignolo, is most illuminating. Landa was a sixteenth-century Franciscan friar who, after spending many years winning the minds and bodies of the Maya for God and Spain, became the provincial of the Franciscan order in the Yucatan peninsula, and also a zealous destroyer of Amerindian books. As a Franciscan provincial, he carried out one of the harshest extirpation campaigns against Amerindian idolatry ever witnessed in sixteenth-century Spanish America. After having been informed that Maya converts had used their knowledge of Christianity to engage in pagan ceremonies in Christian temples, which reportedly involved ritual crucifixions of infants and relapses into ritual cannibalism, in 1562, Landa unleashed all the power of the Church to prosecute the culprits, including the use of systematic torture to extract confessions, causing 158 Mayans to die and some 30 others to commit suicide. Landa, to be sure, collected and burned all the Maya ritual books that he managed to lay his hands on, twenty-seven in all.[24] Yet he simultaneously scoured the Yucatan peninsula looking for stelae from which to draw the history of the ancient kingdom of Mayapan. Landa was convinced that the Maya kept very accurate historical records because they had developed sophisticated calendars and chronologies.[25] It seems that he was able to read Maya sources, and his testimony is confirmed by another contemporary Franciscan, Antonio Cuidad Real (1551–1617), who reported friars capable of reading and writing in Maya script.[26] Landa's scholarship on Maya writing and historiography, which included a list of syllabic phonograms and an understanding that Maya stelae were documents that recorded the deeds of historical figures, was ignored for many generations. It has only been in the twentieth century that scholars have begun to read Maya stelae as historical documents, not as ancient cosmogonies, and to interpret Maya glyphs as Landa had originally suggested.[27]

One problem with Mignolo's interpretation of both Motolinía and Landa is that he assumes that Spaniards thought that *reliability* was a function of the script in which the accounts were written. Yet it seems that for Motolinía, reliability was rather a function of who had penned the book. According to Motolinía, Mexican horoscopes, books of feasts, and accounts of rites and ceremonies were untrustworthy because, unlike the Gospels, the devil and his agents had written them. Historical annals, however, were documents written by Amerindians. It is true that according to Motolinía, Mexican systems of writing left room for conflicting interpretations and contradictory accounts, because they were based on an oral exegesis of "paintings."[28] Yet Motolinía's concern with the relationship between a script that required oral commentary and reliability lay less in his patronizing view of Amerindian scripts and more in his grasp of the age-old politics of ethnicity in the Central Valley of Mexico.

Motolinía knew that there were many competing indigenous historical narratives in circulation. Not unlike the historical records kept by most other peoples, Mesoamerican historical annals were part of elite propaganda, campaigns of dynastic self-aggrandizement and manipulation that routinely included the invention and obliteration of historical data. In fact, according to Joyce Marcus, the need for state propaganda was the prime reason that writing developed in Mesoamerica: "Mesoamerican writing was both a tool and a by-product of this competition for prestige and leadership positions."[29] Motolinía understood that Mesoamerican historical narratives were contradictory, because they presented the views of opposing ethnic groups. He recorded Aculhua and Tlaxcalan versions of the history of central Mexico along with that of the Mexica. But instead of declaring as hopeless the effort of translating local histories into Western historiographical molds, Motolinía appointed himself as final arbiter of which version was the closest to the "truth." Motolinía was convinced that despite their drawbacks, Mexican historical records were reliable, because the natives had developed accurate calendars and systems of chronology, as well as reliable ways of transmitting oral testimonies over the generations.[30]

The sixteenth-century Spanish approach to indigenous scripts was somewhat paradoxical. On the one hand, most authors refused to grant Inca and Mesoamerican systems of writing the same authority as the Latin alphabet, which was considered ideal for transmitting historical data, because it did not depend on any oral exegesis. Yet these same authors did not hesitate to consider the historical information stored in quipus and codices as trustworthy. Bartolomé de Las Casas typifies this attitude. In his *Apologética historia sumaria* (before 1559), Las Casas defended the rationality of the Amerindians against those who sought to portray them as examples of Aristotle's natural slaves. Las Casas set out to prove that the Amerindians had been fully capable of ruling their own individual passions (monastic prudence), as well as their own political communities. Moreover, he argued that the Inca and Aztec societies had been at least as sophisticated politically and religiously as the classical ancient polities. Yet, according to Las Casas, the natives were "barbarians" because they had lacked "writing." This statement flew in the face of Las Casas's own efforts to prove that the natives had achieved all the required institutions for civilization, including social ranks, monarchies, cities, and complex religious cults. Las Casas drew generously from indigenous sources kept in writings that he denied were such. Other authors contemporary with Las Casas make the contradiction explicit. For example, there is the case of the secular Spanish priest Miguel Cabello de Valboa (1530–1608?), whose history of ancient Peru, *Miscelánea Antártica*, written in Quito between 1576 and 1586, remained, like Las Casas's *Apologética historia*, unpublished for many centuries.

Working on the assumption that their lack of writing had cast a veil of obscurity over the true origins of native Americans, and that only indirect forms of historical reconstruction were possible, Cabello de Valboa sought to demonstrate that they were, in fact, the descendants of Ophir, Noah's great-grandchild, and had lost the ability to write.[31] He argued that this lack of writing was the primary cause of the plunge into barbarism of Ophir's heirs and of the spread of idolatry among the Andeans, who literally worshipped springs, lakes, mountains, and rocks as their own ancestors.[32] However, in spite of his denunciations of the Amerindians' lack of writing, Cabello de Valboa also argued that in their quipus, the Incas had stored complete and accurate records of their history, going back eight hundred years before the European arrival.[33] After attempting to conjecture the travails and migrations of the lineage of Ophir, Cabello de Valboa saw no contradiction in also including in his manuscript the history of the Incas "according to the quipus and Indian annals."[34]

For all the caveats about Mignolo's thesis, he is right to argue that sixteenth-century Spanish authors considered indigenous systems of writing primitive. He is also right to point out that one needs only to turn to sixteenth-century Spain and Spanish America to find the first conjectural histories of writing that treat hieroglyphs not as a quasi divinely inspired system of writing but as childish, deeply flawed means of representing speech, a view that scholars have traditionally attributed to the Enlightenment.[35] Mesoamerican scripts, a combination of pictograms, ideograms, logograms, and phonograms, never enjoyed the reputation in Spain that Egyptian hieroglyphs had.

In the sixteenth century and the first half of the seventeenth, symbolic scripts possessed far greater status among the learned than alphabetical writing. Egyptian hieroglyphs (and Hebrew letters) were seen as images that synthesized very economically profound truths about the nature of the cosmos and of God. Informed by a Renaissance Neoplatonic revival that posited the world as a theater of symbols in which images held magical powers and in which objects and peoples were connected by a network of microcosmic and macrocosmic analogies, scholars invested considerable energy both in decoding the occult significance of hieroglyphs and in coming up with new ones. However, in spite of the great authority and respectability accorded to hieroglyphs, Spanish scholars failed to find any Neoplatonic symbolism in Mesoamerican scripts, and by the second half of the seventeenth century, the emphasis on the occult and arcane properties of hieroglyphs had given way to a new interest in the unambiguous, open, and more democratic character of alphabetical writing.[36]

Philology, Collation, and Translation

The work of the Spanish Jesuit José de Acosta typifies sixteenth-century Spanish perceptions of Amerindian scripts. In his *Historia natural y moral de las Indias,* published in Seville in 1590, which went through many reprints and was translated into several European languages, Acosta sought to synthesize several decades of readings of classical and patristic sources and some fifteen years of personal observations in the Indies, Mexico, and, particularly, Peru. Acosta wrote his moral history with several purposes in mind. He included a section on indigenous idolatry to help new missionaries identify and root out what he thought were demonically inspired Amerindian religions. Sections on Inca and Aztec customs and systems of government were written to help colonial magistrates to govern the Amerindians according to their own legal and political traditions, which Acosta believed revealed considerable ingenuity and adaptation to local conditions.[37] Finally, Acosta wrote a history of the Incas and Aztecs to prove that "the opinion of those who held the Amerindians to be men lacking in understanding was false."[38] To disprove these false opinions, Acosta used examples of the Amerindians' advanced scientific understanding. In glowing terms, he described Mexican and Inca calendars, which demonstrated that the Amerindians had known enough astronomy to adjust their years according to the true length of a solar cycle through the ecliptic (365.25 days).[39]

Curiously, in spite of his desire to demonstrate the ingenuity of the natives, Acosta overlooked the similitude between Egyptian and Mexican systems of writing as conceived in the Renaissance; he could have easily cast Mexican glyphs as Egyptian hieroglyphs symbolizing arcane knowledge. A thinker who relished order, Acosta offered a helpful typology of forms of idolatry according to types of devotional objects. He argued that peoples commonly worshipped things (the sun, thunder, rainbows, stones, trees), animals, dead ancestors, or anthropomorphic objects. Drawing on a long euhemerist tradition, Acosta maintained that most Greek and Roman gods were in fact deified heroes, and that most anthropomorphic Peruvian gods were deified ancestors. Acosta found Mexica idolatry something of a curiosity, however, for the Mexica had many gods that seemed monstrous composites without any resemblance to human figures, creatures concocted solely in the imaginations of their worshippers. These Mexican deities, like Egyptian hieroglyphs, were not simple images but had multiple layers of meaning. The image of Tezcatlipoca, the god of penitence and sin, according to Acosta, had countless symbolic details. A golden ear painted with the glyph for speech in

Mexica writing seemed to represent Tezcatlipoca's willingness to hear the pleas of sinners; a mirrorlike object in Tezcatlipoca's left hand stood for his alleged omniscience.[40] However, Acosta never drew a connection between these images and Mexica systems of writing. Had he drawn such connections, Acosta would have seen that some Mexica ideograms resembled Egyptian ones. Although he found these images in Mexica books, Acosta kept the discussion of Mexica idols and of Mexica systems of writing completely separate. But despite his unconscious severing of indigenous representations of Mexica deities from potentially fruitful Neoplatonic interpretations, Acosta did not dismiss the value of Amerindian scripts in recording reliable historical information.

Acosta, it seems, worried that his readers would take as mere fables his accounts of the migrations, dynastic genealogies, customs, and laws of the Incas and Aztecs. He anticipated that readers would raise a number of difficult questions regarding his work. How, for example, was it possible to talk about Aztec and Inca "laws" when these two peoples lacked alphabetical scripts? After all, the difference between customs and laws lay in that the former were transmitted orally and were transient, whereas the latter were written, codified, and thus stable. How could one vouch for the historicity of Amerindian genealogies and alleged migrations? How could one describe the Incas and Aztec states as young, expanding empires if they lacked systems to keep communication flowing between the center and the peripheries? Without straining the credulity of readers, how could one maintain that the Incas and Aztecs had kept verbatim records of ancient speeches?

Faced with these dilemmas, Acosta prefaced the historical sections of his treatise with a lengthy discussion of systems of writing. To convince skeptical readers that keeping historical records was possible even without the use of alphabetical writing, he offered a tripartite classification of methods "to keep the memory of history and antiquities."[41] The best and most economical means, to be sure, was an alphabet, which afforded peoples great flexibility in representing foreign languages and time to spare for learning other arts and sciences. "Cifras or memoriales," conventional symbols that did not represent speech, such as Chinese script, Arabic numbers, and astrological signs, were a second recordkeeping device. "Cifras" allowed peoples of different languages to communicate with one another. Yet they were difficult to adapt to foreign terms, and, moreover, they were extremely time-consuming to learn. Chinese scholars, for example, had great difficulty writing Spanish names and spent their entire lives mastering 120,000 characters, so that they did not have time to pursue any of the scientific and philosophical disciplines.[42] The third form of recordkeeping was through "paintings," a system that Acosta thought "almost all the world has used, for as the second Council of Nicea has argued, painting is the book of idiots who do not know how to read."[43] Acosta did not include quipus in this scheme, but he was certain that these knotted strings of the Incas, along with paintings and other mnemonic devices, had allowed Peruvians to keep accurate historical records as well. "It is incredible what [Peruvians] achieved by these means," Acosta maintained, "for astonishingly quipus can store history, laws, customs, and business transactions as accurately as books."[44]

To satisfy skeptics who argued that lengthy speeches allegedly delivered by ancient warriors and rulers were the invention of imaginative Spaniards, Acosta maintained that the Aztecs had created educational systems to ensure the fidelity of oral transmissions, and that songs were reliable alternative records developed by the Mexica to store historical information. Skeptics "presented with the truth [about these means of accurate oral transmission] could not help but give due credit to the histories [of the Amerindians]."[45] Finally, to address those critical readers ready to pose the embarrassing question of how empires could exist in the New World without systems to relay information between centers and peripheries, Acosta zeroed in on the Mexican and, particularly, Inca institution of couriers, capable of delivering fresh fish to Cuzco in only two days, along, of course, with paintings or quipus.[46]

For all his defense of alternative yet reliable forms of recordkeeping devices, Acosta's history of the Incas proved disappointing. He condensed four centuries of history into some five pages and offered only very sketchy data on the last three generations of Inca rulers. Moreover, Acosta, who had obtained most of this information from an inquiry that the viceroy of Peru, Francisco de Toledo, had recently ordered as part of a larger reform of the viceroyalty, blamed quipus for the scarcity of historical records.[47]

In contrast to his neglect of the Incas, Acosta's attitude toward the Mexica was rather respectful. He devoted an entire book to recording their migrations and dynastic genealogies, going back to the year 820 C.E, and confidently assured readers that "this [account of the ancient history of Mexico] is not unworthy of being written and read, because it is history and not fables and fictions."[48] Acosta's differing attitudes toward quipus and Mesoamerican documents could not have been more striking, and stemmed in part from his awareness of the views of the Catholic Reformation on the historiographical value of images. Acosta also suffered, as Tom Cummins has recently argued, from the Western inability to understand nonmimetic systems of representations such as the quipus.[49] In addition, his trust of Mexican scripts derived from his correspondence with a Jesuit brother in Mexico, Juan de Tovar (ca. 1546–ca. 1626), who acquainted him with the techniques used by Spanish humanists in New Spain.

After working for many years as a missionary in Peru, Acosta spent a few months in Mexico in 1586 before returning to Spain to write his *History*. In Mexico, he met Tovar, who had long worked on local antiquities and who gave Acosta a history of the Aztecs. Acosta, it seems, reviewed the work and began to suspect that it was based entirely on native accounts, for he wrote to Tovar asking two questions: "What certainty or authority does this relation or history possess?" and, "Since the Indians did not have writing, how could they preserve such quantity and variety of matters for so long a time?"[50] Tovar responded quickly, describing Mexican mnemonic and writing systems that had allowed Amerindians to memorize even ancient speeches. He also explained to Acosta how he had gathered his information about the precolonial history of Mexico. The viceroy, "wishing to know these people's antiquities exactly, ordered a collection of the libraries that [the Amerindians] had on these matters." Old sages from Tollan, Mexico, and Texcoco had responded to the order by sending many codices, which the viceroy gave to Tovar. After trying to interpret the documents alone and accepting his ignorance, Tovar turned to the local sages. "It was necessary for the wise men of Mexico, Texcoco, and Tollan to meet with me . . . [and after] talking over and discussing the matter in detail with them, I made a thorough history." Tovar concluded the letter by explaining briefly how Mexican "writing" worked. To be certain that Acosta understood, he included a glossed ritual calendar and a pictographic and logographic manuscript in which the Amerindians had written various Christian prayers, a form of sixteenth-century document that used paintings to record Catholic doctrine, first introduced in Mexico by the Franciscan friar Jacobo Testera.[51] Tovar summarized in a paragraph some fifty years of Spanish humanist techniques for studying Mexican antiquities. Acosta was so satisfied with Tovar's answers that he copied the history compiled by Tovar verbatim.[52]

Tovar's methods were typical of those of sixteenth-century Spanish humanists working on Mexican antiquities. Many Franciscans who came to Mexico had been educated in the universities of Alcalá and Salamanca, which were at the forefront of Spanish humanist culture until the mid sixteenth century. In 1533, the Franciscans founded the college of Santa Cruz of Tlatelolco to train native elites for the priesthood. Before the college sank into oblivion in the face of the growing opposition of the Spanish colonists, the Franciscans managed to train a formidable cadre of indigenous humanists, knowledgeable about grammar, logic, and rhetoric, and capable of writing in Latin, Spanish, and Nahuatl in alphabetic script. Both students and teachers set out to translate classical and biblical texts, religious plays and psalms, and works by Spanish mystics in Latin, Spanish, and Nahuatl. This circle also mined the literary corpus of central Mexico.[53] In 1552, for example, Martín de la Cruz and the Nahua philologist Juan Badiano wrote their *Libellus de medicinalibus Indorum herbis* (or Codex Badiano), a typical Renaissance herbal. The herbal included a text of "pictograms" of indigenous plants and a Latin translation of the testimony offered by local shamans for the therapeutic value associated with each plant.[54]

Works such the *Libellus* were characteristic of the school of Santa Cruz. The most celebrated of them all is perhaps the Florentine Codex, a multivolume encyclopedia of Nahua lore that took more than twenty-five years to produce (1557–83), and that went through numerous drafts but was never completed. Although Bernardino de Sahagún was responsible for the Florentine Codex, the process of collation, translation, and interpretation of indigenous sources was a collaborative effort in which numerous indigenous philologists participated. Sahagún conceived the encyclopedia as a Renaissance polyglot text with parallel columns in Nahuatl, Latin, and Spanish. Although in the last multilingual version of the encyclopedia (ca. 1579), Mexican scripts lost their quality of "text" and appeared as illustrations to the written word, the column written in Nahuatl in Latin script still occupied the central position in all drafts.[55]

Not only Dominicans (Durán), Franciscans (Motolinía, Sahagún), and Jesuits (Tovar) but city councils and universities sought to translate, collate, gloss, and annotate indigenous documents written in Mesoamerican scripts. In 1558, the city council of Mexico City commissioned Francisco Cervantes de Salazar (ca. 1514–ca. 1575), a professor of rhetoric who was soon to be rector of the University of Mexico, to write a history of the city. Cervantes, who had published and glossed the works of several important Spanish humanists in Spain and Mexico, immediately set out to collect and study native sources. The council summoned native scribes, who created a codex that Cervantes later "translated."[56] This was not an isolated event. The will to believe indigenous historical testimony was such that in colonial courts in Mexico, where according to law "two Indians or three women presented as witnesses [were] worth one Spanish man,"[57] Mesoamerican codices were introduced as legal evidence, particularly in land disputes. When the new University of Mexico opened its doors in 1553 under royal and pontifical auspices, three new chairs were added to the traditional European liberal arts, two on native languages (Nahuatl and Otomí) and one on native script, the latter to train court interpreters to read indigenous documents.[58]

If Acosta's history of Mexico and his correspondence with Tovar unveiled the density of techniques employed by sixteenth-century Spanish antiquarians in New Spain, Acosta's sketchy history of the Incas hid, rather than uncovered, similar processes taking place in Peru. As in Mexico, missionaries in Peru used the local systems of writing for teaching catechism and prayers, and Amerindians brought quipus to Christian churches to read them aloud during confessions.[59] As in Mexico, scholars and bureaucrats in Peru also summoned local scribes (*quipucamayos*: the readers and makers of quipus) to "translate" their testimonies into the Latin alphabet.

In 1551, Juan de Betanzos (d. 1576), a Spanish resident of Cuzco, completed his *Suma y narración de los Incas*, which was to remain unpublished for many centuries. Like many other early Spanish colonists, Betanzos married an Inca princess, Doña Angelina Añas Yupanqui (or Angelina Cusimaray). She and her kin told Betanzos their history, recorded in quipus, which he poured into alphabetic writing. Betanzos's account was deeply partisan, designed to advance the dynastic interest of the Inca lineage represented by his Andean relatives. The relevance that Betanzos's *Suma y narración* has for my argument, however, is that Betanzos understood his task as one of translation, not even one of glossing and commentary. Betanzos argued that his history superseded all previous ones written by Spaniards, because his, unlike theirs, was grounded on knowledge of the language and access to local witnesses and scribes. Casting himself as "a truthful and faithful translator," Betanzos declared: "I have been informed not only by one but by many [scribes; among them] those [who kept annals] of the greatest antiquity and credit." Unlike other Spanish chroniclers, Betanzos did not even edit the indigenous testimonies he collected. He, for one, did not seek to cast Inca myths of origins and Inca lineages into orderly European dynastic genealogies and biblical chronologies. Moreover, Betanzos's Spanish prose included many terms of validation typical of Quechua, suggesting that he had translated the testimony of his informants verbatim. The end result was a book that faithfully captured the Amerindians' view of the past.[60]

Betanzos was not an isolated figure. Twenty years after him, Pedro Sarmiento de Gamboa (1532?–1608?) also strove to write an authoritative history of the Incas, *Historia índica* (1572), based on the briefing of dozens of local scribes in Cuzco, Xauxa, and Guamanga. Sarmiento de Gamboa claimed to have interviewed quipucamayos, whose testimony he had verified before a notary and representatives of twelve different Inca lineages, for he thought that a single trustworthy narrative would finally emerge from comparison of the many alternative histories kept by each of the Cuzqueño rival lineages.[61] These representatives discussed the narrative publicly and suggested changes to it.[62]

Betanzos and Sarmiento de Gamboa were part of a larger historiographical pattern. In the mid seventeenth century, the Jesuit Bernabé Cobo (1580–1657) maintained that all the significant Spanish histories of precolonial Peru written in the sixteenth century (most of which, by the way, were left unpublished) had followed the same procedure, namely, one based on the extensive and intensive briefing of Amerindian witnesses and scribes. Cobo highlighted three of these compilations for their depth and significance.[63] The first had been compiled in Cuzco in 1559 by Polo de Ondegardo (d. 1575), at the prompting of Viceroy Marquis de Cañate and Archbishop Fray Jerónimo de Loaysa. The second was compiled at the request of Viceroy Toledo and had two components: a first, large set of interviews of provincial elites from 1570 to 1575, whose premeditated goal was to prove that the Incas had been tyrants, whom the Spaniards had therefore been right to depose; and a second set conducted by Sarmiento de Gamboa around 1572. Cristobal de Molina, chaplain of a hospital for Amerindians in Cuzco, undertook the third great compilation of indigenous histories under the auspices of the bishop of Cuzco, Sebastián de Lartaún, around 1574. These compilations, with the exception of the tightly scripted interviews with provincial Andean elites during Viceroy Toledo's visits, represented the views of the Inca elites in Cuzco.[64]

In light of the numerous contradictions among the historical accounts gathered from the natives, it is surprising that the compilations that represented the views of Cuzco were deemed reliable by the Spaniards. Like the rulers of the ethnically contested and crowded Central Valley of Mexico, the nobles of Cuzco fought among themselves. Although they all came from the same ethnic group, they were politically divided into many competing lineages, or *panacas*. Each panaca furiously vied for power, both before and after the Spanish Conquest, and lineage politics in the Inca state determined many contesting views of the past.[65] Yet in spite of the contradictory nature of the evidence collected, Spaniards did not dismiss the study of Inca antiquities as hopeless; rather, they sought to bring "order" to the narrative. Spanish chroniclers apportioned credit selectively to favor their own Inca clients and their own political agendas (e.g., Betanzos; Viceroy de Toledo's controlled interviews of local witnesses). Spanish authors also forced Andean historiographical sensibilities that allowed for many parallel views of the past into a single chronology to fit the biblical account and European tastes. In an attempt to translate Inca accounts of the past into the European idiom of dynastic genealogies, for example, Spaniards converted the names of some Inca social and political hierarchies into historical figures. Today, there is scholarly consensus that at least the first eight Inca rulers of eleven described in Spanish chronicles were not really historical figures.[66]

But despite these manipulations to make the Inca past fit European historiographical models, Spanish authors showed a willingness to let the indigenous peoples "speak." To do so, they developed techniques to create and validate historical knowledge. Pedro Cieza de León was one of the many sixteenth-century Spanish chroniclers in Peru who strove mightily to pour the contradictory information he obtained from Andeans into available European historiographical molds.[67] He also typified the efforts of Spaniards to develop criteria to apportion credit among the many contradictory versions of the past he encountered in Cuzco.

Cieza de León, who left Spain in 1535 to join the growing ranks of soldiers of fortune in search of riches and glory in South America, journeyed from Panama to Cuzco, a trip that took him fifteen years (1535–50) to complete. Cieza kept diaries of his travels, and upon returning to Spain, he drew on his notes to write a multivolume history of the Andean peoples, of the events surrounding the Conquest of Peru, and of the bloody civil wars among the conquistadors that ensued from the Conquest. In the first part of his work, *La crónica del Perú*, which appeared in Seville in 1553, Cieza described the lands and peoples he had visited. He also hinted at the formidable civilizing force of the Incas. Most nations to the north of the former Inca empire appeared as bestial savages, given to cannibalism, sodomy, and devil worship. However, the closer Cieza got to Cuzco, peoples appeared more civilized, a testimony to the virtues of the former empire of the Incas.[68] Cieza admired the Incas so much that he devoted one of the four parts of his history to them. Entitled *El señorío de los Incas*, it remained unpublished for centuries. In it, however, Cieza spelled out in great detail the underlying historiographical critical principles he followed.

Cieza's descriptions of non-Inca peoples in his *Crónica* are atemporal natural histories of manners and customs. Only occasionally does he hint that these Andeans had a past.[69] When it came to the Incas, however, Cieza assumed they had a history that was worth knowing, and so he set out to write it. One of Cieza's main preoccupations in his *Señorío* was to show that Inca recordkeeping systems were trustworthy. Only alphabetical writing could preserve memory, he thought, and its absence made the reconstruction of the past extremely difficult.[70] Yet, for Cieza, the Incas' ability to keep "records of all the things we now hold to be certain" was a source of wonder and bewilderment.[71] The Incas had used two recordkeeping devices: quipus, to store vital statistics and tax records, and songs, to store historical narratives. Inca quipus seemed "exact and dependable," and kept "with all truth and accuracy, without fraud or deceit."[72] Their songs were also reliable, made so by the high social standing, learning, and well-cultivated memories of those charged with their keeping.[73] Quipus were also sometimes used for historical records, Cieza noted. His history of the deeds of eleven Inca rulers from Manco Capac to Huayna Capac (the father of Atahualpa and Huascar, the Inca leaders whom the Spaniards had confronted) is presented as uneven, for example, because there were differences in the volume of available quipus on each. Quipu "writing" had only been invented under the ninth Inca, Inca Yupanqui (or Pachacuti Inca), and Cieza was therefore able to cover his reign and those of the next two Incas, Tupa Inca Yupanqui (or Tupac Yupanqui) and Huayna Capac, in much greater detail than the history of all the preceding eight Inca monarchs.[74]

As a matter of principle, Cieza privileged the testimony of *orejones*, upperclass Incas who pierced holes in their earlobes as a mark of nobility, over that of plebeians. A man typical of his age, Cieza believed that commoners were utterly unreliable as historical informants, because they had a natural tendency to transform the past into "fables and novels."[75] Although the testimony of the nobility was inherently more valuable, however, it was not all equally valuable either. Throughout, Cieza favored the reports of orejones over those of the provincial indigenous nobles. When elucidating the origins of the name "Viracocha," given by the natives to the conquering Spaniards, for example, Cieza pitted the testimony of the provincials of Cacha against that of the orejones of Cuzco, accepting the testimony of the latter as more credible.[76] Again, Cieza chose the names of the mythical ancestors of the Inca rulers, who had allegedly emerged from caves in a mountain in Pacariqtambo, according to the Cuzco version, even though he knew that many other names were in circulation in the provinces.[77] But even though Cieza did not give much credit to the testimony of provincial elites, he nevertheless refused to pass judgment on the credibility of their historical testimonies. Confronted with the oral testimony of the Cana to the effect that their great ancient leader Zapana had once battled Amazons, Cieza said that only God could know whether this was true.[78]

Cieza not only weighed the testimonies of indigenous elites, he also apportioned credit when the accounts of Spaniards and Amerindians conflicted, systematically according more weight to testimony of orejones than to that offered by the Spaniards, who, according to Cieza, frequently distorted history to justify their depredations. He disregarded Spanish charges that the Incas had sacrificed thousands of children to their gods and engaged in various other savage practices, for example, saying, "I know from the testimony of elderly orejones that the Incas were free of the sin [of sodomy], and that they did not have other bad customs such as cannibalism or engage in public vices." Claims of Inca cannibalism and sodomy were spread by some Spaniards to justify their predatory behavior.[79] Although he put great value on the testimony of eyewitnesses and derided Spanish armchair authors, such as López de Gómara, who had never visited America, Cieza was careful to check the testimony of witnesses against material evidence.[80] Here, again, he proved more prone to disregard the testimony of Spaniards than that of orejones. Some Spaniards, for example, had argued that one of Christ's apostles had visited Peru, and that he had left a temple in his honor in the province of Cacha. Cieza went to Cacha and observed the idols in the temples and concluded that the story of the apostle's visitation was false, for none of the idols there resembled any of the apostles.[81] Numerous ruins of postal relays he found along his path, on the other hand, confirmed the testimony of orejones about an efficient postal service under the Incas.[82]

Cieza thought so highly of the orejones that he allowed them to be the ultimate judges of the validity of their own numerous conflicting accounts. He was confronted with so much contradictory information about the ninth to the eleventh Incas (Inca Yupanqui, Tupa Inca Yupanqui, and Huayna Capac) that he argued that no human was capable of "writing down [in alphabets] all that has been written [in quipus about them]." To be sure, Cieza was aware that the testimony of orejones was sometimes conflicting and contradictory. The solution for Cieza consisted in using only what the orejones themselves called "most credible."[83] After summoning and interviewing representatives of the leading Cuzqueño Inca elite on the history of the Inca empire, Cieza acknowledged that there were many conflicting historical narratives, for each lineage (panaca) was charged with exalting the memory of its own dead ancestor. Unruffled by the historiographical contradictions, and in order to use the testimonies he had collected, Cieza made the conscious decision to substitute a structural, atemporal analysis of the Inca empire for the orderly narrative of dynastic genealogies he had originally set out to compile.[84]

Cieza sought to explain away the more fabulous aspects of Inca history. Take, for example, his accounts of the three mythical ancestors of the Inca said to have emerged from mountain caves in Pacariqtambo. According to the myth, Ayar Cachi had special powers that included the ability to throw stones into the clouds and to knock down mountains with his slingshot. Tricked by his own two brothers, Ayar Cachi once was left buried in a cave, but an earthquake that altered the Andean landscape set him free. Faced with such accounts, Cieza argued that the brothers were in all likelihood three ancient warriors, either from Pacariqtambo or from some other faraway place, who had conquered the neighboring lands. As for the preternatural powers of Ayar Cachi, Cieza explained them as the skills of a trickster, a demon with the power to manipulate nature.[85] Cieza recounted how the sixth Inca, Inca Roca, had had his ears pierced to become an *orejón*. The pain was so intense that Inca Roca fled from Cuzco to a mountaintop, where he put his ear to the ground to soothe it, in a place that had recently been struck by lightning. His ear bled, and he heard a subterranean current. He ordered a hole dug at the spot, from which sprang the river dividing Cuzco. Inasmuch as underground rivers do indeed exist, Cieza thought that the story was plausible.[86]

The writings of Cieza and myriad others demonstrate that in Peru, no less than in Mexico, Spanish antiquarians thought of their work as a "translation" of indigenous testimonies stored in quipus, songs, and other recordkeeping devices. So when Acosta's *Historia natural y civil* appeared, antiquarians interested in Inca history felt compelled to respond. The Inca Garcilaso de la Vega, the son of an Inca Cuzqueño princess and a Spanish conquistador left for Spain at the age of twenty to train both as a soldier and as a scholar. Dissatisfied with Acosta's history and other available printed accounts of the Inca past, he decided to write his own, based on indigenous sources.

Garcilaso spent some twenty years collecting information on the Incas to supersede the printed accounts offered by Spaniards. Until his *Comentarios reales de los Incas* appeared in Lisbon in 1609, Europeans had access to only very limited accounts of the Inca past. In 1552, Francisco López de Gómara (1511–1564) had published his *Historia de la Indias y de la conquista de Mexico*, but this title was misleading, for López de Gómara had little to say about Amerindian antiquities, including those of Mexico, whose myths of origins and records of dynastic lineages he quickly retailed.[87] Likewise, on grounds that the Incas had lacked an alphabet, which was what made people human, López de Gómara provided only one very short chapter on Inca foundation myths.[88] Although much more sympathetic to them than López de Gómara, Cieza did not include a history of the Incas in his 1553 *Crónica*, and his *Señorío* was destined to remain unpublished until the late nineteenth century.

Agustín de Zárate's 1555 history of the discovery and conquest of Peru was also shallow on Peruvian antiquities. Sent out to audit the Peruvian treasury by the emperor Charles V, Zárate (b. 1514) used his time to accumulate information about the civil wars among the Spanish conquistadors then wrecking Peru. He described Andean foundation myths as sacred histories that had become garbled because the Incas lacked alphabetical writing.[89] Although Zárate thought that Inca quipus kept records of the history of "many ages," he only referred to the Incas' most recent past, the deeds of Huayna Capac, Atahualpa, and Huascar.[90]

The history of Jerónimo Román y Zamora (1536–1597), a Dominican friar, published in 1575 was not much of an improvement over those of López de Gómara, Cieza, or Zárate. In the sections devoted to America in his *Repúblicas del mundo*, Román y Zamora offered a summary of Bartolomé de las Casas's *Apologética historia sumaria* (ca. 1559), but his history of the Incas was disappointing. Like Zárate, Román y Zamora praised the accuracy of indigenous recordkeeping devices.[91] Yet he could deliver no more than a perfunctory list of the first eight Inca rulers, and only brief references to the deeds of the ninth Inca, Inca Yupanqui, whom Román y Zamora considered the real civilizing hero of the Andes, rather than Manco Capac.[92]

Finally, in 1601, the royal chronicler of the Indies, Antonio de Herrera y Tordesillas (d. 1625) published the first four "decades" of his massive *Historia general de los hecho de los castellanos* (1601–15), covering events surrounding the Conquest from 1492 to 1531. In the face of swelling European discontent with the conduct of Spaniards in the New World, Herrera was more interested in describing the Spanish military conquest of the Indies and the Spanish crown's attempts to bring justice and law to the new frontier than in discussing Amerindian antiquities. Herrera's sources included both unpublished chronicles such as Cieza's *El señorío de los Incas*, which he ransacked for details, and unpublished official papers. Yet when it came to the history of the Incas and the Aztecs, Herrera had little to add to the information from López de Gómara and Acosta.[93]

Garcilaso read these histories, including José de Acosta's, and decided to write one that would supersede them all. He explicitly cast his history as a commentary and gloss on the available printed Spanish accounts, thus the title of his work, *Comentarios reales de los Incas*.[94] Margarita Zamora has argued that Garcilaso thought of his work as a philological commentary on Quechua terms misunderstood by previous Spanish authors, including a commentary on terms that Andeans used to describe the sacred, such as *huaca*, which Spaniards had often interpreted as evidence of Inca polytheism. Although I agree with Zamora, it seems to me that Garcilaso's employment of the term *comentarios* was also intended as a reference to his glossing of prior Spanish historical sketches, drawing extensively on the unmediated testimony of the Incas' own poems, songs, and quipus.[95]

Although, according to the seventeenth-century Jesuit Bernabé Cobo, Garcilaso "hardly deviated" from the information on Inca antiquities provided by the three major sixteenth-century Spanish inquiries (those of Polo de Ondegardo, Viceroy Toledo, and Martín de la Cruz), Garcilaso insisted that his commentaries were based on personal recollections of twenty years' worth of conversations with his mother's kin, particularly with his uncle, a member of a noble Cuzqueño lineage, whom Garcilaso describes as "that great archive."[96] Garcilaso often introduces transcriptions of long paragraphs of his uncle's version of the Inca past, a text clearly invented but intended to convey the unmediated nature of his information. Garcilaso also maintained that he had access to news from Cuzqueño and provincial classmates in Peru, who, responding to his constant pleas from Spain, had interrogated, transcribed, and sent information stored by quipucamayos.[97] Finally, Garcilaso acknowledged his debt to a Peruvian Jesuit, Blas Valera, who like himself had been born to Amerindian and Spanish parents and had therefore had access to unmediated indigenous testimonies. Parts of Blas Valera's manuscript in Latin on Peruvian antiquities had barely survived the English raid on Cadiz in 1596 and were given to Garcilaso by Pedro Maldonado de Savedra, a Jesuit member of the circle of antiquarians in Cordoba to which the Peruvian mestizo belonged.[98]

Garcilaso's methodology led him to compose a book that although written by a self-confessed "Indian" was destined to become a European classic. In it, some four hundred years of Inca dynastic history parade in all their splendor and exquisite detail, including the deeds and battles of each of the eleven Inca monarchs up to Huayna Capac, the last legitimate ruler of the empire, as well as the civil wars between Atahualpa and Huascar. As I have already described in Chapter 1, Garcilaso's appeal lay in his ability to cast the Inca past in an idiom familiar to the Europeans. The Inca state appeared as a classical virtuous polity, with well-kept dynastic genealogies, and the Inca religion was presented as a rational prefiguration of Christianity, not unlike that achieved by pagan moral philosophers.[99]

It is curious that dissatisfaction with the available printed Spanish versions of the history of Mexico also surfaced in New Spain at about the time when Garcilaso published his history of the Incas. As I have already mentioned, Acosta provided European audiences with the most complete account of

some six hundred years of the history of migrations and travails of those nations who had come to dominate central Mexico, including the peoples of
Mexico — Tenochtitlan, Tlatelolco, Texcoco, and even Tlaxcala, the allies of
Cortés and the nemesis of the Mexica. Acosta had made available the collation and translation of indigenous sources undertaken by Jesuits like Tovar
and Dominicans like Durán. Clearly, Acosta seemed to have superseded all
other writings published by Spaniards on Mexican antiquities, including the
accounts of López de Gómara and Román y Zamora. His work appeared to
be the culmination of some fifty years of Spanish scholarship on central
Mexico. Juan de Torquemada, however, did not think so.

Like Garcilaso, Juan de Torquemada, a Franciscan friar born in Spain, but
who moved to Mexico early in his youth, became dissatisfied with available
Spanish printed sources on the history of Mesoamerica. He maintained that
writers such as López de Gómara, Acosta, and, more recently, Herrera had
not had access to the writings of Andrés de Olmos (ca. 1491–1571), Motolinía,
Bernardino de Sahagún, and Gerónimo de Mendieta (1525–1604), the leading sixteenth-century Franciscan antiquarians, who had collected and studied numerous indigenous sources. As a Franciscan, Torquemada did have access to these authors and also to many indigenous documents, including the
writings of Alva Ixtlilxochitl and of other indigenous chroniclers who independently or under the auspices of the Franciscans had translated Mexican
pictograms and logograms into alphabetic writing. In 1615, Torquemada's
Monarchía indiana appeared in Seville in three volumes. Torquemada's second volume was merely a rewriting of the sections on Mexica religion and
political institutions that he found in the unpublished manuscript of
Bartolomé de Las Casas's *Apologética historia sumaria* (ca. 1559). His own
contribution lay in arguing that Mexica religion, but not that of previous civilizations of central Mexico, was the product of demonic machinations,
whereas Las Casas's had argued that Amerindian idolatry was the consequence of innate postlapsarian fear and weakness operating on rational
human minds. Torquemada's third volume was devoted to chronicling the
history of the Franciscans in Mexico from the time of their arrival there.[100] It
was in the first volume of *Monarchía indiana*, however, that Torquemada was
most original, for in it he set out to supersede all available printed accounts
of the Mexican past.

Torquemada's critique focuses on the assumption of writers such as Acosta
that civilized societies had appeared in Mexico only about six hundred years
prior to the European arrival, as the outcome of a series of ancient northern
migrations into a valley originally occupied by the wild, uncivilized

Chichimecs. Drawing on numerous sources, Torquemada argued that many cycles of civilization had in fact preceded these migrations, and that the peoples whom the Spaniards had found in Mexico (the Mexica, Tlaxcalan, and Texcocan) were relatively recent arrivals. Giants, Toltecs, and other peoples had once dominated central Mexico and had created complex and grandiose civilizations. Torquemada took it upon himself to reconstruct those cycles, particularly the Toltec. He also sought to make transparent the process through which he had apportioned credit to competing indigenous versions of local history.

For Torquemada, as for Cicero, history was philosophy by example. It was also about telling the truth. Discovering the truth was time-consuming, however, because it necessitated painstaking gathering of information, and creating and validating historical knowledge also required great wisdom. Maturity and great learning were needed to weigh evidence, to apportion credit prudently, and to locate events in their right chronological order. Finally, finding the truth required independence, putting aside self-interest and the search for personal rewards.[101]

To be true to the history of central Mexico, Torquemada suggested various narrative strategies. There were chronological gaps in the history of ancient Mexico, many of them caused by the destruction of indigenous sources by zealous friars during the first decades of the Conquest, but inventing data to fill in such lacunae was a strategy better suited to poets than to historians. A reliable and trustworthy history of Mexico required strict adherence to "either what is written or what is transmitted by tradition," making a jumpy and sometimes confusing narrative unavoidable, given the scarcity of sources. Torquemada's lack of narrative control and disorderly style, for which he would be criticized in the following centuries, was in fact a self-conscious technique that vouched for the reliability of his history.

The second constraint on style imposed on the narrative was Torquemada's insistence that the history of Mexico follow a strict chronological order. He condemned authors like López de Gómara and Herrera for including native history only parenthetically, as an aside, to spice up other accounts. Histories such as López de Gómara's and Herrera's, he argued, were the result of a limited access to indigenous sources. These authors had written in Spain, "where they were unable to resolve the doubts that efforts to write the history of the natives engender."[102]

Torquemada repeatedly demonstrated the drawbacks of writing history away from primary indigenous sources. The case of the accounts offered by López de Gómara, Acosta, and Herrera of the marriages and descendants of the first Mexican monarch is illuminating. When the Mexica were still a subordinate nation in the valley of Mexico, they had requested various neighboring rulers to give them a bride for their first elected monarch, Acamapichtli, "Handful of Reeds" (r. 1376–95 in the Codex Mendoza). One after another, their neighbors rejected the Mexica invitation. Finally, one ruler acquiesced and gave Acamapichtli a bride, who, however, turned out barren. The Mexica monarch soon obtained a new bride from another neighboring ruler, from whom he finally got two sons. The confusion originated when Spanish historians sought to identify the names of Acamapichtli's wives, sons, and neighboring rulers. According to Torquemada, the first wife of Acamapichtli was Ilancueitl, given to the Mexica by the ruler of Cohuatlychan. Although barren, Ilancueitl had never returned to her father and therefore had to put up with Cozcatlamiahuatl, Acamapichtli's second wife, given to the Mexica by the neighboring ruler of Tetepanco as a sign of goodwill. Ilancueitl helped raise Cozcatlamiahuatl's second son, Huitzilihuitl. Acamapichtli's first son, Tlatolzaca, became the founder of the Mexica nobility. Torquemada used this example to highlight the errors of previous historians. López de Gómara, for example, had presented Ilancueitl as Acamapichtli's servant, charged with raising Tlatolzaca. Lopéz de Gómara had also argued that Acamapichtli had twenty wives. Lopéz de Gómara's error was the consequence of his distance from the sources, "not knowing history from its roots." Lopéz de Gómara had failed to realize that there was a scale of credibility in the multiple indigenous versions, and that some sources were more reliable than others. Acosta was also distant from the "roots" of Mexican historiography; he had argued that Acamapichtli married a bride offered by Culhuacan. Torquemada chided Acosta for accepting this indigenous account on the grounds that when the Mexica had elected Acamapichtli, they were not even near Culhuacan. Herrera, whom Torquemada insisted had merely drawn from others, had followed Acosta in this, falling blindly into the same error.[103]

Distance from primary sources had made these historians commit an even more serious mistake, which was to assume that the Mexica were the original inhabitants of central Mexico, rather than the last in a series of civilizations. Unlike the previous civilizations of central Mexico, which had developed virtuous religious worship, the Mexica were Satan's chosen people. Moreover, their accounts of their origins were utterly unreliable. Torquemada argued that these accounts were efforts at self-aggrandizement by newcomers attempting to present themselves as the most ancient. Historians, he concluded should privilege the sources of those Nahua peoples who had migrated to the

Central Valley of Mexico before the Mexica, namely, the Aculhua of Texcoco and the Tepanecs of Tacuba and Azcapotzalco[104] (Figs. 2.4, 2.9, and 2.10).

Torquemada argued that the history of the Central Valley of Mexico was particularly difficult to write because there were many contesting versions by rival ethnic groups in circulation. The plurality of accounts complicated efforts to bring chronological order into the material, because there were many available dates for the same event, as well as contradictory sequences of events. The history of a single group, let alone that of the entire region, spawned many contradicting accounts. Many versions of the origins of the Mexica existed, which explained the differences in the narratives of Lopéz de Gómara, Acosta, and Herrera. Torquemada maintained that his own version was trustworthy, however, because he had had access to the source held by the most reliable scribes.[105] Given this plurality of accounts, if writing history was in and of itself time-consuming, writing that of Mesoamerica was even more exacting. "After unraveling the garbled confusion [of chronologies]," Torquemada sighed, after some six years of painstaking labor collating indigenous sources, "I felt I had left the labyrinth of Crete."[106] According to Torquemada, the multiplicity of accounts was the natural outcome of scripts that depended on the oral exegesis of "rabbis and scholars." Politically savvy peoples willfully took advantage of the nature of these scripts to edit and manipulate interpretations of the past.[107]

Torquemada offered numerous examples of how the politics of ethnicity in central Mexico promoted historical distortions. The Mexica and the Tlatelolcan, the two ethnic groups who shared Tenochtitlan, for instance, had two opposite versions of who had first elected a king. The Tlatelolcan maintained that they had elected a king the year before the Mexica, a version that, according to Torquemada, Acosta had wrongly followed. Yet an impartial version of the history of Tenochtitlan offered by the outsider Aculhuas maintained that the Mexica had been first to elect a king. It was patriotism, Torquemada argued, that had made the Tlatelolcan distort the truth: "Emotions [such as patriotism] should not be mixed with truthful histories, whose majesty and gravity should never be violated."[108] Ethnic pride worked in even more subtle ways. The Mexica, for example, had versions that cast Acamapichtli, their first elected monarch, as a warrior who had conquered neighboring peoples. According to Torquemada, this was patently false, for the Mexica under Acamapichtli were a subordinate ethnic group incapable of expanding. Acamapichtli had ruled in peace for twenty-one years, however, laying the groundwork for the future prosperity and power of the Mexica (Fig. 2.4 and Plate 12).[109]

Ethnic politics and a script that was open to easy editing during its exegesis notwithstanding, Torquemada believed that Mesoamerican sources held the truth about the past of the region. Torquemada often privileged the written testimony of the natives, even if it sometimes contradicted that of the Spaniards. On the origins of Amerindians, for example, Torquemada dismissed theories that took the natives to be stranded Carthaginians, because, according to the indigenous sources, they had come from the north, over land bridges connecting America with Asia.[110] But it is perhaps in the sections where he covered the events surrounding the Spanish Conquest of Mexico that Torquemada most clearly demonstrated his willingness to believe indigenous written accounts. Torquemada again took López de Gómara and Herrera to task for using only Spanish sources and excluding Amerindian testimony recorded both in pictograms and in the Roman alphabet in Nahua narratives, "so well written that I wish I could imitate them one day," which had fortunately been collected by Bernardino de Sahagún, who had spent some sixty years exploring the secrets of the land and language of the Mexicans. "The error [of López de Gómara and Herrera]," Torquemada argued, "lay in making inquiries and gathering information [on the Conquest] only using Spanish witnesses and not looking for the testimony of the Indians . . . who [after all] were the ones upon whom the events of the Conquest fell and who kept very good knowledge of those experiences [because] they recorded them as history, first using figures and characters and later alphabetical writing."[111]

Consistent with this view, Torquemada introduced the Amerindians' version of Moctezuma Xocoyoltzin's death. Spanish accounts claimed that the Aztec monarch died as the result of a stone thrown by an Amerindian. Moctezuma had languished for two days, refusing to be treated, and before expiring had asked to be converted to Christianity. The Amerindians, however, maintained that the Spaniards had garroted Moctezuma, along with some Tlatelolcan nobles, in the palace where they were hiding, from which their corpses had subsequently been thrown out.[112] Torquemada also presented the alternative indigenous version of the torture and final execution of Cuauhtemoc, the last Aztec ruler, who resisted the Spanish siege of Tenochtitlan.[113]

Torquemada's willingness to believe indigenous testimonies was based on the assumption that their recordkeeping devices were trustworthy. He thus included the speeches of the Chichimec ruler Nopaltzin, preserved in songs and other mnemonic devices.[114] Mesoamerican scripts were so reliable a means of historical recordkeeping that when confronted with claims that appeared outrageous at face value, Torquemada submitted to the authority of the source. Chronicling the history of the end of the Toltec civilization at the hands of savage invading Chichimec tribes from the north, Torquemada recounted how, after first having sent a scouting party, a million Chichimecs descended on the valley. "This number, I fear, appears incredible, " he explained, "yet it is not my imagination that begets these numbers but they are numbers that I have found in their writings that I assume are accurate and not lying."[115]

Images as Sources in the Early Modern European World

I have belabored the point that, notwithstanding caveats about the sophistication of indigenous writing systems, sixteenth-century Spanish scholarship on Mexican and Peruvian antiquities, culminating in the writings of Torquemada and Garcilaso, held native documents to be reliable. These views were, to be sure, not peculiar to Spain, a country that is often depicted as isolated from larger European intellectual trends. As early as the sixteenth century, European humanists began to discuss how the literary records of Rome's first five centuries had disappeared after the sack of the city by the Gauls in 390 B.C.E. European humanists realized that after the sack, Roman and Greek historians had resorted to other available public written records (annals of the clergy and of magistrates) and to other forms of storing memories, such as songs and oral accounts, to reconstruct the earliest Roman past. Although there was much skepticism about the fabulous histories of early Rome that had survived, until the early eighteenth century, historiographical discussions were not centered on the *reliability* of the sources in alternative recordkeeping devices used by later Roman and Greek historians to reconstruct the earliest Roman past. At the time when Spanish antiquarians were "translating" the testimony of Native Americans preserved by non-alphabetical means, European humanists were also drawing on epic songs and poems from oral traditions to write the histories of their own countries.[116]

Renaissance Europe was not wedded to the ideology of literacy; it was closer to the Middle Ages than to our own time in its attitude to unwritten testimony. In his magisterial account of the impact of literacy in England in the Middle Ages, Michael Clanchy has argued that in the wake of the Norman invasion, literacy became central to the business of governing, but that documents in alphabetical script were more often than not considered unreliable. Before the Norman invasion, land titles and claims to nobility had been validated by the ownership of symbolic objects (swords, knives, and seals) and by the ability to summon numerous trustworthy witnesses in courts of law. The Normans, however, sought to undermine the Anglo-Saxon aristocracy by demanding from it written records in proof of claims to land and nobility. Needless to say, written charters proliferated, as did forgeries. A state bureaucracy, including notaries, developed to validate the new written claims. But even then written documents were not considered reliable. Courts still admitted witnesses and symbolic objects to validate written titles. For many centuries, possession of symbolic objects such as swords, knives, and seals carried as much weight as written charters in cases involving landed property. Although Clanchy traces a history that is peculiar to England, it may be assumed that sensibilities about writing would not have differed widely in the rest of Europe, including Spain, notwithstanding Spain's higher rates of literacy than England during this period.[117]

In Catholic countries, the association of nonalphabetical recordkeeping devices with the reliability of testimony had its own peculiar development in the sixteenth century, which helps explain the Spanish fascination with Mesoamerican pictograms and logograms. As already mentioned, Walter Mignolo has argued that Francesco Patrizi's *Della historia dieci dialoghi* (1560) constituted an isolated challenge to the ideology of alphabetical writing as the only warranty of truth. Yet it is clear that Patrizi was no isolated figure. He belonged to a larger tendency in the Catholic Church to exalt the historiographical value of images in theological debates with iconoclastic Protestants. The Italian scholar Gianfranco Cantelli has suggested that Mexican scripts played a significant role in these debates. For example, Gabriele Paleotti (1524–1597), the archbishop of Bologna, in his *Discorso intorno alle imagini sacre e profane* (1581) insisted that images preceded letters in the postdiluvian era, when humans had lost their ability to write. Using Mexican scripts as evidence, Paleotti insisted that Egyptian hieroglyphs were historically more primitive than alphabets. According to Cantelli, Paleotti's major reformulation of Renaissance histories of writing did not seek to undermine the value of images as reliable means of communication. On the contrary, Paleotti sought to present painting as a more "natural," and thus more efficient, form of transmitting information than alphabetical writing. Paleotti and other members of the Catholic hierarchy insisted that paintings were the most adequate books for the illiterate, and that although they harbored the danger of idolatry, they also held important advantages. Images were a "natural" form of language, whereas alphabets required prior acceptance of conventions.[118]

Catholic Reformation ideas about the pedagogical usage of images had some practical consequences for the survival of local indigenous scripts, particularly in Mexico, after the arrival of alphabetic writing in the New World. Although I subscribe to the idea that whether native scripts survived or disappeared largely depended, both in Mexico and Peru, on political calculations in Amerindian communities, the attitudes of the European conquerors may have helped retard the pace of the obliteration of local scripts. The incorporation of local scripts for purposes of conversion may have played a significant role, particularly in Mexico.

Friars, by and large, thought that Native Americans were by "nature indifferent to internal things and forgetful of them, so [that] they must be helped by means of external appearances."[119] Needless to say, the friars created visual devices to help their charges memorize the basics of Christian doctrine (Fig. 2.1).[120] Fray Jacobo Testera, one of the first Franciscans to arrive in Mexico after the Conquest, was so desperate to get his Christian message across that he had live cats and dogs thrown onto bonfires to teach the natives the sufferings awaiting them in hell. He also put Nahua logograms to good use by creating a genre of codices that today bears his name.[121] Testerian manuscripts made use of phonograms to teach the natives to pray in Latin, among other things. In the seventeenth century, the Franciscan Juan de Torquemada offered a succinct description of how friars like Testera taught the "Pater Noster" to their charges: "The sound that . . . most resembles the word *Pater* is *pantli*, which is represented as a small flag. . . . For *Noster*, the closest sound they have is *nuchtli*, which among us is called 'tuna' [that is, prickly pear cactus, *Opuntia tuna* or *Opuntia ficus-indica*], and in Spain, fig of the Indies. . . . Therefore, after the small flag, the Amerindians draw a 'tuna.' . . . They continue in like fashion to the end of the prayer."[122]

Missionaries also used native glyphs to ease problems of communication that arose during confession. The friars found at least nine different linguistic groups in central Mexico. Since only a few friars were able to master more than one indigenous language, the missionaries encouraged the natives to bring their sins written down in Mesoamerican scripts; like Chinese ideograms, Mexican pictograms and logograms allowed speakers of different languages to communicate with one another.[123] In the new churches, built with the bricks and stones of the old pagan temples, the friars tolerated the presence of indigenous hieroglyphs carved on façades and walls.[124] Mexican pictograms were also presented in treatises of rhetoric as good mnemonic devices to complement Renaissance palaces of memory (Fig. 2.2). In 1579, the year the Jesuit Mateo Ricci landed in Goa on the way to China, where he would deploy the pagan art of memory to hasten conversion of the heathen,

FIGURE 2.1. A Franciscan compound in Mexico. Within the compound, the natives are taught Christian doctrine, music, and writing, tended in infirmaries, given the sacraments (baptism, the Eucharist, penance and confession, matrimony, and the anointing of the sick), and buried. Under the letter *P* (upper left corner), Pedro de Gante and Amerindians "discuss all subjects" (*discunt omnia*), using what appear to be pictograms and logograms. From Diego Valadés, *Rhetorica Christiana* (Perugia, 1579).

the Franciscan friar Diego de Valadés (b. 1533), who had served many years in the province of Mexico, published his *Rhetorica Christiana*, a manual for Christian preachers in the New World, in Perugia. In the sections on memory, Valadés discussed the mnemonic value of Mesoamerican scripts and suggested that Mexican calendars could also be used as memory aids, although did not explain how.[125]

Spanish colonialism in America in the sixteenth century was thus far from being solely an effort at cultural extermination. A more critical reassessment is needed of the complex dynamics of indigenous and Spanish interactions in the New World, particularly in Peru and Mexico. Like William Jones and other British orientalists in India who studied local languages and sources and translated them into English, numerous sixteenth-century Spanish friars, colonists, and bureaucrats collected, collated, and translated Amerindians' historical recollections. To be sure, Spaniards in the New World, as much as the British in India, forced the local versions of the past they encountered into Eurocentric historiographical models. Yet sixteenth-century Spanish historians in the New World exhibited greater sensibility and greater willingness to listen to the voices of non-European "subalterns" than would be the case later in the eighteenth and nineteenth centuries.

Curiosities, Renaissance Humanists, and Amerindian Scripts

In the Renaissance, Europeans avidly sought to collect Native American documents written in pictograms and logograms.[126] In the sixteenth and seventeenth centuries, especially in Italy, cabinets of curiosities could show a variety of Mesoamerican annals and divinatory calendars, along with samples of Amerindian ceramics, textiles, and featherwork. The Medici were particularly fond of things Mexican and put together an impressive collection through the sixteenth century. By the late 1580s, the third grand duke of Tuscany, Ferdinand II (1549–1609), had acquired Bernardino de Sahagún's Florentine Codex and hired Lodovico Buti to paint frescos representing the New World in the Uffizi Palace. Ferdinand ordered Buti to draw his models from the polyglot, "illustrated" texts assembled by the Franciscan a few years earlier in Mexico.[127] In 1603, the Italian naturalist Ulisse Aldrovandi (1522–1605?) gave his cabinet of curiosities, full of objects from the New World, as a legacy to the city of Bologna, and it was later opened to the public as a museum. Between 1665 and 1677, the city received two more cabinets containing "Americana": Count Valerio Zani's and Ferdinando Cospi's. Believing it to be a *libro della China* (a book from China), Zani (d. 1696), who was a pa-

FIGURE 2.2. A chart on mnemonic images that stand for letters. In Renaissance palaces of memory, rhetoricians distributed striking mental sculptures along imagined courtyards and chambers to remind themselves of the order and content of speeches. Images of letters were hung on mental sculptures to clarify further the content of the passage committed to memory. In this mnemonic chart, the iconography is mostly indigenous and the images appear to be addressed to rhetoricians preaching in Indian languages. The images in the chart bear a striking resemblance to Mesoamerican pictograms and logograms and represent Otomí, Tarascan, or Nahuatl words; A = *achásami* (Tarascan) = man; C = *cotocaoeni* (Otomí) = non-turkey fowl; P = *pohhaí* (Otomí) = owl. (Thanks to David Tavárez who identified the words in the chart for me.) From Diego Valadés, *Rhetorica Christiana* (Perugia, 1579). Unfortunately, Valadés does not discuss the chart at all.

tron of travelers, acquired a Mixtec ritual-divinatory calendar, which he gave to Cospi, the marquis of Petrioli, who in turn gave it to the Bologna museum. By the late seventeenth century, Bologna boasted one of the greatest collections of Native American objects, including the Mixtec book, now called the Codex Cospi.[128]

Mesoamerican indigenous books often changed hands in the culture of deference and courtly patronage that determined the fate of curiosities in early modern European collections. The history of the so-called Codex Vindobonensis, or Vienna Codex (Fig. 2.8), typifies the ways in which Mesoamerican books circulated. Upon his arrival on the coast of Veracruz in 1519, Cortés sent to Emperor Charles V (r. 1519–56) an indigenous book that recorded the dynastic genealogies of the Mixtec from the eighth through the mid fourteenth centuries. The emperor, in turn, offered it as a present to his brother-in-law, Manuel I, then king of Portugal (r. 1495–1521). In 1521, Manuel gave the annals to Giulio de' Medici (1478–1534), the future Pope Clement VII, along with a Mexican blanket of parrot feathers and a set of indigenous bells. Upon the pope's death, Ippolito de' Medici (1509–1535) inherited his uncle's estate, including the Mesoamerican book. But Ippolito himself died a year later. In 1535, one of Ippolito's creditors, the German cardinal of Capua, Nicolaus Schomberg, asked to be paid in items from the deceased's estate and thus got the annals. Schomberg died soon afterward, and in 1537, his estate, along with the Mesoamerican annals, went to Germany, where the exact location of the Mixtec dynastic genealogy for the next hundred years remains a mystery. In 1650, however, it resurfaced in the cabinet of curiosities of Prince Wilhelm of Saxe-Weimar. By 1677, it was in the hands of Wilhelm's son, the duke of Saxe-Eisenach, who that year presented it to Emperor Leopold I. The latter deposited it in his library, the Imperial Library of Vienna, where it has been ever since.[129]

Despite their status as curiosities, Mesoamerican books were considered reliable historical sources in both Europe and New Spain. In 1553, André Thevet (1502–1590), soon to be royal cosmographer to the king of France, obtained a set of documents that the viceroy of New Spain, Antonio de Mendoza (r. 1535–49), had recently ordered painted, recording Aztec annals from 1325 C.E. to the Spanish Conquest in pictograms and logograms, including tributary lists from towns subordinated to the Aztecs and descriptions of assorted indigenous customs and laws. After falling prize to a French privateer en route to Spain, this so-called Codex Mendoza wound up in the hands of Thevet, who drew on it for his books on cosmography and biographies. In 1587, three years before his death, and with his scholarly reputation in decline, Thevet sold the Codex to Richard Hakluyt, then chaplain to the English ambassador in Paris. A staunch supporter of a policy of Atlantic maritime expansion, at a time when England accepted Spanish hegemony in the New World, Hakluyt had set out to compile a collection of English travel accounts, and he acquired the Codex Mendoza in hope of finding in it strategic information about the Spanish empire in America. Samuel Purchas, an Anglican pastor, who inherited Hakluyt's papers, subsequently published the Codex Mendoza (Figs. 2.4 and 2.5a and Plate 12), for the first time, in 1625, as part of a multivolume universal history and compilation of travel accounts entitled *Hakluytus Posthumus, or Purchas His Pilgrimes*.[130]

Purchas thought that just as humans were superior to animals because they had understanding and speech, and thus the ability to dominate animals by use of communication and reason, some groups of humans "excelled" others, who were "Brutish, Savage, [and] Barbarous," solely because the former were able to communicate through writing. The want of letters animalized peoples like the Amerindians, who seemed "in comparison of [Europeans who had writing] as speaking Apes."[131] Implicit in Purchas's formula lay the assumption that literate Europeans had the right to dominate Amerindians in the same way that humans had the right to dominate animals. Nonetheless, Purchas thought that Inca "Quippos in stones or Threads" and Mexican "Pictures" were forms of writing.[132] Consistent with his definition of Mexican pictograms as writing, Purchas printed the entire Mendoza collection, along with an English translation of the accompanying Spanish glosses. Purchas not only relied on Spanish interpretations of Mexican sources but used the Codex Mendoza as his documentary foundation for the sections on Mexico of his history of the world.[133]

Purchas's exaggerated yet vacuous rhetoric about the value of alphabetical writing in essence resembles the attitude of sixteenth-century Spanish humanists to Mesoamerican scripts and annals. Like the Spaniards on whose scholarship he drew, Purchas also limited himself to translating Amerindian accounts of events.[134]

Conjectural Histories of Writing

After conjectural histories maintaining that writing evolved gradually from primitive painting to alphabets began to appear in Europe in the late seventeenth and early eighteenth centuries, Amerindian scripts ceased to be valued as repositories of reliable accounts.[135] Since the sixteenth century, Spanish scholars had characterized nonalphabetical scripts as merely the early stages in the gradual ascent of reason toward the mastery of the visual representation of speech. However, the novelty of the new conjectural histories of writing lay rather in presenting nonalphabetical scripts as untrustworthy. More important, too, conjectural histories deployed systems of writing to demonstrate the evolution of the human mental faculties. Amerindian documents were used to demonstrate the progress of the human spirit through various mental stages rather than as reliable historical records.

The use of Amerindian scripts, and in particular Mesoamerican pictograms, to shed light on the Old World's history began as early as the sixteenth century. Perhaps the Italian scholar Monsignor Michele Mercati (1541–1593) offered the first full-fledged statement. In *De gli obelischi di Roma* (1589), Mercati set out to clarify the meanings of the hieroglyphs carved on ancient Egyptian obelisks recently unearthed from local ruins by Domenico Fontana, architect of Pope Sixtus V's ambitious renovation of Rome. As Gianfranco Cantelli has shown, Mercati drew on the scholarship of his colleague Paleotti, who in his *Discorso intorno alle imagine sacre et profane* had offered a conjectural history of writing that treated hieroglyphs as primitive, yet reliable forms of writing. Mercati, who thought that alphabetical writing was not a human but a divine invention, sought nevertheless to explain the origin of Egyptian hieroglyphs as a postlapsarian human creation that had begun as primitive picture-writing, not unlike that used by the Mexica and the Ethiopians. Egyptian hieroglyphs, however, had later evolved into forms of symbolic writing, a means devised by cunning priests to keep arcane and sophisticated knowledge away from the masses.[136]

In 1626, the Italian antiquarian Lorenzo Pignoria (1571–1631) also turned to Mexican books to shed light on the history of Egypt, but he reached very different conclusions from those of Mercati. Well known among European antiquarians for his interpretation of the "Isiac table," a stela with Egyptian hieroglyphs dating back to Ptolemaic times, Pignoria was a staunch follower of Annius de Viterbo, a late-fifteenth-century forger who had sought to persuade Europeans that they were the descendants of the Egyptian hero Osiris. Pignoria was determined to prove that Egyptians had done more than just colonize Europe, and that they had also created the Hindu, Chinese, Japanese, and Mesoamerican civilizations. In 1626, to prove that Asian and American deities derived from analogous Egyptian ones, Pignoria adduced statues and paintings in the cabinets of curiosities of friends and patrons. In the case of America, he also drew on a copy made in Italy in the 1560s by Pedro de los Ríos of a compilation of pictograms of Mexica gods, ritual calendars, and histories, the original of which has since been lost. Now known as the Codex Ríos (or Vaticanus 3,738), this included Italian glosses, and Pignoria followed these and the images of the book to show that the Mexica were familiar with many ancient Egyptian scientific and religious concepts (see, e.g., Fig. 2.3), including the idea of a nine-sphere cosmos, the Chain of Being, the Trinity, the Flood, and the devil. To prove the Egyptian origins of the Mexica, Pignoria also compared their systems of writing, which he assumed were both hieroglyphical. Pignoria found confirmation of the symbolic nature of Mexican writing in the Codex Ríos. As with Egyptian writing, some symbols, according to the authors of the glosses to the Codex, held deeper symbolic significance: thus, a deer represented a thankless man, and a lizard copiousness of water; a stone next to wilted maize stood for sterility, whereas green corn stalks signified bountifulness.[137]

If Pignoria's comparison of Mexica script to Egyptian hieroglyphs was unusual, his attempt to establish a conjectural history of Egyptian migrations was nothing new. In his *Oedipus aegyptiacus*, published between 1652 and 1654 in four stout folio volumes, Athanasius Kircher (1602–1680) had sought to trace Egyptian migrations on the assumption that most pagan religions had originated in Egypt. Kircher thought that only two ancient peoples, the Hebrews and the Egyptians, had enjoyed a privileged insight into the structure of the cosmos, the former through God's own dispensation and the latter through their own independent and pious accumulation of knowledge. Just as God had encoded his work in symbols, writing the books of nature and revelation in sacred hieroglyphic characters, the pious Egyptians (and Hebrews) had understood that objects and writings always had deeper symbolic meanings. Kircher mustered geometry, mathematics, music, alchemy, medicine, astrology, and architecture to prove that Egyptian texts were polysemic, adumbrating the teachings of the Bible. Migrations and demonic manipulation, however, had made peoples forget the original Egyptian and Hebrew sacred knowledge. According to Kircher, scripts were proof that the descendants of the Egyptians had strayed from the truth. Unlike the Egyptians, who had stored profound theological and philosophical insights in their hieroglyphs, the Chinese, Hindu, Mexican, and other descendants of the Egyptians had, however, lost their capacity to write symbolically. In Kircher's account, Mexican scripts are interpreted as mere pictograms (see Fig. 2.4), if useful as historical evidence.[138]

As part of their larger efforts to trace the history of writing or peoples, Mercati, Pignoria, and Kircher focused their attention on the similarities and differences between Mexican scripts and Egyptian hieroglyphs. They were not, however, interested in weighing the credibility of records written in

FIGURE 2.3. Similarities between the Mexica deity Homocoya (taken from the Codex Ríos) and Osiris. According to Lorenzo Pignoria, Homocoya was "the creator of everything," First Cause, and the Trinity. Pignoria explained this resemblance to Christian ideas as the product of either a blurred reflection of natural reason or demonic deception. From Lorenzo Pignoria, "Seconda parte delle imagini de gli dei indiani," in Vicenzo Cartari, *Imagini de gli dei delli antichi*, 2d ed. (Padua, 1626). Courtesy of the Biblioteca Nacional, Madrid.

primitive scripts. Apportioning credit to documents written in nonalphabetical scripts was a preoccupation that came to dominate the late seventeenth century, a period that Paul Hazard has characterized as one of *crise de la conscience européenne*. This crisis of European consciousness originated in, among other sources, the multiple skeptical attempts of "freethinkers" to challenge the validity of the Bible as reliable universal history. Richard Simon's higher criticism presenting the Pentateuch as the product of multiple ages and scribes went hand in hand with the efforts of Spinoza to cast the Bible as the mythic-historical records of just one provincial people, the Jews. There were other intellectual developments as well. New naturalistic accounts of the origins of civil society explained the emergence of human institutions without any recourse to providential metanarratives. Moreover, the discovery, study, and elucidation of ancient sources and chronologies of Egyptians, Chaldeans, Phoenicians, Greeks, and Romans, combined with the arrival of new ones, particularly from China, cast doubt on the reliability of the entire biblical chronology. Even more seriously, the biblical Creation was itself called into question by the revival of ancient pagan doctrines positing the eternity of matter and the publication of Isaac La Peyrère's *Praeadamitae* in Amsterdam in 1655, which insisted that humans had inhabited the earth before Adam.[139]

Pious scholars reacted furiously to these attacks. A favorite strategy among scholars to bolster the authority of the Bible consisted in challenging all alternative chronologies, including those of the Egyptians and Chinese. In the process, nonalphabetical scripts were cast as primitive, unreliable record-keeping devices. The Anglican divine Edward Stillingfleet (1635–1699), was typical of this new breed of intellectuals bent on dismissing nonbiblical universal chronologies. In his *Origines sacrae* (1662), Stillingfleet sharply summarized the ideas of modern "atheists" as a tripartite challenge to the Bible, which included "the irreconcilability of the account of Times in Scripture with that of the learned and ancient Heathen Nations; the inconsistency of the belief of the Scriptures with the principles of reason; and the account which may be given of the Origin of things from the principles of Philosophy without the Scriptures."[140] To be sure, Stillingfleet spent part of his voluminous treatise proving the consistency between "principles of reason" and "the belief of the Scripture" and the inconsistencies in the doctrine of the eternity of matter. More important for my purposes, Stillingfleet sought to address those critics who maintained "the irreconcilability of the account of Times in Scripture with that of the learned and ancient Heathen Nations." His strategy was simple. On the one hand, he cast doubt on the credibility of all an-

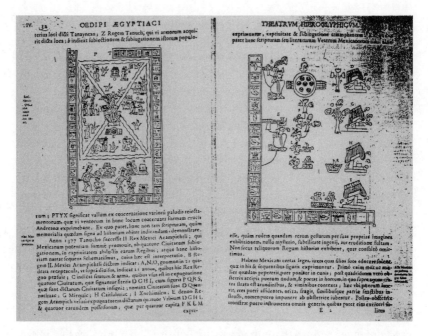

FIGURE 2.4. Athanasius Kircher's copy of pages of the Mendoza collection edited by Purchas. The image on the left records events from years 2 House (1325, *upper left*) through 13 Cane (1349, *upper center*) that led to the foundation of the city of Tenochtitlan in a lake (see also Plate 12). The bottom of this image recounts the military campaigns that the first elected Mexica monarch, Tenoch ("Nopal Stone") waged on the towns of Culhuacan ("Place of those with ancestors") and Tenayuca ("Ramparts"). The image on the right describes twenty-one years of the reign of Tenoch's alleged heir, Acamapichtli ("Handful of Reeds"), who appears here conquering the neighboring towns of Cuahnahuac ("Beside the Trees"), Mizquic ("On the Mesquite"), Cuitlahuac ("On the Water-Excrement"), and Xuchimilco ("Flower Field"). Torquemada would have disagreed strongly with this sequence of events. According to Torquemada, the first Mexica monarch was Acamapichtli, not Tenoch. Moreover, under Acamapichtli, the Mexica were still a subordinate ethnic group with no power to make war on their neighbors. Kircher concluded that Mexica script differed considerably from Egyptian hieroglyphs. These pages exemplify how ideograms and calendrical signs combined to create sophisticated historical narratives. From Athanasius Kircher, *Oedipus aegyptiacus* (Rome, 1652–54).

cient historical accounts that seemed to challenge the Bible. On the other hand, he emphasized the credibility of Moses, the alleged author of the Pentateuch, whose learning and wisdom vouched for his credibility.

Of all the available accounts of heathen nations, Stillingfleet concentrated his attention on those of the Greeks, Chaldeans, Phoenicians, and Egyptians. Throughout, he dismissed heathen alternative chronologies as either fakes or the products of unreliable or misunderstood calendrical systems; he also sought to undermine the character and credibility of heathen historians. Stillingfleet argued that heathen histories were false because internal analyses demonstrated "monstrous confusion [and] ambiguity" in them; contradictions surfaced as soon as the accounts were checked against one another; the chronologies were the product of nations bent on patriotic self-aggrandizement. More important, Stillingfleet dismissed them because of the "defect, weakness and insufficiency" of the recordkeeping devices with which they had been kept.[141]

Stillingfleet set out to prove that only alphabetical writing was capable of keeping reliable historical records. After the Flood, most nations had lost their original, God-given ability to write, because, as in contemporary English colonies, the isolated tended to revert to barbarism. Stillingfleet therefore offered a conjectural history of writing in which Egyptian hieroglyphs appeared as a stage even more primitive than speech itself, a recordkeeping device "clogged with two inconveniences very unsuitable to the propagation of knowledge which were obscurity and ambiguity." Only alphabetical writing was more "lasting than words, more firm than memory, more faithful than tradition."[142] Moses was trustworthy because he alone had had access to reliable Jewish historical records. The Jews alone put a premium on the exact mechanism of transmission of traditions.[143]

In France, the question of the Bible's credibility as a universal history was conveniently couched as a debate about the credibility of the sources upon which later Greek and Roman historians had chosen to reconstruct the history of early Rome. As already noted, during the Renaissance, it was conventionally argued that Greek and Roman historians had reconstructed Rome's origins and the first five centuries of Roman history from nonliterary sources, including family memoirs and songs (carmina) and the lists of pontiffs and magistrates (the fasti), as well as other public documents. In the early eighteenth century, the reliability of these sources came under close scrutiny by the Académie des inscriptions et belles-lettres. The debate this time pitted pious scholars against skeptical "freethinkers." The abbé Antoine Anselme (1652–1737) began the exchange with two memoirs defending the credibility of Moses and the Pentateuch, read to the members of the Académie in 1715 and in 1720. In the first memoir, Anselme maintained that the Jews had uninterrupted written accounts that went back to Creation, from which Moses had drawn. Even without access to such an uninterrupted written tradition, Moses could have drawn information from other equally reliable sources, including statues, inscriptions, temples, and the architecture of cities. Songs and myths also stored trustworthy historical information, although in a garbled fashion.[144]

Freethinkers at the Académie, such as Louis-Jean Levesque de Pouilly (1691–1750), challenged Anselme's views. In 1722, Levesque de Pouilly delivered a memoir in which he called into question each and every one of the recordkeeping devices that Anselme had cited to defend the credibility of the Pentateuch. Querying the reliability of sources such as family memoirs, inscriptions, and mythology, he suggested that recordkeeping devices gained in credibility as they evolved. The annals of the magistrates and pontiffs and of the neighboring peoples of Rome, from which later historians had drawn their information to reconstruct the early history of Rome prior to the sack of the city by the Gauls, were primitive, untrustworthy records.[145] Such primitive recordkeeping devices and orally transmitted information led to distorted recollections: "The histories that are trusted to the memory of man are altered in the mouths of each of those who successively transmit them. The more these [types of oral] histories distance themselves from their origins, the more foreign accretions are added to them and the fewer things in them we can trust, until any trace of truth disappears from them entirely."[146] Only the written testimony of witnesses might be trustworthy, but even then, historians needed to be careful of their character and motivations.[147]

The debate continued within the Académie and included members as prominent as Nicolas Fréret, who came to the support of the use of oral traditions, particularly mythology, as an important source for reconstructing obscure eras. According to Fréret, mythology garbled popular historical recollections of significant social and cultural events. The role of the historian, he argued, was to unveil the historical meaning of those recollections.[148] The last word in the debate, however, came from an outsider to the Académie, Louis de Beaufort (1703–1795), who agreed with Levesque de Pouilly that the credibility of all nonalphabetical scripts was suspect. So, too, was the credibility of Greek and Roman historians such as Dionysius of Halicarnassus and Quintus Fabius Pictor, who had allegedly reconstructed the history of Rome from nonliterary sources.[149]

In Italy, much ink was also spent in discussion of the reliability of nonalphabetical sources. Giambattista Vico produced various editions of his *Scienza nuova* from 1725 to 1744 to do battle with freethinkers bent on destroying the historical authority of the Bible. Vico was concerned that new modern historical narratives left no room for God in their accounts of the origins of human social institutions. By insisting that history revealed regular and lawful patterns, Vico sought to create a new science to demonstrate the workings of an indirect Providence operating though the law of unintended consequences. Like Stillingfleet, Vico solved the problem posed by alternative heathen chronologies by positing a radical distinction between the chronology and credibility of the Bible and the untrustworthiness of alternative heathen historical narratives. Again like the Anglican divine, Vico maintained that the Pentateuch was the result of an uninterrupted written historical tradition, and that nonbiblical chronologies were unreliable, because they were those of peoples who had lost the ability to write after the Flood. Moreover, like Stillingfleet, Vico maintained that the historiography of the heathen nations was the unreliable product of patriotic self-aggrandizement.[150]

Like Stillingfleet, Vico was concerned with finding forms to create and validate historical knowledge, but he went about it differently. Vico did not attempt to demonstrate the credibility of Moses or prove the consistency of the account offered by the Pentateuch. For Vico, humans could never have access to the mind of the Creator, hence God was unintelligible and certainty about the laws of nature unreachable. Truth was to be found in disciplines such as geometry and history, created by human beings. Like geometry, human social institutions were built upon conventions created by human beings themselves and had a history. The history of such principles, Vico maintained, "ought to be found within the modifications of our very own human minds."[151] However, two impediments had to be overcome to create the science of history, namely, *la boria delle nazioni* and *la boria de' dotti*: the conceit of nations and the conceit of the learned. Greeks, Chaldeans, Scythians, Egyptians, and Chinese boasted of "having been the first founders of the humanity of the ancient world."[152] The conceit of scholars assumed that ancient peoples were as learned as the scholars themselves, and that ancient myths and hieroglyphs therefore stood for sophisticated knowledge stored allegorically both in speech and paintings.

Vico pierced through the self-aggrandizing narratives of ancient heathen nations and through layers of accumulated commentary on myths and hieroglyphs by academics to find that the minds of nations, like those of individuals, developed in stages. Ancient Egyptian hieroglyphs held no mystic meanings, and Greek myths were not sophisticated philosophical allegories.

Hieroglyphs and myths were the product of primitives who projected themselves and their fears onto the cosmos using figurative, not abstract, rational thought.

According to Vico, the history of the heathen (gentiles) could only be indirectly reconstructed through the study of myths, oral tradition, and linguistics. That of the Jews, however, was directly accessible in the Bible, because they had not degenerated into childlike poetic primitives after the Flood, and had therefore never lost track of their history.[153] Vico found in the very chronology of the Egyptians a clue to understanding the stages of the development of the mind of the heathen. The Egyptians had classified their own history into three ages: the age of gods, the age of heroes, and the age of man. Each age, Vico maintained, had witnessed the development of a corresponding system of writing: hieroglyphic, or sacred; symbolic, or figurative; and epistolary, or vulgar.[154] The human mind went through similar stages, as did writing, which evolved from primitive hieroglyphs to alphabets (the epistolary stage). In the age of gods, humans were so limited that they expressed themselves in monosyllables, and words consisted simply of endless lists of deities. Later, this age witnessed the development of songs recounting the myths of gods and goddesses. The names and songs of deities sought to signify particular events in the past of the primitives. In the age of heroes, the gentiles still spoke in songs and poetry, but now they kept their garbled historical recollections in myths of heroes and heraldic signs. The final age, that of men, at last witnessed the arrival of prose, of alphabetical writing, and of the ability to think abstractly without recourse to figures and tropes.

As he sought to undermine the credibility of the historiography of all ancient nations but the Jews, Vico paradoxically went about creating a new science to "recover the underlying truth" (*i motivi del vero*) in "vulgar traditions" and languages.[155] Not only did myths preserve clues about the events of the past, but the history of important social changes also lay hidden beneath words.[156] Vico's *Scienza nuova* was a blueprint on how to interpret myths and words as reliable historical records. Like fossils and ruins, words and myths were material evidence upon which to reconstruct the past. So, too, were writing systems, which encapsulated the development of human mental faculties.

Vico demonstrated that conjectural histories of writing did not simply call into question the reliability of "primitive" scripts, but described the progress of the human mind. Conjectural histories of writing as histories of the mind, in fact, first appeared in Restoration England, a society traumatized by the English Civil War, for which "enthusiasts"—zealous religious reformers and dabblers in Neoplatonism and the occult — were widely blamed. In an effort to discredit the Egyptian sources from which enthusiasts allegedly drew their inspiration, Egyptian and Mexican scripts were treated as manifestations of early stages of mental development. In 1668, the English scholar John Wilkins (1614–1672) unveiled his "real characters" and "philosophical language." Wilkins sought to create a script that would allow individuals from different nations to communicate with one another without equivocation, a recorded language isomorphic with nature, resembling the structure of the world itself. There was nothing new about his quest. Beginning with the Renaissance, Neoplatonists had thought that Egyptian hieroglyphics were a philosophical language. A mechanical philosopher and a founding member of the Royal Society, Wilkins, however, had little sympathy for enthusiasts and Neoplatonism. Far from being a "philosophical language," he argued, Egyptian hieroglyphs were useless. "But there is no reason to doubt whether there be any thing in these [Egyptian hieroglyphics] worth the inquiry," Wilkins concluded, "the discoveries that have been hitherto made out of them being but very few and insignificant. They seem to be but slight, imperfect inventions, suitable to those first and ruder Ages; much of the same nature with that Mexican way of writing by Picture." According to Wilkins, Egyptian hieroglyphs were identical to Mexican pictograms, the script of "first and ruder Ages."[157]

In France, conjectural histories of writing as histories of the mind appeared not to attack enthusiasts but to contradict the alleged exaggerations of the Jesuits regarding the accomplishments of China. In a memoir presented to the Académie des inscriptions in 1718, Nicolas Fréret sought to deflate European representations of Chinese erudition. Along with Montesquieu, Fréret had the opportunity to learn Chinese ideograms from Arcadio Huang, a Chinese scholar who arrived in Paris in 1711 to help catalogue the Chinese holdings of the Royal Library. After taking a course with Huang for no more than two years, Fréret found that the Jesuits had exaggerated the complexity of Chinese writing and civilization. French Jesuits in particular had contributed throughout the seventeenth century to the creation of an image of a millenarian Chinese civilization led by old sages. This image, among other things, challenged the authority of the Bible, for the Chinese boasted chronologies more ancient than any the Judeo-Christian sources could offer and appeared to live happily under a naturalistic moral system without any need of religious revelations. The prestige of China in Europe reached such heights that, by the second half of the seventeenth century, reputed scholars such as Leibniz thought that Chinese writing was the long-sought "philosophical language," a script to record things according to natural taxonomies. In his memoir, however, Fréret located Chinese writing low on the evolutionary scale, reducing the some 70,000 ideograms to 214 "radicals" and proving that Chinese metaphysics had never been complex enough to devise a philosophical language. Fréret based his attempt to prick the bubble created by the Jesuits on the assumption that scripts proceeded through evolutionary stages. He thought that the mind evolved teleologically, gaining greater power of abstraction, from Mexican pictograms to Chinese characters to alphabetical writing.[158]

The most significant conjectural history of writing as a philosophical history of the mind, however, was not Fréret's but that of William Warburton, Anglican bishop of Gloucester (1698–1779). Hidden in the pages of his elephantine *The Divine Legation of Moses*, Warburton presented the Europeans with one of the most influential eighteenth-century conjectural histories of writing. Like Wilkins, Vico, and Fréret, Warburton cast his history of writing as a study of the evolution of human mental faculties. But unlike his intellectual predecessors, Warburton wrote his history to bolster the authority of the ancient Egyptians. In his convoluted treatise, Warburton sought to defend the credibility of the Pentateuch based on internal evidence. According to Warburton, most contemporary defenses of the Pentateuch (e.g., Stillingfleet's) had focused on the character of Moses. An internal defense, however, might not only be more compelling but also put future debate to rest. If only it could be proven that the Pentateuch had been written under the auspices of Providence, without having to defend first the character, judgment, and learning of Moses, then the authority of the Bible would forever be saved.

Warburton sought to prove that unlike other great ancient legislators, Moses had given laws to the Jews that did not include the doctrine of a future state of rewards and punishments. If this were indeed the case, Moses' dispensation ran counter to the accumulated political insights of pagan nations, including the Egyptians, from whom not only the Greeks but Moses himself had derived their learning. The wise had always known that laws did not suffice to create social contracts and civilized governments. Only religion, by controlling morality, could civilize societies. Understanding this, ancient legislators had invented religious dispensations that struck fear into people's hearts and offered them either punishment or rewards in the afterlife. Moses had not had recourse to these ancient forms of civic religion when he gave laws to the Jews, however, making his dispensation seem truly providential.[159]

Albeit convoluted, the logic of Warburton's thesis built on the very arguments that freethinkers had offered to erode the credibility of the Bible: the account by Hobbes of the transition from the state of nature to civil society; the claims of English deists such as John Toland (1670–1722) that all ancient peoples had drawn their laws and learning from the Egyptians; and Spinoza's insight that in the Pentateuch there were no references to the doctrine of future rewards. Paradoxically, Warburton found his most important opponents in the camp of his potential allies. Pious men such as Stillingfleet had done a splendid job of undermining the credibility of Egyptian historiography and paring down Egyptian chronologies to make them fit the biblical narrative. In 1728, in *The Chronology of Ancient Kingdoms,* Isaac Newton had used hair-splitting etymologies and astronomy to take 500 years off the traditional record of Greek history in order to deny Egyptians their vaunted antiquity. Newton had also rejected the credibility of any historian before Herodotus. Ultimately, Newton's chronology, like Stillingfleet's theories, was designed to bolster the historical credibility of the Bible. Warburton took on Newton and all those who had sought to deny that Moses drew his learning from the Egyptians.[160]

To restore Egypt's much-denied antiquity to it, Warburton paradoxically turned against the tradition, typified by Vico, that used conjectural histories of writing to undermine the value of Egyptian sources. The ancient Egyptians had necessarily been a people of fantastic antiquity, Warburton argued, because Egyptian hieroglyphs had a long and complicated history, and pictograms such as those found in Siberia and the New World were the earliest stage of writing (Fig. 2.5). When Moses lived among the Egyptians, they had already developed alphabets and secret symbols, and it took time for primitive pictographic hieroglyphs to have evolved into sophisticated alphabets and "tropological" secret symbols.

Classical tropes such as synecdoche, metonymy, and metaphor were the mechanisms that Warburton chose to explain the transformation of writing from its most primitive pictographic origins. Like the Mexica, Old World peoples had first been compelled to write in pictures. But as painted communication became time-consuming and burdensome, some nations began to use parts of pictures to represent events (e.g., two hands and a shield and a bow to signify a battle). The use of synecdoche gave way to metonyms, and parts of objects began to be used to represent the whole (e.g., an eye to signify God's omniscience). Later, metaphors allowed nations to draw analogies between seemingly unrelated objects (e.g., a serpent in a circle to represent the universe, because the serpent's spots signified the stars). The most primitive extant Egyptian hieroglyphs were both metonymical and metaphorical,

 PLATE I.

A Mexican Picture History of the 51 years Reign of their Monarch Tenuch. From Purchas.

a

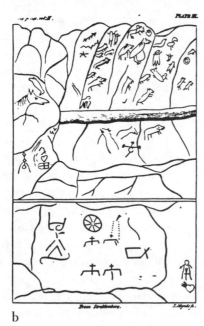

PLATE II.

From Strahlenberg.

b

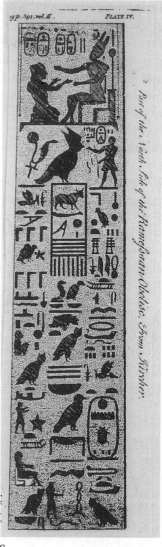

 PLATE IV.

Part of the 14th Side of the Ramesean Obelisk. From Kircher.

c

FIGURE 2.5. Scripts used by Bishop Warburton to illustrate the "tropological" development of writing and the mind: (a) Mexica annals describing events after the foundation of Tenochtitlan; (b) pictographic characters found in Siberia; (c) Egyptian hieroglyphs from an obelisk; (d) pictographic writing of the Huron and Iroquois. Unlike Samuel Purchas and Athanasius Kircher, Warburton made no attempt to read Aztec script, which he merely used to illustrate the development of the mental faculties. From William Warburton, *The Divine Legation of Moses*, 2d ed. (London, 1738–42).

which proved their great antiquity. The ancient Egyptians had let their imaginations run wild, however, and embodied their knowledge of nature in even more arcane metaphors, in the process creating sacerdotal symbols that kept the mysteries of their religion secret from the masses. Moreover, the Egyptians soon broke altogether with the hieroglyphic pattern that named things, not words and used conventional signs to represent words. Furthermore, Hermes, secretary to an Egyptian king, invented signs to represent sounds and to keep state affairs secret. According to Warburton, the Egyptians at the time of Moses had at their disposal a gamut of writing systems, ranging from hieroglyphic proper to sacerdotal-symbolic to epistolic and hierogramatic (Fig. 2.6).[161]

The philosophes were indifferent to Warburton's original intent of defending the authority of the Bible; however, they did embrace his conjectural history of writing. Only section 4 of book 4 of Warburton's *Divine Legation* was translated into French in 1744.[162] The French translation was soon recy-

FIGURE 2.6. The development of conventional signs and alphabets according to Bishop Warburton: (a) the evolution of Chinese ideograms from pictograms to conventional signs; (b) the emergence of alphabetical script in Egypt from hieroglyphs. From William Warburton, *The Divine Legation of Moses,* 2d ed. (London, 1738–42).

cled in Condillac's *Essai sur les origines des connaissances humaines* (1746) and by D. J. Jaucourt for the articles "Hiéroglyphe" and "Ecriture" in the *Encyclopédie* (1755). The attraction of Warburton's conjectural history of writing lay in his developmental history of the evolution of mental faculties. Warburton made the thrust of his argument explicit when he linked the history of writing to a conjectural history of language. Writing evolved from primitive pictograms to alphabets and secret tropological symbols to signify the piecemeal acquisition of mental faculties that permitted greater abstraction. According to Warburton, spoken languages also went through parallel developments corresponding to the tropological evolution of writing. People used first gestures and actions and later forms of speech, dominated successively by figures such as apologias, fables, similes, parables, riddles, pleonasms, and metaphors.[163]

Natural Histories of the Mind

Beginning in the late seventeenth century, students of the mind transformed medieval faculty-psychology into a historical discipline.[164] Locke's *Essay Concerning Human Understanding* (1690) initiated a tradition that by the eighteenth century became canonical: upon birth, the mind was a blank slate, which slowly filled up with ideas gained through the senses and mental reflection. This tradition maintained that nations recapitulated the experience of individuals, who slowly acquired mental faculties as ideas were gradually accumulated and compared. Like children, "primitives" had blank slates for minds, to which new faculties were added piecemeal. The historicization of faculty-psychology was so popular among eighteenth-century savants and literati that even Rousseau, among the harshest critics of the ideology of progress, thought that his noble savages lacked imagination, estimative power, and memory. "In all nations, progress of the mind has been precisely proportioned to the needs that peoples had received from nature," he argued in his *Discourse on the Origins and Foundations of Inequality Among Men* (1755). Because he has no needs, the savage's imagination suggests "nothing to him . . . he is so far from the degree of knowledge, that he can have neither foresight nor curiosity . . . his projects, as limited as his views, barely extend to the end of the day. Such is even today the degree of foresight of the Carib: in the morning he sells his bed of cotton and in the evening he comes weeping to buy it back, for want of having foreseen that he would need it for the coming night."[165]

For all his much-vaunted originality in capturing the dynamics of the primitive mentality, Vico's ideas were rather similar to Rousseau's. According to Vico, primitives were mute, speaking through gesture and drawings, overtaken by passions, and thus incapable of abstraction and so "buried in the body" (*seppellite ne' corpi*) that for them the cosmos became a mirror of themselves.[166] Warburton's primitives were like Rousseau's and Vico's, incapable of abstraction, first communicating themselves through the language of gestures and pictures and slowly later gaining articulate language and rational thought. Behind all these views lay the assumption that the mind of the primitive lacked most mental faculties, although to be fair to Vico, he thought that primitives had an excess of imagination. The idea that the minds of "primitives" were empty affected even figures on the fringes of the Enlightenment such James Burnett, Lord Monboddo (1714–1799), one of the last defenders of the Ancients over the Moderns in the battle of the books.[167] In 1773, Monboddo thought that "man [is] formed, not however at once, but by degrees, and in succession: for he appears at first to be little more than a vegetable, hardly deserving of the name of a zoophyte; then gets sense, but sense only, so that he is yet little better than a muscle; then he becomes an animal of a more complete kind; then a rational creature, and finally a man of intellect and science, which is the summit and completion of our nature."[168]

Along with histories of writing as conjectural histories of the mind, the eighteenth century also witnessed the explosion of philosophical histories of language. Vico and Warburton linked the history of writing and speech tightly, and so did Condillac. Most conjectural histories of language, however, focused exclusively on speech. The world offered a hierarchy of languages that ran the gamut from the primitive-concrete to the civilized-abstract. Eighteenth-century conjectural historians of language drew from two parallel yet slightly different traditions, one focused on grammars, and the other on vocabularies. The first tradition maintained that grammars reflected the structure of the world itself (patterns of causation, relations among objects, systems of classification). When a language deviated from this ideal grammatical structure (Latin in the Middle Ages, universal grammars in the seventeenth century), it demonstrated a failure on the part of its speakers to grasp the structure of the universe. The second tradition insisted that ideas matched an objective reality; the failure of languages to have signs to represent those ideas, therefore, reflected the quality of the minds of the speakers. Eighteenth-century historians of language added complexity to these two views by historicizing them. According to most eighteenth-century historians of language, languages were systems to analyze ideas, and grammatical structures reflected the development of peoples in the process of gaining analytical power over time. In these historical narratives, humans characteristically appeared as first communicating with one another through gestures, then through monosyllables, and finally through articulated speech. The separation of subject from predicates and the appearance of verbs, inflections, prepositions, and pronouns all spoke of the gradual development of the power of analysis of ideas and abstraction.[169]

Grammars, vocabularies, and writing systems became alternative forms of evidence that replaced traditional literary sources (now perceived to be unreliable) to reconstruct the history of the gradual development of the mental faculties and, implicitly, that of Europe's obscure ages. In this context, Amerindian scripts became items of collection to shed light on the natural history of the mind. In the Renaissance, Amerindian documents in indigenous scripts were items of collection used to acquire reliable information about the histories of local peoples. In the eighteenth century, Amerindian documents were valued for their evidentiary power to reconstruct a philosophical history of the mind.

The views of the great French eighteenth-century classicist and orientalist Jean-Jacques Barthélemy (1716–1795) typify this transition. In the 1740s and 1750s, Barthélemy astounded European scholars by deciphering the value of Palmyran and Phoenician letters through an evolutionary and comparative approach similar to that proposed by conjectural historians of writing. Barthélemy assumed, for example, that the Phoenician alphabet derived from Egyptian cursive writing, which in turn had derived from Egyptian hieroglyphs. In the same evolutionary vein, Barthélemy thought that Mexican pictograms were primitive scripts that, had the Spanish Conquest not occurred, would have become either Egyptian hieroglyphs or Chinese ideograms. "It is clear," Barthélemy argued in a memoir addressed to the French minister Bertin around 1770, "that if the [Mexican] empire had subsisted for a few more centuries, their writing, through successive progress, would have become totally hieroglyphic, such as that of the Egyptians and Chinese."[170] Barthélemy urged the minister to sponsor the collection and publication of Amerindian documents on the grounds that "if one wants to be instructed in the progress of the human spirit among these Amerindians, one should collect all the manuscripts that escaped the barbarity of the first bishop of Mexico [who had burnt them]."[171] Barthélemy's main interest in collecting Mexica documents became the study of the evolution of the faculties of the mind. Unlike sixteenth-century Spanish authors, he did not show much interest in using the sources to clarify details of the past of central Mexico.

Amerindian Sources in Eighteenth-Century
European Historiography

In the course of the eighteenth century, European authors interested in the American past contributed to the development of conjectural histories of writing and the mind. In this section, I trace how these views converged to cast doubt on the credibility of Amerindian sources.

As early as 1688, European editors began to question the reliability of indigenous sources and testimonies. The English translator of Garcilaso's *Comentarios reales*, Sir Paul Rycaut (1628–1700), a Fellow of the Royal Society, argued that Garcilaso's history of the origins of the Incas under Manco Capac was in all probability a fable, "divers truths mixed with abundance of fictions and foolish inventions." Rycaut drew a clear connection between literacy and the trustworthiness of historical traditions. "How then can be expected that these illiterate creatures," he argued, "should be able to give an account of their extraction of matters which passed in those [obscure] ages of which the learned parts of the world acknowledge their ignorance and confess themselves to be in the dark [even though they had writing]?" Lack of writing had led Peruvians to be "so simple and credulous" that they actually believed they came from lakes, mountains, fowls, and even the sun, as their foundation myths maintained.[172]

Writing and literacy became a central concern both for those who admired and for those who disliked Garcilaso's history. For Jean-Frédéric Bernard, the editor of the 1737 French translation of *Comentarios reales*, Garcilaso could have done an even more convincing job of presenting the Inca state as a great classical society if the Incas had developed writing. Quipus were not truly writing, in his opinion, so the history of the great capital of the Incas, Cuzco, had been lost forever. Unlike Rome, Cuzco had not kept records of its own greatness: "[With] methods so weak [as songs and quipus], it has only been possible to have but a superficial knowledge [*entendre fort loin*] of the history of its monarchy." "I dare say," Bernard concluded, "that [had the Incas had historical records] this New World could have challenged that of the ancients."[173] The 1744 French editor of Garcilaso did not, however, think so highly of the Incas, and he reorganized the entire structure of the *Comentarios reales* on the grounds that Garcilaso had completely lacked method and system. The chaotic confusion of the work lay in the nature of the recordkeeping devices used by Garcilaso. "Having been able to learn the history of his ancestors only by means of tradition, for [his ancestors] did not have writing, [Garcilaso] could not help but to write a most confusing work, so garbled that it is hardly possible to follow the facts."[174] The editor also argued that quipus were the reason the Inca had limited knowledge of the abstract sciences, including geometry and astronomy, for science was based on the transmission of accumulated insights over time. The Incas, the editor argued, knew enough to keep track of solstices and important agricultural dates, but not enough to understand the cause of eclipses. Illiteracy itself was the reason why the Incas had failed to develop abstract knowledge.[175]

Skepticism about Amerindian scripts as reliable means of storing information increased. Amerindians were incapable of keeping historical records, the abbé Raynal asserted. Quipus, he argued in 1770, were merely systems of numerical calculations. Uncertainty in the transmission of information was characteristic of Amerindian systems of writing, and in such uncertainty lay the nature of the Amerindian systems of government. "Among such [illiterate] peoples, the witness that accuses, the law that condemns, the judgment that decides are all as uncertain as the memory of men, as vague as their ideas, as arbitrary as their inclinations. Even the most prudent laws [when not written down] undergo insensible changes as they lack precision and stability."[176] Illiteracy and untrustworthiness, Raynal maintained, were at the root of the Amerindian penchant for political tyranny.

Jean-Benoît Schérer, the German diplomat who in 1777 furiously denounced de Pauw for calling into question the credibility of classical sources on Egypt and of Jesuit testimonies on China, was less adamant about defending the reliability of quipus. Schérer suggested that Garcilaso's history was unreliable because it was based on information drawn from oral traditions. "Quipus," Schérer argued, "[are not really writing systems], and they therefore can never transmit to posterity the history of a country. Garcilaso, who descended in direct line from the Incas, and who for the first time introduced us to the knots of different colors used [in Peru], did not record the history of his country but [only] the oral traditions of his ancestors."[177]

It is curious that precisely when Amerindian scripts were losing credibility as systems capable of transmitting reliable information, the first and last representation of quipus as more than devices used to store and manipulate numerical data appeared in Europe. In 1750, Raimondo di Sangro (1710–1771), prince of Sansevero, published his *Lettera apologetica*, a book penned to defend the plausibility of Françoise de Graffigny's *Lettres d'une Peruvienne* (1747), a novel about the letters allegedly written in quipus by an Inca princess, Zilia. In the novel, Zilia, after having been taken prisoner by the Spaniards and later ransomed by the French, writes first in quipus and later in alphabetical script to her beloved Aza, an Inca prince.[178] Sansevero's "defense" of Graffigny's novel consisted of a treatise about quipus that was much more than just an attempt to understand the ways quipus stored information. As a critic of Sansevero later suggested, the prince had written as a freethinker seeking to undermine the authority of the Bible by toying with ideas such as the eternity of the world and by backing the credibility of alternative chronologies. Be that as it may, Sansevero was a committed Neoplatonist who read quipus as though they were Egyptian hieroglyphs, that is, as allegorical figures that stored deep symbolic meanings.

Drawing on a manuscript made available by a Jesuit who had recently arrived from Chile, Sansevero concluded that there were two kinds of quipus. One type, well known to Europeans, stored numbers by means of knots representing decimal positions (Fig. 2.7); the second type had been kept secret.[179] This second system was syllabic and based on the woven representation of forty master words (*parole maestre*). Sentences were written (woven in this case) by the permutations of the different syllables of forty master words (see Plates 1 and 2). Knots underneath a figure signified the position of the syllable in the master word (three knots = third syllable). The Neoplatonic aspect of the system that Sansevero obtained from the Jesuit lay in the choice of figures. The master word "Pachacamac" (Pa-cha-ca-mac), God, creator of the Universe, for example, was represented as a yellow circle, signifying the eternity and luminosity of the deity. The yellow circle, in turn, had an inner circle whose four colored quarters each represented one of the four elements: red (fire), blue (air), green (water), and black (earth).[180] The Neoplatonic reverberations of an image that identified God with the sun were obvious. The system also implied that the Incas had been privy, not only to monotheism, but also to a sophisticated view of the cosmos in which four elements were responsible for change, generation, and corruption in the sublunary sphere. The Neoplatonic content of the symbolical representations of the master words was even more obvious in the case of the figure used to signify the master word "Viracocha" (Vi-ra-co-cha), the human incarnation of Pachacamac. Viracocha was a pink knot followed by Pachacamac's circle. The pink knot stood for a human figure and the circle for Viracocha's divinity. The striking thing about this quipu is that it implied that the Inca had already prefigured Christ.[181] The remaining thirty-eight master words and their corresponding quipus reinforced the sense that the Inca were, like Kircher's Egyptians, a very pious and advanced civilization, which had mastered the deepest religious mysteries.

Sansevero's system, which had originally been concocted in the Andes in

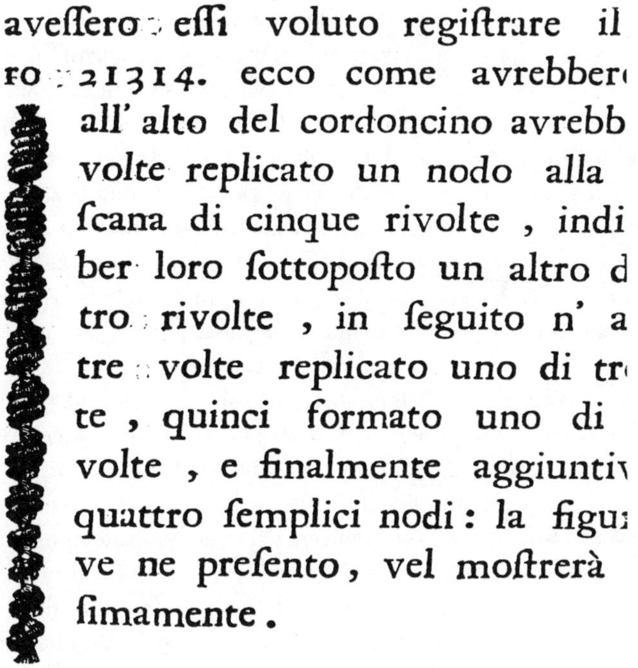

aveſſero ꞉ eſſi voluto regiſtrare il
ro ꞉ 21314. ecco come avrebber
all' alto del cordoncino avrebb
volte replicato un nodo alla
ſcana di cinque rivolte , indi
ber loro ſottopoſto un altro d
tro ꞉ rivolte , in ſeguito n' a
tre ꞉ volte replicato uno di tr
te , quinci formato uno di
volte , e finalmente aggiunti\
quattro ſemplici nodi : la figu
ve ne preſento , vel moſtrerà
ſimamente .

FIGURE 2.7. Representation of the number 21,314 in a quipu according to Raimondo di Sangro, prince of Sansevero. Each turn of a knot represents a decimal position; thus, five turns stand for the tens of thousands, four for the thousands, three for the hundreds, two for the tens, and one for single units. The quipu in the illustration contains two knots of five turns, one of four, three of three, one of two, and four of one: 21,314. The system allows for complex mathematical calculations; combined with colors, it is also useful for keeping elaborate records and classifications. From Sansevero, *Lettera apologetica* (Naples, 1750). Courtesy of the Edward Ayer Collection, Newberry Library, Chicago.

the first half of the seventeenth century by Italian and mestizo Jesuit follow-ers of Kircher, was greeted apparently with absolute silence. After all, Sansevero had gone against all the learned consensus of his age.[182] He was denounced by inquisitors in Rome for seeking to undermine the authority of the Bible by bolstering the authority of nonalphabetical scripts.[183] His views of quipus as woven versions of Egyptian hieroglyphs codifying Neoplatonic verities undermined the views of philosophes who insisted that both written and spoken languages developed through stages. For the leading conjectural historians of the time, Inca quipus did not represent syllabic scripts, let alone religious mysteries, but primitive stages in the development of the mind.

The hostile reception of Sansevero's views speaks volumes about a dominant intellectual culture unwilling to reformulate teleological views of the history of writing and the mind. It could well have also been part of a growing scholarly discontent with Spanish glosses of indigenous sources. Sansevero insisted that he had obtained the manuscript from a Jesuit who had lived in Spanish America (Sansevero did not mention that the original manuscript was ciphered), and it is plausible that a scholarly community wary of the value of Spanish documents regarded these views as delusional ramblings.

There is evidence that by the 1760s, Spanish glosses to indigenous documents had become the prime target of skeptical scholars. Once the glosses became suspect, the document itself was declared useless, for scholars assumed that the original indigenous interpretations had forever been lost. Cornelius de Pauw typifies this trend. His *Recherches philosophiques sur les Américains* (1768–69) was not a typical eighteenth-century history of Amerindians written to shed light on the obscure and fabulous ages of Europe. Instead, he set out to prove that peoples who lived under extreme climatic conditions were degenerate beings. De Pauw was convinced that Laplanders, African blacks, and Native Americans lived in regions of the world that had caused dramatic changes in their bodies and souls, making them unfit for civilization.[184]

De Pauw's dislike for developmental views of history made him hesitant to adapt Warburton's dominant views of the history of writing. He called to task those "savants who have pretended" that scripts unfold from picture writing to alphabets. In the hypothetical case that the Incas and Mexicans had progressed in their development, however, their scripts would have taken different paths. Quipus, he argued, like any other primitive system made of conventional signs, would have become alphabets, whereas Mexican "paintings," mere pictorial representations of objects, would have turned into Egyptian-style hieroglyphs. Painting-writing and signs of convention, De Pauw concluded, evolved differently. To highlight his criticism of Warburton's theories, De Pauw insisted that ancient Egyptians had obtained their epistolary script (alphabet) from foreigners and not through the slow modification of hieroglyphs.[185]

For all his disagreements with Warburton, however, de Pauw was quick to link the history of writing with statements about the development of mental faculties. For example, he firmly linked quipus with the "primitive" mental stages of peoples who lacked memory. Convinced that the American climate had wiped out the will, foresight, and memory of the natives, de Pauw contended that quipus had been designed to help the natives "to remember in the afternoon what they did in the morning."[186] Quipus were thus mere mnemonic devices to assist peoples who had barely acquired memory. Mesoamerican systems of writing were also indicative of the poor mental faculties of Amerindians: "Mexicans had made almost no progress in the art by means of which the memory of things past and historical events are perpetuated."[187] Their manuscripts spoke of the poverty of their taste, of their inability to draw mimetically accurate representations of the world, and of their ignorance of perspective and chiaroscuro.

The fact that Inca quipus and Mesoamerican pictograms and logograms were representative of peoples with inferior mental qualities made them unreliable as recordkeeping devices. According to de Pauw, Garcilaso had built his entire history of the Incas on the oral testimony of his uncle, who had in turn read it from quipus. Building on such shaky ground, Garcilaso had traced the history of the twelve Inca rulers back to the year 1131 C.E. If the Romans, who knew how to read and write before Romulus and Numa, had left posterity a fabulous history of their first five centuries, how could one believe that the oral testimonies of Garcilaso's uncle were any more credible? Echoing the views of the 1744 editor of Garcilaso's work, de Pauw maintained that Garcilaso's history had turned out to be "a work undigested, pitiful, [and] fundamentally ill reasoned," largely because of the Incas' lack of writing.[188] From such speculations, it followed that the history of Peru before the arrival of the Europeans "does not contain any confirmed fact . . . nor does it have any incontestable truth."[189]

The case of the history of Mexico before the European arrival was slightly more complicated. De Pauw blamed the alleged obscurity surrounding the history of Mesoamerica on the Spaniards. Their glosses of indigenous sources such as the Mendoza collection were pitiful: "I do not advise anybody to rely on those [interpretations]."[190] Spanish interpreters insisted that the historical part of the paintings represented the annals of nine Mexica monarchs. However, the paintings in isolation, de Pauw argued, could just as well represent the deeds of Moctezuma Xocoyoltzin and his eight concubines. De Pauw found the same problem with the interpretation of dates in indigenous documents and highlighted the inconsistencies of the interpretations of calendars and dates of migrations offered by Spaniards. The interpretations were flawed because the Spaniards had failed to realize the internal consistency of the indigenous claims. How could they have accepted that the natives had accurate calendars when the natives were ignorant of almost everything else?[191]

The history of European interpretation of the dynastic genealogies of the Mixtec in the Vienna Codex is another telling example of how the questioned authority of the Spanish glosses was partially responsible for the gradual loss of credibility of the Amerindian documents. In 1679, Peter Lambeck (1628–1680), curator of the library of Emperor Leopold I, published a catalogue of the holdings that included seven Persian manuscripts and *unius incomparabilis Mexicani, literis picti Hieroglypicis coloratis.*[192] Lambeck promised to study this "priceless, incomparable" rare codex in more detail after reading what authors such as Ole Worm (1588–1654) and Georg Horn (1620–1670) had written on the subject of Mexican scripts, and after reading and studying Purchas's edition of the Codex Mendoza, with its accompanying Spanish glosses,[193] but he died before making good on this. In 1769, the new curator of the Imperial Library, Adam František Kollár (1718–1783) did read Purchas and discovered that the two codices were "leagues apart" (for one thing, they used two different iconographic conventions and very different sets of pictograms and logograms, one Mexica, the other Mixtec). Purchas's edition of the Codex Mendoza was, moreover, at several removes from the indigenous original. In fact, it was an English translation of Spanish glosses, which, in turn, were allegedly a translation of a Nahuatl commentary. This process of sequential translation was not only cumbersome but also unreliable. Kollár did not offer any interpretation of the Vienna Codex, which he refused to study, on the grounds that he, unlike Lambeck, was "not wise enough [to read it]" and that he had "not seen the Muses of Mexico even in a dream."[194]

Unlike Kollár, William Robertson was not shy about interpreting the Vienna Codex in his 1777 *History of America* (Fig. 2.8). After a brief iconographical analysis using Purchas's edition of the Codex Mendoza and the recent edition in Mexico of a slightly different sixteenth-century set of Aztec tributary records, *Matrícula de tributos,* published in 1770 by the cardinal of New Spain, Francisco Antonio de Lorenzana, Robertson concluded that the Vienna Codex was also a tribute roll.[195] Robertson's profound misunderstanding of Mixtec dynastic genealogy was not merely the result of a scholarship that had not yet developed the intellectual resources necessary to interpret indigenous documents. It originated rather in Robertson's facile and superficial assumptions about the indigenous documents he encountered, stemming from his lack of interest in the information in the documents in the first place.

It would be difficult to claim that Robertson was uninterested in indige-

FIGURE 2.8. Illustrations that William Robertson took at random from the Vienna Codex. Robertson concluded that figures A and C were shields and bales of mantles similar to those represented in Francisco Antonio de Lorenzana's edition of the *Matrícula de tributos* and in Samuel Purchas's edition of the Codex Mendoza. Robertson read figure D as numerical signs representing quantities in the tribute roll. It is in fact a calendrical sign that in the original codex stands either as a date or as the name of a ruler. From William Robertson, *The History of America* (London, 1777).

nous sources. He made widely available both illustrations and information about the Vienna Codex that had been available only to circles of antiquarians acquainted with the publications by Lambeck and Kollár. Robertson also introduced the European public for the first time to the Codex Borbonicus, a ritual divinatory-calendar at that time in the library of the Escorial but removed to Paris in 1826.[196] For all his zeal at identifying new Amerindian sources, however, Robertson's interest in Mesoamerican codices resembled Barthélemy's rather than Torquemada's. Robertson was interested in using the documents to write a philosophical history of the mind, not to inquire into the natives' own version of their past.

The first three books of the *History of America* retrace the voyages of "discovery," to show the technical superiority of the Moderns over the simple navigational skills of the Ancients and to demonstrate the civilizing role of commerce, only possible among highly advanced sea-faring societies. Book 4 is entirely devoted to the "rude" natives of America. Robertson, who thought that the works of the Ancients were not good guides for interpreting Americans, proposed a new genre: a natural history of the human mind. "In order to complete the history of the human mind and attain a perfect knowledge of its nature and operations," he argued, "we must contemplate man in all those various situations wherein he has been placed. We must follow him in his progress through the different stages of society . . . we must observe, at each period, how the faculties of his understanding unfold."[197] In typical eighteenth-century fashion, his natural history of the mind assumed that the minds of "savages" were empty, without speculative reasoning, foresight, and will.[198] Like Rousseau, he offered the story about the forgetful Carib who sold his hammock in the morning only to realize at night that he needed it back to sleep.[199] Such minds were, of course, untrustworthy. Savages who claimed to be very old were not to be believed, since, "most of them are unacquainted with the art of numbering, and all of them are forgetful of what is past, as they are improvident of what is to come."[200]

Robertson considered, however, that "man cannot continue long in this state of feeble and informed infancy . . . the powers of his nature, as well as the necessity of his condition, urge him to fulfill his destiny."[201] Thus he went on to classify the savages in a hierarchy of moral and political progress. The peoples of the Isthmus, Brazil, and the Caribbean were placed at the bottom, whereas the more independent and courageous North Americans and Chileans, inhabitants of more temperate regions, were given a higher standing.[202] Mexicans and Peruvians were no "savages"; they belonged in a different category. Hence, Robertson used a separate book to study them. In book 7, Robertson set out to describe the "positive" and "negative" traits of Aztecs and Incas, as on a balance sheet. He was torn, so he said, between those things that made Incas and Aztecs comparable to "highly polished peoples" and the other practices that made them resemble savages. In a typical display of epistemological "moderation," he argued that readers themselves should decide where to locate Peruvians and Mexicans on the scale of development.[203] He, to be sure, had already reached conclusions of his own: "In their highest state of improvement [the] power [of Mexicans and Peruvians] was so limited, and their operations [of their minds] so feeble, that they can hardly be considered as having advanced beyond the infancy of civil life."[204]

This conclusion helps us navigate through Robertson's seemingly contradictory usage of Mexica and Inca documents. In a superficial reading of the *History of America*, one might get the impression that Robertson thought that the codices might yield useful historical information. In a long digression on the possible Asiatic origin of the Americans via the Bering Strait, for example, he, like Torquemada, argued that annals of the Mexica indicated that they came from the north across a strait. "This account of the population [coming via the Bering Strait]," Robertson argued, "coincides with the traditions of the Mexicans concerning their own origin, which imperfect as they are, were preserved with more accuracy, and merit greater credit, than those of any people in the New World."[205] Moreover, he deplored the loss of almost all codices at the hands of superstitious Spaniards, forcing historians to rely on untrustworthy oral traditions.[206] Conceding that Mexican "picture-writing" might have included some "signs of convention" to represent abstract ideas, Robertson thought that Aztec glyphs were on their way to becoming a true alphabet.[207]

But all these statements are deeply misleading, for Robertson thought little of the codices as historical documents. Besides using the Aztec annals to support the thesis of the Asiatic origins of the Americans, Robertson employed Mexica manuscripts only once throughout the four volumes of his history, and only to dismiss as "exaggerated" accounts of the great antiquity of the Nahua.[208] He thought, in fact, that "the Mexican paintings, which are supposed to have served as annals of their empire, are few in number, and of ambiguous meaning."[209] Robertson systematically excluded the Amerindian version of the Conquest.[210] His description of the massacre of Panuco, for example, was entirely based on Cortés's own letters, although he openly flaunted his knowledge of an alternative native account recorded by the Franciscan Torquemada.[211] Robertson had only scorn for authors like Torquemada and Clavijero who had followed native sources to the letter. He found them to be "whimsical credulous" men with a "propensity for the marvelous" and their works "improbable narratives and fanciful conjectures."[212] Robertson was absolutely convinced that Mexica writing was after all "little more than a species of picture-writing, so far improved as to mark their superiority over the savage tribes of America; but still so defective, as to prove that they had not proceeded far beyond the first stage in that progress which must be completed before any people can be ranked among the polished nations."[213] In less than two pages, he demonstrated that Inca quipus were wrong, for they had recorded absurd, garbled chronologies and "contributed little towards preserving the memory of ancient events and institutions."[214]

Again, the difficulties that Robertson had believing the Mexica and Incas stemmed from the ideas he had about the nature of their minds. He chose to follow Warburton's account of the evolution of writing, because the Anglican bishop, "with much erudition and greater ingenuity," had traced through scripts "the successive steps by which the human mind advanced." "He is the first," Robertson declared, "who formed a rational and consistent theory concerning the various modes of writing practices by nations, according to the various degrees of their improvements."[215] The historicization of faculty-psychology led him to believe that the Mexica had not acquired enough foresight. Accounts that claimed that Tenochtitlan had had some 200,000 inhabitants and that the Mexica had resisted the siege of the city for three months were clearly exaggerations. Robertson thought that the provisions required to feed all those people during the siege were so great that it would have demanded "much foresight and arrangement to collect" them. The accounts were clearly wrong, because the Mexica were "naturally so improvident, and so incapable of executing a complicated plan, as the most improved Americans [savages]."[216]

The end result of these views is that Robertson set the clock of the historiography on Mesoamerica back to the period before Torquemada. Paying no attention whatsoever to the scholarship of the early-seventeenth-century Franciscan, who had lengthened the history of central Mexico to allow for numerous cycles of civilization, Robertson collapsed the history of the region and studied only the deeds of the Mexica (Aztecs). Moreover, Robertson's analysis was structural not diachronic; he described the institutions of the Mexica but had little to say about their migrations and dynastic genealogies. As shown in Chapter 1, Robertson included the Mexica not because he was interested in their history but because he needed them to shed light on Europe's own obscure ages.

Whereas de Pauw, Barthélemy, and Robertson came to value native records as evidence of the development of the human mind, rather than for the sake of the historical information they provided, Alexander von Humboldt can scarcely be said to have participated in this epistemological reorientation. Reviewers, particularly in England, denounced Humboldt for according too much authority to indigenous sources, for credulously believing Spanish glosses, and for drawing unwarranted conclusions from the glosses and sources. From the complaints of the reviewers, it would seem that Humboldt's approach harked back to Renaissance paradigms. This was in fact the case. Unlike previous eighteenth-century European historians of the New World, Humboldt was operating in the wake of a massive Spanish American historiographical reaction that was to some extent instrumental in restoring the credibility of indigenous sources. Yet a closer reading of Humboldt's *Vues des cordillères* reveals that he was also a conjectural historian of the mind. Humboldt's views, therefore, are a good point at which to end this chapter, for they allow us to see two different views of the value of indigenous sources, coexisting in a single capacious mind.

Based on the research of antiquarians whom he had encountered on his trip to Mexico and the writings of exiled Jesuits in Italy, Humboldt rejected Robertson's conclusions about the history of Mexico. Robertson's *History of America*, Humboldt argued, was "admirable for the sagacity with which it has been compiled, but too much abridged in the part relating to the Toltec and Aztecs." To make up for Robertson's silence, Humboldt included dynastic genealogies from the Toltec to the Mexica.[217] Taking his cues from Torquemada, Humboldt concluded that the history of the Central Valley of Mexico could be documented all the way back to the seventh century C.E., although he also concluded that the annals of the Toltec were as "uncertain as those of the Pelasgi and the Ausonians."[218] Humboldt blamed the uncertainty, in part, on the fact that the Toltec sources were not original, but versions kept by later invaders who came to replace the Toltec as the dominant power of central Mexico.[219]

Although he did not take its chronology seriously, Humboldt deduced from a plate in the Codex Ríos depicting the ages of the world according to Aztec tradition (Fig. 2.9) that the first age, when the people were giants, had lasted 5,206 years and ended in famine; the second had lasted 4,804 years and ended in fire, with all humans being transformed into birds; the third had lasted 4,010 years and had ended in hurricanes, with humans becoming apes; and the fourth had lasted 4,008 years, terminating in floods, with all people becoming fishes. According to Humboldt this Aztec chronology derived from a Central Asian myth, from which the Hindus had also taken their history.[220] As for the 18,028 years recorded in the Mexica document, Humboldt maintained, drawing on the writings of the seventeenth-century Texcocan noble Alva Ixtlilxochitl, that they were not annual but monthly cycles, corresponding therefore to only a few hundreds of years. Humboldt cited the case of Hindu chronologies to justify his interpretation, for according to scholars, the alleged four million "years" of the Hindu represented only 12,000 real years.[221] For all his shortening of Nahua mythical chronologies to a mere fourteen hundred years, however, Humboldt did believe that the Mexica had kept complete and accurate records, "[with] the greatest order and [revealing] an astonishing minuteness in the recital of events," since at least 1091 C.E., the year they had left their northern home of Aztlan.[222]

FIGURE 2.9. Cycles of history or "solar ages" according to Mexica chronology. The document, drawn under Spanish patronage, should be read from bottom up and from right to left. The right order and even the number of the ages (either four or five) created heated controversy among colonial scholars. From Alexander von Humboldt, *Vues des cordillères* (Paris, 1810). Courtesy of the John Carter Brown Library, Brown University, Providence, R.I.

Humboldt also adduced in evidence a "hieroglyphical history of the Aztecs from the deluge to the foundation of the city of Mexico" published in 1699–1700 by Giovanni Francesco Gemelli Careri (1651–1725), an Italian world traveler, who had obtained it in Mexico from a local antiquarian, Carlos de Sigüenza y Góngora. Robertson thought that Gemelli Careri's "map" (Fig. 2.10) was a fake, fabricated by Spanish friars bent on proving the truth of the Bible by means of alternative non-European documentation. Humboldt dismissed this on the grounds that he had found many copies of the same map in Mexico, which, unlike Gemelli Careri's, showed no evidence of European iconographic influences. Humboldt interpreted the map according to the glosses in Italian first offered by Gemelli Careri and concluded that it was a document that supported, not the historical narrative of the Bible, but the existence of a widespread common myth of origins. The map showed that, like the Hindus, Chinese, and Semites, the Mexica explained the existence of marine fossils on mountaintops through the fiction of a universal flood and saw their mythical ancestors as the survivors of this flood (Coxcox for the Mexica, Noah for the Semites).[223] Although he took all these myths to be "childish fables," Humboldt thought that the map accurately recorded the migrations of the Mexica since at least the year 1038 C.E. (a date he obtained from his careful reading of the late-eighteenth-century antiquarian Antonio de León y Gama [1735–1802]), contradicting his own earlier assertion that the Mexica had kept accurate records since the year 1091 C.E.[224] Finally, Humboldt introduced his readers to an alternative version of the annals of the Mexican "empire" offered by the Codex Telleriano-Remensis (so called because it had once been in the possession of Archbishop Tellier of Rheims), which he had found in the Royal Library in Paris.[225]

Humboldt had little to say on Inca history, largely because during his trip to the Andes, unlike in Mexico, he did not find local antiquarians from whose research to draw. The striking differences in the way Humboldt handled Peruvian and Mexican antiquities show the derivative nature of most of his work, a fact that has gone largely unnoticed. But be that as it may, the fact still remains that Humboldt's *Vues* restored some of the depth of the Mexican past, which had recently been shortened and edited out of recognition.

Humboldt did not merely, however, make the research of Spanish American antiquarians in New Spain widely available to Europeans. In seeking to write a philosophical history of America, he used Amerindian sources to shed light on the natural history of the human mind through a conjectural history of writing not much different from those of Vico, Fréret, and Warburton. He found Mexica pictograms and logograms, "these hieroglyphical paintings which Robertson has so aptly denominated picture writing," primitive, signifying the initial unfolding of the Amerindians' mental faculties.[226] Echoing Warburton, Humboldt argued that figurative writing like that of Mexico characterized all primitive peoples.[227] All reports that suggested that Amerindians could have developed alphabets, he dismissed as unreliable.[228]

But the Mexica had not only used pictograms but logograms and phonograms as well. For Humboldt this was evidence that the peoples of central Mexico were advancing teleologically toward the discovery of the alphabet. Such developmental history, not surprisingly, allowed Humboldt to offer some speculations on social psychology. The peoples of central Mexico, he concluded, had not developed alphabets because they were changeless orientals, "[adhering] to their manners and customs with the same invincible obstinacy as the Chinese, the Japanese, and the Hinds."[229] Humboldt's willingness to embrace romantic stereotypes of Asia and apply them to Mexico was contradictory, because he himself argued some hundred pages later that

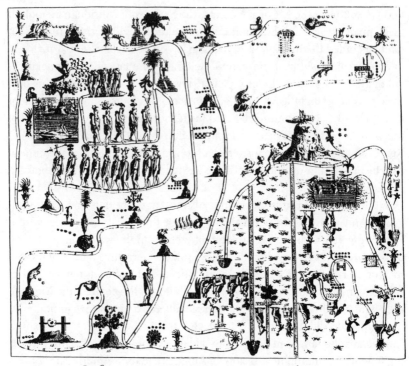

Histoire hiéroglyphique des Aztèques,
depuis le Déluge jusqu'à la fondation de la Ville de Mexico

FIGURE 2.10. Pictorial history of Mexica migrations from the departure from Aztlan to the founding of the city of Tenochtitlan, known as the Mapa Sigüenza, first made public in Giovanni Francesco Gemelli Careri's *Giro del Mondo* (1699-1700). The dots along the route represent 52-year cycles. According to the glosses, the Mexica descended from Coxcox, a survivor of a flood. Coxcox's fifteen mute descendants regain speech from a dove as they set out on their wanderings. This document exemplifies how Amerindian scripts and calendars were deployed to create detailed historical records. From Alexander von Humboldt, *Vues des cordillères* (Paris, 1810). Courtesy of the John Carter Brown Library, Brown University, Providence, R.I.

religion in Mexico had changed dramatically in the wake of the Aztec invasions, transforming the benign cults of past Amerindian civilizations into the gory practice of human sacrifice.[230]

In any event, Humboldt repeatedly drew lessons on social psychology from indigenous sources. When compared to Egyptian hieroglyphs, Mexica scripts, for example, "[reflected] on the progressive steps which the human mind appears to have followed in the invention of graphic means fitted to express ideas; we see that the nations of America were very distant from that perfection which the Egyptians obtained."[231] By the same token, Humboldt thought that Amerindian sources under Spanish patronage were "superior" to precolonial ones, because the former revealed a greater mimetic capacity to observe and represent reality, "the progress of the arts toward perfection."[232] Humboldt sometimes was not derivative and advanced theories of his own. For example, he suggested that certain Nahua precolonial documents (representing the extension of communities and land tenure disputes) had originated as a result of the Nahua judicial system, which required communities to represent their cases before magistrates. Under European colonial rule, communities at first represented themselves before the Spanish magistrates and kept the genre of cadastral maps alive; later, however, lawyers arrived and began to serve as intermediaries between the state and the Amerindians and the drawing of maps ended.[233]

After dismissing Humboldt's entire historiographical approach to Amerindian antiquities, the British reviewer of *Vues* commended Humboldt for his efforts at collecting indigenous sources, because Amerindian documents were useful for completing the history of the development of the human mental faculties. From the beginning, Humboldt himself maintained that he had collected and studied documents and ruins because they were "interesting to the philosophical study of man."[234] "[The] investigations of monuments erected by half-civilized nations," he insisted, "have another kind of interest which we may call psychological; presenting to us a picture of the uniform progress of the human mind."[235] Humboldt was no Torquemada. For him, the mere deciphering of "shapeless writing of the Mexicans" represented but "little gain" for the sciences. The most important aspect of the enterprise of collecting and studying native sources lay elsewhere. Through the "study of the symbolic and sacred characters," Humboldt concluded, "philosophers, [when presented with] the uniform progress of the language of signs in parts of the earth the most remote from each other, [will gain] an image of the first unfolding of the faculties of man."[236]

CHAPTER 3

Historiography and Patriotism in Spain

From 1795 to 1801, Pedro de la Estala (1757–1815), who had previously edited twenty volumes of sixteenth- and seventeenth-century Spanish poetry and translated Aristophanes' *Plutus* and Sophocles' *Oedipus Rex*, published a 43-volume compilation of travel accounts.[1] At first, the erudite Estala limited himself to translating Joseph La Porte's *Le voyageur françois*, published in Paris between 1766 and 1795 in forty-two volumes. Employing the conceit of fictional letters sent by a philosophical traveler to a curious *salonnnière* back in Paris, La Porte offered a seamless narrative. Although Estala kept La Porte's organizing principle of fictional letters, he started a compilation of his own after finishing the translation of La Porte's fifth volume. His dissatisfaction with La Porte might well have originated in Estala's acquaintance with sources unavailable to the French author, namely, a vast number of unpublished Spanish travel reports, particularly dealing with the New World. But Estala also initiated his own compilation because his interpretations conflicted with those offered by La Porte. La Porte, for example, presented the Mexica and the Inca societies as somewhat modified classical polities, completely oblivious to the calls by authors such as Cornelius de Pauw and William Robertson to abandon classical tropes for representing the Amerindians.[2] Estala, however, was too much a man of his time not to pay heed to these new views. In a patriotic attempt to defend Spain against charges of having committed genocide in the New World, he paradoxically set out to read sixteenth-century Spanish reports on the New World using the critical techniques and conjectural philosophical reconstruction of the history of the New World offered by the likes of de Pauw and Robertson.

Estala began his survey by borrowing de Pauw's dismal view of the New World. America was portrayed as a cold, wet, degenerating environment, and the natives as effeminate, monstrous, insensitive creatures. Whereas for de Pauw these views were linked to an attack on Spanish colonialism, Estala linked them to a patriotic defense of the nation. De Pauw gave the impression that the Europeans had found an almost empty land, barely populated.

"It is therefore the greatest absurdity," Estala commented, "to follow the reports of fanatics . . . who claim that in the New World there were a great many millions of [original] inhabitants who were exterminated by the Spaniards."[3] De Pauw's new art of reading served Estala's patriotic purpose well. To oppose the Inca Garcilaso de la Vega's accounts of Peru under the Incas as a land teeming with people, for example, Estala subjected Garcilaso's history of the Incas to forms of internal criticism. There was a contradiction, Estala argued, between Garcilaso's representation of the grandeur of the Incas and his description of Inca technologies, including Inca quipus (a most inadequate system of writing), the absence of cities (with the exception of Cuzco, the capital), and backward forms of agricultural production. They all indicated that the Incas were primitives, not a populous civilized nation.[4] According to Estala, the Inca tribute system described by Garcilaso was harsher than that used by the Spaniards. How then could the population have been greater under the former than under the latter, if, as most authors argued, the demographic collapse that followed the Conquest was due to Spanish brutality? "Those who [like Garcilaso] have written on the population of Peru at the time of the Incas," Estala concluded, "have suffered the grossest mistake by establishing the original inhabitants in the millions without having the flimsiest shred of evidence to support their arbitrary assertions."[5] Estala argued, by the same token, that early reports of the grandeur of the Aztecs were also exaggerations, particularly because ruins of their allegedly great palaces, temples, and buildings had not survived: "There is no [material evidence left] in Mexico that supports any of what our own historians have maintained. With their pardon, I don't believe one half of what they say."[6] Supporting de Pauw's call for early Spanish testimony and traditional travel accounts to be discarded, Estala cited de Pauw's article in the *Encyclopédie*.[7] Perceptual distortions caused by lengthy sensory deprivation, he explained, had led Cortés and other early Spanish witnesses to overrate the accomplishments of the Aztecs and the Incas. In the first phase of colonization in the Caribbean, the Spaniards had encountered the most primitive people on earth, and they had thus naturally been prone to exaggerate when decades later they came across the slightly more advanced peoples of Mesoamerica. In this they resembled contemporary travelers to the Pacific who, after months on the high seas, found even the savages of Tahiti endearing.[8]

Estala embraced de Pauw's art of reading because he was a patriot seeking to defend Spain against centuries of northern European innuendo. But by brushing earlier reports aside, Estala appeared to be undermining his own patriotic agenda, for, after all, he was accepting the new emerging characterization of Spanish witnesses as ignorant. There were also other contradictions haunting Estala's defense of Spain. He was so eager to prove that the Mexica rulers had been tyrants, for example, that at one point he set out to demonstrate that they had behaved like oriental satraps. Dominant contemporary representations of the "Orient," however, forced Estala to accumulate evidence directly contradicting his other statements regarding the material and cultural poverty of the Mexica. In his account of Moctezuma Xocoyoltzin as an oriental despot, Estala drew on Cortés's description of the palaces, zoos, seraglio, and splendor of Moctezuma's court. Estala also introduced the testimony of Cortés and other early Spanish witnesses on the great Mexican markets, the grandeur of Mexica architecture, and the accuracy of Mesoamerican calendars.[9]

Estala's compendium typifies the contradictions and tensions in most eighteenth-century Spanish accounts of the New World. Had he chosen to follow La Porte, he would have been compelled to admit that contemporary Amerindians seemed wretched when compared to their gloriously civilized ancestors, thus making inevitable the conclusion that Spain had misbehaved in America. Estala therefore embraced de Pauw. But de Pauw's ideas were a double-edged sword. On the one hand, de Pauw's negative views of America as a cold, humid place might help clear Spain's name, because they suggested that the New World had originally been empty. On the other hand, de Pauw's new art of reading raised the specter of Spanish philosophical incompetence. Moreover, the urgent need to defend Spain against foreign calumnies led Estala to draw promiscuously from the range of available depictions of Amerindians. He thus simultaneously portrayed the Mexica and the Incas as primitives (and early Spanish accounts of them as credulous or perceptually misguided) and cast their rulers as oriental despots, surrounded by splendors characteristic of more "advanced" societies.

Estala's work should be understood in the context of a rising tide of northern European criticism of the Spanish "mind." Criticism of Spain, to be sure, was not new. Since the Middle Ages, Europeans had represented Spain as a threatening frontier where Jews and Arabs roamed undisturbed. With the consolidation of the formidable Spanish overseas empire, at the outset of the Reformation in the sixteenth century, Spain was both admired and despised. In the course of the wars of secession in the Netherlands, the figure of the intolerant, greedy, cruel Spaniard, dedicated to killing Amerindians and the Dutch, came to life in the hands of Protestant printers. It was only in the late seventeenth century, however, that the Spanish "mind" came in for detailed scrutiny and that Spaniards were represented not only as cruel bigots but also as ignoramuses, natives of a country firmly controlled by superstitious friars. Moreover, in the writings of its European critics, Spanish colonialism became a caricature of itself, a foil used by political economists to demonstrate the charms of the laws of nature and the dangers of disobeying them.[10] Estala, as well as many others in eighteenth-century Spain, wrote in order to correct such gross misrepresentations.

The history of eighteenth-century Spanish New World historiography has already been written, but this chapter sheds new light on a literature that is already vast.[11] In addition to bringing to bear a significant amount of new archival research, it places some well-known texts, and a few little-known ones, in new contexts and offers new interpretations. Of all European countries, I argue, Spain led in breaking with antiquated interpretations of the American past. In the process, many new institutions were created, among them the Spanish Royal Academy of History, founded in the early eighteenth century, one of whose main preoccupations was to write new critical natural and civil histories of the New World. Many of the developments attributed to the German objective historian Leopold von Ranke were first elaborated in passionate historiographical debates in Spain. Spanish authors privileged "primary" sources (which they called "public") over printed ones because they thought that the latter were biased, written with the intention of moving the audience to support specific agendas. Such emphasis on the study of "public" documents led to the creation in the 1780s of the Archive of the Indies, one of the largest colonial archives ever assembled.

The chapter is divided into several sections, which develop separate but related arguments. In the first section, I describe the reception in Spain in the 1740s and 1750s of the work of Lorenzo Boturini Benaduci (1702–1755), an Italian antiquarian who put together a great collection of Amerindian codices while living in Mexico. Boturini ended up in Spain without his collection but determined to write a new history of America, based largely on the insights of Giambattista Vico. After many years of trying, Boturini died without seeing his new history through to completion. I argue that the Italian's failure to carry out his new historiographical proposals should ultimately be located in numerous gaffes he committed as courtier, not in Spain's intellectual backwardness, as has been alleged by Italian historians such as Franco Venturi. This section identifies two distinct patriotic styles of scholarship dominant in eighteenth-century Spain.

In the second section, I demonstrate that at the time when Boturini brought his project for sweeping historiographical renewal to the attention of the Spanish crown, numerous Spanish authors were already proposing radical new reforms. I use these proposals to characterize the Spanish Enlightenment as a patriotic movement. Resistance to the negative representations of the "Spanish mind" by other Europeans and the realization that colonial empires were lost or won by those who controlled the description of lands and peoples moved authors to place urgent calls for the renewal of Spanish historiography, cartography, and botanical studies. Intellectuals became adamant about the need to produce new histories of colonization and discovery, as well as the need to control the naming of plants and places if the empire of Spain in America was to survive.

The Royal Academy of History, I argue in the third section, was the institution charged with carrying out these new ambitious calls for historiographical renewal. For some twenty years, the members of the Academy feverishly accumulated sources and indulged in protracted methodological debates. Little came of all this activity, however, because the Academy was stymied by the need to compete with a rival body, the Council of the Indies, for access to information about the colonies.

In the fourth section, I analyze the failure of the Royal Academy to complete and publish an annotated translation of William Robertson's *History of America*. Although this episode has been studied before, it has also been misunderstood. I locate the episode in the context of a confrontation among three distinct historiographical paradigms then vying for the support and attention of the Spanish crown. Some members of the Academy, led by its director, the Asturian Pedro Rodríguez, count of Campomanes (1723–1803), embraced the new northern European historiography on the New World with only slight modifications. A second group, led by Catalan Jesuits in exile in Italy, likewise denounced previous Spanish historiography as unreliable and dismissed Amerindian writings. Yet this second group also defended the record of Spanish colonization in the Indies, which Campomanes's party rejected. The third project, representing a tradition of scholarship unique to Valencia, originated with Gregorio Mayans y Siscar (1699–1781) during the debates over Boturini's radical historiographical proposals and later carried to completion by the Royal Chronicler of the Indies, Juan Bautista Muñoz. Dismissing Campomanes's new French and English intellectual fashions as shallow, derivative, and unpatriotic, the Valencians sought rather to restore the humanist traditions of Spanish Renaissance figures such as Juan Luis Vives (1492–1540). Although the recovery of the Spanish Renaissance exercised every eighteenth-century Spanish mind, the Valencians' particular brand of scholarship privileged erudition and philology.

It was only towards the late eighteenth century that the Spanish crown mustered the political will to discipline the rival institutions and the Archive of the Indies was founded. Of the three competing paradigms, the Valencians partially won, for Juan Bautista Muñoz was the force behind its creation. Muñoz's set up the archive to write a multivolume history of America, but only one volume ever appeared. Despite all the efforts and resources invested in the eighteenth century to write new histories of America, the record of publication in Spain was dismal. Rivalries among different corporations and groups of courtiers, usually representing different geographical regions, condemned most writings to the obscurity of private and public archives, where many of them still await publication.

The Travails of Lorenzo Boturini

On April 25, 1745, Lorenzo Boturini Benaduci, an Italian of patrician origins, submitted a plan to write a new history of the Mesoamerican past to the Council of the Indies in Madrid. "It has been proven," Boturini maintained in the final paragraph of his proposal, "that [my] outline is *new* in the sources it uses . . . *new* in its method and interpretations . . . and *new* in its utility."[12] Boturini's own words well capture the boldness of his "Idea de una nueva historia general de la America Septentrional," but not everything in his proposal was new. He presented his proposed history as the first to be entirely based on the painstaking gathering, collation, and interpretation of indigenous sources, which it was not (see, for example, the discussion of Juan de Torquemada's writings in Chapter 2). Moreover, Boturini was methodologically derivative, drawing most of his ideas from the Neapolitan scholar Giambattista Vico. Nonetheless, the council debated Boturini's "Idea" for many years, mulling over the consequences for Spain of allowing him to fulfill his vision. In the end, however, Boturini's proposal foundered.

Franco Venturi has argued that Boturini had both allies and enemies in Madrid, but that the ultimate reason for the failure of his proposal was the refusal of both his foes and his friends in Spain to embrace Vico. According to Venturi, Boturini's story typifies secular Spanish traditionalism.[13] Nicola Badaloni, the translator of Boturini's proposal into Italian, follows Venturi uncritically, concluding that "the context and the polemic surrounding the first edition of [Boturini's] *Idea* are a confirmation of the state of decadence of Spanish culture during those years."[14] Venturi and Badaloni notwithstanding, I maintain that the reason why Boturini's proposal was left unfulfilled lies elsewhere. Boturini had both opponents and supporters. But the opposition, led by a party of Aragonese courtiers, did not stem from the alleged backwardness of Spain but from the perception that Boturini was openly insulting Spain. Boturini's supporters, however, were also patriots. I argue that two versions of patriotism were at loggerheads, and that Boturini's *supporters* won. Boturini managed to publish his first work and obtained the post of Royal Chronicler despite the furious opposition of the Aragonese. Later, however, he proved unable to overcome the opposition, because he alienated key supporters. In the following pages, I also identify the main problems with which eighteenth-century Spanish historiography on the New World had to contend, as well as two patriotic styles of scholarship that emerged to address these problems.

Boturini's 'Idea de una nueva historia general de la América Septentrional'

Boturini arrived in Madrid in 1744 after many ordeals, including his incarceration in Mexico City. Born in 1702 in northern Italy to noble Milanese parents, Boturini went when young to Vienna to serve at the court of Charles VI (r. 1711–40), moving around for years within the Holy Roman Empire. Forced to leave the Viennese court in 1734 when the Spanish Bourbon king Philip V (r. 1700–46) threatened to punish and confiscate the property of any Italian serving under the Habsburgs, Boturini wandered about the courts of Portugal and Madrid until 1735, when he went to Mexico to take care of some financial affairs for the countess of Santibañez, the wealthy heiress of the former Mexica emperor Moctezuma Xocoyoltzin. Boturini was a courtier but also a pious and a curious man. Once in Mexico, he became a passionate devotee of Our Lady of Guadalupe and set out to prove that the miracle of the Virgin had been recorded in writing. As I discuss in Chapter 5 in greater detail, the tradition of the miracle of Our Lady of Guadalupe had long been surrounded by doubts in the absence of written documentation. Boturini set out to prove that the Amerindians had recorded the miracle in their own pictograms and logograms, and in so doing, he slowly began to get involved in the study of Mesoamerican antiquities. By 1742, he had gathered one of the greatest collections of indigenous sources ever assembled. Yet he also embarked on an illegal project.[15]

In 1738, Boturini sent to Jesuit friends in Rome a request to be allowed to "crown" the sacred image of Our Lady of Guadalupe. Such requests, however, had to be processed through official channels. In the case of the Indies, requests for the coronation of sacred images had first to be approved by the secular bureaucracy in Madrid, for since the Conquest, the pope had surrendered control over the affairs of the Church in the Indies to the Spanish monarch through the institution of *patronato real*. In the summer of 1740, Boturini unexpectedly got a papal brief approving the coronation of the sacred image. He then first went to the archbishop to clear the brief, but the prelate repeatedly turned him down. Boturini then sent the Roman document for approval to the magistrates of the local Audiencia (council and high court of New Spain), who in March 1742 acquiesced. Armed with the blessing of the Audiencia, Boturini sent a circular to parishes, authorities, and wealthy and prominent patrons over the entire viceroyalty requesting contributions. Jewels and cash began to flow in, but the plan was cut short by the arrival of a new viceroy in October 1742. Informed by the local authorities at Veracruz about Boturini's proposed coronation, the new viceroy, Pedro Cebrián y Agustín, Comte of Fuenclara (1687–1752), ordered an immediate investigation. In November 1742, Boturini was arraigned to explain his activities, and soon it became clear that he had not only circumvented the laws of *patronato* but had also entered Mexico illegally. Boturini was imprisoned in December 1742 and all his property was seized, including his collection of antiquities and indigenous codices, which the viceroy suspected had been gathered in the same way as the contributions for the coronation. In the course of the following year, the viceroy conducted a far-reaching investigation, gathering testimonies as far away as the Philippines, Guatemala, and California in an effort to clarify whether Boturini was an embezzler. In October 1743, after it became apparent that Boturini had acted in good faith, the viceroy sent the Italian back to Spain for a final ruling. But Boturini's travails were hardly over. The English captured the vessel bound for Spain off the coast of Cadiz. Boturini was set free in Gibraltar sometime in early 1744 but had to surrender the only indigenous document he had managed to save from his collection. Fortunately for Boturini, his judicial file was also confiscated by his captors, which gave him time to drum up support in Madrid as well as to write a book.

In April 1745, Boturini presented his new historiographical proposal to the Council of the Indies in Madrid, along with a request that his collection be returned to him. To understand what happened next, we need first to review briefly the content of his proposal, which opened with a set of shocking statements. The historical records of the Amerindians of Mexico, he argued, were among the richest ever assembled by any people in history. They were accurate, reliable, voluminous, and seemed to confirm every single detail of the biblical narrative, including Genesis, the Flood, the Diaspora after the destruction of the tower of Babel, and the total solar eclipse that plunged the earth in darkness at the death of Christ.[16] Boturini argued that of the many civilizations that had risen and fallen in central Mexico, the Toltecs had independently developed a system of writing, and that by 660 C.E. the Toltecs had assembled a sacred book recounting the history of their migrations, their laws, their customs, and the workings of their calendars. Boturini suggested that the records of the Toltec were reliable, because Huematzin, the Toltec Moses, drew his information from the "wisdom of the vulgar" that was "hidden in the hieroglyphs of the gods."[17] Without ever citing Vico, Boturini maintained that the key to understanding the Mesoamerican past lay hidden in the language, fables, songs, and theater of Mesoamerica's peoples, and that Huematzin knew it. Since language and myths constituted alternative historical records to traditional literary sources, the past of Mesoamerica could not only be traced in the numerous pictograms and logograms available but also in the words the Amerindians had used to name their deities and calendrical signs. The past could also be reconstructed by studying Amerindian myths.

Boturini's reference to *new* sources in his outline was a reference to the vast, unexplored new continent of data stored in names and myths. Citing the Roman writer Varro, not Vico, Boturini maintained that after the Flood, the history of gentiles had gone through three ages: divine, heroic, and human.[18] In the divine age, individuals spoke through gestures and monosyllables and recorded important historical events in the names of their deities. Boturini claimed that etymological analysis of the names of thirteen Mexican deities showed them to encode the story of the postdiluvian wanderings of ancient Amerindians. The names revealed that the mute primitives had first lived promiscuously in the open; that they fled to caves to engage in monogamous relationships after mistaking physical phenomena (for example, thunder) as the manifestation of angry gods who were fed up with their wayward behavior; and that a few unrepentant savages had, however, kept up their promiscuous, sinful pairings, creating a race of miserable bastards. Those who became monogamous out of fear of the gods flourished and established both virtuous families and virtuous worship. A new age, the age of heroes, dawned on America when the race of bastards realized that if they were to survive, they would have to surrender their rights to those who had prospered. In the new heroic period, as the original founding families were swelled by the arrival of the slothful bastards, new laws became operative. Laws of truce and embassies were created when wars for control of lands and peoples erupted between rival communities. Fortunately for historians, the heroes had encoded their travails in stories of wondrous transmutations of heroes into deities and animals, as well as in heraldic emblems. According to

Boturini, the Amerindians had books equivalent to Ovid's *Metamorphoses* and Virgil's *Aeneid* and *Eclogues*, as well as tales of their own Ulysses and Hercules, and these could be interpreted to reconstruct the past. Meso-american heraldry preserved the history of the battles of the heroes and the history of agriculture and land tenure in the second age.[19] Finally, according to Boturini, Mexico witnessed the rise and fall of many groups during the age of heroes, including the Giants, Olmecs, and Xicalanca (or Xilanca). The Toltecs had also flourished in this period, and after 100 B.C.E., they had cre-ated an extremely accurate calendar that took into account the real duration of the tropical year.[20]

According to Boturini, when Huematzin wrote the sacred book of the Toltecs in C.E. 660, he inaugurated the human age. Writing and the estab-lishment of monarchical governments marked the transition to the third age. Boturini saw the reconstruction of the events from the Deluge to the end of the age of the heroes (3,362 years) in the history of Mesoamerica as his most original contribution. "These events have not been narrated by any other [European] author before. [I am therefore the first to do so,] and this period has become exclusively my own."[21] He devoted a mere five pages to the human age, even though most of the Mesoamerican documents in his col-lection allegedly belonged to it. According to Boturini, the human age wit-nessed the decline of the Toltecs and the appearance of new empires, monarchies, and republics in central Mexico, including the Chichimecs, the Tlaxcalan-Tepanecs, the Mexica, and the Teochichimecs. As for the history of the Conquest, Boturini insisted that although much had been written about this, the perspective of the Amerindians, who had left voluminous writ-ings, had unfortunately been forgotten.[22] Boturini's outline ended with a de-tailed listing of the Amerindian writings in pictograms, logograms, and the Latin alphabet that he had collected during his years in Mexico.[23]

Although he lifted this entire historiographical paradigm from Vico with-out acknowledgment, Boturini, in fact, stood Vico on his head. As I have al-ready shown, Vico had sought to demonstrate that the histories and chro-nologies of the Chaldeans, the Phoenicians, and particularly the Egyptians were untrustworthy. For Vico, hieroglyphs were the product of poetic, prim-itive minds, and the Bible was the only reliable continuous historical record. Paradoxically, Boturini used Vico to give Mesoamerican sources a historio-graphical status similar to that enjoyed by the Bible. By revindicating the use of words and myths as reliable historical evidence, Boturini cast the sacred book of the Toltecs as the American equivalent of the Bible. If Moses wrote the Pentateuch drawing on the continuous written traditions of the Jews,

Huematzin had written his book based on an equally reliable set of sources. It is clear that Boturini misunderstood Vico's intention. Unlike Vico, for example, Boturini thought highly of hieroglyphic writing. He took the German Jesuit Athanasius Kircher to task for having declared that Mexican hieroglyphs were manifestations of "rustic minds," an idea with which Vico would have agreed wholeheartedly. "On the contrary," Boturini declared, "[the hieroglyphs] of the first and second ages [in Mesoamerica] and even some of the third age encode noble secrets of popular wisdom, symbolic science, and high issues of gentile theology."[24]

The Council of the Indies welcomed Boturini's proposal and assigned a magistrate to review it. Such a positive reception was an indication of a rising consensus in Spain that the traditional historiography of the land and peoples of the New World was in need of radical revision. In November 1745, along with his review, José Borrull, a former professor of law at the University of Salamanca and former magistrate of the high court and council (Audiencia) of Granada, returned a recommendation that Boturini be given the title of "general writer of New Spain" (*escritor general de la Nueva España*), a salary to go back to Mexico, the right to reclaim his collection, and unlimited access to all the archives in the viceroyalty. Borrull also recommended that the council allow Boturini's proposed coronation of Our Lady of Guadalupe to proceed.[25] The council convened in December 1745 and approved all of Borrull's suggestions, with the exception of the coronation, which was rejected on the grounds that the king himself was about to create an *Iglesia colegiata*, or chapter of canons without cathedral, on the very spot at which the miracle had occurred. The council also approved the publication of Boturini's manuscript.

Between December 1745 and May 1746, however, something happened. After meeting twice in May 1746 to discuss Boturini's appointment, the council withdrew its original support. It now concluded that the person best qualified to interpret the documents was not the Italian, but a Mexican Indian, Antonio López, a Nahua interpreter working for the Audiencia of New Spain, who had compiled an inventory of Boturini's collection at the request of Viceroy Fuenclara. The council declared that López seemed better prepared to deal with Mesoamerican pictograms and logograms than Boturini, and that an Academy of History should be created in Mexico under López's leadership.[26] With opposition mounting, Boturini had to publish before it was too late, and his *Idea de una nueva historia general de la América Septentrional* appeared in print in June 1746, only days after the council convened to withdraw its support.

To make some sense of the council's sudden change of heart, we need first to look at the content of Borrull's official review, as well as at the many congratulatory prefaces, written on Boturini's behalf, that were appended to the *Idea*, most likely to help defray the costs of printing. Borrull not only saluted Boturini as the first person capable of understanding Mesoamerican documents, he also cast Spanish scholarship in a very negative light, maintaining that the likes of José de Acosta, the Inca Garcilaso de la Vega, Antonio de Herrera y Tordesillas, and Antonio de Solis had written about Amerindian antiquities "so superficially that instead of satisfying the curiosity of the reader they only excited it further." According to Borrull, no Spaniard had studied the origin, migrations, government, policies, customs, religion, languages, hieroglyphs, and paintings of the natives with "any [degree of] seriousness."[27] This daring statement was complemented by an even more daring suggestion. Boturini, he claimed, was the first to offer a serious study of Amerindian antiquities precisely because he was a foreigner, for Spaniards in the New World had been more interested in exploiting mines and getting richer than in studying the local past. "Boturini," Borrull maintained, "has not gone to the Indies to discover material mines . . . but to unearth those buried by [our] oblivion." "This is not surprising but it is rather common," he continued, "for many foreigners are solely motivated by curiosity and selflessness and visit various countries to observe in each that which is most singular. I conclude therefore that only [the foreigner Boturini] is capable of carrying out the new historiographical proposal [under review]."[28]

This gross and inaccurate attack on early Spanish observers of the New World came from the pen of a powerful Spanish magistrate, and everyone who wrote prefaces for the *Idea* backed it. An endorsement by the Carmelite friar Juan de la Concepción, written in January 1746, reinforced all of Borrull's ideas. A member of the Spanish Academy (of Language), Concepción argued that Boturini was about to do away with centuries of "[Spanish] negligence and forgetfulness." It was Spanish scholarly negligence, he argued, that had been responsible for depicting the Amerindians as savage.[29] Moreover, Concepción maintained that, with Boturini, Italians, not Spaniards could claim to be both the material and historiographical discoverers of the New World.[30] As they paraded their poetical skills in the various sonnets, epigrams, and poems appended to the *Idea*, Boturini's friends did not lose the opportunity to present the Spaniards as voracious plunderers of America's gold and riches, in sad contrast to the Italian pioneers Columbus, Vespucci, and Boturini, discoverers of lands and antiquities. "Boturini," exclaimed Antonio Emmanuel Campoy Morata, a magistrate in the Royal Council, in a Latin sonnet, "[with your scholarship] you are recovering for the kingdoms of the Indies some of the riches that others stole while motivated by an execrable, voracious thirst for gold."[31]

Clashing Patriotic Agendas

A book prefaced with such views was bound to face opposition. A group of courtiers, to be sure, did its utmost to persuade the council to overturn its prior ruling and to derail the forthcoming publication.[32] Although some Mexican Creoles complained that Boturini was receiving exaggerated praise, Aragonese made up the party that led the charge against Boturini.[33] To understand the nature of the arguments leveled by the Aragonese against Boturini, we need first to consider their leader, the courtier and senior librarian of the Royal Library, Blás Antonio Nasarre y Férriz (1689–1751).

Nasarre was part of a larger erudite movement that emerged in Spain beginning in the late seventeenth century to write a critical ecclesiastical history based on the careful scrutiny of archives, a movement inspired by the historiography of the French Maurists Jean Mabillon and Bernard de Montfaucon, the Italian Ludovico Antonio Muratori (1672–1750), and the Bollandists of Antwerp responsible for the *Acta sanctorum*. Like the French Benedictines, those involved in the movement to rewrite the history of the Spanish Church in rigorous yet pious terms enjoyed enthusiastic royal support. The Bourbons, the new Spanish dynasty that had replaced the Habsburgs after the War of the Spanish Succession (1701–14), had embarked on a program of cultural and economic renewal. The Spanish crown had much to gain from historiographical efforts to strengthen royalist currents within the Spanish Church and therefore encouraged patriotic clergy, including not only Jansenists but also Spanish Jesuits, to raid archives for evidence of Spain's ecclesiastical independence from Rome during the Visigothic and Mosarabic past.[34] Many initiatives were launched from the Royal Library, led by Nasarre, to organize the ecclesiastical archives of Castile and study in detail the rich manuscript holdings of the Escorial.[35] Two important institutions linked to the reformist impulses of the Bourbons also received crucial support from Nasarre, namely, the Academy of History and a periodical devoted to critical reviews of current literature, the *Diario de los literatos españoles* (1737–42). Created to give impulse to new patriotic yet critical historical narratives, the Academy of History met at the Royal Library from its inception in 1736 until well after Nasarre's death in 1751.[36] The *Diario*, headed by the Aragonese Juan Martínez de Salafranca (1697–1772), the Catalan Leopoldo Jerónimo Puig (d. 1763), and the Castilian Francisco Manuel de la Huerta (d. 1752) also enjoyed Nasarre's patronage. It sought to create a review journal in Spain like the *Journal des Scavans* and *Mémoires de Trevoux* in France or *Philosophical Transactions* in England. The editors of the *Diario* and Nasarre represented a wing of the Spanish intelligentsia bent on rooting out superstition in Spain and strengthening the state. Thus, for example, the *Diario* undertook the defense of Benito Jerónimo Feijóo y Montenegro (1676–1764), a Benedictine whose *Theatro crítico* (1726–39) and *Cartas eruditas* (1742–60) introduced the literate public in Spain to the ideas of Descartes and Newton in order to put an end to popular "delusion and ignorance."[37]

It was this party of courtiers that sought to derail the publication of Boturini's *Idea*. The Aragonese opposed Boturini because they were patriots revolted by the insults piled by Boturini's supporters on early Spanish observers of the New World. It would be extremely simplistic to argue that in the ensuing debate, Aragonese patriots were pitted against cosmopolitan Moderns. The debate was far more complex, for the supporters of Boturini were also Spaniards and wrote their prefaces largely out of love for their embattled nation. Two opposing views of patriotism thus came into conflict in these debates.

In 1737, a debate erupted in Madrid between two camps of courtiers, the Aragonese, led by the editor of the *Diario*, Martínez de Salafranca, and the Valencians, led by Gregorio Mayans y Siscar, a leading eighteenth-century humanist, soon to become one of Boturini's staunchest supporters in Spain.[38] In an article published in the pages of *Acta eruditorum* in Leipzig in 1731, Mayans offered a survey of what he thought was the sorry contemporary state of Spanish erudition, implicitly and explicitly criticizing the type of scholarship represented by Feijóo.[39] In 1737, the article by Mayans came to the attention of the editors of the *Diario* via Nasarre. Martínez de Salafranca thereupon set about taking Mayans to task for having argued in a foreign journal that Spain was a wasteland as far as jurisprudence, historiography, poetics, and, generally, good taste were concerned, offering the example of Feijóo's scholarship to confute this.[40] Mayans, however, thought that the *Diario* and Feijóo stood for shallow, derivative, and unpatriotic scholarship, passively and uncritically aping French fashions.[41] According to Mayans, Spain needed to return to the rigor and erudition that had characterized sixteenth-century Spanish humanists of the stature of Juan Luis Vives, Antonio de Nebrija (1444?–1522), Antonio Agustín, Francisco Sánchez de las Brozas (1523–1601), and Benito Arias Montano (1527–1598), as well as to the prose and poetry of writers such as Miguel de Cervantes Saavedra (1547–1616) and Luis de León (1528?–1591). Spain did not need the French fashions of the philosophes.[42] The debate over the publication of Mayans's article in *Acta eruditorum* revealed two opposing conceptions of how best to defend Spain. On the one hand, Mayans maintained that a truly patriotic defense had to begin with the acceptance that contemporary Spain was a mere caricature of its greater sixteenth-century self. Scholars needed to build on local traditions and not to be afraid of denouncing past and current Spanish shortcomings. The Aragonese led by Nasarre and Martínez de Salafranca, on the other hand, thought that to embrace foreign modernity was the only way for Spain to regain its lost strength; they also maintained that scholars should not denounce the nation openly.

Manuel Martínez Pingarrón (fl. 1740–50), assistant librarian under Nasarre, expressed his astonishment that any Spaniard could support an Italian who drew on Vico and "other authors" to "discredit our nation."[43] For the Aragonese, the problem lay in the innuendoes implicit in Boturini's narrative and claims. How, in two centuries of colonial rule, could Spaniards have failed to notice any of the wondrous sources Boturini claimed to have collected? To argue that Boturini was the first to assemble a great collection of indigenous sources implied, as Boturini's supporters made explicit in their prefaces and sonnets, Spanish carelessness and negligence. When asked to evaluate the parts on calendrics of Boturini's work, the court mathematician and naval officer Jorge Juan y Santacilia thought it very hard to believe that Boturini had in fact been the first collector of Mesoamerican documents. A powerful courtier, the Jesuit Andrés Marcos Burriel (1719–1762), intervened and vouched for the Italian, using examples closer to home: "[In Spain] there has been and there still is so much negligence in the inquiry of our true antiquities that for this reason many manuscripts are being and have been lost. If in Spain there is hardly a church or family archive that is well organized, how could then we expect in the Indies things to be different? Little can we demand of such curiosity [of ours in the Indies]."[44]

According to the Aragonese, there was another important criticism implicit in Boturini's narrative, and it referred to the devastating effects on the human spirit inflicted on its colonial victims by Spanish colonialism. How could cultures as advanced as those presented by Boturini have become so pathetically depressed only a few years after the Spanish Conquest? If the Amerindians had once been the superb astronomers that Boturini claimed, then it followed that somebody had to be blamed for the poverty and ignorance into which their contemporary descendants had been plunged. Was

Spanish colonialism really to blame, or were accounts like Boturini's simply fantasies? Clearly, the Aragonese thought that Boturini's grandiose representations of the Mesoamerican past were exaggerations. Boturini's supporters, however, put the onus on the colonial system, largely in order to highlight the urgent need for reform. The views of the Jesuit Burriel, who along with Mayans sought to shield Boturini from the attacks of the Aragonese, illustrate the way this worked.

Burriel could have easily followed the example of the French mathematician Charles-Marie de La Condamine and voiced his skepticism of accounts that depicted the Amerindians of the past as highly civilized. In 1745, in his *Relation abregée*, La Condamine had suggested that the Amerindian indolence and stupidity that he had allegedly encountered on his trip to the Andes had not been caused by the ill-effects of Spanish colonialism, for even those natives who lived in the Amazon basin, far from the deleterious effects of Spanish rule, were bestial. The Amerindians, La Condamine concluded, were stupid by nature. Burriel was perfectly familiar with La Condamine's work. In fact, he was the most prominent supporter in Spain of Ulloa and Juan y Santacilia, the two naval officers who accompanied the French academicians on their expedition to the Andes. There is no denying that Burriel was a patriot. He supported Ulloa and Juan y Santacilia largely because he thought that their new travel reports "would fulfill the expectations of Europe [at the same that they] would bring incredible glory to the nation."[45] He single-handedly persuaded the crown to hire engravers and acquire paper, prime hides (for bookbinding), and new printing types overseas to guarantee the quality of the publication of their accounts.[46] Yet for all his patriotism and intimate knowledge of the works of La Condamine, Burriel embraced Boturini's representations of a highly civilized Amerindian past. "Had the Spaniards conquered China," Burriel argued "today there would be skeptics questioning the prodigious antiquities and sciences of the Chinese Empire."[47] Burriel lashed out against Spanish behavior in the New World in order to revamp the Spanish colonial economy. Along with Ulloa and Juan y Santacilia, he thought that cliques of corrupt and exploitative Creoles controlled the colonies (and the Amerindians).[48]

The Aragonese opposition to Boturini was not blinded by its own brand of patriotism. The Aragonese criticism of the *Idea* was both penetrating and persuasive, and it raised important epistemological and historiographical questions as well. To undermine Boturini, the Aragonese called attention, for example, to the fact that the *Idea* made no reference whatsoever to Vico. Boturini underestimated his audience and presented the theory of the three ages and the discovery of alternative historical evidence in names and popular poetics as his own. The Aragonese knew better, however, and denounced Boturini as a plagiarist. "My enemies [*émulos*]," Boturini bitterly complained to Mayans, "preach on every street corner that my *Idea* is lifted from Vico."[49] The charge of plagiarism was to haunt Boturini in the years to come, suggesting that the issue of authors' rights had already become important in Spain.

The Aragonese also criticized Boturini's and Vico's philosophy of history. Working under the positivist paradigm that history was about rigorously discerning the "truth," and not about speculating about its meaning, all the Spaniards involved in the debate thought, in the words of Martínez Pingarrón, that "the system of Vico, if I am not wrong, is imaginary, proof of a gigantic fancy [*entendimiento giganteo*]. It resembles Plato's *Republic* [in that it is ideal]."[50] Even Boturini's allies would repeatedly recommend that he not attempt to reconstruct the divine and heroic ages and concentrate solely on the human age, drawing on his extensive collection of indigenous writings.[51] Modernity arrived in Spain, as Francisco Sánchez-Blanco Parody has argued, with Bacon, not Descartes. The new knowledge that developed outside the purview of the universities in academies, salons, and other officially sponsored institutions was not interested in the kind of rationalism and system-building typified by Vico. From the beginning, reformers in Spain embraced Baconian empiricism and developed a strong distaste for metaphysical speculations.[52] The Aragonese rejected Boturini's sweeping generalizations. A true follower of Vico, Boturini had peppered the *Idea* with all sorts of classical allusions to Ovid and to ancient Roman and Greek historians. In one passage, for example, he dismissed with supreme confidence the views of Livy and Dionysius of Halicarnassus to the effect that Roman laws derived from Greece. As part of a larger argument in which he sought to prove that most theories about the origins of Native Americans were flawed because they emphasized historical descent and cultural borrowings, Boturini insisted that most peoples developed independently of one another: the Romans had crafted their laws without any Greek influence, he contended, and the Amerindians had evolved in isolation from the rest of the world after the Deluge.[53] The Aragonese, however, thought that this approach to the origins of Roman law was unpersuasive and speculative.[54]

Another criticism of the Aragonese was aimed at Boturini's version of natural law. Boturini embraced Vico because the Neapolitan scholar had offered an alternative jurisprudence to that of Hugo Grotius (1583–1645), one in which there was still room for the indirect workings of Providence in history. In 1750, in an address to the Valencian Academy, Boturini argued, like

Vico, that the systems of natural law of Grotius, Hobbes, and Samuel Pufendorf (1632–1694) were too secular. In them, the origins of most legal systems appeared as the working out through history of human self-interest.[55] Societies evolved because individuals grew increasingly dependent on the labor of others.[56] These secular narratives of the origins of law had opponents within Spain. Mayans, for example, felt drawn to Boturini largely because he shared the Italian's criticisms of these systems. In his evaluation of Boturini's address to the Valencian Academy in 1750, Mayans argued that for all the absurdities in Vico's (and Boturini's) historiographical proposal, the Italian was right in seeking alternatives to the new, impious secular theories of natural law. According to Mayan, systems of law derived not from selfish individual calculations but from God-given, innate human faculties such as the cardinal and theological virtues, which operated independently of reason (faith, charity, prudence, temperance, justice, and fortitude). Charity, for example, moved parents to form families, because they took pity on their offspring. Mayans postulated that the sinful nature of man caused many to plunder the virtuous to survive. Governments, he argued, emerged out of efforts to discipline the sinful and to bring justice and peace. National communities were families writ large, in which kings were fathers who practiced charity to the weak and the orphaned; who looked after the defense of the group; and who rewarded the just and punished the slothful. This Augustinian interpretation of human nature might have found sympathetic ears in a bureaucracy bent on creating a centralizing monarchy. Yet the Aragonese rejected both Mayans's and Boturini's critiques of Grotius.[57]

It is possible that the Aragonese disdained the natural jurisprudence of Boturini and Mayans because they thought that this jurisprudence had problematic consequences for the centralizing state they sought to represent. We know, for example, that Boturini rejected the opening of free trade between the colonies and Spain on the grounds that the operation of the state should not be left to the laws of nature but to the absolute will of the monarch. "How little these people know of the law of nature and nations," Boturini communicated to Mayans, "for the government and the prince has the faculty to determine what things to prohibit or to tax."[58] If we are to believe that the Aragonese kept abreast with the ideas of the French Physiocrats, Boturini's Augustinian justification of absolute monarchy might have sounded extreme in an age that advocated that monarchs follow the laws that nature had established for the economy, not combat them. But the opposition of the Aragonese to the natural jurisprudence of Boturini and Mayans could also have originated in fear that some of their ideas seemed to weaken rather than strengthen the absolute power of the state. In his Valencian address of 1750, for example, Mayans insisted that meting out justice within communities passed first not through the state but through corporate, private sovereignty: "[Only] when the force of the [large original] families is not sufficient is public force necessary to contain and punish the unruly citizen."[59]

The final criticism leveled by the Aragonese against Boturini focused on the nature of the sources the Italian had used. Was Boturini's collection as extraordinary as the Italian alleged? The librarian Martínez Pingarrón urged Boturini to explain why most of the indigenous documents in his celebrated and impounded collection were actually made of European paper.[60] As soon as a catalogue of Boturini's collection was made available in 1746, the Aragonese began to cast doubt on the credibility of the entire collection. How could sources written on European paper be ancient documents dating back to Huematzin in the seventh century? This was indeed an important question, and one that, to my knowledge, was left unresolved. As recent censuses of Mesoamerican sources have demonstrated, only a handful of extant codices can be considered pre-Hispanic. Most of the sources that the public likes to consider "authentic" were in fact drawn by Amerindian scribes under Spanish patronage and by indigenous communities struggling to reinvent their past in new colonial conditions.[61] It is no wonder, therefore, that careful observers like the Aragonese began to question the antiquity of documents that appeared to be recent colonial creations. The Aragonese were successful at highlighting the problematic origins of the collection, and when the court mathematician Juan y Santacilia was given the task of evaluating Boturini's treatise on Mesoamerican calendrics in 1748, he questioned whether the documents were not forgeries. The powerful Burriel had to intervene again to assure Juan y Santacilia "that [the authenticity] of Boturini's archive cannot be denied."[62]

The weight of all the charges that the Aragonese brought against Boturini was formidable. It was a wake-up call for the magistrates of the Council of the Indies. In May 1746, only five months after having warmly embraced Boturini, the council prudently withdrew its unanimous support. In December 1746, however, it backpedaled and reconfirmed Boturini as the official historian of the New World. Clearly, the council was split.

Boturini's 'Ciclografía'

In January 1747, an elated Boturini wrote to Mayans, the nemesis of the Aragonese, to inform him of the council's new resolution. Dizzied by the possibilities ahead, Boturini listed all his future projects to Mayans: a critical apparatus to clarify the meaning of many Amerindian paintings and manu-scripts and interpret the glyphs and symbols of the age of gods and heroes; an essay on the errors of all previous European historians; a treatise on the ori-gins of the Amerindians; a massive project of translation, that, although ex-pensive, would put into Castilian the Nahua writings of those Amerindian authors who were most trustworthy. Boturini also wrote Mayans for advice. How to avoid the charges of plagiarism? Should he insist in writing about the ages of the gods and the heroes? As for the history of the human age, should he write a general account or just offer separate narratives for each empire? What Spanish authors should he spare from criticism to avoid being accused of being anti-Spanish?[63] This letter initiated a fruitful exchange between Mayans and Boturini, which over the years came to fill several volumes.

Mayans replied swiftly. In February 1747, he recommended that Boturini avoid references to Vico's divine and heroic ages, as well as any comparative analysis with Greco-Roman mythology. Mayans was highly skeptical about the usefulness of Vico's historiography and recommended that Boturini focus on those periods for which the Italian had accumulated substantial written documentation. After eviscerating Boturini's entire historiographical proposal, Mayans proceeded to offer some positive advice. Boturini, he ar-gued, should write general, not particular histories; should introduce a trea-tise on the origin of the Amerindians to make the history "entertaining"; and, more important, should seek to publish the sources, even those he could not interpret, so that others could later do so. As for avoiding charges that he was anti-Spanish, Mayans suggested he avoid writing a separate treatise on the shortcomings of previous historians. "Reprehend in passing those authors who misunderstood [the past]," Mayans advised Boturini. "Since the criti-cisms will be scattered in various sections of the treatise and will never [jamás] be together, they will be less odious."[64]

In the years to come, Boturini met Mayans's advice halfway. Although he finally decided to concentrate on the study of the human age by writing a treatise on Mesoamerican calendrics, so as to lay the basis for a full under-standing of the indigenous annals, Boturini remained committed to Vico's philosophy of history. In March 1747, he replied to Mayans, insisting that "knowledge of [the ages of the gods and the heroes] is the key to [under-standing] the rest."[65] Boturini's stubborn insistence in elucidating the history of the first and second ages prompted Mayans to warn the Italian again. Boturini's speculative criticism of Livy and Dionysius of Halicarnassus on the origins of Roman laws, Mayans maintained, was the cause of too much gos-sip and criticism at court.[66]

Boturini greeted Mayans's advice with silence, and sometime after March 1747, he again lost his appointment, revealing the depth of the split within the council. The post that Boturini had thought he firmly controlled in December 1746 was in fact still up for grabs. Upset, Boturini's allies took the case before the recently anointed King Ferdinand VI (r. 1746–59) for final arbitration. In July 1747, the king handed down a verdict that confirmed Boturini as Royal Chronicler in the Indies and ordered the immediate return of his collection.[67] But not even in the wake of the king's ruling did things get any better. The Aragonese still managed to block Boturini's repeated requests for the post and salary of magistrate in the Audiencia of New Spain in order to pay for the scribes, painters, and translators he needed to carry the new history through to completion. Moreover, Boturini never got his collection back. Be that as it may, Boturini remained busy over all these months of uncertainty, completing the first of fifteen projected volumes, a treatise on Mesoamerican calendrics and chronology that would finally bring order to the many confusing references to Mesoamerican dates in both Spanish and indigenous sources. In July 1748, he reinitiated contact with Mayans, and until April 1749, Boturini and Mayans engaged in weekly epistolary exchanges seeking to polish the *Ciclografía*, Boturini's treatise on Mesoamerican chronology.[68]

Boturini's treatise proved difficult yet insightful. He began by showing how Mesoamerican calendars had evolved. The Amerindians, he argued, had first divided the year by observing the seasons. Gradually, however, they introduced more subtle divisions by turning their gaze to the stars. At this point, Boturini sought to blend the scholarship of Vico with that of the abbé Noël-Antoine Pluche, who in 1742 had maintained that the signs of the zodiac encoded the history of important agrarian and social developments in the Mediterranean world. Boturini argued that the Mexicans had first developed a "zodiac" of fifteen constellations, bearing the names of deities, which stood for major sociological and historical transformations. Boturini had already devoted large sections of his previous book, the *Idea*, to reconstructing the social history of Mesoamerica through an exegesis of the names of Mesoamerican deities.[69]

It was in the process of gathering evidence on the evolution of Mesoamerican calendars that Boturini committed his first serious mistake: he launched an attack on the person and writings of the Jesuit José de Acosta, author of the influential *Natural and Civil History of the Indies*. The mistake lay not in the attack itself, about which nobody in Spain really cared, but in what it revealed about Boturini's psyche. His backers, for the first time, did not like what they saw and began to ponder the consequence for Spain of endorsing a person who appeared insane. They began to withdraw after years of unflagging support.

In 1590, Acosta had argued that it was doubtful whether the Amerindians knew how to adjust their calendars to the real duration of the year (365.25 days). More important, Acosta also maintained that the Mexican Amerindians, unlike those of Peru, had not counted their months using lunar cycles, for their months lasted only twenty, not thirty days.[70] Boturini, however, thought that the Amerindians had developed ways to adjust their calendars (for example, by leap years). Curiously, and notwithstanding evidence to the contrary, he also thought that the Amerindians of Mesoamerica had lunar months, for according to him, knowledge evolved gradually and through empirical accumulation. Boturini considered that the Amerindians had of necessity observed the cycles of the moon as they accumulated evidence about the motion of the sun. In fact, there were indications that the natives had once organized their months after lunar cycles; the word *metzli*, which signified month in Nahua, was also the name the natives gave to the moon. Moreover, in 1699–1700, the Italian traveler Gemelli Careri (see pp. 227–30 below) had published an indigenous calendric wheel (Fig. 4.3) that had mysterious references to the cycles of the moon. Boturini concluded that the twenty-day Mexican month had to fit somehow within the thirty-day lunar cycle, a proposal that in order to work required a mathematical feat more complex than squaring the circle.[71] Although all the evidence seemed to indicate he was wrong, Boturini stubbornly held fast to his hypothesis. Moreover, he concluded that behind Acosta's denials lay an insult to the observational capacity of the Amerindians, and he devoted an entire section of the *Ciclografía* to calling into question the credibility of Acosta's entire historical oeuvre.[72] Boturini set out to undermine Acosta's version of the history of Mexico by demonstrating the shallowness of the Jesuit's sources, which he identified, using Torquemada for support, as a single, unreliable indigenous document (the Duran-Tovar manuscript). Boturini also criticized Acosta's account of Inca calendars, citing the Inca Garcilaso de la Vega to prove that the Incas had based their monthly cycles on the sun, not the moon.[73]

When the Jesuit Burriel, hitherto one of his staunchest supporters, read Boturini's new manuscript and noted Boturini's strenuous efforts to prove that Mesoamerican monthly cycles were in fact lunar, he began to question the credentials and reliability of the Italian.[74] It was not that Burriel felt that Boturini was attacking the Jesuits by undermining Acosta, as Boturini would later repeatedly contend. What Burriel feared most was that Boturini might well be delusional. Burriel had seen how Boturini pestered court mathematicians and astronomers for months for proof that a twenty-day cycle could be somehow linked to lunar cycles.[75] By September 1748, Burriel began to question the wisdom of supporting the Italian. If left to his own devices, Burriel confided to the court mathematician Juan y Santacilia, Boturini might eventually produce an account that would be the laughingstock of Europe. Burriel wrote to Mayans in fear that the work of Boturini might turn out to be like the fake lead tablets "discovered" in Granada in the late sixteenth century that narrated the foundation of the Spanish Church by the apostle James. The tablets had brought shame on Spain and the laughter of European authors of the likes of Pierre Bayle (1647–1706), who had scoffed at Spanish historians' credulity and blind patriotism.[76] Burriel agonized in his correspondence with Mayans: "How can we make sure that the monuments [that constitute Boturini's collection] are not lost [to Spain] and, that [at the same time] we don't sponsor the publication of new [absurdities]?"[77] Burriel faced a dilemma. If the court withdrew its support, the Italian would take his collection and his ideas to other European courts, and if he produced a valuable work after all, some other country would take credit, and Spain would lose both face and Boturini's collection to boot. Burriel's patriotism took precedence over any personal loyalties, and he recommended that Juan y Santacilia propose in his official report that the crown extend only conditional support to Boturini. The Italian should be paid a salary, Burriel suggested, to be reevaluated once he finished work. Should Boturini's labors turn out to be reputable, Spain would reap the glory. Should they be found worthless, however, Spain would retain Boturini's collection in restitution of his salary.[78]

But beyond its obsessive interest in Amerindian lunar cycles, Boturini's *Ciclografía* proved to be a tour de force. It brought order to some two hundred years of European confusion about Mesoamerican calendrics. Every author had until then postulated his own list and order of calendrical signs for days, months, and years. Moreover, there were many versions of when the Mexican year had begun, and of how the Amerindians had adjusted their calendars. Boturini postulated five considerations. To account for the different seemingly contradictory versions of the name of the year at the beginning of each 52-year cycle, the Mesoamerican "century," Boturini contended that the Amerindian centuries were in fact part of larger 208-year cycles. Every 52-year cycle began within the larger cycle with one of four possible different year signs. Moreover, he argued that every ethnic group had preferences for different leading year signs. To account for the contradictory references to mechanisms of adjusting the calendars and the many versions of the order of the months and the date in which the year began, Boturini postulated the existence of two separate calendars, one civil and one ritual, each with identical monthly series, but slightly different. The civic calendar always began on a date corresponding either to February 1 or February 2 and was adjusted by adding one extra day every four years. The ritual calendar, on the other hand, had a different movable starting date and was adjusted differently, namely, by intercalating thirteen days at the end of every 52-year cycle. The many confusing references to indigenous dates and calendars in Spanish sources could easily be clarified this way, Boturini argued, and he provided tables for converting Amerindian dates into European ones.[79]

This extraordinarily complex piece of scholarship, to which Mayans contributed mightily, was destined not to come to light. Nor did it help Boturini obtain his overdue salary or long-sought appointment as magistrate to the Audiencia of New Spain. There is no simple explanation for the chilly reception that the manuscript of the *Ciclografía* received. Upon its completion in April 1749, the manuscript went through three separate evaluations, testimony that there was now a reigning skepticism as to the quality of Boturini's scholarship. The Council first sent the *Ciclografía* to one of Boturini's allies, the magistrate José Borrull, who had written the council's original report on the *Idea*. Borrull thought it appropriate to ask Mayans for help and requested that the latter write the evaluation for him. Mayans offered a spirited defense of the trustworthiness and loyalty of the Italian. Although many were skeptical of Boturini's claim that he was the first to have noticed the accuracy of Mesoamerican calendars, Mayans urged skeptics not to dismiss the Italian. It could not be denied, Mayans contended, that Spaniards had shown little interest in studying the lands and peoples they encountered. As for the charge that Boturini was an enemy of Spain because his narrative insinuated Spanish colonial wrongdoing, by highlighting the contrast between the past grandeur of the Amerindians of Mesoamerica and Peru and their wretched present state, Mayans argued that Spaniards were wrong to try to hide the fact that Spain had done to the Amerindians what the Turks had done to the Greeks — reduced them to a lower state of civilization from a higher one.[80]

This evaluation did not evoke much sympathy, and in June 1749, the *Ciclografía* went to the Royal Cosmographer, the Jesuit Pedro Fresnada, for a new review. After a few months, Fresnada approved the technical aspects of the work, but he refused to vouch for the accuracy of the premises on the grounds that he was no expert on Amerindian antiquities.[81] So, in August 1749, the *Ciclografía* went to a third referee, the Royal Chronicler of the

Indies, Miguel Herrero de Ezpeleta.[82] It seems to have sailed by this new reviewer, for it was finally approved in October 1749.[83] Yet it never went to press. Until he died in July 1755, Boturini struggled unsuccessfully to publish his *Ciclografía*. Why?

I have argued that the debate elicited by Boturini's works in Spain remained throughout a dispute over the best strategy for defending the nation. For Mayans, Borrull, and Burriel, three of Boturini's staunchest allies, the best defense consisted in openly accepting past mistakes while embracing forms of scholarship that tapped into age-old local traditions, particularly the humanist-philological approach that Boturini typified. For the Aragonese, on the other hand, patriotism meant embracing the new foreign, modern scholarship, while rejecting any open discussion of Spanish errors. Although the Aragonese rejected Boturini on epistemological and historiographical grounds too, their main problem with him remained the criticisms of Spain implicit in his argument. Of these two strategies, the one espoused by Burriel, Borrull, and Mayans initially carried the day. The *Idea* was published, and Boturini was declared Royal Chronicler in the Indies, despite all the obstacles thrown in his way by the Aragonese. Boturini failed to notice, however, that his obsession with the nature of Mesoamerican months was undermining his support at court. Moreover, in 1750, his closest ally in the Council of the Indies, the magistrate Borrull, died. Although Nasarre also died the following year, the Aragonese continued to oppose Boturini as a team, this time under the leadership of a council member by the name of Bamfi.[84] Finally, Boturini also managed to alienate Mayans. In September 1751, Boturini encouraged his friends to write polemical broadsides against Feijóo, supposedly to bolster Mayans's image at court. Mayans was infuriated, because this could only hurt him. The best way to survive at court, Mayans lectured Boturini, was not to attract attention.[85] In the wake of this incident, the correspondence between Boturini and Mayans came to a halt. According to Mayans, Boturini was responsible for his own plight. "Boturini rightly endures the effects of persecution," Mayans confided to the librarian Martínez Pingarrón in 1751. "[All this] would have never happened had he followed my advice, namely, to dissimulate."[86] Although brought up as a courtier, Boturini did not have the necessary skills to succeed in an environment characterized by cabals and backstabbing. "Poverty has killed him," Mayans declared in September 1755 when Burriel informed him of Boturini's death.[87]

There is more to the history of the reception of Boturini's work in Spain than meets the eye. Far from being merely a blind rejection of Vico by decadent and ignorant courtiers, as Venturi and Badaloni would have us believe, the Spanish reception reveals a lively and complex intellectual milieu, perfectly capable of sophisticated critical assessments. Ultimately, Boturini was defeated by his own mistakes, for he managed to alienate key allies when he most needed them. More important, the reception accorded Boturini's work shows that there were two distinct styles of patriotic scholarship contending for the attention of the Spanish public. On one hand, the Aragonese, who controlled important cultural institutions such as the Royal Library and the influential *Diario*, advocated the embrace of foreign modernity but rejected any open attack on Spanish shortcomings. On the other hand, writers such as Mayans argued that Spanish scholars should not be afraid of denouncing past mistakes. However, they rejected the embrace of foreign intellectual fashions and argued that the way to rebuild Spain's former glories was to tap into the rich history of Spanish humanism.

Empires Are Lost or Won in the Struggle over Naming and Remembering

Boturini's insistence that a *new* history based on *new* sources should replace the old enjoyed widespread acceptance in Spain, the Aragonese notwithstanding. Calls in Spain for a new historiography that would replace the old, which was allegedly plagued by erroneous assumptions and misrepresentations, preceded by many years the works of de Pauw, Raynal, and Robertson. Partial criticism of Spanish historiography of the Indies began perhaps with Andrés González de Barcia (1673–1743), an influential figure, member of the Royal Council and Royal Treasury and magistrate of the Council of Castile and the Council of War. During the 1720s and 1730s, Barcia undertook the editing of Spanish classics on the history of the New World dating from the sixteenth and early seventeenth centuries that had long been rare and inaccessible, a task that was completed by a nephew of the same name in the 1740s.[88]

Barcia's editorial campaign was part of a larger effort in both official and private circles to reacquaint both national and foreign audiences with the Spanish scholarship of the long sixteenth century, a century that many assumed best reflected the intellectual accomplishments of Spain. Barcia was one of the founding members of the Spanish Academy (of Language) created in 1711 by the new Bourbon dynasty to recover some of the prestige Spanish had enjoyed as a language of learning.[89] Juan de Iriarte (1701–1771), one of the leading members of this Academy, made the official policy explicit when he maintained in 1747 that the priority of the learned should be "to make available our classical authors; to write apologies of our language; to defend ourselves against foreign innuendos that either deny our nationality by making us African or Asian or circumscribe the number of our good authors to two or three. [Foreigners] affirm that all Spanish science can be reduced to two verses and four syllogisms. [We then should] praise the great men of our nation by resurrecting their memories."[90] Most learned Spaniards throughout the eighteenth century shared the editorial priorities of Barcia and Iriarte. Critics like the brothers Rafael and Pedro Rodríguez Mohedano called on the nation in 1769 not to let its glories go unnoticed, for having been "forgotten even by nationals, it is not surprising that foreigners pass them by either through ignorance, dissimulation, or silence."[91] To refute Montesquieu's mocking remark that Spanish books and libraries had "romances on one side and scholastics on the other, [revealing that] the whole [was] assembled by some secret enemy of human reason," José Cadalso (1741–1782), a typical representative of the so-called Spanish Enlightenment, argued in 1772 that "the charge that our books are limited to novels and scholastic treatises is unfounded." "Compare the dates of our literature with that of the French regarding dead languages, rhetoric, mathematics, navigation, theology, and poetry," Cadalso argued. "[I]t clearly shows the greater antiquity, numbers, and merit of our authors."[92] The literati worked untiringly to rescue the past intellectual accomplishments of Spain from oblivion. They edited and published hundreds of works, with such success and support that, in the words of Ivy Lilian McClelland, "a really comprehensive bibliography of publications [of editions and reprints of older Spanish works in the eighteenth century would] form such a large collection that it would require a volume of its own to contain it, and the history of scholastic editorship in that century another."[93]

Scholars often published long patriotic genealogies tracing key discoveries of the new European sciences back to the Spanish Renaissance, and expeditionary botanists and naturalists saw themselves as heirs to the renowned sixteenth-century Spanish natural historians Francisco Hernández, Nicolás Monardes (ca. 1512–1588), Gonzalo Fernández de Oviedo (1478–1557), and Acosta.[94] Rabid neoclassicists, who sought to extirpate all traces of baroque theater from the stage, and whom the public considered Francophile (afrancesados), framed their reforms of taste on the basis of long-forgotten Spanish drama.[95] Nasarre, Boturini's nemesis, for example, was an ardent follower of French neoclassical tragedy and comedy. Yet he was also tired of the continuous complaints of the Italians and the French about the lack of verisimilitude and complete disregard for the unities of time, action, and space that allegedly characterized Spanish drama. Particularly incensed by the appearance in Paris in 1738 of a periodical devoted to the analysis and criticism of Spanish theater, Nasarre edited samples of Cervantes's drama, *Ocho comedias y ocho entremeses* (1615), to prove that Cervantes had already criticized Spanish baroque theater using neoclassical terms. According to Nasarre, baroque theater was a deviation from a long neoclassical national tradition that had been thoroughly informed by the rules of Aristotle's *Poetics* and by the Latin theater of Plautus and Terence. According to Nasarre, Spanish theater had anticipated all the theoretical insights of Molière and Corneille. In the same way that Petrarch had drawn on Catalan, Aragonese, and Provençal medieval poets, Nasarre argued, Molière and Corneille had drawn on sixteenth-century Spanish dramatists.[96]

In seeking to recover the glorious Spanish past, Spanish scholars paradoxically also set out to reclaim the glories of the Arabs. Although little or nothing has been written on the history of eighteenth-century Spanish orientalism, it is clear that the literati found in the intellectual and technical accomplishments of the Arabs of medieval Spain allies to fend off northern European attacks on the Spanish mind.[97] There were numerous calls throughout the eighteenth century to introduce the teaching of Arabic as a learned language in the universities.[98] Every defense of Spain against northern European attacks also included the required section on the great intellectual achievements of the Arabs.[99] Moreover, the first serious studies of Arab intellectual history in the Iberian peninsula took place in the eighteenth century under the leadership of Michel Gharcieh Al-Ghaziri, a Maronite Christian cleric who went by the Hispanic name of Miguel Casiri García (1710–1791). Between 1760 and 1770, Casiri edited the *Bibliotheca arabico-hispana escurialensis*, an annotated bibliography of the holdings of Arabic manuscripts in the library of the Escorial.[100] The scholarship of the Arabs and of the Spanish Renaissance became an endless source of inspiration and pride for the eighteenth-century literati in their struggle to silence the ever-louder northern European criticisms of the Spanish mind.

It is no wonder therefore that Barcia embarked on a vast editorial operation to recover rare old sources on the land and peoples of the New World. Barcia held Spanish scholarship on the Amerindian past in high regard. In his new edition of Torquemada's *Monarchía indiana* (1615), for example, he argued that it was exemplary scholarship, the product of years of selfless, painstaking labor. Through a careful collation of the original manuscript and of a few copies that had survived the loss of the bulk of the first edition in a shipwreck,

Barcia restored sections that had been excised.[101] Barcia's new edition of Gregorio García's *Origen de los Indios del Nuevo Mundo* (1607) also typified his satisfaction with the quality of sixteenth-century Spanish antiquarian insights into the New World. García's treatise on the origins of the Amerindians dealt with one of the greatest philosophical enigmas, Barcia maintained. The mystery did not lie in the path taken by the Amerindians to reach America but in the state of arrested development in which the Europeans had found them. Although, according to Barcia, the Amerindians were ancient arrivals in America, they had clung to "singular customs that cannot be found among any other nation on the face of the earth, either surviving or extinct."[102] García had solved the mystery. Long before Buffon or de Pauw, he had argued that the Amerindians had degenerated to adapt to the climate and conditions of the New World.[103] Trusting García's erudition, Barcia saw fit to add only a few parenthetical notes.[104]

This satisfaction with Spanish historiography turned into patriotic anguish, however, when Barcia confronted the status of Spanish scholarship on the history of the Indies *after* the Spanish Conquest. Historiographical negligence and inept editorial policies might, he believed, contribute to the loss of Spain's colonies to rival European powers, some of which had published misleading histories claiming historical precedence over Spanish discoveries and assigning foreign nomenclature to places Spaniards had first named.[105] Naming places, Barcia argued, was the first step toward actual colonial possession.[106] In a treatise in which he set out to reconstruct the history of Spanish colonization in Florida to stop the symbolic loss of this territory to the English, Dutch, French, Swedes, and Danes, Barcia argued that Garcilaso's *La Florida* (Lisbon, 1605), although a good first step toward the history of the Spanish colonization of the peninsula, had many weaknesses, including limited access to sources.[107] Based on numerous new archival discoveries, Barcia sought to reconstruct the original names the Spaniards had used in Florida. This concern with the symbolic and actual loss of Spanish colonial frontiers to other European powers was also manifested in Barcia's efforts to compile bibliographies on the history of the European colonization of East Asia and the New World. Barcia's new edition of Antonio León Pinelo's *Epitome de la biblioteca oriental y occidental* (1629) was an entirely new work; he transformed León Pinelo's slim 143-page bibliography in quarto of European travels and colonization of the West and East Indies into three stout folio volumes.[108]

But Barcia's criticism of the Spanish historiography of the colonial expansion was soon extended to accounts of the pre-Hispanic period too. By the time Boturini published his *Idea*, there was mounting discontent with alleged Spanish neglect of the study of New World history. In 1751, the Royal Chronicler of the Indies, the Benedictine Martín Sarmiento (1695–1772), declared that as a result of a complete lack of interest in the natural and civil histories of the Indies, Spain was losing its colonial territories to other European powers, both symbolically and in fact. In a proposal to complete a great geographical survey of imperial Spain written in 1751, Sarmiento maintained that Spanish cartography, botany, and historiography needed to be revived in order to compete in the international battle over naming. Owing to Spanish negligence, Sarmiento argued, the names of places, plants, and discoverers of territories were being altered every day by rival European powers in new maps, taxonomies, and histories.[109]

It is curious that the patriotic Spanish intelligentsia chose to follow French complaints about Spanish ignorance of the lands and peoples of America. The French had long argued that Spanish America was a territory barely explored, largely because Spaniards had been so busy plundering it. In 1714, for example, Louis Feuillée argued that Spanish America was "a vast land about which we ought to know more but which remains almost unknown."[110] The editors of the 1744 French translation of Garcilaso denounced Spain for its lack of philosophical curiosity and expressed amazement that La Condamine had been the first to describe the plant quinine. "This [alone]," the editors maintained, "is enough to make us see Peru as a land where the sciences have not yet penetrated at all." They explicitly condemned Spain for having abandoned "regions of the world where it would be perhaps possible to make discoveries in all the areas of knowledge."[111] This state of affairs did not surprise the French, who regarded Spaniards as superstitious and bestial. In 1771, for example, Zacharie de Pazzi de Bonneville, who paradoxically defended the value of sixteenth-century Spanish historiographical testimonies against de Pauw's criticism, confidently demanded: "Does anybody know of any other nation, more brutish [*abrutie*], more ignorant, more savage, and more barbarous than Spain? I defy that person to name it."[112] Joseph La Porte argued in 1777 that Spain was a land of superstitious people dabbling in judicial astrology, cabala, and other "Arab chimeras," and uncritically following Aristotle "whose tenebrous philosophy, empty of sense, suits their taste."[113]

This wholesale attack on Spain as a non-European frontier, or as the "other" in Europe, at times took on comical proportions.[114] In Spain, however, it generated great anxiety, which created the political will to send out many scientific expeditions. In the second half of the eighteenth century, the monarchy launched a crusade to map the colonies and to establish clear boundaries with competing European powers, as well as to catalogue the botanical and physical resources of the empire. Countless expeditions arrived in America headed by foreign experts, or by Spaniards trained in French and German schools, to improve the output of mines by introducing technical innovations; to challenge the commercial monopoly of Dutch and British merchants by discovering cloves and cinnamon in the tropical forests of America; to collect statistical and historical data in order to reorganize the colonies on a more rational basis; to create alternative educational institutions to the universities to train civil servants; and to help reform public health so as to improve, within a mercantilist paradigm, the economy.[115] There was, to be sure, a utilitarian streak behind all these expeditions by which the Spanish Bourbons struggled to revamp the empire. Yet a strong nationalistic undercurrent underlined all efforts: cartography and taxonomy were to help preserve the Spanish names of plants and places, and the new expeditions were to prove to northern Europeans that Spaniards were reliable philosophical observers.[116]

The Royal Academy of History and the History of the New World, 1755–1770

Calls for renovation of the historiography of the Indies also accompanied this crusade. In fact, one of the most erudite men in Spain, the Benedictine Martín Sarmiento, was appointed by the Bourbons in 1751 to revitalize the moribund post of Royal Chronicler of the Indies after two previous historians, Luis de Salazar (incumbent from 1691 to 1734) and Miguel de Herrero y Ezpeleta (incumbent from 1736 to 1750), had failed miserably. But for all his reputation as the greatest living scholar, Sarmiento also proved quite ineffective, and he quit in 1755, citing too many other responsibilities. The crown then decided that an institution, the Royal Academy of History, rather than an individual, would do the job best,[117] and starting in 1755, the Academy struggled to bring new life to the historiography of the New World.

Two major methodological debates took place within the Academy. They demonstrate how in tune Spain was with the dominant historiographical European currents of the day, for most of the criticism of Spanish colonial historiography that was advanced by the likes of de Pauw was first articulated by the Academy.

The First Debate

The first debate occurred in 1756, immediately after the Academy obtained the title of chronicler. Three members were charged with circulating position papers: Ignacio de Hermosilla y Sandoval, Francisco de Ribera, and José Marcos Benito. Participants in the discussion focused on at least three questions. Should the Academy compile a geographical atlas and natural history of the Indies before attempting to write a civil history? Should the Academy build on the works of previous Spanish historians and naturalists or dismiss them entirely? And, finally, should the Academy be concerned with Amerindian antiquities and indigenous sources at all?

The first question with which the academicians grappled stemmed straight from the anxieties expressed earlier by Barcia and Sarmiento regarding Spanish losses to other European powers in the symbolic battle over naming and remembering.[118] Hermosilla y Sandoval, also a member of the Council of the Indies, insisted that the Academy should not be concerned with natural history and should write only a civil history. He also argued that the Academy should delegate research into ecclesiastical, military, and political history to three different members, who would later meet to weave together a single general narrative.[119] Francisco de Ribera, who was also secretary to the king and court mathematician, maintained rather that a survey of the geography and natural history of each colony was the first priority, for it would help the crown assess its colonial resources accurately. For Ribera, "history" was the endless Baconian accumulation of data on natural history. The only historicity Ribera allowed in his plan was that the survey of names of borders and political and ecclesiastical units should also include changes over time.[120] Finally, Marcos Benito, professor of humanities at the University of Salamanca, met Hermosilla and Ribera halfway and argued that civil and natural histories were both badly needed.[121] For all his support for the writing of a natural history, Marcos Benito predicted, however, that there would be "many obstacles to writing a good natural history of the Indies, for we would get [the information from written] papers, not from [our own] eyewitness observations."[122] In another paper, read before the Academy in November 1756, Marcos Benito insisted that geography and natural history involved "things that have to be witnessed, otherwise, when one depends on the testimony of others, even if credible [inteligentes], one is bound to make many mistakes."[123]

The question over what sources to use and on whether to build on previous Spanish scholarship was also a central concern of the academicians. From an examination of the position papers and the minutes of the

Academy's meetings, it is possible to conclude that there was almost absolute consensus among all participants as to the poor quality of previous Spanish historiography, as well as regret over the negligence shown by previous chroniclers. In August 1756, the academician Antonio Hilarión Domínguez de Riezu deplored "the negligence [*incuria*], omission, and carelessness of our previous chroniclers." Domínguez de Riezu blamed this state of affairs on the difficulties previous historians had had in obtaining access to official sources, and thus to reliable information.[124] Antonio de Herrera y Tordesillas and Pedro Fernández del Pulgar (d. 1697) in particular were two seventeenth-century chroniclers who came in for sustained criticism. Their writings were depicted as no more than undigested compilations of unreliable facts. Fernández del Pulgar, whose manuscripts lay languishing in archives, was often cited by those who wanted to highlight the perils of ignoring geography and of rambling narratives.[125] Of all the academicians who participated in this debate, Marcos Benito was the only one who urged his colleagues to build on previous Spanish scholarship. He insisted that the civil history of the Indies should simply continue Garcilaso's *Historia general del Perú*, Solis's *Historia de la conquista de México*, and Herrera's only reliable *Década*, the first, devoted to the deeds of the Spanish conquistadors in the Caribbean. As for the Philippines, Marcos Benito agreed that the Academy should start from scratch. He also insisted that all the histories had to be based on the study of official papers housed in the Archive of Simancas, the Royal Library, the Council of the Indies, and the Casa de Contratación in Seville. As far as natural history was concerned, Marcos Benito maintained that the Academy should simply build on the works of Spaniards such as Francisco Hernández, José de Acosta, Gregorio López (1542–1596), Francisco Ximénez (1560?–1620), and Nicolás Monardes, and of foreigners such as Willem Piso (1611–1678), Ulisse Aldrovandi, Joseph Pitton de Tournefort (1658–1708), and Carolus Linnaeus (1707–1778), with the caveat, of course, that since it would be merely a derivative compilation, not firsthand reporting by academicians, it was likely to be riddled with mistakes.[126]

The third question with which the academicians grappled focused on the viability of antiquarian research into the Amerindian past. Here deep skepticism colored the views of most participants. Hermosilla, for example, maintained that the academicians should not even attempt to write the history of the Amerindians. According to Hermosilla, writing the history of the "obscure ages" was in and of itself a highly speculative exercise and required an apparatus of erudition from which most readers would shy away. The task of the chronicler, Hermosilla lectured his peers, was to educate the lay public, not to communicate with other scholars. The study of the history of the obscure ages in America presented the additional problem of having to deal with sources written in nonalphabetical scripts that were indecipherable. "It can [safely] be said," Hermosilla concluded, "that we don't have the necessary documents upon which to draw in order to write this kind of history."[127] Ribera, on the other hand, took a slightly more positive stance and argued, following Boturini's lead, that "diligent search of the recollections stored in [the hieroglyphs] of the Mexicans ought to be the way to restore a history that has been abandoned."[128] Ribera agreed with Hermosilla, however, that should the Academy choose to write the history of highland Mesoamerican and Andean societies, the difficulties would be insurmountable because of inability to read indigenous systems of writing. According to Ribera, the solution lay in writing a history of the Amerindians that instead of relying on Native American sources would draw upon information scattered in Spanish sources. In an independent position paper, Vicente García de la Huerta, also a member of the Spanish Academy, maintained that, by arguing that indigenous systems of writing had until now proved indecipherable, Ribera and Hermosilla gave Amerindian sources too much credence. According to García de la Huerta, indigenous sources were worthless, irrespective of whether it might one day be possible to read them. Building on disparaging references in Juan de Solórzano y Pereira's *Disputationem de indiarum iuere* (1629–39) to Inca quipus, García de la Huerta argued that quipus kept extremely shallow historical records. The information the Incas had stored in this way went back to a mere thirty years prior to the European arrival.[129]

The Council of the Indies and the Academy

In December 1756, after requesting clarifications from Hermosilla, Ribera, and Marcos Benito, the Academy approved a modified version of Ribera's proposal that gave precedence to the writing of natural histories over civil histories. The academicians agreed to work on an "atlas" of the New World. The record of what transpired subsequently is scant and confusing. The Council of the Indies, it seems, returned the plan to the Academy for further deliberation. On December 18, 1760, three years after the original debate took place, Agustín de Montiano y Luyando, director of the Academy and a member of the Royal Council, resubmitted the three proposals to the Council of the Indies, along with his own, a mildly revised version of Hermosilla's. Montiano reversed the priority of the first plan and called upon the Academy to write a civil history instead of a natural history. The Council of the Indies thereupon procrastinated until February 1762, when Manuel Pablo Salcedo penned a summary and evaluation that cavalierly dismissed *all* the proposals submitted by the academicians, including Montiano's.[130] Finally, in September 1764, eight years after the process had begun, the council sent the Academy a set of official guidelines. It is clear that the Academy and the council were not on good terms.

María Teresa Nava Rodríguez has argued that the conflict between the two institutions lay in differences of perspective. The Council of the Indies demanded knowledge that was immediately useful, whereas the Academy emphasized erudition.[131] This interpretation is, however, difficult to sustain. The two "official" proposals sent by the Academy to the council varied wildly in perspective. The first blueprint of 1756 emphasized utility and advocated the writing of an atlas emphasizing natural history. Montiano's plan of 1760 made the priority of the Academy the compilation of erudite civil histories. Moreover, there were hardly any ideological differences between the members of the Academy and the council. The plan put forth in Salcedo's 1762 evaluation of the proposals of Hermosilla, Ribera, Marcos Benito, and Montiano was in all respects identical to, if not more far-reaching than, theirs. Whereas Hermosilla and Ribera insisted that "the Academy ought not to continue [the work of] any [previous] historian of the Indies and ought to begin a history from scratch [*emprehender de raíz esta historia*]," Salcedo argued that all previous Spanish histories of America and its peoples were unscientific and hence worthless.[132] "Spanish [historians] enjoy praising heroes [and they dwell on insignificant details such as describing their knife fights and battles]," Salcedo argued, "but [these same historians] are silent on the origins of wars; the causes and outcomes of victories; the impact of economic systems, laws, and mores that are introduced [with each conquest]." According to Salcedo, this interest in the insignificant aspects of the lives of heroes was "good for entertaining children [but useless] to instruct Men in matters of State, Government, and Commerce."[133] Salcedo took Marcos Benito to task for having suggested that the Academy build on the histories of Garcilaso, Solís, and Herrera. "To continue the histories of the Indies that have been printed to this day," Salcedo contended, would represent "an opprobrium for the Spanish nation and would go against the spirit of the laws of the Indies. All of the sages of Europe maintain that all the available [Spanish] histories of the Indies have very substantial problems of style, organization, and content. Why should the Academy build on such flawed histories?" Although the Academy had never approved Marcos Benito's plan, Salcedo insisted that so as "not to authorize the dishonor of the Spanish nation," the council prohibit the Academy from rehashing earlier histories.[134] Although Salcedo dismissed all the plans on the grounds that they did not follow the laws of the Indies, which regulated the activities of the Chronicler and Cosmographer of the Indies, his proposal was simply a derivative compilation. Salcedo advised the council to ask the Academy to do it all: produce a geographical atlas of the entire colonial empire, including the Philippines, and write both natural histories of each of the three natural kingdoms and four separate civil histories, dealing respectively with political, military, ecclesiastical, and naval events.

The Council of the Indies approved Salcedo's plan and in 1764 issued clear guidelines for everyone involved in studying the Indies. To the Cosmographer, a post controlled by Jesuits at the Imperial College of Madrid since 1628, the council assigned the study of the geography and cartography of America. The council charged the Jesuits with compiling treatises on maritime routes; tables of dates and hours to observe eclipses in each locale (useful for gathering accurate information on longitude); general geographical "descriptions" (which would include general maps of North and South America and the Philippines, fluvial maps of ports, and topographic maps of cities, villages, mountains, mines, ports, and bays); and an encyclopedia with entries on mountains, rivers, cities, mines, volcanoes, and ports indicating their location (longitude and latitude), shape, surface, and any other available data.[135] The council gave the chronicler, that is, the Academy, the task of writing the natural and civil histories of the continent, including three separate natural histories (animal, vegetable, and mineral) for each locale, province, and region; four civil histories (political, ecclesiastical, military, and naval) for each of the four areas of the Spanish colonial empire (the Caribbean, Mexico, Peru, and the Philippines); and various separate treatises on the customs, laws, and origins of the natives. The council also asked the Academy to assemble a compendium of facts that would allow anyone to put together different narratives by an almost mechanical permutation of information. Finally, the council mandated "that neither the natural nor [the civil] histories should continue [the histories of] Antonio de Herrera and [of] any other [previous Spanish] author. [The histories] ought to be written anew."[136] In the guidelines, the council gave the Jesuits and the Academy access to confidential papers, inasmuch as they were sworn to secrecy.

The fact that it took eight years for the council to come up with such unrealistic guidelines indicates that there were tensions between the corporate bodies dealing with or studying the Indies. The problem, it seems, was one of overlapping corporate jurisdictions and access to colonial secrets. For all the rhetoric about allowing academicians and Jesuits access to closely guarded documents, the council actually restricted access to confidential information at every possible step. In fact, the original appointment of the Academy as the official historian of the Indies met with stiff resistance from the council. The crown offered the Academy that role in 1744 but had to wait until the Benedictine Sarmiento unexpectedly resigned in 1755 to make good on its promise.[137] In the same way that the struggle between parties of courtiers brought the writing of Boturini's history to a halt, the jurisdictional fight between the Academy and the council guaranteed that none of the Academy's ambitious plans would ever come to fruition.

The Second Debate

After the council issued the guidelines, the Academy again embarked on protracted methodological debates about how to fulfill its duties. This time, the problem for the Academy lay in devising ways of collecting and organizing information. In December 1764, Martín de Ulloa, who was also a magistrate of the Audiencia of Seville, insisted that the Academy should delegate duties to seven of its members to complete the writings of each of the three natural histories and four civil histories requested by the council. Ulloa suggested first completing the seven histories of the Caribbean, leaving those of Peru, Mexico, and the Philippines for later. He proposed to draw information both from archival and published sources and from carefully designed colonial surveys. As for how to gather the information for the compendium of facts that the council had requested, Ulloa argued that the entries should be material purged of "negligent credulity, blind ignorance, malignant biases, twisted intelligence, and defective inquiry."[138] The new director of the Academy (elected in November 1764), Pedro Rodríguez, count of Campomanes, however, raised doubts as to the wisdom of launching archival searches and colonial surveys without first exploring what had been printed both in Spain and overseas. In January 1765, Campomanes invited the Academy to deliberate on how to proceed and what documents to use.[139]

The day after Campomanes addressed the Academy, Felipe García de Samaniego, who was also a canon of the cathedral chapter of Pamplona, a member of the Royal Council, and an expert linguist in the Academy, suggested that as a reference tool the Academy first compile an annotated bibliography of all available sources, organized according to a sliding scale of credibility. Dismissing Barcia's revised edition of León Pinelo's *Epitome* as inadequate, García de Samaniego maintained that a bibliography had to be organized based on a descending scale of trust: from eyewitnesses to compilers of witnesses' reports to erudite historians to translators to mere plagiarists. García de Samaniego also argued that since not even eyewitnesses were entirely trustworthy, academicians should seek to draw their information from physical remains, which, he said, "are superior in class and quality to any literary source, no matter how original or coeval [to the event] the literary source is."[140] He proposed compiling information in files on sculpture, paintings, buildings, quipus, hieroglyphs, and furniture. The entries for the files would come from the critical sifting of literary sources, both published and archival, and from cabinets of curiosities. The Academy agreed to follow García de Samaniego's proposal.

Academicians sifted literary sources to create the files García de Samaniego proposed until October 1765. Then, under the nagging insistence of Ulloa not to put off the task assigned it by the council in order simply to compile a reference tool, the Academy embraced a new hybrid plan, an awkward one that included parts of Ulloa's and García de Samaniego's proposals.[141] The institutional structure adopted by the Academy to meet the demands of the council was called the Committee of the Indies (Junta de Indias), consisting of academicians each charged with one of the seven different histories (natural and civil) of each of the four regions of the empire. Although it was to last for many years as an empty shell, the committee in fact enjoyed a very short life, largely because of the vastness of its task. In addition to reading dozens of literary sources, each of the seven members of the committee was to compile a huge database, organized alphabetically as an encyclopedia. Just as Garcilaso's *Comentarios reales* had been reorganized in 1744 by its French editors into a compendium of separate entries on, among other things, the astronomy, natural history, and political and moral philosophy of the Incas, the members of the Committee of the Indies now converted colonial texts into hundreds of encyclopedic entries. Each of the seven members of the committee was assigned a text, according to his area of expertise, from which to create files (*cédulas*). Having been allotted the natural history of Caribbean animals, for example, Alonso María de Acevedo had to develop files on each of the animal species cited in Gonzalo Fernández de Oviedo's *Sumario de la natural historia de las Indias* (including descriptions of the various indigenous peoples). Acevedo also, however, had to fill out entries on dozens of other subjects as he read Oviedo. The index approved by the committee was overwhelming, requiring that the academicians create files on, among other things, geographical accidents; genealogical trees; secular and ecclesiastical authorities; Church councils and cathedral chapters; miracles; utensils and furniture; travel reports and diaries; laws, decrees, and briefs; battles, treaties, and rebellions; the forms and virtues of plants; geographical distribution of fauna and flora; quipus and hieroglyphs; sacred, civil, and private buildings; ruins; crafts and trades. The list went on and on.[142] Unable to reconcile the council's twin demands that it compile a huge database and simultaneously write the natural and civil histories of the Indies, the Academy chose to do the former.

In October 1766, Domínguez de Riezu, one of the members of the Committee of the Indies, addressed the Academy in despair. Only a year after having started work, Domínguez de Riezu said, the committee was already in disarray: two of its seven members had resigned and three others had stopped attending its meetings. Domínguez de Riezu explained to the Academy that he had been assigned the civil maritime history of the Indies, and hence José de Veitia Linage's *Norte de la contratación de las Indias* (1672), a treatise on colonial Spanish commercial and maritime laws. After having compiled 1,115 entries on "chronology," 260 on "diplomacy" (on briefs and decrees), 80 on fleets and armadas, 60 on admirals, captains, and officers of the navy, and countless others on individual pilots, Domínguez de Riezu said, he was still far from having finished Veitia's text.[143] He therefore begged the Academy both to shorten the list of categories and to enlarge the committee. In response, the Academy tinkered a little with the categories, but in April 1768 new grievances were heard, this time from Lorenzo Diéguez, its secretary until 1769. Again the Academy introduced slight new modifications, but the project continued to drift. By 1777, Domínguez de Riezu was in a position to announce with a mixture of pride and dismay that so far he had compiled 3,850 useless files.[144] After ten years of work, the committee had yet to write one of the seven histories.

Work was hampered not only by the Academy's own choices but also by the uncooperative attitude of the Council of the Indies. Since September 1764, when the council had first sent it the guidelines, Martín de Ulloa had taken the lead in pressing the Academy to demand access to information from the colonial authorities. When, in October 1765, the Academy concocted the hybrid plan that brought García de Samaniego and Ulloa's proposals together by creating the Committee of the Indies, it also authorized the committee to draw up a list of queries for colonial authorities.[145] In November 1765, the committee accordingly compiled lists requesting information on every conceivable subject.[146] At this point, the committee decided that it was within its purview to demand very high critical standards. It asked the authorities to decide for themselves what popular traditions to include in their answers to the queries and to leave out traditions "that contain references to strange or incredible events, unless [the authority] can cite powerful reasons to include them."[147] Should they find two or more contradictory reports on the same subject, the authorities were asked to spell out the reasons why they had chosen one rather than the other. The committee also instructed the colonial authorities to specify the source from which they drew their information in each case. In the case of Amerindian antiquities, the academicians relaxed their demands a little and admitted that inasmuch as the Amerindians lacked writing, "we cannot pretend to more assurances" than what was recorded in popular oral traditions. Yet even here the academicians demanded rigor. Should the authorities find indigenous recordkeeping devices with information "at variance with what has already been reported in our histories," they were asked to make transparent the process of interpretation, "specifying the underlying principles followed in the translation."[148]

In February 1766, on grounds that by imposing such strict guidelines, the academicians were virtually asking the colonial authorities to do their job for them, the Council of the Indies angrily denied the Academy the right to collect information in the Indies.[149] When the Academy asked that same month that Boturini's collection of indigenous sources be moved to Madrid, the Council again denied the request.[150]

Two important methodological debates took place in the Academy between 1755 and 1770. Neither led anywhere. The Academy was never able to produce or publish a new history of the Indies, despite the growing public demand in Spain for one. For some twenty-five years, it faced the opposition of a Council of the Indies that was afraid of losing corporate control of information about the New World. The Academy also made poor methodological choices, seeking to organize dozens of literary sources into hundreds of encyclopedic entries, which, in turn, led to the compiling of thousands of useless files. But for all the energy that was wasted, the activities of the Academy demonstrate that well before de Pauw or Robertson, Spanish scholars were calling into question the entire corpus of sixteenth- and seventeenth-century literature on the Indies. Moreover, those scholars were part of the larger European movement that in the eighteenth century saw fit to deny the value of Amerindian sources. In the next section I discuss a slightly more productive period in Spanish historiography on the New World, which, among other things, led to the creation of the Archive of the Indies.

The Archive of the Indies

There was no dramatic improvement in Spanish historiography of America in the last quarter of the eighteenth century. Squabbles between jealous institutions over who should control access to information about the colonies, among factions representing different regions, and among courtiers with conflicting views on patriotism went on unabated. The disputes between the Aragonese and Boturini's supporters brought the Italian to his knees. The rift between the Academy of History and the Council of the Indies spawned endless unproductive methodological debates. In the 1770s and 1780s, in particular, there was a new round of arguments about how to write patriotic histories. This time, however, they left more than a legacy of wasted energies. Partly in response to the policy of centralization pursued by the new Bourbon dynasty, particularly under Charles III (r. 1759–1788), a new institution, the Archive of the Indies, was founded to bring together and preserve documents relating to the history of Spanish America. Neither was the desire for a single central repository of information about the colonies the sole reason for the creation of the archive. With the failings of eighteenth-century Spanish historians of the New World becoming more and more obvious, and with northern European criticism of Spanish behavior in the Indies mounting, official circles in Spain increasingly saw the need for fresh histories. Anticipating many of the epistemological and historiographical ideas of Leopold von Ranke, a Valencian faction led by Cosmographer Royal Juan Bautista Muñoz argued, moreover, that to be objective, such histories would have to be drawn from public sources.

In the following pages, I explore the debates surrounding the foundation of the Archive of the Indies, beginning with the decision of the Academy of History to translate Robertson's *History of America*. A section of the Academy that espoused the new scholarship of northern Europe, led by its director, the Asturian Pedro Rodríguez, count of Campomanes, fought to have Robertson translated, but these efforts were frustrated when an anonymous reviewer demonstrated Robertson's anti-Spanish biases to the powerful minister of the Indies, José de Gálvez (1720–1787). In the wake of this affair, the Valencian party led by Muñoz took the post of Royal Chronicler of the Indies away from the Academy.

In the 1780s, Muñoz set out to consolidate all primary colonial documents under a single roof, and I argue that he was largely responsible for offering the epistemological and historiographical justification for creating the

Archive of the Indies. Muñoz also set out to write a new history of America, although only one of the series of volumes he proposed was ever produced. Campomanes's faction did its utmost to prevent the publication of Muñoz's history, and he also had to contend with a third party vying for the crown's attention, a group of Catalan Jesuits in exile in Italy. Along with my account of Muñoz's scholarship, I discuss the works of two Catalan Jesuits, Juan Nuix (1740–1783) and Ramón Diosdado Caballero (1740–1810?), who in the 1780s produced histories of America that sought to counter foreign criticisms of Spain, which in the contemporary political and intellectual context might conceivably have overshadowed both Campomanes's and Muñoz's efforts. It is significant, however, that despite all the opposition he faced, Muñoz was able to carry out his plan to create the Archive of the Indies.

The Reception of Robertson's 'History of America'

On August 8, 1777, Ramón de Guevara y Vasconcelos addressed the Academy of History, urging it to approve a translation of Robertson's *History of America*, which had recently been published in Edinburgh. Guevara y Vasconcelos presented Robertson as an erudite scientific historian who had been able to see through the barrage of foreign invective aimed at Spain. Robertson's efforts, characterized by the painstaking collection of new documents, demonstrated that the Spanish crown had sought to treat the Amerindians justly. According to Guevara y Vasconcelos, Robertson's description of the debate between Juan Ginés de Sepúlveda (1490–1573) and Bartolomé de Las Casas typified the Scot's lack of biases. Guevara y Vasconcelos, who was then working with the Academy on an edition of the works by the sixteenth-century humanist Sepúlveda, Las Casas's nemesis, praised Robertson for not succumbing to Las Casas's negative portrayals of the Spanish colonization of America. Had Robertson enjoyed access to the Archive of Simancas, Guevara y Vasconcelos argued, he would have clarified even further "the good conduct of the government and of the Spanish nation [in America], the reprehensible conduct of a few private individuals notwithstanding."[151] But Robertson was not only to be praised for his temperance. According to Guevara y Vasconcelos, he was also both a superb stylist and a great philosopher. Like Cicero's, Robertson's narrative was fluid, sober, elegant, and moving. Like Tacitus, he had investigated the past to inquire into the causes of political events. Guevara y Vasconcelos clinched his argument for the urgency of a translation by referring to Robertson's praise of Campomanes, the director of the Academy. According to Robertson, Guevara y

Vasconcelos argued, Campomanes's treatises on the promotion of popular industry (1774) and of education (1775) revealed both a philosopher and a citizen actively involved in public life. Moreover, Campomanes had grasped the principles of political economy, advocating free trade despite "the opinions of the vulgar and national prejudices"[152]

Guevara y Vasconcelos considered that a detailed review of each book of Robertson's *History* was warranted, "to give a better idea of the whole and of its wonderful method. [The history] brings together distant events and scattered materials that have been submerged in the chaos and labyrinth of countless [other] obscure and cumbersome works."[153] In book 1, devoted to the progress of European navigation, beginning with the Ancients, Robertson, Guevara y Vasconcelos maintained, had matched the depth of his earlier essay on the progress of the economy and the rise of political balances in medieval Europe, appended as introduction to the *History of Charles V*. However, book 4, which dealt with Amerindians and the Americas, was perhaps "the most curious, interesting, and novel part" of Robertson's history. In it, Guevara y Vasconcelos contended, Robertson had risen above the "swarm of compilers of events and dates," drawing on the narratives of "the few philosophical travelers who have visited America, [to deliver] the best observations that his penetration [was capable] of discovering."[154] Book 8, on Spanish American societies, was, however, "the most useful," in Guevara y Vasconcelos's opinion. It also showed the "advancement of enlightenment relative to previous centuries" introduced by the recent reforms of the Spanish Bourbons.[155] The evening when Guevara y Vasconcelos read his address, the Academy voted unanimously to extend membership to Robertson for having demonstrated throughout his career a "predilection for our national history."[156] The Academy also approved Guevara y Vasconcelos's proposal that Robertson's *History of America* be translated into Spanish, on the grounds that the work would be "useful and enjoyable to the public."[157]

Guevara y Vasconcelos and the Academy were particularly impressed by book 4 of the *History of America*, in which Robertson depicted the Americas as colder and wetter than the Old World and set out to prove that the Amerindians belonged to the most primitive stages of social and mental development. As already noted, too, when it voted unanimously to sponsor a translation of Robertson's work, the Academy was busy completing an edition of Juan Gines de Sepúlveda's historical works, motivated by the serendipitous discovery of two of Sepúlveda's unpublished manuscripts, "Historia de Carlos V" and "De Orbe Novo."[158] The biases that motivated the Academy to offer an annotated Spanish edition of Robertson's *History* can be better understood if we first look at the Academy's edition of Sepúlveda's work.

In the mid sixteenth century, Sepúlveda, a prominent Spanish humanist trained at Bologna, had engaged the Dominican Bartolomé de las Casas in a famous debate about the Spanish Conquest. In 1780, in an effort to reach a broad European audience, and with the official backing of the Spanish crown, the Academy made Sepúvelda's writings available in Latin. This was an odd thing to do, because Spain's disreputable image in northern Europe rested largely on the contempt for Amerindians that Sepúlveda and his ilk had promoted. Sepúlveda had depicted Amerindians both as savages, whose horrible crimes against nature, including cannibalism, justified waging war on them (*justis belli causis*), and as natural slaves.[159]

Las Casas had won the debate as far as the Spanish court was concerned, because he called for monarchical power in the colonies to be strengthened, and for the power of the burgeoning class of would-be colonial grandees to be curtailed. Sepúlveda's writings had officially been condemned to oblivion. Paradoxically, however, in the rest of Europe, Sepúlveda's ideas were held to represent Spanish official views, largely because of the wide publicity accorded in Protestant countries to Las Casas's description of Spanish colonization in the New World. Now, however, despite the widespread perception in northern Europe that Las Casas's opponents were evil, the Academy nevertheless set out to offer a new edition of Sepúlveda's works.

The Academy considered Sepúlveda a great humanist, one of "the most distinguished learned men who flourished in sixteenth-century Spain." His views on the Amerindians, the Academy further argued, were never intended as a charter to expropriate and kill Native Americans, but as an Aristotelian analysis of the proper relation between the ruler and the ruled. "Foreigners have held [Sepúlveda's book] in low esteem even though they have never seen it. Its publication will show the good intentions that moved Sepúlveda to write it and the quality of his thinking, praised by some universities and learned men in and outside Spain."[160] The biography by Francisco Cerdá y Rico (1739–1800) that prefaced the four-volume edition, for example, included Sepúlveda's unpublished glosses and notes to Aristotle's *Politics* "to demonstrate [Sepúlveda's] profound knowledge of the Latin and Greek languages."[161] Sensing, however, that its publication would only help to reinforce northern European biases against Spain, the crown rejected inclusion of Sepúlveda's *Demócrates segundo, o, De las justas causas de la guerra contra los indios*.[162] The Academy nonetheless edited Sepúlveda's unpublished correspondence with Melchor Cano in which the arguments of *Demócrates* were laid out. The biases of the academicians regarding the Amerindians were made perfectly clear when in the process of research for this edition they came across many manuscripts by Las Casas on Amerindian antiquities, including his *Apologética historia sumaria,* but chose to leave them unpublished.[163]

Footnoting Robertson's 'History'

The Academy set out to translate Robertson's history with the same sense of excitement and mission that it brought to its edition of Sepúlveda. Every week, the academicians met to discuss passages that Guevara y Vasconcelos had rendered into Spanish, and soon they found themselves discussing how to obtain reliable information to clarify Robertson's views. Campomanes asked the surviving members of the old Committee of the Indies for the files they had once assembled, and a commission of three (Domínguez de Riezu, Guevara y Vasconcelos, and José Miguel de Flores) was appointed to reorganize these and evaluate their usefulness.[164] As the collective reading of the translation proceeded, Campomanes drew up a new list of authors for the academicians to read, reviving the ineffectual method of research used by the committee.[165] In early December 1777, the Academy created a new commission, consisting of Antonio de Capmany y de Montpalau (1742–1813), Joseph de la Concepción, José Miguel de Flores, and José de Guevara y Vasconcelos (Ramón's brother), to hold extra weekly meetings to speed up the process of revisions.[166] Finally, a few days before the year ended and less than four months after Ramón de Guevara y Vasconcelos's plea, the Academy addressed a memorandum to the crown and the Council of the Indies announcing the completion of a tentative translation and justifying its usefulness. In their brief to the crown, the academicians maintained that in the court of European public opinion, all Spanish historiography was perceived to be untrustworthy because it was tainted by chauvinism. The best defense was, therefore, to make available an annotated translation of a book written by a foreigner who had emphasized Spanish efforts to bring law and justice to the colonies, as well as the wisdom and benefits of the new Bourbon colonial reforms.[167] According to the Academy, all that was left to do was to add some annotations, for which information needed to be assembled.

In a letter sent to the minister of the Indies, José de Gálvez, the same day that the Academy sent its brief to the crown, Campomanes requested access to confidential information. He argued that many of the errors in Robertson's original history, particularly in geography, colonial commerce, and population statistics, were owing to lack of appropriate documentation. The Academy, Campomanes reminded Gálvez, had a right to access to information "necessary to fulfill its duties, for without well researched facts the truth cannot be properly assessed."[168] Campomanes informed Gálvez that the Academy had assigned three members (Guevara y Vasconcelos, Ignacio de Hermosilla, and Antonio Mateos Murillo) to do research in the various secretariats of the council and promised that they would not remove original documents from any of the archives. Once Gálvez approved the request, the secretary of the Academy, Flores, immediately handed the Council of the Indies a list of requests.[169] Most of the information requested concerned the size and income of the Church in colonial Spanish America.[170] It is not clear why the Academy chose to focus on the colonial Church. It is highly unlikely, however, that it was part of the Academy's plan to append notes that would exalt the civilizing role of the Church in the Indies, for Campomanes had long demonstrated that he was no friend of the clergy.

By the time Campomanes threw his considerable weight behind the publication of a Spanish version of Robertson's *History*, he had already earned something of a reputation as radical freethinker. In a series of highly controversial works published between 1765 and 1769, he laid the ideological foundations for a monarchical assault on the religious orders and the Church in general. In *Tratado de la regalía de amortización* (1765), he maintained that although the right of the Church to hold property had been curtailed in Visigothic times, the clergy had continued to accumulate wealth as landlords. In northwestern Europe, the result of such ecclesiastical money-grubbing had been the Protestant Reformation. In Spain, however, the unchecked growth of the power of the Church had led to depopulation and economic decline. Based on Visigothic historical precedent, Campomanes argued, the monarch had the right to prohibit the Church from acquiring further property. In 1767, in a treatise written to justify the expulsion of the Jesuits from all Spanish territories, Campomanes presented the followers of Ignatius of Loyola as an order responding solely to the mandate of the father-general and dedicated to exalting the temporal power of the pope. The Jesuits had not only encouraged rebellions against the monarchy in Spain but had also eroded the power of the secular Church in the American colonies and created missions that were virtually autonomous republics, particularly in Paraguay. In 1769, in *Juicio imparcial sobre el monitoreo de Roma*, Campomanes launched a fierce attack on the temporal authority of the pope and declared that the civil sovereign, based on historical precedent and reason, had a right to rule over both the civil and ecclesiastical bureaucracies. The king therefore had the authority to manage the wealth and appointments of the Church. Moreover, inasmuch as there was a single sovereign for both the Church and the state, the clergy and laity should be treated as equals before the law and the former should not enjoy a separate set of corporate rights. According to Campomanes, the authority of the Church lay only in the spiritual realm; it was within the purview of the state to enforce Church doctrine and persecute heretics.

Campomanes's attack on the Church was part of a larger plan for economic and cultural renewal. By going after the landed wealth of the Church, he sought to lay the basis for a republic of virtuous, entrepreneurial citizens, giving priority to the promotion of Spanish industry, rather than agriculture. A mercantilist rather than a follower of Adam Smith or the Physiocrats, Campomanes sought the opening of unrestricted trade only between American and Spanish ports (until the early eighteenth century only Cadiz and two Spanish American ports were allowed to conduct Atlantic trade). He also envisioned the Indies as fantastic markets for potential Spanish industries, as well as a source of raw materials. For example, he envisioned prosperous fisheries and vicuña peltries blossoming in Tierra del Fuego and Peru respectively.[171] But for these reforms to work, manufacturing in Spain needed to be reorganized. In his *Discurso sobre el fomento de la industria popular* (1774) and *Discurso sobre la educación popular de los artesanos y su fomento* (1775), Campomanes called for the abolition of guilds, the importation of foreign craftsmen, and the creation of patriotic societies that would make useful technical knowledge available at the local level. Within a matter of ten years (1765–75), Campomanes provided a blueprint for the complete reorganization of Spanish religion, culture, politics, economics, and colonial trade; a blueprint that was to be closely followed by Charles III. By the time the Academy set out to complete the translation of Robertson's *History of America*, Campomanes had become a powerful figure indeed. He was not only the director of the Academy but also a leading magistrate on the Council of Castile (and its president beginning in 1783) and a member of the Royal Council.[172]

In Robertson, Campomanes found confirmation of most of his reformist ideas, as well as a soul mate with an erudite bent for discerning the reasons for the rise and decline of nations. In a series of letters that started only days after the Academy approved the translation of the *History of America*, Campomanes praised Robertson for his moderation and impartiality toward Spain and for his ability to focus on the comparative study of customs, ages, and governments. Campomanes declared himself impressed by Robertson's ability in previous works to identify the cause of the collapse of Rome, as well as the causes of the subsequent ascent of Europe, from the Middle Ages to the sixteenth-century commercial expansion to east and west.[173] In a letter written in March 1778, Campomanes revealed that he had been the spirit behind Guevara y Vasconcelos's address to the Academy. Campomanes presented Robertson as a modern Tacitus (C.E. 56– ca. 120), who had elegantly and economically narrated events, focusing exclusively on the political and economical forces guiding them. Robertson, Campomanes maintained, had said more in a few books than previous historians had in scores of confusing volumes. Histories solely interested in narrating "battles, catastrophes of public figures, conquests, the destruction of cities, provinces or empires" were worthless. To be useful, history needed to educate by identifying the causes of historical changes and events, ignoring popular and nationalist biases.[174] Robertson responded with delight to Campomanes's flattery and declared that although he had been raised under "a form of government and a religious system very different" from those of Spain, he had sought to be aware of his own prejudices. Through a careful reading of Spanish historians and of the legal codes of Spain, Robertson said, he had striven to be impartial. "I reiterate my care for the honor of the [Spanish] nation," Robertson concluded, "which I have respected more than some other foreign writers because I have sought to know it better."[175] Correspondence between Robertson and Campomanes continued over the years.[176]

Once the collective discussion of the translation concluded in the very last days of 1777, and once the Council of the Indies had approved the search for documentation to clarify the activities of the colonial Church in January 1778, a commission of the Academy began to work on the notes. The academicians Joseph de la Concepción, José and Ramón de Guevara y Vasconcelos, Antonio de Capmany, José Miguel de Flores, and Antonio Mateos Murillo met twice a week from January to April 1778 to complete the assignment. In April, the commission announced that the forthcoming annotated translation was almost finished. Although Robertson had sought to be impartial, traces of condemnatory language remained in the original, and the commission had to tone it down. The notes that sought to elucidate themes such as the income of the colonial Church, the dynamics of the secular and religious clergy, and the conflict between Peninsulars and Creoles were done. All that was left to do was to write the preface and to finish the notes on colonial trade and population statistics, stalled by the slowness of the Council of the Indies to deliver information.[177]

If, by the end of April 1778, the relationship between the Council of the Indies and the Academy was tense, in November 1778, it deteriorated completely. For reasons that would later become clear, Gálvez had sent the translation to an outsider for review, and the anonymous reviewer denounced it as anti-Spanish propaganda. On November 26, 1778, Gálvez wrote Campomanes a memo asking whether the director of the Academy had actually had time in his busy schedule to read Robertson. The review he commissioned indicated that Robertson had at every turn insulted Spain. Was not the role of the Academy to "vindicate the truth of history [and] to honor our nation by doing justice to the Conquest and [the Spanish] government of America"? Was it not the duty of the Academy to defend "the reputation of the conquistadors, whose good memory we shall strive to maintain, out of gratitude, duty, and policy"? "[It is the duty of the Academy]," Gálvez reminded Campomanes, "to impugn anything that is offensive and goes contrary to the national glory [*faustos*]."[178] A month later, on Gálvez's advice, Charles III suspended publication of the Spanish edition and banned the English edition throughout the empire. Moreover, the king took away from the Academy the responsibility of writing the history of the Indies. The new appointee would debunk "the false premises of Robertson."[179] Clearly, something had gone terribly wrong for the Academy.

The Anonymous Review

To this day, the events leading to the royal decree barring the translation and the circulation of Robertson's *History* remain surrounded by mystery. Historians have attributed it to the fact that Spain entered the war of the American Revolution in 1779. According to this interpretation, Guevara y Vasconcelos's translation was suspended in 1778 because it would have been unthinkable for a nation gearing up for war against Britain to sponsor the works of a British citizen. Robertson's *History* is thus depicted as a casualty of Anglo-Hispanic hostilities.[180] The real reason for the demise of the Academy's patriotic project, however, lies in a reader's report that landed on the desk of the minister of the Indies sometime in November 1778. To my knowledge, this report has not heretofore been studied, and it therefore merits attention.[181]

In the preface to his *History*, Robertson argued that it was trustworthy because it was based on the extensive reading of primary sources and new documents. "If these are the sources from which [Robertson] has drawn his information" the anonymous reviewer jeered, "then any Chinese philosopher can write on the deeds of the Romans and offer a new interpretation of the history of Europe."[182] Behind this sarcastic remark lay a proprietary view of the history of Spanish America. The reviewer implied that since the archives and sources were located in Spain, only Spaniards could write a truly new history of the Indies. But the quarrel of the reviewer with Robertson was not merely that the Scot had enjoyed limited access to colonial documentation. The thing that upset the reviewer most was the way in which Robertson had chosen to interpret the facts.

In book 1, devoted to the history of navigation from the ancients to the rise of Portuguese and Spanish maritime expansion in the fifteenth century, the reviewer argued, Robertson had failed to acknowledge any of Strabo's references to "Spanish" navigation to the western coast of Africa in antiquity. Robertson had also failed to note that the Canary Islands had been discovered during the Aragonese commercial expansion of the fourteenth century, not in the fifteenth century. More worrisome, however, was Robertson's carefully differentiated portrayal of the Portuguese and the Spanish fifteenth-century expansion to Africa. According to the reviewer, in Robertson's narrative, the Portuguese appeared as friendly merchants and the Spaniards as slave raiders: "Robertson sought to create a beautiful representation of the Portuguese as a foil to his sketch [of the Spaniards] in slanderous colors."[183] In book 2, Robertson had also made a number of inaccurate statements about Columbus's voyages of discovery. Robertson cast the Spaniards as ignorant, cowardly, and ungrateful, saying, among other things, that the Spanish pilots who accompanied Columbus on his first voyage had panicked and sought to take the ships back to Spain, and that Ferdinand had not honored the crown's original agreement with Columbus. This list of complaints assembled by the reviewer revealed that he was perfectly aware that even seemingly harmless accounts involved interpretations. The reviewer countered the narratives that presented Spanish pilots as ignorant cowards with his own. It was Columbus, he argued, who had learned from Spanish pilots to navigate on the high seas. "[They]," the reviewer argued, "had more skill, more nautical knowledge, more character, and more prudence than the Admiral [himself]." As for Ferdinand's stripping Columbus of his rights, it had been justified by Columbus's own tyrannical attitudes while governor in the Caribbean.[184]

The reviewer also identified Robertson's anti-Spanish bias in books 3, 5, and 6 (on the Spanish discovery and early colonization of the Caribbean, Mexico, and Peru), where he consistently portrayed *all* the conquistadors as "cruel, greedy, ambitious, and inhuman."[185] Robertson never even considered that the massacres of Amerindians allegedly committed by Cortés and by Pizarro might have been acts of self-defense by soldiers in danger of being captured and sacrificed, or even eaten. In book 8 (on the colonies), the reviewer identified a plethora of problematic statements advanced by Robertson — inter alia, that he said that the Spaniards based their rights to conquest solely on Pope Alexander VI's bull of 1493 granting Spain dominion over the New World in exchange for converting the Amerindians to Christianity; that the majority of the secular clergy in the colonies were ignorant, because most came from Spain, where they had failed to get appointments to even the most miserable parishes; that the religious, although brighter, had left Spain to run parishes in America in order to avoid a wretched life of corporal self-punishment and unbearable discipline in the cloisters, and were corrupt because they engaged in political and economic activities; that Church taxes bled the economy white and caused depopulation and poverty; that the crown had absolute control over the wealth and appointments of the colonial Church through the institution of *patronato real* and therefore received most of its revenue from the Church; that idleness and bad climate had led to the degeneration of Creole patricians; that colonial universities had failed to produce a single author of note; and that the Amerindians were the most miserable and despised members of colonial society. Again the reviewer was appalled by what appeared to be Robertson's willful distortions. The rights of Spain in the Indies, he argued, were not based on any papal bull but on discovery, "pacification," and settlement. The expansion and stability of the Spanish empire in America had rested squarely on the shoulders of the secular and religious clergy, who therefore could have hardly been ignorant and impious. Finally, the Amerindians were citizens of their own republics and had wealthy and powerful lords of their own, who were recognized and honored by the Spanish rulers.

It is very telling that the reviewer, like the Academy, paid scant attention to those sections in Robertson's history devoted to the Amerindians' past. The reviewer spent only a few paragraphs analyzing the biases in books 4 (on the nature of the continent and the Amerindians) and 7 (on Inca and Mexica political, religious, and economic institutions) of Robertson's *History*. "The political, military, civil, and religious institutions attributed by Robertson to the natives [described in books 4 and 7]," the reviewer argued, "did not exist and have never existed."[186] Not only were Robertson's descriptions of indigenous polities imaginary but his criticism of sixteenth-century Spanish historiography was unfounded. In a highly atypical passage for his age, the reviewer argued that sixteenth-century Spanish historiography on the Indies was complete and accurate, and that being exclusively based on the testimony of witnesses, it was deeper and richer than any extant history of the ancient world.[187]

When this report reached Gálvez, the Academy's translation was doomed. Gálvez had been instrumental since the 1760s in bringing about colonial reforms along the lines proposed by Campomanes, but unlike Campomanes, he could not stomach any of Spain's many foreign critics.[188] We know, for example, that Campomanes corresponded with the abbé Raynal precisely in the years when the latter was piling insults on Spain in the pages of his *Histoire philosophique*, declaring: "[N]ever has a nation been idolatrous of its prejudices to such a degree as the Spaniards. . . . never has unreason [*la déraison*] been so dogmatic, so closed and so subtle [as in Spain]." Campomanes nonetheless sent information the abbé requested on the Spanish Caribbean.[189]

Gálvez could not stand such tolerance of foreigners who insulted Spain. "I have often seen Gálvez, minister of the Indies, burst into violent passion at the mere mention of [Raynal]," reported the secretary to the French ambassador to the Spanish court, Jean François Bourgoing. "[He has treated] those who have endeavored to introduce some surreptitious copies [of Raynal's *Histoire philosophique*] into the Spanish colonies in the light of criminals guilty of high treason against God and man."[190] It is no wonder that Gálvez reacted furiously to the anonymous review and ordered the Academy to end the translation. But who was the author of the report and what party did he represent?

I have found no trace of the identity of the reviewer. Based on the handwriting, it is possible to maintain that the author might have been Juan Bautista Muñoz, at the time Royal Cosmographer of the Indies, for the penmanship of the report and Muñoz's handwriting are almost identical (Fig. 3.1). Moreover, Muñoz was a Valencian patriot who had grown skilled at taking books by foreign authors apart, especially those that Campomanes liked. Finally, Muñoz's main contribution to the historiography of the Indies was his insistence that any new history of the Indies needed to be based on an abundance of public sources only available in Spanish archives. The reviewer, we should recall, ridiculed the shallowness of Robertson's sources and suggested that only Spanish historians could have access to the documentation that was needed. Yet some of the ideas in the anonymous review run counter to the historiographical principles that Muñoz most cherished. Muñoz, unlike the reviewer, was a staunch critic of sixteenth-century Spanish observers and historians of the New World. Moreover, like Mayans,

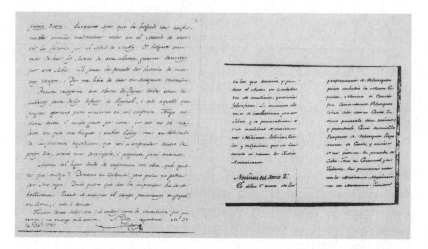

FIGURE 3.1. Handwriting in a personal letter from Juan Bautista Muñoz, Royal Cosmographer of the Indies, to Antonio de Cavanilles (courtesy of the Real Jardín Botánico, Madrid), compared with that of the anonymous report that derailed the Spanish translation of William Robertson's *History of America* (courtesy of the Fundación Universitaria Española, Madrid). The penmanship in the two documents appears similar, perhaps indicating that Muñoz was the author of the report, but the report itself runs counter to some of Muñoz's historiographical principles, suggesting some other author.

Muñoz was against any rhetorically virulent and explicit defense of Spain. There is, therefore, the distinct possibility that someone else may have penned the report.

When the Academy was readying the translation, a third historiographical agenda was then emerging, namely, that sponsored by Catalan Jesuits in exile. It is hard to imagine that Gálvez, a persistent critic of the role of the Jesuits in the Indies, would have delegated review of the translation to Jesuit exiles. Yet Gálvez did keep in touch with some patriotic Jesuits and supported their studies of the New World. Given its rhetorical virulence and the defense of sixteenth-century Spanish historiography in the report, the community of Catalan Jesuits might well have penned it.

Juan Nuix's 'Riflessioni imparziali'

In 1780, in Venice, Juan Nuix published *Riflessioni imparziali supra l'umanita degli spagnuoli nell' Indie contro i pretersi filososofi e politici*. Nuix, a

Catalan living in Italy since the expulsion of the Jesuits, wrote the book to defend Spanish colonialism and historiography against the attacks of Robertson and Raynal.[191] It sailed by the censors in the Council of the Indies, and two separate translations appeared in succession, one in 1782, edited by a member of the Royal Council, Pedro Varela y Ulloa, and another in 1783, by Joseph Nuix, Juan's brother.[192] The Spanish edition sponsored by the crown opened with an essay by Varela y Ulloa, in which he first offered a searing critique of traditional forms of colonialism, not unlike that put forth by Raynal. After describing military campaigns in foreign lands, from Alexander the Great to Genghis Khan, as butcheries, Varela y Ulloa went on to claim that Spanish colonialism was unique. The crimes attributed to Spain in the Indies had been committed by private individuals, who did not represent the nation as a whole, and who had acted as they did while surrounded by hungry cannibals. Moreover, compared with the atrocities committed by other European colonial powers, the actions of the Spaniards looked like misdemeanors.[193] Varela y Ulloa's effort to portray Spanish colonialism as uniquely benign captured the essence of Nuix's thesis well.

Nuix's defense of the record of Spanish colonialism opened with passages that sought to bolster his credibility by stressing that he was a Catalan, and that Catalans had not really participated in the Spanish colonization of the Indies, so that he could not be accused of being partisan.[194] He then articulated a five-pronged defense of Castilian colonial behavior in America, seeking to demonstrate the unreliability of the sources used by Robertson and Raynal, and of their interpretations. Nuix first set out to prove that charges of Spanish cruelty to Amerindians were exaggerations, originally put into circulation by writers such as Las Casas, whose reports on the destruction of the Indies were at the root of most foreign criticisms of Spain. According to Nuix, Las Casas was of Flemish origin, which explained why he had sought to undermine Spain. Las Casas also often contradicted himself, Nuix argued, and no impartial jury could trust such "an inept" witness.[195] Foreign historians who had echoed Las Casas's allegations were not credible either, not even Robertson, whose moderation had prompted him to dismiss Las Casas. Robertson had selected and reinterpreted the testimony of Spanish witnesses when recounting various colonial massacres. Instead of quoting them, moreover, Robertson had manipulated the testimony of witnesses to depict the Amerindians as passive victims of Spanish cruelty. History was not a matter of interpretation, however, but of faithfully presenting the testimony of witnesses, and in that respect, Robertson lacked credibility.[196]

In order to prove that Spaniards in America had not behaved like greedy barbarians, Nuix argued that the alleged depopulation caused by the Conquest was the product of factors outside human control. The infantile susceptibility of the natives to disease, for example, was why epidemics had wiped them out. The barrenness of the Americas and the idleness of the originally small number of natives had moved the conquerors to create economies based on mining and large estates. Such economies, along with the foreign monopoly on colonial trade, not Spanish cruelty and greed, Nuix contended, were responsible for having slowed both markets and population growth.

Nuix asserted, furthermore, that far from being a charter to rule the Native Americans, Alexander VI's bull of 1493 had merely sought to encourage the Spaniards to convert them to Christianity. Spain's sovereignty in the New World did not rest on any papal bull — the authority of which might be contested, or even ridiculed — but on natural law and the law of nations. For this thesis to work, however, Nuix had to embrace the same derogatory view of the Amerindians as Robertson and Raynal, whose credibility he had questioned. When the first Europeans arrived in America, they had found it almost uninhabited, Nuix maintained, because the Native Americans were savages, and empty land belonged to the first nation that claimed it. The Spaniards had merely followed the precepts of natural law when they declared sovereignty over the entire continent. Yet there was problem with this logic, because Spain clearly did not occupy all the land in the Americas. Other European powers could, then, turn the same principle of natural law against Spain. Nuix therefore argued that international law gave sovereignty over unoccupied lands to "nations" so that they could keep lines of trade and communication open between settlements. Again, Nuix showed himself aware of potential flaws in his logic, for the Amerindians could have countered by deploying the same argument. Even though their lost lands might have been "empty," as Nuix argued, Amerindians could nonetheless claim sovereignty over them in terms of the need to keep open communication between settlements. Nuix, however, maintained that the Amerindians were not nations but families of wandering savages, to whom the laws of nations did not apply.

This preoccupation with secularizing Spanish claims in the New World is yet another link between the thinking of the Catalan Jesuits and the views espoused by the anonymous reviewer of Robertson's history. Unlike Muñoz, who argued that Spaniards had based their claims on Pope Alexander VI's bull of 1493, both Nuix and the anonymous reviewer insisted that this story had been devised by foreigners to ridicule and contest Spanish sovereignty in the Indies. Nuix's third, fourth, and fifth lines of defense were all well-worn arguments that the anonymous reviewer also deployed. Nuix maintained that if violence had in fact been committed, men whom the remoteness of the colonial frontier had turned into barbarians were responsible for it. Moreover, the inevitable frontier violence had quickly been brought under control by the expansion of the Spanish state, which introduced fair and humane laws. Nuix also argued that the violence visited on Amerindians and blacks by other colonial powers had been far worse than that committed by Spain. Finally, Nuix maintained that Amerindians had benefited from the Conquest through the introduction of Christianity and of European science and technologies.

In the middle of this uncompromising defense of the rights and doings of Spain in America, Nuix, like the anonymous critic, launched into a defense of sixteenth-century Spanish observers and historians. The new philosophical histories were not really histories but brief summaries of events that in fact called for volumes, Nuix argued.[197] He quickly dismissed Raynal's claims that Spanish historians were unscientific. "I have been luckier than Raynal," Nuix declared. "I have found among the Spanish authors of the sixteenth and seventeenth centuries real philosophers, although they might not be fashionable today."[198] As for Robertson's argument that new documentary sources located in archives were required to truly understand the past, Nuix observed sarcastically: "I have found it fitting for my purpose not to consult the secret papers of [the archive of] Simancas. My subject is public and well known. All I need are the widely available and accessible Spanish literary sources."[199] Finally, Nuix argued that all that was positive in Robertson's *History* came from Spanish sources. "When the Scot follows the Spanish historians," Nuix maintained, "he is one of the best historians of our century. When [in his rush to be] a philosopher he does not follow [our historians], he is no historian at all."[200]

Inasmuch as Nuix's entire theoretical edifice was built on the premise that the Amerindians were degenerate primitives, he dismissed Spanish testimonies that claimed that the continent had originally been densely populated. Like Pedro de la Estala, discussed at the start of this chapter, Nuix could not avoid contradiction. Notwithstanding all his efforts to discredit Robertson for having manipulated the testimony of Spanish witnesses, Nuix set out to explain why early colonial observers had got it all wrong.[201] Taking a leaf out of de Pauw's book, Nuix argued that the early colonists had found the Indies a "barren land, hard to cultivate, and covered by forests, for there were not enough people to clear them away."[202] Those reporters who claimed to have seen populous nations did so out of "fear associated to danger and the desire of glory, which prompted them to multiply and exaggerate the objects they saw."[203] Indulging in the casuistry deployed by de Pauw, Nuix argued that the testimony of early observers was worthless because it conflicted with the laws of political economy.[204]

Ramón Diosdado Caballero

Another Catalan Jesuit also sought mightily to defend the record of Spanish colonialism in America from exile in Italy and fell into the same contradictions. Ramón Diosdado Caballero confronted a hostile intellectual environment in exile, in which the influence of Spain in Italy was repeatedly decried.[205] He therefore spent the rest of his adult life setting the record of his homeland straight. In Rome, in 1793, for example, he published *De prima typographiae hispanicae aetate specimen*, a reference tool listing the first editions of books published in Spain from 1451 to 1500. In it, Diosdado sought to demonstrate to the Italians that no "nation in the fifteenth century [could boast] so many cities with the printing press [than Spain]." Moreover, the industriousness and vitality of late medieval and early modern Spain, Diosdado argued, had caused Spaniards to take the new technology to the peoples of the New World, as well as to the Philippines and Japan. Italy itself had benefited from this global civilizing effort, for it was Spaniards, not Italians, Diosdado contended, who had introduced the printing press to Naples and Ferrara.[206] Outraged by the suggestions of Italian scholars that the great Spanish painter José de Ribera (1591–1652) had been born in Naples, Diosdado wrote a treatise in 1795 that reclaimed Ribera for Spain.[207] It is no wonder, then, that Diosdado also spent so much effort defending the historical record of Spanish colonialism.[208]

Diosdado first made his views public when plans for a Spanish translation of Francisco Clavijero's *Storia antica del Messico* (1780–81) were announced in 1784. Diosdado had read his Jesuit brother's work and concluded that Clavijero was treacherously and intentionally providing ammunition to the critics of Spain. According to Diosdado, the Creole Jesuit described a glorious Amerindian past but said nothing about the role of Spain in the pacification of Amerindians with voracious appetites for human flesh. Like the Aragonese critics of Boturini, Diosdado maintained that such views of the past necessarily implied criticism of Spain. No reader could avoid drawing the conclusion that Spanish colonialism had transformed formerly civilized Amerindians into miserable, ignorant creatures. To halt the publication of the *Storia*, Diosdado wrote three volumes of "observations," now lost, in which he refuted many of the points made by Clavijero on the alleged grandeur of the Mesoamerican past. Although Diosdado's manuscript itself was deemed too partisan for publication, the Catalan succeeded in derailing publication of the translation of Clavijero's book.[209]

An analysis of those sections of Diosdado's manuscript that have survived shows that he grappled with the problem of apportioning credit to Spanish and indigenous testimonies in the same ways that Nuix did. Although he constantly strove to defend sixteenth-century Spanish historiography, as part of his larger defense of Spanish colonialism, Diosdado was faced with having to admit that there were Spanish testimonies to the grandeur of Amerindian ancient polities. To clear the name of Spain of charges of having committed atrocities in the Indies, Diosdado, like Nuix, nonetheless claimed that America had originally been sparsely populated, inhabited only by a handful of primitive savages. This paradox led Diosdado to challenge the perceptions of eyewitnesses as collective psychological delusions. On the first Spanish expedition to the coast of Mexico in 1517, for example, which had departed from the wild Antilles, Francisco Hernández de Córdova had found a town on the coast of Yucatan that he called Gran Cairo (Great Cairo). In fact, Diosdado argued, it was merely a collection of adobe houses. "Those who understand how powerful is the force of desire to transform things, specially when the object that was left behind [that is, the Caribbean] was insignificant," Diosdado explained, "should excuse our discoverers, . . . for, on good faith, they greatly exaggerated" the wealth and cultural attributes of the inhabitants of the Yucatan peninsula. Like Pedro de la Estala, Diosdado argued that early Spanish visitors to the New World had exaggerated because they had suffered sensory deprivation during decades of living in the primitive Caribbean. To confirm his thesis that all sixteenth-century Spanish witnesses magnified their descriptions of the grandeur of the Mesoamerican civilizations, Diosdado recounted the case of soldiers in Cortés's party who had reported a "silver palace" at the sight of the whitewashed adobe house of the petty ruler of Cempoala. "The much-sought-after El Dorado," he concluded, "is an irrefutable proof of the great ease with which reason deludes itself when the will is vehemently predisposed [to see things]. [Early reporters] substituted palaces, gardens, gold, and silver for miserable houses, thickets, copper, and whitewash."[210]

With the same enthusiasm and care with which he read Clavijero, Diosdado also read Count Gian Rinaldo Carli's *Lettere americane* (1780). In a series of detailed notes on the work of the Italian political economist,

Diosdado summarized Carli's views on Spanish witnesses and on the grandeur of ancient Mexico and Peru. As we saw in Chapter 1, Carli argued that Spanish witnesses were reliable because they wrote in hostile circumstances, with many rivals seeking to undermine their credibility. According to Carli, Spanish witnesses were also credible because they were ignorant and could not have invented the complex Amerindian political and social institutions described in their writings. Diosdado engaged Carli at every step in denying the Spaniards' ignorance, but he was not willing to vouch for the reliability of their accounts of the societies they had encountered.[211]

Diosdado was equally skeptical of the value of indigenous sources. According to him, they were worthless. Clavijero, for example, had followed the authority of Amerindian sources that denied that Cortés, in his march to Tenochtitlan, had sent Amerindian emissaries from Cempoala (Totonecs) to announce his peaceful intentions to the inhabitants of Tlaxcala, traditional enemies of the Mexica. In the Spanish version of events, the Totonec ambassadors had been mistreated, and Cortés had waged war on Tlaxcala as a consequence. According to the "painted" annals left by the Tlaxcalan, however, the Totonec ambassadors had never been mistreated. Diosdado expressed bewilderment that Clavijero had chosen to follow the indigenous sources. "The fact that there is nothing on the [peaceful] embassy of Cempoala in the Tlaxcalan annals does not undermine at all the truth of the event. The ancient memories of the peoples of Tlaxcala are limited to a set of ridiculous paintings similar to the equally worthless ones kept by the Mexica."[212] Diosdado, like Torquemada, thought that there were numerous conflicting ethnic accounts, and that some Amerindian versions were more credible than others. If the annals of Tlaxcala were of little value, those of the Mexica were even less trustworthy.[213] When later Muñoz had to evaluate Diosdado's manuscript, he concluded that Diosdado went even further than Raynal and de Pauw in denying the possibility of knowing anything about the indigenous past prior to the European arrival.[214]

Some twenty years after successfully frustrating the publication of Clavijero's history in Spain, Diosdado published a defense of Cortés in Rome under the auspices of a local Spanish College.[215] Raynal, Robertson, de Pauw, and other enemies of Spain had harped on the many crimes allegedly committed by Cortés and his soldiers in the Tenochtitlan campaign. Seeking to clear Cortés of charges of unnecessary cruelty, Diosdado went about apportioning credit selectively in a detailed reading of the available sources, including those written by Bernal Díaz del Castillo (1496–1584), Torquemada (representing the indigenous perspective as compiled by the Franciscan

Bernardino Sahagún), and Cortés himself. Diosdado presented the massacres as the inevitable result of various forms of Amerindian deceit. In Diosdado's hands, they became just acts of retaliation on the part of Spaniards surrounded by savages hungry for human flesh. Diosdado privileged the testimony of Spanish witnesses and dismissed the Amerindian testimonies compiled by Sahagún. In fact, he dismissed the entire corpus of indigenous sources collected under Franciscan patronage, on the grounds that the natives, who were in any case liars by nature, had been compelled under duress to say whatever they thought the friars wanted to hear.[216] Diosdado insisted that the Mesoamerican annals were very inaccurate and reminded his readers that Torquemada had struggled for years to find his way through a labyrinth of contradictory Mesoamerican chronologies. Conveniently overlooking Torquemada's own arguments that the contradictions were the result of deliberate ethnic political manipulations, Diosdado concluded that the disagreements in the sources revealed the poverty of indigenous knowledge.[217]

Diosdado selectively undermined the reliability of Spanish perceptions. On one hand, he defended the testimony of conquistadors like Cortés to clear Spain of having committed atrocities. On the other hand, he dismissed Spanish testimonies as to the complexity of the indigenous civilizations of central Mexico. Cortés himself, the subject of Diosdado's hagiography, had written many letters to Charles V waxing eloquent about the wonders of Mexico, the grandeur of the palaces, the wealth and extent of the indigenous markets, and the formidable size of the cities he encountered. Once again, however, Diosdado concluded that this and other descriptions were hallucinations on the part of adventurers who had been exposed for too long to the insignificant indigenous material culture of the Caribbean. By Caribbean standards, anything the Spaniards found in Mexico appeared fabulous.[218] As for the numerous references in Cortés and Bernal Díaz to great indigenous fortifications and towers, Diosdado argued that they were simply a convoluted way of describing parties of Amerindians inaccessibly entrenched in the mountains (towers) or in rugged territory (fortifications).[219]

There is no way to know whether Nuix or Diosdado had anything to do with writing the anonymous report that caused Gálvez to seek the prohibition of the translation of Robertson's history. The resemblances between the report and the writings of Nuix and Diosdado are, however, striking. This scholarship was characterized by a virulent defense of the historical record of Spanish colonialism in the Indies. It also sought to shield sixteenth-century Spanish observers and historians from criticism. Inasmuch as their defense of Spanish colonialism was grounded in a negative view of America and its peoples, these scholars had to dismiss reports by Spanish witnesses whom they badly wanted to defend. For all their criticisms of writers like Robertson and Raynal, these scholars had no choice but to deploy the same views of the American continent, the same techniques of reading sources, and the same skepticism about the value of indigenous documents as their enemies. In the end, both the party of Campomanes and that of the Catalan Jesuits proved derivative; each in its own way drew most of its methodological insights from the dominant school of northern European scholarship. There was, however, a third party, represented by Muñoz, that articulated an alternative position.

Juan Bautista Muñoz

After earning a doctorate in theology and teaching for five years at the University of Valencia, Juan Bautista Muñoz was made Royal Cosmographer of the Indies, a post left vacant in 1767 in the wake of the expulsion of the Jesuits. The Academy of History, led by Campomanes, had applied for the post the year of the Jesuit expulsion,[220] but in 1770, with the help of a circle of influential Valencian courtiers, Muñoz succeeded where the Academy had failed, although he was unqualified as a mapmaker.[221] By the time both the Academy and Muñoz applied, the Spanish Navy had transformed Spanish colonial cartography through a series of modern observatories and countless maritime expeditions. The post was about to be phased out, which occurred in 1784.[222] Muñoz, therefore, fulfilled his duties of cosmographer not as a mapmaker but by doing erudite work and envisioning an alternative *patria* to that of Campomanes.[223]

The year the Academy was working on the notes for the translation of Robertson's *History*, Muñoz confronted Campomanes for the first time. In 1778, the Italian Cesareo Giuseppe Pozzi (1718?–1782), a Benedictine former professor of mathematics at the Sapienza in Rome, and a retainer of the papal nuncio in Spain, published *Saggio de educazione claustrale per li giovani* (1778), a treatise on education for friars that echoed many of Campomanes's pedagogical views. The Council of Castile, where Campomanes was a leading figure, decided to promote a translation.[224] Suddenly, however, a treatise denouncing Pozzi, not unlike the one written against Robertson later that year, appeared. Muñoz's exposé of Pozzi threw the plans of the council into disarray. It sparked a process that began with the recall of all available copies of Pozzi's *Saggio*, further sale of which was prohibited, and ended with an inquisitorial trial of the Italian.[225] Since the confrontation with Pozzi (and therefore with Campomanes) was over matters of substance, including visions of Spain, it merits our attention.[226]

Muñoz argued that Pozzi partook of a recent Italian fashion "that, without any knowledge of Spanish literature and drawing in evidence accumulated from reading books we perhaps ourselves disparage, has imposed on us the sobriquet of ignoramuses and corrupters of good taste." Pozzi, Muñoz complained, had begun to mock the "backwardness of Spanish erudition" as soon as he arrived in Spain.[227] Yet, according to Muñoz, certain sectors at court were dazzled with Pozzi. Members of the Royal Council, for example, began to promote a translation. Like Mayans, who could not stomach derivative authors who aped French intellectual fashions, Muñoz set out to show the ignorance of Pozzi's followers, who had failed to notice that Pozzi was a fraud. In a few pages, Muñoz demonstrated that the Italian was a plagiarist who had lifted entire passages from fashionable French pedagogical treatises. Moreover, according to Muñoz, Pozzi was also peddler of fashionable impieties.

Pozzi had insisted that education be about identifying and shaping the natural impulses of the child. According to Muñoz this was a doctrine, derived from Rousseau's *Emile*, that saw human nature as inherently good.[228] Drawing on the sixteenth-century Spanish Augustinian tradition represented by Juan Luis Vives and Luis de León that Mayans had sought to resurrect, Muñoz argued that human nature was sinful and that the role of education as well as of legislation was to discipline and root out from "the heart of man the evil to which he is inclined from childhood."[229] Pozzi had also maintained that the teaching of Christian doctrine should be delayed until children had acquired the use of reason. To introduce children to religion too late, Muñoz countered, would be devastating to the social fabric, for one could not wait for the "passions, which erect strong hurdles to any belief that opposes them, [to be] unleashed." Religious indoctrination, not reason, was needed to restrain the innate evil tendencies of children before they got out of hand.[230] Finally, following the rather fashionable views of contemporary political economy, Pozzi had presented virtues and vices as the product of contingent, changing social consensus, according to which self-interest was perceived to be vicious if it hurt the community or virtuous if it benefited the whole.[231] Muñoz insisted that these views were antithetical to Christianity. Drawing again on St. Augustine, Muñoz argued that cardinal virtues (faith, hope, and charity) were innate and at war with equally innate human vices, in a perpetual confrontation over absolute values of good and evil.[232]

One is tempted to cast Muñoz as a traditionalist waging a losing battle against modernity. But Muñoz in fact stood for a *different version* of modernity from that represented by Campomanes. In fact, he represented the culmination of the project spearheaded earlier by Mayans, Boturini's staunchest ally, who advocated a return to the erudition and values of sixteenth-century Spanish humanism. The project of the Valencian erudite was Augustinian to its core, closer to the views of seventeenth-century French Jansenists than to those of Voltaire or Rousseau. Like that of Campomanes, the Valencian's project seemed functional to the interest of the Spanish monarchy, in that it justified absolutism and the creation of a royalist Church. Far from being secular, however, it envisioned a return to Erasmian forms of piety and inward spirituality that shunned baroque ritual.[233] It was also a project that in the name of Baconian empiricism refused to embrace any learned system, either ancient or modern. In a manuscript addressed to a Dominican by the name of Martínez, a professor of the University of Salamanca, Muñoz rejected Martínez's passionate calls for theologians to embrace the new sciences of Descartes and Newton in the same way that St. Thomas Aquinas had embraced Aristotle. "[Martínez] has not been able to pin me down either as modern or as Aristotelian," Muñoz maintained, "because I have always sought to keep myself free from parties. I have guided my theology [solely] according to the words of God and the authority of the Church. In the natural sciences, I have followed reason and experience [alone]."[234] This was precisely the spirit that had moved Mayans not to accept Boturini's version of Vico's philosophy of history.

The Valencian project was also patriotic to its core. Muñoz could not stomach Pozzi's facile disparagement of Spain, because it was oblivious of centuries of Spanish erudition. Like Mayans, however, Muñoz denounced the shallowness and derivative nature of most contemporary Spanish scholarship. In 1778, in the same letter in which he described the campaign against Pozzi to his close Valencian friend Antonio José Cavanilles (1745–1804), who was then busy naming the flora of the Spanish empire after Spanish great men while on a fellowship to study botany in France, Muñoz argued: "I see no reason why we should glory [in the state of our learning], [particularly] if we compare [Spain] with other nations. In other times, we were able to compete. Nowadays, our knowledge is still immature [*agráz*], generally speaking." Like Mayans, Muñoz had no fear of denouncing Spain's shortcomings. Muñoz blamed the immaturity of contemporary Spanish letters on the same men who had promoted Pozzi — namely, the members of the Council of Castile, who had refused to create an Academy of Sciences modeled on the French Academy and establish a literary committee (*junta literaria*) to promote Spanish humanism.[235]

Why Create Archives?

Muñoz was an erudite like Mayans, with high critical standards, which led him to reject all previous Spanish and, more generally, European histories of the New World. Muñoz's rejection, however, was very different from those of de Pauw, Raynal, and Robertson. According to Muñoz, the trouble with all previous histories of the Indies was not so much that they were based on the testimony of ignorant, unreliable witnesses as that they lacked a solid documentary foundation. If anybody in Europe should be either praised or denounced for introducing a positivist obsession with painstaking archival research as a precondition for writing history, it is Muñoz. In the course of some twenty years of physically exhausting labor, he put together one of the greatest collections of carefully chosen documents and manuscripts on the New World and the Spanish colonies in Asia, some 150 volumes in all, which are now housed at the Royal Academy of History and the Royal Library in Madrid.[236] Muñoz also persuaded Gálvez and the Council of the Indies to create the Archive of the Indies.[237]

From the moment he received the assignment to write the history of the New World, Muñoz saw it in patriotic terms. "The writing of the history of the Indies," he informed Charles III in 1779, "has been neglected to the detriment of the honor and interest of the nation." "Foreigners, more often than not, unjustly attack the actions of Spain, belittle our discoveries, and censure even the sage and beneficial policies and laws of our monarchs."[238] However, Muñoz tempered his patriotism by heeding the secular demand to do away with all previous Spanish historiography. Patriotism and the writing of a new history were, in his view, intimately related, for the truth about the deeds of Spain in the New World could only emerge after the painstaking accumulation of new sources. "The history of Spain is a wreck [*esta en mantillas*]," Muñoz confided to Juan Antonio Mayans y Siscar (1718–1801), Gregorio's brother, in 1782. "It will not be possible to write this history without first publishing collections of the many manuscripts that are now being consumed by insects and resisting the injuries of time."[239] "The true history of the Indies," Muñoz maintained, "will only surface through the analysis of the authentic documents that have not been used yet."[240] The sheer accumulation of information would demonstrate that the charges raised by the enemies of Spain were simply innuendo, deliberate manipulation of the truth, and biased interpretation of the available information. "To end with all these," Muñoz informed Gálvez in 1783, "the only art that is needed is to examine and describe the events from all sides and refer to things simply as they happened, without hiding or silencing anything."[241] Again, like Mayans, Muñoz wanted the "truth" to speak for Spain.

Muñoz considered that his project, if it were to be persuasive and effective, needed to be erudite, not simply a rancorous apologia for Spain. His style completely lacked the aggressive tone that characterizes the writings of most Catalan Jesuits. Unlike the rancorous and satiric style used by Nuix and Diosdado, Muñoz's is self-consciously subdued. He sought in this way to gain the sympathy of European readers. "Urbanity and decorum are not opposed to a truthful and complete narration of historical events," Muñoz argued in 1783, striving to explain the logic behind his patriotic historiographical strategy to his Valencian friend Cavanilles. "The one who has little love for truth does not present it in a way that is well received. I am determined to bring to light a history that is worthy of this name, not a tirade, not a satire, not a [vociferous] apologia."[242] Muñoz dismissed as useless the writings Nuix and Diosdado, on grounds that "they, with more goodwill than judgment and instruction, have opposed [to foreign tirades against Spain] their own. Although they have demonstrated the biases of the malicious [enemies of Spain], they were unable to articulate a persuasive defense, [so much so] that they have not even managed to silence their enemies on those points in which they are right. One should come to expect such failure from declamatory and self-righteous [exísticos] writings."[243] Muñoz opposed the publication of Diosdado's "observations." Although he found some merit in the Catalan's criticisms of Clavijero, particularly regarding the latter's exaggerated reliance on indigenous sources and derivative scholarship, Muñoz declared the observations unsuitable for publication. Diosdado hurled insults to foreigners promiscuously. "A writer has to be moderate," Muñoz lectured Diosdado, "not to create suspicion that his principles come from places other than the love of truth."[244] "Even when [combating] heretics and freethinkers," Muñoz concluded, "it is better to use urbane expressions, great moderation, and not to injure anybody's character. . . . This should be done in the pursuit of the truth and for the cause of the nation."[245]

Muñoz set out to complete a new history that would replace all that had been written before, particularly Antonio de Herrera y Tordesillas's *Historia general de los hechos de los castellanos*, known as the *Décadas* (1601–15). Although he decided to follow Herrera in reconstructing the activities of Spain in America only from 1492 to 1555, Muñoz did not think of the

Décadas as anything more than "a diary made up of excerpts, [a quilt] made up of scraps," lacking completely in argument and philosophical depth.[246] In the preface to his *History of the New World*, Muñoz dismissed all sixteenth-century histories of the New World. He publicly ridiculed Sepúlveda's *Orbe Novo*, published by the Academy under the leadership of Campomanes, as disorganized and derivative, a compendium drawn from the works of Gonzalo Fernández de Oviedo. *Orbe Novo*, Muñoz maintained, "is so badly put together, so pitiful, so lacking in things of importance, and so full of errors . . . that had I not read it, I would have doubted that such work came from [the hands of Sepúlveda], such an erudite author."[247] Senility was to blame here, Muñoz contended. Muñoz also criticized the writings of Pietro Martire d'Anghiera (1457–1526), who had enjoyed privileged access to information from the Indies that tantalized Muñoz. Despite his training in Italy, Muñoz argued, Anghiera's *De Orbe Novo* was an "undigested compilation lacking in order and accuracy."[248] López de Gómara also came in for criticism. According to Muñoz, he was a good stylist but had enjoyed limited access to sources and "credited [too many] absurdities [*patrañas*]."[249] Muñoz applauded Herrera for his learning and efforts as collector of primary sources. Herrera's *Décadas* were the only place where many sources that had disappeared could still be consulted. Yet, as noted, Muñoz dismissed the *Décadas* as an undigested collection of "excerpts and scraps" taken from the documents Herrera had so painstakingly collected.[250] Muñoz praised Fernández de Oviedo for his curiosity but decried his ignorance and credulity. He spared only Las Casas's manuscript "History of the Indies" (comp. 1550–63) and Fernando Colón's manuscript life of his father, Christopher Columbus.[251]

Muñoz envisioned himself as a Descartes of American historiography, doing away with previous textual authorities through methodical doubt, and as a Bacon, reconstructing knowledge upon solid foundations based on the painstaking collection of facts. "I have done what in the sciences those few who now deserve the name of inventors or restorers have practiced," Muñoz informed Gálvez in 1783. "I have put myself in a state of methodical doubt, observing in painstaking detail every particular, drawing generalizations from induction, establishing solid and fecund foundations from whence the propositions of a perfect system will emerge."[252]

But Muñoz had more to offer than skepticism and contempt for previous Spanish historiography. He thought that the answer to each and every one of the charges leveled by foreigners against Spain was to be found in the Spanish archives. Although in his first forays into the archives Muñoz despaired, unable to find any logic connecting the thousands of stored documents, he slowly began to uncover order. In the many documents and manuscripts lying unpublished on the shelves of archives and private libraries, Muñoz maintained, there was evidence that Spain had transformed the history of navigation and commerce. The documents also revealed something other Europeans denied: the profound philosophical contributions of Spain. The many unpublished travel reports of the sixteenth and seventeenth centuries, the countless geographical surveys, particularly those sponsored in the later sixteenth century under Philip II, and the various manuscripts on natural history, Muñoz contended, all demonstrated the many contributions of Spain to natural history and geography. The many letters, reports, and trials of colonial bureaucrats, and the prolonged and well-documented discussions surrounding the issue of laws for the colonies, showed the prudence and philosophical depth of Spanish colonial legislation, "a precious monument of human wisdom."[253] The many unpublished ethnological studies of indigenous peoples, Muñoz argued, indicated that colonial laws had been hammered out on the anvil of exquisite anthropological knowledge. The many documents related to the Church demonstrated that the Conquest had never been motivated merely by greed. According to Muñoz, they also revealed that the civilization created by Spain in the Indies was a harmonious whole, in material and spiritual balance. This search for evidence of the wisdom of Spanish legislation and of the wisdom of Spanish observations regarding both humans and natural history was the organizing principle behind the collection of primary documents that Muñoz gathered in the course of twenty years.[254]

After traveling with a band of from three to six scribes to countless archives and private libraries all over Spain and Portugal for some six years, after having supervised the consolidation of colonial documents from different repositories into the new Archive of the Indies, officially created by Gálvez in 1784, and after sidestepping Campomanes's plots for five additional years in Madrid, Muñoz finally completed the first volume of his long-awaited new *History of the New World* in 1791.[255] Muñoz was to see only this volume through publication.

Muñoz's 'History'

Volume 1 of Muñoz's *History* was written in the same moderate skeptical tone and with the same ideas about the New World and its indigenous peoples as those introduced by Robertson in book 4 of his *History of America*. Muñoz portrayed the New World as a cold, wet, barren place that was slowly being transformed by colonists who cleared forests and drained swamps.[256] Like de Pauw, he considered the indigenous peoples of America, who had lived for millennia in isolation, to be arrested in the most primitive stages of social development. Like de Pauw, too, he concluded that of all peoples on earth, the Amerindians were the most "indolent, childish, and distant from human dignity."[257] Like Raynal, Muñoz described the expansion of trade and commerce as a pacifying and civilizing force, and the discovery of America as the transforming episode of European history, much more significant that either the Renaissance or the introduction of the printing press.[258] In book 2, he carefully described the medieval Iberian maritime expansion to Africa that began with trading expeditions to the Canary Islands in the thirteenth century; the growing speculative mood of the fifteenth century about lands across the Atlantic; Columbus's cosmological vision of a shorter maritime route to Asia; and the final decisive support he enjoyed from the learned Spanish Dominicans and the *Reyes católicos* ("Catholic monarchs"), Ferdinand and Isabella. In books 3 to 6, Muñoz narrated the voyages of Columbus and the colonization of the Caribbean to 1500, in the process correcting dates and events obscured by previous historians who had lacked adequate access to primary sources. Steeped in the Ciceronian rhetorical tradition introduced in the late fifteenth century by Nebrija and Vives in Spain, Muñoz decided "to imitate the difficult simplicity of the ancient classics." He therefore did not include any notes that would burden the flow of the narrative with "researches and impertinent disputes."[259] The much-expected references to primary documents would have to wait. He planned to publish them as appendixes after having covered the events of each reign.

Crisis in the Academy

Upon completion, Muñoz's first and last volume was sent to the Academy for peer review. Unexpectedly, the Academy at first welcomed the work. Early in October 1791, the commission assigned to review it, led by Pedro Francisco Jiménez de Góngora y Luján, duke of Almodóvar (1727–1794), saluted Muñoz. His history was recognized as methodologically sound, its description of places as accurate, its prose as precise and fluid, its language as proper and pure. The commission suggested its immediate publication and recommended only the inclusion of an index and appendixes with the primary sources from which Muñoz had derived his most controversial information.[260]

Campomanes reacted furiously to the recommendations of the commission. In November, he urged the Academy to listen to the dissenting views of José de Guevara y Vasconcelos, the brother of the man who fourteen years earlier had translated Robertson's *History of America*. Campomanes's faction did not expect the commission to go against the will of the powerful director, and Guevara y Vasconcelos patched together a review so quickly that he himself admitted that he had not yet read the last third of the book. Campomanes and Guevara y Vasconcelos thought, however, that this was enough to pass judgment. Muñoz's history, Guevara y Vasconcelos argued, had no preface to spell out the structure and historiographical premises of the larger project. The narrative that covered the initial events of the Conquest from 1492 to 1500 in six books was so detailed that to see the project through to completion, no fewer than three hundred books and dozens of volumes would probably be needed. Notwithstanding the long-winded narrative, Guevara y Vasconcelos objected, the volume under review lacked a dissertation connecting developments in astronomy, navigation, and politics to the maritime Atlantic expansion that Columbus's voyages had initiated. It also lacked a dissertation on the origin, laws, and customs of the Amerindians in general and of the Caribs in particular. The title, *History of the New World*, he argued, was misleading, for the volume did not include the history of the Amerindians at all. Guevara y Vasconcelos suggested that this lacuna might indicate gaps in Muñoz's readings and invited Muñoz to look up Columbus's famous letter to Santángel for information on the natural and moral history of the Caribbean. Finally, Guevara y Vasconcelos railed against Muñoz's "pompous expressions, awkward locutions, antiquated idioms, grammatical errors," and various other stylistic defects.[261] The kernel of Guevara y Vasconcelos's criticism was that Muñoz added "nothing substantial to what other historians of the Indies, both national and foreigners have said." According to Guevara y Vasconcelos, the problem lay in Muñoz's shallow philosophical perspective. "Muñoz has written a history," Guevara y Vasconcelos declared, "without the philosophy that characterizes this century," failing to "instruct the reader" with reflections on politics, scientific knowledge, and Amerindian customs.[262] Clearly, Muñoz had refused to imitate Robertson or Campomanes.

José de Guevara y Vasconcelos shared more just than a personal dislike for Muñoz with Campomanes. They brought a completely different philosophical outlook to the writing of the history of the New World. In September 1770, in an address to the Academy and the Royal Council, Guevara y Vasconcelos had already urged the magistrates of the two bodies not to contribute to Spanish "backwardness" (*atraso*) by impeding the diffusion in Spain of the works of Grotius, Pufendorf, Hobbes, Galileo, and Montesquieu. While praising Descartes and Newton for their knowledge and piety, Guevara y Vasconcelos urged the magistrates to do their utmost to prevent the publication of sermons in bad taste. He also urged them to ban baroque tragedy, "which deviating from the objective of the genre inspires love and lovers instead of heroes."[263] Guevara y Vasconcelos and Campomanes were neoclassicists and reformers who clearly wanted more than just a new history of the Indies with solid documentary foundations. They wanted a philosophical history à la Robertson that would put Spain firmly on the map of contemporary European scholarship.

Campomanes approved Guevara y Vasconcelos's reviews and convened the Academy to a collective reading of Muñoz's history. This was a slap in the face for Almodóvar, whose commission had approved the new history, and, taking advantage of the new political and cultural mood gripping Spain in the wake of the French Revolution, the duke began to plot Campomanes's replacement as director of the Academy. Campomanes did not have much of a chance of winning this battle.[264] Although not notably more radical than Almodóvar, who had published an abridged Spanish translation of the first five volumes of Raynal's *Histoire philosophique*, Campomanes, who had gained for himself the title of count, was an upstart of obscure origins facing a powerful grandee.[265] In late December, only a few months after he had lost the presidency of the Council of Castile, Campomanes was removed and replaced by Almodóvar as director of the Academy. The Council of the Indies then ordered the immediate publication of Muñoz's *History*.[266] Finally, Muñoz was admitted as regular member of the Academy in January 1792, delivering an address in which he denounced the entire corpus of Iberian historiography.[267]

Francisco Iturri's Critique

In 1793, Muñoz's much-awaited history finally appeared. With Campomanes out of the running, the only opponents left who were capable of articulating a powerful critique of Muñoz's work were the Spanish American Jesuits in exile in Italy. In 1798, in Madrid, Francisco Iturri (1738–1822), a Jesuit born in Santa Fe, in the viceroyalty of La Plata, published *Carta crítica*, a slim volume devoted to identifying the historiographical underpinnings of Muñoz's history. Iturri insisted that Muñoz had lifted many of his ideas from Robertson and de Pauw, including the notions that America was cold, wet, and barren and that the Amerindians were the most primitive humans on the face of the earth. Muñoz's prologue, Iturri argued, was one of the most critical pieces ever penned against Spanish colonial historiography. It reinforced de Pauw's views of the Spaniards as inept scientific observers.[268] Iturri organized his work as a defense of the historiographical value of Herrera's *Décadas*, seeking to identify contradictions and factual errors in Muñoz's history. The most blatant contradiction was that in book 1, where Muñoz presented the New World as humid and degenerate, whereas in books 3 to 6, recounting Columbus's voyages in the Caribbean, he described it as a temperate paradise. To oppose Muñoz's negative and derivative views of America, Iturri compiled testimonies by numerous sixteenth-century witnesses. These, he argued, had more authority than armchair philosophers did. To prevent "prejudice and self-interest" from seeping into their accounts, historians needed to encounter the New World face-to-face.[269]

The only thing that Iturri's *Carta crítica* had in common with Guevara y Vasconcelos's and Campomanes's criticisms was that all three called attention to Muñoz's complete lack of interest in the Amerindian past. To Muñoz's disparaging view of the Amerindians, Iturri opposed the grandeur of the Incas and Aztecs. Drawing on Mayans's authoritative testimony, he maintained that Mesoamerican calendrics proved the depth of indigenous knowledge, and therefore the sophistication of their civilizations. According to Iturri, Muñoz's ignorance of the Native American past stemmed from his limited linguistic knowledge of Amerindian systems of writing. "Without the information [stored in quipus and hieroglyphs] . . . one will never be able to understand the Indians."[270]

By the time Iturri published his *Carta crítica*, Muñoz had already responded to the charges leveled by Guevara y Vasconcelos that his history totally excluded the Amerindians. Citing the authority of Robertson, Muñoz argued that attempting to reconstruct ages with no literary sources was hopeless.[271] But the fact that Muñoz completely ignored the history of the indigenous peoples of the Caribbean does not mean that he was about to do the same for that of the Mexica and the Incas. Had he written the history of the conquest of Mexico and Peru, he would have probably introduced sections on the Incas and the Aztecs. Muñoz was, for example, responsible for identifying the whereabouts of Bernardino de Sahagún's *Primeros memoriales*, one of the many drafts that preceded the Florentine Codex.[272] Moreover, Muñoz spearheaded efforts to bring Boturini's collection to Spain. It is significant, however, that he only sought to retrieve works by sixteenth- and seventeenth-century indigenous chroniclers that were in Latin script (see pp. 301–5 below).[273]

Muñoz did not think much of Amerindian recordkeeping devices. Despite his admiration for the scholarly accomplishments of the Spanish Renaissance, he did not demonstrate an interest comparable to that of the Renaissance in the information contained in documents written in non-alphabetic scripts. When it came to valuing Andean quipus and Meso-american pictograms and logograms, Muñoz was truly a man of his age. Throughout his career, he revealed only contempt for Mesoamerican sys-tems of writing. In his 1785 report on Diosdado's "observations," he agreed with Diosdado that one of the most serious flaws in the work of Clavijero was that it gave to the "paintings and quipus and other monuments of the Indians . . . more value than what they deserve."[274] In 1794, in a paper read to the Academy of History on the historicity of the miracle of Our Lady of Guadalupe in Mexico, Muñoz, following Boturini, insisted that only the Amerindians had left contemporary records of the miracle in their writings. Unlike Boturini, however, Muñoz presented the Amerindian sources as "dirty papers" (*papeles mugrientos*), creations of minds given to "easy and in-discreet" devotions. "The fantasy of the Indians is feverish and fecund due to enthusiasm," Muñoz maintained, "What can it fail to produce? Can any monster compare to their poetic compositions and paintings? Isn't it possible that these visions [of the miracle] might have been concocted in the brains of these fanatics?"[275] Finally, in 1798, in a short treatise against Iturri, Muñoz argued that it was as absurd to seek "abstraction and sublimeness" in Inca quipus and Mesoamerican hieroglyphs. According to Muñoz, hieroglyphic writing, including that of the Egyptians, typified primitives, not advanced societies.[276]

Conclusion

The debates sparked by the publication of Muñoz's history reveal that there were at least four historiographical projects circulating in Spain in the last quarter of the eighteenth century. Campomanes and his followers were adamant about embracing current European historiographical trends, par-ticularly the variety of scholarship typified by Robertson, in which erudition was subordinated to the larger goal of identifying the secular social, cultural, and political forces that caused nations to rise and decline. Magistrates were to draw lessons as they sought to reform Spain. It is worth noting that Campomanes was Asturian. The second project was that of the Catalan Jesuits. Nuix and Diosdado launched a furious defense of the historical record of Spanish colonialism. For all their criticism of fashionable philosophical and conjectural historians, in seeking to defend Spain against its critics, Nuix and Diosdado embraced de Pauw's bleak portrayal of the New World and its peoples and dismissed any testimony that contradicted this dismal picture. In defending the value and depth of Spanish historiography, the Jesuits rejected eyewitness reports of the populousness and splendors of highland Amerindian societies. The third project, led by Muñoz, deployed the age-old Valencian tradition of humanist erudition in order to justify the creation of new colonial archives. Although, like Campomanes and the Catalan Jesuits, Muñoz drew on the new northern European scientific histories of the Americas to characterize the New World and its peoples, he put more emphasis on careful documentary reconstruction of the deeds of Spaniards in the Americas. In the process, he formulated the epistemological and historiographical arguments that persuaded the Spanish crown to create the Archive of the Indies. Yet another group of provincials, the Spanish American Creole Jesuits in Italy, spearheaded the fourth project. Iturri sought to defend the historicity of Spanish reports of the grandeur of highland Amerindian civilizations. To do so he not only defended the accuracy and reliability of Spanish witnesses and historians but also emphasized the value of Amerindian sources.

The category of patriotism, on the importance of which historians such as José Antonio Maravall and François Lopez have insisted, is needed to bring order to any interpretation of the Spanish Enlightenment.[277] This chapter lends support to the argument of I. A. A. Thompson that a discourse of early modern "Spanish" identity was articulated despite, not because of, Castile.[278] The participation of the periphery in the defense of Spanish conduct in the Indies is particularly striking, not only because Spain was a loose composite of separate kingdoms, but also because much of the periphery had been excluded from what for all practical purposes had been a Castilian colonial adventure in the New World. If Spain was one of the first early modern European national states, it was also one of the weakest. In the late fifteenth century, Ferdinand and Isabella unified Spain and put an end to the social disorder and uninterrupted civil wars that had engulfed Castile, Aragón, and Catalonia for more than a century. As they wrestled the judiciary away from local lords, disciplined the Church, and created a national bureaucracy, the *Reyes católicos* laid the basis for the early modern Spanish state. Yet Spain remained politically and economically divided. The Jewish Castilian bankers and financiers expelled from the peninsula in 1492 were replaced, not by Aragonese or Catalan merchants, but by German, Flemish, and Italian ones; nor were Aragonese or Catalan merchants allowed into the new colonial markets opened in the New World. The conquest of America did not contribute to the economic integration of Spain; the Castilian and Aragonese economies remained distinct and separate, with Aragon, Catalonia, and Valencia tied to the Mediterranean economy, and Castile to America and to Flanders. Political integration was limited too. The Spanish state followed the Aragonese medieval imperial model, bringing together separate political nations under a weak central monarchy, which was forced to respect the local traditions and laws of the independent kingdoms (*fueros*). The fragmentation only worsened in the course of the seventeenth century, particularly after 1640, when Catalonia and Portugal seceded. The economic and political differences across regions were so profound that the so-called "Spanish" decline should in fact be thought of as solely a Castilian phenomenon. Not even under the Bourbons did Spain become fully united. Although some degree of political integration was achieved after the wars of succession in which Castile defeated Aragon, Catalonia, and Valencia, the merchants of these regions had to wait until the second half of the century to begin sharing in Castile's Atlantic colonial economy.[279] Why, then, were representatives of Spain's eastern periphery so interested in defending the history of the deeds of Castilians in America?

The search for a Spanish identity as a project that in the eighteenth century exercised the periphery more than the core has yet to be fully explored. Aragonese opposed Boturini. Catalans were the first to denounce the anti-Spanish biases of Raynal and Robertson. Valencians spearheaded the effort to create a truly patriotic new history of America based on public sources. We now need to turn to those other "provincials," the Spanish American Creoles.

CHAPTER 4

The Making of a "Patriotic Epistemology"

While in exile in Italy and after having read scholars such as Cornelius de Pauw and William Robertson, the Jesuit Juan de Velasco (1727–1792) decided to finish the natural and civil histories of the "Kingdom of Quito" that he had begun to write sometime in the 1750s. Velasco dusted off his notes collected during years of pilgrimages up and down the Ecuadorian Andes to study plants, insects, manuscripts, and indigenous oral traditions. In 1788–89, he submitted for the approval of the Spanish authorities three volumes in which he painstakingly refuted the views of European writers on the Americas. Velasco not only attacked the peddlers of negative representations of the lands and peoples of the New World but also sought to prove the stubborn continuity of the "Kingdom of Quito" in the face of many challenges, including two invasions by the Caran-Shyri (ca. 980 C.E.) and the Incas (ca. 1487 C.E.). Although his history had to wait until the mid nineteenth century to be published, his observations trickled through the presses of late-colonial Quito in the 1790s to inspire local patriots.[1] Misunderstanding his works, nationalists have used Velasco to create the historiographical foundation of Ecuador.[2] It is true that Velasco's history sought to endow the Creole colonial society of Quito with a glorious past. Yet his idealized north Andean ancient polities were not "nations," that is, fraternities of virtuous citizens, but "kingdoms," societies made up of corporate social estates.

Velasco typifies scores of Spanish American antiquarians who both in Europe and in the colonies attempted to refute the views of skeptical northern European authors. David Brading has for many years been perhaps the most astute reader of these Spanish American antiquarians. In *The Origins of Mexican Nationalism*, for example, Brading has studied the work of one of Velasco's Jesuit brethren, Francisco Clavijero, concluding that the latter wrote, not only to refute Cornelius de Pauw, the abbé Raynal, and William Robertson, but also to provide Creole patriots with legitimating historical narratives. According to Brading, Creole patriotism originated in the late sixteenth and early seventeenth centuries when the American-born descendants of Spanish conquistadors complained that the crown was turning its back on its original commitment to foster a class of grandees in the New World. As the monarchy phased out the grants of Amerindian tribute and labor (*encomiendas*) given to the conquistadors in the most economically dynamic areas of Mexico and Peru, Creoles lost the right to be a privileged landed nobility surrounded by communities of Amerindian retainers. The Creoles then turned to the Church, whose secular branch they gradually came to dominate. Ensconced in universities, cathedral chapters, nunneries, and parishes, Creoles produced countless patriotic sermons and treatises that praised the wealth of their ecclesiastical establishments, as well as their own learning and piety, including that of the many New World saints that the Church had canonized, or should have canonized. The historiography that the clerical Creoles produced sought to transform the "colonies" into "kingdoms," part of a loosely federated Spanish universal monarchy, each endowed with a glorious past. Clavijero's history of ancient Mexico was no exception.[3]

Brading has argued that it was this tendency that made Creole historiography unpopular in the nineteenth century, a period of *nation* building. The Creole project of an orderly polity composed of hierarchical social orders in nested subordination failed to attract Mexican intellectuals in the wake of the wars of independence (1810–21). Over the course of the colonial period, the most economically dynamic areas of Mexico, the geographical crescent surrounding the capital, developed more fluid social structures, in which upward social mobility partially did away with the corporate restrictions of the colonial core. It was here that forms of popular liberalism (or republicanism) became deeply rooted and that a social order based on universal participation of male citizens emerged. Mexico's liberalism captured the imagination of most nineteenth-century literate Spanish American elites, who therefore had little taste for Clavijero's musings. The patriotic histories of the Aztecs written in the late-colonial period found little resonance in the postcolonial age, at least until the Mexican Revolution of 1910. It was only after the Revolution that *indigenismo* (the cult among mestizos of things Amerindian) finally rendered the historiography of Creole patriotism more palatable to the republican traditions of popular liberalism.[4] Scholars working on nineteenth-century Peru have echoed Brading's insights into the failure of late-colonial Creole historiography to inspire new generations of nineteenth-century intellectuals. A similar preoccupation with creating postcolonial liberal republics led Peruvian elites to underemphasize the rich colonial historiographical tradition initiated by the Inca Garcilaso de la Vega that sought to reconstruct a classical Inca past for the viceroyalty of Peru.[5]

The views of scholars like Brading have helped guide my readings of the countless works produced by late-colonial Spanish American historians and antiquarians who wrote to criticize the new northern European historiographies of the New World. This chapter and the next explore the epistemological and methodological assumptions that authors such as Velasco and Clavijero brought to bear in their writings. These authors crafted an epistemology that can be called "patriotic." Drawing on the insights of Brading, I argue that patriotic epistemology was a discourse of the ancien régime that created and validated knowledge in the colonies along lines that mimicked and reinforced wider public principles of socio-racial estates and corporate privileges. Seeking to refute northern European histories of the New World and its peoples, these authors also crafted persuasive critiques of the genre of conjectural history. More important, they articulated an original analysis of the epistemological limitations of the "traveler" that foreshadowed many of our contemporary postcolonial insights. In this chapter, I first clarify the rules of the discourse of patriotic epistemology. Then, I explore Creole authors who by the mid eighteenth century began to articulate some key insights of this discourse as they set out to refute biased travel accounts and sought to demonstrate the privileged status of the testimonies of Amerindian and Creole-clerical elites. In the third section, I study the writings of Creole Jesuits in exile who brought this discourse to maturity. The chapter ends with an analysis of how the logic underpinning this discourse helps illuminate the nature of the seemingly contradictory colonial representations of the "Indian," who was both despised and admired.

Patriotic Epistemology: An Overview

The histories of the Incas and the Aztecs written by the likes of Velasco and Clavijero were a reaction to Enlightenment paradigms and techniques developed in philosophical compilations of travel accounts and conjectural histories. It is tempting to argue, therefore, that these histories were simply a return to the methods and attitudes of the Renaissance. Both Velasco and Clavijero, for example, claimed that their accounts were thoroughly grounded in native sources. Already in the early seventeenth century, the Inca Garcilaso de la Vega and the Franciscan friar Juan de Torquemada had claimed privileged access to Amerindian testimonies and sources. But the epistemological agenda of Velasco and Clavijero did not consist merely of taking up where Garcilaso and Torquemada had left off. While the latter two built on a tradition of sixteenth-century Indo-Spanish humanism to show the complexity and historical depth of indigenous polities, the two Jesuits wrote to undermine the epistemological and critical principles of eighteenth-century northern European historians. Along with many others, Velasco and Clavijero developed an approach to the problem of assessing the credibility of testimonies and of validating knowledge that can be called "patriotic epistemology."

The discourse of patriotic epistemology validated the historical knowledge produced only by learned clerical observers and by precolonial and sixteenth-century Amerindian nobles. Like the humanist epistemology deployed by Garcilaso and Torquemada, eighteenth-century patriotic epistemology privileged the testimony of Amerindian oral traditions and written sources, but unlike its sixteenth-century counterpart, it also sometimes dismissed these sources outright. The humanist epistemology of the sixteenth century emerged in an early-colonial landscape of complex indigenous polities that, although demographically and culturally battered, maintained the sharp differentiation between commoners and rulers that had characterized precolonial highland societies. Sixteenth-century colonial intellectuals sought to collect and translate into European historiographical idioms conflicting historical traditions relayed by Amerindian rulers. Over time, however, as those rulers disappeared, this reliance on the testimonies of Amerindian elites began to be questioned. To observers in the late eighteenth century, Amerindian communities looked socially undifferentiated. Although some indigenous elites adapted to the new colonial conditions, taking Castilian names and becoming the new caretakers of Christian temples and saints, the rich tapestry of social hierarchies that had characterized past Amerindian polities underwent considerable simplification.[6] For most late-colonial observers, Amerindian communities seemed homogeneous collectivities of wretched commoners. It was in this context that clerical writers sought to distinguish carefully between sources produced by reliable precolonial and early-colonial indigenous elites and those produced later by unreliable commoners. From this perspective, the Creole clerical project appears as one of restoration, a return to the simpler times in which virtuous Amerindian nobles had embraced the teachings of the Church.

The discourse of patriotic epistemology also privileged the knowledge and credibility of the representatives of the Church. With Amerindian nobles considered virtually an extinct species, representatives of the Church, whose intimate acquaintance with the land and indigenous communities supposedly made them impervious to deception and misrepresentation, now assumed responsibility for reporting credibly on natural and ethnographic phenomena in the Indies.

In the discourse of patriotic epistemology, the foreign observer appeared as nemesis of learned clerical witness. Foreign travelers were portrayed as helpless victims of Amerindian cunning, who in any case paid only short visits to the lands they studied and were therefore unable to discover much about them. They also lacked the time and inclination to develop lasting attachments to communities and were incapable of penetrating beneath the surface of local social phenomena. Travelers were at the mercy of communities that gulled foreigners and laughed at their expense. Moreover, since travelers did not know the Amerindian languages, they were forced to rely on translators and secondhand interpretations.

Patriotic epistemology not only offered an epistemological critique of the perceptual limitations of both Amerindian commoners and philosophical travelers, it also targeted the reliability of Spanish colonists. Late-eighteenth-century clerical authors tended to differentiate between the testimony of the clergy and that of lay colonists, who were often found guilty of bias, whether conscious or unconscious. This clerical critique of the colonists had illustrious antecedents in the sixteenth century, when the religious had constantly fought "greedy" lay colonists. "Spaniards" were far from being a homogeneous group: colonists, clergy, and royal magistrates clashed incessantly over, among other things, the right to control Amerindian lands and labor.[7] Each group in turn was divided. The Church, for example, was an institution in which the seculars fought the religious and Creoles fought Peninsulars over the control of parishes, monasteries, nunneries, cathedral chapters, and universities.[8] These tensions had already sparked historiographical debates between colonists and clerics by the early sixteenth century; parties accused each other of manipulating evidence for the sake of agendas of greed and exploitation.[9] This tension somewhat subsided with the rise of the secular Church in the seventeenth and eighteenth centuries, but by the late eighteenth century, the policies of the monarchy had considerably undermined the judicial, political, and economic power of the secular clergy, setting off an anticlerical wave led by provincial bureaucrats and some local communities. Bureaucrats (intendants, *alcaldes*, and *subdelegados*) sought to take the economic assets of parishes and sodalities from clerical control, as well as to limit the clergy acting as civil magistrates. Some communities also got involved in the anticlerical charge and snarled parish priests in endless litigation over ecclesiastical fees and the latter's rights to punish and discipline.[10] This heightened tension between laity and clergy partly revived former clerical claims to greater credibility.

Mestizos, or *castas*, the products of miscegenation among Amerindians, poor Spaniards, and blacks, were at the bottom of the scale of credibility devised by the discourse of patriotic epistemology and were consistently targeted for criticism by clerical writers. Such interbreeding was thought appropriate only when it involved the upper classes. Whereas the mating of upper-class Amerindian women with high-born Spaniards had been welcomed in the early days of the Conquest, the miscegenation that later united commoners of different races was another matter. Vulgar *mestizaje* was seen as a threat to the existence of idealized hierarchical polities. Mestizos were consistently portrayed as evil and out of control, responsible for introducing vicious lifestyles, including a culture of lies and deception, into Amerindian communities that the clergy sought to keep unsoiled.[11]

The patriotic epistemology described here cannot be ascribed solely to Creoles. Spanish bishops who served terms in the colonies, for example, were among its leading representatives. The discourse of patriotic epistemology appears therefore broadly clerical rather than merely Creole, which is the reason for the awkward, sometimes redundant, term "clerical-Creole."

Clerical-Creole historiography was a reflection of aristocratic, racialized longings of members of ancien régime polities, not modern nation-states. Nineteenth-century national projects in Latin America, to be sure, also offered very limited definitions of citizenship. Yet these exclusionary projects were committed to ending the colonial traditions of corporate privileges and socio-racial estates, the twin principles upon which clerical patriots sought to build utopian colonial kingdoms. But in spite of differences between the historiographies of the colonial and national periods, they remained connected by the concept of the nation-state. Although a recent arrival on the historical scene, the nation-state has managed to present itself as eternal, as Benedict Anderson and Eric Hobsbawn have noted. By helping tailor collective memories, history has been a powerful nationalist legitimating resource, and it is deployed in educational systems and the public sphere to this end.[12] Clerical-Creole historiography helped rescue and preserve narrative traditions that would later give the freshly minted Spanish American nation-states a patina of eternity.

A remarkable distance separates our modern and postmodern sensibilities from the views of these clerical authors, many of whom inhabited strange mental landscapes that have not yet been fully explored. My intention is to provide a reading of late-colonial Spanish American culture that, I hope, will challenge a Eurocentric historiography obsessed with discovering the precursors of modernity in the former Spanish colonies. A secular, liberal, modern interpretation of late-colonial culture tends to offer stereotypical and anachronistic readings of the authors studied, thus making a universal master narrative out of local, provincial European experience.[13] This chapter and the next will make clear the density and originality of intellectual debates in colonial Spanish America. Once the rules of the discourse are understood, the depth and creativity of late-colonial Spanish American authors should become apparent. It is very telling that the bulk of the scholarship critically addressing the epistemological and methodological proposals of the Enlightenment did not come from the British American colonies but from Mexico. Thomas Jefferson, Alexander Hamilton, and Benjamin Franklin did not offer any comprehensive methodological response to the negative views of America proposed by authors such as Buffon, de Pauw, Raynal, and Robertson.

In the next section, I study three mid-eighteenth-century authors, Juan José de Eguiara y Eguren (1696–1763), Mariano Fernández de Echeverría y Veytia (1718–1780), and José Joaquín Granados y Gálvez (1734–1794), who, I argue, first outlined many of the insights of the discourse of patriotic epistemology.

The Making of Patriotic Epistemology: Mexico, 1750–1780

Juan José de Eguiara y Eguren

The arrival in the Indies of works by Nicolás Antonio (1617–1684) and Manuel Martí (1663–1737), two of the most important Spanish neo-Latinists of the late seventeenth and early eighteenth centuries, created a major intellectual upheaval. Antonio and Martí sought to renovate Spanish intellectual life through the diffusion of italianate humanist values. They held the Creole culture of the colonies in contempt, and the 1735 and 1742 (posthumous) editions of Martí's and Antonio's letters, respectively, include remarks denigrating New World peoples. In notes addressed to pupils grappling with whether to migrate to the Indies, Antonio and Martí encouraged their young friends to move instead to Rome, because the Spanish American colonies, with no libraries and no authors of note, had little to offer inquisitive minds. From Quito to Mexico, the clerical establishment reacted with indignation, seeing Antonio and Martí as the culmination of some two hundred years of Peninsular arrogance and misinformation about America. Juan José de Eguiara y Eguren typified the clerical authors who penned angry responses.[14]

A powerful cleric, holder of the chair of theology and dean of the University of Mexico and appointed bishop of Yucatan (a post he declined), Eguiara y Eguren became the most outspoken critic of Antonio and Martí in

America and devoted his life to proving them wrong. In a work that mobilized a vast network of correspondents and provincial intellectuals, Eguiara y Eguren set out to demonstrate that the Spanish American colonies were not intellectually barren. In his *Bibliotheca mexicana*, he assembled a list of published and unpublished works produced in Mexico after the Conquest (with short biographies of the authors). Although the *Bibliotheca* suffered the fate of many of the works it catalogued (only one volume was published), a lengthy preface did come out. As a typical patriot, Eguiara y Eguren used the preface to list the accomplishments of the Creole mind, including the extraordinary feats of memory of a handful of university scholars. He described the exceptional linguistic and academic qualifications of the average parish priest; the many works on mathematics, theology, history, politics, law, rhetoric, grammar, linguistics, and medicine written in Mexico; and the many outstanding libraries available in New Spain. Moreover, Eguiara y Eguren also cited the political and intellectual virtues of the ancient Mesoamerican polities. The novelty of Eguiara y Eguren's thesis lay, however, in his criticism of the epistemological foundations of European knowledge of the Indies. In his preface, Eguiara y Eguren outlined the clerical discourse of patriotic epistemology, emphasizing the inability of outsiders ever to comprehend America.

Eguiara y Eguren zeroed in on Marti's views as part of his larger argument against armchair philosophers and travelers, attacking the genre of travel accounts that since the late seventeenth century had specialized in "orientalizing" Spanish America by presenting the colonies as riddled with corruption, sexual promiscuity, ignorance, cruelty, and pagan superstition.[15] To counter this view and especially to prove that the religion of the colonies was not dominated by survivals of Amerindian idolatry, the biographical sketches in Eguiara y Eguren's *Bibliotheca* dwelt on the piety and morality of the Creole intelligentsia, as well as of learned Native Americans who had served clerical scholars as translators, interpreters, and guides in the sixteenth century or become distinguished parish priests in the seventeenth and eighteenth centuries.

Although Eguiara y Eguren constantly used the testimony of "foreign" authors (including Peninsular Spaniards) to strengthen the credibility of his theses, he acknowledged only travelers who had used learned Creoles as guides. Thus, for example, he cited the testimony of the Italian traveler Giovanni Francesco Gemelli Careri, who had briefly visited Mexico in the late seventeenth century. According to Eguiara y Eguren, Gemelli Careri reported accurately on Mexican antiquities and on clerical educational establishments, largely because he had followed information provided by the great Creole polymath Carlos de Sigüenza y Góngora (1645–1700).[16] Eguiara y Eguren also acknowledged the testimony of "outsiders" with long-term residence in the Indies. Believing that exposure to "the American experience [was] educational," Eguiara y Eguren concluded that foreigners who had lived many years in America were trustworthy.[17] As a matter of principle, Eguiara y Eguren dismissed Peninsular authors who collected their information en route to somewhere else. This, Eguiara y Eguren argued, was the reason for the only partially accurate passages on Mexico in the *Geographía histórica* published in Madrid in 1752 by Pedro Murillo Velarde (1696–1753). Although it described Mexico City's numerous and wealthy educational establishments, which was, of course, music to Eguiara y Eguren's ears, Murillo Velarde's *Geographía* referred slightingly to colonial literary styles and asserted that although Creoles were mentally precocious, they degenerated early. Eguiara y Eguren ascribed these calumnies to the fact that Murillo Velarde had quickly assembled his data on Mexico while en route to Manila.[18]

Only reliance on trustworthy local interpreters could provide solid knowledge about America, Eguiara y Eguren thought, and he accordingly exalted the Amerindian Christian culture that the Franciscans had created in the sixteenth century at the College of Santa Cruz of Tlatelolco. Eguiara y Eguren praised the Latinate Amerindian intelligentsia that once walked the halls of the college for having preserved and translated sources that were the foundation of all trustworthy historical knowledge about ancient Mesoamerica, including that of Franciscans such as Bernardino de Sahagún.[19] This emphasis on the value of local interpreters led Eguiara y Eguren to call into question the work on Mesoamerican scripts by the learned seventeenth-century German Jesuit Athanasius Kircher, who in his *Oedipus aegyptiacus* (1652–54) had argued that Mexican writing was childish. Kircher's interpretation of Mexican writing was wrong, Eguiara y Eguren argued, because it was uneducated. "The opinion of this extraordinarily erudite man would have been different," Eguiara y Eguren maintained, "had he had access to the writings of our indigenous writers or had he found an interpreter who would orally have explained to him those paintings he failed to comprehend."[20] Had Kircher relied on the knowledge of the Amerindian historians of the sixteenth century, he would have not failed to understand the true character of Mesoamerican scripts. According to Eguiara y Eguren, Mexican writing resembled that of the ancient Egyptians in that it was divided into paintings that could be understood by commoners and hieroglyphs whose deep, arcane symbolism could only be comprehended by learned priestly elites.

Throughout the preface, Eguiara y Eguren also implied that the heirs of the Amerindian aristocracy of the precolonial period and the early sixteenth century were the Creoles, making them the only surviving credible interpreters of American realities. Eguiara y Eguren applauded Kircher for having correctly identified the arcane symbolism hidden behind the representation of the Mexica deity Huitzilopchtli, but maintained that the German's interpretation was based on the information he had obtained from Creole Jesuit brethren.[21]

Struggling against the facile characterizations of colonial culture in European literature on the New World, typified by Antonio and Martí, Eguiara y Eguren outlined a patriotic epistemology that denied that transient reporters possessed the ability to come up with insights of any value into the lands they visited, and that privileged the epistemological authority of postcolonial Amerindian nobles and their intellectual heirs among contemporary Creole clerics. A few years later, in a history of Mesoamerica and its peoples, Mariano Fernández de Echeverría y Veytia would develop Eguiara y Eguren's argument.

Mariano Fernández de Echeverría y Veytia

Mariano Echeverría y Veytia was the scion of a powerful bureaucratic family in the city of Puebla. After obtaining a fine education and a degree in law, he toured Europe and eventually settled in Madrid. One day in 1744, an Italian stranger knocked at his door; it was Lorenzo Boturini, who, after having been imprisoned in Mexico, had been sent back to Spain to face charges. For two years, Echeverría y Veytia welcomed the stranger into his household, where Boturini worked on his great historiographical project calling for a complete reconceptualization of the history of Mesoamerica using new sources, the *Idea de una nueva historia general de la América Septentrional.* While at Echeverría y Veytia's, Boturini introduced his host to the fascinating world of Amerindian antiquities. When he was called back to Mexico in 1750, Echeverría y Veytia promised the Italian to send him copies of indigenous documents in his collection that lay sequestered in New Spain. By the time Echeverría y Veytia got around to fulfilling his promise, however, it was too late. Boturini had died. With some of Boturini's ideas brewing in his head, and copies of Boturini's wonderful collection of indigenous sources,

Echeverría y Veytia began to write a history of his own, which remained un-completed at his death in 1780.[22]

Echeverría y Veytia's history of ancient Mexico seems to have been written circa 1769, after many years of studying indigenous sources and grappling with Boturini's ideas.[23] Like Boturini, Echeverría y Veytia was suspicious of theses that emphasized cultural diffusion, and he therefore sought to highlight the independent development of the Mesoamerican civilizations. In Boturini's and Echeverría y Veytia's accounts, the natives developed their great civiliza-tions largely in isolation. According to Echeverría y Veytia, a mere 104 years after the destruction of Babel (ca. 2,133 years after Creation, that is, 1797 B.C.E.), seven Chichimec families had established the city of Huehue-tlapallan near the Colorado River.[24] Along with these Chichimecs, Giants also arrived in the New World. These settled further to the south, only to be wiped out by a hurricane in the year 3,433 after Creation (601 B.C.E.).[25] The northern Chichimecs discovered the length of a year (365.25 days), reformed their calendrical system, and introduced the concept of leap years as early as the year 3,901 after Creation (133 B.C.E.).[26] This empire also became the cra-dle of the civilizations that later emerged in the Central Valley of Mexico, as splinter groups swarmed the south at different time periods. The first wan-derers were the Olmecs, Xicalanca, and Zapotecs, who moved eastward to the Gulf and eventually reached Veracruz by sea. As they moved into the interior, these peoples killed off the few surviving Giants. In the case of the Olmecs, they settled in central Mexico and built the great city of Cholan in 51 B.C.E.[27] Not until the heyday of the Olmecs did an Old World visitor arrive: the apos-tle St. Thomas, whom the natives called Quetzalcoatl. St. Thomas intro-duced the natives to the mysteries of the Trinity, the Crucifixion, and the Resurrection, as well as to the sacraments of baptism, confession, commun-ion, and priestly ordination. He also taught them the concepts of penance (bloodletting, self-flagellation, fasting) and charity, and introduced stern laws to punish homicide, perjury, theft, and adultery. Distance from Rome, how-ever, soon led the priestly corps to distort St. Thomas's original teachings.[28] Development in isolation continued, and a second splinter group swarmed central Mexico. According to Echeverría y Veytia, seven Toltec families aban-doned their parent Chichimec culture after staging a revolt in 583 C.E.[29] The Toltecs, mixed with the Olmecs, Xicalanca, and Zapotecs, built Tollan in 719 C.E., and convened a council of elders around 800 C.E., led by Huematzin, the Toltec Moses, who put together a Pentateuch-like book, the Teoamoxtli, or great book of civil and sacred histories. When news reached the northern empire that Tollan and the Toltecs had collapsed in 1116 C.E. as a result of famine, plagues, and civil wars, the Chichimecs sent parties led by Xolotl to resettle the land. Those Toltec groups who still clung to the land fought back and were crushed. Some, however, intermarried with the newcomers, establishing new dynasties. According to Echeverría y Veytia, three new northern groups, the Tepanec, the Otomí, and the Aculhua, moved down in 1168 C.E. to further complicate the ethnic and dynastic landscape of central Mexico. The last northern group to arrive consisted of seven Mexica families. They settled in central Mexico in 1298 C.E., founded Tenochtitlan in 1327 C.E., and took over the region in 1428 C.E.

Like Boturini, Echeverría y Veytia thought that ancient Mesoamerican sources were abundant and reliable, and that the Chichimecs and Toltecs had kept an accurate recollection of the stories of Creation, the Flood, and Babel, confirming each and every one of the elements of the biblical narrative. Moreover, through a comparative analysis of Amerindian and Old World chronologies, events in the Bible such as the correct date of death of Christ could be elucidated. Echeverría y Veytia shared Boturini's interest in clarifying Amerindian chronologies to shed light on significant biblical events. Cracking the obscurities of Amerindian calendrical systems became a means to settling disputes between the contradictory versions of the Bible (that is, the Vulgate and the Septuagint). Echeverría y Veytia, for example, used references to ancient eclipses in native sources to calculate Christ's true birth date, which he argued had been in the year 4,034 after Creation.[30]

Echeverría y Veytia did not, however, follow Boturini blindly. For one thing, he came up with a slightly different interpretation of Mesoamerican calendrics. More important, he refused to read myths as allegories of ancient social revolutions. Although Echeverría y Veytia explicitly insisted that the analysis of the meaning of words was a resource yet to be tapped, his use of etymology was rather different from Boturini's. Echeverría y Veytia implicitly rejected Boturini's evolutionary metanarrative of society and the mind.[31] The postlapsarian savages who in Boturini's *Idea* coined the names of gods to express dramatic changes in social conditions are nowhere to be found in Echeverría y Veytia's history. Nor are there any heroes whose poetic expressions in hieroglyphs, myths, and songs reveal the tensions of their class-ridden societies. Rather, for Echeverría y Veytia, the history of Mesoamerican polities was one of a decline from monotheism to polytheism. Full-fledged humans, whose natural reason had once led them to design accurate calendars and to worship a single, abstract deity, evolved into superstitious brutes. So convinced was Echeverría y Veytia of the relatively recent appearance of "idolatry" and "superstition," that he maintained that although the

Chichimec reform of the calendar dated back to 133 B.C.E., the pagan names of the twenty days and eighteen months of a typical Mesoamerican calendar were relatively recent.[32] Echeverría y Veytia believed that idolatry had appeared in Mexico only around 750 C.E., some 2,500 years after the foundation of the city of Huehuetlapallan,[33] and that it had been deliberately introduced by merchants and priests seeking to attract pilgrims to struggling urban centers.[34] He saw moral decline in ancient Mexico as intimately linked to elite behavior. The concupiscence of a single Toltec ruler, Topiltzin, who violated the taboo against polygamy, for example, led to the sexual corruption of the entire Toltec clerical corps, which in turn led to widespread social corruption and generalized unrest. According to Echeverría y Veytia, the fall of the Toltecs could be blamed squarely on Topiltzin's immoral behavior.[35]

Although Boturini put together one of the greatest collections of written indigenous sources ever to be assembled in Mexico, he ultimately did not pay much attention to them. Boturini thought that the reconstruction of the human age had largely been accomplished, and that his contribution lay in the reconstruction of the age of the gods and the heroes. Echeverría y Veytia was also particularly interested in reconstructing these ages, but he thought that they were not as obscure as Boturini had once argued, for there was abundant written documentation. For Echeverría y Veytia, the source of Boturini's interpretative errors lay ultimately in the physical distance imposed by exile between the Italian and his own formidable collection of literary sources.[36]

The following pages focus on the way in which Echeverría y Veytia elaborated the discourse of patriotic epistemology first presented by Eguiara y Eguren. Unlike Eguiara y Eguren, Echeverría y Veytia did not write explicitly to address European misrepresentations of the New World, and his history had no obvious polemical intent. Yet Echeverría y Veytia's history was organized around a set of critical and epistemological principles that complemented those presented by Eguiara y Eguren. The task of the historian, Echeverría y Veytia argued, consisted in returning a core of reliable precolonial and early-colonial sources to their pristine original condition. According to Echeverría y Veytia, these sources had been altered, mainly by the democratization of access in Amerindian communities under colonial rule to hitherto closely guarded interpretation and sources, the willful manipulation of historical narratives by Amerindian elites, and the transformation of indigenous grammars and vocabularies. Echeverría y Veytia's epistemology condemned as untrustworthy the historical accounts of Amerindian commoners in all periods, as well as those of late-colonial indigenous interpreters, irrespective of their social standing. As he sought to reconstruct the original Amerindian sources, Echeverría y Veytia privileged the scholarship of Amerindian historians such as Fernando de Alva Ixtlilxochitl, a member of the dynastic lineage of Texcoco who, as noted in Chapter 2, had befriended Torquemada, and whose writings Echeverría y Veytia sought to recover and imitate. I argue that the scholarship of these two authors cannot be easily distinguished, and that historians who have sought to present the "Indian" and "Spanish American" populations as two separate and distinct homogeneous monoliths are wrong. At least at the elite level, these two populations shared more than one cultural value. Finally, I argue that Echeverría y Veytia advanced a critique of foreign observers that, although not as coherent and fully developed as Eguiara y Eguren's, nevertheless focused on the epistemological limitations of travelers.

Three Processes of Distortion

Unlike the typical northern European accounts that emphasized the burning of irretrievable Amerindian texts by fanatical Spanish friars, Echeverría y Veytia argued that the destruction of Amerindian books had not led to their eradication; they simply had gone underground. Having witnessed the burning of entire archives housed in the courts of Texcoco and Mexico during and after the Conquest, Mesoamericans decided to conceal their documents, guarding them jealously from strangers. This was all the more justified, Echeverría y Veytia contended, because not even those learned Spaniards who later mastered Nahuatl and studied extant indigenous sources had managed to cast off their persecutory mentality where Amerindian documents were concerned. Torquemada, for example, disqualified the study of the entire genre of calendrical sources on the grounds that they were demonically inspired.[37] The Amerindians knew this and hid their archives. It was at this crucial moment, Echeverría y Veytia argued, that reliable Mesoamerican historical documents began to be misread and misinterpreted.

Building on the methodological writings of Alva Ixtlilxochitl, Echeverría y Veytia maintained that the hiding of documents in Amerindian communities had democratized access to them. This in turn led to anarchy, because commoners who lacked knowledge of the traditional exegesis of Mesoamerican scripts introduced their own spurious readings. Citing a case described by Alva Ixtlilxochitl of an Amerindian upstart from the town of Cohuatepec (Coatepec?) who argued that his hometown was the original cradle of the Aculhuan lineage, Echeverría y Veytia sought to exemplify the modifications and distortions introduced by commoners. Alva Ixtlilxochitl, who represented the views of Texcoco, a rival Aculhuan town, had confronted the commoner with contrary documentary evidence, but to no avail.[38] Echeverría y Veytia cited Alva Ixtlilxochitl's anecdote to make the point that the hiding of sources in the context of the collapse of indigenous social hierarchies had led to profound distortions, which later surfaced in the writings of Europeans.[39]

This approach allowed Echeverría y Veytia to weigh the credibility of sources and to apportion credit to the narratives of Amerindian and European writers. He was, for example, confronted with multiple enumerations of Mesoamerican historical ages. According to the myth of "solar ages," three successive catastrophes had destroyed the earth, and a fourth and final solar age was soon going to end. Boturini had once argued that floods (the sun of Water), earthquakes (the sun of Earth), hurricanes (the sun of Air), and a forthcoming apocalyptic conflagration (the sun of Fire) represented, in that order, the correct succession of ages. Echeverría y Veytia disagreed with Boturini's interpretation of one of Alva Ixtlilxochitl's texts and cited an earlier work by the same author. According to this version, hurricanes, not earthquakes, had followed the Flood. Facing two different accounts by the same author, Echeverría y Veytia chose one partly on rational grounds. According to Echeverría y Veytia, Mesoamerican natives had a cosmology in which the four elements were organized in ascending hierarchical order: Water, Air, Earth, and Fire. Echeverría y Veytia concluded that this cosmology was also the organizing principle of the natives' history, and that the chronological succession of ages should therefore mimic the ascending hierarchical order of the elements. After the Flood (Water), Echeverría y Veytia argued, came the ages of hurricanes (Air), earthquakes (Earth), and the forthcoming final conflagration (Fire).

If reasoned hypothesis served Echeverría y Veytia to elucidate the order of ages, his clinching argument rested on who had authorized each of the accounts presented by Alva Ixtlilxochitl. According to Echeverría y Veytia, a list of Amerindian elders and rulers had vouched for the reliability of the earlier account, whereas the later account did not have such authoritative support. To emphasize the importance of using only authoritative sources, Echeverría y Veytia compared his list of solar ages with the sixteenth-century enumeration of not four but five ages by Francisco López de Gómara, who, Echeverría y Veytia argued, had either been deliberately misled or had used a "vulgar" informant.[40]

According to Echeverría y Veytia (and Alva Ixtlilxochitl), the second

mechanism that introduced distortions in the original core of indigenous primary sources lay in the willful manipulation of the sources by the Amerindian elites. Drawing again on Alva Ixtlilxochitl's writings, Echeverría y
Veytia quoted the example of an elderly informant from a leading family in
the city-state of Tepetlaoztoc who recounted the events surrounding the birth
of the fifteenth-century Aculhua ruler Ixtlilxochitl, father of the philosopher
king Nezahualcoyotl. The elder argued that Ixtlilxochitl had hatched from
an eagle's egg, and that mesmerized by such preternatural birth, the Aculhua
had selected him as their ruler. When challenged by a skeptical Amerindian
historian, the elder responded that he had decided to mislead all those ap-
proaching him, especially if they were Spaniards constantly seeking interviews. Echeverría y Veytia cited this story to argue that deliberate distortion
by tired ruling elites who did not see any concrete advantage in their initial
partnership with Spaniards should be counted as yet another major factor
that had led to the distortion of the original Amerindian primary sources.[41]

Echeverría y Veytia identified yet a third mechanism of distortion of indigenous documents, namely, the failure of later indigenous interpreters to
understand the language of their earlier peers. As James Lockhart has shown,
in the course of the seventeenth and eighteenth centuries, as the indigenous
communities of central Mexico came into closer cultural contact with the
Hispanic world (which included mestizos), sixteenth-century Nahuatl underwent profound transformations. Not only were Spanish words introduced,
but Nahuatl syntax and grammar were also changed.[42] The end result of
these linguistic shifts, Echeverría y Veytia argued, was that later indigenous
interpreters, independently of their social status, could no longer understand
sixteenth-century Nahuatl. Those authors who relied on contemporary
Amerindian translators to read precolonial and sixteenth-century Amerindian
documents were bound to introduce misrepresentations.[43]

That Echeverría y Veytia was so weary of indigenous documents of late-
colonial vintage should not be surprising, because by the time he wrote, central Mexico was flooded with forged documents. Beginning with the
Conquest, colonial magistrates had accepted documents recorded in
ideograms, logograms, and paintings in litigation, and courts had hired specialized interpreters to translate them. Lawsuits about indigenous dynastic
rights and control of communal lands, and Amerindian denunciations of
overzealous and exploitative *encomenderos*, or provincial crown bureaucrats,
were often presented in the form of traditional indigenous paintings, which
were later glossed by court interpreters and scribes. In fact, a substantial per-
centage of the extant Mesoamerican codices are of such provenance. When

the Amerindian demographic collapse of the sixteenth and seventeenth centuries century finally bottomed out in the mid eighteenth century, the number of land disputes in central Mexico skyrocketed. With greater pressure on scarce resources, Amerindian pueblos began to fight to halt the loss of land to Spaniards and mestizos and armed themselves with false charters (*títulos primordiales*),[44] which have recently attracted scholarly attention. Mesoamerican communities used forged *títulos* to identify their origins with the building of Christian churches or visitations by patron saints, reflecting a profound change in historical consciousness. Local Amerindian notaries and scribes sought in these charters to recreate what they thought were the languages and visual forms of the sixteenth century, while endowing communities with new historical narratives.[45] Such efforts to reproduce sixteenth-century forms led to obvious anachronisms. Urban charter-forging factories became quite sophisticated, however, deliberately aging paper and introducing extinct grammatical forms of classical Nahuatl.[46]

"I have drawn my history from documents with the required authority, solidity, and trustworthiness," Echeverría y Veytia declared, citing the mechanisms that had led to the distortion of Amerindian primary sources to discredit rival interpretations. He dismissed all previous European accounts. "My sources are the same [sources] upon which [many Spanish] and foreign authors have based theirs. [They, however] have disfigured and dislocated the sources."[47] Typical of this approach to the criticism of previous European accounts and of Amerindian sources of late-colonial provenance was his study of Quetzalcoatl among the Olmecs.

Echeverría y Veytia's thesis that Quetzalcoatl was none other than St. Thomas the apostle, on a visit to Mexico some sixty years after the death of Christ, was directly contradicted by historians such as Torquemada and Antonio de Herrera y Tordesillas, who identified this elusive figure as a Toltec who had flourished around 800 C.E. Torquemada had drawn uncritically on the bewildering array of contradictory indigenous sources, Echeverría y Veytia countered, leading him to characterize Quetzalcoatl contradictorily as both a sage and a villain, a pious priest and a cunning magician. Herrera, for his part, had used erroneous etymologies to identify Quetzalcoatl as a deity, the "god of the air," rather than as the historical figure that he was. Echeverría y Veytia concluded that Torquemada and Herrera had been misled by informants who were either ignorant or deliberately deceptive.[48]

According to Echeverría y Veytia, it was treacherous to build on written indigenous documents of the colonial period to prove that St. Thomas had visited Mesoamerica. Although he cited the testimony of a handful of priests who claimed to have seen Amerindian "books" with the mysteries of the faith painted in them, Echeverría y Veytia sought to avoid such shaky evidence. He thus refused to introduce as his sole evidence a manuscript penned in Mexico in the 1670s by the Jesuit Manuel Duarte, who had interpreted an Amerindian "map," a large cotton sixteenth-century canvas, which most likely was drawn in a pueblo in Oaxaca as part of a land litigation process, as an allegorical rendition of the history of St. Thomas's migration to America. According to Duarte, the map also included St. Thomas's teachings, namely, the stories of Creation, Eden, the Fall, the Crucifixion, and the Resurrection. Duarte even managed to identify the Virgin Mary among the cast of characters overflowing the giant cloth. Echeverría y Veytia obtained a copy of this bizarre manuscript (it had been given as a gift along with the map to Sigüenza y Góngora) while searching through the papers of Boturini's collection. Unable to find the map itself to check whether it was truly ancient or a later Amerindian concoction, Echeverría y Veytia decided not to pay much heed to Duarte's manuscript. He suspected the map to be a worthless colonial document.[49]

To ascertain the real identity of Quetzalcoatl, Echeverría y Veytia privileged iconography, etymology, and cultural and material artifacts over European and indigenous colonial literary sources. A comparative etymological analysis of the names for Thomas in Hebrew and Nahuatl, Echeverría y Veytia argued, revealed that St. Thomas and Quetzalcoatl were the same person, for both referred to a "learned twin."[50] Moreover, an engraving on the supposed tomb of St. Thomas discovered by the Portuguese in Mylapore, India, depicted what appeared to be a quetzal, or "American peacock," as though St. Thomas's followers in India had decided to memorialize him symbolically with the Amerindian name he had acquired in Mexico (Fig. 4.1). But the ultimate proof of St. Thomas's visit, Echeverría y Veytia maintained, lay in the many cultural and material artifacts he had left behind, including a host of Mesoamerican religious institutions that eerily resembled Christian ones; handprints on stones; and the many ancient crosses that had marked the Mesoamerican landscape prior to the European arrival.[51]

Fernando de Alva Ixtlilxochitl

Besieged by spurious interpretations and documents of suspicious provenance, Echeverría y Veytia relied on a select group of sources that he thought were trustworthy — namely, the histories written by sixteenth-century Amerindian historians from ruling families who had been conversant with

FIGURE 4.1. Alleged tomb of St. Thomas the Apostle in Mylapore, India. Echeverría y Veytia identified the bird on top of the cross as a quetzal, a logographic representation of Quetzalcoatl, St. Thomas's supposed Nahuatl name. From Manuel Duarte, "El apostol Santo Tomás en el Nuevo Mundo" (1670s).

the native languages and scripts. These historians were typified by Fernando de Alva Ixtlilxochitl, whose writings guided most of Echeverría y Veytia's history. Although that his various accounts in Spanish sometimes contradicted one another,[52] Alva Ixtlilxochitl had subjected his findings to the evaluation of Amerindian town councils, which had vouched collectively before notaries for their reliability.[53]

Little is known about the evolution of Alva Ixtlilxochitl's writings. His Texcocan (Aculhua) perspective claims a long-enduring Toltec-Chichimec dynastic lineage for the rulers of this city-state. Alva Ixtlilxochitl was an extraordinarily thorough researcher. He collected and preserved studies by other Aculhuan sixteenth-century historians, such as Juan Bautista Pomar's *Relación de Texcoco* (1584) and the letters and *Memorial* (ca. 1557) of the governor of Texcoco, Hernando Pimentel, as well as the works of non-Aculhua historians, such as the *Historia de la conquista de México* (1548) by Tadeo de Niza de Santa María (Tlaxcalan).[54] Alva Ixtlilxochitl also assembled accounts from several indigenous communities that often contradicted one another. It is possible that the several narratives he left were merely compilations of these many competing accounts he was trying to reconcile.[55] Be that as it may, when he died, Alva Ixtlilxochitl left a smooth and continuous narrative history in Spanish that sought to prove that all the peoples of Mexico had common Chichimec-Toltec roots.[56] The history moved teleologically, plotting the ascent of the Aculhua of the city-state of Texcoco until, in the fifteenth century, they gave the world the philosopher-king Nezahualcoyotl, allegedly one of the most noteworthy rulers ever to appear in Mesoamerica.[57] Alva Ixtlilxochitl's *Relaciones* consistently cast the Texcocan rulers as the faithful allies of the Spaniards, dismissing Texcocan leaders who took the side of the Mexica as illegitimate.[58] Texcoco actually rose to power and fame only in the fifteenth century, after a long subordination to Coatlichan, a city-state whose rulers alone could legitimately claim "ancient" Aculhua lineage.[59] As Enrique Florescano has argued, Alva Ixtlilxochitl's history was written from the perspective of native ruling families who, in the great turmoil that followed the Conquest, justified their rights to the tribute of Amerindian commoners by producing legitimating historical accounts.[60]

Typical of several Amerindian ruling families of Mexico, Texcoco, and other powerful city-states of precolonial central Mexico who chose to assimilate the European conquerors by intermarrying with them, Alva Ixtlilxochitl was culturally a Creole. Not only was he the first to portray Quetzalcoatl as an ancient Olmec sage who resembled a Christian apostle, an idea that seventeenth- and eighteenth-century Creoles like Echeverría y Veytia later developed, but he may have also been behind the Creole patriotic cult of Our Lady of Guadalupe.[61] He enjoyed excellent relations with the secular Church and dedicated one of his unpublished manuscripts to the archbishop of Mexico, Juan Pérez de la Serna (d. 1631), who took refuge in Teotihuacan, an Amerindian town under the jurisdiction of Alva Ixtlilxochitl's family, when fleeing from a mob in Mexico City in 1624.[62] Moreover, Alva Ixtlilxochitl's brother Bartolomé (fl. 1634–41) was a learned seventeenth-century parish priest who wrote several doctrinal works in Nahuatl.[63] Fernando de Alva Ixtlilxochitl typified the fashion among indigenous elites of adopting

Spanish names to distinguish themselves from Amerindian commoners in the new colonial society.[64] After being appointed governor of several Amerindian towns, Alva Ixtlilxochitl was later given a position of interpreter in the courts of New Spain.[65] His antiquarian research left a lasting imprint on colonial historiography, which has not yet been fully assessed. Thus, for example, Alva Ixtlilxochitl's Texcocan-Aculhuan bias was adopted by Torquemada, through whom it came to dominate the colonial historiography of New Spain.[66]

Alva Ixtlilxochitl's second lasting impact came from his efforts as a collector. Diego de Alva, Fernando's son and heir to the governorship of Teotihuacan, donated Alva Ixtlilxochitl's collection to Sigüenza y Góngora sometime in the late seventeenth century, after the latter helped to block a challenge from commoners in Teotihuacan seeking to deny upper-class "mestizos" such Alva Ixtlilxochitl the right to rule the town.[67] One of the most influential Creole polymaths of the colonial period, Sigüenza used Alva Ixtlilxochitl's writings to correlate Amerindian and European calendars through the study of ancient astronomical phenomena.[68] When Sigüenza died, Alva Ixtlilxochitl's collection ended up in the archives of the Jesuits. Parts of it eventually surfaced among Boturini's collections and were therefore available to Echeverría y Veytia. Although Echeverría y Veytia was weary of the multiple and contradictory accounts left by Alva Ixtlilxochitl, he adopted the latter's Texcocan-Aculhuan perspective, dwelling endlessly on the deeds of Texcocan rulers. Echeverría y Veytia's incomplete history of ancient Mexico, for example, concludes with a eulogy of the philosopher-king Nezahualcoyotl.

For all practical purposes, Alva Ixtlilxochitl and Echeverría y Veytia inhabited identical cultural and historiographical worlds, and their lives challenge attempts to draw radical distinctions between the "Indian" and "Creole" populations of Mesoamerica. Both enjoyed close links with the Creole-clerical establishment, both supported the thesis that St. Thomas the Apostle visited Mexico, both were significant players in the spread of the Creole cult of Our Lady of Guadalupe, and, finally, both saw Mesoamerican history as having developed largely in isolation from the Old World.

Along with the writings of Alva Ixtlilxochitl, Echeverría y Veytia also used the works in Nahuatl of other sixteenth-century Amerindian historians, including those by the Tlaxcalan Diego Muñoz Camargo (ca. 1529–1599), whose account of the arrival of the Olmecs, Xicalanca, and Zapotecs on the Gulf coast Echeverría y Veytia repeated.[69] It is therefore plausible to argue that Echeverría y Veytia sought to create a single narrative that would integrate the numerous, sometimes contradictory, histories offered by Amerindian historians of the sixteenth and early seventeenth centuries, such as Alva Ixtlilxochitl, Muñoz Camargo, Fernando Alvarado Tezozomoc (Mexica) (fl. 1598), and Francisco de San Antón Muñón Chimalpain Cuauhtlehuanitzin (Chalcan).[70]

Giovanni Francesco Gemelli Careri

Echeverría y Veytia contended that the untrained eye could not easily distinguish between reliable sources and spurious ones. Through an analysis of the way Echeverría y Veytia dealt with a peculiar set of colonial indigenous documents, namely, calendrical wheels, I summarize his critical techniques and show that they ultimately prompted him to elaborate an epistemological critique of the value of travelers' testimony.

The understanding of Mesoamerican calendars and chronologies became something of an obsession with Echeverría y Veytia, consuming most of his scholarly energies. Much, of course, rode on the deciphering of Mesoamerican calendrical mechanisms, including the possibility of settling scholarly disputes over the dating of crucial events in biblical history. The translation of indigenous memories into European historiographical models of linear narrative was also at the mercy of calendrical interpretation. Be that as it may, when confronted with a multiplicity of contradictory accounts of Mesoamerican chronology by European witnesses, Echeverría y Veytia fell back on seven calendrical wheels that he found in Boturini's impounded collection, which allowed Echeverría y Veytia to dismiss all previous interpretations, including Boturini's.

When Echeverría y Veytia wrote, there were many conflicting interpretations of the order of the calendrical signs of the years in a 52-year cycle (four that each repeated thirteen times), of the months in an annual cycle (eighteen signs), and of the days in a 365-day cycle (twenty signs, organized in "weekly" series of thirteen). According to Echeverría y Veytia, the origin of this multiplicity of conflicting accounts stemmed from the European attempt to translate the circular indigenous presentation of calendrical signs into a linear series. Echeverría y Veytia used wheel number four of his collection of seven to prove this point (Plate 3). The outer circle represented a 52-year cycle, the native equivalent of a European century; the inner circle stood for a yearly cycle of eighteen months. Aside from the position of the head of the snake surrounding the wheel, there was no obvious way of determining the beginning and the end of either circle.[71] Europeans had chosen the first element of their linear series at random, creating a bewildering variety of interpretations.

Echeverría y Veytia deployed the wheels, clearly of colonial provenance, to unlock the mysteries of Mesoamerican calendrics. He used wheel number five, with its Spanish glosses and paintings in European style, to determine the order of the eighteen months (Plate 4). The wheel moved clockwise (which no precolonial wheel would have done) from "Atemoztli" to five "intercalary" days used to round off the 365-day annual cycle (located in the wheel in an additional nineteenth space that would have never appeared in precolonial wheels). Echeverría y Veytia did not, to be sure, follow the document blindly. A reasoned analysis of the etymology of the names of the months revealed that the wheel offered the only plausible correct order, given the agricultural and weather phenomena the names signified.[72]

Echeverría y Veytia used the wheels to undermine Boturini's *Ciclografía*, a thesis the Italian had first sketched in the *Idea*. Boturini argued that each Mesoamerican century had four possible leading year symbols (Flint, House, Rabbit, and Cane), and that the order of the years therefore differed every century within the larger cycle of 208 years. For Echeverría y Veytia, this led to intolerable chaos in the interpretation of chronological records, and he argued that the natives had always used the same leading sign. The wheels, he maintained, supported his interpretation.

The snake biting its tail in wheel number four (Plate 3) symbolized the eternal continuity of the series of years in a Mesoamerican "century," Echeverría y Veytia contended.[73] It also indicated, however, that Echeverría y Veytia's reasoned hypothesis of a hierarchical succession of yearly signs from Flint (Fire) to House (Earth) to Rabbit (Air) to Cane (Water) was wrong, for the head of snake was over the element Air (Rabbit), not over Fire (Flint).[74] Echeverría y Veytia solved the apparent contradiction by postulating that the Mexica and Toltec had different leading years: the original Toltec calendar began in Flint, but the Mexica calendar did so in Rabbit, to commemorate the year in which they had arrived in central Mexico.[75] Echeverría y Veytia used wheel number one (Plate 5) to demonstrate that the dates of the historical events recorded in the upper section of the wheel (describing the southbound path of migrations of the Mexica) would have been different had natives used a different leading year symbol every 52-year cycle.[76]

Finally, Echeverría y Veytia used wheel number six (Plate 6) to argue against Boturini's ordering of the series of days in a month. The Italian maintained that Crocodile (*cipactli*) was the leading day of every month.

Echeverría y Veytia, however, used the wheel to demonstrate that there was no possible way of determining the initial element of the series, and that the character of the year ultimately determined the leading sign of each month.

Echeverría y Veytia did not blindly follow the evidence of the wheels; after all, he knew that these were colonial sources, which might be spurious. Ultimately, most of his interpretation of Mesoamerican calendrical systems rested on indirect evidence; namely, etymological analyses of indigenous names and reasoned hypotheses. For example, he argued that the leading sign of the days of the month changed according to the nature of the leading sign of the year (Flint, House, Rabbit, Cane) because the natives had an ascending hierarchical view of the four elements.[77] Such guarded reliance on documentary sources forced him to confront a wheel published in the seventeenth century by the Italian traveler Giovanni Francesco Gemelli Careri.

Gemelli Careri visited Mexico in the late seventeenth century as the last leg of a trip that also took him to Siam, China, and Japan. To the account of his travels through New Spain, he appended a series of illustrations from indigenous codices that the Creole polymath Sigüenza y Góngora had given him. It is very difficult to know whether Gemelli Careri's interpretations accurately reflect the antiquarian knowledge available in the colonies. It seems that he both distorted and accurately conveyed information. In any case, he served as a conduit to transmit to European audiences a seventeenth-century Creole historiographical tradition that, beginning with Torquemada, had cast the Mexica as a sort of inverted mirror image of the Hebrews. According to this tradition, the Aztecs and Hebrews were both peoples who had migrated in search of a Promised Land. The latter, however, had worshipped the true God whereas the former, led by Satan, had practiced ritual cannibalism and mimicked many of the rituals of the Catholic Church. Gemelli Careri offered a copy of a map of the migrations of the seven Mexica families (Fig. 2.10) and introduced cabalistic analysis of the names of the ten Mexica monarchs, from "Acamapichtli" to "Quauhtimoc" (Cuauhtemoc) to demonstrate that their names added up to 666, the number of the Beast in the Apocalypse. He also introduced a hydrographic map of the Central Valley of Mexico whose rivers and lakes resembled the shape of the beast, including its horns, belly, and claws (Fig. 4.2b). He obtained all these documents in Mexico. But even as Gemelli Careri accurately relayed this Creole historiographical tradition, he also introduced changes in the interpretation of some illustrations he received from colonial savants. For example, he mistakenly presented a series of paintings of Texcocan monarchs that had belonged to Alva Ixtlilxochitl

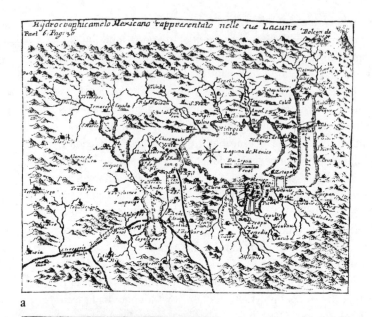

Hydrocvaphicamelo Mexicano rappresentato nelle sue Lacune

a

b

FIGURE 4.2. (a) Rivers and lakes reproduce the shape of the beast in Revelation 13, including its horns, belly, and claws, in this early seventeenth-century hydrographic map of the Central Valley of Mexico, demonstrating that even the Mexican landscape was shaped by the devil. From Giovanni Francesco Gemelli Careri, *Giro del mondo* (Naples, 1699–1700). Courtesy of the John Carter Brown Library, Brown University, Providence, R.I. (b) A portrait of the Texcocan philosopher-king Nezahualcoyotl, that Gemelli Careri wrongly identified as Moctezuma Xocoyoltzin (r. 1502–20 in the Codex Mendoza), citing Carlos de Sigüenza y Góngora as his source. This immediately aroused suspicion about his reliability, because the Mexican Creole polymath would never have made such a mistake.

FIGURE 4.3. Like the wheel shown in Plate 3, this calendrical wheel represents a 52-year cycle and an 18-month annual cycle. Unlike the wheel in Plate 3, however, this wheel gives the phases of the moon in its inner circle, leading Boturini to claim that the 20-day Mesoamerican month was necessarily connected to the cycles of the moon. This wheel also has the serpent moving counterclockwise, but the order of the months is different. Antonio de León y Gama used the two wheels to call attention to the flaws in Francisco Clavijero's *Historia antigua de México*. From Giovanni Francesco Gemelli Careri, *Giro del mondo* (Naples, 1699–1700). Courtesy of the John Carter Brown Library, Brown University, Providence, R.I.

as portraits of Mexica rulers (Fig. 4.1b). It was in this context that Echeverría y Veytia subjected to scrutiny the Italian traveler's interpretation of a calendrical wheel (Fig. 4.3).[78]

Gemelli Careri's wheel explicitly contradicted Echeverría y Veytia's ordering of the eighteen Mexican months. Boturini had accepted Gemelli Careri's calendar wheel, which included representations of lunar phases, along with the signs of the months, but had criticized most of Gemelli Careri's interpretations as simple-minded and misleading. Like Boturini, Echeverría y Veytia refused to believe that Gemelli Careri accurately conveyed Sigüenza's insights into Mesoamerican calendrics. The wheel sported numbers in the inner circle that ordered the months clockwise beginning with Tlacaxipehualixtli (or Cohuailhuitl in Tlaxcalan versions), not Atemoztli, the leading month of the year, according to Echeverría y Veytia.[79] Echeverría y Veytia dismissed this ordering as spurious, a late-colonial concoction and concluded that Gemelli Careri had altered Sigüenza's insights by uncritically following glosses introduced into the document by ignorant scribes.[80]

According to Echeverría y Veytia, Gemelli Careri's shortcomings had little to do with personal flaws and everything to do with his status as traveler. Echeverría y Veytia used Gemelli Careri to highlight the epistemological limitations of foreign travelers. The Italian, he argued, had been doubly removed from the sources, given his limited knowledge of both Spanish and Nahuatl. Equally problematic, he thought, was the fact that he had visited Mexico only briefly.[81]

Echeverría y Veytia fleshed out the emerging discourse of patriotic epistemology first outlined by Eguiara y Eguren. His skeptical attitude toward seventeenth- and eighteenth-century Amerindian sources contrasts sharply, however, with his uncritical embrace of the historiography of sixteenth-century Amerindian historians, culminating in the writings of Alva Ixtlilxochitl. Eighteenth-century Creole antiquarians saw themselves as heirs to the historiographical tradition inaugurated by these latinized upper-class Amerindian scholars of the sixteenth century. Eguiara y Eguren and Echeverría y Veytia both emphasize the crucial role played by learned interpreters acquainted with the extinct languages and historical traditions of the indigenous populations and highlight the epistemological shortcoming of foreign observers.

This late-eighteenth-century patriotic epistemology was not, however, exclusively Creole. The *Tardes americanas* of José Joaquín Granados y Gálvez, a Franciscan from Málaga and would-be bishop of the northern dioceses of New Spain in Sonora and Durango, proves that this discourse was embraced, and even formulated, by acculturated Peninsulars.

José Joaquín Granados y Gálvez

José Joaquín Granados y Gálvez's *Tardes americanas: Gobierno gentil y catolico . . . noticia de toda la historia indiana . . . desde la entrada de la gran nacion tulteca . . . hasta los presentes tiempos* (1778) has failed to attract the attention of scholars largely because it is not easily characterized. Its author was related to José de Gálvez, minister of the Indies and the primary enacter of the Bourbon reforms that sought to "reconquer" the New World from corrupt Creoles and power-hungry Jesuits, and the book is dedicated to him. Paradoxically, however, *Tardes americanas* is a staunch defense of the Creole mind and piety. In it, Granados y Gálvez predictably sought to justify the right of the crown to raise taxes and to transform Creole clerical culture. Yet he also derided those who portrayed Creoles as corrupt and Amerindians as inherently stupid. Making use of typical Creole patriotic tropes, Granados y Gálvez reviewed the many saintly clerical figures who, whether alive or dead, had performed miracles. He also described the vast colonial market in relics of saintly Creoles, which included nails, hair, fingers, noses, and earlobes. As part of his review of this cast of saintly figures, Granados y Gálvez defended the right of Creoles to claim Mexico as the birthplace of Felipe de Jesús (1572–1597), murdered in Japan along with other Franciscans and canonized by the Church. By the same token, Granados y Gálvez highlighted the patriotic significance of the miracle of Our Lady of Guadalupe and exalted the grandeur of the precolonial Mesoamerican past.

Clearly a study of this paradoxical figure is long overdue. My intention here is, however, to focus on the epistemology of *Tardes americanas*, which has two sections, one devoted to precolonial history and the other to the colonial past. Granados y Gálvez uses a fictional dialogue between a Spaniard and an Indian to convey his complex message. Amerindian and Spaniard, in turns, take skeptical positions as they seek to persuade each other. Significantly, the Spaniard repeatedly declares himself unable to write the history of America and its peoples, largely because of the many contradictory accounts he has encountered or because he cannot understand and interpret Mesoamerican scripts.[82] The Amerindian, on the other hand, represents himself as having mastered, not only the writings of Alva Ixtlilxochitl, Alvarado Tezozomoc, Chimalpain Cuauhtlehuanitzin, and other sixteenth-century native interpreters of Mesoamerican paintings, but the ancient books themselves as well.[83] After teaching the Spaniard how to interpret calendrical wheels and to read scenes and dates in indigenous annals, the Amerindian sets out to convince the Spaniard that the documents prove the greatness of the Mesoamerican past (Fig. 4.4).

The Amerindian presents Mesoamerican civilizations as more pious, politically sophisticated, and morally upright than those of classical Rome and Greece. The skeptical Spaniard, however, argues that such literary portrayals find no support in the extant material remains. According to the Spaniard, the few puny ruins of Mexico prove that the Indian's claims are exaggerations. The slothful, miserable, and ignorant nature of contemporary

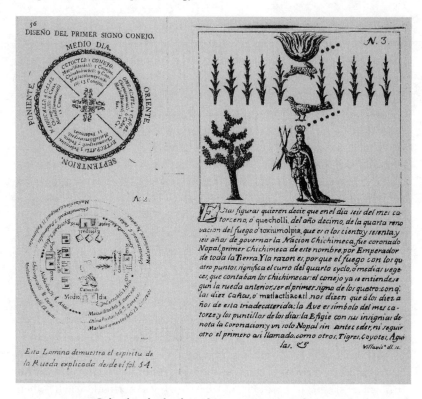

FIGURE 4.4. Calendrical wheels and an entry in an indigenous document allegedly recounting the coronation of Lord Nopal in the year 10 Rabbit, day 6 of the month Quecholli in the fourth Chichimec century (represented by the "bundle" or "bonfire" above). From José Joaquín Granados y Gálvez, *Tardes americanas: Gobierno gentil y catolico* . . . (México, 1778). Granados y Gálvez sought to use these made-up images to show that the Mesoamerican peoples had reliable documentation preserved by accurate systems of writing and chronology.

Amerindians indicates that the thesis of past Amerindian grandeur is merely an idyllic invention.[84] The Indian, as expected, lashes out against the prevalent skepticism of the age and claims that the lack of material evidence cannot be used to deny the truthfulness of any historical written tradition.[85] As for using wretched contemporary natives as negative evidence, the Indian, again as expected, insists that the behavior of living commoners cannot be used to judge the historicity of the hierarchical polities of the past. Over and over, the Amerindian decries the process by which indigenous elites were eliminated, particularly by the weakening or virtual abolition of the sixteenth-century

Amerindian colleges, where a latinized Indo-Christian culture had once flourished.[86]

The Amerindian repeatedly confronts the skeptical Spaniard with a dual scale of credibility, distinguishing between the knowledge of upper-class Native Americans and that of commoners. The Spaniard, for example, doubts whether the Amerindians knew much about geology and meteorology (including an understanding of the workings of volcanoes, subterranean waters, earthquakes, thunder, and lightning). Insisting that his ancestors rivaled classical Greece in astronomy, mathematics, rhetoric, music, theater, and other areas of knowledge, the Amerindian replies that what the Spaniard fails to realize is that the Mesoamerican priestly class kept most of their scientific and religious insights hidden from the masses. The Spaniard mistakenly judges ancient civilizations by the superstitious behavior of contemporary Amerindian plebeians.[87]

The faith of Granados y Gálvez's Amerindian in the written testimony of the ancient elites at times demanded that readers suspend their critical faculties. The Spaniard, for example, challenges the credibility of the dynastic genealogies presented by the Amerindian. How is one to believe that rulers could have lived and governed for 160 years, as the Amerindian claims? The Amerindian counters that physical deterioration triggered by the many changes brought about by colonization (changes in diet, loss of status, alcoholism, and so forth) has considerably shortened the Amerindian life span from hundreds of years to mere decades.[88]

The views that he put in the mouth of the Amerindian show that for Granados y Gálvez there was no clear demarcation between Creoles and upperclass Amerindians. The Indian, for example, takes Creoles to task for failing to find inspiration in the ancient Amerindian rulers, who were sages in the art of statecraft, and he calls on Creoles to copy them, pointing out that these rulers were their own ancestors.[89] Remarkably, the Amerindian regards the continuity between Creoles and the ancient Mesoamerican ruling class as not merely cultural but racial as well. In this Granados y Gálvez was not alone. Doris Ladd has shown that numerous Spanish and Creole grandees in Mexico boasted of their mestizo heritage. The counts of Moctezuma, Javier, and Guara and the duke of Granada in Spain and titled grandees of New Spain such as the Aguayo, Alamo, Jaral, Miravalle, Salinas, Salvatierra, Santa Rosa, Santiago, Valle Oploca, and Valle de Orizaba all claimed descent from precolonial Aztec rulers. The family palace of the counts of Santiago (Calimaya), a block off the Zócalo in Mexico City, used a great precolonial feathered-serpent head as a cornerstone.[90] The historiographical maneuvers that claimed both cultural and racial continuities between the precolonial ruling class and contemporary leading Creole families allowed Granados y Gálvez to cast the Indian, not the Spaniard, as the defender of the colonial order. If he at one point berates the Spaniard for the useless brutality of the Conquest, the Amerindian also consistently praised the justice and prudence of the Spanish crown in the colonies.[91]

Although Granados y Gálvez seems to have had access to Boturini's impounded collection, the pages on Mesoamerican history in *Tardes americanas* are, in fact, derivative, summaries of Boturini's *Idea* and Torquemada's *Monarchía indiana*. Granados y Gálvez's only original contribution was to add a few pages on the history of the Tarascan peoples, which he probably collected during his years of parish work in the dioceses of Michoacan. But for all his lack of originality, Granados y Gálvez, a peninsular bishop himself, ultimately helped hammer out the discourse of patriotic epistemology. Along with his contemporaries Echeverría y Veytia and Eguiara y Eguren, he called into question the epistemological value of foreign observers and defended the credibility of the Amerindian and Creole elites. The three scholars maintained that only learned Amerindians and Creoles who had access to the ancient priestly interpretations of ancient Mexican hieroglyphs could be trusted. Granados y Gálvez's scholarship and that of Francisco Antonio de Lorenzana (1722–1804), archbishop of Mexico, are helpful reminders that, rather than a Creole ideology, patriotic epistemology was a clerical discourse, hammered out by both peninsular and Spanish American Church intellectuals. As will become clearer below, Lorenzana mobilized the considerable resources of his archbishopric to collect, study, and print Amerindian sources. Although he never articulated his own epistemological principles conceptually, Lorenzana, in practice, acted in ways similar to those espoused by Granados y Gálvez. In the next section, we shall see how this discourse of patriotic epistemology developed outside Mexico in the Papal States.

Creole Jesuits in Exile

Hundreds of Jesuits ended up in exile in the Papal States after the Bourbons expelled them from all Spanish territories in 1767 on the advice of such reformers as José de Gálvez, Granados y Gálvez's relative. The expulsion was part of a larger Bourbon effort to "reconquer" the colonies by reconfiguring the geopolitical, economic, and cultural landscape of America. The reforms sought to rein in the hitherto unchecked military and economic presence of

European rivals, who through smuggling, piracy, raids, and direct colonization had pushed Spain aside in the New World. The reforms also sought to
transform the loosely autonomous "kingdoms" of the Creoles into politically
and economically dependent modern colonies. Finally, the reforms were
part of a larger European trend by which fledgling nation-states sought to
curtail the transnational, corporate power of the religious orders. The Jesuits
were among the first casualties of these new policies. Hundreds of Creole
Jesuits soon found themselves impoverished and banished from their homelands and families. It was in this context of hardships that many of them came
across the writings of Buffon, de Pauw, the abbé Raynal, and Robertson.[92]

The extent and depth of the Jesuit Creole reaction to these northern
European writings is still poorly understood. Ever since Antonello Gerbi described the Jesuit reaction as part of a larger "dispute over the New World,"
scholars have concentrated on how the exiled Jesuits responded to European
characterizations of the nature and peoples of the New World. But, as we
have seen, the writings of Buffon, de Pauw, Raynal, and Robertson were not
only diatribes against tropical America, but also methodological and epistemological proposals. Besides writing natural and civil histories that denied
that America was humid and emasculating, the Jesuits also addressed the
methodologies of the Europeans and offered powerful and persuasive critiques of European knowledge of the New World. To do so, they drew on the
discourse of patriotic epistemology outlined above. In this section, I study the
writings of a handful of Creole Jesuits who participated in the debate.

Francisco Xavier Clavijero

Before his exile, Francisco Clavijero, born in Veracruz to Spanish and
Creole parents, was a leader of curricular reform in the Jesuit province of
Mexico, advocating the introduction of types of experimental physics that did
not challenge Aristotelian metaphysics, the ultimate foundation of the
Catholic Reformation theology and natural law.[93] After its publication in
Italian between 1780 and 1781, Clavijero's *Historia antigua de México* was im-
mediately translated into English and German and reviewed widely in
European journals, and modern historians such as David Brading, Anthony
Pagden, Charles Ronan, Benjamin Keen, Fernando Cervantes, and Enrique
Florescano have all applied their critical skills to Clavijero's writings.[94] It is,
however, difficult to understand why Clavijero's history became so popular,
for, as Ronan has argued, the Mexican Jesuit was derivative and even deceptive. Like Granados y Gálvez, Clavijero made misleading statements to the

effect that he had consulted ancient Mesoamerican texts and sixteenth-century Native American historians. Exile limited Clavijero's research only to published works, including those by Boturini, Eguiara y Eguren, Francisco Hernández, Samuel Purchas, and, especially, Torquemada, whose baroque *Monarchía indiana* (1615) Clavijero rewrote in terms enlightened eighteenth-century European audiences could understand.[95] Clavijero could have studied unpublished Mesoamerican codices stored in Italian libraries but did not. Thus, for example, although the so-called Codex Cospi, a Mesoamerican ritual calendar, was housed in the public library of Bologna, where Clavijero lived, he seems to have consulted it only perfunctorily. Clavijero, it is clear, did not uncover any new primary sources, but rather produced new interpretations of the Mesoamerican past.

Brading and Cervantes have maintained that Clavijero ended the Franciscan interpretative stranglehold on Creole historiography, which for two centuries had given unchecked agency to the devil in Mesoamerican history. Pagden has argued that Clavijero's originality lay in his creative use of the work of Montesquieu. According to Pagden, Clavijero sought to present Mesoamerican civilizations as long-enduring and evolving in splendid isolation, civilizations capable of creating writing systems, architectural styles, calendars, and currencies that, although different from those of the Old World, were equally complex and equally valuable.[96] Be that as it may, methodologically speaking Clavijero's ancient history belonged in the tradition of patriotic epistemology.

Clavijero's history consists of a preface on sources, ten books on precolonial history and the Conquest, and a separate volume of "dissertations." Book 1 is a treatise on the boundaries of the Aztec empire and on the fauna and flora the Europeans most likely encountered upon arrival. Book 2 briefly discusses the cycles of civilizations in Mesoamerica, beginning with the Toltecs and the Chichimecs led by Xolotl and culminating with the migration south of the Mexica. Book 3 describes the complex dynastic histories of the ethnically contested space of the Valley of Mexico after the arrival of the Mexica, including the rise and fall of the Tepaneca of Azcapotzalco. Book 4 is primarily devoted to the ancestors of Alva Ixtlilxochitl, that is, to the efflorescence of the Aculhua of Texcoco under the leadership of the philosopher-kings Nezahualcoyotl and his son Nezahualpilli. Book 5 describes the consolidation of the Mexica as the dominant ethnic group in the land under the leadership of Moctezuma Ilhuicamina (r. 1440–69 in the Codex Mendoza), the ninth "king" of the Mexica. Building on Torquemada's study of Mexica religion, book 6 is a lengthy encyclopedic description of Mexica rituals, deities, and religious institutions. In equally encyclopedic fashion, book 7 covers the more secular dimensions of Mexica culture, that is, the legal, political and economic aspects, poetry, rhetoric, games, music, language, writing, and calendrics. Books 8 through 10 deal with the Conquest and the many battles that culminated in the fall of Tenochtitlan and the capture of Cuauhtemoc (r. 1520–24), the last Mexica monarch. The multivolume project concludes with nine "dissertations," essays purporting to correct errors in the histories of Buffon, de Pauw, Raynal, and Robertson, which for the most part rework material already covered in the previous volumes thematically and for polemical purposes.

Such encyclopedic study of Mexica history and culture was remarkable for its refusal to indulge in speculation. Whereas Echeverría y Veytia's narrative begins in 1797 B.C.E. with the Chichimecs at Huehuetlapallan, Clavijero's begins around 500 C.E., with the Toltecs, paying almost no attention to the Giants, Olmecs, and Xicalanca that had captured the attention of Boturini and Echeverría y Veytia. Clavijero's history also lacks the standard Creole learned reconstruction of St. Thomas's visit to the New World. Clavijero's surveys of Mexica religion and culture fall under the rubric of natural history and lack any broader interpretative framework. It is only in the "dissertations" that Clavijero advances interpretations and seeks to impose meaning on his material. The dissertation on Mexican religion, for example, argues that the Mexica were more pious than ancient Romans and Greeks. The dissertation on human origins in the New World postulates hypothetical land bridges with Africa to explain how tropical fauna and flora might have reached America and speculates that since widely dispersed Amerindian peoples preserved similar historical recollections of great floods, arks, Noah-like figures, and lengthy migrations, their common origin might have been postdiluvian. Clavijero reasoned that inasmuch as pre-Columbian Amerindians had been ignorant of iron smelting and cattle domestication, they must have arrived in the New World right after the Flood. Had these technologies been available to them when they left Central Asia, they would have brought them along, given their obvious utility. But for all the use of hypothetical reconstructions, Clavijero remained cautious, guarding against any "systems," or grandiose philosophical interpretations.

Clavijero's constant refusal to speculate was part of his larger critique of the philosophical method of Buffon, de Pauw, Raynal, and Robertson. In the dissertations, Clavijero demonstrates the countless tensions and contradictions incurred by these northern European authors, who, Clavijero argued, had been more interested in building systems than in cataloguing facts. In his earlier writings and particularly in his approach to reforming philosophy in New Spain, Clavijero had already demonstrated a predilection for the eclecticism and empiricism of Francis Bacon.[97] The encounter with the genre of philosophical histories of America only deepened his commitment to a variety of Baconianism.

Clavijero's history reveals his painstaking efforts to get the "facts" right. For example, he spent considerable effort determining the original architectural appearance of the Great Temple of Tenochtitlan. When Clavijero set out to write his history, there were two iconographic traditions available to represent the temple. The first was introduced by Giovanni Battista Ramusio in Venice in 1550 to go with the written account of the temple by the Anonymous Conquistador (Fig. 4.5a). The illustration surfaced one hundred years later in Kircher's influential *Oedipus aegyptiacus* (Fig. 4.5b). The second tradition was based on a 1580 image of a generic Mesoamerican temple by the Franciscan Diego Valadés (b. 1533) and appeared in compilations of travel accounts such as Bernard Picart's *Cérémonies et coutumes religieuses des peuples idolâtres* (Amsterdam, 1723–28) and A.-F. Prévost's *Histoire générale des voyages* (Paris, 1746–61). The popularity of this tradition was such that the illustration was even reproduced in the 1770 Mexican edition of Cortés's *Cartas de relación* by the archbishop of Mexico, Lorenzana (Fig. 4.6). Based on detailed readings of available eyewitness accounts and careful calculations, Clavijero partially rejected the first tradition and completely rejected the second one. Clavijero worked out his own hypothetical reconstruction and offered his own illustration of the temple (Fig. 4.5c).[98]

Clavijero deployed a similar careful reading of sources to reconstruct many other aspects of Mexica precolonial society. Although he did not have access to any of the documents in the collections of Sigüenza and Boturini, Clavijero did have access to some published indigenous sources. In the seventeenth century, for example, Samuel Purchas and Melchisédec Thévenot had edited a modified version of the so-called Codex Mendoza, and Clavijero knew it. Although Clavijero believed that the historical section of the Codex contained many inaccuracies and reflected only one of many alternate versions of Mexica migrations and dynastic genealogies (something Boturini had already pointed out), he nevertheless used sections of the codex to reconstruct the legal and educational institutions of the Mexica.[99] More impressive, however, was Clavijero's use of another indigenous codex, the *Matrícula de tributos*, a sixteenth-century tributary roll of similar provenance to the Codex Mendoza. Made available in 1770 by Lorenzana, this Mexica logographic and ideographic text was a major breakthrough in European his-

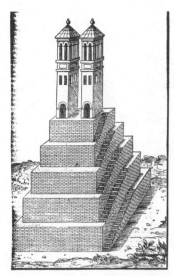

a

b

c

FIGURE 4.5. In *Delle navigationi et viaggi* . . . (Venice, 1556), Giovanni Battista Ramusio depicted the great temple of Tenochtitlan, (a). Courtesy of the Edward Ayer Collection, Newberry Library, Chicago. This portrayal resurfaced as (b) in Athanasius Kircher, *Oedipus aegyptiacus* . . . (Rome, 1652–54). Francisco Clavijero subjected these illustrations to a critical analysis through a detailed parallel reading of written accounts by witnesses. Although he concluded that this iconographic tradition was the most accurate, he came up with his own version of the temple, (c), in his *Storia antica del Messico* (Cesena, 1780–81). Courtesy of the Department of Rare Books and Special Collections, Princeton University Library.

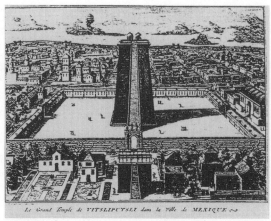

a

b

c

FIGURE 4.6. The temple of Tenochtitlan as depicted in (a) Bernard Picart, *Cérémonies et coutumes religieuses des peuples idolâtres* (Amsterdam, 1723–28), and (b) Francisco Antonio de Lorenzana, in Hernán Cortés, *Historia de Nueva-España . . .* (Mexico, 1770). Courtesy of the John Carter Brown Library, Brown University, Providence, R.I. Clavijero dismissed this iconographic tradition and argued that it had originated in a generic image of a temple, (c), from Diego Valadés, *Rhetorica Christiana* (Perugia, 1579).

toriography on Mesoamerica, because for the first time a document in indigenous script was published in its entirety with only relatively minor distortions (Lorenzana added putti here and there) (Plates 7 and 8). Clavijero made extensive and creative use of this source to map the geographical boundaries of the Aztec empire. To do so, he first interpreted the meaning of the many symbols that stood for names of towns, a major feat, given the fact that Lorenzana's edition failed to include many of the Nahuatl glosses in Latin script that in the original spelled out the names (Fig. 4.7a). Such careful deciphering allowed Clavijero to reconstruct the boundaries of the Aztec polity, formulate a natural history of precolonial Mexico, and locate the many ethnic "kingdoms" that had existed in central Mexico upon the European arrival (Fig. 4.7b).[100]

Clavijero's creative analysis of available European and indigenous published sources was done with a sharp critical eye that deployed traditional humanist techniques of reading. He consistently privileged eyewitnesses over secondhand reporting, even if the chronicler was as learned as José de Acosta. Thus, in books 8 through 10, Clavijero dismissed Antonio de Solis's narrative of the Conquest as secondhand, biased speculation and privileged Cortés's letters to Charles V.[101] He repeatedly voiced skepticism about the accuracy of the reports of Bernal Díaz del Castillo, largely because the Spanish soldier had written his recollections at an advanced age, years after the actual events had taken place. Clavijero also weighed the biases and motivations of eyewitnesses. He dismissed some of Díaz del Castillo's reports of battles on the grounds that Díaz del Castillo had held grudges against Cortés, which colored his narrative.[102] By the same token, Clavijero gave little credence to Gonzalo Fernández de Oviedo's ethnographic descriptions on the grounds that Oviedo simply hated the natives.[103] Clavijero considered most accounts by sixteenth-century Spanish witnesses reliable because they were numerous, did not contradict one another, and were "public," that is, addressed to social superiors who would have not tolerated lies or deception. Cortés's letters, for example, were trustworthy because the emperor Charles V, to whom they were addressed, would have punished Cortés had they not been.[104] When eyewitness accounts were not available, Clavijero privileged the testimony of those chroniclers who were closer in time to the event and who were most learned.[105]

As with accounts of witnesses, Clavijero subjected narratives of past ages to rigorous critical standards (Fig. 4.8). His treatment of Torquemada typifies Clavijero's approach to historical sources. In less than two pages devoted to a description of the fall of the Toltecs and the arrival of the Chichimecs in

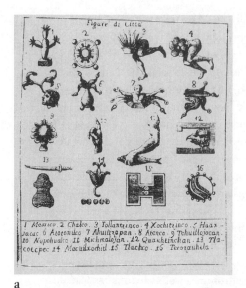

FIGURE 4.7. Images from Clavijero's *Storia antica del Messico* showing him to have been a careful reader of published Amerindian codices: (a) logographic signs for the names of Mesoamerican towns that Clavijero took from the *Matrícula de tributos* and Purchas's edition of the Codex Mendoza; (b) map of the extension of the various Mesoamerican polities and empires on the eve of the European conquest drawn by Clavijero using the *Matrícula de tributos*. Courtesy of the Department of Rare Books and Special Collections, Princeton University Library.

central Mexico, for example, Clavijero found at least five major contradictions or errors in Torquemada's narrative. Having found in Toltec annals a monstrous-looking figure embracing a group of Toltec dancers, Torquemada concluded that the devil had been responsible for the ruin of the Toltecs. Clavijero argued that the figure was simply an allegory of the famines and epidemics that had destroyed the Toltecs. Torquemada presented the Chichimec invaders led by Xolotl as cave dwellers but also offered a description of the Chichimec "city" of Amaquemecan. Clavijero zeroed in on the logical impossibility of presenting the Chichimecs as both urban folk and nomadic cave dwellers. Torquemada argued that the name "Chichimec" derived from *techichimani*, a creature that sucks animals' blood. Clavijero considered this an unwarranted etymology and claimed that the name derived from the group's place of origin, Chichiman. Torquemada maintained that a million Chichimecs had made up Xolotl's invading army. Such a figure, Clavijero argued, was not only absurd from the perspective of the logistics involved but also impossible given the amount of land that it would have taken to sustain a million roaming Chichimec hunters. Finally, Torquemada asserted that the Chichimecs had arrived eleven years after the fall of Tollan. Clavijero maintained that this chronology was preposterous, and that at least a century must have intervened, because the Chichimecs found only ruins when they first arrived in the lands formerly dominated by the Toltecs.[106] For page after page, Clavijero made the inconsistencies and contradictions in Torquemada explicit, finding Torquemada gullible and credulous.[107] It is clear that Clavijero was as astute a reader as de Pauw. Like the northern European authors whose accounts they were contesting, patriotic epistemologists such as Clavijero also drew a clear distinction between "internal" and "external" forms of evidence. Clavijero dismissed Torquemada largely using the new European art of reading that de Pauw had helped to popularize.

Clavijero extended this critical rigor to the analysis of indigenous sources. Precolonial records were trustworthy because they were abundant, he argued. The Amerindians had been familiar with many systems of recordkeeping, including hieroglyphs and quipu-like devices, as well as songs and speeches. The sources were also reliable because the Amerindian rulers had instituted laws to punish lying scribes.[108] Clavijero was often willing to bend over backward to believe preternatural accounts in precolonial narratives, such as descriptions of supernatural events, including the resurrection of an Amerindian princess, and signs predicting the arrival of the Spaniards.[109] But he nevertheless detected biases and contradictions in indigenous accounts of the Conquest.[110] He criticized Boturini, for example, not only for his reliance

lacronologia delle pitture antiche. Non resta dunque altro ri-
piego, se non quello di dire, che quella celebre capitale si fon-
dò nel 1325. dell'era volgare: e questo fu senz'altro il sen-
timento del Dott. Siguenza ; perciocchè Gemelli, il quale non
ebbe in questo soggetto altra istruzione, se non quella, che gli
fu data da quel Letterato messicano, mette tal fondazione nell'
anno 1325. il quale dice, fu, II. Calli, (b) Se prima fu d'un
altro parere, lo cambiò poi accorgendosi, che non s'accorda-
va bene con quel principio certo d'essere stato I. Acatl l'anno 1519.

§. III.

Su la Cronologìa de' Re Messicani.

E' difficile il mettere in chiaro la cronologìa de' Re Messicani a cagione della discordanza degli Autori. Noi ci servi-
remo d'alcuni punti certi per rintracciare gl'incerti. Per dare
ai Lettori qualche idea della varietà delle opinioni basta met-
ter gli occhj su la seguente tavola, nella quale accenniamo
l'anno, in cui secondo l'Acosta, l'Interprete della Raccolta
di Mendoza, ed il Siguenza cominciò a regnare ciascuno dei
Re: (c)

	Acosta	L'interpr.	Siguenza	
Acamapitzin.	1384.	1375.	3. Maggio	1361.
Huitzlihuitl.	1424.	1396.	19. Aprile	1403.
Chimalpopoca.	1427.	1417.	24. Febbr.	1414.
Itzcoatl.	1437.	1427.		1427.
Motezuma I.	1449.	1440.	13. Agosto	1440.
Axajacatl.	1481.	1469.	21. Nov.	1468.
Tizoc.	1477.	1482.	30. Ottobre	1481.
Ahuitzotl.	1492.	1486.	13. Aprile	1486.
Motezuma II.	1503.	1502.	15. Sett.	1502.
				Aco-

(b) Abbjamo altrove accennata l'equivocazione di Gemelli nell'avere scritto:
l'anno 1325. della creazion del Mondo, in vece di scrivere : *dell'era volgare*.
(c) Gli anni messi nella tavola secondo l'interprete della Raccolta di Mendoza son quelli che si leggono nell'edizione di Tedi Purchàs, la quale non
abbiamo potuto trovare.

FIGURE 4.8. A page from Clavijero's *Storia antica del Messico*
demonstrating his careful reading of Indian and European sources on
Amerindian chronologies. Clavijero juxtaposes the dates of ascension of
Mexica rulers according to the Codex Mendoza, Acosta, and Sigüenza y
Góngora in a single table, seeking to show the contradictions among
them. Courtesy of the Department of Rare Books and Special Collections, Princeton University Library.

on overarching philosophical systems but also for his willingness to believe all Amerindian accounts.[111] For the same reason, he criticized Torquemada and even Acosta (whom Clavijero respected most).[112] Clavijero was aware of the politics of ethnicity in central Mexico and how different indigenous groups had manipulated historical memories to suit their own ethnic agendas.[113]

Clavijero's somewhat critical analysis of precolonial and sixteenth-century sources turned into absolute skepticism, however, when it came to later colonial sources. His handling of the *Matrícula de tributos*, the codex Lorenzana made public in 1770, typifies his attitude. Clavijero summarily dismissed the interpretation of the *Matrícula* in the Spanish glosses, which he attributed to the archbishop's aides, and in any case to someone "ignorant of the antiquities and the Mexican language [Nahuatl]." For Clavijero, the danger of the *Matrícula* lay in the fact that the spurious interpretations were validated by the prestige and social standing of the editor, the archbishop of Mexico.[114] Lorenzana said that three Amerindian interpreters had helped him: Carlos de Tapia Zenteno, a parish priest and professor of Nahuatl at the University of Mexico and at the cathedral seminary, who was the author of Nahuatl and Huastec grammars, *Arte novissima de la lengua Mexicana* (1753) and *Noticia de la lengua Huasteca* (1767); Domingo Joseph de la Mota, also a parish priest and a Nahua noble, author of *Mes Fructuoso* (1755); and Luis de Neve y Molina, holder of the chair of Otomí at the cathedral seminary and author of the Otomí grammar-dictionary *Reglas de la orthografía, diccionario, y arte de la idioma Othomí* (1767).[115] In the absence of an explanatory introduction by Lorenzana, however, it is unclear what role these three interpreters (who also appear to have helped Lorenzana clarify indigenous terms for his edition of Cortés's *Cartas de relación*) played in his edition of the *Matrícula*, and especially whether they were responsible for the odd omission of many of the original Nahuatl glosses in Latin script. Lorenzana also kept all of the mistaken original glosses in Spanish, which consistently mistranslated the signs for quantities in the tributary roll (see Plates 7 and 8).[116] Whatever the source of the flaws, later scholars like Clavijero who were familiar with the logographic and ideographic conventions of the Nahua concluded that Lorenzana had been misled by his Amerindian interpreters. Although Clavijero did not elaborate on the reasons for the failure of Nahua interpreters to understand the Nahuatl glosses, later commentators liked to argue that the changes undergone by classical Nahuatl during the colonial period had rendered late-colonial Amerindian interpreters unable to comprehend the language of their ancestors. Clavijero remained skeptical of the value of all late-colonial indigenous documents and advised future historians to be "cautious" when drawing information from "modern paintings." He lashed out at Boturini for having given credit to sources produced by ignorant, credulous modern Amerindians that were "popular among the rabble [*vulgo*] of New Spain."[117]

Considering that most "illustrious ancient [Indian] houses" had been forced into miserable conditions and degraded to the level of the most "infamous plebes,"[118] Clavijero — like Echeverría y Veytia, Eguiara y Eguren, and Granados y Gálvez — had reason to mistrust late-colonial sources. Notwithstanding a campaign by Ramón Diosdado Caballero to stop the publication of Clavijero's history in Spain on the grounds that it was anti-Spanish, Clavijero was no critic of the Spanish colonial regime as such. Although he denounced the conquistadors' crimes, he contended that they had been committed by private individuals, and that Spain ought rather to be judged by the behavior of its public representatives, namely, the officers of the crown, who had quickly stepped in to curb private excesses.[119] For Clavijero, the main error of the colonial system lay in policies that had impoverished the indigenous elites.[120]

Like Granados y Gálvez, Clavijero posited racial continuity between precolonial Amerindian elites and leading contemporary Creole families and regretted that this type of *mestizaje* had taken place only on a limited scale. His illustrations of the genealogical trees of Mexica rulers and of precolonial and colonial rulers sought graphically to convey the message of cultural and racial continuities between precolonial and colonial Creole elites (Fig. 4.9). It is from the perspective of the growing erosion of indigenous social hierarchies that we can understand why Clavijero considered that histories produced by Amerindians in the colonial era, like the testimony of most commoners, were worthless and unreliable.

Not only did Clavijero call into question the testimony of Amerindian commoners, he was also deeply skeptical of writings by foreigners and travelers, who, he said, peppered their books with fables to dazzle and entertain their audiences and generalized on the basis of isolated observations.[121] Clavijero found the testimony of only two foreign authors worth believing: Gemelli Careri's and Boturini's.[122] For Clavijero, the main trouble with foreign observers was their limited knowledge of indigenous languages. Thus, for example, Buffon's estimate of the number of species in the New World was related to the French naturalist's failure to understand native taxonomies. Had Buffon known Nahuatl and, more important, had he spent time in Mexico, he would have realized that species he placed into a single category

a

b

FIGURE 4.9. (a) Moctezuma, the last Mexica emperor, surrounded by the four leading Spanish conquistadors. Clavijero sought in this illustration in his *Storia antica* to show the continuity between the Amerindian and Spanish American rulers of Mexico. Courtesy of the Department of Rare Books and Special Collections, Princeton University Library. (b) A historical tableau of Inca rulers and Spanish viceroys of Peru, from Antonio de Ulloa, *Relación histórica de viage a la America meridional* (Madrid, 1748). Courtesy of the John Carter Brown Library, Brown University, Providence, R.I.

were in fact separate and distinct. Based on facile armchair analogies drawn from the works of Francisco Hernández, the sixteenth-century naturalist sent by Philip II to compile a natural history of America, Clavijero noted, Buffon had reduced the number of species of quadrupeds in Mexico. Unlike Buffon, however, Hernández had spent many years in Mexico and had used the taxonomic categories that the natives themselves had devised.[123]

Clavijero likewise argued that ignorance of native languages was responsible for most of the mistakes made about Mexican writing by foreign authors such as de Pauw, Kircher, and Purchas. To their claims that Mexica script was merely pictographic and childish, Clavijero counterposed the arguments of Valadés, Sahagún, Torquemada, and Acosta, who had lived in America. He concluded that only the testimony of the Franciscan and Jesuit clerics was reliable, because they knew the native language well and had held in their hands far more codices than the few to which the linguistically ignorant de Pauw, Purchas, and Kircher had been exposed.[124]

According to Clavijero, linguistic limitations also bedeviled those who chose to visit the New World instead of speculating at home. For example, Clavijero considered that for all C.-M. de La Condamine's prestige as a scientific traveler, he was not a reliable witness, because he had not spent sufficient time in the Indies and, worse, lacked a working knowledge of Quechua. During his trip to the Andes, La Condamine, like most travelers, had relied on interpreters, and this had led to misrepresentations.[125] Long periods of residence in America and close contact with the natives through mastery of their language were for Clavijero the prerequisites for writing about the New World.

Clavijero's criticism of the value of testimony by travelers and foreign system builders also extended to many Creoles. Clavijero could not deny that many Creoles shared de Pauw's dismal view of the natives as degenerate, effeminate brutes. Place of origin, in and of itself, did not guarantee the reliability of someone's testimony. When it came to assessing the credibility of ethnographic testimonies, Clavijero maintained that the reports of any learned cleric had more value than those of greedy, exploitative colonists.[126] Aware that his ideas were unfashionable, Clavijero deliberately assigned greater credit to the testimony of missionaries than that of lay observers. Learned, otherworldly, disinterested men, the missionaries had assembled valuable testimony about indigenous societies.[127]

The master narrative of clerical-Creole patriotic epistemology is revealed in the way Clavijero formulated and validated historical knowledge. Developing many of the tropes that Eguiara y Eguren, Echeverría y Veytia, and Granados y Gálvez had first articulated, he privileged certain testimonies and excluded others, rejecting the evidence of foreigners, travelers, greedy colonists, and indigenous commoners as untrustworthy but treating that of early colonial native nobles and learned clergy with the greatest respect. This pattern repeated itself in the works of other Jesuits in exile. Juan de Velasco's history of the kingdom of Quito is no exception.

Juan de Velasco

Like Clavijero, Juan de Velasco, who was born in Quito, sought to reformulate the Jesuit curriculum in line with new developments in experimental philosophy. While working toward ordination, Velasco conceived of the project of writing a natural history of the territory within the jurisdiction of the high court (Audiencia) of Quito, the land that Creoles liked to refer to as the "kingdom" of Quito. In exile in Faenza, Velasco was asked by his superiors to finish the history but fell ill. It was only after other Creole Jesuits such as Clavijero had published histories of their "fatherlands," and after the Spanish crown had offered pensions to exiled scholars who produced works to defend the battered honor of Spain, that Velasco finally completed his history. Although Velasco's history was well received by the Royal Academy of History in Madrid, it remained unpublished until the mid nineteenth century.[128]

Velasco modeled his history on Clavijero's. The first volume, delivered in 1788 to the Spanish minister Antonio Porlier, was a collection of polemical essays against Buffon, de Pauw, Robertson, and Raynal, and a natural history of Quito consisting largely of a catalogue of Quechua terms for the local fauna and flora. The second volume consisted of a history of precolonial Quito and of the Spanish Conquest. Velasco departed from Clavijero and in 1789 introduced a third volume with a history of colonial developments up to 1767, the year of the Jesuit expulsion. Like Clavijero, Velasco presented his history as a measured, critical reading of both indigenous and Spanish sources. Velasco found that the extant accounts of the events that led to the Conquest of Peru were contradictory. He therefore sought to present a synthesis by weighing competing testimonies and assessing the credibility of rival accounts.[129] Velasco also turned his attention to the precolonial period, where multiple and conflicting versions vied for attention.

The historiography of precolonial Quito was, to be sure, greatly underdeveloped compared to that of Mexico. The Spaniards had encountered no logograms or pictograms there. Moreover, the European perspective on the history of the Andean peoples had been unduly concentrated on the Inca past — that is, on the deeds of the Cuzco elites. Velasco asserted, however, that the peoples of the northern Andes had invented quipu-like devices, similar to those of the Incas, and that their past and dynastic genealogies had therefore been reliably preserved. Building on manuscripts by Spanish clerics and colonial Amerindian nobles, Velasco sought to endow the region with a venerable history.[130] He maintained that Quito had witnessed four distinct historical periods, each interrupted by the arrival of an invader. The ancient kingdom of Quito, led by the primitive Quitus, had been overthrown by the Cara-Shyri, who, after landing on the Pacific coast, had conquered the highlands around 980 C.E. The more advanced Cara-Shyri (who in each and every respect appeared as lesser copies of the Incas) paved the way for the arrival of the Cuzco-based polity. The Cara-Shyri surrendered in 1487 C.E. to the Incas, but not without first creating blood alliances with the invaders, inaugurating the third era of the kingdom of Quito. The fourth and final era, that of the Conquest, had begun with the capture of the Inca ruler Atahualpa in 1532 by the Spaniards. Velasco argued that the documents available — and therefore the credibility of testimonies — for each one of these four eras was inversely proportional to its historical length: the long-enduring past of the original peoples of Quito was enveloped in a thick fog of fable and myth; that of the Cara-Shyri, although partially recorded in "writing," was also surrounded by confusion; and although the records of the Incas were better preserved, they were dwarfed by Spanish accounts of the Conquest.[131] Velasco therefore spent only a few pages on ancient Quito, two chapters on the Cara-Shyri, a book on the Incas, and almost a volume narrating the Conquest of Peru and the ensuing civil wars between rival Spanish factions.

Evolutionary views of writing and reliability notwithstanding, Velasco did not share the epistemology of northern European philosophical historians. In Velasco's eyes, prolonged residence in the Indies and religious training rendered an observer credible. Velasco harshly criticized outsiders like Buffon, de Pauw, Raynal, and Robertson for having denied that eyewitnesses enjoyed privileged perceptions, as well as for suspecting the testimony of the religious. He cast himself as a moderate, willing to accept even the negative characterizations of some of the animals of America by northern European critics of the continent.[132] Yet, for all his moderation, Velasco chastised the philosophical historians for their love of systems, which blinded them to contrary evidence, for their tendency to generalize from isolated facts, and for their audacity in passing judgment on a continent they had never visited.[133] Like Clavijero, Velasco appended several essays seeking to prove the errors and contradictions of the Europeans' purportedly scientific accounts of America.

Falling back on early modern idioms developed by John Locke, among others, that held that the experience of the marvelous was only relative to the observer, Velasco assembled a catalogue of natural phenomena typical of the kingdom of Quito that in the eyes of Europeans could have been construed as fables.[134] Velasco's natural history sought to dazzle European readers by taking them to task for their exaggerated skepticism, which he considered the mask of a narrow provincialism.[135] It is from this perspective that we need to understand an aspect of Velasco's natural history, not present in Clavijero's, that has puzzled later observers: the apparent contradiction between Velasco's enlightened rhetoric and his "credulity," namely, his constant reference to wonders and monstrosities.[136]

For Velasco, as for Clavijero, the epistemological limitations of outsiders stemmed from their lack of mastery of Amerindian languages. Velasco offered Quechua taxonomies to catalogue the flora and fauna of Quito using the same assumptions that had moved Clavijero to introduce Nahua taxonomies for Mexico, namely, to show that linguistic shortcomings lay behind the tendency of European naturalists to find fewer species in the New World. For all their philosophical training and experimental instruments, travelers like La Condamine and Antonio de Ulloa, Velasco maintained, were ultimately unreliable witnesses.[137] Short visits to foreign places and linguistic ignorance (although La Condamine and Ulloa had stayed in the Andes for some ten years), according to Velasco, made travelers dependent on informants. La Condamine, who did not know Quechua, had failed to realize that the natives liked to tailor their behavior to meet expectations. He thus wrongly concluded that the Amerindians were naturally stupid. Velasco, who was being raised by Amerindian wet nurses when La Condamine visited Quito, recalled how the Amerindians joked among themselves every time they deceived the French. In fact, the Amerindians thought that La Condamine was the naive and stupid one.[138] According to Velasco, La Condamine's ignorance of the language made him easy prey to manipulation, leaving him without the critical tools to weigh the credibility of his informants.

Velasco presented himself as a follower of the epistemology of José de Acosta. The sixteenth-century Jesuit had distinguished his writings from the huge corpus of books on the New World by emphasizing not only his learning but his *long* firsthand acquaintance with the land and peoples that he described, including the knowledge of Amerindian languages.[139] Acosta's emphasis on mastering Amerindian languages and living in close, intimate proximity to Amerindian communities led Velasco to privilege religious over secular clergy (parish priests) and lay observers. Although aware of the eighteenth-century critique of the biased missionary observer, he thought that only religious observers were reliable eyewitnesses.[140] According to Velasco, the religious were learned and therefore able to fend off the tricks of self-delusion and superstition. They also knew the local languages well and were therefore able to gain the confidence of the indigenous peoples.[141]

Like Clavijero, Velasco held mestizos in contempt and spent more time lashing out against them than articulating a critique of the colonial regime. Any reader of Velasco's third volume, a typically Creole history of the colonial period, with descriptions of prodigious miraculous images and of Creole and Amerindian saintly figures, cannot help noticing its tragic focus on the endless successions of earthquakes, plagues, and rural and urban uprisings that Quito suffered in the eighteenth century, aggravated by the ruinous Bourbon reforms. For all the tragedy, Velasco nevertheless was very timid in his criticism of colonial government and chose to hide his grievances. He criticized the economic reorganization of the empire that led to the crisis of the local woolen industry only when attacking those travelers and foreigners who had presented Creoles as inherently indolent and corrupt. The alleged apathy of Creoles, he argued, was the result of commercial lack of incentives, not an inborn, climatically determined trait.[142] Velasco closed his history of the Conquest by claiming that the riches of the gospel and civilization brought about by the Conquest had offset any Spanish cruelty to the Amerindians. Moreover, like Clavijero, Velasco maintained that all cruel acts had been the responsibility of private individuals, and that the crown had intervened on behalf of the Amerindians.[143] Yet for all his lack of criticism of Spain, Velasco projected his anger onto the mestizos, as if the blurring of racial and social hierarchies had caused the decline of Quito.

Velasco had great respect for the Amerindian and white elites but very little for mixed-blood commoners, for whom he reserved the harshest passages in his multivolume history. He presented the great 1765 urban uprising in Quito as directed against the colonial authorities and the new taxes introduced by the Bourbons as a plot of the mestizo plebes whose anger had fortunately been defused and channeled by the local patrician Creoles.[144] The Amerindians had been corrupted, Velasco alleged, by the disappearance of the native ruling class and the evil effects of contact with urban commoners, particularly *castas*, who had introduced them to their vices, including idleness, alcoholism, and theft.[145] Of all vices, the tendency to lie, in particular, Velasco contended, characterized all mixed bloods. In fact, Velasco's criticism of mestizos was part of a larger critique of the value of the testimony of commoners.[146]

Plates

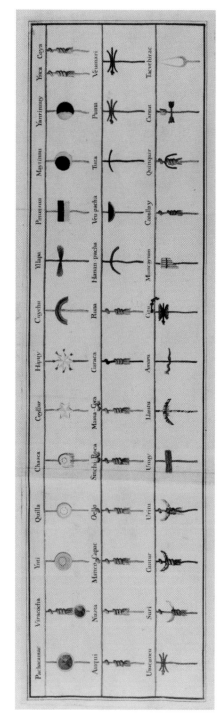

PLATE 1. The representation in quipus of forty master words (*parole maestre*). From Raimondo di Sangro (Sansevero), *Lettera apologetica* (Naples, 1750). Courtesy of the Edward Ayer Collection, Newberry Library, Chicago.

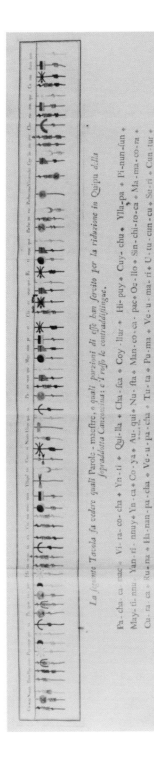

La seguente Tavola fa vedere quali Parole-maestre, o quali porzioni di esse han servito per la riduzione in Quipu d'lla sopradetta Canzoncina; e'l resto le contraddistingue.

Pa - cha - cu - mac + Vi - ra - co - cha + Yn - ti + Qui - lla + Cha - fca + Coy - llur + Hi - puy + Cuy - chu + Ylla - pa + Pi - nun - fun +
May - ti - nnu   Yan - ri - nnuy+ Yn - ca + Co - ya + Au - qui+ Nu - fta+ Man - co - ca - pac+ Oz - llo+ Sin - chi - to - ca + Ma - ma - co - ra +
Ca - ra - ca + Ru - na + Hi - nan - pa - cha + Ve - u - pa - cha + Tu - ta + Pu - mi + Ve - u - ma - ri + U - tu - cun - cu + Su - ri + Cun - tur +
U - ti - ru + U - nuy + Lla - u - tu + A - ma - ru + Ci - tu + Mun - cay - nim + Ca - to - llay + Quin - quir + Can - tut + Tac - ve - hi - rac +

A pronunciar le suddette parole si dee tener la maniera Spagnuola, secondo la quale si trovano scritte; vale a dire, s pronuncian
Chi-glia la parola Qui-lla, e May-ti-gnu la parola May-ti-nnu; e così tutte le altre simili.

PLATE 2. Poem in Quechua recorded in syllabic script. From Raimondo di Sangro (Sansevero), *Lettera apologetica* (Naples, 1750). Courtesy of the Edward Ayer Collection, Newberry Library, Chicago.

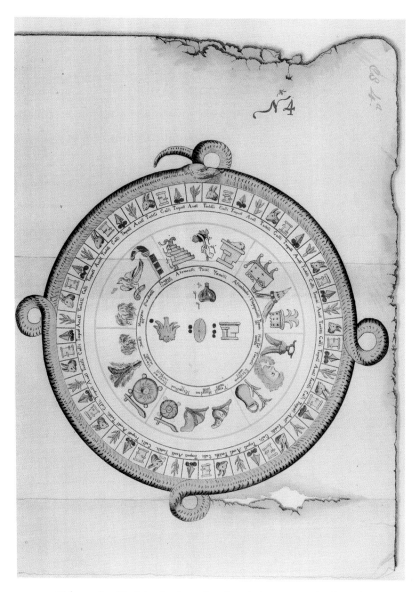

PLATE 3. Echeverría y Veytia's wheel number four. In its outer circle, this colonial calendrical wheel shows a 52-year cycle in which four signs, those of the rabbit, house, cane, and flint, are repeated thirteen times each. The inner circle represents the eighteen months of the Mesoamerican year. The only indication of where the series of years and months begins is the head of the snake around the wheel. The snake also shows that the wheel runs clockwise. From Mariano Fernández Echeverría y Veytia, *Los calendarios mexicanos* (Mexico, 1907).

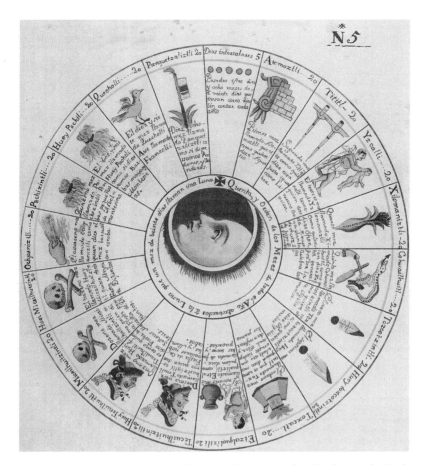

PLATE 4. Echeverría y Veytia's wheel number five. This colonial calendrical wheel, most likely by the seventeenth-century Tlaxcalan priest Manuel de los Santos y Salazar, belonged to Boturini. It represents the order of the eighteenth months of the year, moving clockwise from Atemoztli to five "intercalary" days. Echeverría y Veytia used the wheel to support his interpretation of the order of the months, which he ultimately derived through etymological analysis of the name of the months. From Mariano Fernández Echeverría y Veytia, *Los calendarios mexicanos* (Mexico, 1907).

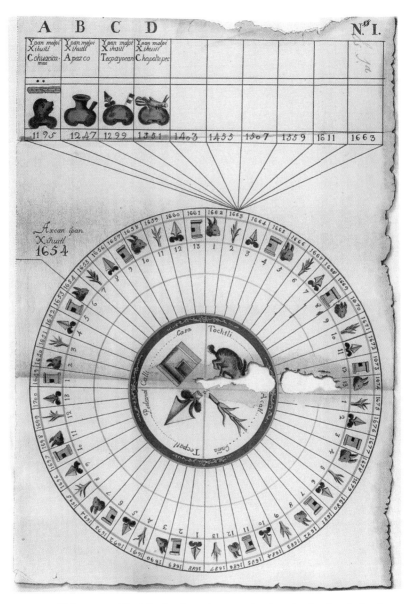

PLATE 5. Echeverría y Veytia's wheel number one. A colonial calendrical wheel representing a 52-year cycle and the dates in years of places where the Mexica celebrated the end of a "bundle of 52 years" or "century." Echeverría y Veytia interpreted the "bundles" as "2 Cane," the year in which the listed towns were founded in different "centuries." This reading allowed Echeverría y Veytia to claim that the leading sign every year always remained constant. From Mariano Fernández Echeverría y Veytia, *Los calendarios mexicanos* (Mexico, 1907).

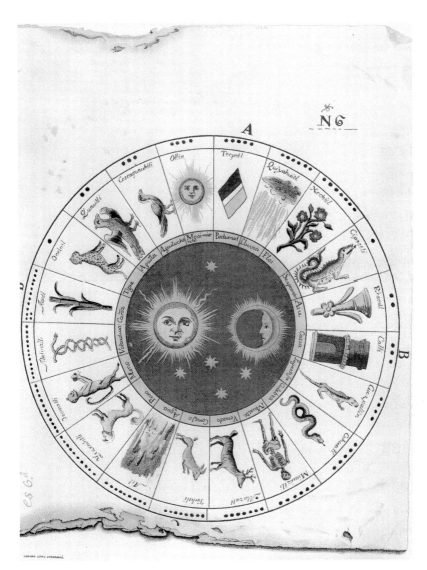

PLATE 6. Echeverría y Veytia's wheel number six. A colonial calendrical wheel representing the series of twenty days of the Mesoamerican month. With the twenty day signs, a parallel series of thirteen numbers creates 260 permutations, the basis for the ritual calendar. Echeverría y Veytia used the calendar to claim that *cipactli* (crocodile) was not the leading day of every month. From the wheel alone, there was no possible way to determine where the series began. Echeverría y Veytia used an alleged hierarchical order of the elements to determine the order of the leading days of each month. From Mariano Fernández Echeverría y Veytia, *Los calendarios mexicanos* (Mexico, 1907).

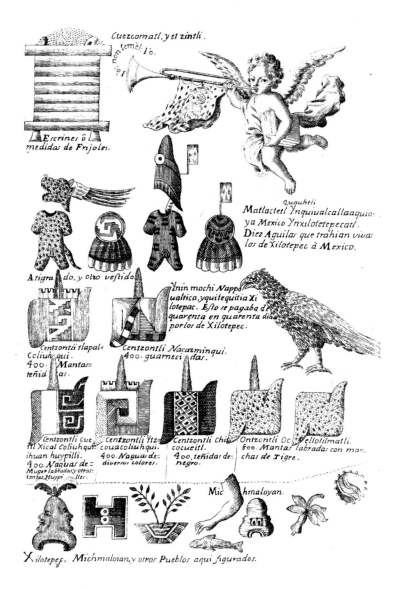

Cuezcomatl, y et zintli.

nontemi. 10.

Escrines ô medidas de Frijoles.

Ququhtli
Matlactetl Ynquiuailcallaaquia-
ya Mexico Ynxilotetepecatl.
Diez Aguilas que trahian viuas
los de Xilotepec à Mexico.

A tigrado, y otro vestido.

Inin mochi Nappo
ualtica, yquitequitia Xi
lotepac. Esto se pagaba d'
quarenta en quarenta dia
por los de Xilotepec.

Centzontli tlapal=
Coliuhqui.
400. Mantas=
teñidas.

Centzontli Nacazminqui.
400. guarneci das.

Centzontli Cue
tl Xical Coliuhqui
ihuan huypilli.
400. Naguas de=
Muger labrada y otros
tantas Huypilles.

Centzontli Ytz=
coua coliuhqui.
400. Naguas de:
diuersos colores.

Centzontli Chi
cocueitl.
400. teñidas de:
negro.

Ontzontli Oc Ellotilmatli.
800. Mantas labradas con man-
chas de Tigre.

Michmaloyan.

Xilotepec. Michmaloian, y otros Pueblos aqui figurados.

PLATE 7. A page of the *Matrícula de tributos* from Francisco Antonio de Lorenzana, "Fragmentos de un mapa de tributos . . . ," in Hernán Cortés, *Historia de Nueva-España* . . . (Mexico, 1770). Courtesy of the John Carter Brown Library, Brown University, Providence, R.I.

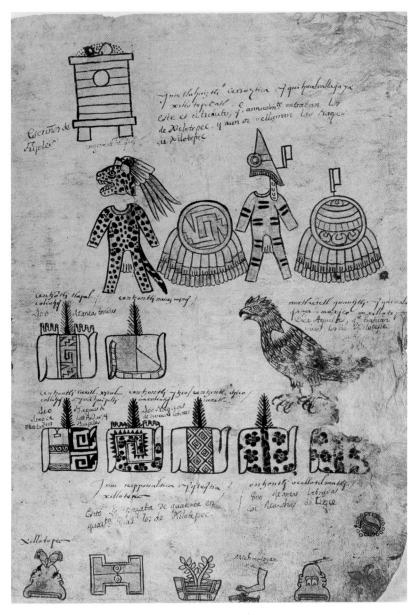

PLATE 8. Same page of the *Matrícula de tributos* as in Plate 7 from a facsimile of the early sixteenth-century original. Courtesy of Akademische Druck- u. Verlagsanstalt. Lorenzana's edition introduced slight iconographic changes and even a putto holding a trumpet with the archbishop's coat of arms. Although this is not the case with this page, Lorenzana copied all the Spanish glosses but only part of those in Nahuatl in Latin script. The original Spanish glosses consistently misread the logographic and ideographic signs for quantities. This prompted many Creoles, including Francisco Clavijero, to claim that the Amerindian interpreters who helped Lorenzana could not read sixteenth-century Nahua glosses, and that the edition was therefore untrustworthy.

PLATE 9. The Fall and the Tree of Wisdom from the Codex Borgia, which Lino Fábrega interpreted as a repository of patriarchal traditions handed down by Noah.

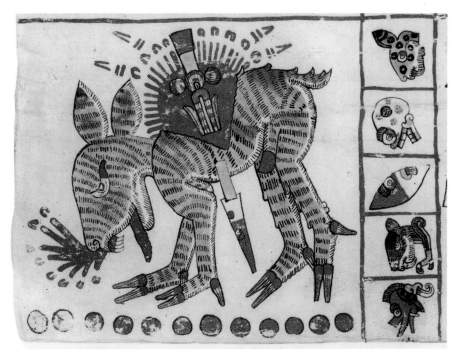

PLATE 10. Prefiguration of Christ as a "sacrificial Lamb" from the Codex Borgia.

PLATE 11. The Flood, and the date when it occurred (during the fall season), when Scorpio was the ascendant constellation, from the Codex Borgia.

PLATE 12. The founding of Tenochtitlán by the Mexica. From the Codex Mendoza. A portrayal lacking Christian patristic influences. Reproduced with permission of the Bodleian Library, Oxford, MS. Arch. Selden. A. 1, fol. 2r. For an explanation of this page, see caption of Figure 2.4 (p. 100).

Velasco and Clavijero followed very similar strategies. Both sought to undermine the reliability of foreign authors and travelers, both emphasized the trustworthiness of religious witnesses, and both focused on the importance of observers knowing the local Amerindian languages. Juan Ignacio Molina, one the other hand, departed significantly from these views.

Juan Ignacio Molina

Juan Ignacio Molina (1740–1829), the author of *Saggio sulla storia naturale de Chili* (1782) and *Saggio sulla storia civile de Chili* (1787), stands out among the Creole Jesuits who wrote natural and civil histories of their homelands in exile because he refused to embrace several key aspects of the discourse of patriotic epistemology. Unlike Velasco and Clavijero, Molina organized his histories of Chile around the testimony of European travelers. He was "not disposed to question the account of respectable writers, several of whom have been eyewitnesses of what they describe."[147] Drawing on his own personal experience, Molina also used the writings of travelers like Amédée Frézier, Louis Feuillée, Antonio de Ulloa, and Lord George Anson (1697–1762) to bolster his own credibility.[148] Molina's surprising departure from the Creole Jesuit critique of the epistemological limitations of the foreign traveler was related to the fact that Chile had traditionally fared well in most European travel accounts. Chile had long been a peripheral colonial outpost, sparsely populated by Spaniards, a land whose climate most learned travelers found benign, and whose original Araucanian inhabitants were portrayed as courageous republican warriors. Unlike Peru or Mexico, Chile received positive reviews from European travelers. The early-eighteenth-century account of the South Seas by the French engineer Frézier typifies this tendency. Whereas Frézier portrayed Chile as an Alpine, temperate land inhabited by heroic Araucanians, he presented Peru as corrupting, a land of concupiscence, paganism, and effeminate idleness.[149] It is understandable, therefore, that Molina did not choose to criticize foreign accounts. In fact, he deliberately cast his book as a learned complement to the early-eighteenth-century natural history of the Minim friar Feuillée.[150] His embrace of accounts by foreign witnesses was, however, tempered by a forceful critique of armchair philosophers and system builders such as de Pauw. Throughout his history, Molina refused to consider "vague conjectures and hazardous hypotheses."[151] Like Clavijero and Velasco, he decried de Pauw's tendency to generalize from isolated examples, particularly because de Pauw had never set foot in the New World.[152] Molina's contempt for systems caused him to introduce

Linnaean taxonomy into his work only grudgingly, for such taxonomies, Molina argued, were artificial. He followed Linnaean classifications largely because they were popular, not because he thought they were useful.[153]

The genre of natural and civil histories deployed by Clavijero, Velasco, and Molina does not exhaust the repertoire of writings by the exiled Creole Jesuits. Among the dozens of manuscripts that survive, the remainder of this section focuses on the writings of two Creoles from New Spain, Pedro José Márquez and José Lino Fábrega.[154] Although Márquez and Fábrega did not add anything significant to the discourse of patriotic epistemology, their works give us greater insight into the nature of the Creole histories of the Amerindians. They also highlight the vitality and creativity of the Creole Jesuit diaspora in Italy.

Pedro José Márquez

Pedro José Márquez (1741–1820) experienced exile while still a young novice and peaked intellectually years after Clavijero, Velasco, and Molina. Unlike his fellow Jesuit exiles, who lived in provincial cities in the Papal States, Márquez was sent to Rome, where he came into contact with the great antiquarian tradition of the city. Before he turned his attention to the study of Mexican antiquities, Márquez published several studies on Roman antiquities and on aesthetic theory.[155] In 1804, he published his only two works on ancient Mexico: an annotated Italian translation of the 1794 Mexican edition of Antonio de León y Gama's work on Mesoamerican calendars and a study of two ruins first described in Mexican periodicals in the 1780s and 1790s.

Márquez sought to demonstrate the depth and quality of the Creole intellect by making León y Gama's brilliant treatise on Amerindian chronology widely available in Italy.[156] Using precolonial Mesoamerican codices stored in Bologna and the Vatican, Márquez supported in parenthetical notes most of the conclusions reached by León y Gama, and in a short essay appended at the end, he argued that Mesoamerican civilization had ancient origins.[157] The great recorded antiquity of the Amerindians, its seems, allowed Márquez to play a role in contemporary European debates on universal chronology. According to the censor of the translation, the Roman cleric Michele Carrega, Márquez was known in Rome for deploying precolonial Mesoamerican codices to bolster the credibility of the Mosaic chronology, then under attack.[158]

The second treatise that Márquez published in 1804 was more clearly linked to the discourse of patriotic epistemology. In a dedication to the "most noble, illustrious, and imperial" city of Mexico, Márquez argued that Europeans had long been fed misleading accounts of the New World. He also argued that the intelligentsia of Mexico had the responsibility of setting the glorious historical record of their own "ancestors" (antenati), the Amerindians, straight.[159] Márquez thought that most written indigenous sources had either been burned or hidden. So to reconstruct the great accomplishments of his "ancestors" the Amerindians, he assembled both eyewitness accounts and descriptions of material remains. One half of the treatise was devoted to the study of two recent archeological discoveries in Mexico. The other half consisted in a compilation of the reports by Cortés and the Anonymous Conquistador on the breathtaking spectacle of the precolonial Mexican cities and architecture taken from the 1565 Venetian edition of Ramusio's Delle navigationi et viaggi.

Building on a serendipitous discovery by a colonial officer who had been charged with eradicating illegal tobacco crops on the Gulf coast of Mexico, Márquez first introduced Italian readers to a pyramid in Papantla (Fig. 4.10). Márquez's description sought to prove the pyramid's many similarities to the architecture of ancient Mediterranean civilizations. The pyramidal form itself, Márquez argued, indicated the descent of Egyptians and Mexicans from common Babylonian roots. The stairs, on the other hand, Márquez maintained, resembled those of Roman and Greek amphitheaters, with the central wider set for seating and the two lateral flights for circulation. Finally, the niches of the pyramid, he argued, were similar to those of the temple of Janus in Rome, a quadrangular temple in which each wall represented a season and had twelve niches to signify the months of the year. Márquez counted 378 niches in the pyramid by adding a hypothetical seventh layer to the original six-story structure. He contended that the niches had been built to house the Mesoamerican calendar's signs for the 365 days of the year, plus the 13 days added at the end of every 52-year cycle to adjust to the real duration of the sun's journey through the ecliptic (365.25 days).

In this treatise, Márquez also included a study of the ruins of Xochicalco made public in 1791 by the Creole polymath José Antonio de Alzate y Ramírez (1737–1799).[160] The ruins occupied an entire terraced mountain, which Alzate y Ramírez identified as a fortified "castle," surrounded by a ditch with a pyramid on top (Fig. 4.11). At the base and inside the mountain, there lay a network of neatly arranged tunnels and rooms. According to Alzate y Ramírez, on top of the mound, inside a walled area, there had once been a five-story pyramid, which the owners of nearby sugar plantations had destroyed in their search for stones for mills. Alzate y Ramírez offered a hy-

FIGURE 4.10. The pyramid of Papantla, from Pedro Márquez, *Due antichi monumenti di architettura messicana* (Rome, 1804). Márquez argued that this structure had many similarities with monuments in the classical world, including the temple of Janus, amphitheaters, and Egyptian pyramids.

pothetical reconstruction of the pyramid, drawing on eyewitness accounts. Like Alzate y Ramírez, Márquez argued that the mound and the pyramid reflected the sophistication of Mesoamerican peoples, their knowledge of subterranean geometry, mechanics, and pulleys to move boulders, and their mastery of techniques to build domes and arches, allegedly one of the most important architectural signs of civilized life.[161] Betraying his view of the "original" Amerindian religions as benign, Márquez concluded, however, that the structure was no "castle," but a temple. His efforts to transform Alzate y Ramírez's castle into a temple also reflected his skepticism of Spanish accounts of the scale of human sacrifice in late Mesoamerican religion. Márquez agreed with Alzate y Ramírez that the pyramid had originally lacked stairs, but he insisted that it had been built by the long-enduring Toltecs and reflected a stage of religious development in which flowers (thus the name Xochicalco, from *xochitl*, flower), not humans, were offered to the gods, for stairs were used in later temples to fling sacrificial victims down.[162]

But how to account for the disappearance of such splendid civilizations? The answer for Márquez, as well as for Clavijero and Velasco (and Alzate y Ramírez), lay in the transformation of societies that had once sported splen-

FIGURE 4.11. The ruins of Xochicalco, from Pedro Márquez, *Due antichi monumenti di architettura messicana* (Rome, 1804). Márquez copied the illustrations from José Antonio de Alzate y Ramírez's study of the ruins published earlier in Mexico. The pyramid on the upper right is a hypothetical reconstruction by Alzate y Ramírez based on eyewitness accounts; only the lower base of the pyramid survived. Márquez maintained that the complex was a temple from earlier stages of Mesoamerican religious development because it did not have a flight of stairs, which allegedly were only needed to fling sacrificial victims down. Alzate y Ramírez studied the ruins and concluded that the structure was a fortified "castle." He also refused to speculate on the meaning of the carved hieroglyphs.

did courts, books, and scholars into societies of commoners, "destined to represent in the great comedy [that is, theater] of the world the plebe."[163] Drawing on a well-worn trope already used by Clavijero (and Alzate y Ramírez), Márquez compared the transmutation of the ancient Mexicans into the pitiful contemporary Amerindians to that of the Greeks under the Turks. The fact that there was a gap between the greatness of classical antiquity and the purported wretchedness of contemporary Greeks served Creoles to bolster the credibility of their historical accounts, for, to be sure, no one called into question the achievements of ancient Greece.

Márquez's writings on Mesoamerican antiquities somewhat modified the discourse of patriotic epistemology by introducing the study of archeological sites and material remains as a complement to interpretation of indigenous writings. Márquez did not, however, relinquish the use of indigenous written sources. In fact, like Boturini, Echeverría y Veytia, Sigüenza, and many others before him, he used indigenous documents to bolster the credibility of the Bible. This latter aspect of the Creole patriotic epistemology was most clearly articulated by José Lino Fábrega, another young novice at the time of the Jesuit expulsion.

José Lino Fábrega

Like Márquez, José Lino Fábrega lived close to powerful clerical circles in Rome. Sometime in the 1780s, Fábrega came under the protection of Cardinal Borgia, who gave him carte blanche to study a precolonial codex in the cardinal's private library, a *tonalamatl*, or sacred-ritual calendar, known ever since as Codex Borgia. Under this auspicious patronage, Fábrega scoured Roman libraries, with impressive results. In the Vatican, he unearthed another precolonial ritual calendar, the Codex Vaticanus 3,776 (of similar provenance to the Codex Borgia), and a sixteenth-century colonial compilation of indigenous rituals and migrations with Italian glosses known today as the Codex Ríos (or Vaticanus 3,738) (the document Lorenzo Pignoria had used in the early seventeenth century to point to the doctrinal similarities between Mexico and Egypt). In the holdings of the cardinal's library, Fábrega also identified a rare copy, by the Italian painter Antonio Basoli, of the Codex Cospi, yet another ritual calendar, of the same family as the Codex Borgia and the Codex Vaticanus 3,776. The original of this was housed in the public library of Bologna and had been cited but not studied by Clavijero. Single-handedly, Fábrega managed to identify an entire collection of related precolonial sources. With such a wealth of sources, he then set out to gloss his patron's codex, the most complete *tonalamatl* available.

Fábrega's study of the Codex Borgia, penned between 1792 and 1797, has to my knowledge failed to attract any scholarly attention, but it is an extraordinary document.[164] Fábrega followed two Creole tropes, namely, that Mesoamerican civilizations were ancient polities that had evolved in splendid isolation, and that Mesoamerican religious beliefs and rituals resembled Christian ones. He brought these two themes together without postulating satanic influences or apostolic visitations. Alva Ixtlilxochitl (and Echeverría y Veytia), among others, had long offered solutions to a tension inherent in the twin but contradictory theses of ritual resemblance and the long-enduring isolation by suggesting an early apostolic visitation. Other authors, such as Torquemada and Gemelli Careri, had explained the religious similarities as the product of mocking satanic inversions. Clavijero had dismissed both theses and focused exclusively on the theme of long-enduring isolation to highlight the creativity of Mesoamerican polities. Fábrega built on Clavijero's insight.

According to Fábrega, the Codex Borgia, a "masterwork of the Mexican genius," was an extremely accurate calendar. It demonstrated that the Mesoamerican peoples had not only identified within minutes the exact duration of the sun's movement through the ecliptic but also a host of other planetary and stellar cycles of 1,040, 1,460, and 3,380 years each.[165] In fact, according to Fábrega, the codex revealed that the natives knew that 12.5 days had to be intercalated in every 52-year cycle (not 13 as Boturini, Echeverría y Veytia, Clavijero, and Márquez had suggested) and that 7 days had to be deducted every 1,040 years, because a tropical year lasted not 365.25 but 365.243 days. The codex also revealed a knowledge of the story of Creation; the fall of Lucifer; the immortality of the soul and its ascent (or descent) through cosmic levels (that is, purgatory, limbo, and the many circles of hell); the expulsion of Adam and Eve from the Garden of Eden and the origins of human mortality, sinfulness, and ascetic self-mortification; the Great Flood; future deliverance by a new Savior; and the final apocalyptic conflagration.[166] These echoes of the Bible, Fábrega contended, were not the result of apostolic visitations or demonic manipulations but of the perpetuation of knowledge bequeathed by Noah to those of his progeny who eventually migrated to Mexico.[167] The Codex Borgia thus stored a "complete set of the historic and prophetic traditions" that went back to the Flood.[168]

Although Fábrega said that to avoid repeating the mistakes of conjectural historians, he had shunned all speculative reading of the images of the Codex Borgia,[169] he in fact at every step advanced bold interpretations, as seen in Plates 9–11. He read the image shown in Plate 9 as depicting the Fall of Man, triggered by failure to heed the injunction to keep away from the Tree of Wisdom. The image in Plate 10 prefigured the Savior as a "sacrificial lamb." The symbol of running water next to a temple in Plate 11 stood for the Flood; the temple itself was the Ark; the individual crouched within the temple was Noah; and the smoke coming out of the temple represented the origins of religious sacrifice. The zodiacal sign of Scorpio next to the temple indicated, moreover, that the Flood had occurred in autumn.[170]

These prophetic and historic traditions had, however, been distorted and manipulated almost beyond recognition owing to the nature of the medium that Noah chose to transmit his teachings, namely, figurative writing. Thus, for example, the figure of the heart, which had originally been used by Noah to represent the abstract concept of sacrifice, was later construed literally, paving the way for human sacrifice. Innate human passions had also promoted literal readings of the original patriarchal hieroglyphic symbols.[171]

Although Fábrega explained the religious resemblance between Christian and Amerindian religions that had haunted Creole scholars in the past negatively, as the failure of the natives to transmit Noah's original dispensation, his account of the consequences of long-enduring isolation was far more positive. Ever since the migrations triggered by the destruction of the Tower of Babel, Fábrega argued, the peoples of the New World had remained isolated, with the continent becoming a place of social curiosities, where Europeans upon arrival encountered "all the types of government imagined by man" and "polities established since time immemorial on fundamental and sage laws." Fábrega maintained that the Incas, for example, had developed a form of "communal economy" not to be found anywhere else in the world. He also contended that the ancient civilizations of America had built sumptuous buildings and bridges, and created outstandingly accurate calendars without recourse to iron tools, beasts of burden, telescopes, or any other instrument "known to us," and without any outside help. In a single stroke, Fábrega turned the logic that had motivated the skepticism of authors such de Pauw, Raynal, and Robertson upside down. Whereas northern Europeans thought that the absent technologies called into question the verisimilitude of Spanish accounts, for Fábrega, the absences indicated that in their isolation, the peoples of the New World had followed alternative paths of development, different from those sanctioned by philosophical historians.[172]

Like other Jesuit authors, Fábrega criticized de Pauw, Robertson, and

Raynal, who, he said, "instead of either publishing the already known indigenous documents or searching for new ones have relied on anonymous accounts by those who are little accurate or by those biased by the ridiculous system [hypothesizing] the degeneration of nature in America."[173] Operating within the clerical-Creole discourse of patriotic epistemology, Fábrega privileged precolonial indigenous documents. Confronted with these "inestimable monuments" predating the Conquest of Mexico, Fábrega maintained, "the authority of any other historian who says otherwise is nullified."[174] Fábrega was deeply skeptical of all writings by sixteenth-century Spanish authors on Mesoamerican religions, because they had drawn misleading analogies between Mexican and Old World deities, on the assumption that the Mexicans were descendants of Chaldeans, Egyptians, or Greeks, and had assumed the satanic origins of Amerindian religion.[175] European sources were problematic because most authors had used commoners or impostors as interpreters, not the keepers of Amerindian religious knowledge.[176]

I have only scratched the surface here of the vast scholarship put forth by the Creole Jesuits in exile. My intention has been solely to draw attention to the way they created and validated historical knowledge by bringing the discourse of patriotic epistemology to maturity. In the concluding section of this chapter, I study late-colonial representations of the Amerindians and how these representations, although seemingly ambivalent and contradictory, can be accounted by the same ancien régime logic that governed the discourse of patriotic epistemology.

Manco Capac: The Ultimate Sage

Those seeking to understand representations of the "Indian" in colonial Spanish America cannot help but be puzzled, for these representations are deeply ambivalent, often oscillating between apparent respect and outright racism. A recent study by William Taylor has sought to make the contradictory character of these late-colonial representations explicit.[177] Strict hierarchical views of society allowed the Creole clergy simultaneously to depict Amerindians as wretched and as the creators of great ancient polities. To understand the connections between the values of the ancien régime and these contradictory representations, we need to turn to the Bourbon reforms and the debates they engendered in the eighteenth century about the nature of the Indian.

In the wake of the Bourbon reforms aimed at reviving Spain's moribund colonial empire, the bodies and minds of Native Americans were scrutinized much as they had been by sixteenth-century European colonists and missionaries. It began to be asked, among other things, whether the old mechanisms of labor coercion were appropriate to the nature of the Amerindian. One institution in particular attracted attention, the *repartimiento de mercancías*, in which magistrate-entrepreneurs advanced credit and marked-up goods to the natives in order to force them to sell their labor for cash. This institution, along with the infamous system of forced rotational labor (*mita*), had long been sanctioned on grounds that the natives were lazy by nature. For a while, the thesis of the naturally lazy native and the need for forced distribution of credit and goods triumphed in the eighteenth century, particularly in Peru. But when the great pan-Andean uprising led by José Gabriel Condorcanqui, Tupac Amaru II (1740?–1781), rocked the viceroyalty of Peru in 1781, the colonial authorities had no choice but to abolish the *repartimiento*. With the abolition, the debate over the nature of the Amerindians acquired new urgency.[178] Alejandro Malaspina (1754–1810), the leader of the largest expedition sent by Spain to its colonial possessions, wrestled, for example, with the all-consuming question of how to involve the Amerindians in the newly emerging commercial circuits. He wanted not only to use the Amerindians for cheap labor but also to expose them to the alleged civilizing effects of commerce. Malaspina concluded that the crown could not afford to dismantle its baroque religious institutions in the colonies, because the Amerindians' religious practices were their only tenuous link to the market, where they bought candles, images, and other religious paraphernalia.[179]

As in the past, the debate over the nature of the Amerindian body and soul was closely related to historiographical discussions. In the late sixteenth and early seventeenth centuries, the staunchest defenders of forced labor systems linked the alleged natural laziness of the Amerindians to the statecraft of their ancient rulers. The Jesuit José de Acosta and the jurist Juan de Solórzano y Pereira (1578–1655) argued in 1577 and 1629–39 respectively that the rulers of Mexico and Peru knew the debased nature of their subjects and legislated accordingly. Moctezuma Xocoyoltzin and Manco Capac, Acosta and Solórzano y Pereira maintained, had been able to transform degenerate Amerindians into the citizens of great polities because they gave their subjects no respite. To prevent them from slipping back into their preferred state of laziness, they had even made them pick one another's lice.[180]

These views did not go away with the Enlightenment; in fact they were repeated by philosophes such as Montesquieu and Francesco Algarotti (1712–1764) (the popularizer of Newton in Italy). Drawing on Aristotle's insight to the effect that good magistrates needed to tailor their laws to the climate of the land they ruled, Montesquieu argued that rigorous rulers who would not let people slip into indolence were needed in humid climates. "There are countries," he argued, "where the excess of heat enervates the body and renders men so slothful and dispirited that nothing but the fear of chastisement can oblige them to perform any laborious duty." The "spirit" of the Inca and Aztec "law" indicated that the ancient rulers of the Americas, who like those of China had had lazy subjects, had devised the appropriate legislation, according to Montesquieu.[181] In 1753, in an essay exalting the great civilization that Manco Capac and the Incas had created in the Andes, Algarotti maintained that Manco Capac had succeeded despite the degenerate character of the natives. Based on the testimony of La Condamine, Algarotti argued that the Amerindians of Peru were stupid and indolent by nature. How, then, could Manco Capac and the other Inca rulers have created a great civilization with such material? According to Algarotti, Manco Capac's success proved "the miracles that legislation can bring about."[182]

The debates over the character and nature of the Amerindians that Spanish America witnessed in the second half of the eighteenth century drew upon the same principles. An anonymous report written during Malaspina's visit assessed the effect on Peru of the abolition of the forced distribution of credit and goods after the Tupac Amaru rebellion and suggested that to halt the decline of entire branches of industry and commerce, forced distribution should be revived in a new form, under the control of the crown in order to avoid abuse. Moreover, to bring Amerindians into the commercial circuit, baroque worship also had to be stimulated. As Manco Capac had long ago realized, the writer maintained, forced labor was the only thing that could persuade the indolent Peruvian natives to engage in market transactions. To oblige the Amerindians to work, Manco Capac had therefore devised institutions such as the *mita* and public floggings, which had made the Incas prosperous and civilized.[183] Antonio Pineda, a member of Malaspina's expedition, came to similar conclusions in the case of Mexico.[184]

José Hipólito Unanue (1755–1833), one of the leading figures of the Enlightenment in the viceroyalty of Peru, approached the Amerindians of Peru from much the same perspective as Acosta, Solórzano y Pereira, Algarotti, and Malaspina. The sublimity of the Andean landscape paralyzed the natives, Unanue argued, and their excessive sensitivity made them melancholic, but if the Spanish authorities would only follow the example of the Incas, a great, civilized society might nonetheless be created. Unanue accordingly recommended "therapeutic" floggings to cure the Amerindians of their indolence.[185]

a

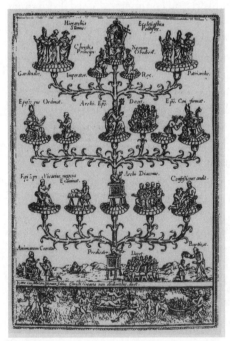

FIGURE 4.12. To teach Amerindians about the civil and ecclesiastical hierarchies in European societies, the Franciscans used images like these, neatly encapsulating the values of the ancien régime in colonial Spanish America, which was organized in terms of corporate privileges based on socio-racial estates. From Diego Valadés, *Rhetorica Christiana* (Perugia, 1579).

b

How could it be, however, that although the natives were degenerate, their former rulers, who had been Amerindian too, after all, were models of statecraft? The answer to this paradox lay in the same logic that gave coherence to the discourse of patriotic epistemology. Creole antiquarians similarly derided the credibility of contemporary Amerindian evidence but simultaneously held precolonial and early-colonial Amerindian sources in the highest esteem. The difference between these two types of evidence, they argued, was that the former came from commoners and the latter from the aristocracy. Under the ancien régime, the gulf between the two classes was deemed so immense that they were sometimes thought to belong to different races. As Paul Freedman (1999) has recently shown for the late Middle Ages, the discourse of social estates contemplated immense bodily and mental differences between peasants and nobles. The application of a comparable logic in colonial Spanish America (see, for example, Fig. 4.12) both enabled the exclusion of the precolonial native rulers from the stereotype that Amerindians were lazy degenerates and gave coherence to the discourse of patriotic epistemology.

Whose Enlightenment Was It Anyway?

Recent surveys of the Enlightenment have called into question earlier portrayals of this "rebirth of 'paganism'" as a secular, liberal critique of ancien
régime religious and political values launched by a handful of great writers
such as Voltaire and Diderot. Dorinda Outram, for example, has offered a
different framework in which the Enlightenment is seen as revolving around
controversies about gender, religion, government, science, and the exotic, in
the context of the rise of new forms of sociability. This broadening of the
concept of the Enlightenment to include all those involved in building
the "public sphere" — a critical marketplace of ideas that forced state and
Church to find new languages of legitimization — is salutary, but it nonetheless remains Eurocentric.[1] Although Outram has gone out of her way to acknowledge that there were many "publics" outside Britain, France, and
Germany, including those in the British and Spanish American colonies,
Greece, Italy, and eastern Europe, the controversies she studies are those that
preoccupied the great minds of northern Europe.[2] Outram has justified her
choice by pointing to the marketplace. Cheap books, newspapers, and periodicals homogenized and globalized the public sphere; the questions and
controversies of the world were those that haunted northern European scholars and intellectuals.[3]

This approach to the Enlightenment is limiting and only partially right.
The emergence of educated publics in Scotland, France, and Germany led
to the development of a new art of reading and genres that called into question the value of traditional sources in writing the history of the New World.
These new genres, in turn, framed public discourse in Spain (and the Papal
States) and the Spanish American colonies. But the language and rules of
northern European discourses and controversies were not passively trans-
ferred to the New World, Spain, or the Papal States. The themes that were
significant to the public in Spanish America had less to do with building new
religious and political languages than with constructing alternative, critical

epistemologies. The Spanish American Enlightenment was a dual process of creating such discursive space and consolidating a public sphere.[4]

It would, of course, be easier to disassociate the discourse of "patriotic epistemology" from the Enlightenment. I have, after all, described it as a project whose criteria of assessing and validating knowledge reinforced the corporate privileges of ancien régime polities. Moreover, it was a clerical construct, thoroughly informed by religious values, the antithesis of modernity. But to measure Enlightenment from this perspective would be to return to the paradigms Outram has challenged.

This chapter draws its inspiration from the works of Joseph M. Levine, who has shown the importance of antiquarian debates in reconstructing eighteenth-century cultural history.[5] Here, I examine the discourse of patriotic epistemology in Spanish America through analysis of three antiquarian controversies that took place in the 1780s and 1790s in the viceroyalty of New Spain. Unlike the authors described in the previous chapter, the participants in these debates worked in a rarefied environment characterized by rapid institutional and cultural change brought about by the Bourbon reforms, which challenged the Church's monopoly on knowledge. The reforms opened up, often by fiat, a public sphere in the colonies that made the discourse of patriotic epistemology slightly less clerical. However, they did not substantially alter its logic and content.

The debate triggered by the discovery in the central plaza of Mexico City of a number of ancient monuments, including the famous "Solar Stone," demonstrates that the Spanish American Enlightenment was not merely a belated reflection of ideas first tried out in Europe. Representatives of the Enlightenment in New Spain who participated in the debate were explicitly attempting to develop a critique of Eurocentric epistemologies. Their critique was organized around questions and preoccupations that reflected the colonial status of the region. The practical political dimensions of the Spanish American Enlightenment are examined in the second section of this chapter through analysis of the debate that took place in the 1780s and 1790s in New Spain over the whereabouts and final destination of Lorenzo Boturini's collection. I contend that it never left Mexico, despite all the efforts of the crown, because the Creole intelligentsia successfully plotted to keep it at home. The third section of the chapter returns to the debates over the stones found in the plaza of the capital of New Spain, focusing this time on participants who can hardly be characterized as members of the Enlightenment. Using the long overlooked works of José Ignacio Borunda, I reconstruct the clash between old and new forms of scholarship in Spanish America, maintaining that the traditions of the Baroque did not disappear but had a lasting and powerful influence in the late-colonial period. In the fourth and final section, I turn to yet another antiquarian debate, this one triggered by the discovery of the ruins of Palenque in the 1780s and 1790s. Palenque pitted a "philosophical" methodology based on the insights of the northern European social sciences against a patriotic, "baroque" paradigm. The debate introduces the reader to the rich culture of the Spanish American Baroque through an analysis of the scholarship of those involved in the study of the ruins and sheds light on the lasting religious preoccupations of the Creole-clerical elites of Spanish America. Finally, the debate shows how Creoles deployed the discourse of patriotic epistemology to undermine the authority of foreigners who dared to get involved.

The Stones: Interpreting the Spanish-American Enlightenment

From August 1790 to June 1792, excavations for public works projects undertaken by the viceroy, Juan Vicente de Guemes Pacheco de Padilla, second count of Revillagigedo (r. 1789–94), introduced the citizens of Mexico City to a series of remarkable archeological discoveries. Giant boulders were revealed, which had to be lifted with pulleys or blown to pieces. Two monuments in particular attracted the attention of the local literati: the monstrous figure of an Aztec deity, known today as Coatlicue, which went to the university for further study (Fig. 5.1a), and a huge wheel carved in stone, the so-called Solar Stone, which was assigned to the cathedral chapter for display (Fig. 5.2).[6] When the boulder carved with the Aztec deity attracted a stream of curious Amerindian visitors to the university, the authorities, fearful of encouraging a pagan revival, buried it again.

The discovery of these stones set off a wave of learned speculation, notably by José Antonio de Alzate y Ramírez and Antonio de León y Gama, two leading luminaries of the Mexican Enlightenment. The two men's approaches differed substantially. Prompted by the criticisms of his nemesis, Alzate y Ramírez, León y Gama sought to interpret the stones, producing one of the most epistemologically sophisticated texts to appear in the Atlantic world in this period. Conversely, Alzate y Ramírez, representative of a less rigorously scholarly aspect of the Enlightenment in Mexico, refused to speculate about the meaning of the stones. But when the epistemologies of these two authors are compared, their differences vanish. León y Gama's

a

b

FIGURE 5.1. Nahua aesthetics. (a) One of the many stones found in the central plaza of Mexico City from 1790 to 1792, now known to represent the Aztec deity Coatlicue. According to Antonio de León y Gama, it was a composite of the hieroglyphic attributes of at least seven Mesoamerican deities. José Ignacio Borunda also interpreted it as a montage of hieroglyphic signs, which he read as logograms that were veiled allegories of historical events. From Antonio de León y Gama, *Descripción histórica de las dos piedras* (Mexico, 1792). (b) Colonial representation of Tlaloc, "god of the rain," that originally belonged to Fernando de lva Ixtlilxochitl. From Giovanni Francesco Gemelli Careri, *Giro del mondo* (Naples, 1699–1700). Courtesy of the John Carter Brown Library, Brown University, Providence, R.I. León y Gama used these illustrations to argue that the Indians had mastered the principles of mimetic representation, and that the figure of Coatlicue was the product of deliberate distortion, not ignorance of aesthetic principles.

FIGURE 5.2. The Solar Stone found in Mexico City, which Antonio de León y Gama contended was a semi-annual calendar plotting the main festivals of the sun. The sockets in the perimeter (marked *xzpqysqp*) had once held the gnomons of a sundial that measured solstices and equinoxes, he argued. At the center of the wheel, he read the day sign Ollin Tonatiuh and the dates when the four solar ages ended. The first circle contained the twenty signs of the days of the month, which León y Gama assumed ran counterclockwise. The symbol for the Milky Way was in the outer circle of the wheel, topped by the sign of the year 13 Cane. From Antonio de León y Gama, *Descripción histórica de las dos piedras* (Mexico, 1792).

interpretative scholarship was ultimately geared to proving that foreigners who knew America only superficially could never decode Amerindian scripts. Alzate y Ramírez, for his part, refused to advance any interpretation of Mesoamerican hieroglyphs as part of his larger critique of theories and systems, provoked by the new histories and accounts of America and its peoples, but he articulated one of the most thorough and forceful critiques of the epistemological limitations of foreign travelers, going so far as to found periodicals to review and expose their writings.

In December 1790, in his capacity as editor of the *Gacetas de literatura*, Alzate y Ramírez announced the discovery of the two stones, which might, he said, have belonged to the Great Temple of Tenochtitlan. He suggested that the monstrous-looking figure might be a representation of Huitzilopochtli, the Mexica god of war and death. Alzate y Ramírez doubted whether the meaning of the carved hieroglyphs could ever be cracked, but he suggested that carved stones from Aztec temples that had been reused in other structures in the city be used for comparative purposes. In August 1791, in *Gaceta de México*, Ocelotl Tecuilhuitzintli dismissed Alzate y Ramírez's suggestion that the stones had once belonged to the Great Temple. For Tecuilhuitzintli, the wheel was a calendar that confirmed Clavijero's interpretations, and the monstrous-looking figure was a composite of three deities: Teotlacanexquimilli (the headless and limbless god of darkness), Tlazolteotl (a Venus-like goddess of pleasure), and Tlateuctli (the punisher of adultery). The calendar wheel might represent either a 52-year cycle or an annual cycle, or even be a record-keeping device that stored historical information dating back at least a millennium, Tecuilhuitzintli thought, but whichever it was, it proved that those who called ancient Mesoamericans savages were wrong. The calendar wheel would outlast and dwarf the followers of Newton and Descartes who speculated on vortices and gravitation while denying the glorious past of the American continent.[7] Alzate y Ramírez immediately replied in the pages of *Gaceta de México* to Tecuilhuitzintli's charge that he had confused the calendar wheel with the sacrificial stone. As for the monstrous-looking figure, Alzate y Ramírez refused to engage his critic and speculate further about its meaning, on the grounds that speculation "is not an occupation that suits my genius; I never set out to walk in darkness."[8]

Antonio de León y Gama's 'Descripción histórica'

But Ocelotl Tecuilhuitzintli and Alzate y Ramírez were not the only ones interested in the new discoveries. In January 1792 and again in May of that year, *Gaceta de México* offered subscriptions to a forthcoming treatise that would set the record straight and would give the lie to European skeptics bent on denying the civilized status of the ancient Mexicans.[9] Sometime in June 1792, the much-announced treatise appeared: Antonio de León y Gama's *Descripción histórica y cronológica de las dos piedras*, an in-depth study of the two stones. *Descripción histórica* was a labor of love, the result of years of painstaking research and familiarity with indigenous sources. It is a text difficult to summarize, given its many argumentative lines and its extreme complexity. León y Gama, a poorly understood and largely overlooked figure of the Spanish American Enlightenment, yet one of its brightest luminaries, used the stones as a window through which to study Mesoamerican chronology, calendrics, and mythology.[10] Like Boturini and Mariano Fernández de Echeverría y Veytia, León y Gama aspired to correct all previous interpretations.

Given the numerous interpretations of Mesoamerican calendrics, León y Gama, like Boturini and Echeverría y Veytia, gave precedence to original indigenous documents. Whereas Echeverría y Veytia used reasoned hypothesis and colonial indigenous wheels as his ultimate reference, León y Gama privileged Nahuatl annals in Latin script by sixteenth-century Amerindian interpreters such as Fernando de Alvarado Tezozomoc, Francisco de San Antón Muñón Chimalpain Cuauhtlehuanitzin, and Cristóbal del Castillo (1526–1606). León y Gama also privileged two indigenous sources written in Mesoamerican scripts: the Codex en Cruz ("crosslike annals" — hence the name — that recorded in traditional logograms and pictograms several 52-year cycles of central Mexican history, including events after the Conquest) and the Tonalamatl Aubin (a ritual calendar of early colonial provenance, part of Boturini's impounded collection, named after its nineteenth-century French owner, Aubin). The first four sources (Alvarado Tezozomoc's, Chimalpain Cuauhtlehuanitzin's, and Castillo's annals and the Codex en Cruz) contained entries on precolonial and colonial events that combined references to three indigenous calendars at once. They gave dates using three separate calendrical counts: in years (according to the 52-year cycle), in days (according to the 260-day ritual cycle), and in months (according to the 18-month annual cycle). Any worthy interpretation had to correlate each triple calendrical entry with the Gregorian calendar. Moreover, an interpretation had to correlate all sources with one another, a particular challenge given that Alvarado Tezozomoc, Chimalpain Cuauhtlehuanitzin, Castillo, and the author of the Codex en Cruz belonged to different ethnic groups with calendrical variations of their own. This multi-ethnic system led to confusion. For example, the date of Cortés's arrival in Mexico, November 9, 1519, in the Julian calendar appeared recorded in Castillo's annals (Texcocan) as year "1 Cane" (in the 52-year "century" count), day "1 Cane" (in the 260-day ritual calendar), and the 13th of the month Quecholli (in the 18-month annual count). In Mexica annals such as Alvarado Tezozomoc's, however, the same date appeared as year "1 Cane," day "4 Eagle" (4 Cozcaquauhtli), the 16th of the month Quecholli. To make things more complicated, even within a single calendrical system there were contradictory references. Castillo, for example, had recorded the fall of Tenochtitlan (which according to the Julian calendar happened on August 12, 1521) in the year "3 House," day "1 Snake." Had Castillo been consistent and followed his own Texcocan calendar, the fall of the city should have corresponded to day "4 Snake," not "1 Snake." Such inconsistencies had bedeviled previous students of Mesoamerican chronology.

León y Gama showed that none of the available interpretations, including those advanced by Gemelli Careri, Echeverría y Veytia, Boturini, and Clavijero, could make sense of any of the dates in these Amerindian sources. Chimalpain Cuauhtlehuanitzin and Alvarado Tezozomoc, for example, maintained that Moctezuma Xocoyoltzin's ascension to the throne corresponded to year "10 Rabbit," day "9 Deer," and the seventh of the month Tozoztontli in the Amerindian counts (1502 C.E. in the Julian calendar). León y Gama showed that if one were to follow the different models of Clavijero, Gemelli Careri, Boturini, and Echeverría y Veytia, it was impossible to correlate year "10 Rabbit," day "9 Deer" with the seventh of the month Tozoztontli.[11] These models could not even reconcile a date within the same calendrical system, much less make different ethnic calendric variations correspond with one another. So, to clear the air, León y Gama first criticized all previous interpretations of the order of days (in a 260-day ritual count), months (in an annual count), and years (in a 52-year count). Drawing on Echeverría y Veytia, León y Gama argued that the origins of all the confusion lay in the efforts of Europeans to get orderly linear series out of wheels that did not have clear beginnings or ends.

The problem of all European interpreters, León y Gama suggested, stemmed from their inability to detect spurious colonial documents. For example, León y Gama maintained that the order of the months in Gemelli Careri's wheel was the most accurate (Fig. 5.3a), but that the colonial interpreters of the wheel had tinkered with the original, changing the direction in which the wheel had to be read (counterclockwise in the original) and substituting the sign of the month Tozoztontli (month of "the lesser vigil/fast") for the sign of month Quecholli ("Flier"). In Gemelli Careri's wheel,

Tozoztontli appeared represented by the hieroglyph of a pierced bird (instead of flayed human skins appropriate to identify a month of fasting and human sacrifice), and a flayed human skin (instead of a pierced bird) represented the month Quecholli. Clavijero had sought to make adjustments by changing the direction of Gemelli Careri's wheel but was unable to detect that the hieroglyphs of the two months had been switched (Fig. 5.3b). Not surprisingly, Clavijero remained puzzled by the gap between the etymologies of these two months and their respective hieroglyphs.[12] This inability to detect spurious colonial sources was one of the most important charges León y Gama leveled against Clavijero and others, including Echeverría y Veytia. Clavijero, León y Gama argued, copied the Franciscan Diego Valadés's wheel of the months in an annual cycle (Fig. 5.4a), changing only its direction but preserving symbols that were clearly of colonial provenance (Fig. 5.4b). The symbols of the months in Clavijero's wheel did not correspond at all with those on the recently discovered Solar Stone (Fig. 5.4c).[13]

Using Cristóbal del Castillo's sixteenth-century interpretation of the Tonalamatl Aubin and the ritual calendar itself (as well as the calendar stone), León y Gama set out to provide his own analysis of Mesoamerican calendars and annals. After having postulated an interpretation of the correct order of the series of days and months, León y Gama tackled the difficult issue of correlating the multiple ethnic versions of the calendar with European Julian and Gregorian chronologies. Citing obscure references in Torquemada and Acosta, he argued that the Mesoamerican 52-year cycle began with the winter solstice, at midnight on December 26, when the Pleiades were ascendant in the sky over Mexico City. León y Gama maintained that since the natives had only 365 days in their annual cycle, they had alternately added twelve or thirteen extra days at the end of every 52-year cycle to compensate for the day lost every four years. Thus every new cycle coincided again with the date of the winter solstice, and every 104 years the Amerindians caught up with the real duration of the tropical year.[14] All references in Amerindian sources therefore required the addition of as many days as needed to compensate for the years left unintercalated in a 52-year cycle. To do so, it was also necessary to identify the ethnic provenance of the Amerindian source with which an author was working. Moreover, European dates also needed corrections. All dates in the Julian calendar required nine extra days.

Using these techniques, León y Gama managed to correlate references in sources to the day of Moctezuma Xocoyoltzin's coronation and the day of the Spanish landing. The contradictory reference to *ce cohuatl* (day "1 Snake") as

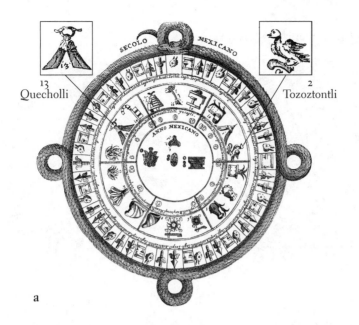

13
Quecholli

2
Tozoztontli

a

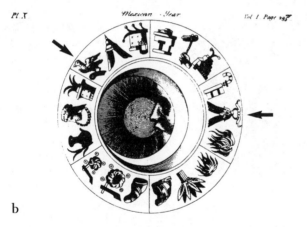

b

FIGURE 5.3. (a) The order of the eighteen months of the
Nahua annual cycle. According to Antonio de León y
Gama, Clavijero modified the direction of the wheel but
failed to switch the images of Quecholli, # 13 in (a) and
Tozoztontli, #2 in (a). Giovanni Francesco Gemelli Careri,
Giro del mondo (Naples, 1699–1700). Courtesy of the John
Carter Brown Library, Brown University, Providence, R.I.
(b) A modified version of Gemelli Careri's 18-month annual
wheel from Francisco Clavijero's *Storia antica del Messico*
(Cesena, 1780–81). Courtesy of the Department of Rare
Books and Special Collections, Princeton University Library.

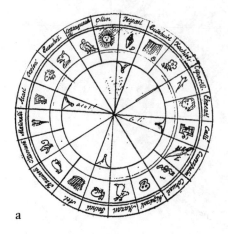

a

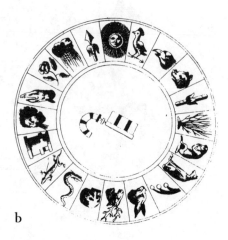

b

c

FIGURE 5.4. Three different versions of a 20-day month calendric wheel. (a) From Diego Valadés, *Rhetorica Christiana* (Perugia, 1579). (b) From Francisco Clavijero, *Storia antica del Messico* (Cesena, 1780–81). Courtesy of the Department of Rare Books and Special Collections, Princeton University Library. (c) From Antonio de León y Gama, *Descripción histórica de las dos piedras* (Mexico, 1792). Clavijero copied his wheel from Valadés, keeping the same images of clear colonial provenance, and changing only the direction of the signs. The images of the signs of the days in (a) and (b) differ markedly from those of the precolonial version found in the Solar Stone (c).

the day of the surrender of the Aztec city of Tenochtitlan, however, proved more challenging. León y Gama had already demonstrated that in the 260-day ritual count of the Tonalamatl Aubin, all days were "accompanied" by other signs, corresponding to other counts in addition to the three already discussed (annual, ritual, and monthly). The nine signs of the "lords of the night" in the Tonalamatl Aubin (Fig. 5.5), for example, did not overlap with signs of a ritual cycle. In each new thirteen-day "week" of the ritual count, the same day sign was followed by a different accompanying sign or "lord of the night," making it possible for Amerindian annalists to give a date simply by including the day sign and its accompanying lord of the night.[15] This was the case with references to the date of the final surrender of Tenochtitlan, which according to Amerindian sources occurred in the day "1 Snake" (*ce cohuatl*), with its accompanying lord of the night, "Water." No calendric model, including León y Gama's, however, could correlate day "1 Snake," lord of the night "Water," with the European date (August 12, 1521, in the Julian calendar, but August 21 in the corrected Gregorian count). To circumvent the problem, León y Gama argued that the reference to "1 Snake/Water" was metaphoric. The reference to "1 Snake," he maintained, alluded to the last of the five "idle" days (*nemontemi*) of the 365-day calendar, the most ominous of all, and therefore to a disastrous turning point in history, not an actual date. The reference to the lord of the night "Water" was also metaphorical. It sought to signify the rainy day when the capital of the Aztecs fell after a three-month siege.[16]

If most date references by Nahua annalists fit perfectly after León y Gama subjected them to adjustments and metaphoric interpretations, there were others that could not be so easily accommodated. To save his model in the face of such challenges, León y Gama argued that some Amerindian annalists were wrong. He used astronomy to prove it. Like Carlos de Sigüenza y Góngora, León y Gama sought to correlate dates in Amerindian annals with the Gregorian calendar using references to eclipses and other stellar phenomena in the indigenous sources. Many annals, for example, had identified two solar eclipses during the reign of the Mexica ruler Axayacatl ("Face of Water") (r. 1469–83 in the Codex Mendoza). One was a complete eclipse the day following Axayacatl's triumph over the Matlazinca; the other was partial and marked Axayacatl's death. The dates of the eclipses in indigenous sources were difficult to pinpoint. Three different annals to which León y Gama had access contradictorily asserted that the first eclipse took place in 1476, 1478, and 1479. Only one of the three sources identified the day as "1 Movement" (*ce Ollin*). As for the second eclipse, only one of the three annals referred to it at all, placing it in the year 1481. Using available tables that traced back the motions of the moon relative to the sun, León y Gama identified several eclipses that had in fact occurred in Mexico between 1476 and 1481. He then concluded that two eclipses, one in 1477 and the other in 1481, had been complete. It was the eclipse of 1481, not that of 1477, as one of the annals maintained, however, that had fallen on the day "1 Movement." León y Gama therefore assumed that the annalists, Domingo Hernández Ayotzin and two anonymous others, had switched the date of one eclipse and mistaken the year of the other. Of all the indigenous sources that dated eclipses

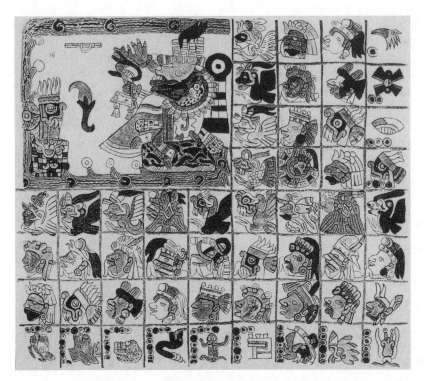

FIGURE 5.5. The dominant signs in the sixteenth week of the ritual calendar Tonalamatl Aubin. As in a typical ritual calendar, the dominant sign of the thirteen days of the "week" is in the upper left corner. The thirteen day signs are located in the bottom line and in the upper four squares of the outer right column. The lines and columns in between represent "accompanying" ritual cycles, including the cycle of the nine "lords of the night" immediately to the left of and above the squares that house the day signs. León y Gama used the Tonalamatl Aubin and Cristóbal del Castillo's interpretation extensively to recreate the many cycles of the calendar. León y Gama also used the image in the periphery of the upper left corner to argue that the sign Ollin Tonatiuh is frequently accompanied by the sign of the Milky Way, as in the case of the Solar Stone. It also supported his thesis that most images in Mesoamerican sources referred to simplified hieroglyphic attributes of deities, as is the case of the figure of Tlaloc in the upper left corner and in the images of the lords of the night.

during the reign of Axayacatl, only one was trustworthy: Chimalpain Cuauhtlehuanitzin's annals.[17] The point behind such an erudite exercise was that not all precolonial Amerindian sources were reliable. According to León y Gama, historians had to weigh the credibility of Amerindian documents, precolonial as well as colonial. This skeptical attitude toward precolonial and early colonial annals, despite their having been written by Amerindian nobles, was a new departure. Like the northern European authors that he himself despised, León y Gama did not credit sources simply because they had been written by upper-class native scribes. He subjected Amerindian annals to the test of internal logical analysis. It is in this more than any other sense that León y Gama can safely be classified as a figure of the Enlightenment.

Supplied with a wealth of information, and such a demonstrable command of most available precolonial and early colonial Nahuatl sources, León y Gama set out to study the stones, which he used to highlight the creativity of the Amerindians. By insisting that the natives had in fact lacked iron tools and sophisticated technologies, León y Gama transformed the stones into a cause for wonder.[18] Like Fábrega and Clavijero, he turned the tables on European critics by highlighting the Amerindians' accomplishments despite their limited technologies. The stones, León y Gama contended, demonstrated the exquisite ability of the Amerindians to work granite without iron tools. They also proved that they had known a great deal about mechanics (because pulleys had been required to move the boulders just a few meters), geometry (indicated by the perfect circular cuts of the Solar Stone), and astronomy.

Yet for all the accomplishments of the natives, the monstrous-looking stone (Fig. 5.1a) seemed to indicate that the Mexica had a poor command of aesthetic principles. León y Gama, however, maintained that the monolith was a composite of hieroglyphs of deities, not a distorted rendition of the human body. Citing an illustration of the deity Tlaloc published by Gemelli Careri, León y Gama argued that the natives had developed the ability to render the bodies of deities (Fig. 5.1b) exquisitely. It followed, therefore, that aesthetically repulsive representations were montages of many hieroglyphs of deities, the result of deliberate choice by natives well acquainted with the rules of fine art.[19]

Drawing on the Tonalamatl Aubin and on a careful reading of Torquemada's volume on Mesoamerican religions, León y Gama managed to identify the hieroglyphs of at least seven deities in the sculpture. Teoyaomaqui, a goddess charged with collecting the souls of warriors who died in sacred battles and of sacrificial victims to take them to the enchanting heavenly house of the

Sun, was represented in the sculpture by the breasts and the collar of hands around the neck. The "bags" of copal incense (in fact, representations of hearts), located in the collar next to the hands, stood for the ritual offering by warriors to the goddess before battle. Huitzilopochtli appeared as the "mask" on top of the figure, as well as being represented in the skulls on the belt. The snake-woven skirt, León y Gama argued, stood for Cohuatluye (Huitzilopochtli's mother) and the snake and feathers underneath the skirt represented Quetzalcoatl. On the base of the sculpture, there lay the hiero-glyphic attributes of Miclanteuhtli, the lord of the netherworld, and Tlalxicco, the netherworld, to which the souls of those who did not die in bat-tle were carried away.[20]

The second stone was equally problematic and difficult to understand (Fig. 5.2). León y Gama concluded that the monolith was a calendar that plotted several important dates associated with the cult of the sun in a 260-day ritual count. It recorded dates in three separate ways: through (1) large and (2) small gnomons stuck in the sockets around the outside of the wheel, identified in Figure 5.2 as *xzys* and *ppqq*, and (3) through dates carved on the wheel proper. The holes around the wheel, León y Gama argued, in one of the most speculative sections of the essay, were the sockets of gnomons, whose shadows had helped measure the path of the sun through the ecliptic between two solstices (*xzys*) and between two equinoxes (*ppqq*).[21] The carved wheel itself recorded important religious dates in a calendar corresponding to the year "13 Cane" (found at the top of the wheel) of a 52-year count. The symbols in the outer circle of the wheel, León y Gama maintained, repre-sented the Milky Way and the image in the center of the wheel, a clawed sun with an open mouth, Ollin Tonatiuh (Solar Movements), a day-sign of the ritual count. That the symbols of the Milky Way and Ollin Tonatiuh were usually together, León y Gama asserted, was attested by the fact that they appeared joined in the same page of the Tonalamatl Aubin as the ruling "zo-diacal" sign of the thirteenth "week" of the ritual count (Fig. 5.5).[22] Ollin Tonatiuh, in turn, Leon y Gama argued, was a representation of the four solar ages, for the dates of the end of each of these ages were located in the corners of the image. Dismissing Echeverría y Veytia's and Boturini's inter-pretations of the order of the solar ages, León y Gama maintained that the dates and the succession of ages in the stone coincided with those found in an anonymous document in Nahuatl in Alva Ixtlilxochitl's collection.[23] León y Gama also managed to find many other calendrical symbols allegedly rep-resenting dates in honor of the sun in a semi-annual ritual cycle.

José Antonio de Alzate y Ramírez's Misgivings

Despite its impressive rigor, this extraordinary text met with a chilly reception, and León y Gama failed to attract subscribers for a second volume, and it was thus left unpublished. Moreover, León y Gama's *Descripción histórica* soon came under attack by Alzate y Ramírez, the editor of *Gacetas de literatura*, who had pronounced himself unable to speculate on the meaning of the stones.

Before reviewing Alzate y Ramírez's critique, we need to turn briefly to the origins of the animosity between Alzate y Ramírez and León y Gama. Alzate y Ramírez, a secular priest, belonged to the same educated petit bourgeois class as León y Gama, but unlike León y Gama, he was a wealthy man and enjoyed international recognition. As the only child of a prosperous family of bakers, he had the resources to subsidize several periodicals over the course of his lifetime. The French Académie des sciences considered at least one of Alzate y Ramírez's works on the natural history of New Spain, and in 1771, the Académie granted him the title of corresponding member.[24] In contrast, León y Gama was a middling bureaucrat burdened by responsibilities and a large family. His efforts to gain a measure of international recognition ultimately failed, and this failure was the source of his lasting dislike of Alzate y Ramírez.

In 1772, sending the French astronomer Joseph-Jerôme Le François de Lalande (1732–1807) data on an eclipse to correct information previously sent by Alzate y Ramírez, León y Gama called Alzate y Ramírez's astronomical observations sloppy and shaming to the Creole nation — just the sort of thing, he said, that led some foreigners to see Mexicans "as irrational creatures, others as incapable, and the great majority as monsters [*faunos*] or savages."[25] Delighted by the unexpected arrival of valuable information, Lalande wrote back and asked León y Gama for information on the satellites of Jupiter seen from Mexico and on tides, as well as for an accurate map of New Spain.[26] León y Gama responded with information on tides at distant coastal sites, and Lalande replied requesting data on comets, promising to reward León y Gama's efforts with acknowledgment in his forthcoming treatises.[27] Lalande never fulfilled his end of the bargain to my knowledge, and León y Gama was saddled with Alzate y Ramírez's lasting enmity.

León y Gama and Alzate y Ramírez first clashed in public in 1789 and 1790 in a debate about the interpretation of a celestial light that appeared on the northern horizon of New Spain, the aurora borealis.[28] Because this debate got personal and nasty, it comes as something of a surprise that in June

1792 Alzate y Ramírez advanced only a lukewarm critique of León y Gama's description of the two stones. Alzate y Ramírez argued that León y Gama had failed to propose a general interpretation of Mexican hieroglyphs, and that another antiquarian was about to offer an alternative reading of the stones, a veiled reference to the work of José Ignacio Borunda. León y Gama's public response was also restrained and challenged Alzate y Ramírez's friend to publish.[29] Alzate y Ramírez replied this time with a lengthier critique of the shortcomings he found in Leon y Gama's treatise. To better understand Alzate y Ramírez's second critique we need to examine Alzate y Ramírez's career as a patriot and as an antiquarian.

More than any other scholar, Alzate y Ramírez pushed the anti-Eurocentric dimensions of the discourse of patriotic epistemology to its limits. He launched *Gacetas de literatura* in 1788 with the intention, among other things, of subjecting foreign accounts on New Spain to public scrutiny. The reviews in *Gacetas de literatura* sought to demonstrate the epistemological limitations of outsiders in comprehending the nature and history of the New World. Alzate y Ramírez's approach was typified by his criticism of the travel writings of Joseph La Porte and Lord Anson and of a treatise on gold and silver amalgams by Baron Ignaz von Born (1742–1791). In 1788, Alzate y Ramírez declared that in the compilation of travel narratives by La Porte, the French editor had treated New Spaniards worse than Eskimo "savages." In particular, Alzate y Ramírez zeroed in on those passages by La Porte that presented colonials in New Spain as lascivious, corrupt, ignorant, and superstitious. Alzate y Ramírez also condemned the Frenchman's many factual mistakes of natural history and geography.[30] Seeking to expose the lies of travelers to the Mexican public, Alzate y Ramírez also took on Lord George Anson, who had depicted Spanish Americans as cowards, so incapable of defending the colonies that in Anson's estimation the entire viceroyalty of Peru could be conquered by a 1,500-man naval force. Alzate y Ramírez introduced evidence from an unpublished memoir describing the siege of Manila by the English where a contingent of Mexican commoners (the Philippines were economically and politically linked to New Spain) had outsmarted the aggressors. Contrary to Lord Anson's assertions, this episode showed that even the rabble of New Spain, the "feces" (*heces*) of Mexico, was capable of routing the English, and that "even the rotten members of the Spanish nation maintained their noble lineage."[31] In 1790, Alzate y Ramírez blasted Baron Ignaz von Born's history of silver mining, which was even more outrageous than the books of La Porte and Anson. Although he appeared to be praising the Creole inventor in his account of the discovery of the technique of amalgamating mercury with silver in Spanish America, Born depicted it as having occurred by mere chance and called for scientific study of the process so that it could be put to better use in European mines. Besides his numerous factual historical errors, including the name of the discoverer of amalgamation, Born described the colonists as rabidly opposed to the Spanish crown's introduction of rational reforms in mining.[32] Alzate y Ramírez took issue with each and every one of Born's points.[33]

In notes commissioned by the Spanish printer Antonio de Sancha for the failed Spanish edition of Clavijero's history, Alzate y Ramírez echoed the Jesuit's conclusion that foreign travelers tended to be ignorant of native languages, gullible, and easily manipulated by savvy locals.[34] Alzate y Ramírez's critique of foreign accounts was, however, also part of a larger critique of system builders. From this perspective, he critically scrutinized the natural and civil histories of the viceroyalty of New Granada written by the Italian Jesuit Filippo Gilii (1721–1789),[35] whom he cast as a follower of conjectural historians such as Buffon. Subordinating observation to their systems, such armchair philosophers concluded on the flimsiest of evidence that the New World had only recently emerged from the ocean, and that the Amerindians were thus newcomers. The facts showed, however, that Buffon was wrong. Amerindian monuments proved that the natives had ancient roots, and the higher mountain peaks of America showed that the New World had emerged much earlier than Europe. The many mistakes in Gilii's text, beginning with the title, *Saggio di storia americana; o sia, Storia naturale, civile e sacra de'regni, e delle provincie spagnuole di Terra-ferma nell'America meridionale*, suggested that he had never actually visited Panama, Colombia, and Venezuela, which he claimed to describe, and his generalizations about cowardly *castas* (mestizos or mulattos) and drunken Amerindians showed his predilection for system building. Not all Amerindians and mestizos were alike.[36]

Having read Clavijero's analysis of the contradictions and inconsistencies in the writings of the likes of de Pauw, Buffon, and Robertson, Alzate y Ramírez firmly linked his attack on system builders to his patriotism. By so doing, he created a discourse that presented New Spain as a land whose natural wealth showed the folly of all philosophical generalizations. Like the Jesuit Juan de Velasco (whose work he did not know), Alzate y Ramírez insisted that patriotic natural historians should identify the "curiosities" of the land to debunk European system builders. Alzate y Ramírez made a career out of discovering natural phenomena that contradicted the natural "laws" devised by European naturalists, particularly by taxonomists such as Linnaeus.[37]

Between 1788 and 1790, Alzate y Ramírez engaged Vicente Cervantes (1755–1829), a Spanish naturalist charged with teaching Linnaean taxonomy at the new Royal Botanical Garden, founded to challenge the clerical-Creole control of the faculty of medicine at the University of Mexico. In a debate conducted in the pages of rival Mexican periodicals, Alzate y Ramírez derided the Linnaean classifications propounded by the newcomer Cervantes for their inability to capture the uniqueness of Mexican species; their tendency to group fauna and flora not according to "virtues" but according to misleading, sometimes microscopic, resemblances; and, finally, their corrupting influence on youth because of their inordinate attention to the sexual characteristics of plants.[38] Alzate y Ramírez used the singularities of many of the fauna and flora of Mexico to throw in disarray the neat logic of Linnaeus and his Spanish disciple and to highlight the incompetence of foreigners ever to comprehend Mexican reality.[39]

Alzate y Ramírez on Xochicalco

Alzate y Ramírez's dislike of foreign "systems" also surfaced in his forays as an antiquarian. In the pages of *Gacetas de literatura*, he often introduced reports of ancient ruins. Among all these reports, *Descripción de las antigüedades de Xochicalco*, a study of the ruins found in Xochicalco (later used by the Jesuit Pedro José de Márquez), stood out. Although Alzate y Ramírez claimed that he had originally written the work around 1777 and that it had been translated into Italian, suggesting therefore that Clavijero might have derived his ideas from reading it (Alzate y Ramírez had no modesty), he published it in 1791 as a supplement of his *Gacetas de literatura* to commemorate the visit of Alejandro Malaspina's scientific expedition to Mexico.[40] Be that as it may, Alzate y Ramírez set out to expose foreign representations of ancient Mexicans as "innuendo" and "sinister views."[41] The entire treatise was framed as a polemic against foreign skeptics such as de Pauw, Raynal, and Robertson, whose "internal" readings of sources led them to suppose that reports of high population density and the military prowess of the Aztecs were refuted by the ease of the Conquest, that accounts of the grandeur of precolonial Mexican cities were undermined by the wretchedness of contemporary Amerindians, and that the reports of the courtly deportment of the Aztecs were called into question by the extent and barbarity of Aztec human sacrifices. Alzate y Ramírez also framed his work as a reply to comments made by naturalists such as Buffon and Jacques Christophe Valmont de Bomare (1731–1807) to the effect that the Mesoamericans were recent arrivals and that precolonial

Mexico had therefore been thinly populated. Finally, Alzate y Ramírez sought to contest Lalande's assertions that the precolonial Mexicans had known no astronomy.[42]

Alzate y Ramírez rejected as spurious the contradictions identified by the skeptics. The Conquest, he argued, had not been easy; the Spaniards had fought with hundreds of thousands of Amerindians as allies. As for the allegedly widespread practice of human sacrifice, Alzate y Ramírez maintained, it was simply an exaggeration by biased parties who did not understand that these practices were typical of all ancient societies. Taking on the northern European critics at their own game, Alzate y Ramírez — who, like the northern Europeans, had rejected Amerindian literary sources on the grounds that they were undecipherable — used precisely the alternative, non-literary evidence (that is, material remains) proposed by the critics to refute them. On the charges leveled by Buffon, Valmont de Bomare, and Lalande, Alzate y Ramírez argued that the ruins of Xochicalco, a fortified castle with ditches, terraces, a pyramid, and subterranean pathways, proved them wrong (Fig. 4.11). The ruins demonstrated that the ancient inhabitants of Mesoamerica had known mechanics (only pulleys could have moved the boulders), military engineering (given the fortifications in the mound), subterranean geometry (in the arched tunnels and vaulted rooms inside the mountain), and astronomy (the castle was perfectly aligned relative to the four cardinal points). Like Clavijero, León y Gama, and Fábrega, Alzate y Ramírez also maintained that these accomplishments were all the more remarkable in that the Amerindians had enjoyed limited technologies and lacked iron tools.[43]

In his description of the "castle" of Xochicalco, Alzate y Ramírez addressed one of the contradictions identified by the European skeptics, namely, that the wretched, meek contemporary Amerindians gave the lie to reports of grandiose ancient societies. As a typical Creole patriot, Alzate y Ramírez argued that the behavior of contemporary Amerindian commoners, "negligible plebes" (ínfima plebe), should not be used to judge the accomplishments of the ancient Amerindian ruling elites.[44] Like many Creole patriots before him, Alzate y Ramírez carefully distinguished between the glorious stratified Amerindian societies of the past and the wretched, miserable communities of the present. This transformation, he maintained, was the result of the metamorphosis of Amerindian polities into homogeneous collectives of commoners. In his notes to Clavijero's history, Alzate y Ramírez set out to demonstrate that "contamination" by urban mestizos had led to the corruption and decline of Amerindian communities.[45]

The blurring of social distinctions in indigenous communities, according to Alzate y Ramírez, rendered the testimony of all contemporary Amerindians worthless. He himself, however, offered a hypothetical reconstruction of the pyramid that seemed to have existed on top of the castle mound based on the statements of anonymous witnesses, who may or may not have been Amerindians. Yet he also derided the value of the testimony of the Amerindian authorities of the town of Tetlama, who informed him that underneath the mountain of Xochicalco, there lay a network of tunnels that reached the capital, and that the ghost of an old Amerindian lived in them. Alzate y Ramírez dismissed the testimony of these "noble" Amerindian informants as "ridiculous fictions" (*patrañas*) and "popular errors," typical of "imaginations inhabited by phantasms."[46]

Alzate y Ramírez did not behave like a typical Creole antiquarian when judging Amerindian testimonies. He was prone to dismiss indigenous oral testimonies as well as the written evidence found in the monoliths and pyramids that he himself had contributed to discovering. His skepticism of systems kept him from advancing an interpretation of the hieroglyphs he found in Xochicalco, and at this level, he resembled the skeptical northern European critics of the Americas. But Alzate y Ramírez was a patriot and turned the tables on the Europeans by using these alternative, nonliterary forms of evidence (the ramparts, tunnels, and pyramids of Xochicalco) to prove the critics wrongs. It is at this point that we must return to an analysis of Alzate y Ramírez's critique of Antonio de León y Gama's study.

Alzate y Ramírez's Critique of León y Gama

In some ways, Alzate y Ramírez's criticism was petty. For example, he devoted a large part of his argument to challenging León y Gama's mineralogical classification and calculations of the weights of the two stones. But Alzate y Ramírez also raised points of greater significance. He first denounced León y Gama for having shown an exaggerated preoccupation with "systems," echoing the same criticism he had used against León y Gama during the debate over the nature of the aurora borealis. This time, Alzate y Ramírez cast León y Gama as a follower of philosophical historians and pedantic antiquarians. After poking fun, like Voltaire, at biblical scholars whose entire historical systems rested on a few etymologies, Alzate y Ramírez contended that etymologists like León y Gama were responsible for having created conjectural histories of the origins of human institutions that blurred the distinctions between humans and animals. In an indirect reference to Rousseau and his followers, Alzate y Ramírez maintained that these conjectural historians-cum-etymologists derived the origins of humans from parrots, monkeys, or dogs based simply on the similarities of animal and human sounds. León y Gama's scholarship, Alzate y Ramírez argued, belonged in this speculative world. Claiming that no two past scholars, independent of their social standing and learning, had managed to agree on the interpretation of simple Nahuatl words, Alzate y Ramírez argued that any interpretation of Mesoamerican calendrics and scripts was hopeless, including those advanced in León y Gama's *Descripción histórica*. Alzate y Ramírez insisted that he was unable to interpret any of the hieroglyphs on the stones.[47]

Alzate y Ramírez's second criticism was also designed to expose León y Gama's alleged fondness for systems. Alzate y Ramírez argued that the only way to see whether the Solar Stone was a sundial was to conduct an experiment. Alzate y Ramírez urged León y Gama to put gnomons in the sockets of the Solar Stone to see whether the shadows marked solstices and equinoxes as he had predicted. Alzate y Ramírez's third criticism was of León y Gama's racial characterization of Cristóbal del Castillo, the Amerindian historian whose annals and calendric interpretations were the foundation upon which most of León y Gama's system rested. Alzate y Ramírez maintained that Castillo had not been an Amerindian but a mestizo. Thus he implicitly called into question the reliability of León y Gama's entire oeuvre, for mestizos enjoyed little or no credibility among the clerical elites of colonial Spanish America.[48] Alzate y Ramírez, the great critic of speculative theories, paradoxically closed his essay by demanding from León y Gama "a key," a system (!) for understanding Mesoamerican scripts, that is, "the rules by means of which all figures [hieroglyphs] should be interpreted."[49]

León y Gama's Reply

Alzate y Ramírez's tirade prompted León y Gama to respond with an even more remarkable second treatise on Mesoamerican antiquities, which, as noted, unfortunately failed to attract subscribers and was left unpublished. In the second installment of his *Descripción histórica*, León y Gama interpreted four other stones found in the plaza of Mexico between January 1791 and June 1792. One, León y Gama contended, was yet another solar calendar, whose 128 circles represented the days that intervened between the beginning of the year and the most important festival of the sun in the Mexica calendar, one that fell sometime in mid May (Fig. 5.6a). The figures carved on the walls of the cylinder signified the dancers of fifteen outlying towns, whose names León y Gama made out by interpreting their logograms. Every year in mid May, León y Gama argued, dancers from nearby towns had worshipped the sun as a reminder of their subordination to the Mexica.[50] The other three stones, according to León y Gama were aesthetically repulsive montages of attributes of deities: Huitzilopochtli and Tlacahuepancuexcotzin (Fig. 5.6b); Quetzalcoatl (Fig. 5.6c); and Tlaloc, god of the rain. The second part of the *Descripción histórica* also included a survey of all the stones to be found in the capital (Fig. 5.7); an essay on Mesoamerican arithmetic and mathematics; and a paper in which he sought to prove geometrically (not experimentally as Alzate y Ramírez had demanded he do) that the gnomons of the first Solar Stone were, in fact, part of a sundial. It is, however, the introductory essay that I find significant for the purposes of this chapter. In it, León y Gama replied to each and every one of the charges leveled by Alzate y Ramírez.

León y Gama responded to Alzate y Ramírez's contention that Cristóbal del Castillo was a mestizo by contrasting the latter with contemporary *castas*. Mestizos, he argued, did not have the command of Nahuatl exhibited by Castillo. By and large, they sought to forget their indigenous roots, including their maternal language. Only a native, descendant of the great Nezahualcoyotl, legendary monarch of Texcoco, could have had both the command of classic Nahuatl, so full of metaphors, and the knowledge of astronomy and calendrics that Castillo displayed. Alzate y Ramírez, León y Gama concluded, had clearly lacked any contact with mestizos. Had Alzate y Ramírez rubbed shoulders with them, as León y Gama had during his thirty-six years working at the high court, he would have realized that mestizos did not work as interpreters in local tribunals. Moreover, had Alzate y Ramírez known his history better, he would have realized that it was perfectly normal for upper-class natives like Cristóbal del Castillo to adopt Hispanic names. Moreover, had Alzate y Ramírez done his calculations, he would have discovered that Castillo had most likely been born prior to the invasion of the Spaniards in 1519.[51] The fact that León y Gama spent several pages belaboring the point that Castillo was no mestizo speaks volumes about the fact that belonging to the lower racial estates in colonial Spanish America undermined the worth of one's historical testimony.

To the criticism that his work lacked a "general key" to interpreting Amerindian scripts, León y Gama responded with a remarkable essay in which he set out to demonstrate that only a limited few were capable of handling original Amerindian primary sources, because reading indigenous documents required an exquisite command of local natural history, Nahuatl, and

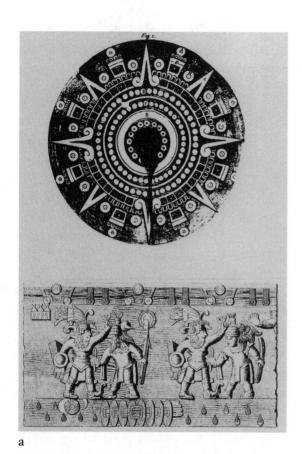

a

b

c

FIGURE 5.6. Images from three other stones found in Mexico City between 1790 and 1792 and interpreted by León y Gama in the second, unpublished part of his *Descripción histórica*. (a) Semi-annual calendar plotting the dates of one of the most important festivals of the sun, in which "dancers" from fifteen subordinated towns were summoned to "worship" both the sun and the Mexica. (b) Symbolic attributes of Huitzilopochtli. (c) Symbolic attributes of Quetzalcoatl. Collection Goupil-Aubin, MS 97. Courtesy of the Bibliothèque Nationale, Paris.

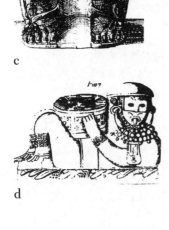

FIGURE 5.7. Hitherto unpublished carvings from stones found scattered in Mexico City in diggings and in the foundation of buildings. According to Antonio de León y Gama they stood for: (a) the calendric day sign 8 Cane (the day the Great Temple was finished during the reign of Ahuitzotl); (b) the symbolic attributes of the deities *cipactli* (calendrical sign), Cohuatl, Ehecatl, and Mizquiztli; (c) Izquitecatl, god of wine; (d) Tezcatzoncatl, god of wine; (e) the calendric day sign 1 Snake; (f) Tezcatlipoca, god of providence; (g) the calendric day sign 2 Monkey; (h) Cihuateotl, a goddess who honored women who died in labor; (i) a frog (given by the authorities to the San Carlos Academy of Art); (j) an eclipse in which the sun is devoured by a creature called the *tequanes*; (k) a wolf (given by the authorities to the San Carlos Academy of Art); and (l) the calendric day sign 5 Crocodile (*cipactli*). Collection Goupil-Aubin, MS 97. Courtesy of the Bibliothèque Nationale, Paris.

Mesoamerican calendrics. In making this point, he, like Alzate y Ramírez, launched an assault on the shallowness of the knowledge of foreign authors. But to appreciate this aspect of his epistemology, we need briefly to review another public debate in which León y Gama participated and in which he first articulated his views on the limited ability of "outsiders" to understand the past and the nature of the New World.

Lizards and Epistemology

In 1782, Dr. José Flores (1751–1824), the *protomédico* (first physician) of the Audiencia of Guatemala, published a treatise claiming to have discovered that the raw flesh of lizards of the Amatitlan region cured cancer, triggering a medical controversy in the capital of the viceroyalty of New Spain.[52] Dr. José Vicente García de la Vega, a distinguished professor of medicine at the University of Mexico, went Flores one better, asserting that not only cancer but other diseases, too, could be treated with the flesh of certain lizards found in the vicinity of Mexico City, which did not, moreover, need to be eaten raw but could be mixed into unguents or ingested in pill form.[53] In a confidential report to the city council, which was charged with regulating medical practice in the capital, Dr. Manuel Antonio Moreno and Dr. Alejo Ramón Sánchez recommended, however, that it outlaw the use of lizard flesh, the "acrid" particles of which had proven in many trials to be poisonous rather than miraculous, they said. At this point, León y Gama stepped in with his *Instrucción sobre el remedio de las lagartijas*, urging that the city council not forbid this cure. Contrary to García de la Vega's claim, however, León y Gama contended that since the curative power of lizards did not reside in any "subtle animal spirit" but in the organic attraction between the flesh of the lizard and the tumor, the lizard flesh did, indeed, have to be eaten raw. Citing Newton, he depicted the lizard as an animal "lodestone" that "attracted" splinters on the outside and tumors inside. As for Moreno and Sánchez's warning, he countered that the trials they had conducted were unreliable and flawed: they had either administered the wrong lizard to their patients or had mishandled those that were curative. Drawing on the works of Francisco Hernández, the sixteenth-century savant sent by Philip II to compile a natural history of the New World, León y Gama maintained that several distinct species of lizards, some of them indeed poisonous, existed in central Mexico. To identify them as well as their virtues, great care and great knowledge was needed. León y Gama conceded that the two physicians might have given their patients the curative species but mishandled it. For the cure to work, he argued, many precautions needed to be taken. Once the right lizard was caught, it had to be fed only with the appropriate local insects; all female lizards, particularly pregnant ones, had to be discarded; finally, the lizard had to be treated gently, for if irritated it could become poisonous.[54] The amount of knowledge that these techniques demanded from physicians was extraordinary. Doctors needed to know the natural history of the area in order to identify, feed, and treat the curative lizards properly.

Flores, the physician who had first claimed that raw lizard flesh cured cancer, had not "discovered" anything, León y Gama said. He had simply rediscovered a remedy (*remedio nuevamente descubierto*) long known by the ancient Amerindians, confirming the wealth and complexity of ancient Amerindian herbal and medical lore.[55] The message of León y Gama's *Instrucción* was that only those who knew the local fauna and flora in all their exquisite detail and intricacy could be trusted to use the lizards.[56] The *Instrucción* gives us an outline of León y Gama's epistemology. First, he was a humanist engaged in the *rediscovery* of the insights, medical and otherwise, of the ancient Mesoamericans. Second, he thought that only a tiny learned elite was privy to those insights. When Alzate y Ramírez asked León y Gama to deliver a system to interpret Mesoamerican scripts, he responded just as he did in the debate over the curative power of the lizards. Those who lacked the linguistic skills and the appropriate understanding of the bewildering details of Amerindian lore were condemned to remain in the dark.

A General Key to Mesoamerican Hieroglyphs?

In the unpublished second installment of *Descripción histórica*, León y Gama ridiculed Alzate y Ramírez for seeking a ready-made set of rules for reading Mesoamerican scripts. Indigenous primary sources, León y Gama argued, ranged from widely accessible historical documents to arcane repositories of secret knowledge. He offered a few examples. Codex *Histoire mexicaine (1221–1594)*, on the one hand, indicated that the Tenochtitlan flood had occurred in the year "8 Flint" (1500 C.E.) (Fig 5.8a). Although it, too, in equally rough fashion, placed the Tenochtitlan flood in the year "8 flint," the Codex en Cruz (Fig. 5.8b), on the other hand, dated other events using a finer grid. For example, it recorded the *days* on which the legendary monarch of Texcoco, Nezahualcoyotl (1402 C.E.), his son Nezahualpilli (1464 C.E.), and the ruler Cuauhcaltzin (1502 C.E.) had been born. Moreover, the Codex en Cruz dated the death of Ahuitzotl and the ascension of Moctezuma Xocoyoltzin (1502 C.E.) providing not the sign of the day but of its accompanying "lord of the night." Codex *Histoire mexicaine (1221–1594)*, León y Gama argued, assumed of the reader a very general working knowledge of annual calendrical cycles, whereas the Codex en Cruz demanded from its audience exquisite knowledge of several types of ritual counts. Besides differences of calendrical knowledge, the two codices included pictographic narratives with different degrees of detail that demanded equally different knowledge of reading scripts from the audience. Codex *Histoire mexicaine (1221–1594)*, for example, used the symbol of water to describe a flood in 1500 C.E., whereas the Codex en Cruz recorded not only the date but also the location of the flood, the city of Tenochtitlan, with precision. Moreover, the entry on the flood in the Codex en Cruz included information on the deity responsible for the flood (Chalchihuitlicue) and on the help the Mexica received from the subordinate towns of Texcoco and Tlacopan. The difference between references in documents of the likes of Codex *Histoire mexicaine (1221–1594)* and the Codex en Cruz, León y Gama argued, was not merely a matter of calendrical accuracy and narrative detail; the codices were intended for two different audiences. Sources such as Codex *Histoire mexicaine (1221–1594)* had been written for the masses, because they required only a superficial acquaintance with writing techniques and astronomical knowledge. Sources such as the Codex en Cruz, on the other hand, were addressed to more knowledgeable and sophisticated audiences, for they demanded familiarity with the hieroglyphs of deities and towns, as well as an exquisite command of multiple calendrical counts. The scale of accessibility in Amerindian primary sources, León y Gama maintained, did not stop with these two types of documents. A third type of source, such as the ritual calendar Tonalamatl Aubin, could only be read by highly trained religious specialists (Fig. 5.5). With hundreds of symbols and obscure references to celestial phenomena and deities, sources such as Tonalamatl Aubin demanded from their intended audience complete command of both theological subtleties and celestial physics.[57]

Complicating this system of different documents for different audiences, there was the additional problem of the nature of the logograms and pictograms used by the Amerindians to record their annals. According to León y Gama, logograms and pictograms often alluded to local objects accessible only to a privileged few. An extensive knowledge of local natural history, León y Gama argued, was needed to understand the logograms of town names. The names of towns in such documents as the Codex Cozcatzin and the Codex Azcatitlan could not be read without a vast knowledge of the natural history of central Mexico (Fig. 5.9a). The names of Cimatlan, Tollan,

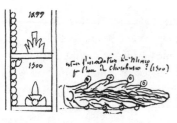

a

b

FIGURE 5.8. Entries recording events that took place in the Central Valley of Mexico around 1500 C.E.: (a) *Histoire mexicaine depuis 1221 jusqu'en 1594*; (b) Codex en Cruz. The copies belonged to León y Gama, who used these entries to exemplify the ascending scale of complexity and accessibility of indigenous sources. Differences in narrative complexity and calendrical accuracy between (a) and (b) are apparent, an indication that they were intended for two different audiences. The entries in the Codex en Cruz exemplify how Aztec script worked. In 1402 C.E. (1 Rabbit, signified by a rabbit's head and one circle), day 1 Deer (a day symbol linked to a deer's head and one circle), Nezahualcoytl ("Fasting Coyote" = a coyote's head and the symbol of a priest's fasting circle) was born (cradle) in the town of Texcoco ("Place of Pot/ Alabaster Stone" = pot on top of a mountain). In 1464 (11 Flint) day 12 Snake, Nezahualpilli ("Fasting Lord" = head and fasting circle) was born (cradle) in Texcoco ("Place of Pot"). In 1500 (8 Flint), Tenochtitlan ("Nopal Cactus on Stone") was flooded (water running over houses; according to León y Gama Chalchihuitlicue is also represented) and received help (represented by two porters, whom León y Gama identified as help from Texcoco and Tlacopan). In 1502 (10 Rabbit) day 11 Rabbit, Cuauhcaltzin ("Caged Bird" according to León y Gama) was born. That same year on a day presided over by Xipe Totec (a lord of the night according to León y Gama), Ahuitzotl ("Water Beast/Otter?") died (mummy bundle) and Moctezuma Xocoyoltzin ("Angry Lord the Younger") took over. Collection Goupil-Aubin, [a] MS 89 (1–2), fol. 24 and [b] MS 88 (5), fols. 71, 74, 77. Courtesy of the Bibliothèque Nationale, Paris.

and Papatztaca, in the Codex Cozcatzin, and Huexotzinc, in the Codex Azcatitlan, were written with logograms and pictograms depicting local shrubs, trees, and flowers. According to León y Gama, some logograms were simply too idiosyncratic and undecipherable, as in the case of references in the Codex Cozcatzin to the town of "Teyahualco," whose rebus image León y Gama challenged anyone to explain (Fig 5.9b). Even more upsetting for those such as Alzate y Ramírez who sought a shortcut to the interpretation of Amerindian documents was the fact that some towns with somewhat similar Nahua names were identified with the same logograms in different documents. This, León y Gama argued, was the case with Atempa in the Codex Cozcatzin and Atenco in the *Matrícula de tributos* (Fig.5.9c).

But if to read the names of towns in Amerindian primary sources at times required knowledge beyond the reach of common mortals, the reading of the names of rulers presented even more challenges. According to León y Gama, the signs scribes used to refer to rulers did not merely allude to the sound of their names but also to some aspects of their moral character. The fact that the logogram of the ruler Cuauhcaltzin in Codex en Cruz was a caged eagle (Fig 5.8b), León y Gama argued, was of little consolation for those who knew that the logograms of the last Mexica monarch, Cuauhtemoc, the Aculhua lord Cuauhtletcohuatzin, and the lord of Coyuacan, Cuauhpopocatzin, in other sources were also eagles. The eagles that represented the names of all the above rulers, however, showed subtle differences; their beaks appeared either shut, open, or giving off smoke, and their eyes gazing up or down. According to León y Gama such subtle distinctions were allusions to some aspect of the moral character of these rulers that had been understood only by a handful of retainers. The logic behind these correlations, therefore, lay now beyond the grasp of any mortal, including late-colonial native scholars.[58]

In his response to Alzate y Ramírez, León y Gama suggested that foreigners were condemned to be unable to read indigenous sources. His analysis of the self-referential complexity of the Mesoamerican writing systems led León y Gama to deny subtly that "outsiders" would ever be able comprehend them. For example, he ridiculed the ideas of Athanasius Kircher on the nature of Mexican scripts. Kircher had declared that Mesoamerican hieroglyphs were completely transparent childish representations, unlike the mysterious symbols used by the Egyptians, which hid sophisticated arcane knowledge. To exemplify this, Kircher had used a page from the Codex Mendoza, edited by Samuel Purchas, representing the baptism of a four-day-old Indian child (Fig.5.10a). The age of the child was given by four circles, standing for days (Fig. 5.10b). According to León y Gama, Kircher had, how-

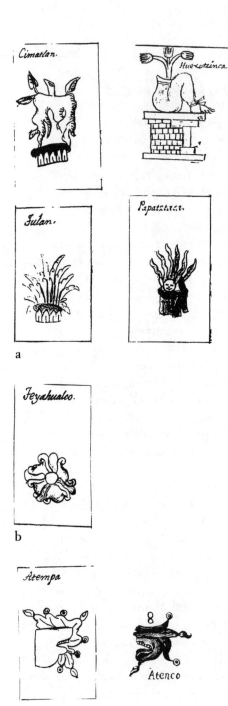

FIGURE 5.9. Pictograms for Meso-american towns in indigenous sources used by León y Gama to demonstrate the difficulty of establishing general rules for the reading of Mesoamerican scripts. (a) Ideograms of towns whose names in rebus refer to local plants. Codex Cozcatzin and Codex Azcatitlan. Collection Goupil-Aubin, MS 89 (3), fol. 34 (#4) and MS 89 (5), fol. 66, 68, 74. Courtesy of the Bibliothèque Nationale, Paris. (b) Ideogram of Teyahualco whose logic León y Gama could not make out. Codex Cozcatzin. Collection Goupil-Aubin, MS 89 (5), fol. 69. Courtesy of the Bibliothèque Nationale, Paris. (c) Two similar rebus signs standing for two completely different towns. Codex Cozcatzin. Collection Goupil-Aubin, MS 89 (5), fol. 64. Courtesy of the Bibliothèque Nationale, Paris. Some images show how phoneticism and pictography combined in Aztec script. The symbol for the Huexotzinca (Codex Azcatitlan) is made up of a rump [*tzin*], which stands for the adjective "little," and a tree = "Little Tree." The teeth in the images for Atempa and Atenco (Fig. 5.9c) stand for *tlan*, also an adverbial particle ("near"). The proper way of reading the images would therefore be "near Atempa/ Atenco." Francisco Xavier Clavijero, *Storia antica del Messico* (Cesena, 1780–81). Clavijero took the image from Lorenzana's *Matrícula de tributos*.

ever, failed to understand the bewildering complexity of the signs. Behind the seeming simplicity of the round sign of the day (which León y Gama maintained was the sign for months), for example, there lay subtle philosophical principles that had allowed the natives to draw distinctions with other round signs used to represent days and years. The sign for the months (actually days), León y Gama argued, also hid a world of complex mathematical rules and operations. Moreover, the image of the river into which the baby was submerged was the glyph that represented the goddess Chalchihuitlicue.[59] Clearly, this page from the Codex Mendoza demonstrated that there was nothing "transparent" about Mesoamerican scripts, and that Kircher was a recklessly ignorant commentator on things American.

Alzate y Ramírez was never able to respond to the second installment of León y Gama's *Descripción histórica*, because it was never made public. But for all the differences between them in style and learning, however, Alzate y Ramírez and León y Gama were ideological twins. They occupied extremes in the spectrum of the Spanish American Enlightenment, but their views on epistemology turned out to be almost identical. When it came to assessing foreigners' understanding of the past and nature of the New World, León y Gama and Alzate y Ramírez were both patriots. Alzate y Ramírez cast León y Gama as a system builder enamored of philosophical speculations. Such criticism stemmed from Alzate y Ramírez's dislike of travel accounts and conjectural histories of the New World. Alzate y Ramírez disliked de Pauw, Buffon, and Linnaeus because their systems forced America into prefabricated molds. Alzate y Ramírez's visceral rejection of foreign systems framed the way he approached natural history, seeking at every turn to collect curiosities in order to prove that the laws of nature unearthed in Europe were narrowly provincial. This visceral rejection also framed his entire understanding of Mexican antiquities. Fearful of systems, Alzate y Ramírez consistently refused to advance any interpretation of the hieroglyphs found both in Xochicalco in 1777 and in the central plaza of Mexico City in 1791. León y Gama, on the other hand, did not cast his criticism of the knowledge of outsiders as a critique of philosophical systems. Unlike Alzate y Ramírez, he was willing to engage and to deploy theories. León y Gama's more philosophical turn of mind, however, did not make him less a patriot than Alzate y Ramírez. In the debates over the curative power of lizards' flesh and the interpretation of the stones, León y Gama insisted that Amerindian medical and historiographical knowledge was self-referential and contingent, and

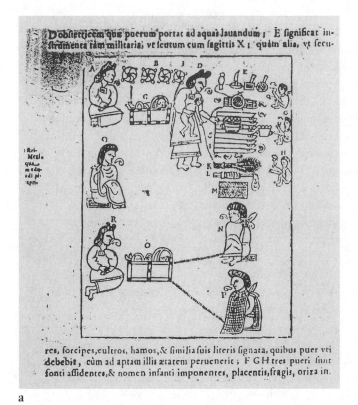

a

b

FIGURE 5.10. León y Gama used these images to highlight the epistemological limitations of foreign interpreters such as the Jesuit Athanasius Kircher. (a) Copy of a page from the Codex Mendoza narrating the "baptism" of a four-day-old child, used by Kircher to highlight the transparency and simplicity of Mesoamerican scripts, very unlike Egyptian hieroglyphics. From Kircher, *Oedipus aegyptiacus* (Rome, 1653–54). (b) Symbolic attributes of annual, monthly, and daily cycles, according to León y Gama. Collection Goupil-Aubin, MS 97. Courtesy of the Bibliothèque Nationale, Paris. In seeking to prove Kircher's ignorance, León y Gama mistook the ideogram for "day" (b, Fig. 13) for an ideogram for "month," arguing that the four little circles around the circumference signified the mathematical operation of multiplication. According to León y Gama, the colors and forms of the symbols corresponded to deep insights into the nature of time.

thus addressed to a tiny elite of learned individuals. In exposing the ignorance of foreigners such as Kircher, León y Gama highlighted the extraordinary competence required in Nahuatl linguistics and local natural history to read and understand Amerindian historical sources.

León y Gama and Alzate y Ramírez were ideological twins in another, less obvious way: they both deployed the new art of reading of the Enlightenment. As noted, this art of reading was characterized by a skeptical probing of the internal consistency of texts and the search for alternative, nonliterary forms of evidence. Unlike the northern European critics who did not care to interpret Amerindian scripts and who dismissed all Amerindian sources, León y Gama extended the new techniques of reading to Amerindian precolonial documents (which other patriotic epistemologists had read uncritically) in order to determine a core of authoritative, unimpeachable authors. His study of fifteenth-century eclipses in central Mexico, for example, showed that the entries in many Nahua annals were untrustworthy. Only the works of the Nahua annalist Cristóbal del Castillo emerged unscathed from this rigorous scrutiny. León y Gama, therefore, turned Castillo's works into the bedrock of his own history. Alzate y Ramírez, on the other hand, was somewhat more traditional. He judged Castillo's reliability on the basis of his racial and social standing, rather than on the internal consistency of his writings. Alzate y Ramírez sought to discredit León y Gama by suggesting that Castillo was a mestizo commoner. But Alzate y Ramírez was utterly familiar with the new art of reading of his age, and he deployed it against the northern European critics of the Americas. Like the skeptics of the age, Alzate y Ramírez refused to interpret Mesoamerican scripts and dismissed all precolonial written sources outright. Again, like his European foes, Alzate y Ramírez sought more reliable, alternative, nonliterary forms of evidence, which he found in Xochicalco. But by using Xochicalco's ramparts, tunnels, terraces, and pyramids, Alzate y Ramírez proved each and every one of the Europeans' views of the Amerindian past wrong.

The debate over the meaning of the stones typified the nature of the Enlightenment in Spanish America in general and in New Spain in particular. It was a debate conducted entirely in the public sphere. Like the debates over the curative power of lizards' flesh and over the merits of Linnaean taxonomy, the discussion in Mexican periodicals of the meaning of the stones was characterized by an all-consuming concern for assessing the power of outsiders to comprehend local realities. This debate had little or nothing to do with seeking new religious and political languages of legitimization. Historians have so far directed their attention to finding traces of ideas first developed in Europe in order to characterize the Spanish American Enlightenment. Although valuable, these efforts have paradoxically rendered invisible one of the most richly creative aspects of the movement in a colonial setting, namely, the discourse of patriotic epistemology.

Why Did Boturini's Collection Never Reach Madrid?

Alzate y Ramírez and León y Gama turned their epistemological insights into political capital when they sought to dispute the monopoly that Europeans began to acquire over the new academic institutions that the Bourbon monarchy established in Spanish America. Dozens of botanical and cartographic expeditions visited the colonies in the second half of the eighteenth century. In Bogota, Mexico City, and Lima, some of these expeditions turned into institutional efforts that lasted many years. The Botanical Garden (1788); an academy to train painters and masons in the new neoclassical taste (Academia de la Nobles Artes de San Carlos, 1781); a hospital to train learned surgeons (Real Escuela de Cirugía, 1768); and a college to educate miners in subterranean geometry and mineralogy (Colegio de Minería, 1792) were some of the new royal establishments created in New Spain to challenge the monopoly of the Church over education.[60] Most of these institutions were staffed and led by Peninsulars. Both Alzate y Ramírez and León y Gama had harbored hopes of getting chairs in the new college of mining, but as soon as the Basque mineralogist Fausto de Elhuyar (1755–1833) arrived to direct the college, they were deliberately excluded from the lists of potential candidates, who unsurprisingly all turned to be Peninsulars.[61] Debates such as the one conducted by Alzate y Ramírez over the merits of Linnaean taxonomy formed part of a Creole organized resistance to the founding of new chair of botany for physicians at the recently opened Botanical Garden, which operated outside the purview of the clerically controlled University of Mexico.[62] I argue in the following pages that the failure of the Bourbon regime in the 1780s and 1790s to bring Boturini's collection to Spain was another manifestation of Creole resistance. Creoles like Alzate y Ramírez and León y Gama conspired to keep indigenous documents in Mexico.

Seeking to centralize colonial documentation, the Spanish crown sent several requests and even an expedition (Malaspina's) in the course of the 1780s and 1790s to bring to Madrid all available indigenous codices, particularly those impounded from Boturini in 1742. Had the requests of the crown and of the visiting expedition been heeded, the great collections of Mesoamerican codices now in Mexico, Paris, Berkeley, New Orleans, and Texas would in all probability be housed today at the Royal Academy of History in Madrid. A Creole conspiracy, however, rendered the efforts of the crown futile, but it served to keep many of these Mesoamerican codices in Mexico for only a few more years By the early nineteenth century, an undertow of indigenous codices began to flow out of Mexico toward Europe and the United States. Significantly, the trickle started when the discourse of patriotic epistemology in historiography began to give way to liberal and republican ideologies.[63]

Some twenty years ago, John B. Glass reconstructed the many attempts of the Spanish crown, particularly in the 1780s and early 1790s, to recover all or parts of Boturini's collection. Many edicts ordering local authorities to assemble and send to Spain the many volumes that had once belonged to the Italian scholar were consistently met with silence or were simply poorly carried out. Glass has attributed the problems to errors committed by the person who drafted the official lists requesting specific documents, namely, the Royal Chronicler of the Indies, Juan Bautista Muñoz, and also to the state of complete disarray in which Boturini's collection was found in the 1780s. The collection had left the premises of the viceregal palace and moved around for years, losing several of its volumes in the process. It went first to the archbishopric, where Archbishop Lorenzana used it for his edition of the *Matrícula de tributos*. Later, it moved to the university, where it was kept with holdings that had belonged to the Jesuits before their expulsion. By the time the authorities sought to return the collection to the viceregal archives, Glass has argued, they had lost track of the whereabouts of many of the documents.[64]

In addition to the problems attending a traveling archive on which Glass has focused, confusion seems also to have originated in the profusion of copies of indigenous documents then circulating in Mexico. When antiquarians such as Echeverría y Veytia, Granados y Gálvez, and León y Gama gained access to the collection, they made copies of several documents, which later could not be distinguished from the originals. Of the annals by Alvarado Tezozomoc and Alva Ixtlilxochitl that finally made it to Spain, most were copies that had belonged to Echeverría y Veytia, not Boturini. In addition to Echeverría y Veytia, Granados y Gálvez, and León y Gama, the larger roster of late-eighteenth-century antiquarians devoted to copying indigenous sources included the Peninsular navy officer Diego García Panes (1730–1811), who used many of the codices assembled by Boturini to complete an illustrated version of Echeverría y Veytia's ancient history of Mexico. A tireless collector, García Panes inter alia commissioned what is now known as the Lienzo de Tlaxcala, a copy of the pictograms decorating the chambers of the municipal building in Tlaxcala, narrating that city's participation in the Conquest. He was also responsible for bringing a copy of Sahagún's monumental Florentine Codex back to Mexico.[65]

This list of antiquarians should also include the mysterious figure of Juan Santelices Pablo, the most important broker of antiquities, curiosities, and books in late-eighteenth-century Mexico and the owner of the largest cabinet of curiosities-cum-library.[66] Then, by the turn of the nineteenth century, the leading antiquarian in Mexico was José Antonio Pichardo (1748–1812), a member of the order of San Felipe Neri, who inherited his collection of indigenous documents in part from León y Gama. Pichardo was Alexander von Humboldt's principal guide when the latter began to navigate the stormy waters of Mesoamerican historiography while visiting New Spain. The list could go on; suffice it to say that in 1790 a local periodical listed at least eleven large collections of antiquities and natural curiosities in the capital.[67] The number of indigenous codices (including originals, copies, and forgeries) circulating in late-eighteenth-century Mexico and Guatemala (more on this region later) was so large that it is plausible to argue that most holdings of colonial Mesoamerican codices in such institutions as the Bibliothèque Nationale in Paris, the Bancroft Library in Berkeley, California, Tulane University in New Orleans, the Nettie Lee Benson Library in Austin, Texas, the National Museum of Anthropology in Mexico, and the Royal Academy of History and the Library of the Royal Palace in Madrid can ultimately be traced to this period and to one or another of the antiquarians mentioned above.

Glass insists that those charged with collecting the documents were paralyzed by confusion and unclear requests from Spain, and that after many years of trying, the Council of the Indies and the Royal Academy of History managed to collect only a handful of indigenous sources; without exception, all were annals in Spanish either by Alvarado Tezozomoc or Alva Ixtlilxochitl. These annals were highly esteemed sources, but the crown in the end got only copies, not the originals. Glass does not seem surprised by the fact that Bourbon efforts to recover Boturini's collection finally retrieved some *thirty-two* volumes, most of which were filled with material unrelated to the original lists of requests. As Glass acknowledges, the entire process of collecting and selecting the documents remained throughout firmly under Creole control, first by a group at the university and later, owing to the faculty's utter "inefficiency," by a community of scribes at the Franciscan headquarters in the capital.

Pace Glass, there is, however, abundant evidence that the delays and inefficiencies were part of a vast Creole conspiracy to keep indigenous sources in Mexico. Whenever Muñoz drafted a list of documents in Madrid, the order was treated lightly. Take, for example, the case of Alzate y Ramírez, who was ordered to collect documents prior to the arrival of Alejandro Malaspina's expedition to Mexico, the largest scientific expedition ever assembled in Spain, which emulated and even dwarfed that of Captain Cook. As the expedition circumnavigated the world, visiting Spanish colonial outposts in both the Atlantic and the Pacific, local authorities and literati were asked to gather data on the economy, demography, politics, and history of the colonies.[68] Thus, prior to Malaspina's arrival in Mexico, an order was sent to reassemble Boturini's collection, something the crown had been ordering to no avail since 1784. This time, the crown hoped that the members of the expedition would get personally involved, speeding up the process. Alzate y Ramírez's reply to the official request is significant: he advised Malaspina to stop looking for Boturini's collection, on the grounds that it was "useless" outside Mexico. In an ironic gesture, Alzate y Ramírez suggested that the Italian Malaspina instead use the illustrations in Clavijero's history, then only available in an Italian edition.[69]

When nothing came of Malaspina's request, Arcadio Pineda, the member of the expedition charged with scouring and combing local archives, set out to visit cloisters and libraries once the expedition arrived. Pineda soon declared himself helpless and frustrated, however, for he had found no trace of indigenous documents in the archives. Moreover, all the documents that had once belonged to Boturini's collection, he maintained, seemed to have completely vanished.[70] In fact, while the expedition was visiting Mexico, the entire collection had been moved to the Franciscan headquarters, and the members of the cloister had made their own sweep of local repositories. Malaspina finally departed with thirty-two volumes of historical documents that the Franciscans put together between 1790 and 1792, the so-called Colección de Memorias de Nueva España. The collection included copies of some of the documents Muñoz had originally requested, particularly annals in Spanish by sixteenth-century Amerindian annalists such as Alvarado Tezozomoc and Alva Ixtlilxochitl. There were, however, no annals written in Nahuatl in Latin script and no sources in Mesoamerican scripts in the entire collection. Why?

The answer lies in the preface by the Franciscans charged with assembling and selecting the documents, Francisco García Figueroa and Manuel de la Vega, and in an evaluation of the indigenous historical paintings by the interpreter of the local tribunals, Vicente de la Rosa y Saldivar. In the preface to the collection, García Figueroa and de la Vega maintained that no indigenous document (in Nahuatl in Latin script or logograms) was included because they were all worthless, "trivial, obscure, and dry [pieces]."[71] The Franciscans maintained that their decision was ultimately based on the expertise of the interpreter de la Rosa, who in fact wrote a lengthy essay assessing each and every one of the available codices, annals in both Latin and Mesoamerican scripts, in which he found garbled chronologies and utter confusion. De la Rosa advised the authorities to use Torquemada's history instead. Torquemada's work, he declared, was already a neat, chronologically organized summation of indigenous documents.[72]

García Figueroa and de la Vega's decision not to include any indigenous sources, except the writings in Spanish by Alvarado Tezozomoc and Alva Ixtlilxochitl, is puzzling because it was taken precisely at the time when León y Gama's *Descripción de las dos piedras* demonstrated their historiographical value. Moreover, it was a decision taken immediately after scores of copies of the Italian edition of Clavijero's history had arrived in Mexico. There are two plausible scenarios that help explain this puzzling editorial decision. One is that the editors and the interpreter really thought that the documents were worthless. I have been arguing in this chapter that the clerical-Creole discourse of patriotic epistemology looked with suspicion on indigenous sources of later colonial provenance, for such sources could have been produced by misinformed commoners. De la Rosa, the interpreter, seems to have followed this logic, because he praised Torquemada's history as a reliable compilation of ancient Amerindian sources, while identifying most documents in Boturini's collection as of colonial provenance. This logic, however, is nowhere made explicit in de la Rosa's essay.

The second plausible scenario is that the Franciscan editors and the interpreter deliberately misled the Spanish authorities. Such a scenario is confirmed by a letter sent by León y Gama to his Jesuit friend in Italy Andrés Cavo (1739–1803), who was then translating León y Gama's *Descripción* into Latin for publication in Italy, in August 1796. Apparently prompted by Cavo's continuous requests not to let Amerindian codices leave the country, León y Gama responded that a plot to keep the indigenous documents at home had already been set in motion. León y Gama noted how many Amerindian documents had left in 1792 (and in 1780), "[when] all the [holdings] of the university were taken to Spain," and how, in order to keep some at home, he and the university librarians had managed to declare many Amerindian sources useless as "things that could not be understood."[73] León y Gama's letter to

Cavo, Alzate y Ramírez's ironic response to Malaspina, the refusal of the Franciscan editors to include any indigenous source in Mesoamerican script in the thirty-two-volume collection that Malaspina took to Spain, and the constant delays with which orders to collect indigenous sources were greeted between 1784 and 1792 all suggest a Creole conspiracy to keep Mexican codices in New Spain.

Our Lady of Guadalupe as Neoplatonic Seal and Mesoamerican Glyph

Unlike Alzate y Ramírez and León y Gama, who, patriotic epistemology notwithstanding, evidently shared the mind-set of the late-eighteenth-century literati of northwestern Europe, there were many Spanish American antiquarians whose concerns and methodologies cannot adequately be captured under the rubric of the Enlightenment. In this section I study the work of José Ignacio Borunda, whom Alzate y Ramírez and Voltaire would have characterized as a "pedantic antiquarian," given to etymological flights of fancy. Operating within the discourse of patriotic epistemology, he penned texts that reveal a deeply influential aspect of colonial culture in Spanish America: the "baroque," a world dominated by images and occult sympathies and resemblances. Borunda was one of the many antiquarians who sought to interpret the stones found in the central plaza of Mexico between 1790 and 1792. Although his work proved at the time to be far more influential than anything either Alzate y Ramírez and León y Gama ever wrote, historians today dismiss Borunda as mad and incomprehensible.

In three of the stones, Borunda immediately found (Figs. 5.1, 5.2, and 5.6a) confirmation of many of the ideas he had been developing for more than thirty years while working for local tribunals. Like Boturini, Borunda thought that the history of the New World sorely needed a new narrative, and, more important, a new methodology, one based on the allegorical interpretation of terms. Borunda had come to realize that all previous colonial historians, whether of Amerindian or European descent, had distorted the history of Mesoamerica beyond recognition. Applying his radically new methodology to the three stones, Borunda produced a new history that sent the body politic reeling when it was made public in 1794 by one of Borunda's friends, the Dominican friar Servando Teresa de Mier (1765–1825), in a sermon commemorating the miraculous appearance of Our Lady of Guadalupe. Using Borunda's ideas, Mier argued that the story of the miracle was false, rendering the secular and ecclesiastical authorities in his audience speechless. The authorities, who were grappling with the spread of the French Revolution to the New World in Saint Domingue (Haiti), decided that enforcing religious traditions was more valuable than promoting skepticism. They initiated legal proceedings against both Borunda and Mier, which led to the silencing of Borunda for life and to Mier's expulsion and imprisonment in Spain. Mier fled Spain, however, to become one of the most picturesque and influential figures in Mexico during and after the wars of independence.[74]

Most historians have either ignored Borunda or have cast him as an incoherent lunatic.[75] David Brading, who has written by far the best study of Mier's particular brand of Catholic republicanism, and who has otherwise shown exquisite sensibility when dealing with Creole sources, has argued that "apart from a few wild etymologies," Borunda "brought nothing new . . . save his completely baseless assertions [about St. Thomas and Our Lady of Guadalupe]."[76] Edmundo O'Gorman, who published an annotated edition of primary sources on Mier's conviction, including Mier's sermon and documents impounded from Borunda by the prosecution, has characterized Borunda's views as an "indigestible bundle [*fárrago*] of disconnected ideas."[77] Why has Borunda been so easily dismissed? The answer lies in the complexity of Borunda's methodology, the obscurity of his chef d'oeuvre, the *Clave general de geroglíficos americanos* (General Key to American Hieroglyphs), which is the Mexican equivalent of Champollion's Egyptian work, and the complete lack of attention to the rest of his writings. In the following pages, I study Borunda's ideas and the culture that made them possible, with the ultimate purpose of identifying some cultural properties of the Spanish American baroque.

José Ignacio Borunda's 'Clave general de geroglíficos americanos'

When Boturini's collection was ordered sent to Spain in 1790, the crown also asked that a local expert assess the documents. A month after the first stones were found in the central plaza, Borunda introduced himself as the expert the authorities needed. In documents submitted with his application for the position, Borunda very coherently and very clearly (indicating that he was not mad) outlined a new historiographical proposal, in which he castigated all previous attempts at writing the precolonial history of New Spain.[78]

According to Borunda, all sixteenth-century indigenous and Spanish interpreters got the facts of the ancient history of Mesoamerica wrong owing to essential problems of cross-cultural communication. Amerindians, he argued, had sinned on the side of orthography and Spaniards on the side of what he called "orthology." Newcomers to the art of putting down sounds in the Latin script, the natives had altered "the original voices" of Nahuatl terms when they moved away from their traditional scripts (orthographic miscommunication). The failure of the Spaniards, on the other hand, consisted in having changed the pronunciation of Amerindian voices as they grappled with the new alien languages ("orthological" miscommunication). Gaffes in "orthology" and orthography, Borunda argued, had come together to alter the original sounds of the names of places, rulers, and deities. The changes were significant, Borunda maintained, because Amerindian knowledge (historical and otherwise) was stored in words, veiled as verbal allusions and metaphors. An unacknowledged disciple of Boturini, and thus of Vico, Borunda argued that words were crucial "documents" for any historical reconstruction. Place-names in particular, he asserted, were allegorical references to historical events. By changing the original toponymy through orthological and orthographic mistakes, Amerindians and Spaniards alike had contributed to making impossible any etymological-cum-allegorical study of Nahuatl words.

Borunda identified yet another mechanism of historiographical distortion associated with the first colonial encounter. Individuals trained to read documents and names, he argued, had disappeared during the early phase of the Conquest. The Amerindian interpreters used by the first missionaries had not previously been exposed to the secrets stored in metaphors and veiled allegories, and their translations were merely literal allusions, not an exegesis of occult knowledge.

By highlighting the many processes of miscommunication and distortion of the original Amerindian sources, Borunda's skepticism outdid anything patriotic epistemologists had advanced before. As noted, Alzate y Ramírez had refused to advance any interpretations of Mesoamerican hieroglyphs, and had therefore dismissed all Amerindian pictographic and logographic sources. He had never argued, however, that the dozens of Nahuatl annals and writings in Latin script into which sixteenth-century Amerindian elites had poured their original sources in translation were not to be trusted. Even León y Gama, whose internal reading of indigenous documents exposed many annals as untrustworthy, would have considered it unthinkable to reject the vast corpus of early colonial Amerindian writings. Borunda, on the other hand, dismissed all these sources as though he were a faithful follower of Cornelius de Pauw.

Borunda was not, however, a thoroughgoing radical skeptic. He maintained that there were alternative mechanisms for reconstructing the original sources. After working for twenty-seven years in the courts, he said, he had become familiar with one particular variety of sixteenth-century Amerindian documents, namely, land titles. Borunda claimed that these documents were so numerous that through careful collation it was possible to identify the original place-names and thus the logic behind the orthographic and orthological distortions introduced in the encounter.[79] Borunda also identified another mechanism to recover the original terms and their hidden historiographical meanings, namely, the behavior of "pure" Amerindian communities "unsoiled" by contact with mestizos. These communities retained the original place-names, and their elites still mindlessly practiced secret ceremonies that alluded to the original meaning of the allegories stored in names. Through what we Moderns call ethnography, and through the careful collation of land titles, Borunda claimed to have completed a "Geographical History," a dictionary of reconstructed original geographical terms, along with an analysis of their allegorical significance.

Borunda first used his method in another document, addressed to the viceregal authorities in 1788, in which he claimed that the location of mercury mines could be identified through reconstruction and etymological analysis of the toponymy of Mexico. Borunda wrote his proposal at a time when the authorities were facing the continuous military disruption of supplies of mercury (used for amalgamation of silver) from Almadén in Spain, and therefore were sponsoring surveys to locate local supplies. In the document Borunda insisted that place-names stored the history and "cause of everything."[80] Etymological analysis of place-names revealed that mercury mines were to be found in the north of New Spain. According to authors such as Echeverría y Veytia, the name of this place was Huehuetlapallan. Borunda, who assumed that "orthologic" and orthographic distortions had transformed the primitive name, reconstructed it as Huehuetlapa, which, in turn, he translated as "abundant in mercury."[81] Somewhere in the north of the viceroyalty, he thus concluded, there lay large mercury mines.

Such linguistic manipulations typified Borunda's methodology. There is also the example of Cuernavaca, a town near Mexico City. Borunda first restored the name "Cuernavaca" to its alleged original, "Cuaunauac." He then split the word into several root particles given the purported agglutinative character of Nahuatl. "Cuaunauac," he maintained, was the sum of the words *nau* (which he translated either as "fontanel," a boneless space in the forming skull, or as "cardinal point"); *atl* ("water"); and *cuautla* ("bushes"). It was also the sum of the words *nauac* (which according to most grammarians stood for the adverb "near," but that Borunda thought signified "fence" or "wreath," or "wreath of spines" when associated with the word *uitztli*) and *cuautla* ("bushes"). At this point Borunda subjected each of the particles to an allegorical analysis. *Nau*, fontanel or cardinal point, and *atl*, water, he argued, signified the sinking of the earth. *Nauac*, on the other hand, stood for the wreath of spines that had tormented Christ. The name "Cuaunauac," Borunda concluded, had been used by the natives of Mexico to signify the geological catastrophe that had been visited on Mesoamerica in the wake of Christ's passion and crucifixion.[82]

Basing himself on such tortuous, painstaking analysis of hundreds of Nahuatl place-names, Borunda claimed that all previous histories of Mesoamerica and its peoples were in error. Dates and events, he argued, were wrongly attributed and recorded; so too were references to migrations and the rise and fall of nations. Groups that were assumed to have disappeared were still there; peoples who were thought to be ethnically distinct belonged in fact to the same nation.

Sometime before the stones were found in the central plaza of Mexico City, Borunda had established that the peoples of central Mexico used to live in mountains to the south; sierras, not lacustrine valleys, were the natural habitat of the Amerindians. To reach this conclusion Borunda argued that *alteptl*, the term that most Mesoamerican city-states used to define themselves as people, signified "mountains with water."[83] Giants, Borunda contended, had inhabited the ancient capital of the southern sierras before its destruction by a geological catastrophe that engulfed the earth at the time when Christ expired on the cross. In the wake of the catastrophe, St. Thomas had visited the survivors and taught them the mysteries of Christianity. Over time, they had turned their back on the apostle's original teachings, however, corrupting the rituals and dogmas of the Church. Eventually in 430 C.E., these apostates settled in the Central Valley of Mexico near the lakes and founded a new capital. Using hairsplitting etymologies characteristic of the baroque culture, Borunda at a single stroke cavalierly dismissed centuries of accumulated learning: a very modern gesture indeed.

Borunda on the Stones

To his own amazement Borunda discovered that the three stones found in Mexico City's central plaza confirmed and amplified much of the historical narrative he had already retrieved from the allegorical study of place-names. Borunda maintained that Mesoamerican writing was thoroughly logographic; every image in a source was a rebuslike transparent reference to a term, which, in turn, was a veiled allusion to a historical episode. When the first missionaries destroyed Amerindian religious documents that contained images of animals on the assumption that they were idolatrous references to animal deities, they had in fact destroyed logograms that allegorically hid historical references. Such basic misunderstanding of Mesoamerican scripts, he contended, meant that the new codices produced under colonial patronage were unreliable and worthless. Moreover, according to Borunda, the natives had recorded their historical deeds on stone, not paper. Thus, when the conquistadors leveled the temples of Tenochtitlan, they destroyed the Mesoamerican archives. Anticipating this, however, the Mexica chose to bury their most precious historical documents during the siege of their capital. The three stones unearthed in Mexico in 1790 and 1791, Borunda argued, were those precious documents.[84]

Borunda concluded that the Solar Stone recorded crucial dates in universal history from the day of Creation to the year 5,280 (1,280 C.E.) (Fig. 5.2), and that the stone León y Gama had read as another calendar to commemorate the most important festival of the sun in mid May was in fact a monument that recorded the foundation of the Great Temple of Tenochtitlan (Fig. 5.6a). The impounded manuscript of Borunda's *Clave general* does not include the process by which he reached such conclusions.[85] The manuscript, however, contains his reading of the monstrous-looking stone that León y Gama had interpreted as a montage of the hieroglyphic attributes of several deities.

Borunda argued that this boulder (Fig. 5.1a) recorded in careful detail the events that had led to the destruction of the ancient capital in the sierras and to the foundation four hundred years later of the city among the lakes of the Central Valley of Mexico. The head of the monster was a "crab," or *tecusitli* in original Nahuatl reconstructed à la Borunda. The amphibian animal was itself a reference to the reestablishment of the ancient mountain capital in the lacustrine environment of the Central Valley. Moreover, the analysis of the root particles of crab, *sitli* (grandmother) and *tecutli* (master), stood allegorically for God's preordained destruction of the ancestral capital.[86] This reading of the elements of the stone as logograms combined with an allegorical interpretation of the historiographical significance of the reconstructed Nahuatl term allowed Borunda to gain insight into the details of the past. The base of the stone, for example, sported among other things a crouched female figure with skulls on her hands, elbows, and knees; a body that was a circle with a quartered square inside; and a necklace and a mouth with fangs. The crouched individual, Borunda argued, was known in Mexico as "frog," a clear reference to the amphibian character of the new capital. The skulls, *cuaxicalli* allegedly in reconstructed original Nahuatl, signified the original volcanic landscapes where the ancient capital had first been established. To reach this conclusion, Borunda split *cuaxicalli* into two root particles, *xicalle* ("container") and *cuaitl* ("mountain peak")." The circular body with a quartered square for its belly represented the quarters and canals of the new capital. The skulls of "coyotes" hanging from the limbs and hands of the individual stood for the mixed racial descent (Mexica and Otomí) of the inhabitants of the new capital, for *coyotl*, he argued, was used by the natives as an allegory of *mestizaje*. The necklace (*cuscatl*, or "ruby") and the mouth with the fangs of a serpent (*tlalpalli*) were references to the time in which the new capital was established. Borunda maintained that this occurred in the months between spring and winter, because the ruby necklace stood for the rubylike nature of the sun in the spring and the four fangs of a serpent stood for the four barren months of winter.[87]

Such extraordinarily convoluted methodology and unlikely historical narrative would, one might imagine, have failed to convince serious observers of Mesoamerican culture. Yet Borunda enjoyed a reputation as a leading linguist and antiquarian in Mexico. Although wrapped in the fanciful world of baroque scholarship, there was something very modern about Borunda's theses. With the stroke of a pen and the gusto of a radical skeptic, Borunda tore down the building of Spanish American historiography on the Aztecs. Such reckless disrespect for tradition, I suspect, made him attractive to new generations of innovative scholars. Even Alzate y Ramírez made veiled positive references to Borunda when he chastised León y Gama for having failed to produce a general key for reading and interpreting Mesoamerican scripts. The fact that the erudite Mier, charged with giving the commemorative sermon for the anniversary of the miracle of Our Lady of Guadalupe, approached Borunda for expert advice demonstrates that Borunda was not considered a crackpot.

So why did Borunda soon come to be seen as a deranged antiquarian? The answer lies in his interpretation of the image of Our Lady of Guadalupe, which he "read" as he read the stones, namely, as a montage of logograms that stood for Nahuatl terms that hid past historical events. The reading of the image as a montage of symbols that could be read was nothing new in Mexico. Borunda's radicalism lay in the conclusions he reached. Detouring into the Spanish American Baroque, the following pages show how scholars read Christian icons as Mesoamerican scripts and vice versa.

Christian Icons and Nahua Glyphs

By the time Borunda applied his methodology to the image of Our Lady of Guadalupe, the reading of Nahua glyphs as Christian icons and of Christian images as Nahua glyphs had long exercised the imagination of the learned. For example, when in 1729 the Discalced Carmelites celebrated the canonization of their patron, the sixteenth-century Spanish ascetic St. John of the Cross, they commissioned the leading Creole scholar Cayetano de Cabrera y Quintero (d. 1775) to design the impresas, or emblems, for the triumphal arch.[88] Cabrera y Quintero chose eagles as the allegorical creatures to portray St. John. An eagle gliding to the sun stood for the mystical ascent of the saint's soul through the heavenly spheres. Cabrera y Quintero thus complemented the allegories available to pious Europeans with a Christianized version of a traditional Nahua glyph. The Mexica had traditionally complemented the logogram representing the name of their capital, Tenochtitlan, a nopal (cactus) on a stone, with an eagle perched on top of it to emphasize the prophetic nature of their settlement (Fig. 5.11a; Plate 12). During their migration south to the lakes of the Central Valley of Mexico, they had been told by an oracle to settle at the place where they found an eagle perched on a nopal. The glyph seems, however, to have undergone a change under Christian influence, for by the late sixteenth century, it included a snake (Fig. 5.11b).[89] The addition might have well been related to a demonological exegesis of the original glyph among circles of Nahua scribes brought up by the Franciscans in millenarian, patristic, and classical traditions. Be that as it may, Cabrera y Quintero determined that the eagle with its wings spread devouring a serpent had nothing to do with the life of St. John of the Cross. Rather, it pointed to a resemblance to the cross, which indicated that the glyph could be used as an impresa in the triumphal arch to shield the city against evil spirits (Fig. 5.11c).[90]

In 1750, at the metropolitan cathedral, the Dominican friar Antonio Claudio de Villegas (b. 1700), professor of theology and censor for the Inquisition, concluded that the same glyph was a prefiguration of the Church in New Spain. After quoting Pliny the Elder at length on eagles' habit of nesting on "ethites" ("eagle stones," common in lakes) and interpreting the appropriate prophecies and biblical passages, Villegas concluded that the Mexican Church was an eagle "nesting" on the ancient pagan temples of stone. Just as Pliny had shown in his *Natural History* that ethites enhanced the reproductive power of eagles and gave solid foundation to their nests, Villegas argued, the Mexican Church was fecund and anchored

a

b

c

FIGURE 5.11. The founding of Tenochtitlan by the Mexica. (a) A portrayal lacking Christian patristic influences. From the Codex Mendoza. Reproduced with permission of the Bodleian Library, Oxford, MS. Arch. Selden. A. 1, fol. 2r. (b) A portrayal revealing likely Christian patristic influences. From Diego Durán, *Atlas de la historia de las Indias y islas de tierra firme* (Mexico: Librería Antiquaria, 1963). (c) The coat of arms of the City of Mexico. The eagle with its wings unfurled was often read by Creole clerics as a Neoplatonic seal that could be deployed as a "fortification" to keep evil spirits away, because it looked like a cross. From Pedro José Márquez, *Due antichi monumenti* (Rome, 1804).

solidly in the midst of lakes.[91] Mariano Antonio de la Vega, the Jesuit dean of the College of San Pablo at Puebla, interpreted the glyph differently. In September 1752, he wrote that the eagle and the serpent stood for the archangel Michael slaying a dragon. De la Vega concluded that the Aztecs had prefigured the defeat of their own idolatrous practices in the hieroglyph. "The heavens gave [the natives of] Mexico another eagle," he reflected in convoluted prose, "as a clear symbol of the victory [of God] . . . over [their own] infernal and serpentine troops."[92] The exegesis of the symbol of Tenochtitlan that Villegas and de la Vega put forth shows that introducing the image of the snake to the eagle perched on the nopal cactus allowed the clergy of Mexico to advance a demonological interpretation of the Amerindian past.

It was the image of Our Lady of Guadalupe, however, that exercised the minds of the learned seeking to assimilate Mesoamerican scripts to local colonial religious icons (Fig. 5.12). According to tradition, the Virgin had appeared several times in 1531 to a Nahua commoner, Juan Diego, on the small hill of Tepeyac. The Virgin told Juan Diego to request the archbishop to build her a chapel. The latter did not believe Juan Diego, however, who was thus twice obliged to return empty-handed to the Virgin. Finally, the Virgin ordered him to collect some flowers in his cape (*tilma*). When he visited the wary bishop for the third time, he unfolded his cape and, to everybody's surprise, the image of the Virgin appeared printed on it. According to tradition, after this miracle, the authorities built a chapel to house Juan Diego's cape and sponsored the cult of Our Lady of Guadalupe. A small chapel was built near the base of the hill Tepeyac, where an ancient Aztec goddess, Tonatzin, had long before been worshipped. At first, Franciscan missionaries, influenced by iconoclastic, Erasmian tendencies, did not promote the cult, but after the Council of Trent (1545–63), the local ecclesiastical authorities enthusiastically integrated veneration of the Virgin into Mexican devotional practice. When the Virgin successfully controlled the waters during a flood in Mexico City in 1629, the cult began to spread rapidly among Creoles. Yet it was only after 1648, when Miguel Sánchez (1594–1674) — a serious student of St. Augustine — explained the Neoplatonic meaning of the image, that the Creoles finally grasped its significance.[93]

In a sudden illumination, Sánchez realized that the description offered by St. John in chapter 12 of the Apocalypse (Rev. 12:1–9) was a prefiguration of the image of Our Lady of Guadalupe. St. John describes a pregnant woman crowned with stars who is threatened by a multiheaded red dragon, the devil, seeking to devour her child as soon as she gives birth to it. God, however,

FIGURE 5.12. Our Lady of Guadalupe protecting Mexico City as a "shield" against the plague. From Cayetano de Cabrera y Quintero, *El escudo de armas de México* (Mexico, 1746). Religious icons were deployed as Neoplatonic seals to keep evil spirits away; correct interpretation of them was therefore crucial. Many such icons were interpreted as Mesoamerican writing, particularly that of Our Lady of Guadalupe, which attracted much scholarly attention; intellectuals vied with one another to evoke the symbolic meaning of every detail of the image.

takes up the child to heaven, hides the woman in the desert, and sends an army of angels, headed by the archangel Michael to destroy the dragon. The parallels, according to Sánchez were obvious: The image of Our Lady of Guadalupe, along with the angel supporting her, represented the defeat of the kingdom of darkness of the Aztecs. Sánchez thought that there were other prefigurations at work in the story of the miracle. The encounter of Moses with God in Sinai, for example, anticipated the encounter of the Virgin with (and her message of deliverance to) Juan Diego at Tepeyac. In fact, Sánchez thought, the image was a unique divine creation. Inasmuch as God had never painted an image himself until the day of the miracle, the portrait of Our Lady of Guadalupe on Juan Diego's cape was clearly the most important icon in Christendom, for all other religious images in the world were mere human creations.[94] Sánchez offered interpretations of every detail of the painting. The moon beneath the Virgin represented her power over the waters; the Virgin eclipsing the sun stood for the New World, whose torrid zone was temperate and inhabitable; the twelve rays of the sun surrounding her head signified Cortés and the conquistadors, who had defeated the dragon; and the stars on the Virgin's shawl were the forty-six good angels who had fought Satan's army (Sánchez used cabalistic means to calculate the number of good angels).[95] Sánchez's interpretation inaugurated a literature of exegesis that took on clear millenarian and messianic tones, a literature in which contemporary Mexicans appeared as God's new chosen people. In the imagination of Creole scholars, Mexico became the place to which the pope and the monarchy would eventually retreat after being ousted from Europe by the forces of evil.[96]

Throughout the seventeenth and eighteenth centuries, Creole intellectuals sought to understand the "signatures" of the image of Our Lady of Guadalupe. Since the Madonna appeared standing on the moon, and the moon had control over both the tides and the sphere of water, many thought that the Virgin had dominion over floods.[97] Every time the capital was flooded, which happened often, thousands of anguished citizens took to the streets to parade her image; to their relief, the waters always subsided.[98] The image of Our Lady of Guadalupe also acted as a "shield" during the devastating plague of 1736–37, saving hundreds.[99]

As the enthusiasm of Creoles for the historical significance of the image and its Neoplatonic protective virtues mounted, it soon became clear that the story was plagued with contradictions. The most formidable challenge facing the advocates of the historicity of the miracle was that not a single document recounting the episode dating back to 1531 could be found in the ecclesiasti-

cal archives. The clergy sought to mitigate this lack by interviewing the elderly and scouring local archives for indirect evidence that Juan Diego, for example, had truly existed. The learned also collected and investigated Amerindian sources in the hopes that indigenous codices contemporary to the
events would confirm the story. Boturini, who assembled his famous collection while seeking to bolster the historical credibility of the miracle, typified
this approach.

Another strategy was to claim that the image itself was the much-sought
paper trail. In an introduction to a history of the miracle written in 1688 by
the Jesuit Francisco Florencia, Gerónimo de Valladolid insisted that since
the image was "writing printed on paper," there was no need of written testimonies of the miracle. "What need do we have of the much-missed documentary evidence," asked Valladolid rhetorically, "if we have the original
scripture from the hand of God himself?" Valladolid contended the image
'had been "written" in a traditional Mesoamerican script because God had
sought to communicate with the natives of Mexico. He was convinced that
the image was a hieroglyph "in the form and style used in the ancient past by
the natives for whom [God] wrote it in the first place."[100] In their struggle to
defend the historicity of the miracle, Creole scholars presented the image as
God's "document" and repeatedly used aesthetic and technical analyses to
prove that the cloth could have been "written" only by God.

In 1755, Miguel Cabrera (1695–1768), the most prestigious contemporary
painter of New Spain, was summoned by his patron, the archbishop, along
with five other artists, to pass judgment on the nature of the miraculous
image. After examining the quality and artistry of the materials and after deciphering the esoteric meaning of an eight on the robe of the virgin (it signified that the image of Guadalupe was the eighth wonder of the world),
Cabrera concluded that the image itself was proof enough that the miracle
had in fact occurred. Inasmuch as the image was aesthetically perfect, and
the cloth had lasted for two centuries without showing any sign of deterioration, Cabrera contended that God himself had indeed painted it, and that
contemporary observers had therefore felt no need to document the miracle.
The history of the miracle, he argued, had been written in a sacred script.
"The painting [of the Virgin]," José González del Pinal, a member of the recently created chapter of canons without cathedral, the Colegiata of
Guadalupe, argued in the preface of Cabrera's treatise, "manifests at once
what many pages of a book would have taken to explain."[101] Cabrera himself
argued that God had here employed "the language of the Indians. . . . who
did not know any script other than symbolic expressions or hieroglyphs."[102] In

a sermon delivered in 1756, Juan José de Eguiara y Eguren, who in his *Bibliotheca mexicana* denied that transient foreign observers would ever be able to comprehend American realities, argued that God had spoken to Juan Diego using images, the books "that the ignorant use to instruct themselves." "The image of Guadalupe," he explained, "is a book written in flowery, golden letters." The Virgin, Eguiara y Eguren continued, "wise, prudent and loving, [sought to accommodate herself] to the style of the country and of the Mexicans, and because the natives had used paintings, symbols and hieroglyphs, instead of letters, she likewise . . . painted her prodigious image [in] hieroglyphs and symbols."[103]

Like many other baroque Creole scholars who had previously sought to interpret the painting, Borunda set out to read the image as a Mesoamerican hieroglyph. But this time, he brought to bear his new critical techniques. Borunda argued, for example, that the crescent underneath the Virgin was the logogram of "moon," *meitzli* in Borunda's reconstituted original Nahuatl. Borunda then broke *meitzli* down into its alleged root components, *itzli* ("cutting edge") and *metl* ("maguey plant"), a somewhat veiled allusion to the use of the maguey as whip. The word *meitzli*, he argued, was an allegory for punishment, particularly the geological catastrophe with which God had punished the Giants. The grayish color of the moon in the painting, on the other hand, was a reference to the eclipse that had darkened the earth after the death of Christ. According to Borunda, the slightly darkened crescent on which the Madonna stood in the image of Our Lady of Guadalupe was a logogram-cum-allegory representing the geological catastrophe that occurred in Mexico the day Christ died.[104]

By means of such philological and allegorical techniques, Borunda reached conclusions that were to startle the public of the capital when the Dominican Mier later delivered them. Borunda argued, for example, that the robe of the Virgin that folded on top of the moon stood for a folded scroll similar to those on which the oriental patriarchs of the Christian Church had written the Bible.[105] Moreover, the eight on the robe (interpreted before as a sign indicating that the image was the eighth wonder of the world) was a Syrian-Chaldean letter, similar also to those used by the oriental patriarchs of the Church.[106] In light of this new evidence, Borunda concluded that the traditional narrative of the miracle was wrong. The Madonna had never appeared to Juan Diego, and her image had never been printed on the Indian's cape. Rather, St. Thomas had left the image in Mexico after having established the Oriental Church. The image was not a preternatural creation by God the scribe, he argued; it was merely a human document penned by St.

Thomas to teach the mysteries of Christianity to the Amerindians. Again, Borunda deployed typical baroque religious scholarship to advance modern views and to undermine the authority of tradition.

Paradoxically, Borunda deployed his new methodology on the image to defend the cult against the increasing number of skeptical attacks. The narrative of the miracle of Our Lady of Guadalupe had long been under close scrutiny by the "insolent criticism" of a few enlightened skeptics.[107] Critics pointed to many inconsistencies in the story, not least among them being that the cape on which the image was painted did not correspond in size or shape to the capes used by natives at the time of the Conquest. To make things worse, the Creole physician José Ignacio Bartolache (1739–1790), in a work published posthumously by his wife in 1790, unintentionally showed through microscopic and chemical analyses that the material of the cloth was not maguey, the plant used by commoners to make their capes, but *iczotl*, which was used exclusively by Aztec nobles. The findings of Bartolache thus undercut the account that the Virgin had appeared to an Amerindian commoner.[108] Borunda's solution to the dilemma was both elegant and bold: St. Thomas had brought the printed cape with him when he came from the Orient, he argued.

As we have seen, after Mier delivered the sermon inspired by Borunda, the religious authorities brought charges against both Mier and Borunda. The prosecution, led by the Creole cleric José Fernández de Uribe (1741?–1796), exonerated Borunda on grounds of insanity. Mier, however, was condemned to exile and prison in Spain.[109] Although the prosecutors argued that even the most outrageous scholarship was acceptable if it was pursued in silence, they recommended that Borunda's manuscripts be locked up. Mier's sermon had, however, caused a crisis among the pious, challenging a tradition that had already reached the status of "apostolic."[110] It was heretical and thus punishable.

Trial documents show that the prosecution charged Borunda with lack of patriotism, inasmuch as he had dismissed all previous Spanish American and native historiography, much like the "erudite but delirious" Buffon and de Pauw. Moreover, the prosecution claimed, Borunda had invented a special geological catastrophe for America that did nothing but confirm Buffon's and de Pauw's most negative views of the continent.[111] There is some evidence that León y Gama participated in the trial against Borunda. In an unfinished manuscript on the history of the cult of Our Lady of Guadalupe, León y Gama echoed the views of the prosecutor Uribe and denounced the revisionist history of Bartolache and Borunda as heretical.[112]

Borunda's scholarship has been unfairly haunted by the stigma of incoherence. His methodology and historiographical vision were part of the larger cultural tradition of the Spanish American Baroque, a world in which religious images were both read as hieroglyphs and interpreted as Neoplatonic seals with magical virtues. The world of Borunda coexisted uncomfortably with that of León y Gama and Alzate y Ramírez in late-eighteenth-century New Spain. The turmoil created by Borunda's radical historio-graphical conclusion opens a window on the aggressive modernity of the Spanish American Baroque and the profoundly conservative nature of the Spanish American Enlightenment. Unlike most other Creole historians, Borunda dismissed all previous historiography, including that of the sixteenth-century Amerindian interpreters. The enlightened León y Gama, on the other hand, cast Borunda as a heretic when the latter threatened to tarnish Mexico's most cherished religious traditions. It is perhaps characteristic of the Spanish American Enlightenment that Borunda, the baroque scholar, was ultimately portrayed as a follower of the northwestern European authors who offended national pride with their bold new historical speculation about the land and peoples of the New World. Borunda, his critics maintained, built on the conclusions reached, and the methodologies used, by conjectural historians such as Buffon and de Pauw. Like them, Borunda dismissed the value of *all* sixteenth-century colonial sources and contended that the New World had a separate geological history. As Borunda's case makes clear, the dominant preoccupation of the Spanish American Enlightenment was maintaining control over the creation and validation of historical and philosophical knowledge about the New World. At least in Mexico, criticism ended when threats to political stability began.

José Antonio Maravall has characterized baroque culture as the product of exuberant yet conservative imaginations.[113] The brief survey of the literature on the devotion of the image of Our Lady of Guadalupe presented here would seem to prove Maravall right. But, can we really characterize baroque culture in Spanish America as "conservative," the manifestation of a traditional spirit? Borunda's fanciful etymologies that undercut centuries of accumulated learning on historiography and devotional practices prove otherwise. The literature about devotional practices reviewed here shows that with the stroke of a pen and a few daring interpretations of words and images, every writer advanced bold new theories that undermined tradition. The epistemology and methodologies of the Baroque sought to unsettle tradition but failed to study the Amerindian past. With the exception of Carlos Sigüenza y Góngora, who devoted much energy to the elucidation of Mesoamerican calendars and chronologies, the seventeenth-century clergy had better things to do. In the intervening years between the publication of Torquemada's *Monarchía indiana* (1615) and Eguiara y Eguren's *Bibliotheca mexicana* (1756), the clerical elites of New Spain are remarkable for their silence concerning the study of the Amerindian past. Why? Kenneth Mills and William Taylor have recently suggested that baroque religiosity implied "something of an escape from history." Through a comparative study of altarpieces, Mills and Taylor have argued that sixteenth-century altars in Mexico had historical narratives as their organizing principle (paintings of Christ and statues of Church fathers and saints that point to intellectual and institutional genealogies), whereas seventeenth-century altars did away with history as they sought to dazzle and engage the emotions rather than the intellect.[114] Whether the seventeenth-century silence on Amerindian history is part of the Spanish American Baroque's escape from history is something that can only be elucidated by further research. What is clear, however, is that as soon as scholars such as Borunda began to apply baroque epistemologies to the study of the Mesoamerican past in the second half of the eighteenth century, radically new narratives began to surface.

The Ruins of Palenque

The antiquarian controversy surrounding the discovery of the Mayan ruins of Palenque provides a case study of the paradoxical encounter of the Baroque and Enlightenment in Spanish America. Ramón Ordóñez y Aguiar (d. ca. 1840) was the engine behind the European discovery of Palenque. Ordóñez y Aguiar's exaggerated claims about Palenque's significance for universal history and biblical chronology were largely responsible for an early flurry of official Spanish expeditions. But given the allegorical methods in his historiography, and the fact that the expeditions failed to find evidence for Ordóñez y Aguiar's claims, the Spanish authorities lost interest in the ruins. I study the debate over the significance of Palenque between the official responsible for the expeditions, the president of the high court of Guatemala, the magistrate José Estachería, and Ordóñez y Aguiar. It pitted a historiographical paradigm informed by philosophical and conjectural reconstructions of the past against the scholarship of the Baroque.

There is another controversy in the history of the European discovery of Palenque that merits our attention. Ordóñez y Aguiar confronted not only Estachería but also Pablo Félix Cabrera, an Italian resident in Guatemala. Cabrera and Ordóñez y Aguiar were members of an academy of literati in

Guatemala City devoted to the study of Palenque and Mayan texts. Although the acknowledged leader of the academy was Ordóñez y Aguiar, Cabrera departed slightly from the teachings of the master. The embattled Creole priest deployed the discourse of patriotic epistemology to crush and discredit the knowledge and techniques of the Italian. The bitter struggle between Cabrera and Ordóñez y Aguiar demonstrates that patriotic epistemology was an all-pervasive discourse that in the colonies cut across cultural divides.

Although much has been written on the discovery of Palenque, little is known of the world of ideas and the culture that made the discoveries possible. The reason for this historiographical vacuum has partly to do with the difficulty involved in understanding unfamiliar mental landscapes. Paz Cabello Carro, for example, has recently reproduced a cache of primary sources on the discovery in an anachronistic demonstration of the "modernity" of Spanish culture, using as evidence the Spanish authorities' commitment to the "archeological" study of Palenque in Chiapas and to that of Pompeii and Herculaneum near Naples. The historiographical vacuum also stems from the difficulty of getting at the relevant sources, which are housed in Berkeley, Paris, Chicago, New Orleans, Madrid, Seville, London, Guatemala City, and Mexico City.[115] This widely scattered distribution has not only contributed to keeping the wealth of eighteenth-century Spanish American intellectual debates hidden but also exemplifies the fate of the great collections of indigenous sources put together by most eighteenth-century Spanish American antiquarians. By mid nineteenth century, they had begun to be exported from the region.

The Parish Priest and the Governor

In late 1784, José Ordóñez y Aguiar, brother of Ramón and vicar of a parish in Chamula, went to Guatemala City to visit his friend the Dominican provincial Tomás Luis de la Roca. Roca considered that the news brought by his friend had to be relayed to the president of the Audiencia of Guatemala, the magistrate José Estachería. When Estachería welcomed Roca and the vicar, he was left speechless, for Ordóñez y Aguiar had information regarding the discovery of an ancient city on the eastern slopes of the province of Chiapas that might rewrite the history of the Western Hemisphere. Drawing on information conveyed by his brother Ramón, a secular priest then residing in Ciudad Real, the capital of Chiapas, José maintained that there was a city in Chiapas that had once been a hub of a global economy linking exiled Romans, Hittites, and Carthaginians in America to the Old World. The city had once presided over vast gold mines, endless supplies of spices, and a network of canals and ports. All evidence indicated that the city was Solomon's legendary Ophir and that it held the key to the origins of the Amerindians, as well as to many ancient texts, including the Bible. Ramón, who never visited the ruins himself, had long sought to attract the attention of the authorities in Chiapas. He partially succeeded, and a couple of local functionaries in Ciudad Real, Fernando Gómez de Andrade and Esteban Gutiérrez, visited the ruins in 1773, but they made little of them. This time, however, the powerful Estachería was willing to invest considerable resources in the study of Palenque.[116]

Estachería immediately ordered the functionary closest to the ruins, José Antonio Calderón, alcalde of the hamlet of Palenque, to quickly survey the "fragments" of this "most populous city" and to interview the neighboring natives on the traditions surrounding the ruins. In a letter dated November 1784, Estachería urged Calderón to act swiftly. Much was riding on compliance with the order, Estachería argued, because interpretation of the monuments "could shed light on the annals of ancient and modern history "and the discovery had the potential to bring untold honor to the Spanish nation.[117]

Whether the lowly bureaucrat was moved by the patriotic rhetoric of the powerful Estachería we do not know, but it took Calderón only two weeks to fulfill the order, a record of sorts in the labyrinthine world of the Spanish American colonial bureaucracy. The report of the expedition must have confirmed to Estachería that the Spanish nation was about to reap the glory of introducing the world to a momentous discovery, for Calderón described a city with great palaces, arched hallways, and multistory towers and with sprawling neighborhoods that extended for miles. After three days of conducting interviews in the rain and of opening trails in the jungle, Calderón declared that the ruins had once been the site of a great court that ruled over the entire province of Tabasco. Although the natives refused to tell him anything, inscriptions in the city palace, he argued, indicated the probable Roman origins of its first inhabitants, for a figure in one stucco relief wore shoes adorned with crescents similar to a motif used by the Roman elites as described by Plutarch (Fig. 5.13a). Calderón also suggested that the inhabitants might have been Spaniards who fled immediately after the Moorish invasion of the Iberian Peninsula or even ancient Carthaginians. In closing his report, Calderón reminded Estachería of his efficiency in the past in putting down rebellions by brutish Amerindians in the region. Clearly, he saw no contradiction between his glamorous portrayal of the past and his efforts to discipline the wretched Amerindians of the present.[118]

a

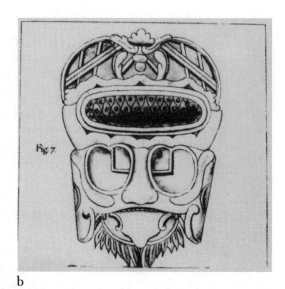

b

c

FIGURE 5.13. Images used to argue the Roman origins of the original inhabitants of Palenque, drawn by Spanish expeditions sent to study the ruins in the 1780s: (a) Palenquians wearing "Roman" shoes adorned with crescents, according to José Antonio Calderón; (b) Jupiter, according to Antonio del Río; (c) Pegasus, according to del Río. From Paz Cabello Carro, *Política investigadora de la época de Carlos III en el área maya* (Ediciones de la Torre, Madrid, 1992).

Having obtained swift independent confirmation of Ordóñez y Aguiar's claim, Estachería was now almost ready to inform the authorities in Spain. However, he first sent an expeditionary party led by one of the most competent functionaries in the land, Antonio Bernasconi, member of a leading Italian family of architects. When the provincial authorities decided to leave Antigua after a devastating earthquake in 1773, they hired Bernasconi to build Guatemala City, the new capital, on neoclassical principles. Among other things, Bernasconi designed the cathedral, the central plaza, and the equestrian statute of Charles III in the new capital.[119] The choice of the eminent architect to lead the expedition shows that Estachería attached great importance to the discovery. Moreover, he personally assumed the task of drawing up the research program for the expedition.

Antonio Bernasconi's Expedition to Palenque

Estachería asked Bernasconi to focus attention on four distinct areas. The first was to collect iconographic information (including making casts of carved boulders) to help determine the antiquity of the original inhabitants by comparative means. Bernasconi was therefore prompted to study the architectural orders of Palenque with the ancient classical authors in mind. Estachería's second request of Bernasconi was to identify the nature of the economy that had supported the city. The Italian architect was asked to find buildings used by the Amerindians to store treasure, not food, for only a city with metal currency and a mint could be considered civilized. As part of the study of the past political economy of the city, Bernasconi was also asked to scour the land for traces of paved roads, for no great city in the rain forest could have thrived with only muddy trails. By the same token, Estachería requested Bernasconi to explore the rivers nearby to see whether they were navigable, and whether ports could be found on their shores. In the third guideline, Estachería ordered Bernasconi to identify the reasons that had led to the destruction of the city. Bernasconi was to look for caches of iron weapons that could indicate a great invasion by an armed force. Likewise, the Italian was asked to study the multistory tower of Palenque carefully. Should he find walled-up windows in the tower (as Calderón's report had suggested), it would be an indication that the locals had resisted an invasion. Traces of volcanic eruptions, on the other hand, might indicate that the city had come to a more violent end. Estachería prompted Bernasconi to dig into the mounds covered by the jungle to look for lava. In the fourth and final guideline, Estachería asked Bernasconi to come up with a detailed scale map of the city, its buildings (baths, temple, jails, treasuries, and so forth), and the surrounding ditches and walls. Calderón had found a large round stone on the shore of the river dividing the city, and Estachería asked Bernasconi to determine whether it had simply been a millstone or was part of something more elaborate. He also asked Bernasconi to report on whether the foundations of the buildings in Palenque were adequate to their volume and weight, for only a civilized people would have known how to calculate this.[120]

When Bernasconi turned in the results of his survey in mid June, after spending some three months in the field, Estachería felt he had been misled by Ordóñez y Aguiar and Calderón. Claims that Palenque was the biblical Ophir and that the city might have once housed communities of hardy Romans and entrepreneurial Carthaginians were not borne out by the testimony of the more credible Bernasconi.[121] The Italian architect found the ruins of some twenty-two houses within a radius of some three miles (five miles to the west), indicating that the city had indeed been a sprawling community. Moreover, Bernasconi reported that the foundations of most extant buildings, particularly those of the tower and the palace, were sturdy; that the subterranean chambers of the palace had domes; and that there were arches to be found in an aqueduct, two stone bridges, and the surrounding houses. Such evidence of civilized existence, however, contrasted with the absence of most of the things Estachería had expected would be found in a great commercial hub. Bernasconi reported that he had failed to find paved roads in and out the city; treasury chambers in the palace; nearby ports for seaworthy vessels (the closest port was some twenty miles away, due north on the lake of Catazaja, which in turn drained into the sea on the coast of Campeche, and was only good for canoes with carrying capacities of up to about five hundred pounds); metal currency and gold mines (the area was only rich in cacao, vanilla, and dyes); complex machinery (the stone by the river described by Calderón had never been part of a mill, let alone part of some other more sophisticated mechanical device); traces of sudden destruction (there were no volcanic ashes in the mounds and no caches of iron weapons either; nor there were any fortifications in and around the city); and an orderly layout for the distribution of houses (there were no streets). Finally, an analysis of the collected iconography suggested that the inhabitants had been Amerindians.[122]

Estachería shared the mind-set of the enlightened European conjectural historians of the period. The research program he drew up for Bernasconi clearly derived from contemporary social science. For Estachería, a great civilization emerged only if certain conditions were met. Since Palenque did not satisfy most of the criteria associated with being a "commercial society," the pinnacle of progress, he simply wrote it off. Finally, Estachería privileged the testimony of Bernasconi, a learned Italian, over that of Calderón, a lowly local bureaucrat. Calderón's allegations seemed like exaggerations when contrasted with the skeptical tone of Bernasconi. Estachería would have no more of the ruins.

Estachería's conclusions and Calderón's and Bernasconi's reports reached Madrid in March 1786 and were sent to the Royal Chronicler of the Indies, Juan Bautista Muñoz, for review. Muñoz praised Estachería for his efforts and agreed with the magistrate's conclusions. The city was ancient but had been built by Amerindians who, unlike their contemporaries (or those at the time of the Conquest), had been somewhat civilized and knowledgeable of architecture. Muñoz, however, thought that more could be done to investigate the ruins. They clearly showed that the sixteenth-century Spanish witnesses had been accurate in their reports of urban life in Mesoamerica. In addition, the ruins also seemed to contain material evidence that contradicted traditional accounts of the origins of civilized life in Mesoamerica, for the legendary Toltecs, supposedly the mainspring of ancient civilized life in Mesoamerica, had left remains that did not correspond to those found in Palenque. Muñoz sifted through the reports of Calderón and Bernasconi identifying passages that clashed with what was known about Toltec, Mexica, and Inca architecture. Calderón and Bernasconi had described a spiral staircase in the tower and "windows" in the palace and surrounding houses. They had also made references to baked bricks and clays and some type of cement, as well as to heraldic seals, including one with a fleur-de-lys at the entrance to the subterranean chambers of the palace. But the most surprising reference in the reports, Muñoz argued, had been to the existence of arches and domes. Bernasconi had described the arches in the subterranean chambers as "Gothic." Were there truly spiral staircases, arches, windows, cement, bricks, and heraldic seals in Palenque as Calderón and Bernasconi contended? Muñoz recommended another expedition to check these facts. He also suggested that the expedition collect samples of building materials to be sent to Spain. From the answers to these questions, Muñoz argued, much could be learned about the internal history of Mesoamerica, but not about the history of the world, "as the enthusiasm of the first reports [mistakenly suggested]."[123] Muñoz's patron, the minister of the Indies, José de Gálvez, immediately ordered the skeptical Estachería to put together a third expedition.

Antonio del Río's Expedition to Palenque

After delaying for months, Estachería reluctantly complied with Gálvez's instructions, assigning the leadership of the expedition to Captain Antonio del Río (1745–1789?), an artilleryman, whose ability to carry out a successful mission was doubted by both Estachería and del Río himself.[124] The latter in any case set out with only a handful of queries posed by Muñoz and no master plan to guide his research.

Del Río arrived in early May and spent a month clearing the jungle with a team of Amerindians summoned by the local authorities. In the two weeks left to him, he then conducted "archeological" digs, thinking that jewelry and coins buried in the ground might throw some light on the place. In the course of his search, he knocked down every conceivable kind of structure, including ramparts, walls, niches, ceilings, floors, doors, and graves in the tower, houses, palace, and temples. After causing such havoc, he concluded that some walls were in fact made of "the hardest mix of plaster and small stones" (cal y canto).[125] To make sure that Muñoz got a good sampling of the stucco of wall and pillar ornaments, he tore heads, limbs, and hieroglyphs off several reliefs.[126] To his chagrin, he had to stop after opening a hole some eight feet deep in one of the walls of the tower, because he realized that the building might be coming apart, but he informed Muñoz that the hole revealed that the space between the central staircase of the tower and the outside wall was filled with sand and small stones.[127] Muñoz need not content himself merely with samples of stucco, stone, and clay, del Río noted. The buildings could easily and cheaply be taken apart and shipped to Spain, to the nation's lasting glory.[128]

Along this exquisitely detailed narrative of the damage he had done to Palenque, del Río included speculations as to the origins of the ancient inhabitants. Noting that a friend of his in the city of Merida knew of similar ruins in Yucatan that had been abandoned long before the Spaniards arrived, del Río concluded that Palenque belonged to a distinct architectural regional style. The tower supported the hypothesis that the place had been a Roman colony, he said, because the natives could have not built it on their own.[129] There was also some iconographic resemblance between images in the wall reliefs of the palace and Roman portraits of Jupiter and Pegasus (Figs. 5.13b and c).[130] Moreover, Palenque had been established in a bucolic landscape, rich in fruits and exotic fauna and flora but with no iron and metals nearby, a place conducive to a "quiet life, of more solid happiness than that available today in the concentrated luxury of the largest and most cultivated centers."[131] Del Río's Romans were republicans. Citing a 1638 manuscript by the Dominican Jacinto Garrido that concluded based on etymology that the Amerindians were descended from parties of stranded navigators of different European nations, and calling attention to the many wall reliefs in the palace sporting "Greek crosses," De Río also suggested that the Amerindians of Palenque might have once received Greek or even Phoenician visitors.[132]

In July 1788, thirteen months after del Río's return, Estachería sent five crates containing the spoils of his expedition to Spain, along with a report, which did not, however, answer any of Muñoz's questions about arches, vaults, spiral staircases, windows, and heraldic seals.[133] It is revealing that the events surrounding the discovery of Palenque have been firmly linked to the name of del Río to the complete exclusion of everything and everyone else. Estachería's finely reasoned program, Bernasconi's competent fieldwork, and Calderón's first survey were all superseded by del Río's report, a piece of bureaucratic incompetence. In 1822, in the first published edition of del Río's report, Henry Berthoud blamed the failure to make such a wonderful document public on the Spanish character. The failing, he argued, was demonstrative of "[the Spanish] peculiar apathy . . . as far relates to any vestiges of antiquity." In the same preface, Berthoud attributed the discovery of Palenque to del Río.[134]

After receiving del Río's report, the Spanish authorities decided to let the matter rest until some twenty years later, when they sent Guillermo Dupaix (ca. 1750–ca. 1818), a French officer in the Spanish army, to Palenque as part of a larger official study of extant Mesoamerican ruins. In the meantime, however. Ramón Ordóñez y Aguiar was not about to give up. Bernasconi's report notwithstanding, Ordóñez y Aguiar continued to press Estachería, this time with an indigenous source that allegedly identified Palenque as an ancient multinational city. Estachería summarily dismissed the document as incoherent and untrustworthy.[135] To escape "terrible persecution," Ordóñez y Aguiar left Ciudad Real (Chiapas) in 1788 and moved to Guatemala City, where he continued his philological studies and his campaign to put Palenque on the map.[136] It was here that he met Pablo Félix Cabrera, beginning a new chapter in the debate over Palenque's significance.

In Guatemala City, the spurned Ordóñez y Aguiar surrounded himself with a small circle of disciples. Along with José Miguel de San Juan, leader of the city council (regidor) and of the guild of merchants, and Pablo Félix Cabrera, Ordóñez y Aguiar created an "academy" that met periodically to discuss his philological findings. In 1792, through the powerful San Juan, Ordóñez y Aguiar sought unsuccessfully to gain access directly to the king. In the process, he made public for the first time a study of the ruins of Palenque in light of a colonial-era Tzeltal Maya document known as the Provanza de Votán, which Ordóñez y Aguiar held told of the origin of the founders of the city in detail. The comity of the Guatemala City academy was shattered in 1794, however, when Cabrera drew on Ordóñez y Aguiar's ideas without proper acknowledgment in a study of an ancient Mayan medal dedicated to the king. Angered, Ordóñez y Aguiar began to spread rumors of plagiarism, leading Cabrera to bring criminal libel charges against him. As part of the ensuing trial, Ordóñez y Aguiar produced a second manuscript, this time an allegorical, etymological study of the Popol Vuh, in which he sought to prove that this "Indian bible" was a modified version of the Pentateuch.

In the following pages, I study the activities of the Guatemala City academy and the works of Cabrera and Ordóñez y Aguiar. The theories spawned at the academy and the manuscripts of Cabrera and Ordóñez y Aguiar are windows on the baroque world of Spanish America. Moreover, the debate between the two sheds light on the spread and cultural significance of the discourse of patriotic epistemology. To discredit his Italian rival, Ordóñez y Aguiar depicted Cabrera as an epistemologically naive foreigner whose knowledge of Native American languages was limited.

Interpreting Palenque

Sometime in November 1792, the three members of the Guatemala City academy began to put together a dossier on the significance of the discovery of Palenque to be sent to Spain. The *regidor* José Miguel de San Juan may have told the other two academicians that an acquaintance of his in Madrid could get the king himself to listen. For this purpose, Ordóñez y Aguiar dusted off a manuscript that he had written for Archbishop Cayetano Monroy y Franco, and Cabrera wrote a dissertation on a Mayan medal that had been delivered to the academy by two officers of the mint. Finally, San Juan attached to the dossier a cover letter describing the activities of the academy and summarizing the insights of Cabrera and Ordóñez y Aguiar.

In the document originally intended for the eyes of Archbishop Monroy y Franco, Ordóñez y Aguiar interpreted the significance of the ruins of Palenque using del Río's report.[137] After chastising del Río for the quick manner in which he had conducted the survey and criticizing him for having suggested that the Romans, Greeks, or Phoenicians had merely been visitors, whose technical knowledge of architecture had been partially understood by the Amerindians who built the city, Ordóñez y Aguiar set out to prove that

Palenque was nothing less than the legendary Ophir, described in the Bible, to which King Solomon had once sent his fleets for gold and spices. Throughout, Ordóñez y Aguiar emphasized the many influences evident in the ruins. Moorish traces were to be found in the rings of the walls of the subterranean chambers in the shape of torch holders typical of mosques. The Moors had also left their mark in the tower, which resembled a minaret. Roman influences were to be found everywhere, particularly in the so-called palace, which Ordóñez y Aguiar contended was a Roman temple, because it was both located on top of a mound, close to the sky, and had subterranean chambers. The Romans had celebrated Jupiter in high open spaces and worshipped Pluto underground, Ordóñez y Aguiar noted, so it stood to reason that the temple was Roman. Moreover, the carved stucco over the entrance to the underground rooms, he argued, represented two Roman deities, Proserpina and Ceres (Fig. 5.14a). The Romans had also left behind an aqueduct. The Hebrews had left their signature in the size of the stones used in the buildings: huge, to signify magnificence. The palace-temple also resembled the legendary temple of Jerusalem. Finally, Ordóñez y Aguiar argued that the Egyptian influence was overwhelming, found in the use of animal shapes as script; in portrayals of Osiris (Fig. 5.14b); in crosses, which since antiquity had signified "torment"; in images of deified serpents; in the word "Tzeltal" itself (the name of the ethnic group in the Lacandon forest, where Palenque was located), which in Egyptian reportedly stood for "good spirit." And the list went on.

Having proved the multiethnic character of the place, Ordóñez y Aguiar set out to demonstrate that the city had once been a commercial entrepôt. Palenque, he argued, had been visited by great fleets that traded using metal currency. Del Río and Bernasconi had reported neither gold mines nor treasure chambers in Palenque, but Ordóñez y Aguiar simply attributed this to the mendacity of the natives. His argument was typical of the Creole literati: when the local Amerindians told him that no mines existed in the area, del Río ought to have realized that they were afraid that they would be put to work if they revealed the truth.[138] Quite apart from gold mines, there was in any case evidence of the commercial character of the city, the size of which spoke for itself. By most counts, including del Río's, Palenque was several miles long and wide. Could a city this large have survived without a brisk international exchange of commodities?[139] Ordóñez y Aguiar complained, too, that del Río had failed to mention in his report that a port on the banks of the river Usumasinta was located only three miles from the center of Palenque. The Usumasinta drained into Lake Catazaja, twenty miles to the north,

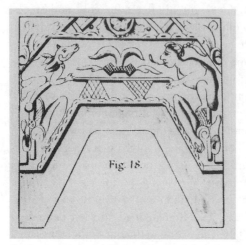

a

b

FIGURE 5.14. Images from Palenque read by Ramón Ordóñez y Aguiar as evidence that the city had once been an ancient multinational entrepôt: (a) Proserpina and Ceres; (b) Osiris. In Greco-Roman mythology, Proserpina (Persephone), personifying the change of the seasons, spends half of the year on Olympus and the other half underground in Hades. Ordóñez y Aguiar contended that the cloth stamped with three hearts held by "Osiris" was a genealogical reference to Votán III, discussed in the Tzeltal Maya document known as the Provanza de Votán. From Paz Cabello Carro, *Política investigadora de la época de Carlos III en el área maya* (Ediciones de la Torre, Madrid, 1992).

which in turn drained into the Gulf of Mexico. Moreover, the painter attached to del Río's expedition, Ricardo Almendáriz, had found an intact cache of logwood, also called *palo de campeche* (the wood of Campeche), in the port on the banks of the Usumasinta. Logwood was both the main export of the area and the source of a dye, and it was well known to any student of the Bible that Solomon's fleets had obtained a dye called *thino* from Ophir, which the great French biblical scholar Dom Augustin Calmet (1672–1757) had shown was the dye called *sesthim*, or "incorruptible tree," by Moses in the Pentateuch. This "incorruptible tree," Ordóñez y Aguiar explained, was clearly logwood from Palenque.[140]

Interpreting the Provanza de Votán

To the wealth of material corroboration found in the city itself, Ordóñez y Aguiar added his pièce de résistance, the Tzeltal Maya codex known as the Provanza de Votán, which, he contended, indisputably identified Palenque with Ophir. Now lost, and only a few pages long, this document allegedly described the mixed ethnic origins of the inhabitants of this most ancient postdiluvian city, and its rise and fall, in exquisite detail, by means of veiled references.[141] Through allegorical interpretations of Tzeltal terms, Ordóñez y Aguiar determined that the Provanza was a first-person account by one Votán III, of the nation of the Chivin, or "Snakes," telling how he had left home in search of his ancestors, whom Ordóñez y Aguiar identified as the Hittites (Heveos or Hivites), because after Babel the Hittites had left Libya, and their name in ancient Phoenician signified "snake." Ordóñez y Aguiar identified this Votán ("heart" in Tzeltal), with Osiris, also depicted in plaster images in Palenque (Fig. 5.14b). In his search for the "roots of heaven," Votán visited the Chivin four times, on trips that took him to Spain, Rome, Jerusalem, and, finally, Babel, the "root of heaven." On his way back from Babel, he went first to check the "holes of the snakes," which, according to Ordóñez y Aguiar, metaphorically stood for all the places the Hittites had colonized on the African coast. Then he visited the "thirteen snakes," or thirteen Canary Islands, which had served the Hittites as outposts in their Atlantic expansion. Votán went on to tell of the arrival of seven Tzequile families after his return home, and of how they had taught the original Snakes/Hittites manners, including the use of utensils, dishes, tablecloths, and spittoons. The Tzequile, in turn, learned about monarchical rule and religion from the Snakes, Votán teaching them to worship the "Snake."

Ordóñez y Aguiar held that these Tzequile were Carthaginians, and that the Aztecs — known in Chiapas as "Tzequile" — were the descendants of the Tzequile-Carthaginians. In Ordóñez y Aguiar's view, the Provanza de Votán clearly proved that the first inhabitants of America had been postdiluvian descendants of Noah's son Ham, who had arrived by sea from the east, not from Asia via the Bering Strait. Palenque, the great multiethnic metropolis ruled by Votán III, Ordóñez y Aguiar concluded, had thus been both the first city in America and the Ophir of the Bible.

Pablo Félix Cabrera's 'Theatro crítico americano'

Pablo Félix Cabrera might have had very little to add to Ordóñez y Aguiar's narrative had it not been for the discovery of two medals of obscure origin that allegedly told the story of the rise and fall of Palenque. The academicians assigned Cabrera to interpret one of the medals, and Ordóñez y Aguiar generously lent the Italian his manuscript. Cabrera worked diligently, and by the time San Juan wrote to his contact in Spain, the Italian had not only interpreted the medal but was on his way to finishing a larger work, the *Theatro crítico americano*.

Theatro critico sought to present a radically new history of the origins of the Amerindians and to defend the credibility of ancient sources, including Diodorus Siculus, Plato, Strabo, Aristotle, and the Bible, whose authority Cabrera perceived as under siege by pre-Adamites and *philosophes*. The work was also a thoroughgoing critique of sixteenth-century historiography on precolonial Mesoamerica and an assault on the propensity of Spaniards not to believe their most lucid informants. Finally, the *Theatro crítico* sought to put together a panoply of methodologies, including the comparative study of medals and images, a euhemerist study of Mexica and ancient deities, and an analysis of Mesoamerican calendrics and ancient chronologies.[142]

Building on Ordóñez y Aguiar's allegorical exegesis of the Provanza de Votán, Cabrera maintained that the first inhabitants of America had been Hittites, led by Hercules Tyrius, who had arrived on Hispaniola sometime in 380 B.C.E., 1,200 years after the Hittites had colonized the coast of Africa and the Canary Islands. According to Cabrera, Votán III, the founder of Palenque, was the third in the genealogy of the Hittites in Hispaniola, so Palenque must have been settled circa 290 B.C.E. A few years after the foundation of Palenque, which Cabrera argued corresponded to the Toltec city of Amaquemecan, Votán left for the Old World. While visiting Spain and Rome, he spread the news of the existence of Hittite colonies in the New World, and a stream of Roman and Carthaginian settlers began to arrive. This migration,

Cabrera contended, had ended with the defeat of the Carthaginians by the Romans in the First Punic War, which he dated to 256 B.C.E.. The defeated Carthaginians in the Old World thereupon demanded that the settlers in New World return. A few heeded the order, but most stayed. This refusal, he asserted, spelled the end of Palenque-Amaquemecan, which by 200 B.C.E. had begun to collapse as a result of internal feuding. Fearing that Carthage would send a punitive expedition, the Hittites began to plot to expel the Carthaginians from the city, and internal struggles ensued. In the aftermath of these wars, the surviving Tzequile-Carthaginians, the Toltecs, migrated north until 175 B.C.E., when Tollan was founded.

Cabrera's radical reinterpretation of Mesoamerican history ran into two significant chronological and historiographical hurdles. First, most sources, including Torquemada and Clavijero, maintained that the Toltecs (actually, the Chichimecs) had left Amaquemecan in the year "1 Flint," that is, sometime in 596 C.E. Second, all sources agreed that the Toltecs had come from the north, not the southeast. Cabrera discounted all previous European accounts of the origins of the Toltecs, for Moctezuma Xocoyoltzin himself had told Cortés that his ancestors came from the peninsula of Yucatan. After a careful exegesis of speeches by Moctezuma found in Cortés's *Cartas de relación*, Cabrera proved to his own satisfaction that neither Cortés nor any of the Spaniards who came after him had been paying attention, for Moctezuma had clearly said that his ancestors had come from the southeast, not the north.[143] As for when the Toltecs had left Amaquemecan, Cabrera drew up calendrical tables that showed that "1 Flint" also corresponded to the year 181 B.C.E., fitting perfectly into his chronology of the fall of Palenque.[144] References in Amerindian codices to maritime voyages, he argued, alluded to crossing, not the Gulf of California, as both Torquemada and Clavijero maintained, but the Atlantic Ocean. Moreover, the codex that Gemelli Careri had published in 1700 (also known as Mapa Sigüenza), which most scholars thought referred to the southward migrations of the Mexica from North America (Fig. 2.10), was a map that recorded the Hittite colonization of the western coast of Africa circa 1,500 B.C.E.[145] All this chronological tinkering, Cabrera argued, made sense if Toltec references to the visit of the legendary Quetzalcoatl-St. Thomas were to be believed.[146]

But for Cabrera's new historiographical model to work, more than chronological tinkering was needed. Solid proof from iconography was required. The analysis of one of the images in the palace of Palenque typified Cabrera's approach (Fig. 5.15a). According to Cabrera, the image depicted a human sacrifice, the punishment that Isis meted out to Typhoon for having killed Osiris. Drawing on an age-old euhemerist tradition, Cabrera assumed that myth of Osiris recounted the story of two brothers, one, Osiris, who had spread civilization in the Mediterranean world and America through the use of force and persuasion, and the other, Typhoon, who, enraged by jealousy, murdered and cut Osiris into pieces, which he hid or scattered. Osiris's sister and wife, Isis, did not rest until she found all the parts of Osiris's body, with the exception of the penis. In despair, Isis paid homage to her brother-husband's missing part by inaugurating a cult of the phallus and sacrificing Typhoon to the gods. According to Cabrera, the image found in the palace of Palenque summarized the myth of Osiris in all its gory detail, depicting the sacrifice of Typhoon by Isis. Typhoon appeared sitting on a sacrificial altar, beneath which lay Osiris's missing penis.[147]

There was nothing new about such freewheeling iconographic analysis. With the possible exceptions of Bernasconi and Estachería, everyone involved in the study of Palenque, from Calderón (who thought that one of the shoes in an image in a stucco relief indicated the Roman origins of the city) to del Río (who drew on images in Palenque to determine the Roman, Greek, and/or Phoenician roots of its first inhabitants) to Ordóñez y Aguiar (who found Ceres and Proserpina guarding the entrance to the subterranean chambers of the palace), had speculated wildly. The truly new element introduced by Cabrera is his analysis of a mysterious medal given to the academicians sometime in 1791 by officials of the local mint.[148]

The medal was remarkable, for according to Cabrera it succinctly narrated the rise and fall of Palenque (Fig. 5.15b). One side of the coin sported in the foreground a snake coiled around a tree. Six other trees, including one of a different kind with a bird on top of it flanked the tree. On the other side of the coin, there were also seven trees, one of them a stunted bush, and a man kneeling and about to be devoured by two monsters. Cabrera found in the images on the coin confirmation of the story of the seven Snake-Hittite and seven Tzequile families alluded to in the Provanza de Votán. The snake on one side stood for the ethnic group of the Hittites and the trees for the seven families of Snakes and Tzequiles who migrated to the New World. The tree with a bird on top of it stood for the Toltec-Tzequile group that would eventually bring Palenque down. The stunted tree, or bush, in turn, was a reference to the surviving Toltecs. The monsters devouring the man stood for the factional feuding that had engulfed Palenque in the wake of the order from Carthage for the settlers to return home.[149]

San Juan summarized the speculations of Cabrera and Ordóñez y Aguiar in two letters to his courtier friend Sesma written in December 1792 and

a

b

FIGURE 5.15. Images used by Pablo Félix Cabrera to support of his thesis that Amerindians were of Hittite-Carthaginian origin. (a) Isis sacrificing Typhoon, with Osiris's penis lying beneath the sacrificial altar. From Paz Cabello Carro, *Política investigadora de la época de Carlos III en el área maya* (Ediciones de la Torre, Madrid, 1992). (b) The "Mayan" medal given by two officers of the mint to Ramón Ordóñez y Aguiar's academy of antiquarians in Guatemala City. Cabrera contended that this medal allegorically depicted the Hittite and Carthaginian families that had founded and then destroyed Palenque. From Pablo Félix Cabrera, *Teatro crítico americano* (London, 1822).

January 1793. After characterizing Guatemala as a purgatory where he had been sent to serve, the magistrate quickly went over the key arguments of Ordóñez y Aguiar's treatise and Cabrera's study of the medal. He presented each and every insight as the product of an academy working collectively.[150]

Nothing, it seems, came of the efforts to win support in Madrid. On June 2, 1794, however, Cabrera sent the medal itself to the king of Spain, along with two copies of his *Theatro critíco*.[151] Ordóñez y Aguiar immediately began spreading the rumor that the Italian had committed plagiarism. How Ordóñez y Aguiar managed to ruin the credibility and credit of Cabrera in only twenty days will forever remain a mystery, but on June 23, 1794, Cabrera stood in front of local magistrates claiming to be bankrupt and pressing criminal charges against Ordóñez y Aguiar for libel. The Italian asked the authorities get a copy of the manuscript that Ordóñez y Aguiar, alias "Cuenca," had addressed to Archbishop Monroy y Franco to demonstrate that he had never committed plagiarism.[152]

A Biblical Exegesis of the Popol Vuh

In the course of the trial, Ordóñez y Aguiar came up with a second manuscript, a work that Cabrera himself referred to once as a labor of love, which had taken the Creole priest some thirty years to produce.[153] It was his long-awaited "Historia de la creación del mundo conforme al sistema americano," an interpretation of ancient Mesoamerican history based on analysis of the ruins of Palenque and exegesis of two Amerindian documents, the Provanza de Votán and the Popol Vuh. "Historia de la creación" was originally a manuscript in two parts, each devoted to the analysis of one of the two indigenous texts.[154] Fortunately for the historian interested in the culture of the literate Spanish American elites of the late eighteenth century, the parts that are missing (the exegesis of Provanza de Votán) can be reconstructed through documentation found elsewhere. Volume 1, which survives in its entirety, however, introduced subjects that had not previously been discussed. In it, Ordóñez y Aguiar sought to prove that the Popol Vuh, a jewel of Mayan religious and historical thought, was a distorted copy of the Pentateuch.

There are many things remarkable about Ordóñez y Aguiar's "Historia de la creación." The analysis of the Popol Vuh itself is an important window on the religious culture of late-colonial Spanish American clerical elites. Also, the debate conducted in its pages against Cabrera reveals yet another example of patriotic epistemology in action. Yet the most significant aspect of the text is that in the process of writing, Ordóñez y Aguiar preserved the only extant version in Quiché of the Popol Vuh, copied in Chichicastenango between 1701 and 1703 by the Dominican Francisco Ximénez (ca. 1666–1722). It was through his endless labor as a collector of Mayan documents and through his contact with the Dominican provincial Roca that Ordóñez y Aguiar located Ximénez's manuscripts, calling attention to their significance. It is likely that the Popol Vuh, along with many other indigenous manuscripts, would have disappeared in the absence of Ordóñez y Aguiar and other patriotic antiquarians. It was the discourse of patriotic epistemology in historiography, I argue, that was largely responsible for the preservation and survival of most extant collections of indigenous colonial codices. When anticlericalism temporarily triumphed in Guatemala in 1830 and monasteries were closed, the Popol Vuh was taken to the university library, and in the 1850s, it was spirited away to France by the abbé Brasseur de Bourbourg (1814–1874). By then, the days of Creole-clerical conspiracies to keep indigenous sources at home seem to have been long gone. Many copies of the Popol Vuh can now be found in Chicago, Paris, and San Francisco, a testimony to the antiquarian efforts of Ordóñez y Aguiar.[155]

The surviving parts of Ordóñez y Aguiar's "Historia de la creación" are difficult, often convoluted, and therefore easy to reject as the product of a feverish mind. Like Borunda, Ordóñez y Aguiar has been quickly dismissed by historians as someone "moved by a nationalist spirit but who, bogged down by a scholastic uncritical vision of the world stood in direct contradiction to the age of Enlightenment."[156] Such facile characterizations have prevented historians from *reading* the text, which although published has remained to this day largely unexplored.

Ordóñez y Aguiar's overall intention in "Historia de la creación" was to present the main historiographical insights in Cabrera's *Theatro crítico* as derivative. To this end, he rehearsed each and every one of the arguments advanced by Cabrera: that the history of Mesoamerica had been completely misunderstood by previous historians; that the first Amerindians had come from across the Atlantic; that Palenque was the first settlement in continental America, colonized by Hittites from Hispaniola; that indigenous sources like the Provanza de Votán showed that after the Hittites, waves of Tzequil-Carthaginian settlers (among others) had arrived; that the Tzequil-Carthaginians were, in fact, the Toltecs, who, in turn, had led the destruction of Palenque before moving north to central Mexico; and that the Mexica traditions regarding the origins of their Toltec ancestors had been dismissed or misunderstood by all European observers, beginning with Cortés. To this paradigm, "Historia de la creación" added the Popol Vuh.

According to Ordóñez y Aguiar, the Popol Vuh proved that Palenque had once been a great global entrepôt. Although the text showed that the religious traditions handed down from Noah to Moses had also arrived in America through the Hittites and Carthaginians, these Mosaic traditions had undergone profound changes as a result of exposure to other Old World religious forces, including Zoroastrianism and Roman paganism. The distortions, Ordóñez y Aguiar argued, had to do with the nature of the scripts in which Noah handed down his knowledge. The secret arcane knowledge preserved in "mute hieroglyphs" by Noah slowly lost its symbolic dimension through repeated translation into articulate languages and scripts.

Yet there was still a way to reconstruct the kernel of Noah's arcane knowledge, which lay buried in texts such as the Popol Vuh. Ordóñez y Aguiar found the crucial methodological procedure for his argument that the Popol Vuh was a distorted variant of the Pentateuch in translating Maya-Quiché terms into the alleged original language of the Hittites, Maya-Tzeltal. Like his contemporary Borunda, Ordóñez y Aguiar first reconstituted each Quiché word into its alleged Tzeltal original, broke the word into its constituent parts, and then read each term allegorically. Like Boturini and Vico, Ordóñez y Aguiar thought that words and hieroglyphs concealed references to key historical events.

The multiple linguistic manipulation of terms allowed Ordóñez y Aguiar to prove among many other things that entire sections in the Popol Vuh were, in fact, passages lifted from the Bible. Some passages, for example, described several attempts by deities to invent human beings. After having first created humans out of mud, after having failed to obtain from them the appropriate pious behavior, and after having destroyed them, the gods convened again to create a male body out of wood and a female one out of *sibac*. The Dominican Francisco Ximénez, who first compiled and translated the Popol Vuh, had originally rendered the Quiché term *sibac* as the name of a local plant, *espadaña*. Ordóñez y Aguiar, however, disagreed. *Sibac*, he argued, was in fact *si-bac* in Tzeltal, a composite of two words: *si* for "wood" and *bac* for "bone." *Si-bac*, Ordóñez y Aguiar concluded, showed that this time the gods had made the female, Eve, out of the "bone" of the wooden male, Adam. Like the first humans, whom the gods destroyed through a hurricane, the wooden creatures were also wiped out and transformed into monkeys by a blaze of fire. According to Ordóñez y Aguiar, this section of the Popol Vuh indicated that the natives were privy to the ideas of the Pentateuch but had distorted them as a result of contact with age-old cosmopolitan religious traditions, including that of the Pre-Adamites (which preserved the thesis of multiple creations) and those of Pythagoreanism and Zoroastrianism (in which the doctrine of metempsychosis considered the transmutation of humans into animals to be plausible). The reference to destruction by fire because of lack of piety, on the other hand, was garbled history. It showed that the natives had once known about the punishment visited by God on Sodom and Gomorrah for their sins.[157]

It would be tiresome to go over the numerous examples in "Historia de la creación" that reconfigured the meaning of the Popol Vuh; suffice it to say that Ordóñez y Aguiar found evidence that long sections of the Quiché text recapitulated the narrative of the fall of Lucifer.[158] Ordóñez y Aguiar also found in the Popol Vuh multiple references to the mysteries of the Gospels, indicating that the natives had been exposed not merely to the Pentateuch but to Christianity as well.[159] Throughout the "Historia de la creación," it is assumed that St. Thomas the Apostle visited America and taught the natives Christianity.

The alleged references in the Popol Vuh to two distinct historical times, that of the Hittites and Carthaginians and that of St. Thomas, allowed Ordóñez y Aguiar to introduce one of the most radical and tantalizing elements of his work, namely, a missionary proposal. According to Ordóñez y Aguiar, the Amerindians remembered both their ancient Hittite and Carthaginian ancestors and the more recent visit of St. Thomas. Inasmuch as both the Carthaginians and St. Thomas had promised to return, when the Spaniards arrived, the Amerindians did not know whether to consider them the heirs of the vengeful Carthaginians or followers of the benign St. Thomas. The Spanish settlers had failed to notice this dual tradition, however, and had therefore failed to take advantage of it, instead adopting strategies of colonization that led to catastrophe. Had the first Spaniards known that there were two separate and distinct historical traditions, one that would provoke resistance and rebellion (against the returning Carthaginians and their punishing expeditions) and one that would encourage meek accommodation (in support of the returning missionaries of St. Thomas), the conquistadors and friars would have presented themselves as the heirs of St. Thomas. The conversion of the continent could have been characterized by the willing and sweeping rational acceptance of the Gospels.[160] Such calls for missionary accommodation and tolerance, however, jarred with other passages by Ordóñez y Aguiar justifying not only the destruction of all idols but also outright religious persecution.[161]

For all the novelty of his approach to age-old missionary controversies, the central thrust of Ordóñez y Aguiar lay somewhere else. "Historia de la creación" was a treatise that sought to highlight the serious interpretative blunders of sixteenth-century Spanish and Amerindian historians. According to the Creole cleric, prior historians, including sixteenth-century Amerindian interpreters, had failed, in the first place, to identify the original language of the continent, namely, Maya-Tzeltal, which had ancient roots presumably in Phoenician, the language of the Hittites. Furthermore, they had failed to comprehend the symbolic allegorical references stored in the native languages. Like his contemporary Borunda, Ordóñez y Aguiar argued that those Amerindians who had held the key to the metaphors locked in the original terms had disappeared with the Conquest. Colonial Amerindians were ignorant and thus oblivious of the meaning of their historical traditions.[162]

According to Ordóñez y Aguiar, only a handful of Spanish American authors had glimpsed beneath the veil of allegories stored in the indigenous languages, including Francisco Ximénez, the Dominican who had compiled and translated the Popol Vuh. But Ordóñez y Aguiar thought that not even the learned Ximénez had been able to grasp the ultimate significance of the indigenous sources, because Ximénez failed to understand that Quiché terms had first to be translated into Maya-Tzeltal.[163]

But for all the criticisms he leveled against incompetent early colonial chroniclers and plebeian contemporary Amerindians, Ordóñez y Aguiar reserved his harshest comments for foreigners such as Cabrera. Perhaps simply because he was, like Cabrera, an Italian, Ordóñez y Aguiar piled scorn on Lorenzo Boturini, whose method he characterized as undisciplined speculation that had ultimately led to the utter corruption of historical facts. Ordóñez y Aguiar used Boturini to exemplify the perils of an imagination gone astray, the same imagination that had led Amerindians to distort the Pentateuch beyond recognition.[164] An upstart with limited linguistic credentials, Boturini had relied on commoners, rather than Amerindian aristocrats, for an understanding of local historical traditions.[165] Foreigners like Cabrera and Boturini traded in abstractions and lacked a practical knowledge of the natives. The Italians' ignorance was revealed in their condemnation of the bishop of Chiapas, Francisco Núñez de la Vega (1632–1706), for burning twenty ancient idols representing figures from the Mayan calendar after a pastoral visit to Soconusco in 1691. Had they been aware that the great Mayan-Tzeltal rebellion of 1713, which came within an inch of massacring or expelling all the Spaniards in Chiapas, might have been averted had the clergy taken away the Amerindians' idols, Cabrera and Boturini would have realized that Núñez de la Vega had been right to act as he did. It was this inability of the Italians to weigh the actions of missionaries such Núñez de la

Vega in the context of local developments that reflected their ignorance and misunderstanding of the real Amerindians.[166] There is much evidence that the "Historia de la creación" was intended to expose the naiveté and epistemological inability of foreigners ever to understand the Americas.[167]

Cabrera does not seem to have replied to Ordóñez y Aguiar's tirade. In November 1796, however, Ordóñez y Aguiar complained bitterly that Cabrera was seeking to hurt his reputation and credibility by raising doubts about his social and racial origins. He denied that he was a mestizo bastard who had fabricated a name to hide his lowly origins and replied in kind: according to documents he had unearthed in the archives, Cabrera was a swindler who had been expelled twice from the viceroyalty of Mexico. Worse, he was a lowly Italian commoner who hid his origins under a false Hispanic name and the title of "Don."[168]

The debates sparked by the discovery of Palenque captured in a nutshell the tensions and paradoxes of a colonial culture poised between Europe and the patriotic aspirations of its own disenfranchised literary elites. Estachería and Ordóñez y Aguiar came from two separate worlds, which failed to communicate. The president of the high court of Guatemala partook of the ideas and methodologies of the European Enlightenment, which privileged material evidence over literary sources. He interpreted the ruins of Palenque in the same way that the likes of William Robertson and the count of Campomanes would have done. A set of expectations about the behavior of "commercial" societies organized the research program he had Bernasconi pursue, but when he found that Palenque did not fit this mold, Estachería abandoned any further study of the ruins, Antonio del Río's expedition notwithstanding. Ordóñez y Aguiar, on the other hand, privileged philology and the study of indigenous literary sources. But unlike León y Gama and the Jesuits in Italian exile, Ordóñez y Aguiar dismissed all previous historiography entirely. As aggressively modern as Borunda, he insisted that Amerindian history was recorded in veiled verbal allegories that no one, native interpreters included, had correctly deciphered since the Conquest. His tortuous and painstaking etymological analyses assumed great familiarity with native languages, and he indulged in grandiose speculations about the history of Mesoamerican linguistic affiliations.

Ordóñez y Aguiar's portrayal of foreigners in general — and Boturini and Cabrera in particular — as epistemologically naive was grounded in his allegedly intimate knowledge, as a Mesoamerican savant himself, of Amerindian languages. In their efforts to rewrite the history of the New World on principles other than those offered by the new conjectural historians of northwestern Europe, he and other Creole scholars of the various schools of thought described in this book found common cultural ground in such patriotic epistemology.

Ordóñez y Aguiar's epistemological and methodological world belonged, like Borunda's, to the culture of the Baroque. Their work was characterized by hairsplitting etymologies and allegorical interpretations of images and words. These are mental resources that scholars have readily associated with early modern attempts to bolster authority and tradition in a world threatened by rapid economic and political change. As a new breed of radical skeptics set out to undermine the Bible, the baroque clergy plunged into a world of allegorical exegeses, searching for certainty and relief. In Spanish America, it seems, these techniques did not serve the cause of tradition; rather, scholars like Borunda and Ordóñez y Aguiar used the allegorical method to question centuries of accumulated learning. True, Borunda and Ordóñez y Aguiar applied this baroque method to Mesoamerican sources to bolster the authority of the Bible, whose chronologies and accounts found confirmation, they believed, in Amerindian documents. Yet Borunda and Ordóñez y Aguiar proved remarkably daring when, with reckless modernity, they brushed aside all traditional colonial historiography. Whether their accounts were wrong is beside the point. It is their willingness to question authority that should preoccupy us. The intellectual and cultural histories of colonial Spanish America have more often than not been captured in shibboleths. Perhaps a second look at the radical modernity of the Spanish American Baroque could in the same critical spirit of the patriotic epistemologists reviewed in this book begin decentering the Euro- and Anglocentric models that dominate the field.

Ordóñez y Aguiar continued in his crusade to make Palenque known to the world. In 1808, he resurfaced as an informant to Guillermo Dupaix, a French-born officer in the Spanish army who between 1805 to 1808 conducted a survey of antiquities in the territory of New Spain, including Palenque. When he visited Ciudad Real, Dupaix was conducted to the cathedral chapter to talk to Ordóñez y Aguiar, who showed him his cabinet of antiquities and the copper medal that Cabrera had once sought to interpret. Guided by Ordóñez y Aguiar, Dupaix included the medal in his survey, agreeing that it told the story of the migration and settlement of "a nation."[169] The spirit of Ordóñez y Aguiar hovers over all the descriptions of the images and monuments of Palenque that Dupaix later offered.[170] Dupaix's expedition ended abruptly, however, when the citizens of Ciudad Real, led by representatives of their leading corporations (including, in all likelihood, Ordóñez y Aguiar and the other members of the cathedral chapter), chased the Frenchman away after news arrived in 1808 that Napoleon had invaded Spain.[171]

The epistemological debates that characterized eighteenth-century Atlantic historiography on the New World did not go away. Drawing on the compilation of travel narratives by the Spanish Pedro de la Estala, John Pinkerton [1758–1826], for example, repeated in 1811 in the third edition of his *Modern Geography* the tiresome complaint that all Spanish accounts were unreliable.[1] This type of criticism, however, waned in Europe in the wake of Alexander von Humboldt's forceful defense of the reliability of early colonial Spanish chronicles. But in Spanish America memories were harder to erase. On the eve of the wars of independence, the pages of Mexican periodicals carried both articles dismissing the glorious reconstructions of the Aztecs' past as unreliable and replies questioning the skeptics. When the wars exploded, rival parties managed to turn an argument over rights of political representation at the Cortes of Cádiz (1810–1814) into a historiographical dispute, in which issues of credibility and authority became paramount.[2] It is no wonder that when these exchanges were taking place, a peninsular prelate, Benito María de Moxó y Francolí (1763–1816), penned in Mexico around 1805 yet another treatise that went over the tenets of patriotic epistemology. Drawing on the writings of Francisco Clavijero, Moxó y Francolí insisted that although biases often distorted the perception of witnesses, witnesses and facts were preferable to armchair philosophers and elaborate theoretical systems. Pitting the testimony of learned clerical writers against foreign observers, Moxó y Francolí maintained that only the former could be trusted. Like José Joaquín Granados y Gálvez, that other peninsular bishop turned patriotic epistemologist, Moxó y Francolí noted that travelers were often manipulated by savvy peoples and armchair observers by local cunning or ignorant informants. According to Moxó y Francolí, only the clergy who had intimate knowledge of the language of the Amerindians and who therefore had easy access to their communities could see through their lies. Using these epistemological insights, Moxó y Francolí denounced Voltaire for calling into question the credibility of early Spanish accounts over the extent of Amerindian ritual cannibalism, Juan Ginés de Sepúlveda for his sweeping generalization of the Amerindians as hopeless, changeless savages, and Cornelius de Pauw for his characterization of the natives as weak, insensitive creatures.[3]

To trace the fate of the discourse of patriotic epistemology in nineteenth-century Latin America one needs to abandon historiographical sources and seek it in the debates over how to write national literatures. The views of Ignacio Altamirano (1834–1893) are a case in point. A leading Mexican liberal, a literary critic, and a novelist himself, Altamirano sought to define what constituted a "Mexican" literature. He was part of a larger movement of Latin American novelists who in the second half of the nineteenth century insisted that plots highlighting national landscapes, problems, and taxonomies and toponyms would do the job.[4] He, however, also argued that the writing of Mexican literature should be left to Mexicans because when European and Anglo novelists had sought to represent local customs they had by and large produced "an endless succession of foolish scenes (cávila de cuadros disparatados)." According to Altamirano, the writing of Mexican novels had a dual purpose: to educate the masses through morally uplifting plots, on the one hand, and to set the record straight against foreign misrepresentation and innuendo, on the other.[5]

The struggle of Latin American intellectuals to correct what they considered to be stereotypes about Latin America circulating among the North Atlantic public survived through the nineteenth century. In fact, it still continues. Shibboleths haunt even the friendliest foreign observers of things Latin American; in fact they haunt Latin Americans themselves. Latin American writers have done their utmost to orientalize the region through the literary conceit of "magical realism" and through histories that emphasize inordinate social conflict and collective secular failure. Some fifty years ago in La disputa del Nuovo Mondo (1955), Antonello Gerbi studied many of the authors and texts that have been the subject of this book. After having spent many years in Peru, Gerbi decided to trace the origins of many of the negative views of Latin America he found still popular in Europe. With no sympathy for such denigrating perspectives, Gerbi, however, reproduced many in his own writings. A case in point is his treatment of the works of those Spanish American clerics who replied to Buffon, de Pauw, Raynal, and Robertson. Gerbi, for example, summarily dismissed whole sections of Francisco Clavijero's history as "grotesque and ridiculous."[6] Worse, he considered that the literature of most Spanish American authors was worthless, for the authors reacted "belligerently, angrily, and resentfully to Buffon's and de Pauw's notions, but without producing any organic corpus of argument and factual data to oppose them. They reply to the all-embracing condemnations with disjointed dithyrambs. To the serious problems raised by Buffon they make no reference at all, and de Pauw is only mentioned for his more scandalous aspects and wilder exaggerations."[7] The enlightened reader might be tempted to dismiss patriotic epistemology as a chauvinist discourse, a relic of a strange but defunct world. I beg to differ. As far as interpretations like Gerbi's are consumed uncritically, and as far as audiences in the United States are only offered stories of violence, resistance to exploitation, instability, and corruption in Latin America (a narrative conceit authorized in part by cultural geographies that characterize the region as "non-Western"), there are going to be storytellers like myself to recreate alternative worlds.

Notes

The following abbreviations are used in the notes:

AC   Archivo Campomanes, Fundación Universitaria Española, Madrid

ACMG   Archivo Colonial del Ministerio de Gobernación (Guatemala City)

AGI   Archivo General de Indias, Seville

AGN   Archivo General de la Nación, Mexico

AHM   Archivo Hispano Mayasiano, Colegio Mayor de Corpus Christi, Valencia

AJPT   Archivo de los Jesuitas de la Provincia de Toledo, Colegio San Ignacio de Loyola, Alcalá de Henares, Spain

AMN   Archivo del Museo Naval, Madrid

AMNA   Archivo del Museo Nacional de Antropología, Mexico

ARAH   Archivo de la Real Academia de Historia, Madrid

ARJB   Archivo del Real Jardín Botánico, Madrid

BN-M   Biblioteca Nacional, Mexico

BN-P (GA)   Bibliothèque Nationale, Paris, Collection Goupil-Aubin.

BN-S   Biblioteca Nacional, Madrid, Spain

BP   Biblioteca del Palacio Real

EAC-NB   Edward E. Ayer Collection, Newberry Library, Chicago

HBC-B   Hubert Howe Bancroft Collection, Bancroft Library, University of California, Berkeley

LAL-TU   Latin American Library, Tulane University, New Orleans

NYPL   New York Public Library

INTRODUCTION

1. Maravall, *La cultura del barroco*.

2. See, e.g., Appiah; Chatterjee; Chakrabarty; Clifford; Cohn; Cooper; Dirks; Duara; Hall; McClintock; Prakash, ed.; Pratt; Said; Stoler; Young.

3. This idea has enjoyed widespread currency in Latin America, a region whose intellectuals have embraced the term "Latin" since the nineteenth century precisely to make the point that it has closer cultural ties with continental Europe than the United States does. It would be a lost opportunity of mutual understanding and dialogue if this assertion were simply dismissed as an elitist construct typical of aristocratic writers such as the Uruguayan José Enrique Rodó, whose *Ariel* (1900) first most coherently articulated this point.

CHAPTER 1: TOWARD A NEW ART OF READING AND NEW HISTORICAL INTERPRETATIONS

1. Adam Smith, *Wealth of Nations*, 308.
2. Engel, 1: 357.
3. Raynal, *Histoire philosophique* (hereafter *HP*), 2d ed. (1774), vol. 3, bk. 6, ch. 1, p. 3.
4. Raynal, *HP* (1781), vol. 3, bk. 6, ch. 20, pp. 255–56.
5. See, e.g., Shaftesbury, 1: 344.
6. L. Davis and C. Reymers, "Preface," in Juan and Ulloa, *Voyage to South America*, iv.
7. Shaftesbury, 1: 297.
8. Daston, *Classical Probability in the Enlightenment*.
9. Manuel, 65–69.
10. Rousseau, n. 8, pp. 84–86. For all the rhetoric of novelty deployed by writers like Rousseau, readers should not assume that skepticism about travelers' reports and calls to include philosophers in expeditionary crews actually began in the mid eighteenth century. These views go back to at least to debates of the Royal Society in the mid seventeenth century about the natural history and resources of British America. Karen O. Kupperman, personal communication.
11. Feuillée, *Journal* (1714).
12. Frézier, "Préface," in *Relation*, viii–xii.
13. Feuillée, "Préface," in *Journal* (1725), vii.
14. Shapin and Schaffer. See also Daston, "Marvelous Facts."
15. B. Smith, *European Vision*, 6–7, 14, 36.
16. Frézier, "Reponse à la préface critique," in *Relation*.
17. Frézier, "Préface," in *Relation*, xii.
18. Frézier, "Des Indiens du Pérou," in *Relation*, 248; see also 185–86.
19. La Condamine, *Relation abregée*, 53.
20. La Condamine, "Mémoire sur anciens monumens," 435–56.
21. Lucian, 64–68.
22. Pagden, *European Encounters*, ch. 2
23. Popkin, *History of Skepticism*; Kahn.
24. Grafton, *Forgers and Critics*.
25. Franklin, pt. 2. See also Shapin, *Social History*.
26. Baudoin, iii and *passim*.
27. Bernard. On Perizonius's critical rules, see Erasmus, 76.

28. Davis and Reymers, "Preface," in Juan and Ulloa, *Voyage to South America*, iv.

29. Feuillée, *Journal* (1714), Epitre (unpaginated).

30. Green, "Preface," in *New General Collection*, ix.

31. Daston, *Classical Probability*, 306–42.

32. Voltaire, "Qu'il faut savoir douter," in *Oeuvres historiques*, 312–13.

33. Ibid., 314. Later in 1757, Voltaire would explain that the Spaniards overstated the number of cannibals to justify their atrocities in the New World; see Voltaire, *Essai sur les moeurs*, 2: 344–45, 361.

34. Buffon, "Variétés dans l'espèce humaine," in *De l'homme*, 309.

35. Harris, "Preface," in *Navigantium* (1744–48) (unpaginated).

36. Harris, "To the Reader," in *Navigantium* (1705) (unpaginated). For Spanish America, see his rather meager synthesis, "Some notes relating to the general history of that part of the West-Indies under the dominion of the Spaniards," vol. 1, ch. 12, pp. 748–51, based on the reports of Alexandro Ursino, a Roman who had lived in Peru and Chile for thirty-four years; of Pedro Ordoñes de Cevallos, a Spanish priest; and of Lopez Vez, a Portuguese.

37. Green, "Preface," in *New General Collection*, vii.

38. Prévost. After Prévost died, four more volumes came out, three under the editorship of Querlon. For Prévost's methodological views, see the "Avertissements" to volumes 1, 3, 5, 8, 10, and the "Avant-propos" in vol. 12, where he announces a new method, different from Green's. For a synthesis of Prévost's methodological changes over time, see Querlon's "Discours préliminare" in vol. 18.

39. Harris, "Introduction," in *Navigantium* (1744–48), ii.

40. Harris, "To the Merchants of Great-Britain," in *Navigantium* (1744–48) (unpaginated), and "Introduction," vii–viii.

41. Brosses, *Histoire*.

42. Rouband, "Préface," in *Histoire generale*, ii–iii.

43. Pauw, "Des Patagons," in *Recherches philosophiques sur les américains* (hereafter cited as *RA*), pt. iii, sec. ii (1: 281–82). I have used the 1770 edition. *Recherches* was originally published in 1768–69.

44. Pauw, "Défense des 'Recherches philosophiques sur les américains,'" in *RA*, vol. 3, ch. 25. John Hawkesworth and Buffon also summarized the evidence for and against giants by comparing and contrasting travel reports. They, however, drew the opposite conclusion — namely, that Patagonian giants did exist. Hawkesworth, 1: ix–xvi; Buffon, "Sur les Patagons," in *De l'homme*, 358–68.

45. The physical mechanical models proposed by Descartes and Newton predicted two widely different shapes for the earth and could only be tested by sending parties to the pole and the equator to measure the motion of pendulums and the length of a degree of the earth's curvature. With the measurement performed by the expedition to Lapland led by Pierre-Louis Moreau de Maupertius, the debate was settled in Newton's favor in 1737. On the debate and the Franco-Hispanic expedition to the Andes, see Lafuente and Mazuecos.

46. Gumilla, pt. 1, ch. 2, pp. 17–18, and ch. 25.

47. La Condamine, *Relation abregée*, 168.

48. Ibid., 101–13.

49. Ibid., 52–53.

50. Pauw, "Des hermaphrodites de la Floride," in RA, vol. 2, pt. iv, sec. iii, pp. 107–9.

51. Pauw, RA, pt. iv, sec. iii (2: 116).

52. Pauw, "Du génie abruti des américains," in RA, vol. 2, pt. v, sec. i, pp. 169–94.

53. Garcilaso, Histoire des Incas Rois (1774), 2: 39–40.

54. Ulloa, "Resumen histórico del origen y succesión de los incas y demás soberanos del Perú con noticias de los sucesos más notables en el reyno de cada uno," in Relación histórica, vol. 4, pt. 2, pp. x–xiv.

55. Pauw, RA, vol. 2, pt. v, sec. i, pp. 195–203, esp. 200–201

56. Pernety, Dissertation sur l'Amérique, in R.A., 3: 19–22, and 3: 32–44 ("Du sol de l'Amérique").

57. Pauw, "Défense des 'Recherches philosophiques sur les américains,'" in RA, vol. 3, ch. 3, pp. 12–13, and "De l'état de l'Amérique au moment de la découverte, et de son état actuel," in ibid., ch. 12, pp. 54–57.

58. Pernety, Examen.

59. Pazzi de Bonneville, ch. 12, pp. 65–67, "Que beaucoup de découvertes son dues au hazard."

60. Ibid., ch. 14, p. 76; see also ch. 1, p. 10.

61. Pauw, "Préface," in Recherches sur les Egyptiens et les Chinois, vi.

62. Guignes, Mémoire.

63. Pauw, Recherches sur les Egyptiens et les Chinois. See also the English edition, Philosophical Dissertations.

64. Mémoires concernant l'histoire, les sciences, les arts, 2: 356–74, 408–12, and 16: 218–65; Voltaire, "Lettres chinois."

65. Etienne Fourmont, Meditationes sinicae, inquibus 1° consideratur linguae philosophicae atque universalis natura 2° lingua sinarum mandarinica, tum in hieroglyphis, tum in monosyllabis suis . . . talis esse ostenditur 3° datur eorundum hieroglyphorum . . . lectio et intellectio (Paris: Musier, 1737); id., Linguae Sinarum Mandarinicae hieroglyphicae grammatica duplex, Latinè, et cum characteribus Sinensium: Item Sinicorum Regiae Bibliothecae librorum catalogus, denuò, cum notitiis amplioribus et charactere Sinico (Paris: Josephi Bullot, 1742); Antoine Gaubil, Observations mathématiques, astronomiques, géographiques, chronologiques et physiques, tirées des anciens livres chinois ou faites nouvellement aux Indes, à la Chine et ailleurs, Tome II. III (Paris: Rollin, 1732); id., Histoire de Gentehiscan et de toute la dinastie des Mongous ses successeurs, conquérans de la Chine; tirée de l'histoire chinoise (Paris: Briasson [etc.], 1739); id., Le Chou-king, un des livres sacrés des Chinois, qui renferme les fondements de leur ancienne histoire, les principes de leur gouvernement & de leur morale (Paris: N. M. Tilliard, 1770); id., Correspondance de Pékin, 1722–1759 (Geneva: Librairie Droz, 1970); Thomas Shaw, Voyages de Monsr. Shaw, M.D. dans plusieurs provinces de la Barbarie et du Levant: contenant des observations géographiques, physiques, philologiques et melées sur les royaumes d'Alger et de Tunis, sur la Syrie, l'Egypte et l'Arabie Petrée (The Hague: J. Neaulme, 1743).

66. Schérer, ch. 10, 219.

67. Gerbi, La disputa, 188–90.

68. Pauw, "Amérique," 1: 344–54.

69. Pagden, *Lords*, 163–77.

70. Feugère, 5. Raynal, "Extrait des Observations curieuses de l'abbé Lambert sur l'Asie, l'Afrique et l'Amérique," in Grimm, 1: 221; and Raynal, "Sur la Histoire générale, civile, naturelle, politique et religieuse de tous les peuples du monde par M. l'abbé Lambert," ibid, 1: 432. Raynal's criticism of Lambert focuses among other things on the latter's "absolute lack of order" and "lack of discernment at choosing sources," particularly his credulity regarding Jesuit reports. See also Raynal's "Sur un Voyage de Turquie et de Perse par M. Otter," in ibid, 1: 161, in which he mocks Otter for not doing anything philosophical with his scattered and unsystematic observations. This evaluation constrasts with "Sur l'Histoire naturalle de l'Islande, du Groenland et du détroit de Davis par M. Anderson," ibid, 2: 154, in which Anderson appears as a philosophical traveler "disabusing the public of the fabulous absurdities [accumulated by travelers who have reported on these faraway places]"

71. Feugère, 103–16, 184–85.

72. Raynal, *HP* (1770) 1: 76.

73. Ibid., 6: 188–89.

74. Ibid., 3: 34–5.

75. Ibid., 3:110.

76. Ibid., 3: 110–18, 138–39, 147–49.

77. Raynal, *HP* (1774), vol. 3, ch. 9, pp. 43–44, and ch. 11, pp. 53–54. In the third (1781) edition, Raynal expanded his criticism of Spanish American colonial sources on the Mexica and added many new pages that follow de Pauw's critical remarks very closely; see Raynal, "Idée qu'on doit se former du Mexique avant qu'il fut soumis à l'Espagne," in *HP* (1781), vol. 3, bk. 6, ch. 20, pp. 243–57. In this edition, Raynal also modified his approach to China to fit de Pauw's views and introduced a long section summarizing de Pauw's negative representation of Chinese society; see ibid., 1: 138–53.

78. Raynal, *HP* (1774), 3: 128–32.

79. Ibid., 3: 114–27.

80. Ibid., 3: 127–28.

81. Brading, *First America*, 432–41.

82. Manuel, ch. 1.

83. Meek, ch. 2.

84. I tend to agree with Sabine MacCormack, who, implicitly taking issue with Frank Manuel, has argued that although the study of Greco-Roman paganism and Amerindian antiquities did overlap, they remained essentially two distinct traditions, which had parted ways by the mid eighteenth century. Classical pagan and Amerindian analogies were the result of learned Christian efforts to show the common biblical origins of both peoples, whose myths preserved blurred, distorted recollections of biblical history. Once the authority of the Bible as an authoritative historical text came under attack in the eighteenth century, the functionality of these analogies unraveled. See MacCormack, "Perceptions of Greco-Roman and Amerindian Paganism," esp. 79 and 119.

85. I follow the 1788 fifth edition of *History of America* (hereafter *HA*), in *Works of William Robertson*, 9: 81

86. Ibid., 10: 280–81.

87. Ibid., 9: 58.

88. Ibid., 10: 315.

89. Francis Bacon, *Novum Organum*, in *Works*, vol. 4, bk. 1, aphorisms lix–lx, pp. 60–61.

90. Brosses, *Du culte des dieux fétiches* (Geneva, 1760), p. 200; quoted in Manuel, 206.

91. Ferguson, pt. ii, sec. 1, pp. 79–80.

92. Robertson, *HA*, in *Works*, 10: 315.

93. Ibid., 9: 53. Robertson, however, thought highly of Antonio de Ulloa and Jorge Juan y Santacilia and included them in a list of reliable observers, along with La Condamine, J.B.T. de Chanvalon (*Voyage a la Martinique* [1763]), and the Spanish Jesuit Miguel Venegas (*History of California* [1759]). See Robertson, *HA*, in *Works*, 9: 378–81.

94. Ibid., 9: 187–88.

95. On eighteenth-century "commercial" humanism, see Pocock, 103–23, and all the contributions in Hont and Ignatieff.

96. Robertson, "A View of the Progress of Society in Europe," in *History of Charles V*, in *Works*, vol. 4. For a more detailed study of Robertson's "commercial" humanism, see O'Brien, esp. 58–60. For more general descriptions of seventeenth- and eighteenth-century views on commerce and the taming of the passions, see Hirschman.

97. Burke to Robertson, quoted in Stewart, "Life of Robertson," in *Works*, 1: lix–lx.

98. Robertson, *HA*, in *Works*, 9: 50–1.

99. Erasmus, 74–98, 114; Manuel, 90–93. For a sketchy history of historical criticism at the University of Edinburgh during Robertson's formative years, see Sharp.

100. Robertson, *HA*, in *Works*, 9: 75–76.

101. Ibid., 10: 316.

102. Ibid., 317–18.

103. Carli, pt. 1, letter i, p. 4; letter ii, pp. 7–8; letter iv, pp. 18–29; letter v, pp. 36–42. In the late seventeenth century, the Benedictine Jean Mabillon had introduced the idea that only "public" sources were reliable; see Barret-Kriegel, *Défaite de l'érudition*, 158–75.

104. Carli, pt. 1, letter xv, p. 122; letter xvi, pp. 122–24.

105. Erasmus, 67–74.

106. Rousseau, 19, 42.

107. De Pauw believed that eighteenth-century contemporary evidence could not be used to describe the New World upon the arrival of the Europeans, because three centuries of colonization had completely transformed the landscape. Many of de Pauw's views on climatically induced degeneration in the Indies had already been articulated in the sixteenth and seventeenth centuries. See Cañizares-Esguerra, "New World, New Stars."

108. Pauw, *RA*, 1: 102–3; 197–98; 317–18.

109. Ibid., 1: 1–24, 52, 89.

110. Ibid., 1: 38.

111. Ibid., 1: 44–45.

112. Ibid., 1: 54.

113. On gender and late-eighteenth century discourses of excitability, see Barker-Benfield.

114. Pauw, *RA*, 1: 43, 53.

115. Ibid., 1: 64–66.

116. Ibid., 1: 68–69.

117. Ibid., 1: 70.

118. Gerbi, *La disputa*, chs. 1, 3.

119. For more details on Buffon's conjectural history of the earth and human migrations, see Sloan; Eddy; Roger, chs. 7–8, 22.

120. Buffon, "Variétés dans l'espèce humaine," in *De l'homme*, 308–11.

121. Buffon, "Animaux communs aux deux continents" in *Selections*, 2: 133–37. For an early-eighteenth-century rendition of St. Augustine's concept of original sin in the context of a cataclysmic history of the earth, see Antonio Vallisneri, *De'corpi che su monti si trovano, della loro origine; e dello stato del mondo avanti il diluvio, nel diluvio, e dopo il diluvio* (1721). Vallisneri argues that "[the destruction and carnage caused by the deluge] without any doubt contributed much to destroying the perfect harmony of [men's] blood and to disturbing the regular movements of their spirits and their humors. Thus the very principles of generation were impaired, and thus those defects and those unhealthy dispositions were passed on to their unborn children, and penetrated them so very deeply that this hereditary misfortune lasts even to now and will last to the end of all time, since we all come from that infected lineage, though it is now enormously multiplied and divided throughout the world." Quoted in Rossi, 78–79.

122. Buffon changed his views. In 1749, in "Variétés dans l'espèce humaine" (*De l'homme*, 308–11), Native Americans appear as newcomers and normal human beings. In 1761, in "Animaux communs," however, they are depicted as having become effeminate in consequence of the humid and degenerating effect of the New World's environment (*Selections*, 2: 130). In 1777, in "Additions à l'article 'Variétés dans l'espèce humaine,'" Native Americans are again portrayed as newly arrived, normal human beings, with the exception a handful of nations in the Amazon basin allegedly emasculated and made insensitive by the humidity of the area (*De l'homme*, 369–72). Buffon's 1777 about-face was the result of his reading de Pauw and his dislike of what he regarded as de Pauw's exaggerations and "credulity."

123. Manuel, 210–27.

124. Raynal, *HP* (1770), vol. 6, bk. 17, pp. 192–96. Raynal adds some disquisitions of his own to geological history in 6: 189–92.

125. Ibid., vol. 3, bk. 6, pp. 19–21; bk. 7, pp. 137–38.

126. Raynal, *HP* (1774), vol. 3, bk. 6, ch. 7, pp. 24–25.

127. Robertson, *HA*, in *Works*, 9: 1–215, 347–57.

128. Ibid., 10: 321.

129. Ibid., 351.

130. Kames, vol. 3, bk. 2, sketch 12, p. 157 (America full of wonders), pp. 144–45 (arrested development), p. 148 (scarce population), p. 154 (no shepherd state), p. 157 (gap in series of development), p. 169 (Aztec paradoxical behavior), p. 178 (Inca political paradox).

131. Kames, vol. 3, bk. 2, sketch 12, p. 157.

132. Kames, "Preliminary Discourse Concerning the Origin of Men and of Languages," in *Sketches*, vol. 1, bk. 1, pp. 24, 44–50. See also vol. 3, bk. 2, sketch 12, p. 141.

133. Bolingbroke, *Letters on the Study and Use of History*, in *Historical Writings*, 49. Bolingbroke derived his views from Louis-Jean Lévesque de Pouilly's "Dissertation sur l'incertitude de l'histoire des quatres premiers siècles de Rome." The term "obscure" derives from the classification offered by the Roman historian Varro, who divided history into obscure, fabulous, and true.

134. Sharp, 33–35.

135. Hume, vol. 1, ch. 1, pp. 1–2. Hume first published the history of the Stuarts, followed by that of the Tudors. It was only in 1761, in the fourth volume of the original edition, that he broached early English history.

136. Ferguson, pt. ii, sec. 1, p. 76.

137. Ibid., p. 80.

138. Brosses, "Mémoire sur l'oracle de Dodone," in *Mémoires de litterature tirés des registres de la Académie Royale des Inscriptions et Belles-Lettres* 35 (1770): 97; quoted in Manuel, 203.

139. Mackintosh, 33, 34–35.

140. On the Scottish stadial conjectural histories, see Meek; Höpfl.

141. Armitage, esp. 67–69.

142. Pauw, *RA*, 1: 3–4.

143. Pauw, *Philosophical Dissertations on the Egyptians*, 1: 10.

144. Pauw, *Recherches philosophiques sur les Grecs*, ix.

145. Raynal, *HP* (1781), 1: 3.

146. Daston and Galison; Daston, "Objectivity and the Escape from Perspective."

147. Schaffer.

148. Outram, 21–24, 89–94; Goodman, ch. 6.

149. Robertson to Gibbon quoted in Alex Stewart, "Life of William Robertson," in *Works*, 1: xlix.

150. Stewart, "Life of William Robertson," 1: lxiv, lxvi.

151. Sher.

152. Smitten, "Shaping of Moderation."

153. Robertson, *History of Scotland*, in *Works*, 1: cxxx.

154. Sher, 100–102.

155. Walpole to Robertson quoted in Stewart, "Life of Robertson," 1: xxvii–xxviii (emphasis in the original).

156. Stewart, "Life of Robertson," 1: xlix.

157. Ibid., 1: lxiii, lxvi. On how Robertson's moderation shaped his judgments about natives and Spaniards in America, see Smitten, "Impartiality in Robertson," esp. 58–64. Smitten attributes Robertson's impartiality to his upbringing in Lockean epistemology (which emphasized probability over certainty) and Stoic moral philosophy (evil and good always coexist).

158. Sher, 287–96.

159. Sher, 121.

160. "Article II: Review of Humboldt's Personal Narratives," *Monthly Review* 88 (Mar. 1819): 234.

161. "Article VIII: Review of Humboldt's Researches Concerning the Institutions and Monuments of the Ancient Americans," *Quarterly Review* 15 (July 1816): 453–54.

162. Ibid., 446, 450.

163. "Article I: Review of Humboldt's Personal Narratives," *Monthly Review* 79 (Jan. 1816): 17.

164. "Article III: Review of Humboldt's Personal Narratives," *Monthly Review* 90 (Sept. 1819): 24.

165. "Article II: Review of Humboldt's Personal Narratives" *Monthly Review* 88 (Mar. 1819): 236.

166. Guignes,"Recherches sur les navigations des Chinois." De Pauw ridiculed these views in *RA*, 2: 293–4.

167. Humboldt, *Researches*, "Introduction," 1: 31–33; "Monuments of America," 1: 35–36; "An Aztec hieroglyph manuscript preserved in the library of the Vatican [plate xiii]," 1: 184–85.

168. Ibid., "Introduction," 1: 2–3, 23; and "An Aztec hieroglyph [plate xiii]," 1: 146–48.

169. Ibid., "Introduction," 1: 14; and "Rock of Inti-Guaicu [plate xviii]," 1: 249–50.

170. Ibid., "Introduction," 1: 5–6.

171. Ibid., 3–5

172. Humboldt, "Considerations preliminaires," in *Examen critique*, 1: 7–8.

173. Humboldt, "Préface," in *Examen critique*, xv; see also xii.

174. Humboldt, "Considerations preliminaires," in *Examen critique*, 1: 5–6.

CHAPTER 2: CHANGING EUROPEAN INTERPRETATIONS OF THE RELIABILITY OF INDIGENOUS SOURCES

1. Durán, 2: 556.

2. Colston.

3. Charles Cullen, "Translator's Preface," in Clavijero, *History of Mexico*, iii, iv.

4. Ibid., iv.

5. "Review of the *History of Mexico* by L'Abbe Francesco Saverio Clavigero [Francisco Xavier Clavijero] translated from the Italian by Charles Cullen," *London Review and Literary Journal*, Aug. 1787, 16.

6. Ibid., 17.

7. Macri.

8. Ascher and Ascher; Brotherston, *Book of the Fourth World*, 193–211. On other Inca systems of storing information, see Zuidema, "Bureaucracy"; Cummins.

9. "Article VIII: Review of Humboldt's Researches Concerning the Institutions and Monuments of the Ancient Americans," *Quarterly Review* 15 (July 1816): 453

10. "No digo los perversos consorcios de los Indios, ni canto los muy grandes fraudes, o las fieras mentiras con las que más de una vez me engañaron, incauto, y me dijeron embustes, aun evitándolo yo con gran cuidado, tacto y esmero; y cuántas veces recibí falseadas las fuerzas y nombres de algunas plantas, por usar falaces informes de un intérprete; que heridas hubo que curar cautamente a veces con arte médica y con los auspicios de Cristo" (Francisco Hernández, "Poema a Arias Montano," in *Obras*, 7: 30).

11. Hernández, *Antigüedades*.

12. On sixteenth-century perceptions of Indians as untrustworthy, see "Relación de Quito," in Jiménez de la Espada, 2: 225. See also Pagden, *Fall*, 44.

13. Mignolo, *Darker Side*, 45, 104–5, 138.

14. Ibid., 129–40.

15. Ibid., 83.

16. Ibid., ch. 2. In *Reglas de ortografía en la lengua castellana* (Salamanca, 1517), Alonso de Nebrija argued that writing evolved from paintings to alphabets, and that hieroglyphs and emblems were not a good way of recording the past, because they held ambiguous and ambivalent meanings (Mignolo, *Darker Side*, 42, 44–45).

17. Mignolo, *Darker Side*, 165–67

18. Ibid., 93. Alva Ixtlilxochitl, *Obras históricas*, 1: 527; Chimalpain Cuauhtlehuanitzin, *Relaciones originales*, 20–21.

19. My evaluation of Mignolo's work owes a great deal to Grafton's "Rest vs. the West."

20. Brading, *First America*, 278.

21. Mignolo, *Darker Side*, 188, 187–202.

22. Sahagún, 1: 105–7. On the humanist underpinnings of Sahagún's work, see Bustamente.

23. Mignolo, *Darker Side*, 74–75. On the rich diversity of precolonial and colonial written genres, see Brotherston, *Book of the Fourth World*; id., *Painted Books*; Mundy; Boone; Lockhart.

24. On the events that lead to Landa's campaign and the Maya's perspective of events, see Clendinnen, *Ambivalent Conquests*.

25. Landa, 54–55, 145–46.

26. Ciudad Real, 2: 392.

27. Landa, 148–49. On Landa contributions, see Marcus, 87–93. Marcus argues that Landa's list of Maya's phonograms "has proved to be a boon for today's epigraphers" (p. 93) and maintains that in the mid twentieth century, there was a shift in Maya epigraphy away from reading stelae as records of local cosmogonies and toward considering them historical texts, as Landa had suggested (pp. 5–7). See Landa, 54–55.

28. Motolinía, "Epístola proemial en la cual se declara el origen de los primeros pobladores e habitadores de la Nueva España," in *Memoriales*, 5.

29. Marcus, 15 ff.

30. Motolinía, 13–14, 5, 9. On the pictographic conventions that allowed the Nahuas and the Mixtecs to put together complex written historical narratives, see Boone.

31. Cabello Valboa, pt. 2, chs. 1–2.

32. Ibid., pt. 1, ch. 11, pp. 72–73, and pt. 3, ch. 6, pp. 235–36.

33. Ibid., pt. 3, ch. 6, pp. 239–40.

34. Ibid., "Al pio y curioso lector," 8.

35. Mignolo, *Darker Side*, 44–45.

36. For exceptions, see Valadés, pt. 2, ch. 27, pp. 93 [233]; and n. 137 below. On the Renaissance cult of hieroglyphs over alphabetical writing, see Hudson, chs. 1–2; Iversen.

37. Acosta, *Historia natural*, bk. 6, ch. 1, p. 390; ch. 12, p. 408; ch. 15, pp. 412, 414.

38. Ibid., bk. 6, ch. 1, p. 389.
39. Ibid., bk. 6, chs. 1 and 2.
40. Ibid., bk. 5, ch. 9, pp. 330–31.
41. Ibid., bk. 6, ch. 4, p. 394.
42. Ibid., bk. 6, chs. 5 and 6.
43. Ibid., bk. 6, ch. 4, pp. 394–95.
44. Ibid., bk. 6, ch. 8, p. 402.
45. Ibid., bk. 6, ch. 7, p. 400.
46. Ibid., bk. 6, chs. 10 and 17.
47. Ibid., bk. 6, ch. 19, p. 418.
48. Ibid., bk. 7, ch. 1, p. 437.
49. Cummins.
50. The correspondence between Acosta and Tovar can be found in Kubler and Gibson, 77–78.
51. Ibid., 77–78.
52. In 1578, Tovar had sent to Spain the original humanist "translation" of the documents that the scribes of Tollan, Mexico City, and Texcoco had interpreted for him. So when Acosta arrived in Mexico in 1586, Tovar handed him a slightly different history, his *Segunda Relación*, based on the history compiled by the Dominican Diego Durán (on whom, see p. 60 above), a relative of his, which, by and large, followed the same historical version that Tovar had obtained earlier.
53. The most prominent native philologists of Santa Cruz were Antonio Valeriano, governor of Tlatelolco for thirty years, a professor of Nahuatl and Latin, who participated in the making of the Florentine Codex and translated Cato into Nahuatl; Martín Jacobita, professor and rector of the college and Sahagún's collaborator; Alonso de Bejarano, professor and Sahagún's collaborator; Pedro de San Buenaventura, Sahagún's collaborator; Hernando de Ribas, who translated Juan de Gaona's *Coloquios de la paz* (1582) into Nahuatl and helped Alonso Molina write *Vocabulario Nahuatl*; Francisco Bautista de Contreras, who translated Diego de la Estella's *Libro contra la vanidad del mundo* into Nahuatl; Martín de la Cruz and Juan Badiano, who wrote *Libellus de medicinalibus indorum herbis* (1552); Esteban Bravo; Juan Berardo; and Diego Adriano. The Augustinians created colleges of liberal arts in Tiripitío, Michoacán, and Mexico City where groups of natives learned Latin, Greek, and even Hebrew. Vasco de Quiroga, the humanist bishop of Michoacán, similarly founded a college in Pátzcuaro. See Baudot; Osorio Romero, *Enseñanza*, xxxiv–xxxviii, xlv–xlix; Gruzinski, *Colonización*, 65–68; and Garibay.
54. Cruz and Badiano; Glass and Robertson, 115; Robertson, *Mexican Manuscript*, 156–58.
55. On the history of the Florentine Codex, see Robertson, "Sixteenth-Century Mexican Encyclopedia"; Ricard, 41–44; D'Owler and Cline; Bustamante.
56. The original codex seems to have included descriptions of the 20-day, 18-month, 260-day, and 52-year cycles of the Mexica calendar, as well as "pictograms" of gods, ceremonies, customs, portraits of rulers, and blanket designs. It is now lost, but copies and/or glosses of sections of it, known as the codices Magliabecchiano, Museo de América, Ixtlilxochitl, and Costumbres of Nueva España, have survived. See Glass,

"Survey," 14; Glass and Robertson, 155–56. On Cervantes, see Millares Carlo, ch. 1; Kohut, "Implantación del humanismo."

57. Pagden, *Fall*, 44.

58. Glass, "Survey," 18; Humboldt, *Researches*, pl. xii, 1: 143.

59. Duviols, 305; Acosta, *Historia natural*, bk. 6, ch. 8, pp. 402.

60. Betanzos, "Dedicatoria al Viceroy Antonio de Mendoza," in *Suma* (unpaginated). See also MacCormack, *Religion*, 108, 111, 118 ff. For Quechua terms of validation, see Salomon, "Introductory Essay," in *Huarochirí Manuscript*, 32–33. Betanzos's Inca wife, Doña Angelina, appears under two different last names in two equally authoritative sources: as Añas Yupanqui in Burns (pp. 26, 31) and as Cusimaray in MacCormack (pp. 81, 108).

61. Sarmiento de Gamboa, 212–13. I thank Susan Niles for this reference. See also Urton, 63–70.

62. Alvaro Ruiz de Navamanule, "Fe de la probanza y verificación de esta historia," in Sarmiento de Gamboa, 276–79.

63. Cobo, bk. 2, ch. 2, pp. 98–101.

64. On the historiography surrounding Viceroy Francisco de Toledo's reforms and the carefully controlled interviews of provincial elites that he conducted, see Brading, *First America*, ch. 6.

65. On colonial historiographical manipulations by indigenous elites, see Urton.

66. On the debates over the historicity of the Inca rulers in Spanish chroniclers, see Zuidema, "Myth and History"; Rowe, "Constitución Inca"; Rowe, "Probanza de los Incas"; Urton, 5–8; MacCormack, *Religion*, 118.

67. MacCormack, *Religion*, 83–84.

68. Cieza de León, *Crónica*, chs. 13 and 38.

69. Ibid., ch. 12, p. 104 (on the past of the peoples of the Nore valley of Antioquia that could be reconstructed from material evidence: burial sites and ruins); ch. 24, 138, and ch. 41, p. 196 (on the songs of the peoples of Quimbaya and Latacunga as record-keeping devices to store information of their past).

70. Ibid., ch. 105, p. 368. Cieza de León could only speculate about the origins of the ruins of Tiaguanuco, because the natives lacked alphabetical script.

71. Cieza de León, *Señorio*, ch. 9, p. 51; id., *Crónica*, ch. 58, p. 220.

72. Cieza de León, *Señorio*, ch. 12, p. 59; ch. 19, p. 78.

73. Ibid., ch. 12, p. 58.

74. Ibid., ch. 9, p. 52; ch. 31, p. 110.

75. Cieza de León, *Crónica*, ch. 47, pp. 218–19.

76. Cieza de León, *Señorio*, ch. 3, pp. 39–40.

77. Ibid., ch. 6, p. 42.

78. Ibid., ch. 4, p. 34.

79. Ibid., ch. 25, pp. 94–95.

80. Ibid., ch. 22, pp. 84–85.

81. Ibid., ch. 5, pp. 38–39.

82. Ibid., ch. 21, p. 84; ch. 9, p. 51.

83. Ibid., ch. 52, p. 154.

84. Ibid., ch. 6, p. 41; ch. 9, pp. 51–52.

85. Ibid., ch. 6, p. 43–44.

86. Ibid., ch. 35, pp. 118–19.

87. López de Gómara, "Cinco soles que son edades" and "Chichimecas, Aculhuaques, Mexicanos, De los reies de Mexico," in id., *Istoria*, fols. cxix–r and cxix–v to cxxi–v.

88. López de Gómara, "Que libraron bien los Indios en ser conquistados" and "La opinion que tienen acerca del diluvio y primeros ombres," in id., *Istoria*, fol. cxxxvii–r (on writing); fol. lxviii–r.

89. Zárate, bk. 1, ch. 10.

90. Ibid., bk. 1, ch. 5, fol. 7r–v (on quipus), and chs. 13–15 (on Huayna Capac, Atahualpa, and Huascar).

91. Román y Zamora, bk. 2, ch. 16 (2: 64–69).

92. Ibid., bk. 2, ch. 11 (2: 7–21).

93. Herrera y Tordesillas. In 1615, Herrera published three new *décadas*, covering events down to 1546. On Herrera, se Brading, *First America*, 203–10.

94. On his "commentary" to the theories of Cieza de León, López de Gómara, and Acosta on the origin of the name "Peru," see Garcilaso, *Comentarios reales*, bk. 1, chs. 5 and 6 (1: 71–76). On his method of commentary, see ibid., bk. 1, ch. 19, 1: 111; and bk. 2, ch. 10 (1: 157–62).

95. Zamora.

96. Garcilaso, *Comentarios reales*, bk. 1, ch. 18 (1: 105). On conversations with his uncle, see ibid., bk. 1, ch. 15 (1: 97–98). See also Cobo, bk. 2, ch. 2, p. 100.

97. Garcilaso, *Comentarios reales*, bk. 1, ch. 19 (1: 109). On Inca quipus, see ibid., bk. 6, chs. 8 and 9. On poems stored in quipus, see ibid., bk. 2, ch. 27.

98. Ibid., bk. 1, ch. 6 (1: 74).

99. On Garcilaso, see Brading, *First America*, ch. 12; and MacCormack, *Religion*, ch. 8, pp. 332–73.

100. On Torquemada, see Brading, *First America*, 275–92.

101. Torquemada, "Prólogo general de toda la Monarchía indiana," in *De los veinte libros rituales*, vol. 1 (unpaginated).

102. Ibid., "Prólogo al libro primero," vol. 1 (unpaginated).

103. Ibid., bk. 2, ch. 13 (1: 105–7).

104. Ibid., "Prólogo al libro segundo," 1: 83–84.

105. Ibid., bk. 2, ch. 1 (1: 85 and 87).

106. Ibid., "Prólogo al libro primero," vol. 1 (unpaginated).

107. Ibid., bk. 1, ch. 11 (1: 34).

108. Ibid., bk. 2, ch. 11 (1: 104).

109. Ibid., bk. 2, ch. 13 (1: 108).

110. Ibid., bk. 1, ch. 10 (1: 32).

111. Ibid., bk. 4, ch. 12 (1: 418).

112. Ibid., bk. 4, ch. 70 (1: 544–45).

113. Torquemada's account of Alvarado's slaughter of the youth of the Mexica nobility was excised from the 1615 edition but reintroduced in the 1723 edition. See Brading, *First America*, 285.

114. Torquemada, *De los veinte libros rituales*, bk. 1, ch. 35 (1: 68).

115. Ibid., bk. 1, ch. 18 (1: 47).

116. Erasmus; Grafton, "Rest vs. The West," 62.

117. Clanchy, 202–57, and *passim*.

118. Cantelli. Thanks to Anthony Grafton for calling my attention to this source.

119. Ricard, 168.

120. A great number of the images used by the Franciscans in sixteenth-century Mexico were published in 1579 in Perugia, Italy. In *Rhetorica Christiana*, Diego de Valadés published the images to highlight the creativity of the Franciscan friars. He included representations of the proper ecclesiastical and civil hierarchies of the Christian republic; the cosmic battles between angels and demons around individuals enchained by sins; a classification of capital sins; individuals protected by angels or progressively won over by demons; different types of torments awaiting sinners in hell; the virtues of monogamy and the evil consequences of adultery; the temptations of demons, represented by blacks (because, according to Valadés, the Indians feared "Ethiopians"); and allegorical representations of the majesty and purity of the Church. See Valadés, pt. iv, ch. 10, pp. 175–83 [403–23], and ch. 13, pp. 205–25 [467–509]. On the linkage between the usage of illustrations and the lack of alphabetical writing, see ibid., pt. ii, ch. 27, pp. 95–96 [237–39], and pt. iv, ch. 13, paragraph N, pp. 221 [501].

121. Ricard, 104–6. A catechism in logograms drawn by the Franciscan Pedro de Gante, most likely ca. 1528, has recently been decoded. The depth of Gante's knowledge of Mesoamerican systems of writing is shown by Cortés Castellanos.

122. Torquemada, *Monarquía indiana*, 3: 102. It took almost a century for the fast-growing publishing industry in Europe to popularize the idea of using phonograms for pedagogical purposes. See Clouston.

123. Valadés, pt. iv, ch. 23, pp. 213–14 [483]; Ricard, 119–20

124. Reyes-Valerio, ch. 14.

125. Valadés, pt. ii, ch. 27, pp. 93–94 [233–35]; ch. 27, p. 100 [247]; R. Taylor; Pagden, *Fall*, 189. On the medieval and Renaissance art of rhetoric and the use of theaters of memory, see Yates; Gombrich, 130–45. On Ricci in China, see Spence, *Memory Palace*.

126. On the Renaissance culture of collecting, see Findlen, *Possessing Nature* and "Possessing the Past."

127. Heikamp, 16, 19–22.

128. Laurencich Minelli. Lorenzo Legati, who cataloged Cospi's cabinet, followed an interesting set of categories to classify curiosities: natural history of humans and animals (including monsters); coins; statues and images of Egyptian and Asian deities (including a description of two Mexican carved knives that he took to be Egyptian); creatures of the sea and water (including fossils); objects of human art. Under the latter, Legati included all samples of "exotic" writing (Chinese, Ethiopian, Arab, and Mexican). Legati described the Mixtec annals but refused to interpret them, on the grounds that there was not enough secondary literature on which to base his conjectures. He limited himself to arguing that some of the figures looked like mathematical signs. See Legati, 191–92 (on Mixtec annals) and 477–78 (Mexican knives).

129. Heikamp, 9; Simons; Glass and Robertson, 235–36.

130. Samuel Purchas, B.D., *Haklvytvs posthumus or Pvrchas his Pilgrimes. Con-*

tayning a history of the world, in sea voyages & lande trauells, by Englishmen and oth-
ers . . . Some left written by M. Hakluyt at his death, more since added, his also perused,
& perfected. All examined, abreuiated, illustrated wth notes, enlarged wth discourses,
adorned wth pictures, and expressed in mapps. In fower parts, each containing fiue
bookes (London: W. Stansby for H. Fetherstone, 1625). Lestringant, 15, 38–39; Keen,
150–55; Robertson, *Mexican Manuscript*, 95–102; Glass and Robertson, 160–61.

131. Purchas, "A discourse," 1: 486–87.

132. Ibid., 1: 492, 494.

133. Purchas, comp., "History of the Mexican Nation." In the second half of the
seventeenth century, Melchisédec Thévenot published the Codex Mendoza in
French as "Histoire de l'empire mexicain, representé par figures." See, e.g., Thévenot,
1696, 2: 1–50.

134. Had Torquemada known of Purchas's edition of the Codex Mendoza, he
would have dismissed it as Aztec propaganda. The collection, for example, presents
Acamapichtli, the first elected Mexica ruler, as engaged in wars of territorial expansion. Torquemada insisted that Acamapichtli ruled in a period when the Mexica
were a subordinate ethnic group in the Central Valley of Mexico, meekly paying
tribute to more powerful groups, and thus with no capabilities of expansion.
Torquemada would have been critical of Purchas's gullibility. The comparison between Torquemada and Purchas is instructive, because it shows that Spanish scholarship in the early seventeenth century far surpassed anything then available in
English. This, however, has often been lost sight of since the eighteenth century by
scholars determined to cast Spain as an intellectual pariah relative to the rest of
Europe.

135. For the most recent statement, see Hudson, ch. 3.

136. Mercati, ch. 11, 86–131. See also Cantelli's modern edition of Mercati's *De gli
obelischi di Roma* (Bologna: Capelli Editore, 1981).

137. Pignoria, esp. 561 (on the similarities of Egyptian and Mexican hieroglyphs).
The first edition of Pignoria's modified version of Catari's *Imagini* appeared in 1615.
On the so-called Codex Ríos, see Glass and Robertson, 136–39, 186–87. On Annius
de Viterbo, see Grafton, *Defenders*, ch. 3. On Pignoria and the Isiac stela, see
Iversen, 85. Pignoria also reflected on the similarities between the Mexican and
Christian religions revealed by the images and glosses of the Codex and concluded
that they were the result of demonic manipulations by "il Demonio Simia di Dios"
(pp. 553, 558). For the interpretation of the symbols of the deer, lizard, and corn,
Pignoria used Ríos's intepretation of images from the cult of Quetzalcoatl; see Codex
Ríos, vol. 1, fol. 7r–v.

138. Kircher, vol. 1, syntagma v, ch. 5 (1: 416–24); vol. 3, diatribe 1, ch. 4 (3: 28–36).
On Kircher's larger intellectual agenda, see Rivosecchi; Godwin; Eco, 144–65. On
Kircher and Mexico, see Keen, 207–8; Kramer; Osorio Romero, *Luz imaginaria.*

139. Hazard. For a detailed account of the challenges to biblical historiography,
see Rossi. On La Peyrère, see Popkin, *Isaac la Peyrère*; Grafton, *Defenders*, ch. 8.

140. Stillingfleet, "Preface to the Reader" (unpaginated).

141. Ibid., bk. 1, ch. 1, p. 15.

142. Ibid., pp. 18–19.

143. Ibid., bk. 2, ch. 2, pp. 132–34.
144. Anselme, "Des monumens"; id., "Seconde dissertation."
145. Lévesque de Pouilly, 21.
146. Ibid., 17.
147. Ibid., 15 n.
148. Manuel, 90–92.
149. Beaufort. I have consulted also the English edition, *A Dissertation upon the Uncertainity of the Roman History During the First Five Hundred Years* (London: T. Waller, 1740).
150. On the larger historiographical context in which Vico wrote, see Rossi, ch. 23 and *passim*; Burke. On Vico's conjectural history of writing, see Hudson, 71–75. On Vico's views of the New World, see Kubler.
151. Vico, *Scienza nuova* 1.3.331; 1.4.349.
152. Ibid., 1.2.125–28.
153. Ibid., 1.2.165.
154. Ibid., Idea, ¶ 32; 1.2.173.
155. Ibid., 1.2.149; Idea, ¶ 34.
156. Ibid., 1.2.240.
157. Wilkins, 12. On philosophical languages, see Slaughter; Knowlson; Eco; Singer.
158. Fréret. On the seventeenth- and eighteenth-century views of China, see Pinot. On changing views on Chinese scripts, see David. On Fréret's training under Huan, see Spence, "Paris Years."
159. Warburton, *Divine Legation*, in *Works*.
160. On Newton's chronology, see Manuel, 85–102. For Warburton's critique of Newton, see his *Divine Legation*, bk. 4, sec. 5 (2: 492–565).
161. Warburton, *Divine Legation*, bk. 4, sec. 4 (2: 387–405; 413–41).
162. Warburton, *Essai*.
163. Warburton, *Divine Legation*, bk. 4, sec. 4 (2: 405–13; 441–52). My interpretation of Warburton's conjectural history of writing is rather different from that offered by Hudson, 59–71. Hudson fails to put Warburton in the larger context of his age. For this larger intellectual context, see Rossi, ch. 33 and *passim*.
164. On medieval faculty-psychology, see Steneck, *Science and Creation*, 130–37; id., "Albert." On eighteenth-century natural histories of the mind, see Wood.
165. Rousseau, 27–28. This story was originally recounted by Jean Baptiste du Tertre in *Historie naturelle et morale des îsles Antilles de l'Amérique, avec un vocabulaire carîbe* (Rotterdam: A. Lers, 1654).
166. Vico, *Scienza nuova*, bk. 2, ¶ 378.
167. For a superb analysis of the relationship between the development of the discipline of history and the "battle of the books" between the Moderns and the Ancients in seventeenth- and eighteenth-century England, see Levine, *Battle of the Books*.
168. Monboddo quoted by Bryson, 68.
169. Aarsleff; Schreyer; Paxman.
170. Barthélemy, 4: 426. On Barthélemy, see David, ch. 8.
171. Barthélemy, 4: 431.
172. Rycaut (unpaginated).

173. Bernard (unpaginated). For Bernard, the Incas were an ideal colonizing power. Unlike the Spaniards, who looted and destroyed, the Incas expanded by gentle consensus.

174. "Préface du Traducteur." In Garcilaso de la Vega, *Histoire des Incas Rois du Pérou* [1744], 1: viii.

175. Ibid., xvi–xvii.

176. Raynal, *HP* (1770), bk. 6 (3: 32); bk. 7 (3: 117). See also Raynal, *HP* (1774), bk. 7 (3: 126–27, 130), in which he argues that in Peru there were compensating mechanisms that kept the Incas from becoming tyrants.

177. Schérer, ch. 4, 118.

178. Graffigny. Letter 5 recounts how the "barbarous" Spaniards take her quipus away. Zilia, however, still in captivity, keeps weaving-writing. Letter 16 recounts Zilia's abandonment of quipus for alphabetical writing.

179. Sangro, *Lettera apologetica*, 192 ff. (quipus as number-crunching devices), 241 ff. (quipus as a secret syllabic written language).

180. Ibid., 246.

181. Ibid.

182. The manuscript from which Sansevero drew has been made available in Animato et al. 1989. The rediscovery of the manuscript has triggered a heated scholarly debate among Peruvianists, focused on the authenticity of the manuscript and on whether the Incas had a syllabic script. The manuscript appears authentic, but the view of Inca syllabic writing is clearly a seventeenth-century invention. In my opinion, the manuscript is more valuable for shedding light on Peru's baroque culture than for understanding Inca scripts. On the current debate, see Domenici and Domenici. Thanks to Daniel Slive for bringing this article to my attention.

183. Sangro, *Supplica*, 118 (reproduces the charges of the inquisitor Abbé L. P. to the effect that Sansevero had denied as "infallible sicura e certisima la Divina Storia del Genesi"); see also pp. 17–18.

184. Pauw, *Recherches philosophiques sur les Américains*, 1: 241–81 (on Laplanders); 1: 172–207; 2: 5–47 (on blacks).

185. Ibid., 2: 204–6.

186. Ibid. 170.

187. Ibid. 197.

188. Ibid. 154–55.

189. Ibid. 174.

190. Ibid. 198.

191. Ibid. 199.

192. Lambeck, 660.

193. Ibid., 661. See also the brief references to Mesoamerican scripts in Worm, 382–83; Horn, bk. 4, ch. 14, pp. 270–74. Horn seeks to prove the analogies between China and Mexico, including systems of writing; he also highlights the contradictions between the versions of Mexica history as described in Purchas's edition of the Codex Mendoza and in Acosta.

194. Vienna Codex (1963), appendix III, 1: 31–32. I follow Adelhofer's translation. Adelhofer attributes to Kollár what is in fact text by Lambeck. Kollár added a com-

mentary, which is the last paragraph in Adelhofer's edition. On the Vienna Codex, see Glass and Robertson, 235–36.

195. Robertson, *HA*, in *Works*, 10: 414.

196. Ibid., 10: 414–16. On the Codex Borbonicus, see Glass and Robertson, 97–98, and Codex Borbonicus.

197. Robertson, *HA*, in *Works*, 9: 49.

198. Ibid., 9: 86–87 (on understanding and foresight); 2: 95–96 (on will).

199. Ibid., 9: 88.

200. Ibid., 82–83.

201. Ibid., 97.

202. Ibid., 238–40.

203. Ibid., 10: 276.

204. Ibid., 270.

205. Ibid., 9: 48.

206. Ibid., 10: 272–73.

207. Ibid., 310.

208. Ibid., 276–77.

209. Ibid., 273.

210. Ibid., 9: 410–15.

211. Ibid., 10: 385–86.

212. Ibid., 8: xvi; 10: 406, 413.

213. Ibid., 10: 302.

214. Ibid., 323.

215. Ibid., 410.

216. Ibid., 383.

217. Humboldt, *Researches*, "Notes," 2: 248; and "Chronological table of the History of Mexico," 2: 248–54.

218. Ibid., pl. vii, 1: 83.

219. Ibid., pl. xxiii, 1: 298.

220. Ibid., pl. xxvi, 2: 15–33; and "Notes," 2: 245.

221. Ibid., pl. xxvi, 2: 27.

222. Ibid., pl. xxiii, 1: 299.

223. Ibid., pl. xxxii, 2: 57–71.

224. Ibid., pl. xxxii, 2: 70.

225. Ibid., pls. lv and lvi. See Quiñonez Keber on the Codex Telleriano-Remensis.

226. Humboldt, *Researches*, pl. xiii, 1: 179.

227. Ibid., pl. xiii, 1: 156–57; 170–76.

228. Ibid., pl. xiii, 1: 151–54.

229. Ibid., pl. xiii, 1: 162.

230. Ibid., pl. xv, 1: 214 ff.

231. Ibid., pl. xiii, 1: 161.

232. Ibid., pl. xxxii, 2: 62.

233. Ibid., pl. xii, 1: 141–44.

234. Ibid., "Introduction," 1: 1–2.

235. Ibid., "Monuments of America," 1: 38.

236. Ibid., pl. xii, 1: 141–44.

CHAPTER 3: HISTORIOGRAPHY AND PATRIOTISM
IN SPAIN

1. Estala. See also Estala's *El Pluto: Comedia de Aristófanes* (Madrid: Imprenta de Sancha, 1794); *Edipo tirano: Tragedia de Sófocles* (Madrid: Imprenta de Sancha, 1793); *Colección de poetas españoles*, 20 vols. (Madrid: R. Fernández, 1786–98).

2. La Porte, vols. 10 (1774, on Mexico) and 12 (1775, on Peru). I have used the 42-volume edition of 1768–95, although La Porte's compilation first appeared in 1766.

3. Estala, vol. 12, letter 162, p. 139.

4. Ibid., letter 163, pp. 147–48.

5. Ibid., vol. 20, letter 339, pp. 156–57; see also ibid., vol. 26, letter 494, p. 209.

6. Ibid., letter 500, p. 308.

7. Ibid., letter 493, p. 206.

8. Ibid., letter 500, pp. 310–12.

9. Ibid., letters 494–95, pp. 208–44. On Western views of the "Orient," see Said.

10. Arnoldsson; Chaunu; Maltby; Juderías; Sarrailh, "Voyageurs français"; García Cárcel.

11. See, e.g., Carbia; Esteve Barba; Brading, *First America*.

12. Boturini, *Idea*, 28.20, p. 111; emphasis in original.

13. Venturi. On the Viconian dimensions of Boturini's work, see also Matute.

14. "[Il] contesto e le polemiche sucitate dalla prima edizione della *Idea*, ci danno sia una conferma dello stato di decadenza della cultura spagnola di quegli anni" (Badaloni, 7).

15. I have reconstructed Boturini's travails in Mexico from AGI, Indiferente general, 398, which contains a voluminous file of the proceedings against Boturini both in Mexico and Spain. His life and adventures in Mexico and Spain have, however, been recounted well in Torre Revello and León-Portilla. My story deviates at times from their accounts, and only in those cases do I refer to the original documents in AGI, Indiferente general, 398.

16. Boturini, *Idea*, ¶ i, *passim* (pp. 31–33); and 14.19–23 (pp. 87–90).

17. Ibid., 21.1 (p. 99).

18. Ibid., 2.1 (p. 33).

19. Ibid., 14.5 (p. 71).

20. Ibid., 20.1–2 (p. 96).

21. Ibid., 21.2 (p. 99).

22. Ibid., 26.1 (p. 105).

23. Ibid., "Catálogo del museo histórico indiano," pp. 113–51.

24. Ibid., 24.5 (p. 103).

25. "Dictamen del fiscal Borrull sobre la *Idea* de Boturini," Nov. 2, 1745, and "Respuesta del fiscal sobre caso Boturini," Nov. 6, 1745, AGI, Indiferente general, 398. Borrull's "Dictamen" was appended to the 1746 edition of Boturini's *Idea*.

26. The inventory reached the council on Aug. 20, 1745, well before the council's sudden about-face. See "Carta al Consejo del Conde de Fuenclara," Aug. 20, 1745; "Acuerdo del Consejo sobre expediente de Boturini," May 14, 1746; and "Resolución del Consejo sobre el expediente de Boturini," May 25, 1746, AGI, Indiferente general, 398.

27. Borrull, "Dictamen," in Boturini, *Idea*, 10.

28. Ibid., 11.

29. Concepción, "Aprovación," in Boturini, *Idea*, 13.

30. Ibid., 14.

31. Campoy, "Eques Boturini Nova Praetiosa Historia Universam Americam Locupletiorem Facit," in Boturini, *Idea*, 28. Curiously, Badaloni's Italian translation does not include the multiple pieces appended to the *Idea*.

32. For the many efforts at derailing the publication and overturning the council's original ruling, see the letter of Andrés Marcos Burriel to Gregorio Mayans, July 30, 1746, in Mayans y Siscar, *Epistolario II*, 289.

33. For the Creole opposition, see Torre Revello, 16. On the Aragonese origins of the party that led the opposition against Boturini, see AHM, vol. 39, Borrull to Mayans, Sept. 28, 1748 (unpaginated). See also Burriel to Mayans, Sept. 13, 1748, in *Epistolario II*, 408.

34. On the movement of historiographical renewal, which in fact began under the Habsburgs in the last quarter of the seventeenth century, see Mestre, *Historia, fueros y actitudes políticas*; Stiffoni.

35. Sierra Nava-Lasa, 35, 80–81.

36. Laurencín, 28. See, however, the comic incident in which Nasarre expelled the academicians from the premises of the Library in a period in which the Academy was in frank decline (Laurencín, 54–55). When Nasarre died, the new senior librarian, Juan Santander y Zorrilla, sought unsuccessfully to throw the Academy out (Laurencín, 70).

37. On Feijóo and more generally on the Spanish Enlightenment as a pedagogical movement devoted to rooting out popular superstition and reeducating the masses as a means to reinvigorating the Spanish economy, see Sarrailh, *Espagne éclairée*.

38. Sánchez-Blanco Parody, 134–50.

39. Mayans, "Nova literaria."

40. The debate between Mayans and Nasarre and the *Diaristas* began with the publication of a review of Mayans's *Orígenes de la lengua española* (1737) in the *Diario*. Mayans responded with a satire, *Conversación sobre El Diario de los literatos de España* (1737). The editors of the *Diario* then replied with an attack on Mayans's article in the *Acta eruditorum*. On the role of Nasarre in the founding both of the Academy of History and of the *Diario* and on the debate between the editors of the *Diario* and Mayans, see Stiffoni, 199–224.

41. Mestre, "Imagen de España."

42. Mayans edited both several well-known and unknown works by leading Spanish humanists of the Renaissance. See, e.g., his editions of Juan Luis Vives's *Opera omnia*, 7 vols. (Valencia: B. Montfort, 1782–90); Francisco Sánchez de las Brozas's *Opera omnia*, 4 vols. (Geneva: De Tournes Bros., 1766); Antonio Agustín's *Díalogos de las armas, i linages de la nobleza de España* (Madrid: Juan de Zúñiga, 1734); Luis de León's *Obras propias i traducciones de latin, griego, i toscano, con la parafrasi de algunos salmos i capítulos de Job* (Valencia: J. T. Lucas, 1761); Cervantes's *Vida y hechos del ingenioso hidalgo Don Quixote de la Mancha* (London: J. & R. Tonson, 1738; The Hague: P. Gosse & A. Moetjens, 1744; Madrid: J. S. Martin, 1750).

Mayans also published part of the *Ars rhetorica* of Antonio Nebrija in his *Organum rhetoricum et oratoriuma* (Valencia: B. Montfort, 1774) as well as Nebrija's *Reglas de ortografía en la lengua castellana* (Valencia: B. Montfort, 1765).

43. Martínez Pingarrón to Mayans, July 16, 1746, in Mayans, *Epistolario VIII*, 262.

44. AGI, Indiferente general, 398, Marcos Burriel to Jorge Juan y Santacilia, Sept. 26, 1748 (unpaginated).

45. Burriel to Ensenada, June 29, 1747, Archivo General de Simancas, Marina 712, in Lafuente and Mazuecos, 227.

46. On Burriel's role in the publication of Ulloa and Juan y Santacilia's travel accounts, see Lafuente and Mazuecos, 219–30.

47. AGI, Indiferente general, 398, Burriel to Jorge Juan y Santacilia, Sept. 26, 1748 (unpaginated).

48. Ulloa confirmed many of La Condamine's dismal views of the Indians, but he blamed Spanish colonialism not nature. The Indians, he argued, had been exploited and transformed beyond recognition by cliques of plundering merchants, idle Creoles, and morally corrupt clergy, both secular and religious (with the exception of the virtuous Jesuits). See Juan y Santacilia and Ulloa, *Relación histórica*, 6.6 (2: 541–66); and Brading, *First America*, 470–72.

49. AHM, vol. 84, Boturini to Mayans, Jan. 10, 1747.

50. Manuel Martínez Pingarrón to Mayans, Feb. 7, 1750, in Gregorio Mayans y Siscar, *Epistolario VIII*, 334.

51. See, e.g., AHM, vol. 142, Mayans to Boturini, Feb. 4, 1747.

52. Sánchez-Blanco Parody, 284–85.

53. Boturini, *Idea*, 26.6–7 (pp. 80–81).

54. Burriel to Mayans, Dec. 3, 1746, in Mayans y Siscar, *Epistolario II*, 309.

55. Boturini, *Oratio ad Divinam Sapientiam*. A Spanish translation has been appended to León-Portilla's edition of the *Idea*. But as Venturi has noticed, this edition has flaws, including numerous deletions of references in the original and errors in the transcription of names.

56. Tuck; Hont.

57. Mayans to Martínez Pingarrón, Feb. 20, 1750, in Mayans, *Epistolario VIII*, 335–36. Mayans sarcastically attacked Nasarre for defending Grotius and for criticizing his address to the Valencian Academy. There is nothing in this letter, however, on Nasarre's views of Boturini's *Oratio*.

58. AMH, vol. 57, Boturini to Mayans, June 19, 1751. See also in the same volume Boturini's letter to Mayans of July 17, 1751 in which he denounces the Freemasons as a "cursed sect" and expresses joy at the attempts of the monarchy to destroy them. "It is necessary," Boturini concluded, "to obey the civil and ecclesiastical authorities according to natural law and divine precept."

59. Mayans, "Juicio aprovando la Oración latina," 5: 395.

60. Martínez Pingarrón to Mayans, Feb. 7, 1750, in Mayans, *Epistolario VIII*, 333.

61. Gibson and Glass, "Census"; Glass, "Survey"; Robertson, *Mexican Manuscript*; Gruzinsky, *Painting the Conquest*; Brotherston, *Book of the Fourth World*; id., *Painted Books*; Mundy.

62. AGI, Indiferente general, 398, Burriel to Juan y Santacilia, Sept. 26, 1748 (unpaginated).

63. AHM, vol. 80, Boturini to Mayans, Jan. 10, 1747.

64. AHM, vol. 142, Mayans to Boturini, Feb. 4, 1747.

65. AHM, vol. 84, Boturini to Mayans, Mar. 7, 1747.

66. AHM, vol. 142, Mayans to Boturini, Sept. 10, 1747.

67. AGI, Indiferente general, 398, count of Montejo to Fernando Triviño (requesting Boturini's judicial file and Boturini's *Idea*), May 31, 1746; Fernando Triviño to count of Montejo (submitting file, except Boturini's *Idea*), June 1, 1746; Resolución final del rey sobre el expediente de Boturini, July 10, 1747. It seems that Triviño, a member of the Council of the Indies and one of Boturini's allies, took the initiative of sending the case to the king on the grounds that the determinations of the council regarding Boturini had been "irregular and capricious." Triviño adds that the council had wavered and changed its mind.

68. The *Ciclografía* was annotated and published in 1949 by Manuel Ballesteros Gaibrois under the title *Historia general de la América Septentrional*. I have used the second edition published in 1990 by the Universidad Nacional Autónoma of Mexico. I prefer the title *Ciclografía* to *Historia general* because this is the name that Boturini himself used in his correspondence with Mayans, and because *Historia general* was the title of the entire multivolume project.

69. Boturini, *Historia general*, ch. 5. See also Pluche.

70. Acosta, *Historia natural*, bk. 6, chs. 1–2.

71. Burriel to Mayans, Aug. 30, 1748, and Sept. 13, 1748, in Mayans, *Epistolario II*, 407–8.

72. Boturini, *Historia general*, 53.

73. Ibid., 54–55.

74. That it had become an obsession can be attested from Boturini's correspondence with Mayans. See AHM, vol. 84, Boturini to Mayans, Jan. 18, 1749. Boturini casts Burriel's comments as part of a Jesuit-orchestrated defense of Acosta's prestige. "[In my work] Acosta will get the [rough] treatment that he deserves [*se llevará su merecido*]." On Feb. 15, 1749, Boturini promises to send Mayans a treatise on "lunations" in which he will complete his demolition of Acosta (*terminaré de darle palos*).

75. Burriel to Mayans, Aug. 27, 1746, in Mayans, *Epistolario II*, 298.

76. Bayle, 2: 74–75 (entry on the Spanish historian Nicolás Antonio).

77. Burriel to Mayans, Sept. 13, 1748, in Mayans, *Epistolario II*, 408.

78. AGI, Indiferente general, 398, Burriel to Juan y Santacilia, Sept. 26, 1748 (unpaginated).

79. Boturini, *Historia general*, *passim*.

80. AHM, vol. 39. Borrull to Mayans, May 3, 1749. For various drafts of the report, see AHM, vol. 645, "Papeles varios de Mayans." The report was published by Mayans in 1773 as "Carta a Félix Yáñez de Lima"; see esp. 390 and 391.

81. AHM, vol. 84, Boturini to Mayans, June 7, 1749; AGI, Indiferente general, 398; Fresnada, "Parecer," Aug. 6, 1748 (unpaginated).

82. AHM, vol. 84, Boturini to Mayans, Aug. 30, 1749.

83. In a letter to Mayans of Sept. 27, 1749, Boturini announced that after having been approved by Herrero de Ezpeleta his *Ciclografía* was about to be sent to a fourth referee. But on Oct. 4, 1749, Boturini declared that the council had finally given him license to publish; see AHM, vol. 84.

84. AHM, vol. 57, Boturini to Mayans, Dec. 5, 1750 (announcing Borrull's death), and Apr. 17, 1751 (blaming Nasarre's death on the negative reception of Nasarre's edition of Cervantes's comedies). On Bamfi as the leading opposition force in the council, see AHM, vol. 57, Boturini to Mayans, Sept. 18, 1751 (Boturini denounces Bamfi for plotting for many years and vows to run him through with a sword).

85. AHM, vol. 57, Boturini to Mayans, Oct. 2, 1751 (in which Boturini admits the need to change and begs Mayans not to abandon him).

86. Mayans to Martínez Pingarrón, Sept. 18, 1751, in Mayans, *Epistolario VII*, 373–74.

87. Mayans to Burriel, Sept. 6, 1755, in Mayans, *Epistolario II*, 604.

88. The following are some of the titles Barcia edited: Herrera's *Décadas* (1725–30); Garcilaso's *La Florida* (1723), *Comentarios reales de los Incas* (1723), and *Historia general del Perú* (1722); Torquemada's *Monarchía indiana* (1723); Gregorio García's *Origen de los indios del Nuevo Mundo* (1729); Antonio de Solís's *Historia de la conquista de México* (1732); Alonso de Ercilla's *La Araucana* (1733); Fernando Colón's *Historia del Almirante Colón* (1749); Hernán Cortés's *Cartas de relación* (1749); Gonzalo Fernández de Oviedo's *Sumario de la natural historia de las Indias* (1749); Alvar Núñez Cabeza de Vaca's *Relación de la jornada que hizo a la Florida con el adelantado Pánfilo de Narvaez* (1749) and *Comentarios* (1749) (on the conquest of the River Plate); Francisco López de Gómara's *Historia de las Indias y de la conquista de México* (1749); Agustín de Zárate's *Historia del descubrimiento y conquista del Perú* (1749); and Francisco de Xérez's *Verdadera relación de la conquista del Perú* (1749). A study of Barcia is long overdue. For a general although incomplete view of Barcia, see Andrés. Not even a good bibliography of his works exists. The entry on Barcia in Aguilar Piñal, 4: 279–82, is incomplete. It shows, however, that Barcia began his editorial career as a playwright. Barcia's edition of the works of Colón, Cortés, Oviedo, López de Gómara, Cabeza de Vaca, Zárate, and Xérez appeared posthumously in Madrid in 1749 under the auspices of Barcia's nephew, who went by the same name. The 1749 edition appeared as a three-volume folio collection under the title *Historiadores primitivos de Indias*.

89. Cotarelo y Mori, "Fundación de la Academia española."

90. Iriarte quoted in Cotarelo y Mori, *Iriarte y su época*, 16.

91. Rodríguez Mohedano quoted in Mestre, "Imagen de España," 63.

92. Charles de Secondat, baron de Montesquieu, *Lettres persanes* (1721), in Gibson, ed., *Black Legend*, 115; Cadalso, 167.

93. McClelland, 122–23.

94. Peset and Lafuente, "Ciencia e historia"; Pascual.

95. Caso; McClelland, 23–26.

96. Nasarre (unpaginated).

97. Ibid. (unpaginated, but corresponds to p. 15).

98. Sierra Nava-Lasa, 28–29 (on Martín Sarmiento's efforts to introduce the teaching of Arabic as part of a larger reform of Spanish universities). Mayans included the seventeenth-century studies of Bernardo José de Aldrete on the influences of Arabic in the Spanish language in *Orígenes de la lengua española por varios autores* (Madrid: J. de Zuñiga, 1737).

99. Cavanilles, 129 (in which Cavanilles not only praises the achievements of the

Arabs but argues that the fact that they had lived in Spain for eight centuries made them Spaniards). See also volumes 12 through 15 of Masdeu's *Historia crítica*, which are devoted to Arab Spain. Even Juan Pablo Forner, who denounced Arab ignorance as the source of the corruption of Greek learning and the origin of the decadent European scholasticism, found time to praise "Spanish" Arabs for their contribution to the natural and mathematical sciences. See Forner, 42–52, 62.

100. Breydy; Casiri.

101. Barcia, "Proemio," in Torquemada, *Primera*. The book in fact appeared in 1725, when the *proemio* was written.

102. Barcia, "Proemio," in García, *Origen* (unpaginated).

103. García, *Origen*, bk 2, ch. 4, sec. 2, p. 56–57; sec. 7, p. 64; and ch. 5, *passim* (pp. 68 ff.). On these ideas, see Cañizares-Esguerra, "New World, New Stars."

104. García, *Origen*, bk. 4, ch. 24.

105. Barcia, *Ensayo cronológico*. Barcia wrote the Chronological Essay under the pen name of Gabriel Cárdenas Cano, one of many he used during his career. In "Introducción a el ensaio cronológico para la historia general de la Florida" (unpaginated), Barcia blamed Sir Francis Bacon's *History of Henry VII* (1622) for promoting the idea that Sebastian Cabot had been the first European to land in Florida.

106. Barcia, "Introducción al ensaio cronológico" (unpaginated).

107. Ibid.

108. León Pinelo.

109. Sarmiento, 85 ff.

110. Feuillée, "Epitre," in *Journal* (1714) (unpaginated).

111. "Préface du second volume." In Garcilaso de la Vega, *Histoire des Incas Rois du Pérou* (1744), 2: v and iv.

112. Bonneville, 61.

113. La Porte, 16: 94. Vol. 16 appeared in 1777.

114. The apogee of this trend was reached in 1783 when the article "Espagne" by Nicolas Masson de Morvilliers appeared in the *Encyclopédie méthodique*. Depicting Spain as the most backward nation in Europe, Masson de Morvilliers asked rhetorically: "What do we owe to Spain? What [knowledge] has Spain [contributed] to Europe in the past two, four, ten centuries? Where are their mathematicians, physicists, naturalists, historians, and philosophers?" The response in Spain was a groundswell of indignation, leading to intense Spanish diplomatic activity to block the publication of the *Encyclopédie méthodique* in France itself. Spaniards also wrote defenses, including, among the most famous, those by the Valencian scholars Antonio de Cavanilles and Juan Pablo Forner. See Masson de Morvilliers 556, 565–66; Cavanilles; Forner; Herr, 219–30.

115. Cañizares-Esguerra, "Spanish America."

116. Pino and Guirao; Clément.

117. On the history of the office from its founding under Philip II to the late eighteenth century, see Carbia.

118. This aspect of the debate has been studied by Nava Rodríguez, ch. 10.

119. ARAH, 9/4161, Hermosilla y Sandoval, "Sobre el método de escribir la historia de las Indias," May 15, 1756, f. 667. In the pages to come, I have identified the professions and institutional affiliations of the members of the Royal Academy using the

"Catálogo de los señores individuos de la Real Academia de Historia," in *Memorias de la Real Academia*, cxxxii–clxi.

120. ARAH, 9/4173, # 4, Ribera, "Proyecto en general para formar la historia universal y la geografía de las Indias," Apr. 29, 1756.

121. ARAH, 9/4173, # 2, Marcos Benito, "Papel en que se pone su idea de escribir la historia de Indias," June 10, 1756 (unpaginated).

122. Ibid.

123. ARAH, 9/4173, Marcos Benito, "Parecer," Nov. 5, 1756, n.p.

124. ARAH, 9/4161, Domínguez de Riezu, "Parecer," Aug. 6, 1756, f. 302v.

125. See, e.g., ARAH, 9/4173, # 4 bis, Hermosilla y Sandoval, "Sobre el método de escribir," and Ribera, "Adición al plan que presenté sobre la historia y geografía de las Indias," July 30, 1756,

126. ARAH, 9/4173, # 2, Marcos Benito, "Papel en que se pone su idea de escribir la historia de Indias," *passim*.

127. ARAH, 9/4173, # 4 bis, Hermosilla y de Sandoval, "Sobre el método de escribir."

128. ARAH, 9/4173, #4, Ribera. "Proyecto en general para formar la historia universal y la geografía de las Indias."

129. ARAH, 9/4173, # 3, Vicente García de la Huerta, "Sobre el modo de escribir la historia de las Indias," Aug. 5, 1756.

130. Manuel Pablo Salcedo's 1762 report, "Sobre el método que ha de seguirse," has been published in Chacón y Calvo. The original document is located in AGI, Indiferente general, 1521.

131. Nava Rodríguez, 561–58 (Nava Rodríguez uses a debate over the approval of a work submitted for publication by José Eusebio de Llano y Zapata to explore the ideological differences between the two institutions).

132. Chacón y Calvo, 309.

133. Ibid., 322.

134. Ibid., 315–16.

135. AGI, Indiferente general, 1521, "Instrucción de lo que ha de observar y guardar el padre ministro Christin Riegger como cosmógrafo del Consejo de Indias en el modo de escribir la historia geográfica de aquellos reinos," June 26, 1762.

136. AGI, Indiferente general, 1521, "Instrucción que se ha de observar y guardar la real Academia de Historia como cronista mayor de Indias, en el modo de escribir la historia natural civil política eclesiástica de aquellos Reinos," Mar. 22, 1762.

137. Nava Rodríguez, 511–26.

138. ARAH 9/4161, Martín de Ulloa, "Sobre el método de escrivir [*sic*] la historia natural y civil de las Indias," fol. 214v.

139. ARH, 9/4161, #10, Pedro Rodríguez Campomanes, "Puntos sobre que parece puede conferenciarse para facilitar el modo de escribir la historia de las Indias," Jan. 10, 1765.

140. AGI 9/4161, Felipe García de Samaniego, "En torno a la formación de una biblioteca de autores de Indias," 316v.

141. On these debates, see Nava Rodríguez, ch. 11.

142. ARAH, 9/4161, "Método y reglas que deberán observarse por los individuos que ha destinado la Academia Real de la Historia a la recolección y coordinación de noticias pertenecientes a la civil y natural de las Indias," fols. 149–58.

143. ARAH, 9/4173, # 20 bis, Domínguez de Riezu, "Papel sobre los trabajos realizados en la Junta de Indias," Oct. 30, 1766.

144. ARAH 9/4161, Domínguez de Riezu, "Papel que da cuenta de la dificultad en ordenar las cédulas," Aug. 29, 1777, fols. 531–32. The *cédulas* compiled by the Academy can still be consulted; see ARAH, 9/4165 (files on natural history); 9/4162 and 9/4163 (files on diplomacy); 9/4168 (files on genealogies; ecclesiastical affairs; portraits; hieroglyphs); 9/4169 (files on Mexican astronomy and calendars; instruments; costumes; maritime history); 9/4170 (files on crafts and trades; politics; nobility); 9/4171 (files on Peru); 9/4166 and 9/4167 (files on chronology); 9/4172 (files on the history of Hispaniola and Paraguay). This huge quantity of material still awaits critical study. I have only reviewed the files on hieroglyphs; most of them come from Boturini's *Idea* and include thirty-seven entries on Mesoamerican deities and on calendrical signs. Under the category "genealogical trees," there are nine describing indigenous "maps."

145. ARAH, 9/4161, "Resoluciones de la Junta sobre pedir infomación a autoridades coloniales," Oct. 11, 1765, fols. 273–80.

146. AGI, Indiferente del Perú, 398, "Instrucciones que envia Academia de Historia a virreyes y autoridades coloniales y obispos pidiendo listas históricas de autoridades civiles y eclesiasticas y descripciones de provincias," Nov. 5, 1765.

147. ARAH, 9/4161, "Apuntamiento de la noticias que habrán de pedirse a los virreyes . . . para escribir con acierto y exactitud la historia civil y natural de las Indias," fol. 647r–v.

148. Ibid., 647 v.

149. AGI, Indiferente del Perú, 398, "Informe del fiscal del Consejo negando expedición de pedidos a colonias para que remitan noticias," Feb. 8, 1766.

150. ARAH, Actas, bk. 4, Feb. 14, 1766. Many thanks to Eloy Benito Ruano, secretary of the Royal Academy, for granting me special permission to consult the Academy's Actas (minutes).

151. ARAH 9/5946, Ramón Guevara Vasconcelos, "Informe acerca de la Historia de América compuesta por Robertson," Aug. 8, 1777, 311v. Guevara's "Informe" was published a month later in the *Gazeta de Madrid*, Sept. 16, 1777.

152. Ibid., 304v.

153. Ibid., 308r.

154. Ibid., 309v.

155. Ibid., 311r.

156. ARAH, Actas, bk. 6, Aug. 8, 1777.

157. ARAH 9/5946, Guevara Vasconcelos, "Informe," note on the margins of 312r (extending membership and approving translation).

158. Sepúlveda. The 1780 edition also contained Sepúlveda's *History of Philip II*, various other appendixes, and a new edition of the complete works of Sepúlveda published in Cologne in 1602. On the history of the Academy's editorial effort, see Gil Fernández.

159. Sepúlveda, *Demócrates segundo*. On Sepúlveda and the debate with Las Casas, see Pagden, *Fall*, ch. 5.

160. ARAH, Actas, bk. 6, Mar. 20, 1778, reproduced in Gil Fernández, doc. # 7, p. 156.

161. ARAH, Actas, bk. 7, Jan. 12, 1781, reproduced in Gil Fernández, doc. # 10, p. 158.

162. ARAH, Actas, bk. 6, May 29, 1778, reproduced in Gil Fernández, doc. # 8, p. 157.

163. The academicians also unearthed the second half of Oviedo's natural history of the Indies and one of Cortes's letters to Charles V; see ARAH, Actas, bk. 6, Aug. 7, 1777, and AC, box 29/30, reproduced in Gil Fernández, doc. # 3, p. 153, and doc. # 15, pp. 161–62. On Las Casas's manuscripts, see AC, box 29/30, reproduced in Gil Fernández, doc. # 14, pp. 160–61.

164. ARAH, Actas, bk. 6, Aug. 29 and Sept. 5, 1777.

165. Ibid., Sept. 19 and Oct. 3, 1777.

166. Ibid., Dec. 19, 1777.

167. Ibid., Dec. 27, 1777. In 1903, Cesareo Fernández Duro published a copy of the document sent by the Academy to the crown arguing that Campomanes had written it on December 19. From a study of the minutes of the Academy, it is clear that the document was written on December 27 by a commission made up of four members (Samaniego, Sánchez, Guevara y Vasconcelos, and Flores); cf., Fernández Duro, 6–7, and ARAH, Actas, bk. 6, Dec. 19, 1777.

168. Campomanes to Gálvez, Dec. 27, 1777, in Fernández Duro, 9.

169. AGI, Indiferente general, 1656, Gálvez, "Orden a las Secretarías del Consejo y a la Contaduría General; también a la secretaría del Perú e Indiferente, para que provean con la información debida a académicos nombrados por la Academia de Historia para completar la ilustración de la *Historia de América* de Guillermo Robertson," Jan. 1, 1778; and José Miguel de Flores, "Sobre las noticias que se solicitan de las dos Secretarías del Real y Supremo Consejo y Cámara de las Indias de cada una por lo perteneciente a su distrito, para la ilustración de la *Historia de América* del Doctor Robertson," Jan. 20, 1778.

170. The Academy asked the council for information on the foundation of bishoprics and archbishoprics, as well as of *audiencias* (high courts-cum-councils) and a few viceroyalties; on the income of the Church from taxes and the sale of bulls; on the number of tributaries in each diocese; on the dignitaries and incomes of cathedral chapters and college churches; on the name, location, and population of each colonial mission; on the numbers of secular priests and religious; on the number of convents, hospitals, and hospices; on the income of a few tribunals of the Inquisition; and news on the most recent Church councils.

171. AC, box 18/19, Pedro Rodríguez Campomanes, "Reflexiones sobre el comercio español a Indias. En que se tratan las leyes, e historia de nuestro comercio, la del asiento de negros y las relaciones de nuestro tráfico con el de las naciones estrangeras en Indias y se da una noticia muy individual de sus colonias; examínanse las causas porque florecen y quales influien a la decadencia de las nuestras y de la marina mercantil española, y se proponen los medios de mejorar el comercio y la navegación" (1762) (unpaginated). On Campomanes's views on colonial reforms, see Muñoz Pérez.

172. Castro; Brading, *First America*, 502–7.

173. BN-S, MS 18.182, Campomanes to Robertson, Sept. 29, 1777. There is a copy of the letter in BP, MS II/2845. The letter has been reproduced by Fernández Duro,

10–11, but he does not identify the location of the original. For Campomanes's own writings, see his *Estudios regalistas* (with the *Tratado de la regalia* in vol. 1 and the *Juicio imparcial sobre el monitoreo de Roma* in vol. 2) and *Discurso*.

174. BP, MS II/2845 and BN-S, MS 18.182, Campomanes to Robertson, Mar. 6, 1778. See also Fernández Duro, 13–14.

175. BP MS II/2845, Robertson to Campomanes, Jan. 31, 1778; cf. Fernández Duro, 12.

176. AC, box 48/118, Robertson to Campomanes, May 5, 1783 (introducing his friend Mr. Liston, newly appointed secretary to the British ambassador in Spain); and AC, box 21/20, Campomanes to Robertson, June 27, 1787 (clarifying Robertson's views on the ordination of Indians as secular priests).

177. ARAH, 9/4161, "Dictamen que ha formado la Junta acerca de la versión castellana de la Historia del descubrimiento de América," Apr. 10, 1778 (unpaginated).

178. AC, box 21/16 bis, Gálvez to Campomanes, Nov. 26, 1778 (unpaginated).

179. Ibid., Gálvez to Campomanes, Dec. 23, 1778 (unpaginated).

180. See, e.g., Esteve Barba, 150–51; Navas Rodríguez, 642–43; Fernández Duro, 14.

181. The report, "Examen de la Historia de América traducida del inglés por Ramón Guevara," can be found at the BP, MS II/2845, f. 47–101, and at AC, box 4/8.

182. BP, MS II/2845, "Examen de la Historia de América," fol. 59r (emphasis in original).

183. Ibid., fol. 61.

184. Ibid., fol. 71r.

185. Ibid., fol. 79r.

186. Ibid., fol. 81r.

187. Ibid., fol. 101r.

188. Brading, *First America*, ch. 21.

189. Raynal quoted in Tietz, 100. On Raynal's requests, see AC, box 38/39, Heredia to Campomanes, n.d.

190. Jean Francois Bourgoing quoted in Lynch, 254.

191. Nuix, *Riflessioni*.

192. The two Spanish editions appeared as *Reflexiones imparciales sobre la humanidad de los españoles en las Indias contra los pretendidos filósofos y políticos. Para ilustrar las historias de MM. Raynal y Robertson,* traducida con notas por Pedro Varela y Ulloa (Madrid: Joachin Ibarrra, 1782); and *Reflexiones imparciales,* añadidas por el mismo autor y traducidas del idioma italiano al español por Josef de Nuix y de Perpina (Cervera: Impr. de la Pontificia y Real Universidad, 1783). On the positive evaluation of Nuix's work at the Council of the Indies, see AGI, Indiferente general, 1656, "Evaluación de Fiscales del Consejo de Indias sobre la traducción hecha por Pedro Varela, oficial de la Secretaría de Marina, de la obra de Abate Juan Nuix, *Reflexiones Imparciales sobre la humanidad de los españoles de Indias,*" Sept. 28, 1781.

193. Pedro Varela y Ulloa, "Discurso preliminar del traductor," in Nuix, *Reflexiones,* xxii–xxiii.

194. Nuix, *Reflexiones imparciales,* "Prólogo del autor," xxxiii–xxxiv.

195. Ibid., 34.

196. Ibid., 43

197. Ibid., "Prólogo del autor," xxxvii–xxxviii.
198. Ibid., xxxvi.
199. Ibid., xxxvi.
200. Ibid., xxxix–xl.
201. Ibid., 121–22.
202. Ibid., 73.
203. Ibid., 122.
204. Ibid., 128–29.
205. On the scholarship of the Spanish Jesuits exiled in Italy, see Batllori.
206. Diosdado Caballero, *Breve examen*, sec. 2, ¶ 8, p. 22, and sec. 5.
207. Diosdado Caballero, *Observaciones sobre Josef Ribera*.
208. See, e.g., BP, MS 1843, Diosdado Caballero, "Excelencia de la América española sobre las extrangeras decidida con hechos." This is a statistical-cameralist study of the commerce, agriculture, industries, and cities of the Spanish colonies, which are compared positively to other European colonies in America. See also Diosdado's overall glowing evaluation of the philosophical wisdom underlying Spanish colonial legislation in AJPT, shelf 4A, box 17, folder 7, "Resumen del extracto de las Leyes de Indias," fol. 1r.
209. On Diosdado's campaign to suppress the Spanish edition of Clavijero in the 1780s, see Ronan, ch. 3. Ronan based his study of Diosdado's campaign largely on information obtained in the 1960s in the Archivo de Indias under the signature Patronato 296. In 1997, I could not find any of these documents under Patronato 296. None of my efforts and those of friendly archivists at the Archivo de Indias succeeded in tracing the whereabouts of the documentation cited by Ronan.
210. AJPT, shelf 4A, box 17, folder 1, observation 1, 3, "Observaciones americanas y suplemento crítico a la historia del ex-jesuita Francisco Clavijero (tercera parte)." My references to the manuscripts by Diosdado located at the AJPT differ from those offered in Ronan. In my visit to the archive in the summer of 1997, I found Diosdado's papers in disarray and, where catalogued, under misleading titles. The person responsible for the archive, Father José Torres García, graciously allowed me to reorganize and give new titles to them. I am solely responsible for the reorganization.
211. AJPT, shelf 4A, box 17, folder 6, "Extractos de *Historia del Perú* de Garcilaso y de *Lettere Americana* de Carli."
212. AJPT, shelf 4A, box 17, folder 1, observation 10, 74.
213. Ibid., observation 14, 100 (on whether Moctezuma knew about the plot of the Cholulans to ambush the Spaniards while they had them as guests in their city). See also ibid., observation 13, 87–88 (on Clavijero's refusal to believe the account of the Tlaxcalans that the Cholulans had mistreated and killed their emissaries sent by Cortés); ibid., observation 19, 163 (on the willingness of Clavijero to believe an Amerindian source that claimed that Alvarado had massacred the Mexica nobility during a festival only because he wanted to get their possessions, not because the nobility had assembled to rise up against their Spanish hosts); ibid., observation 20, 165 ff. (on Clavijero's willingness to believe the indigenous accounts of the killing of Moctezuma by Spaniards).
214. NYPL, Rich Collection, MS 17, "Cargos hechos por el Sr. D. Bautista Muñoz contra el abate Filibero de Parri Palma o sea el Abate Ramón Diosdado

Caballero sobre la Historia antigua de México por el Abate Francisco Xavier Clavijero [Jan. 1786]," 159r–186v. This manuscript has been reproduced in Onis. For Muñoz' s casting of Diosdado as a radical skeptic, see Onis, 80.

215. Diosdado Caballero, *Eroismo*.

216. Ibid., 43.

217. Ibid., 147–49.

218. Ibid., 106.

219. Ibid., 130–31.

220. ARAH, Actas, bk. 4, Apr. 3, 10, 13, and 24, 1767.

221. AGI, Indiferente general, 1521, Francisco Pérez Bayer, "Responde a orden del rey de informar si supiese de algun sujeto habil para el empleo de cosmógrafo," Feb. 17, 1770 (in which the influential Valencian courtier Pérez Bayer introduces Muñoz as the most qualified candidate). On the circle of influential Valencians at court (Francisco Pérez Bayer, Vicente Blanco, and Raimundo Magí), see Ballesteros Beretta, "Don Juan Bautista Muñoz: Dos facetas científicas," 8–9; and Mestre, *Historia, fueros*, 333–34. Muñoz got the job despite having only published a treatise on the usefulness of the new sciences for theology, *De recto philosophiae recentis in theologia usu* (Valencia, 1767).

222. AGI, Indiferente general, 1520, "Real orden declarando inútil el empleo de Cosmógrafo de Indias que ha sido reemplazado por los establecimientos hechos en la marina," Mar. 14, 1784. See also Lafuente and Selles.

223. On Muñoz's request for guidelines and the answer of the navy's top mathematician, Jorge Juan y Santacilia, declaring Muñoz's post superfluous, see AGI, Indiferente general, 1521, Juan y Santacilia, "Informe sobre empleo de cosmógrafo a raiz de la solicitud de empleo para la posición de cosmógrafo de J. B. Muñoz," June 13, 1771. During Muñoz's years as cosmographer, he edited the sixteenth-century work of Luis de Granada, *Sylva locorum communium* (1771) and *Collectanea moralis philosophiae* (1775), to which he appended an essay titled "De scriptorum gentilium lectione, et profanarum disciplinarum studiis ad chrstianae pietatis." Muñoz had already made available Luis de Granada's *Ecclesiasticae rhetoricae* in 1768.

224. On the ideological alliance of Campomanes and Pozzi, see Sánchez-Blanco Parody, 274–75. On the decision of the Council of Castile to translate the book, see Muñoz, *Juicio a Pozzi*, 13.

225. ARJB, división 13, legajo 5, 8, # 3, Muñoz to Cavanilles, June 3, 1778, fol. 1r; and ARAH, 9/6462, Muñoz, "Cartas a un doctor de Salamanca sobre la apología del M. R. Padre Don Cesareo Pozzi. Precede la historia de esta controversia," 68–69 (in which Muñoz maintains that the Inquisition condemned Pozzi's *Saggio* in July 1779).

226. Antonio Mestre has argued that Muñoz was motivated to attack Pozzi because the latter had publicly humiliated as ignorant one of the Valencians at court. See Mestre, *Historia, fueros*, 333–34. That the confrontation was not only with Pozzi but with Campomanes as well is clearly attested by a document written by Muñoz on Dec. 18, 1787, to the secretary of state, Count Floridablanca, requesting protection from Campomanes. Muñoz identified the confrontation over Pozzi's treatise as the source of Campomanes's hatred: "my book against Pozzi's treatise on education irritated Campomanes so much that at the council he publicly made clear his desire to hurt me [*ánimo inclinado a perderme*]." See *Catálogo colección Muñoz*, 3: lxxxvii.

227. Muñoz, *Juicio a Pozzi*, 8, 9.
228. Ibid., 81.
229. Ibid., 82, 96 (on original sin as a justification for the existence of the state).
230. Ibid., 103–4.
231. Ibid., 111,
232. Ibid., 116.
233. Lopez, 149–87.
234. ARAH, 9/6462, 53, Muñoz, "Cartas a un doctor de Salamanca sobre Pozzi."
235. ARJB, división 13, legajo 5, 8, # 3, Muñoz to Cavanilles, June 3, 1778, fol. 1r–v. On how the Valencian botanist Cavanilles transformed taxonomy into a patriotic project while in Paris, see ARJB, división 13, legajo 5, 2, # 11, Juan Andrés to Cavanilles, Aug. 28, 1786, fol. 1r ("I am very pleased to know that you have sought to honor our nation naming its plants after those of ours who have known [botany]. This is an indirect apology of our nation. If you and others could continue doing this, we would not have need of any other apologias"). See also, ARJB, división 13, legajo 5, 2, # 14, Andrés to Cavanilles, May 2, 1987, fol. 1r.
236. For a description of a part of the collection, see *Catálogo colección Muñoz*, which describes in detail the contents of 76 of 95 folio volumes of documentation collected by Muñoz now located at the Academy of History. The remaining 19 volumes can be found today at the Royal Library. The catalogue also includes a short description of 18 quarto volumes, also located at the Royal Library. Muñoz was responsible, too, for pressing the Spanish authorities in Mexico to collect 35 additional volumes known as *Colección memorias de Nueva España* (more on this collection in Chapter 5). The grand total of the collection that Muñoz assembled is 148 volumes.
237. The literature on the founding of the Archivo de Indias is small despite the complexities involved in the mobilization of documents, not to say the many political and cultural dimensions underpinning such an act of centralization. The history of the Archivo de Indias still awaits a complete study comparable to that by Blandine Barret-Kriegel on the centralization of archives in France in the seventeenth and eighteenth centuries in *Académies de l'histoire*. See, however, Gómez Gómez; Solano. The Archive of the Indies, to be sure, was not the first Spanish effort at centralizing colonial information; see, e.g., Manzano; Serrera.
238. ARAH, 9/6462, Muñoz, "Oficio al rey pidiéndole se le permita escribir la historia geográfica de América y que al mismo tiempo se le franquen todos los archivos y bibliotecas con libros y papeles tocantes a este tema," June 8, 1779 (unpaginated). Charles III approved the request on June 17, 1779.
239. Muñoz to Juan Mayans, Aug. 10, 1783, quoted in Mestre, *Historia, fueros*, p. 336.
240. ARAH, 9/6462, Muñoz, "Oficio al rey" (unpaginated).
241. ARJB, división 13, legajo 5, 8, # 9, Muñoz, "Idea de la obra cometida," Nov. 28, 1783, fol. 5 v. This document has been reproduced in Ballesteros Beretta, "Don Juan Bautista Muñoz: La Historia del Nuevo Mundo," 657.
242. ARJB, división 13, legajo 5, 8, # 8, Muñoz to Cavanilles, June 3, 1778, fol. 1v. Muñoz's comments to Cavanilles were part of a larger struggle in Spain over appropriate historiographical styles. The erudite Catalan Antonio de Capmany, acting secretary of the Academy of History, waged a rearguard battle against the publication of

the Spanish translation of the *Critical History of Spain and Spanish Culture* by the Catalan Jesuit Francisco de Masdeu. Masdeu wrote to counter the views of Saverio Bettinelli and Pietro Napoli Signorelli, two Italian scholars who argued that "Spaniards" from Martial and Seneca to Calderón de la Barca and Lope de Vega had contributed to the corruption of Italian good taste. Masdeu originally intended to complete a survey of "Spanish" literature from the Phoenicians to the eighteenth century but unfortunately his life was cut short and he only managed to publish twenty volumes (only two appeared in Italian), bringing his survey up to the Arabs. Back in Spain, however, Capmany worked against the publication of Masdeu's work on the grounds that the Jesuit lacked the propriety required of members of the Republic of Letters. According to Campany, Masdeu's well-intentioned patriotism would only hurt Spain, for to be heard in Europe, Spain required moderate scholarship, not vociferous language insulting foreigners. On this episode, see Saverio Bettinelli, *Del risorgimento d'Italia negli studi nelle arti e ne'costumi dopo il mille* (Bassano: Remondini di Venezia, 1775); Pietro Napoli Signorelli, *Storia critica de' teatri antichi et moderni* (Napoli: Stamperia Simoniana, 1777); Masdeu, *Storia critica dei Spagna e della cultura spagnola in ogni genere* (Fuligno, 1782; Florence, 1787); ARAH, 11/8021, censura # 8, Capmany, "Censura de tomos 5 y 6 de la *Historia crítica de España y de la cultura española* del Abate Masdeu" (ca. 1788); and ARAH, 11/8022, censura # 54, Capmany, "Censura del tomo X de la *Historia crítica de España* del Abate Masdeu" (ca. 1790).

243. ARJB, división 13, legajo 5, 8, # 10, Muñoz, "Razón de la obra cometida," Nov. 16, 1785, fol. 1. Muñoz's "Razón" can also be found at Archivo Histórico Nacional (Spain), Cartas de Indias, box 2, letter # 36. It has been reproduced by Ballesteros Beretta in "Don Juan Bautista Muñoz: La Historia del Nuevo Mundo," 657–60.

244. Onis, 60. On Diosdado's lack of solid documentary foundations, see ibid., 46.

245. Ibid., 99.

246. ARJB, división 13, legajo 5, 8, # 10, Muñoz, "Razón," fol. 4r.

247. Muñoz, *Historia del Nuevo Mundo*, xix.

248. Ibid., xii.

249. Ibid., xviii.

250. Ibid., xxiii.

251. Ibid., viii–ix, xix.

252. ARJB, división 13, legajo 5, 8, # 9, Muñoz, "Idea de la obra cometida," Nov. 28, 1783, fol. 2r.

253. ARJB, división 13, legajo 5, 8, # 10, Muñoz, "Razón de la obra cometida," Nov. 16, 1785, fol. 1v.

254. For the principles organizing Muñoz's collection, see ARJB, división 13, legajo 5, 8, # 9, Muñoz, "Idea de la obra cometida," Nov. 28, 1783, and ARJB, división 13, legajo 5, 8, # 10, Muñoz, "Razón de la obra cometida."

255. On the role of Muñoz on the founding of the archive, see ARAH, 9/6462, Muñoz, "En el que pide se unifiquen todos los archivos de Indias en la Casa de Lonja," Feb. 18, 1784. For a very meticulous narrative of the places that Muñoz visited and the material he gathered during his trips, see Ballesteros Beretta, "Don Juan Bautista Muñoz. Dos facetas científicas," and "Don Juan Bautista Muñoz: La Historia

del Nuevo Mundo." Gálvez died in 1787, and Campomanes used the opportunity to get rid off Muñoz. In 1787 and 1788, events seemed to announce the defeat of Muñoz. In September 1788, however, Muñoz emerged victorious. The new minister charged with the affairs of the Indies, Antonio Porlier, himself a member of the Academy, ruled in favor of Muñoz. With Porlier, the Academy was forced to grant Muñoz membership, as well as to open its collections for consultation. See the various letters dating from this period reproduced in *Catálogo colección Muñoz*, 3: lxxxvi–xcv.

256. Muñoz, *Historia del Nuevo Mundo*, 17.

257. Ibid., 13.

258. Ibid., 20–21.

259. Muñoz, "Ofrece al rey por mano de Porlier los seis primeros de su 'Historia' reseñando el método empleado y los mapas que contienen," July 7, 1791, in *Catálogo colección Muñoz*, 3: xcvii.

260. "Dictamen de los cuatro censores," Oct. 5, 1791, in ibid., 3: xcviii–c.

261. José de Guevara Vasconcelos, "Dictamen," Nov. 10, 1791, in ibid., 3: cx.

262. Guevara, "Dictamen," in ibid., 3: cxiv.

263. ARAH 11/8025, # 10, José de Guevara y Vasconcelos, "Parecer sobre Idea enviada del Consejo a la Academia," Sept. 28, 1770 (unpaginated).

264. On the sudden turn to the right after the Revolution, see Herr, 239 ff. On Campomanes's declining grip on power, see Castro, ch. 7.

265. On Almodóvar translation, see Tietz.

266. On the confrontation between Almodovar and Campomanes surrounding the review, see the documents in *Catálogo colección Muñoz*, 3: cxvi–cxliii.

267. ARAH, 11/8235, Muñoz, "Sobre las dificultades que se ofrecen para ilustrar la historia nacional y algunos medios de vencerlas," Jan. 6, 1792.

268. Iturri, 99.

269. Ibid., 92.

270. Ibid., 120.

271. Muñoz, "Respuesta al voto particular del Sr. José de Guevara," in Fernández Duro, 42–43.

272. ARAH, 9/6462, Muñoz to Gálvez, Apr. 1, 1783, requesting permission to leave Simancas for the Franciscan Convent of Tolosa to copy Sahagún's manuscripts.

273. See the lists drawn up by Muñoz, "Royal Orders" of 1784 and Feb. 21, 1790, in Glass, *Boturini Collection*, 9, 28, 54–55.

274. Onis, 44.

275. Muñoz, "Memoria sobre las apariciones," 693–94.

276. Muñoz, *Satisfacción a la carta*, 11. Muñoz's history appeared in Germany as *Geschichte der neuen Welt* (Weimar: Im Verlage des Industrie-Comptoirs, 1795) and in England as *The History of the New World* (London: G. G. & J. Robinson, 1797).

277. Maravall, "El sentimiento de nación"; Lopez.

278. Thompson, "Castile, Spain"; cf. Koenigsberger, who argues that Spanish "nationalism" until the nineteenth century was an empty shell, the instrument of the Castilian elite, who used it blindly to advance their interests over those of other regions in Iberia and of Castile itself. Although the abstraction of the Spanish "nation" was an ancient rhetorical figure that went back to Roman antiquity and was crafted by both Castilian and non-Castilian intellectuals, particularly early modern historians

who found in Annius of Viterbo's forged chronicles material to imagine a glorious pre-Roman past for the entire peninsula, it remained a discourse with no practical political consequences, limited to a small literate elite. The masses created a confessional protonational identity in seeking to consolidate a homogeneous religious community that excluded Jews and Arabs (and *conversos*). According to Koenigsberger, a common ruler and religion, not history, provided a sense of belonging to a larger community beyond the merely local.

279. Elliott, *Imperial Spain*; id., "Decline of Spain."

CHAPTER 4: THE MAKING OF A
"PATRIOTIC EPISTEMOLOGY"

1. As far as I know, the first mention of Velasco's *Historia* appeared in Quito in the periodical *Primicias de la Cultura de Quito* 2 (Jan. 19, 1792): 17–18.

2. Velasco, 1: 21–23 (Velasco's own account of the evolution of his writings), 1: 360–64 (a summary of the continuity of the kingdom of Quito after assimilating two separate invaders). For a typical nationalist reading of Velasco's history, see Jorge Salvador Lara, "Semblanza," in Velasco, 1: 500–501; Piedad Costales, "El padre Juan de Velasco, historiador de una cultura," in Velasco, 2: 7–80; Juan Valdano, *Ecuador: Cultura y generaciones* (Quito: Editorial Planeta, 1987), ch. 9.

3. Brading, *Origins*. Brading has expanded his thesis of Creole patriotism in *First America*.

4. Brading, *Origins*, pt. 3.

5. Thurner, ch. 1. For a comparative study of popular liberalism in Mexico and Peru, see Mallon. Brading's analysis of nineteenth-century Mexican histories of the Aztecs needs some qualification. Widdifield, ch. 3, demonstrates that Creole historiographical themes resurfaced in painting in the second half of the nineteenth century. See also Tenorio-Trillo, esp. 64–124. Thurner's statements about Peru also need qualification; see, e.g., Méndez; Walker, *Smoldering Ashes*. Walker demonstrates that Inca millenarianism continued unabated among the Creoles of Cuzco, particularly during the period of the Gamarrista Republic (chs. 5–6).

6. On continuity and change among indigenous elites in central Mexico and Yucatan, see Lockhart, ch. 4; Farriss, 96–103, 164–68, 174–92, and 227–55.

7. For an illuminating account of how significant these confrontations were in the early history of colonization, see Clendinnen, *Ambivalent Conquests*.

8. Rubial García.

9. Pagden, *European Encounters*, 56–87.

10. W. Taylor, *Magistrates*. The reforms also undermined nunneries and their role as sources of credit for Indian and Creole elites; see, e.g., Burns, ch. 6.

11. On the threat and characterization of mestizos, see Cope, ch. 1. The threat of *mestizaje* also had a gender component, see Burns, ch. 1 and pp. 119–27.

12. Anderson; Hobsbawn and Ranger. For a critical survey of "modernist" theories that sees the nation-state as a recent creation, see Anthony D. Smith, *Nationalism and Modernism*.

13. Chakrabarty.

14. Efraín Castro Morales pointed out as long ago as 1961 that Eguiara y Eguren was one among many in the mid eighteenth century who mobilized to respond to Martí's demeaning views of the Indies; see Castro Morales. Building on this insight, Ernesto de la Torre Villar has more recently sought to present a broader picture of the range of the clerical-Creole reaction and has also demonstrated that the learned Creoles identified Nicolás Antonio, not only Martí, among their nemeses. See Torre Villar, "Defensa y elogio." For Antonio's and Martí's derogatory views, see Manuel Martí, *Epistolarum libri XII*, 2 vols. (Mantua: Joannem Stunicam, 1735), letter addressed to Antonio Carrillo; and Nicolás Antonio, *Censura de historias fabulosas; obra póstuma. Van añadidas algunas cartas del mismo autor y de otros eruditos. Publica estas obras Don Gregorio Mayans y Siscar* (Valencia: Antonio Bordázar de Artázu, 1742), letter addressed to Juan Lucas Cortés.

15. Eguiara y Eguren, *Prólogos*, 124–25, 203–4, 218–19.

16. Ibid., 82–83, 115.

17. Ibid., 169.

18. Ibid., 165–66, 193, 221.

19. Ibid., 66, 199.

20. Ibid., 77.

21. Ibid., 78.

22. When Echeverría y Veytia died in 1780, his wife gave the authorities of New Spain a set of manuscripts that included histories of four of the most popular religious images in Mexico, a history of the city of Puebla, and, more important, an incomplete history of ancient Mexico. See Moreno Bonett, 173–91.

23. Echeverría y Veytia, *Historia antigua* 1: 243.

24. Ibid., 1: 13–17.

25. Ibid., 1: 19.

26. Ibid., 1: 23, 77.

27. Ibid., 1: 114.

28. Ibid., 1: 133.

29. Ibid., 1: 146.

30. Ibid., 1: 112.

31. Ibid., 1: 65; Echeverría y Veytia, "Discurso preliminar," 319.

32. Echeverría y Veytia, *Historia antigua*, 1: 51–52.

33. Ibid., 1: 167; see also 1: 6 and 28.

34. Ibid., 1: 178–79, 191.

35. Ibid., 1: 193–94.

36. Ibid., 1: 24, 35, 114, 166; Echeverría y Veytia, "Discurso preliminar," 316.

37. Ibid., 302–4.

38. Alva Ixtlilxochitl, *Obras históricas*, 1: 287–88.

39. Echeverría y Veytia, "Discurso preliminar," 307; see also 305.

40. Echeverría y Veytia, *Historia antigua*, 1: 24–26.

41. Alva Ixtlilxochitl, *Obras históricas*, 1: 288; Echeverría y Veytia, "Discurso preliminar," 307–8.

42. Lockhart, ch. 7.

43. Echeverría y Veytia, "Discurso preliminar," 304–5, 319–20.

44. Gibson, *Aztecs*, 287–88.

45. Lockhart, 357–64; Florescano, 110–20; Gruzinski, ch. 3; Haskett. On *títulos primordiales* in the Yucatec-Mayan context, see Restall, 56–58.

46. Lockhart, 410–18; Wood.

47. "Los monumentos de donde las he sacado tienen toda aquella autoridad, solidez y recomendación que es posible en el asunto, y son los mismos en que se han fundado los [muchos] autores nuestros y extranjeros en las noticias que han publicado desfiguradas y dislocadas por falta de explicación o cautela de aquellos nacionales de quienes las hubieron." Echeverría y Veytia "Discurso preliminar," 300.

48. Echeverría y Veytia, *Historia antigua*, 1: 116–17.

49. Ibid., 123–24. Echeverría y Veytia's copy of Duarte's manuscript was published, with related documents, by Nicolás León in *Bibliografía mexicana del siglo XVIII*, under the title "El apostol Santo Tomás en el Nuevo Mundo." For Duarte's allegorical interpretation of the map, see Duarte, 513–20. On the identification of the map as a litigation document pitting two rival towns in colonial Oaxaca, see José F. Ramírez, "Introducción," in Duarte, 366–67.

50. In his unfinished, uncorrected manuscript, Echeverría y Veytia derived the name Thomas (from Hebrew *t'ōm* = twin) from the Greek *didymos* (twin), mistakenly believing the latter word to be Hebrew. He derived Quetzalcoatl from *quetzal* (highly esteemed or revered) + *coatl* (twin) in Nahuatl.

51. Echeverría y Veytia, *Historia antigua*, 1: 136–37; 119–34.

52. Ibid., 1: 25, 49, 114.

53. Alva Ixtlilxochitl, *Obras históricas*, 1: 285–87; 517–21; Echeverría y Veytia, "Discurso preliminar," 309; id., *Historia antigua*, 1: 77.

54. On the writings of Tadeo de Niza de Santa María and Hernando Pimentel, see Gibson and Glass, 353, 355–56. On the several sources studied by Alva Ixtlilxochitl, see Edmundo O'Gorman, 1: 47–85. Other Amerindian analysts contemporary to Alva Ixtlilxochitl such as Domingo de San Antón Muñón Chimalpain Cuauhtlehuanitzin (Chalcan) were also collectors of documents produced by natives. Chimalpain Cuauhtlehuanitzin copied and glossed the chronicles of Hernando Alvarado Tezozomoc (Mexica) and those of Gabriel de Ayala (Texcocan). Chimalpain Cuauhtlehuanitzin also studied and glossed the chronicle of López de Gómara and was a careful reader of Enrico Martínez's *Repertorio de los tiempos e historia natural de Nueva España* (1606). On Chimalpain Cuauhtlehuanitzin, see Susan Schroeder, "Looking Back at the Conquest," 81–94.

55. Alva Ixtlilxochitl, *Obras históricas*, 1: 408, 525.

56. Ibid., 1: 412–13.

57. Alva Ixtlilxochitl, *Historia de la nación chichimeca*.

58. Alva Ixtlilxochitl, *Obras históricas*, 1: 450–517.

59. Gibson, *Aztecs*, 17.

60. Florescano, 126–31. Florescano takes a harsh view of the writings of "mestizos" such as Alva Ixtlilxochitl; he presents them as imitators of European historiographic models, incapable of "[creating] their own authentic discourse" and willfully distorting traditional native historiography (130). Such views reinforce those very colonial discourses Florescano seeks to criticize by reifying the separate and bipolar cate-

gories of "Indian" and "European." On the many histories by sixteenth-century native elites, see Gruzinski, *Painting the Conquest*, ch. 3; Boone; Mundy.

61. O'Gorman, 1: 225. O'Gorman depicts Alva Ixtlilxochitl as collecting stories of the miracles the image brought the pious. He also argues that Alva Ixtlilxochitl collected the Nahuatl play on the encounter of Juan Diego and the Virgin upon which the entire Creole patriotic narrative of the historicity of the miracle of Our Lady of Guadalupe rested. Stafford Poole, however, disagrees and denies Alva Ixtlilxochitl any role in the emergence of the story; see, Poole, 85–87. On the linkage of the cult of Our Lady of Guadalupe and Creole patriotism, see Poole; Brading, *First America*, ch. 16; Lafaye.

62. O'Gorman, 1: 212–13.

63. Schwaller. On the close proximity between Amerindian elites and the Church in Cuzco, see Burns, 15–40, 88–90, 123–27, 149–52.

64. Lockhart, ch. 4.

65. Brading, *First America*, 273. On the late-sixteenth-century colonial practice of appointing Amerindian outsiders as *tlatoanies* (rulers) of Amerindian communities, see Lockhart, 33–35.

66. O'Gorman argues that in the relationship between Torquemada and Alva Ixtlilxochitl, it was the former who drew from the researches of the latter. See O'Gorman, 1: 204.

67. Schwaller, 95, 101. Sigüenza also inherited Bartolomé de Alva Ixtlilxochitl's chantry (Schwaller, 97).

68. Leonard.

69. Echeverría y Veytia, *Historia antigua*, 1: 107–11, 256; Moreno Bonett, 46. On the literature produced by many of these colonial Nahua annalists, see Lockhart, 376–92; Florescano, 120–31. Although the Mayan elites of Yucatan were not as easily assimilated as those of central Mexico, an indigenous historiography resembling that of the Creoles did surface. The works of the mid-sixteenth-century Mayan scholar Gaspar Antonio Chi are a case in point. On Chi, see Karttunen, 84–114; Restall, 144–48.

70. Echeverría y Veytia also knew the writings of the late-seventeenth-century Nahua annalist, Juan Buenaventura Zapata y Mendoza (Tlaxcalan) and drew from the latter's annals for his history of Puebla. See Echeverría y Veytia, *Historia de Puebla*, 1: 35. Lord Kinsborough, a prominent nineteenth-century British editor of Mesoamerican codices and sixteenth-century indigenous writers, refused to publish more than the first 23 introductory chapters of Echeverría y Veytia's incomplete manuscript, leaving out the rest on the grounds that they were merely a copy of works by Alva Ixtlilxochitl, Alvarado Tezozomoc, and Chimalpain Cuauhtlehuanitzin. See Moreno Bonett, 182. On Muñoz Camargo, Alvarado Tezozomoc, and Zapata y Mendoza, see Gibson and Glass, 326–27, 350–51, 378.

71. Echeverría y Veytia, *Historia antigua*, 1: 33, 66–67, 70.

72. Ibid., 1: 46–77, and bk. 1, ch. 6.

73. Ibid., 1: 36.

74. Ibid., 1: 30–31, 42.

75. Ibid., 1: 39.

76. Ibid., 1: 36–38.

77. Ibid., 1: 66–67.

78. Gemelli Careri, vol. 1, ch. 4 (description of map of migrations), ch. 5 (cabalistic analysis of the names of Mexica emperors), and ch. 6 (analysis of calendrical wheel).

79. Echeverría y Veytia, *Historia antigua*, 1: 46, 48–49.

80. Ibid., 1: 71, 33.

81. Ibid., 1: 79.

82. Granados y Gálvez, introduction (unpaginated), 4, 11–12, 23, 228.

83. Ibid., 5–7, 108, 228–30.

84. Ibid., 187–91, 197.

85. Ibid., 191–92.

86. Ibid., 124–29, 194–97.

87. Ibid., 80–84.

88. Ibid., 51–52, 73–75.

89. Ibid., 229–30. This, to be sure, was an unfair criticism, for Sigüenza y Góngora, who thought that the Mexica were Satan's elect, had publicly praised the political virtues of Mexica monarchs in 1680. See Sigüenza y Góngora.

90. Ladd, 21, 235 (n. 28). For leading Creole families in Cuzco who claimed Inca ancestry, see Burns, 162–70, and Lavallé. I owe the reference of the family palace of the counts of Santiago Calimaya to William Taylor, personal communication.

91. Granados y Gálvez, 256–58, 272, 368.

92. Morner.

93. Ronan, ch. 1.

94. Ronan; Brading, *First America*, ch. 20; Pagden, *Spanish Imperialism*, ch. 4; Cervantes, epilogue; Florescano, 190–92; Keen, 292–300. See also Martínez.

95. Ronan, 187–89, 217–21.

96. See n. 94 above.

97. BN-S, MS 12467, Francisco Clavijero, "Vexamen 2. Banquete de la philosophía," 33–72. Clavijero uses the analogy of a banquet to argue that knowledge should draw freely from different "pantries, for according to [Sir Francis] Bacon no pantry holds everything." Clavijero therefore encourages students to learn from scholasticism, atomism, Cartesianism, and Newtonianism. Clavijero drew from Bacon an eclectic approach to natural philosophy as well as a distaste for systems.

98. Clavijero, *Historia antigua*, bk. 6, sec. 10 (pp. 159–62).

99. Ibid., bk. 7 (pp. 202–3, 206–7, 209–11). For criticisms to the Codex Mendoza, see, e.g., ibid., bk. 3, n. 2; bk. 4, nn. 5, 12, and 13; and diss. 2 (pp. 448–53).

100. Ibid., bk. 1 (pp. 1–6); diss. 7 (pp. 558–61).

101. See, e.g., ibid., bk. 9, n. 11 (p. 351) and n. 45 (p. 370).

102. Ibid., bk. 8, n. 26 (p. 315).

103. Ibid., diss. 9, sec. 4 (p. 586).

104. Clavijero's critical principles are summarized in ibid., bk. 6, n. 24 (pp. 161–62); bk. 8, n. 26 (p. 315) and n. 36 (p. 327); diss. 6, sec. 5 (pp. 537–42); diss. 7, sec. 2 (pp. 561–70).

105. See, e.g., ibid., bk. 9, n. 17 (p. 356).

106. Ibid., bk. 2, 52–53; see also diss. 2, sec. 1 (p. 444).

107. Ibid., Prólogo, xxx; bk. 2, n. 18 (p. 56); bk. 3, n. 4 (p. 83); and diss. 2, *passim*.

108. Ibid., Prólogo, xxxiii–xxxiv; bk. 7, sec. 19 (p. 221), sec. 47 (pp. 247–48); sec. 49 (pp. 250–51).

109. Ibid., bk. 5, sec. 10–12 (pp. 137–41).

110. Ibid., bk. 13, n. 32 (p. 324); bk. 9, n. 19 (p. 356).

111. Ibid., Prólogo, xxiii; bk. 6, sec. 1 (p. 149) and sec. 27 (p. 180); bk. 2, n. 9 (p. 51).

112. Ibid., diss. 2, sec. 1 (p. 444); diss. 1, sec. 2. (p. 431).

113. Ibid., diss. 2, sec. 1 (pp. 446–47).

114. Ibid., Prólogo, xxxvii; bk. 7, n. 6 (p. 215).

115. Lorenzana, 176.

116. I have consulted the modern edition, *Matrícula de tributos*.

117. Clavijero, *Historia antigua*, bk. 2, sec. 2 (p. 51) and n. 9 (p. 51).

118. Ibid., bk. 7, sec. 13 (p. 213) and n. 3 (p. 213).

119. Ibid., diss. 5, sec. 1 (p. 509).

120. Ibid., bk. 10, sec. 33 (p. 418); diss. 5, sec. 2 (pp. 518–19).

121. Ibid., diss. 5, sec. 1 (p. 508).

122. Ibid., Prólogo, xxxii–xxxiii.

123. Ibid., diss. 4, sec. 1 (pp. 477–79) and n. 66 (p. 500). On the same theme, see diss. 5, sec. 1 (p. 506).

124. Ibid., diss. 6, sec. 4 (p. 531).

125. Ibid., diss. 5, sec. 2 (p.521); diss. 6, sec. 6 (p. 545).

126. Ibid., diss. 5, sec. 2 (pp. 512–13).

127. Ibid., diss. 7, sec. 2 (pp. 567–68).

128. See Jorge Salvador Lara, "Semblanza del padre Juan de Velasco, historiador del Reino de Quito," in Velasco, 1: 475–501.

129. Velasco, 2: 443–44 (5.13.1–2).

130. On these manuscripts, see ibid., 2: 116 (1.5.15). They are now lost.

131. Ibid., 2, introduction (unpaginated); 2: 81–82 (1.1); 2: 91 (1.2.8) (on Cara-Shyri writing); 2: 92 (1.2.11) (on contradictory and rival chronologies for the Cara).

132. Ibid., 1: 195 (3.4.1); 1: 209 (3.5.12); 1: 183 (3.3.1–22); 1: 181 (3.2.6–16); 1: 216–17 (3.6.1).

133. Ibid., 1: 57 (1.1.10); 1: 171–72 (3.1.5); 1: 256 (4.intro. 2); 1: 314 (4.8.1).

134. On this aspect of early modern epistemology, see Locke 4.15.4. See also Daston and Park, 250.

135. Velasco, 1: 158 (2.8).

136. Ibid., 1: 158–62 (2.8); 1: 163–67 (2.9); 1: 222–24 (3.6.2); 1: 230–32 (3.7.2); 1: 209–12 (3.5.4); 1: 191–92 (3.3.7); 1: 252–55 (3.9).

137. Ibid., 1: 74 (1.3.8); 1: 212 (3.5.17); 1: 434 (Catálogo).

138. Ibid., 1: 342 (6.8.23).

139. Acosta, *Historia natural*, Proemio, 56–57; Velasco, 1: 331 (4.9).

140. Ibid., 1: 307 (4.7.14).

141. Ibid., 1: 222 (3.9.12); 1: 224 (3.9.15); 1: 192–93 (3.3); 1: 331 (4.9.1); 1: 42–43 (4.9.24).

142. Ibid., 3: 120–21 (2.4.27–33).

143. Ibid., 2: 443–45 (5.13).

144. Ibid., 3: 147–52 (2.7).

145. Ibid., 1: 339–40 (4.9.18); 1: 343 (4.9.25); 1: 349 (4.9.36); 1: 357 (4.10.13).
146. Ibid., 1: 224 (3.6.15).
147. Molina, ch. 1 (1: 46).
148. Ibid., Preface (1: xiv–xv). On this, see, e.g., Molina's use of travel accounts to support his claims about Chile's great agricultural productivity (ch. 1, 1: 45–46).
149. Frézier, *Relation*, 218–31, 240–47. On representations of Spanish America in seventeenth- and eighteenth-century travel narratives as a promiscuous and corrupting place, see Cañizares-Esguerra, "Travel Accounts."
150. Molina, Preface (1: x–xi).
151. Ibid., (1: xiv).
152. Ibid., (1: xv–xvii), ch. 1 (1: 73).
153. Ibid., Preface (1: xiii–xiv).
154. For a sense of the extraordinary volume of writings by Creole Jesuits in exile, see the bibliography compiled in Vargas Alquicira, 86–166.
155. Pedro José Márquez, *Delle case di cittá degli antichi romani secondo la dottrina di Vitruvio* (Rome: Presso il Salmoni, 1795); *Delle ville di Plinio il giovane, con un appendice su gli atrii della s. scrittura, e gli scamilli impari di Vitruvio* (Rome: Presso il Salmoni, 1796); *Sobre lo bello en general* (Madrid: Oficina del Diario, 1801); *Dell' ordine dorico, ricerche dedicate alla Reale accademia di S. Luigi di Saragoza Con appendice sopra un' antica tav. di Pozzuolo* (Rome: Presso il Salmoni, 1803).
156. León y Gama, *Saggio*. More on León y Gama's work in Chapter 5.
157. Márquez, "Apendix," 169–82.
158. Carrega, "Approvazione," in *Saggio dell' astronomia*, xii–xiii.
159. Márquez, *Due antichi monumenti*, i–ii.
160. More on José Antonio de Alzate y Ramírez in Chapter 5.
161. This statement was indeed daring, for since the Conquest the natives' alleged failure to have developed arches was used by the Spaniards as a colonialist discourse of legitimization. In a previous work, Márquez had already presented Mesoamerican saunas (*temexcalli*) as evidence that indicated the Indians' mastery of dome-building techniques; see Márquez, *Delle case di città degli antichi romani*, xiv–xv, 362–64. On the discourse of classical architecture to justify colonization in Spanish America, see Fraser.
162. Márquez, *Due antichi monumenti*, 19. On this topic, see also Márquez's notes in Leon y Gama, *Saggio dell' astronomia*, 71 (n. 1).
163. "I Messicani d'adesso sono destinati a fare nella gran commedia del mondo la rappresentanza della plebe" (Márquez, *Due antichi monumenti*, 24).
164. Fábrega.
165. Ibid., 71 (par. 11), 30–34 (pars. 52–61).
166. Ibid., 38–47 (pars. 67–85).
167. Ibid., 44 (par. 80).
168. Ibid., 38 (par. 67).
169. Ibid., 3 (dedication).
170. Ibid., 80–81 (par. 24).
171. Ibid., 39 (par. 69).
172. Ibid., 259–60 (par. 313).
173. Ibid., 11 (par. 15).

174. Ibid., 6 (par. 4) where Fábrega mistakenly identifies the Codex Mendoza as a precolonial source and therefore gives it too much credence. Both Boturini and Clavijero had already declared their skepticism of the accuracy of the historical annals in the codex published by Purchas.

175. Ibid., 12–13 (par. 17).

176. Ibid., 42 (pars. 75–76).

177. W. Taylor, "'. . . de corazón pequeño." See also Walker, "Patriotic Society."

178. On the debates over the abolition of the *repartimiento* and the nature of the Indian, see Brading, *Miners and Merchants*, 47–51, 84–86; MacLachlan and Rodríguez, 261–63. 268–70.

179. Malaspina, 155, 157.

180. Acosta, *Procuranda indorum salute*, bk. 1, ch. 7, 147; bk. 3, ch. 9, 443; bk. 3, ch. 13, 487; bk. 3, ch. 17, 513; Solórzano y Pereira, 1: 176–77. Solórzano y Pereira's work first appeared as *Disputationem de indiarum iure*, 2 vols. (Madrid: Francisco Martínez, 1629–39). It was later enlarged, translated, and published as *Política indiana* (Madrid: Diego Díaz de la Carrera, 1648).

181. Montesquieu, 1: 240, 226, 270.

182. Algarotti, 336.

183. AMN, Colección Malaspina, MS 119, "Caracter, usos y costumbres de los Indios, tributos que pagan al soberano, método de su cobranza y estado de ramo y reflexiones de los repartimientos antiguos y modernos," fols. 180–89.

184. AMN, Colección Malaspina, MS 562, Antonio Pineda, "Viaje de Antonio Pineda desde Acapulco a Méjico y de allí a Guanajuato," fols. 10v, 42v, 128r.

185. Cañizares-Esguerra, "Utopía de Hipólito Unanue."

CHAPTER 5: WHOSE ENLIGHTENMENT WAS
IT ANYWAY?

1. Dorinda Outram builds on insights first developed by Jürgen Habermas. On recent studies of the rise and dynamics of the public sphere, see Calhoun. For "traditional" interpretations of the Enlightenment, see Cassirer; Gay.

2. Outram, 6. Outram's more generous vision draws on Venturi, *Settecento riformatore* (for Italy and eastern Europe) and Aldridge.

3. Outram, 17–18.

4. The contributors to *The Ibero-American Enlightenment*, ed. A. Owen Aldridge, continue to define the Enlightenment from a Eurocentric perspective. The volume makes serious efforts not to exclude "peripheral areas" such as Spain and Spanish America by highlighting the movement's utilitarian and critical dimensions. From this vantage point, the authors in the volume identify a Catholic Enlightenment, in general, and an Ibero-American one, in particular. In an earlier work, Arthur P. Whitaker, a contributor to Aldridge's collection, sought to characterize the Spanish-American Enlightenment in terms of the paradox of Spanish America's "dual role" in the eighteenth century, arguing that Spanish America was both an active participant in the critical utilitarian values of the movement and the movement's principal target of criticism. It exemplified all that had gone wrong with European colonialism. Whitaker does not recognize that in the tensions produced by this dual role lay the

seeds of alternative critical discourses that were not mere copies of northwestern European epistemologies. See Whitaker, "Dual Role."

5. Levine, *Dr. Woodward's Shield*; id., *Battle of the Books*.

6. For a history of the discovery and fate of seven different stones found in the central plaza, see León y Gama, *Descripción histórica*, 1: 8–13; 2: 46 (par. 120); 2: 73–74 (pars. 144–45); 2: 76 (par. 147); and 2: 79 (par. 149).

7. Ocelotl Tecuilhuitzintli, *Gaceta de México* 4, no. 40 (Aug. 12, 1791): 377–79.

8. Alzate y Ramírez, *Gaceta de México* 4, no. 42 (Sept. 1791): 396.

9. *Gaceta de México* 5, no. 2 (Jan. 1792): 14, and no. 9 (May 1792): 88.

10. I have used the 1832 edition by Bustamente. This edition also includes León y Gama's study of other stones found in Mexico City, but it was never published during the latter's lifetime. For a biographical study of León y Gama, see Moreno de los Arcos, "Ensayo biobibliográfico"; id., "Historia antigua de México."

11. León y Gama, *Descripción histórica*, 1: 59–61 (pars. 41–43).

12. Ibid., 1: 47–49 (n. 3).

13. Ibid., 1: 26 (nn. 1–4) and 1: 27 (n. 1).

14. Ibid., 1: 49–55 (pars. 34–39).

15. Ibid., 1: 29–33 (pars. 14–16).

16. Ibid., 1: 81–83 (pars. 49–50).

17. Ibid., 1: 84–89 (pars. 52–56).

18. Ibid., 1: 112–14 (par. 82).

19. Ibid., 1: 36 (par. 21) and 1: 40 (par. 23). León y Gama's views on Aztec aesthetics resemble those recently put forth by Inga Clendinnen. Like León y Gama, Clendinnen is struck by the realism that characterizes Aztec sculptures of vegetables and of small animals and the almost willful distortion of representations of bigger animals and of the human figure. Clendinnen has argued that Mexica selective realistic naturalism sought to capture the essence of small objects, which reportedly resided in their surface appearance. The essence of bigger animals such as leopards and eagles and of humans lay also in their skins (a reason why the Aztecs liked to both flay their victims and wear costumes of fur and feathers and of human skins). Humans and large animals, however, revealed their nature through their behavior rather than their surface appearance. Aztec aesthetic sensibilities, therefore, rejected mimetic representations of these larger objects. See Clendinnen, *Aztecs*, ch. 9.

20. Ibid., 1: 35–44 (pars. 20–29).

21. Ibid., 1: 104–8 (pars. 73–76).

22. Ibid., 1: 100 (par. 67).

23. Ibid., 1: 94–5 (par. 62).

24. Alzate y Ramírez is one of the most studied figures of the Mexican Enlightenment. See, e.g., Peset, pt. 1; Moreno de los Arcos, "Eclesiástico criollo." The papers Alzate y Ramírez sent to the French Académie des sciences were published in *Voyage en Californie* by the abbé Jean-Baptiste Chappe d'Auteroche, who led an expedition organized by the Académie to Mexico to measure the transit of Venus and the satellites of Jupiter in order to calculate longitudes. D'Auteroche received the collaboration of several Creole scholars while in Mexico, including Alzate y Ramírez, León y Gama, José Ignacio Bartolache, and Joaquín Velázquez de León.

25. BN-P (G-A), MS 331, León y Gama to Lalande, Apr. 26, 1772, 7v.

26. Ibid., Lalande to León y Gama, May 5, 1773, 5r.

27. Ibid., Lalande to León y Gama, Sept. 12, 1774, 4r.

28. León y Gama, "Discurso sobre la luz septentrional que se vio en esta ciudad el día 14 de noviembre de 1789, entre 8 y 9 de la noche," *Gaceta de México* 3, no. 44 (Dec. 1, 1789): 432–35, and no. 45 (Dec. 22, 1789): 444–47; Alzate y Ramírez, "Carta del autor de la Gaceta de literatura al discurso que publicó un anónimo en la [Gaceta] política sobre la aurora borcal," *Gacetas de literatura* 1 (Mar. 8, 1790): 301–10; León y Gama, *Disertación física*; Alzate y Ramírez, "Novedad literaria: Disertación (nombrada) física sobre la materia y formación de las auroras boreales," *Gacetas de literatura* 1 (Aug. 16, 1790): 423.

29. León y Gama, *Gaceta de México* 5, no. 13 (July 1793): 124.

30. Alzate y Ramírez," Historia de la Nueva España por el abate La Porte," *Gacetas de literatura* 1 (Jan. 31, 1788): 5–12.

31. Alzate y Ramírez, "Falsedades vertidas por Jorge Amon [*sic*] en la descripción de su viage al rededor del mundo," *Gacetas de literatura* 1 (May 10, 1788): 40 (my emphasis: Alzate y Ramírez described the Mexicans in Manila as commoners of Amerindian descent).

32. Ignaz von Born's treatise first appeared in Vienna in 1786 under the title *Über das Anquicken der Gold- und silberhaltigen Erze, Rohsteine, Schwarzkupfer und Hüttenspeise*. It was translated to English by R. E. Raspe under the title *Baron Inigo Born's New Process of Amalgamation of Gold and Silver Ores, and other Metallic Mixtures, as by his late Imperial Magesty's Command introduced in Hungary and Bohemia* (London: T. Cadell, 1791). The fact that Alzate y Ramírez reviewed it in 1790 indicates the dynamism of the public sphere and the book market in New Spain.

33. Alzate y Ramírez, "Traducción de algunos artículos del estracto del caballero Born acerca de la estracción de la plata y oro con su correctivo," *Gacetas de literatura* 2 (Dec. 30, 1790): 84–90. For a similar rejection of the modernity that Born represented, but this time in early republican Bolivia, see Platt.

34. Clavijero's critique of the epistemological limitations of European travelers is reiterated in Alzate y Ramírez's notes, e.g., bk. 7, n. 55 (BN-M, MS 1679). See Moreno de los Arcos, "Notas de Alzate." The notes are housed in two different repositories, those corresponding to Clavijero's bks. 1 and 2 are in AMNA, MS 176; those for bks. 6–10 are in BN-M, MS 1679; those for bks. 3–5 are missing.

35. Gilii.

36. Alzate y Ramírez, "Noticia del viage en la América por el Abate Gilli y repulsa de sus falsedades," *Gacetas de literatura* 1 (Jan. 10, 1790): 246–54.

37. His research program is laid out in "Ajolotl es muy eficaz su jarabe para la tisis," *Gacetas de literatura* 2 (Nov. 16, 1790): 52–53. On this aspect of Alzate y Ramírez's work and this dimension of Creole patriotism in general, see Cañizares-Esguerra, "Nation and Nature."

38. The many essays by Alzate y Ramírez and Cervantes that appeared between 1788 and 1790 in *Gacetas de literatura* and *Gaceta de México*, respectively, have been reproduced in Moreno de los Arcos, *Linneo en México*. For an interesting account of the controversy over the reception of Linnaean taxonomies in late-eighteenth-century Spain from the perspective of the resistance of the traditional corporate university to the opening of new alternative institutions, see Tanck de Estrada; Lozoya, ch. 2.

39. For examples of this aspect of Alzate y Ramírez's patriotic epistemology, see "Botánica," *Gacetas de literatura* 1 (Feb. 15–Apr. 8, 1788): 20–27. For an example that carries the paradigm into the law of physics, see "Continua la descripción topográfica de México," *Gacetas de literatura* 2 (Oct. 4–8, 1791): 274–75, 278.

40. Alzate y Ramírez, "Descripción de las antigüedades de Xochicalco," 1. There is a long quotation from Alzate y Ramírez's 1777 manuscript in Moreno de los Arcos, "Eclesiastico criollo," p. 12, which varies substantially from the same passage in the 1791 edition, suggesting that there was indeed an earlier manuscript, but I am unaware of its whereabouts.

41. Alzate y Ramírez, "Descripción de las antigüedades de Xochicalco," dedication (unpaginated).

42. Ibid., pp. 2–9 and nn. 8 and 10.

43. Ibid., p. 21.

44. Ibid., p. 3.

45. On the theme of Amerindian corruption induced by proximity to urban *castas* and on the blurring of hierarchies in Amerindian communities, see AMNA, MS 176, nn. 15, 136, and 139 to bk. 1; BN-M, MS 1679, nn. 24, 25, and 32 to bk. 7. Alzate y Ramírez penned an analysis of the "Indians" of central Mexico for Malaspina in which he went over the same tropes: the corrupting effects of urban commoners and *castas* over the original virginal Amerindian communities and the collapse of social differentiation in them. The document, however, has also positive things to say about the mestizos as forceful leaders in Amerindian communities. See AMN, MS 562, Alzate y Ramírez, "¿Cuáles son los caracteres morales y físicos del indio?" fols. 315–323v. This document has been reproduced twice, by Moreno de los Arcos, in Alzate y Ramírez, *Memorias y ensayos*, 154–65, and by González Claverán, "Notas a un documento."

46. Alzate y Ramírez, "Descripción de las antigüedades de Xochicalco," 16–18.

47. Alzate y Ramírez, "Carta del autor a D.N. sobre los caracteres mexicanos," *Gacetas de literatura* 2 (July 13–31 and Aug. 28, 1792): 416.

48. Ibid., 416–18.

49. Ibid., 424.

50. León y Gama, *Descripción histórica*, 2: 46–73 (pars. 121–143). None of the illustrations of León y Gama's second volume have ever been published before. Some have survived in BN-P (G-A), MS 97. Others, it seems, were never drawn. Through cross-references to indigenous codices in the text and the copies of those codices that belonged to León y Gama and that are part of the Goupil-Aubin collection, I have identified most of the remaining images. This reconstruction could be used one day to issue a new complete edition of Leon y Gama's second treatise.

51. León y Gama, *Descripción histórica*, 2: 11–16 (pars. 87–92). But Castillo appears in fact to have been born in 1526.

52. Flores, *Específico*.

53. García de la Vega.

54. León y Gama, *Instrucción*.

55. Ibid., 21, 30.

56. The debate, to be sure, continued. See Moreno and Sánchez, *Carta apologética*, and León y Gama in *Respuesta satisfactoria*. Moreno and Sánchez had

the last word with the public in *Observaciones crítico-apologéticas*. León y Gama did reply but his treatise was left unpublished. It can be read now in HBC-B, MS M-M 125, "Carta que sobre las Observaciones crítico-apologéticas escribía a un amigo D. Antonio de León y Gama." The debate still awaits a sympathetic historian.

57. León y Gama, *Descripción histórica*, 2: 29–32 (pars. 105–9). In the text, León y Gama never identifies the provenance of the examples he cites. After a painstaking survey of the copies of codices he and José Antonio Pichardo owned, I have identified those from which he drew most of his examples. See legend to Fig. 5.8 for detailed archival references.

58. Ibid., 2: 41–45 (pars. 117–19).

59. Ibid., 2: 37–41 (pars. 114–16) and 2: 142–44 (pars. 207–8).

60. For a synthesis and bibliography of these institutional and cultural changes, see Cañizares-Esguerra, "Spanish America."

61. On the substitution of Peninsular for Creole faculty at the Academy of San Carlos, see Brown. On Alzate y Ramírez's and León y Gama's failed bids to get positions as the Colegio de Minería, see Peset, *Ciencia*, 124, 176–89; Ramírez, 86–88.

62. Lozoya.

63. Susan Schroeder describes how Francisco de San Antón Muñón Chimalpain Cuauhtlehuanitzin's manuscripts left Mexico in the early nineteenth century when the liberal ideologue José María Luis Mora exchanged them for a few Bibles from England to enhance literacy at home. Chimalpain Cuauhtlehuanitzin's works thus lay buried for almost two centuries in the London archives of the Foreign Biblical Society; see Schroeder, "Father José María Luis Mora." On Mora, see Hale.

64. Glass, *Boturini Collection*.

65. Although articles on him have been published by Díaz-Trechuelo and Carrera Stampa (see Bibliography), Diego García Panes still awaits comprehensive study. The manuscripts and drawings of his multivolume illustrated history of ancient Mexico, Theatro de Nueva España, are shelved as BN-M, MSS 1745 and 1876 to 1884. Some of the illustrations and captions have been published in García Panes, *Panorama de Anáhuac* and *La conquista*. García Panes typified the cadre of naval officers trained in the new sciences sent en masse from Spain in the wake of the Bourbon reforms to take over the colonial administration. He worked for many years in cartographic surveys and engineering along the Gulf coast of Mexico, where he also dabbled in archeology. The maps that resulted from his surveys have been published under the title *Diario particular del camino que sigue un Virrey de México*.

Most of the volumes of his Theatro de Nueva España are an illustrated version of Echeverría y Veytia's unpublished history based on drawings of indigenous documents in Boturini's collection. The drawings for the volume narrating the Conquest, however, are based on García Panes's own antiquarian research. For example, he drew some images from a document he commissioned from the indigenous authorities of Tlaxcala, the famous Lienzo de Tlaxcala. After repeated efforts to gain financial backing from the viceroy and local corporations in Mexico City, García Panes took his incomplete illustrated history to Spain to seek approval from Juan Bautista Muñoz and thus the imprimatur of the crown. Muñoz advised against publication on the grounds of the unreliability of the narrative, but he gave García Panes a copy of Sahagún's history of New Spain, from which he most likely drew scenes and images of the battles of the Conquest for his Theatro de Nueva España. On the role of García Panes in the origins of the Lienzo de Tlaxcala, see the document written in 1779 by the ruler of Tlaxcala, Nicolas Faustino Mazihcatzin, a graduate in theology and jurisprudence, "Descripción del mapa historiógrapho que se guarda en el arca de privilegios del mui ilustre ayuntamiento de la ciudad e Tlaxcala," *Revista Mexicana de Estudios Históricos* 1 (Jan.–Feb. 1927): 63–90. Mazihcatzin refers to Diego García Panes as Diego Pérez. On the confusing genealogy of the illustrations in the Lienzo de Tlaxcala, see René Acuña, "Estudio Introductorio," in Diego Muñoz Camargo, *Descripción de la ciudad y provincia de Tlaxcala de las Indias y del mar océano para buen gobierno y ennoblecimiento dellas*, facsimile of the MS in Glasgow (Mexico: UNAM, 1981), 9–47. On some similarities between images in the Lienzo de Tlaxcala and García Panes's illustrations, see Jorge Gurría Lacroix, *Códice Entrada de los Españoles en Tlaxcala* (Mexico: UNAM, 1966), 18–19. On Muñoz's negative evaluation of Panes's Theatro de la Nueva España, see AGI, México, 1885, "Informe sobre la obra de Diego Panes, 18 de enero 1791" (thanks to Alison Sandman for getting a copy of this document for me).

66. As far as I know nothing has been written on Juan Santelices Pablo. He was the most important broker of antiquities and books at the time of Malaspina's expedition. On Santelices Pablo, see González Claverán, *Expedición*, 103–4; Pimentel, 245–47.

67. See, e.g., *Gaceta de México* 4 (Apr. 1790): 68–71, and (Aug. 1790): 152–54.

68. On the Mexican phase of the expedition, see González Claverán, *Expedición*. For a general account of the goals, ideas, and itinerary of the expedition, see Pimentel.

69. González Claverán, *Expedición*, 100–101.

70. AMN, Colección Malaspina, MS 562, "Descripción detallada de Nueva España con muchas noticias estadísticas e históricas por Antonio Pineda y de Arcadio Pineda, su hermano," fol. 159v (and fols. 150r and 156v) and MS 563 fols. 329r–v.

71. The original sentence says: "Algunas de estas piezas [en la colección Boturini] pueden servir dignamente a la historia universal [pero hay otras] triviales obscuras y secas, nada correspondientes a la abultada expresión con que se recomendaron en la lista." See AMN, Colección Malaspina, MS 570, "Plan, división y prospecto general de las Memorias de Nueva España que han de servir ala historia universal de esta septentrional América," fol. 7v–8r.

72. ARAH, Colección de Memorias de Nueva España, vol. 1, Vicente de la Rosa Saldivar, "Certificación . . . sobre los mapas del museo del caballero Boturini," and "Juicio que sobre los papeles escritos en ydioma mexicano que se hallan en el museo del caballero Boturini," fols. 87r–120. These documents have been reproduced by Manuel Ballesteros Gaibrois as an appendix in Boturini, *Historia general*, 275–302.

73. León y Gama to Andrés Cavo, Aug. 19, 1796, referring to the removal of part of Boturini's collection to Spain in 1780, reproduced in Burrus, 70–71. León y Gama says that he and the librarians of the university, then entrusted with the collection, sought to make copies of the documents before they left. This earlier transfer seems to be confirmed by a series of documents at AGN, Historia, vol. 35, in which the antiquarian José Ignacio Borunda argues (in 1795) that Diego García Panes took a collection of indigenous sources to Spain. García y Panes in fact went to Spain in search

of patronage for his illustrated Theatro de Nueva España in the early 1780s. The magistrates of the high court took Borunda's denunciation seriously and interrogated García Panes, but nothing seems to have come of it. For copies of these documents, see Torre Revello, 394–96, 399–400.

In his edition of Andrés Cavo's *Historia de México* (Mexico: Editorial Patria, 1949), Ernest J. Burrus mentions the correspondence between Cavo and León y Gama, alluding indirectly to the Colección Cuevas, vol. 30 (Burrus's Prologue, nn. 14, 20, 28, 30–32). The reference, however, corresponds to letters between the antiquarian José Antonio Pichardo and Cavo (also to be found in the Nettie Lee Benson Library, Austin, Texas), which Burrus locates in the same unspecified Roman depository as the correspondence between León y Gama and Cavo in his article "Clavigero and the Lost Sigüenza y Góngora Manuscripts" (1959), which also (n. 38 and p. 84) alludes to the impending publication of the complete correspondence, a collection of twenty letters. However, the only reference to the whereabouts of these letters is that "they are in Rome," and Burrus unfortunately never published them. In "Research Opportunities in Italian Archives and Manuscript Collections for Students of Hispanic History," *Hispanic American Historical Review*, Aug. 1959, p. 446, Burrus refers again to the letters and to microfilmed copies of them at St. Louis University. Microfilmed copies of some (very few, as I discovered to my chagrin) documents on the history of the Jesuits in Mexico assembled (partly in Italy) by the Jesuit Mariano Cuevas in the early twentieth century are in fact at St. Louis University, and finding them there, I thought my detective work had finally paid off. Yet despite the kind help of Dr. Charles J. Ermatinger, the Vatican Film Librarian, and a detailed survey of the microfilm holdings of the Colección Cuevas, I have been unable to locate León y Gama's letters, which might shed further light on the Creole conspiracy.

74. On Mier, see Brading, *Origins*, pt. 2.

75. Keen, 304–5.

76. Brading, *Origins*, 27.

77. Mier, 1: 29 and 2: 65. In line with the prevailing views of Borunda's and Mier's ideas as strange fantasies, the Cuban author Reinaldo Arenas has written a novel on Mier suggestively entitled *Un mundo alucinante* [A Hallucinatory World]: *Una novela de aventura* (Mexico: Editorial Diógenes, 1969), which has been translated by Andrew Hurley under the title *The Ill-Fated Peregrinations of Fray Servando* (New York: Penguin Books, 1994).

78. The documents are in AGN, Historia, vol. 35, and have been reproduced in Torre Revello, 388–94. The next two paragraphs are based on them.

79. Borunda argued that most charters had been written in Gothic script (introduced between 1521 and 1527 by the Franciscan Peter of Ghent, or Pedro de Gante) and that they therefore had to be carefully transcribed according to an "alphabet" he had designed in 1768.

80. BN-M, MS 1387, José Ignacio Borunda and José Mariano Samper, "Descubrimiento legal, histórico y natural del mas célebre mineral de azogue del antiguo imperio mexicano" (1788), folio 446r. Similar arguments were being made in Peru approximately at the same time; see Joseph Manuel Bermúdez, "Discurso sobre la utilidad e importancia de la lengua general del Perú," *Mercurio Peruano* 9 (1793): 185–86.

81. BN-M, MS 1387, Borunda and Samper, "Descubrimiento legal," fols. 445r–447r.

82. Borunda, 236. The original manuscript can be found in the archives of the Basílica de Nuestra Señora de Guadalupe in Mexico City.

83. Borunda, 203–4, 227.

84. Ibid., 200, 202, 223–25.

85. Ibid., 198, 318.

86. Ibid., 204.

87. Ibid., 209–10.

88. As the chronicler of the festivities explained, St. John of the Cross was born in Castile in 1542 to poor hidalgo (lower nobility) parents. Twice saved from drowning by the Virgin when a boy, he had felt the call of God since childhood. He entered the order of the Carmelites but grew dissatisfied with the lax moral behavior of his confreres. To show them the way to moral regeneration, John dwelt in caves, with little to eat, often awakening under a blanket of snow. He routinely scourged himself and always wore chains and a vest studded with nails. To remind himself of the vanity of life, he slept with a skeleton, his only possession. The devil lured him many times into sexual desire, but every time he managed to convert the whore into a pious woman. He was so in touch with God that he levitated in his sleep. The Carmelites, tired of the rebel, sent him to jail, where he lived for about a year deprived of all light and movement. After escaping, he received the support of St. Teresa of Avila, his mentor and patron, and created an order of his own, the Discalced Carmelites. As leader of the order, John lived an exemplary life, which included reviving several deceased nuns. At the end of his days, he radiated a blinding light. After worms had consumed his body, he died without pain in 1591. See Ximénez de Bonilla et al., 1–40.

89. The first representation that I am aware of appears in the Codex Aubin (Codex 1576). See *Historia mexicana*, 48.

90. Cabrera y Quintero, "Aguila Mystica, exaltada en los ápices del Carmelo," in Ximénez de Bonilla et al., 222–24. On sixteenth-century Christian and classical influences introduced to the Nahua literary elite by the Franciscans that might help explain the iconographic change mentioned, see Fernández-Armesto.

91. Villegas.

92. Vega, 11.

93. The literature on Our Lady of Guadalupe is immense. See Maza; Brading, *First America*, ch. 16; Lafaye; Poole. Whether the flood of 1629 marked a turning point in the devotion and whether the devotion was first primarily Creole, as Poole has forcefully suggested, are things that still need further clarification (William Taylor, personal communication). The perception that there are distinct Creole and Amerindian histories of the devotion hinges on the conceit that the identities of these two groups can be sharply elucidated, which I seriously doubt — at least at the level of the elites (see, e.g., Ch. 4 above).

94. Sánchez, 204–9.

95. Ibid., 168 (on the crown of twelve stars); 219 (on the eclipsed sun); 223–4 (on the moon); 226–27 (on the forty-six stars).

96. See, e.g., Carranza; Elizalde Ita Parra, 18, 29–30.

97. Sánchez, 167.

98. Maza, 43–45, also 136 (intercedes in foreign wars), 177 (propitiates rain).

99. Cabrera y Quintero.

100. Gerónimo de Valladolid, "Advertencia," in Florencia, *Estrella del norte de México* (unpaginated).

101. M. Cabrera, 500.

102. Ibid., 521.

103. Eguiara y Eguren, *María santísima*, 484.

104. Borunda, 292.

105. Ibid., 293.

106. Ibid., 276–77; Mier, "El sermón predicado en la Colegiata," in *Obras completas*, 1: 249–50.

107. Complaint by José Fernández de Uribe, the prosecutor, in a sermon delivered in 1777; quoted in O'Gorman, "Estudio preliminar," in Mier, *Obras*, 1: 41.

108. Bartolache y Díaz de las Posadas, appendix. See also Joaquín Traggia, "Dictamen" [1799], in Mier, *Obras*, 2: 232.

109. Fernández de Uribe, "Dictamen," in Mier, *Obras*, 2: 166, 176.

110. Ibid., 2: 164, 169 (on Borunda); 2: 154–64 (on Mier).

111. Ibid., 2: 119, 123–24.

112. BN-P (G-A), MS 320, León y Gama, "Descripción de la sagrada imagen según las relaciones de los indios." See also BN-P (G-A), MS 322, León y Gama, "De la existencia de los gigantes." Creole scholars like Fernández de Uribe and León y Gama, as Edmundo O'Gorman has argued, represented a segment of the Creole intelligentsia that sought to discredit Mier to help prevent news of the French Revolution from undermining the traditions, and thus the authority, of the Mexican Church. See O'Gorman, "Estudio preliminar," in Mier, *Obras*, 1: 38–40.

113. Maravall, *Cultura del barroco*.

114. Mills and Taylor, 141–46, 25-52, and Taylor, personal communication.

115. The following is a list of the location of the documents for reconstructing the history of the discovery of Palenque: AGI, Guatemala 471, Guatemala 645, and Mapas y Planos Guatemala 256–60; BP, MS 2979; ARAH, Colección Muñoz, vol. 91; British Museum, MS 17571; LAL-TU, MS 1796; BN-P (G-A), MSS 216 and 278; EAC-NB, MS 1564; HBC-B, Mexican MS 177; AMNA, MS C.A./226, fols. 123–158r; and ACMG, no signature available.

116. I have reconstructed the chronology of events in this paragraph from different sources; see British Museum, MS 17571, Luis de Roca to Joseph Miguel de San Juan, Jan. 2, 1973, legajo 16, fols. 43–44 (reproduced in Ballesteros Gaibrois, 23–25); AGI, Guatemala 471, José Estachería to José de Gálvez, Guatemala, Feb. 13, 1785, fols. 1–3v (reproduced in Cabello Carro, 103); and AMNA, MS C.A./226, Ordóñez y Aguiar, "Fragmentos al Obispo [Cayetano Monroy y Franco] hacia el año de 1790 sobre el descubrimiento de las famosas ruinas de Palenque," fols. 123–158r (parts are reproduced in Castañeda Paganini, 17–20). Ordóñez y Aguiar offers yet another version of the events in the dedication of the Newberry Library's copy of his "Historia de la creación" (EAC-NB, MS 1564). The chronology is by no means clear. Ordóñez y Aguiar asserts throughout, however, that the original discoverer of the ruins was his granduncle Antonio de Solís, a parish priest, who did not live long enough to make his discovery known. While they were at grammar school together in Ciudad Real,

however, a member of Solís's extended family, Joseph de la Fuente Coronado, spoke of Palenque to Ordóñez y Aguiar, arousing his lasting fascination with the city. Whatever the facts of the matter, there is consensus in all the sources that Ramón Ordóñez y Aguiar played a key part in prompting the Spanish authorities to conduct research on the ruins.

117. AGI, Guatemala 471, Estachería a José Antonio Calderón, Nov. 28, 1784, fols. 1r–1v (reproduced in Cabello Carro, 78).

118. AGI Guatemala 471, José Antonio Calderón to José Estachería, Dec. 15, 1784, fols. 2–11v (reproduced in Cabello Carro, 80–89).

119. On Bernasconi, see Pailles Hernández and Nieto Calleja, 103–5.

120. AGI, Guatemala 471, Estachería to Antonio Bernasconi, "Instrucciones para el reconocimiento de las ruinas de Palenque," fols. 13–21v (reproduced in Cabello Carro, 90–99).

121. AGI, Guatemala 645, # 432, Estachería to José de Gálvez, Aug. 26, 1785 (reproduced in Cabello Carro, 109–10).

122. AGI, Guatemala 645, Bernasconi to Estachería, June 13, 1785 (reproduced in Cabello Carro, 112–15).

123. AGI, Guatemala 645, Juan Bautista Muñoz to marqués de Sonora on the ruins of Palenque, Mar. 7, 1786 (reproduced in Cabello Carro, 118–120, 119 [quotation]).

124. AGI, Guatemala 645, Estachería to marqués de Sonora (Gálvez), Aug. 12, 1786 (reproduced in Cabello Carro, 128–29).

125. ARAH, Colección Muñoz, vol. 91, Informe de Antonio del Río sobre Palenque, June 24, 1787, reproduced in Cabello Carro, 130–47. For examples of these procedures, see Cabello Carro, 131–32, 137, 144.

126. Cabello Carro, 138, 140, 141, 142.

127. Ibid., 139.

128. Ibid., 140–41.

129. Ibid., 133.

130. Ibid., 137–38, 139.

131. Ibid., 133.

132. Ibid., 137, 139–40, 145.

133. AGI, Guatemala 645, José Estachería to Antonio Valdés, July 9, 1788 (reproduced in Cabello Carro, 149–50).

134. Río, vii. This misleading tradition was later perpetuated by John Lloyd Stephens.

135. AGI, Guatemala 654, # 432, Estachería to José de Gálvez, Aug. 26, 1785 (reproduced in Cabello Carro, 110).

136. In EAC-NA, MS 1564 (copy of Ordóñez y Aguiar's "Historia de la creación del mundo conforme al sistema americano"), Ordóñez y Aguiar refers vaguely to the reasons why he left Ciudad Real in 1788. As the member of the cathedral chapter charged with defending the immunity of the secular clergy in the capital of the province of Chiapas, he had been forced by a case to move to the higher court of Guatemala City. Once in the capital of the Audiencia, he pursued yet another vague case for libel against the cathedral chapter of Ciudad Real. According to Ordóñez y Aguiar, in the process he not only had to put up with many "inflammatory broadsides" aimed at him and his reputation but was obliged to spend his fortune on his de-

fense. See EAC-NA, MS 1564, "Dedicatoria al caballero Joseph Miguel de San Juan," 4r–5r. The terms "terrible persecution" to describe the reasons for Ordóñez y Aguiar's forced exile come from a letter by the Dominican provincial De la Roca to San Juan, Nov. 27, 1792, British Museum, MS 17571, fols. 43–44 (reproduced in Ballesteros Gabrois, 25).

137. AMNA, MS C.A./226, Ordóñez y Aguiar, "Fragmentos al Obispo [Cayetano Monroy y Franco] hacia el año de 1790 sobre el descubrimiento de las famosas ruinas de Palenque," fols. 123r–158r. The original longer draft of this document can be found at LAL-TU, MS 1796, which has been wrongly identified as bk. 2 of Ordóñez y Aguiar's "Historia de la creación del cielo y de la tierra" and thus catalogued under the misleading title of "Descripción palencana: Libro II de la Historia del cielo y de la tierra." The manuscript at MNA has also been mislabeled. The erudite José F. Ramírez in 1867 correctly assumed that the document was a letter sent by Ordóñez y Aguiar to a prelate, but he could not identify the bishop's name. From the documentation at the Archivo Colonial de la Gobernación de Guatemala, reproduced in *Anales de la Sociedad de Geografía e Historia de Guatemala* 7 (Mar. 1931): 354–56, we know that "Descripción palencana," was written in 1792 by Ordóñez y Aguiar for Monroy y Franco.

138. AMNA, MS C.A./226, Ordóñez y Aguiar, "Fragmentos al Obispo," 128v.

139. Ibid., 150v–151r.

140. Ibid., 131v–133v.

141. Ibid., 130v–131r, 144v, 155r–157v.

142. The manuscript of *Theatro crítico* is in the British Museum (MS 17571). I have used the English translation by Henry Berthoud published in 1822 along with del Río's report; see Cabrera.

143. Cabrera, 59–63.

144. Ibid., 90–91.

145. Ibid., 81, 89.

146. Ibid., 93–94.

147. Ibid., 39–44.

148. Toward the end of his *Theatro crítico*, Cabrera argued that many precious antiquities, including a silver chalice that might have belonged to St. Thomas, a Hebrew Bible preserved by the Indians in pictograms, and hundreds of ancient coins found in Guatemala, were circulating. Cabrera urged the authorities to collect these antiquities. The two medals in the hands of the academicians, Cabrera argued, were part of a larger cache in the hands of two officers of the royal mint, Juan de Letona and the engraver Pedro Garziaguirre. See Cabrera, 106–11.

149. Ibid., 53–55, 86, 99.

150. British Museum, MS 17571, San Juan to Phelipe de Sesma, Dec. 2, 1792, and Jan. 2, 1793, fols. 19–25 (reproduced in Ballesteros Gaibrois, 27–39).

151. Cabrera, 53.

152. Some of the documentation relating to the trial is in the Archivo Colonial de la Gobernación de Guatemala and has been reproduced in *Anales de la Sociedad de Geografía e Historia* 7, no. 3 (Mar. 1931): 354–56.

153. Cabrera, 32–33.

154. There seem to be several extant copies of Ordóñez y Aguiar's "Historia de la creación." One was reproduced by Nicolás León in *Bibliografía mexicana*; another is at EAC-NB, MSS 1563 and 1564. The copy in the Newberry Library in Chicago is a photographic reproduction of originals in the BN-P (G-A), MS 216 and 278. There is a third copy that I have not consulted at HBC-B, MSS M-M 177. MS 1564 in the Newberry Library has passages not found in Nicolás León's edition, including a dedication to San Juan and a "note to the reader." Unless I refer to sections not found in León's edition, all my citations are to the latter. The full title of the manuscript is indicative, in and of itself, of Ordóñez y Aguiar's aims and methodology: "Historia de la creación del cielo y la tierra conforme al sistema de la gentilidad americana. Theología de los Culebras figurada en ingeniosos geroglíphicos, symbolos, emblemas y metáphoras. Diluvio Universal. Dispersión de las gentes. Verdadero origen de los indios [desde] su salida de Chaldea, su transmigración a estas partes septentrionales, su tránsito por el oceano, [hasta su] derrota que siguieron al llegar al seno mexicano. Principio de su imperio. Fundación y destrucción de su antigua y primera corte, poco há descubierta y conocida con el nombre de ciudad de Palenque. Superstiticioso culto con que los antiguos Palencanos adoraron al verdadero dios, figurado en aquellos symbolos o emblemas que colocados en las aras de sus templos, últimamente degeneraron en abominables ídolos. Libros todos de la mas benerable [*sic*] antigüedad, sacados del olvido unos, nuevamente descubiertos otros, e interpretados sus symbolos, emblemas y metáphoras conforme al genuino sentido del phrasismo americano." For an outline and contents of each of the two parts of the original manuscript, see Ordóñez y Aguiar, 5.

155. For an English translation of the Quiché version and the history of the text, see Popol Vuh. My characterization of nineteenth-century Guatemala as unconcerned with Amerindian history needs qualification. For a more nuanced interpretation of nineteenth-century highland Guatemala, see Grandin.

156. Cabello Carro, 26. Surprisingly, Tedlock omits Ordóñez y Aguiar completely in his history of the manuscript for the English edition of the Popol Vuh.

157. Ordóñez y Aguiar, 28–34.

158. Ibid., 34–46.

159. Ibid., 51, 93.

160. Ibid., 145–52.

161. Ibid., 15, 113.

162. Ibid., 16–17, 39, 64, 68, 75.

163. Ibid., 62, 94.

164. Ibid., 5–7.

165. Ibid., 125–32.

166. Ibid., 9–16. For Boturini's point of view, see his *Idea* 16.14, 19 (pp. 84, 87).

167. Ibid., 10, 27, 39, 101, 143, 181–82, 208.

168. EAC-NB, MS 1564, fols. 230r–31v.

169. Dupaix, 1: 186–88 (188 for quotation).

170. Ibid., 1: 194–261, and 2, figs. 92–125. On the origins of Indians from ancient westward migrations instead of Asian southward ones; and on the peninsula of Yucatan as the original cradle of Mesoamerican civilizations, see 1: 118–19. In 2, fig.

107, Dupaix finds iconographic evidence of Osiris and Mercury (1: 210–11), See also Dupaix's conclusions after his survey of Palenque, 1: 223–33.

171. José Alcina Franch, "Introducción," in Dupaix, 1: 22–25.

CONCLUSION

1. Pinkerton, 2: 299.

2. Cañizares-Esguerra, "Spanish America," 329–33.

3. Moxó, *Entretenimientos*, 1: 78 (Voltaire and cannibalism), 156 (biases of witnesses such as Las Casas), 214–23 (testimony of learned Spaniards versus that of Kircher and Walton over nature of Mesoamerican hieroglyphs), 2: 5 (against systems), 7, 42–43, 49, 94, 309–17 (the clergy, although flawed observers themselves, are better witnesses than travelers), 15–16 (casual observers unable to discover Amerindian lies and cunning), 127 (on Sepúlveda). Moxó, *Cartas mejicanas*, 22 (on witnesses as the most reliable observers), 23–34 (on de Pauw). *Entretenimientos* has been attributed to a relative of Moxó's, the baron of Juras Reales, who used Moxó's manuscript of *Cartas mejicanas* without proper attribution. Although *Entretenimientos* and *Cartas* share similar contents, I find *Entretenimientos* better structured than *Cartas*. It seems that Juras Reales did not limit himself simply to plagiarizing Moxó. He also improved the latter's text. On Moxó, see Vargas Ugarte.

4. Typical of this trend are the Brazilian José Alencar (1829–1877) and the Ecuadorian Juan León Mera (1832–1894), whose theoretical views crystallized in their novels *Iracema* (1865) and *Cumandá* (1879) respectively. For their views on national literature, see Alencar, "Letter to Dr. Jaguaribe," in Alencar, 131–38; and Mera. Although they are provocative, I find the views of Doris Sommer (1991) on nineteenth-century Latin American national novels too focused on gender to the exclusion of both epistemological themes and representations of nature.

5. Atamirano, 73 (quotation); see also 62–63.

6. Gerbi, *Dispute*, trans. Moyle, 201.

7. Ibid., 289.

Bibliography

ARCHIVES AND MANUSCRIPT COLLECTIONS

Alcalá de Henares

Colegio San Ignacio de Loyola
    Archivo de los Jesuitas de la Provincia de Toledo

Berkeley

University of California
    Bancroft Library
        Hubert Howe Bancroft Collection
            Mexican

Chicago

Newberry Library
    Edward E. Ayer Collection

London

British Museum

Madrid

Archivo de la Real Academia de Historia
    Colección de Memorias de Nueva España
    Actas
Fundación Universitaria Española
    Archivo Campomanes
Biblioteca Nacional
    Sala manuscritos
Biblioteca del Palacio Real
Archivo del Real Jardín Botánico de Madrid
Archivo del Museo Naval
    Colección Malaspina

Bibliography

Mexico City

Archivo Museo Nacional de Antropología
Biblioteca Nacional
  Fondos Reservados
Archivo General de la Nación
  Ramo Historia

New Orleans

Tulane University
  Latin American Library

New York

New York Public Library
  Rich Collection

Paris

Bibliothèque Nationale
  Collection Goupil-Aubin

Seville

Archivo General de Indias
  Indiferente General
  Indiferente del Perú
  México
  Guatemala
  Mapas y Planos

St. Louis

St Louis Univerity Vatican Film Library
  Colección Cuevas

Valencia

Colegio Mayor de Corpus Christi
Archivo Hispano Mayasiano

PERIODICALS

Diario de los literatos españoles (Spain)
Gazeta de Madrid
Primicias de la Cultura de Quito
Gaceta de México
Gacetas de literatura (Mexico)

London Review and Literary Journal
Mercurio Peruano
Monthly Review (England)
Quarterly Review (England)

BOOKS AND ARTICLES

Aarsleff, Hans. "The Tradition of Condillac: The Problem of the Origin of Language in the Eighteenth Century and the Debate in the Berlin Academy Before Herder." In id., *From Locke to Saussure: Essays on the Study of Language and Intellectual History*, pp. 146–209. Minneapolis: University of Minnesota Press, 1982.

Acosta, José de. *Historia natural y moral de las Indias.* 1590. Edited by José Alcina Franch. Crónicas de América, 34. Madrid: Historia 16, 1987.

———. *De procuranda indorum salute.* 1588. Edited and translated by Luciano Pereña et al. Corpus Hispanorum de Pace, vols. 23–24. Madrid: Consejo Superior de Investigaciones Científicas, 1984–87.

Aguilar Piñal, Francisco. *Bibliografía de los autores españoles del siglo XVIII.* 8 vols. Madrid: Consejo Superior de Investigaciones Científicas, 1981–95.

Aldridge, A. Owen, ed., *The Ibero-American Enlightenment.* Urbana: University of Illinois Press, 1971.

Alencar, José de. *Iracema.* 1865. Translated from the Portuguese by Clifford E. Landers. New York: Oxford University Press, 2000.

Algarotti, Francesco. "Saggio sopra l'imperio degl'Incas [1753]." In *Saggi,* edited by Giovanni da Pozzo, pp. 329–41. Bari: Gius Laterza & Figli, 1963.

Altamirano, Ignacio. "La literatura nacional (1868)." In *Los novelistas como críticos,* edited by Norman Klahn and Wilfrido H. Corral, 1: 59-76. 2 vols. Mexico City: Ediciones del Norte/Fondo de Cultura Económica, 1991.

Alva Ixtlilxochitl, Fernando de. *Historia de la nación chichimeca.* Ca. 1600–1640. Crónicas de América, 11. Edited by Germán Vázquez. Madrid: Historia 16, 1985.

———. *Obras históricas.* Ca. 1600–1640. Edited by Edmundo O'Gorman. 2 vols. Mexico City: Universidad Nacional Autónoma de México, 1975.

Alvarado Tezozómoc, Fernando de. *Crónica mexicana.* Ca. 1598. 4th ed. Biblioteca Porrúa, 61. Mexico City: Porrúa, 1987.

———. *Crónica mexicayotl.* Ca. 1609. Translated from the Nahuatl by Adrián León. Instituto de Historia, 1st ser., 10. Mexico City: Universidad Nacional Autónoma de México, 1949.

Alzate y Ramírez, José Antonio de. "Descripción de las antigüedades de Xochicalco dedicadas a los señores de la actual expedición marítima alrededor del orbe." In *Suplemento a la Gazeta de literatura.* Mexico City: Felipe de Zúñiga y Ontiveros, 1791.

———. *Memorias y ensayos.* Edited by R. Moreno de los Arcos. Mexico City: Universidad Nacional Autónoma de México, 1985.

Anderson, Benedict. *Imagined Communities: Reflections on the Origins and Spread of Nationalism.* 1983. Rev. ed. New York: Verso, 1991.

Andrés, Gregorio de. "La biblioteca manuscrita del americanista Andrés González de Barcia (m. 1743) del consejo y cámara de Castilla." *Revista de Indias* 47 (1987): 811–31.

Bibliography

Animato, Carlo, Paolo A. Rossi, and Clara Miccinelli, eds. *Quipu: Il nodo parlante dei misteriosi Incas*. Genoa: ECIG, 1989. Reprint, 1994.

Anselme, Antoine. "Des monumens qui ont supplée au defaut de l'ecriture et servi de mémoires aux premiers Historiens." *Mémoires de littérature tirés des registres de l'Académie royale des inscriptions et belles lettres* 4 (1723): 380–98.

———. "Seconde dissertation sur les monumens qui ont servi de mémoires aux premiers historiens." *Mémoires de littérature tirés des registres de l'Académie royale des inscriptions et belles lettres* 6 (1729): 1–13.

Anson, George, Baron. *A Voyage Round the World in the Years 1740, 41, 42, 43, 44, by George Anson, Esq., Commander-in-Chief of a Squadron of His Majesty's Ships, Sent upon an Expedition to the South-Seas.* 1745. Edited by Richard Walter. London: Ingram, Cooke, 1853.

Appiah, Kwame Anthony. *In My Father's House: Africa in the Philosophy of Culture.* Oxford: Oxford University Press, 1992.

Armitage, David. "The New World and British Historical Thought: From Richard Hakluyt to William Robertson." In *America in European Consciousness*, edited by Karen Ordall Kupperman, pp. 52–75. Chapel Hill: University of North Carolina Press, 1995.

Arnoldsson, Sverker. *La leyenda negra: Estudios sobre sus orígenes.* Göteborg: Acta Universitatis Gothoburgensis, 1960.

Ascher, Marcia, and Robert Ascher. *Code of the Quipu: A Study in Media, Mathematics, and Culture.* Ann Arbor: University of Michigan Press, 1981.

Bacon, Francis, Sir. *The Works.* Edited by James Spedding, Robert Leslie Ellis, and Douglas Denon Heath. 14 vols. London: Longman, 1858–74.

Badaloni, Nicola. "Introduzione." In Lorenzo Boturini Benaducci, *Un vichiano in Messico.* Lucca: Maria Pacini Fazzi, 1990.

Ballesteros Beretta, Antonio. "Don Juan Bautista Muñoz: Dos facetas científicas." *Revista de Indias* 3 (1941): 5–37.

———. "Don Juan Bautista Muñoz: La Historia del Nuevo Mundo." *Revista de Indias* 10 (1942): 589–660.

———. "Juan Bautista Muñoz: La creación del Archivo de Indias." *Revista de Indias* 4 (1941): 55–95.

Ballesteros Gaibrois, Manuel. *Nuevas noticias sobre Palenque.* Mexico City: Universidad Nacional Autónoma de México, 1960.

Barcia, Andrés González de. *Ensayo cronológico para la historia general de la Florida . . . desde el año de 1512 que descubrió la Florida Juan Ponce de León hasta el de 1722.* Madrid: Nicolás Rodríguez Franco, 1723.

———. "Proemio." In Gregorio García, *Origen de los Indios de el Nuevo Mundo, e Indias Occidentales.* Madrid: Francisco Martínez Abad, 1729.

———. "Proemio." In Juan de Torquemada, *Primera [segunda, tercera] parte de los veinte i un libros rituales i monarchia indiana.* Madrid: N. Rodríguez Franco, 1723.

Barker-Benfield, G. J. *The Culture of Sensibility: Sex and Society in Eighteenth-Century Britain.* Chicago: University of Chicago Press, 1992.

Barret-Kriegel, Blandine. *La défaite de l'érudition.* Paris: Presses universitaires de France, 1988.

———. *Les académies de l'histoire.* Paris: Presses universitaires de France, 1988.

Barthélemy, J. J. "Reflexions sur quelques peintures mexicaines." Ca. 1770. In id., *Oeuvres*, 4: 425–32. Paris: Bossange Frères, 1821.

Bartolache y Díaz de las Posadas, José Ignacio. *Manifiesto satisfactorio anunciado en la Gazeta de México (Tom. I. Núm. 53): Opúsculo guadalupano.* Mexico City: Felipe de Zúñiga y Ontiveros, 1790.

Batllori, Miguel. *La cultura hispano-italiana de los Jesuitas expulsos.* Madrid: Gredos, 1966.

Baudoin, Jean. "Au Lecteur." In Garcilaso de la Vega, *Le commentaire royale.* Paris: Augustin Courbe, 1633.

Baudot, Georges. *Utopia and History in Mexico: The First Chroniclers of Mexican Civilization (1520–1569).* Translated by Bernard R. and Thelma Ortiz de Montellano. Niwot, Colo.: University Press of Colorado, 1995.

Bayle, Pierre. *A General Dictionary, Historical and Critical.* 10 vols. London: James Bettenham, 1735–41. Originally published under the title *Dictionnaire historique et critique* (1696–97).

Beaufort, Louis. *Dissertation sur l'incertitude des cinq premiers siècles de l'histoire romaine.* Utrecht: E. Neaulme, 1738. Translated as *A Dissertation upon the Uncertainty of the Roman History During the First Five Hundred Years.* London: T. Waller, 1740.

Bellegarde, M. l'abbé de [Jean-Baptiste Morvan]. *Histoire universelle des voyages faits par mer & par terre, dans l'Ancien & dans le Nouveau monde: pour éclaircir la géographie ancienne & moderne.* Amsterdam: P. Humbert, 1708. Microfiche. Louisville, Ky.: Lost Cause Press, 1968.

Bernard, Jean-Fréderic. "Discours preliminaire sur L'Histoire des Yncas." In Garcilaso de la Vega, *Histoire des Yncas.* Amsterdam: J.-F. Bernard, 1737.

Betanzos, Juan de. *Suma y narración de los Incas.* 1551. Edited by Horacio Villanueva Urteaga, Demetrio Ramos, and María del Carmen Martín Rubio. Madrid: Atlas, 1987.

Bolingbroke, Henry St. John, Viscount. *Historical Writings.* Edited by Isaac Kramnick. Chicago: University of Chicago Press, 1972.

——. *Letters on the Study and Use of History.* 2 vols. London: A. Millar, 1752.

Bonnell, Victoria, and Lynn Hunt, eds. *Beyond the Cultural Turn: New Directions in the Study of Society and Culture.* Berkeley and Los Angeles: University of California Press, 1999.

Boone, Elizabeth Hill. *Stories in Red and Black: Pictorial Histories of the Aztecs and Miztecs.* Austin: University of Texas Press, 2000.

Boone, Elizabeth Hill, and Walter D. Mignolo, eds. *Writing Without Words: Alternative Literacies in Mesoamerica and the Andes.* Durham, N.C.: Duke University Press, 1994.

Borunda, José Ignacio. *Clave general de geroglíficos americanos.* Ca. 1792. In *Biblioteca mexicana del siglo XVIII*, edited by Nicolás León, sec. 1, pt. 3, pp. 195–351. Boletín del Instituto Bibliográfico Mexicano, 7. Mexico City: La viuda de Francisco Díaz León, 1906.

Boturini Benaduci, Lorenzo. *Historia general de la América Septentrional [Ciclografía].* 1749. Edited by Manuel Ballesteros Gaibrois. 1949. 2d ed. Mexico City: Universidad Nacional Autónoma, 1990.

Bibliography

———. *Idea de una nueva historia general de la América Septentrional*. 1746. Edited by Miguel León-Portilla. Colección "Sepan Cuantos," 278. Mexico City: Porrúa, 1974.

———. *Oratio ad Divinam Sapientiam. Academiae Valentinae patronam.* Valencia: Typ. Viduae Antonii Bordazar, 1750.

———. *Un vichiano in Messico: Lorenzo Boturini Benaducci.* Italian translation of the *Idea de una nueva historia general de la América Septentrional.* Edited and translated by Nicola Badaloni. Lucca: Maria Pacini Fazzi, 1990.

Brading, David A. *The First America: The Spanish Monarchy, Creole Patriots, and the Liberal State, 1492–1867.* New York: Cambridge University Press, 1991.

———. *Miners and Merchants in Bourbon Mexico, 1763–1810.* Cambridge: Cambridge University Press, 1971.

———. *The Origins of Mexican Nationalism.* Cambridge: University of Cambridge, Centre of Latin American Studies, 1985. Originally published as *Orígenes del nacionalismo mexicano* (Mexico: Septentas, 1973).

Breydy, Michael. *Michel Gharcieh Al-Ghaziri, orientaliste libanais du XVIIIᵉ siècle.* Harissa, Lebanon: Imp. Saint Paul, 1950.

Brosses, Charles de. *Du culte des dieux fétiches, ou, Parallèle de l'ancienne religion de l'Egypte avec la religion actuelle de Nigritie.* . . . 1760. Texte revue par Madeleine V.-David. Paris: Fayard, 1989.

———. *Histoire des navigations aux Terres Australes. Contenant ce que l'on sçait des moeurs et des productions des contrées découvertes jusqu'a ce jour; ou il est traité de l'utilité d'y faire de plus amples découvertes et des moyens d'y former un établisssement.* 2 vols. Paris: Durand, 1756.

Brotherston, Gordon. *Book of the Fourth World: Reading the Native Americas [sic] Through Their Literature.* Cambridge: Cambridge University Press, 1992.

———. *Painted Books from Mexico: Codices in UK Collections and the World They Represent.* London: British Museum Press, 1995.

Brown, Thomas. *La Academia de San Carlos en Nueva España.* Mexico City: Septentas, 1976.

Bryson, Gladys. *Man and Society: The Scottish Inquiry of the Eighteenth Century.* Princeton, N.J.: Princeton University Press, 1945.

Buffon, Georges-Louis Leclerc, comte de. *De l'homme.* 1747–77. Edited by Michèle Duchet. Paris: Maspero, 1971.

———. *Selections from Natural History General and Particular.* 2 vols. New York: Arno Press, 1977.

Burke, Peter. *Vico.* New York: Oxford University Press, 1985.

Burns, Kathryn. *Colonial Habits: Convents and the Spiritual Economy of Cuzco, Peru.* Durham, N.C.: Duke University Press, 1999.

Burrus, Ernest J. "Clavigero and the Lost Sigüenza y Góngora Manuscripts." *Estudios de Cultura Nahuatl* 1 (1959): 59–90.

Bustamente, Jesús. "Retórica, traducción y responsabilidad histórica: Claves humanísticas en la obra de Bernardino de Sahagún." In *Humanismo y visión del otro en la España moderna: Cuatro estudios,* edited by Berta Ares, Jesús Bustamente, and Francisco Castilla y Fermín del Pino, pp. 243–375. Madrid: Centro Superior de Investigaciones Científicas, 1992.

Cabello Carro, Paz. *Política investigadora de la época de Carlos II en el área maya. Según documentacón de Calderón, Bernasconi, Del Río y otros.* Madrid: Ediciones de la Torre, 1992.

Cabello Valboa, Miguel. *Miscelánea antártica: Una historia del Perú antiguo.* 1586. Edited for the Instituto de Etnología, Seminario de Historia del Perú–Incas. Lima: Universidad Nacional Mayor de San Marcos, 1951.

Cabrera, Miguel. "Maravilla americana [1756]." In *Testimonios históricos guadalu panos*, edited by Ernesto de la Torre Villar and Ramiro Navarro de Anda, pp. 494–528. Mexico City: Fondo de Cultura Económica, 1982.

Cabrera, Pablo Felix. See Río, Antonio del, below.

Cabrera y Quintero, Cayetano de. *El escudo de armas de México: Escrito . . . para conmemorar el final de la funesta epidemia de matlazáhuatl que asoló a la Nueva España entre 1736 y 1738.* Mexico City: Viuda de D. Joseph Bernardo de Hogal, 1746.

Cadalso, José. *Los eruditos a la violeta.* 1772. Edited by Nigel Glendinning. Biblioteca Anaya, 76. Salamanca: Anaya, 1967.

Calhoun, Craig, ed. *Habermas and the Public Sphere.* Cambridge, Mass.: MIT Press, 1997.

Campomanes, Pedro Rodríguez, conde de. *Discurso sobre el fomento de la industria popular (1774); Discurso sobre la educación popular de los artesanos y su fomento (1775).* Edited by John Reeder. Clásicos del pensamiento económico español, 2. Madrid: Instituto de Estudios Fiscales, 1975.

——. *Escritos regalistas.* 1765, 1769. Edited by Santos M. Coronas González. 2 vols. Oviedo, Spain: Junta General del Principado de Asturias, 1993.

Cañizares-Esguerra, Jorge. "Nation and Nature: Patriotic Representations of Nature in Late Colonial Spanish America." Working Paper no. 98–31 of the International Seminar on the History of the Atlantic World, 1500–1800, Harvard University, 1998.

——. "New World, New Stars: Patriotic Astrology and the Invention of Indian and Creole Bodies in Colonial Spanish America, 1600–1650." *American Historical Review* 104 (Feb. 1999): 33–68.

——. "Spanish America in Eighteenth-Century European Travel Compilations: A New 'Art of Reading' and the Transition to Modernity." *Journal of Early Modern History* 2 (1998): 329–49.

——. "Spanish America: From Baroque to Modern Colonial Science." In *The Eighteenth Century*, edited by Roy Porter, pp. 814–37. Vol. 4 of *The Cambridge History of Science*, edited by David Lindberg and Ronald Numbers. Cambridge: Cambridge University Press, 2001.

——. "Travel Accounts." In *Guide to Documentary Sources for Andean Art History and Archeology*, edited by Joanne Pillsbury. Washington, D.C.: National Gallery of Art, forthcoming.

——. "La utopía de Hipólito Unanue: Comercio, naturaleza y religión en el Perú." In *Saberes andinos: Ciencia y tecnología en Bolivia, Ecuador y Perú*, edited by Marcos Cueto, pp. 91–108. Lima: Instituto de Estudios Peruanos, 1995.

Cantelli, Gianfranco. *Mente corpo linguaggio: Saggio sull'interpretazione vichiana del mito.* Florence: Sansoni Editore, 1986.

Bibliography

Carbia, Rómulo. *La crónica oficial de las Indias Occidentales: Estudio histórico y crítico acerca de la historiografía mayor de Hispano América en los siglos XVI a XVIII.* Buenos Aires: Ediciones Buenos Aires, 1940.

Carli, Gian Rinaldo, conte. *Le lettere americane.* 1780. Nuova edizione correta ed ampliata colla aggiunta della parte III, prefazione del Abate Isidoro Bianchi. 3 vols. in 1. Cremona: Lorenzo Manini, 1781–83.

Carranza, Francisco Javier. *La transmigración de la iglesia a Guadalupe. Sermón que el 12 de diciembre de 1748 años predicó en el templo de N.S. de Guadalupe de la ciudad de Santiago de Querétaro.* Mexico City: Colegio Real y Más Antiguo de San Idelfonso, 1749.

Carrera Stampa, Manuel. "El 'Theatro de la Nueva España en su gentilismo y conquista' de Diego Panes." *Boletín del Archivo General de la Nación de México* 16 (1945): 399–428.

Casas, Bartolomé de las. *Apologética historia sumaria.* Before 1559. Serie de historiadores y cronistas de Indias, 1. 3d ed. 2 vols. Mexico City: Universidad Nacional Autónoma de México, Instituto de Investigaciones Históricas, 1967.

Casiri, Miguel. *Bibliotheca arabico-hispana escurialensis.* 2 vols. Madrid: Antonius Pérez de Soto, 1760–70.

Caso González, José Miguel. "Ilustración y neoclasicismo." In *Historia y crítica de la literatura española,* edited by Francisco Rico, 4: 195 ff. Barcelona: Crítica, 1991.

Cassirer, Ernst. *The Philosophy of the Enlightenment.* Translated by Fritz Koellin and James Pettegrove. Princeton, N.J.: Princeton University Press, 1951.

Castañeda Paganini, Ricardo. *Las ruinas de Palenque: Su descubrimiento y primeras exploraciones en el siglo XVIII.* Guatemala: Tipografía Nacional, 1946.

Castillo, Cristóbal del. *Historia de la venida de los mexicanos y otros pueblos; e, Historia de la conquista.* Ca. 1600. Edited and translated from Nahuatl by Federico Navarrete Linares. Mexico City: Instituto Nacional de Antropología e Historia, Proyecto Templo Mayor; GV Editores; Asociación de Amigos del Templo Mayor, 1991.

Castro Morales, Efraín. *Las primeras bibliografías regionales hispanoamericanas: Eguiara y sus corresponsales.* Puebla: Ediciones Altiplanos, 1961.

Castro, Concepción. *Campomanes: Estado y reformismo ilustrado.* Madrid: Alianza, 1996.

Catálogo de la colección de Juan Bautista Muñoz. 3 vols. Madrid: Real Academia de Historia, 1954–56.

Cartari, Vicenzo. *Imagini de gli dei delli antichi.* 2d ed. Padua: Pietro Paolo Tozzi, 1626.

Cavanilles, Antonio José. *Observations sur l'article Espagne de la Nouvelle Encyclopédie.* Paris: Alex. Jombert jeune, 1784.

Cervantes, Fernando. *The Devil in the New World: The Impact of Diabolism in New Spain.* New Haven, Conn.: Yale University Press, 1994.

Chacón y Calvo, J. María. "Informe del fiscal del Consejo de Indias D. Manuel Pablo Salcedo: Sobre el método que ha de seguirse para escribir la historia de las Indias." *Boletín de la Biblioteca Menéndez Pelayo,* número extraordinario en homenaje a M. Artigas, 2 (1932): 297–324.

Chakrabarty, Dipesh. "Postcoloniality and the Artifice of History: Who Speaks for 'Indian' Pasts?" *Representations* 37 (Winter 1992): 1–26.

Chandler, James, Arnold Davidson, and Harry Harootunian, eds. *Questions of Evidence: Proof, Practice, and Persuasion Across the Disciplines*. Chicago: University of Chicago Press, 1994.

Chambers, Iain, and Lidia Curti, eds. *The Post-Colonial Question: Common Skies, Divided Horizons*. New York: Routledge, 1996.

Chappe d'Auteroche, Jean-Baptiste, abbé. *Voyage en Californie pour l'observation du passage de Vénus sur le disque du soleil, le 3 juin 1769*. Paris: C. A. Jombert, 1772.

Chatterjee, Partha. *The Nation and Its Fragments: Colonial and Postcolonial Histories*. Princeton, N.J.: Princeton University Press, 1993.

Chaunu, Pierre. "La légende noire anti-hispanique. Des Marranes aux Lumières. De la Méditerranée à l'Amérique. Contribution à une psychologie régressive des peuples." *Revue de Psychologie des Peuples*, 1st quarter (1964): 188–223.

Chimalpain Cuauhtlehuanitzin, Francisco de San Antón Muñón. *Relaciones originales de Chalco Amaquemecan*. Ca. 1603–31. Edited and translated from the Nahuatl by Silva Rendón. Mexico City: Fondo de Cultura Económica, 1965, 1982.

Cieza de León, Pedro. *La crónica del Perú*. 1553. Crónicas de América, 4. Edited by Manuel Ballesteros. Madrid: Historia 16, 1984.

———. *El Señorio de los Incas*. Before 1554. Crónicas de América, 5. Edited by Manuel de Ballesteros. Madrid: Historia 16, 1985.

Ciudad Real, Antonio de. *Relación breve y verdadera de algunas cosas de las muchas que sucedieron al padre fray Alonso Ponce en las provincias de la Nueva España, siendo comisario general de aquellas partes. Trátanse algunas particularidades de aquella tierra, y dícese su ida á ella y vuelta á España, con algo de lo que en el viaje le aconteció hasta volver á su provincia de Castilla*. 1584 onward. 2 vols. Madrid: Imprenta viuda de Calero, 1873.

Clanchy, Michael. *From Memory to Written Record: England, 1066–1307*. Cambridge, Mass.: Harvard University Press, 1979.

Clavijero, Francisco Xavier. *Historia antigua de México*. 1780–81. Prologue by Mariano Cuevas. Colección "Sepan Cuantos," 29. Mexico City: Porrúa, 1964.

———. *The History of Mexico Collected from Spanish and Mexican Historians, from Manuscripts, and Ancient Paintings of the Indians*. Translated by Charles Cullen. 2 vols. London: G. G. J. and J. Robinson, 1787.

———. *Storia antica del Messico cavata da' migliori storici spagnuoli, e da' manoscritti, e dalle pitture antiche degl' Indiani: divisa in dieci libri . . . e dissertazioni sulla terra, sugli animali, e sugli abitatori del Messico*. 4 vols. Cesena: G. Biasini, 1780–81.

Clément, Jean-Pierre. "De los nombres de plantas." In *Ciencia y contexto histórico en las expediciones ilustradas a América*, edited by Fermín del Pino, pp. 141–71. Madrid: Consejo Superior de Investigaciones Científicas, 1988.

Clendinnen, Inga. *Ambivalent Conquests: Maya and Spaniard in Yucatan, 1517–1570*. Cambridge Latin American Studies, 61. New York: Cambridge University Press, 1987.

———. *Aztecs: An Interpretation*. New York: Cambridge University Press, 1995.

Bibliography

Clifford, James. *The Predicament of Culture: Twentieth-Century Ethnography, Literature, and Art.* Cambridge, Mass.: Harvard University Press, 1988.

Cline, Howard F., ed. *Guide to Ethnohistorical Sources.* Vols. 12–15 of *Handbook of Middle American Indians,* ed. Robert Wauchope. Austin: University of Texas Press, 1972–75.

Clouston, A. W. *Hieroglyphic Bibles: Their Origin and History.* Glasgow: D. Bryce and Son, 1894.

Cobo, Bernabé. *History of the Inca Empire.* 1653. Translated and edited by Roland Hamilton from the holographic manuscript in the Biblioteca Capitular y Colombina de Sevilla. Austin: University of Texas Press, 1988.

Codex Azcatitlan. Translated from the Spanish by Dominique Michelet. Edited by Michel Graulich and Robert H. Barlow. 2 vols. Paris: Bibliothèque Nationale de France: Société des Américanistes, 1995.

Codex Borbonicus: Bibliothèque de l'Assemblée nationale, Paris (Y 120): Vollständige Faksimile-Ausgabe des Codex im Originalformat. Graz, Austria: Akademische Druck- und Verlagsanstalt, 1974.

Codex Borgia: Comentarios al Códice Borgia. Facsimile with commentary by Eduard Seler. Mexico City and Buenos Aires: Fondo de Cultura Económica, 1963.

Codex Cozcatzin. Mexico City and Puebla: Instituto Nacional de Antropología e Historia and Benemerita Universidad Autónoma de Puebla, 1994.

Codex en Cruz. Edited by Charles E. Dibble. 2 vols. Salt Lake City: University of Utah Press, 1981.

Codex Histoire mexicaine depuis 1221 jusqu'en 1594. See *Histoire mexicaine depuis 1221 jusqu'en 1594.*

The Codex Mendoza. Edited by Frances F. Berdan and Patricia Rieff Anawalt. 4 vols. Berkeley and Los Angeles: University of California Press, 1992.

Codex Ríos. Religión, costumbres e historia de los antiguos mexicanos: Libro explicativo del llamado Códice Vaticano A, Codex Vatic. Lat. 3738 de la Biblioteca Apostólica Vaticana. Códices mexicanos, 12. Edited by Ferdinand Anders, Maarten Jansen, and Luis Reyes García. 2 vols. Graz, Austria: Akademische Druck- und Verlagsanstalt; Mexico City: Fondo de Cultura Económica, 1996.

Codex Telleriano-Remensis. See Quiñonez Keber, Eloise.

Codex Vindobonensis. See Vienna Codex.

Cohn, Bernard. *Colonialism and Its Forms of Knowledge: The British in India.* Princeton, N.J.: Princeton University Press, 1996.

Colston, Stephen Allyn. "Fray Diego Durán's 'Historia de las Indias de Nueva España e Islas de la Tierra Firme': A Historiographical Analysis." Ph.D. diss., University of California, Los Angeles, 1973.

Cope, R. Douglas. *The Limits of Racial Domination: Plebeian Society in Colonial Mexico City, 1660–1720.* Madison: University of Wisconsin Press, 1994.

Cooper, Frederick. "Conflict and Connection: Rethinking Colonial African History." *American Historical Review* 99 (Dec. 1994): 1516–45.

Cortés, Hernán. *Historia de Nueva-España escrita por su esclarecido conquistador.* 1522–25. Edited by Francisco Antonio Lorenzana. Mexico City: Joseph Antonio de Hogal, 1770.

Cortés Castellanos, Justino. *El catecesimo en pictograms de Fr. Pedro de Gante.* Madrid: Fundación Universitaria Española, 1987.

Cotarelo y Mori, Emilio. "La fundación de la Academia española y su primer director D. Juan Manuel F. Pacheco, marqués de Villena." *Boletín de la Real Academia Española* 1 (1914): 3–38, 89–127.

———. *Iriarte y su época.* Madrid: Sucesores de Rivadeneyra, 1897.

Cruz, Martín de la, and Juan Badiano, eds. *Libellus de medicinalibus Indorum herbis: Manuscrito azteca de 1552.* Facsimile of MS Barb. Lat. 241 in the Vatican Library with Spanish translation. Mexico City: Instituto Mexicano del Seguro Social, 1964.

Cummins, Tom. "Representation in the Sixteenth Century and the Colonial Image of the Inca." In *Writing Without Words: Alternative Literacies in Mesoamerica and the Andes*, edited by Elizabeth Hill Boone and Walter D. Mignolo, pp. 188–219. Durham, N.C.: Duke University Press, 1994.

D'Owler, Luis Nicolau, and Howard F. Cline. "Sahagún and His Works." In *Guide to Ethnohistorical Sources*, edited by Howard F. Cline, 13: 186–207. Austin: University of Texas Press, 1973.

Daston, Lorraine. *Classical Probability in the Enlightenment.* Princeton, N.J.: Princeton University Press, 1988.

———. "Marvelous Facts and Miraculous Evidence in Early Modern Europe." In *Questions of Evidence*, edited by James Chandler et al., pp. 243–74. Chicago: University of Chicago Press, 1994.

———. "Objectivity and the Escape from Perspective." *Social Studies of Science* 22 (1992): 597–618.

Daston, Lorraine, and Katharine Park. *Wonders and the Order of Nature, 1150–1750.* New York: Zone Books, 1998.

Daston, Lorraine, and Peter Galison. "The Image of Objectivity." *Representations* 40 (Fall 1992): 81–128.

David, Madeleine V. *Le débat sur les écritures et l'hiéroglyphe aux XVIIe et XVIIIe siècles, et l'application de la notion de déchiffrement aux écritures mortes.* Paris: Ecole pratique des hautes études, 1965.

Díaz-Trechuelo, María Lourdes. "Diego García Panes: Un autor olvidado." *Anuario de Estudios Americanos* 12 (1966): 723–33.

Dirks, Nicholas B. "Castes of Mind." *Representations* 37 (Winter 1992): 56–78.

Diosdado Caballero, Ramón. *Breve examen acerca de los primeros tiempos del arte tipográfico en España.* Translated by Don Vicente Fontán. Rome: Antonio Fulgoni, 1793. Madrid: Oficina Tipográfica del Hospicio, 1865.

———. *L'eroismo di Ferdinando Cortese confermato contro le censure nemiche.* Rome: Antonio Fulgoni, 1806.

———. *Observaciones sobre la patria del pintor Josef Ribera llamado el españoleto.* Valencia: Benito Monfort, 1828.

Domenici, Viviano, and Davide Domenici. "Talking Knots of the Inka." *Archaeology* 44, no. 6 (Nov.–Dec. 1996): 50–56.

Duarte, Manuel. "El apostol Santo Tomás en el Nuevo Mundo." 1670s. In *Biblioteca mexicana del siglo XVIII*, edited by Nicolás León, sec. 1, pt. 3, pp. 353–532. Boletín del Instituto Bibliográfico Mexicano, 7. Mexico City: La viuda de Francisco Díaz León, 1906.

Dupaix, Guillermo. *Expediciones acerca de los antiguos monumentos de la Nueva España, 1805–1808*. Edited by José Alcina Franch. 2 vols. Madrid: Ediciones José Porrúa Turanzas, 1969.

Durán, Diego. *Historia de las Indias de Nueva España e islas de la tierra firme*. 1581. Edited by M. Garibay. Biblioteca Porrúa. 2 vols. Mexico City: Porrúa, 1967.

Duviols, Pierre. *La Lutte contre les religions autochtones dans le Pérou colonial: L'Extirpation de l'idolâtrie entre 1532 et 1660*. Lima: Institut français d'études andines, 1971. Translated by Albor Maruenda under the title *La destrucción de las religiones andinas: Conquista y colonia*. (Mexico City: Universidad Nacional Autónoma de México, 1977).

Echeverría y Veytia, Mariano Fernández. *Los calendarios mexicanos*. Mexico City: Imprenta y taller de fotograbado del Museo Nacional, 1907.

———. "Discurso preliminar [de la *Historia antigua*]." In Margarita Moreno Bonett, *Nacionalismo novohispano: Mariano Veytia: Historia antigua, fundación de Puebla, guadalupanismo*, pp. 299–320. Mexico City: Universidad Nacional Autónoma de México, Facultad de Filosofía y Letras, 1983.

———. *Historia antigua de México*. Ca. 1769. 2 vols. Mexico City: Leyenda, 1944.

———. *Historia de la fundación de la ciudad de la Puebla de los Angeles en la Nueva España: Su descripción y presente estado*. 1770s. 2 vols. Puebla: Imprenta Labor, 1931.

Eco, Umberto. *La ricerca della lingua perfetta nella cultura europea*. Bari: Laterza, 1993. Translated by James Fentress under the title *The Search for the Perfect Language* (Cambridge, Mass.: Blackwell, 1995, 1997).

Eddy, J. H., Jr. "Buffon, Organic Alterations, and Man." *Studies in History of Biology* 7 (1984): 1–45.

Eguiara y Eguren, Juan José de. "Panegírico de la virgen Guadalupe [1756]." In *Testimonios históricos guadalupanos*, edited by Ernesto de la Torre Villar and Ramiro Navarro de Anda, pp. 480–93. Mexico City: Fondo de Cultura Económica, 1982.

———. *Prólogos a la Bibliotheca mexicana*. 1755. Edited and translated by Agustín Millares Carlo. Mexico City: Fondo de Cultura Económica, 1944.

Elizalde Ita Parra, Joseph Mariano Gregorio de. *Gloria de México en la mayor exaltación y manifestación de la mayor gloria de María Santíssima Señora Nuestra en su triunphante assumpción a los cielos en cuyo mysterio se venera titular de la Sta. Iglesia Metropolitana de dicha ciudad. Sermón panegyrico en el día 15 de agosto de 1743*. Mexico City: Viuda de Joseph Bernardo de Hogal, 1744.

Elliott, John H. "The Decline of Spain." In id., *Spain and Its World, 1500–1700*, pp. 217–40. New Haven, Conn.: Yale University Press, 1989.

———. *Imperial Spain, 1469–1716*. New York: St. Martin's Press, 1964.

Engel, Samuel. "Recherches géographiques & critiques sur la position des lieux septentrionaux de l'Amérique." In *Supplément à l'Encyclopédie*, 1: 354–62. Amsterdam, 1776–77.

Erasmus, H. J. *The Origins of Rome in Historiography from Petrarch to Perizonius*. Assen, Holland: Van Gorcum, 1962.

Estala, Pedro de la. *Viagero universal o noticia del mundo antiguo y nuevo.* 43 vols. Madrid: Imprenta Real, 1795–1801.

Esteve Barba, Francisco. *Historiografía indiana.* 2d ed. Madrid: Gredos, 1992.

Fábrega, José Lino. *Interpretación del Códice Borgiano.* Ca. 1792–97. Texto italiano pareado con traducción al castellano por Alfredo Chavero y Francisco del Paso y Troncoso. In *Anales del Museo Nacional de México,* vol. 5. Mexico City: Imprenta del Museo Nacional, 1899.

Farriss, Nancy M. *Maya Society Under Colonial Rule: The Collective Enterprise of Survival.* Princeton, N.J.: Princeton University Press, 1984.

Feierman, Steven. "Colonizers, Scholars, and the Creation of Invisible Histories." In *Beyond the Cultural Turn,* edited by Victoria Bonnell and Lynn Hunt, pp. 182–216. Berkeley and Los Angeles: University of California Press, 1999.

Ferguson, Adam. *An Essay on the History of Civil Society.* 1767. Edited by Duncan Forbes. Edinburgh: Edinburgh University Press, 1966. Reprint. New Brunswick, N.J.: Transaction Books, 1980.

Fernández-Armesto, Felipe, "Aztec Auguries and Memories of the Conquest of Mexico." *Renaissance Studies* 6, nos. 3–4 (1992): 287–305.

Fernández de Navarrete, Martín. *Colección de los viages y descubrimientos que hicieron por mar los españoles desde fines del siglo XV: con varios documentos inéditos concernientes a la historia de la marina castellana y de los establecimientos españoles en Indias.* 5 vols. Madrid: Imprenta Real, 1825–37.

Fernández Duro, Cesareo, comp. "Informes." *Boletín de la Real Academia de la Historia* 42 (1903): 5–59.

Feugère, Anatole. *Un prècurseur de la révolution: L'abbé Raynal (1713–1796).* 1922. Geneva: Slatkine Reprints, 1970.

Feuillée, Louis. *Journal des Observations physiques mathématiques et botaniques. Faites par l'ordre du Roy sur les côtes orientales de l'Amérique méridionale et dans les Indes Occidentales, depuis l'année 1707 jusque en 1712.* 2 vols. Paris: Pierre Giffart, 1714.

———. *Journal des Observations physiques mathématiques et botaniques sur les côtes orientales de la Amérique Méridionale et aux Indes Occidentales, et dans un autre voiage fait par le même ordre à la Nouvelle Espagne et aux isles de l'Amérique.* Paris: Jean Matiette, 1725.

Findlen, Paula. *Possessing Nature: Museums, Collecting, and Scientific Culture in Early Modern Italy.* Berkeley and Los Angeles: University of California Press, 1994.

———. "Possessing the Past: The Material World of the Italian Renaissance." *American Historical Review* 103 (1998): 83–114.

Florencia, Francisco. *Estrella del norte de México, aparecida al rayar el día de la luz Evangélica en este Nuevo Mundo, en la cumbre del cerro Tepeyacac orilla del mar Tezcucano, a un natural recién convertido; pintada tres días después milagrosamente en su tilma o capa de lienzo, delante del obispo y de su familia en su casa obispal. Para luz en la fé a los indios; para rumbo cierto a los Españoles en virtud; para serenidad de las tempestousas inundaciones de la laguna. En la Historia de la Milagrosa Imagen de Nuestra Señora de Guadalupe de México, que se apareció en la manta de Juan Diego.* Mexico City: Maria de Benavides, viuda de Juan de Ribera, 1688.

Bibliography

Flores, José. *Específico nuevamente descubierto en el reino de Guatemala para la curación del horrible mal de cancro y otros mas frecuentes (experimentado ya favorablemente en esta capital de México).* Mexico City: Felipe de Zúñiga y Ontiveros, 1782.

Florescano, Enrique. *Memory, Myth, and Time in Mexico: From the Aztecs to Independence.* Translated by Albert Bork and Kathryn R. Bork. Austin: University of Texas Press, 1994.

Forner, Juan Pablo. *Oración apologética por la España y su mérito literario. Exornación al discurso del Abate Denina en la Academia de Ciencias de Berlín sobre ¿Qué se debe a España?* Madrid: Imprenta Real, 1786.

Franklin, Julian H. *Jean Bodin and the Sixteenth-Century Revolution in the Methodology of Law and History.* New York: Columbia University Press, 1966.

Fraser, Valerie. *The Architecture of Conquest: Building in the Viceroyalty of Peru, 1535–1635.* New York: Cambridge University Press, 1990.

Freedman, Paul. *Images of the Medieval Peasant.* Stanford: Stanford University Press, 1999.

Fréret, Nicolas. "Reflexions sur les principes generaux de l'art d'ecrire." *Mémoires de littérature tirés des registres de l'Académie royale des inscriptions et belles-lettres* 9 (1731): 328–69.

Frézier, Amédée François. *Relation du voyage de la Mer du Sud aux côtes du Chily et Pérou fait pendant les années 1712, 1713 et 1714. Avec une réponse à la préface . . . du livre intitulé, Journal des observations physiques, mathématiques & botaniques du R.P. Feuillée, contre la Relation du voyage de la mer du Sud, & une chronologie des vicerois du Pérou, Depuis son établissement jusqu'au tems [sic] de la Relation de voyage de la mer du Sud.* Paris: Chez Jean-Geoffroy Nyon, Etienne Ganeau, [et] Jacque Quillau, 1732.

García, Gregorio. *Origen de los Indios de el Nuevo Mundo, e Indias Occidentales.* 1607. Edited by Andrés González de Barcia. Madrid: Francisco Martínez Abad, 1729. Facsimile ed., Mexico City: Fondo de Cultura Económica, 1981.

García Cárcel, Ricardo. *La leyenda negra: Historia y opinión.* Madrid: Alianza, 1992.

García de la Vega, José Vicente. *Discurso crítico que sobre el uso de las lagartijas, como especifico contra muchas enfermedades.* Mexico City: Felipe de Zúñiga y Ontiveros, 1782.

García Panes, Diego. *La conquista (selección de la láminas y textos de los tomos V y VI del Theatro de Nueva España).* Ca. 1790. Edited by José Ignacio Echeagaray and Ernesto de la Torre Villar. Mexico City: Celanese Mexicana/San Angel Ediciones, 1976.

———. *Diario particular del camino que sigue un Virrey de México: desde su llegada a Veracruz hasta su entrada pública en la capital.* Edited by Lourdes Díaz-Trechuelo. Madrid: Centro de Estudios Históricos de Obras Públicas y Urbanismo, 1994.

———. *Panorama de Anáhuac (selección de láminas y textos de los tomos III y IV del Theatro de Nueva España).* Ca. 1790. Edited by José Ignacio Echeagaray and Ernesto de la Torre Villar. Mexico City: Celanese Mexicana/San Angel Ediciones, 1975.

Garcilaso de la Vega, Inca. *Comentarios reales de los Incas*. 1609. Edited by José Durand. 3 vols. Lima: Universidad Nacional Mayor de San Marcos, 1959.

——. *Le commentaire royale, ou L'Histoire des Incas Roys du Pérou*. Translated by Jean Baudoin. 2 vols. Paris: Augustin Courbe, 1633.

——. *Histoire des Incas Rois du Pérou, nouvellement traduite de l'Espagnol et mise dans un meilleur ordre avec des notes et des additions sur l'histoire naturelle*. 2 vols. Paris: Prault fils, 1744.

——. *Histoire des Yncas, rois du Pérou, depuis le premier Ynca Manco Capac, fils du soleil, jusqu'à Atahualpa dernier Ynca: où l'on voit leur établissement, leur religion, leurs loix, leur conquêtes. . . .* Translated by Jean Baudoin. 2 vols. in 1. Amsterdam: J.-F. Bernard, 1737.

Garibay, Angel María. *Historia de la literatura Náhuatl*. Biblioteca Porrúa, 1, 5. 2d ed. 2 vols. Mexico City: Porrúa, 1971.

Gay, Peter. *The Enlightenment: An Interpretation*. 2 vols. Vol. 1: *The Rise of Modern Paganism*. Vol. 2: *The Science of Freedom*. New York: Knopf, 1966–69.

Gemelli Careri, Giovanni Francesco. *Giro del mondo*. 6 vols. Naples: Guiseppe Roselli, 1699–1700.

——. *Viaje a la Nueva España*. Translated by José María Agreda y Sánchez. 2 vols. Biblioteca mínima mexicana, 13–14. Mexico City: Libro-Mex. Editores, 1955.

Gerbi, Antonello. *La disputa del Nuevo Mundo: Historia de una polémica, 1750–1900*. Translated into Spanish by Antonio Alatorre. 2d rev. ed. Mexico City: Fondo de Cultura Económica, 1982. Originally published as *La disputa del Nuovo Mondo: Storia di una polemica* (Milan: R. Ricciardi, 1955). Translated into English by Jeremy Moyle under the title *The Dispute of the New World: The History of a Polemic, 1750–1900*. Rev. ed. Pittsburgh: University of Pittsburgh Press, 1973.

Gibson, Charles. *Aztecs Under Spanish Rule: A History of the Indians of the Valley of Mexico, 1519–1810*. Stanford: Stanford University Press, 1964.

——, ed. *The Black Legend: Anti-Spanish Attitudes in the Old World and the New*. New York: Knopf, 1971.

Gibson, Charles, and John Glass. "A Census of Middle American Prose Manuscripts in the Native Historical Tradition." In *Guide to Ethnohistorical Sources*, edited by Howard F. Cline, 15: 322–400. Austin: University of Texas Press, 1975.

Gil Fernández, Luis. "Una labor de equipo: La *editio matritensis* de Juan Ginés de Sepúlveda." In *Estudios de humanismo y tradición clásica*, pp. 127–62. Madrid: Universidad Complutense, 1984.

Gilii, Filippo Salvadore. *Saggio di storia americana; o sia, Storia naturale, civile e sacra de'regni, e delle provincie spagnuole di Terra-ferma nell'America meridionale, descritta dall'abate Filippo Salvadore Gilij*. 4 vols. Rome: L. Perego erede Salvioni, 1780–84.

Glass, John. "A Survey of Native Middle American Pictorial Manuscripts." In *Guide to Ethnohistorical Sources*, edited by Howard F. Cline, 14: 3–78. Austin: University of Texas Press, 1975.

——. *The Boturini Collection and the Council of the Indies, 1780–1800*. Contributions to the Ethnohistory of Mexico, no. 4. Lincoln Center, Mass.: Conemex Associates, 1976.

Glass, John, and Donald Robertson, "A Census of Native Middle American Pictorial Manuscripts." In *Guide to Ethnohistorical Sources*, edited by Howard F. Cline, 14: 81–241. Austin: University of Texas Press, 1975.

Godwin, Joscelyn. *Athanasius Kircher*. London: Thames & Hudson, 1979.

Gombrich, E. H. "Icones Symbolicae." In id., *Symbolic Images: Studies in the Art of the Renaissance*, pp. 130–145. 1972. 2d ed. Oxford: Phaidon, 1978.

Gómez Gómez, Margarita. "El Archivo General de Indias, génesis histórica de sus ordenanzas." In *Archivo General de Indias: Ordenanzas*, pp. 53–120. Seville: Junta de Andalucia, 1986.

González Claverán, Virginia. *La expedición científica de Malaspina en Nueva España, 1789–1794*. Mexico City: Colegio de México, 1988.

——. "Notas a un documento inédito indigenista de Alzate (1791)." *Quipu* 6, no. 2 (1989): 162–69.

Goodman, Dena. *The Republic of Letters: A Cultural History of the French Enlightenment*. Ithaca, N.Y.: Cornell University Press, 1994.

Graffigny, Françoise d'Issembourg d'Happon-court de. *Lettres d'une Péruvienne*. N.p.: Peineca, 1747. Translated by Francis Ashmore under the title *Letters of a Peruvian Princess*. London: Harrison and Co., 1792.

Grafton, Anthony. *Defenders of the Text: The Traditions of Scholarship in an Age of Science, 1450–1800*. Cambridge, Mass.: Harvard University Press, 1991.

——. *Forgers and Critics: Creativity and Duplicity in Western Scholarship*. London: Collins & Brown, 1990.

——. "The Rest vs. The West." *New York Review of Books* 44, no. 6 (1997): 57–64.

Granados y Gálvez, José Joaquín. *Tardes americanas: Gobierno gentil y católico: Breve y particular noticia de toda la historia indiana . . . trabajada por un indio y un español*. 1778. Facsimile. Mexico City: Miguel Angel Porrúa and Universidad Nacional Autónoma de México, 1987.

Grandin, Greg. *The Blood of Guatemala: A History of Race and Nation*. Durham, N.C.: Duke University Press, 2000.

Green, John. *A New General Collection of Voyages and Travels: Consisting of the most esteemed relations which have been hitherto published in any language . . . in Europe, Asia, Africa, and America . . . so as to form a complete system of modern geography and history exhibiting the present state of all nations*. 4 vols. London: Thomas Astley, 1745–47.

Grimm, Friedrich Melchior, Freiherr von. *Correspondance, littéraire, philosophique et critique par Grimm, Diderot, Raynal, Meister, etc., revue sur les textes originaux, comprenant outre ce qui a été publié à diverses époques les fragments supprimés en 1813 par la censure, les parties inédites conservées à la Bibliothèque ducale de Gotha et à l'Arsenal à Paris*. Edited by Maurice Tourneux. 16 vols. Paris, Garnier frères, 1877–82. Nendeln: Kraus Reprint, 1968.

Gruzinski, Serge. *La colonización de lo imaginario: Sociedades indígenas y occidentalización en el México español, Siglos XVI–XVIII*. Mexico City: Fondo de Cultura Económica, 1991. Originally published as *La colonisation de l'imaginaire: Sociétés indigènes et occidentalisation dans le Mexique espagnol, XVIᵉ–XVIIIᵉ siècle* (Paris: Gallimard, 1988). Translated into English by Eileen Corrigan under the title *The Conquest of Mexico: The Incorporation of Indian Societies into the Western World, 16th–18th Centuries* (Cambridge: Polity Press, 1993).

———. *Painting the Conquest: The Mexican Indians and the European Renaissance.* Translated by Deke Dusinberre. Paris: UNESCO/Flammarion, 1992. Originally published as *L'Amérique de la conquête: Peinte par les Indiens du Mexique* (Paris: UNESCO/Flammarion, 1991).

Guignes, Joseph de. *Mémoire dans lequel on prouve que les Chinois sont une colonie égyptienne.* Paris: Desaint & Saillant, 1759.

———. "Recherches sur les navigations des Chinois du côte de l'Amérique, et sur quelques Peuples situés de l'extremité orientale de l'Asie." In *Mémoires de littérature tiréz des registres de l'Académie royale des inscriptions et belles-lettres* 49 (1772): 27–65.

Gumilla, Joseph. *El Orinoco ilustrado: Historia natural, civil y geográfica de este gran reino y de sus caudalosas vertientes.* Madrid: Manuel Fernández, 1741.

Habermas, Jürgen. *The Structural Transformation of the Public Sphere: An Inquiry into a Category of Bourgeois Society.* Translated by Thomas Burger and Frederick Lawrence. Cambridge, Mass.: MIT Press, 1991.

Hale, Charles A. *Mexican Liberalism in the Age of Mora, 1821–1853.* New Haven, Conn.: Yale University Press, 1968.

Hall, Stuart. "When Was 'the Post-Colonial'? Thinking at the Limit." In *The Post-Colonial Question: Common Skies, Divided Horizons,* edited by I. Chambers and L. Curti, pp. 242–60. London: Routledge, 1996.

Harris, John. *Navigantium atque Itinerarium Biblioteca, or, a Compleat Collection of Voyages and Travels. Consisting of above Six Hundred of the Most Authentic Writers.* 2 vols. London: T. Bennet, 1705.

———. *Navigantium atque Itinerarium Biblioteca or, a Compleat Collection of Voyages and Travels. Consisting of above Six Hundred of the Most Authentic Writers.* 2 vols. 2d ed. London: Woodward, 1744–48.

Haskett, Robert. "Visions of Municipal Glory Undimmed: The Nahuatl Town Histories of Colonial Cuernavaca." *Colonial Latin American Historical Review* 1 (1996): 1–36.

Hawkesworth, John. *An account of the voyages undertaken by the order of His present Majesty for making discoveries in the Southern Hemisphere, and successively performed by Commodore Byron, Captain Wallis, Captain Carteret, and Captain Cook, in the Dolphin, the Swallow, and the Endeavour: Drawn up from the journals which were kept by the several commanders, and from the papers of Joseph Banks, esq.* 3 vols. London: W. Strahan & T. Cadell, 1773.

Hazard, Paul. *La crise de la conscience européenne, 1680–1715.* 2 vols. Paris: Gallimard, 1968.

Heikamp, Detlef. *Mexico and the Medici.* Florence: Edam, 1972.

Hernández, Francisco. *Antigüedades de Nueva España.* 1570s. Crónicas de América, 28. Madrid: Historia 16, 1986.

———. *Obras Completas.* Edited by G. D'Ardois Somolinos. 7 vols. Mexico City: Universidad Nacional Autónoma de México, 1984.

Herr, Richard. *The Eighteenth-Century Revolution in Spain.* Princeton, N.J.: Princeton University Press, 1958.

Herrera y Tordesillas, Antonio de. *Historia general de los hechos de los castellanos en las islas i tierra firme del mar océano ["Décadas"].* 4 vols. Madrid: En la Emplentarea, 1601–15. Critical edition by Mariano Cuesta Domingo (Madrid: Universidad Complutense, 1991).

Hirschman, Albert O. *The Passions and the Interests.* Princeton, N.J.: Princeton University Press, 1977.

Histoire mexicaine depuis 1221 jusqu'en 1594: Manuscrito núm. 40 del Fondo de Manuscritos Mexicanos, Biblioteca Nacional de Francia. Edited and translated from the Nahuatl by Xóchitl Medina González. Serie Etnohistoria, Colección científica, 367. Mexico City: Instituto Nacional de Antropología e Historia, 1998.

Historia de la nación mexicana: Reproducción a todo color del Códice de 1576 (Códice Aubin). Edited and translated from the Nahuatl by Charles E. Dibble. Colección "Chimalistac" de libros y documentos acerca de la Nueva España, 16. Madrid: J. Porrúa Turanzas, 1963.

Hobsbawn, Eric, and Terence Ranger, eds. *The Invention of Tradition.* Cambridge: Cambridge University Press, 1983.

Hont, Istvan. "The Language of Sociability and Commerce: Samuel Pufendorf and the Theoretical Foundations of the 'Four-Stages Theory.'" In *The Languages of Political Theory in Early-Modern Europe,* edited by Anthony Pagden, pp. 253–76. Cambridge: Cambridge University Press, 1987.

Hont, Istvan, and Michael Ignatieff, eds. *Wealth and Virtue: The Shaping of Political Economy in the Scottish Enlightenment.* New York: Cambridge University Press, 1983.

Höpfl, H. M. "From Savage to Scotsman: Conjectural History in the Scottish Enlightenment." *Journal of British Studies* 17 (1978): 19–40.

Horn, Georg. *De originibus americanis.* The Hague: Adraini Vlacq, 1652.

The Huarochirí Manuscript: A Testament of Ancient and Colonial Andean Religion. Edited and translated by Frank Salomon and George L. Urioste. Austin: University of Texas Press, 1991.

Hudson, Nicholas. *Writing and European Thought, 1600–1830.* Cambridge: Cambridge University Press, 1994.

Humboldt, Alexander von. *Examen critique de l'histoire de la géographie du noveau continent et des progrés de l'astronomie nautique aux quinzième et seizième siècles.* 5 vols. Paris: Librairie de Gide, 1836–39.

———. *Researches, concerning the institutions & monuments of the ancient inhabitants of America, with descriptions & views of some of the most striking scenes in the Cordilleras!* Translated by Helen Maria Williams. 2 vols. in 1. London: Longman, etc., Hurst, Rees, Orme & Brown, J. Murray & H. Colburn, 1814.

———. *Vues des cordillères et monuments des peuples indigènes de l'Amérique.* Paris: F. Schoell, 1810.

Hume, David. *The History of England.* 8 vols. Oxford: William Pickering & Talboys & Wheeler, 1826.

Iturri, Francisco. *Carta Crítica sobre la Historia de América de J. B. Muñoz.* In *Francisco Javier Iturri y su "Carta crítica" (1797),* edited by Guillermo Furlong, S.J. Buenos Aires: Libreria La Plata, 1955.

Iversen, Erik. *The Myth of Egypt and Its Hieroglyphs in European Tradition.* Copenhagen: Gec Gad Publishers, 1961.

Jiménez de la Espada, Marcos. *Relaciones geográficas de Indias: Perú.* 3 vols. Biblioteca de Autores Españoles, 183–85. Madrid: Atlas, 1965.

Juderías, Julián. *La leyenda negra: Estudios acerca del concepto de España en el extranjero.* 9th ed. Barcelona: Araluce, 1943. Originally published as *La leyenda negra y la verdad histórica* (Madrid: Tip. de la "Rev. de Arch., Bibl. y Museos," 1914).

Kahn, Victoria Ann. *Rhetoric, Prudence, and Skepticism in the Renaissance.* Ithaca, N.Y.: Cornell University Press, 1985.

Kames, Henry Home, Lord. *Sketches of the History of Man.* 2d ed. 4 vols. Edinburgh: W. Strahan, T. Cadell & W. Creech, 1778.

Karttunen, Frances E. *Between Worlds: Interpreters, Guides, and Survivors.* New Brunswick, N.J.: Rutgers University Press, 1994.

Keen, Benjamin. *The Aztec Image in Western Thought.* New Brunswick, N.J.: Rutgers University Press, 1971.

Kircher, Athanasius. *Oedipus aegyptiacus, hoc est, universalis hieroglyphicae veterum doctrinae, temporum iniuria abolitae, instauratio.* 4 vols. Rome: Vitalis Mascadi, 1652–54.

Knowlson, James. *Universal Language Schemes in England and France, 1600–1800.* Toronto: University of Toronto Press, 1975.

Koenigsberger, Helmut. "Spain." In *National Consciousness, History, and Political Culture in Early-Modern Europe,* edited by Orest Ranum, pp. 144–172. Baltimore: Johns Hopkins University Press, 1975.

Kohut, Karl. "La implantación del humanismo español en la Nueva España: El caso de Francisco Cervantes de Salazar." In *Pensamiento europeo y cultura colonial,* edited by Karl Kohut and Sonia V. Rose, pp. 11–47. Frankfurt and Madrid: Vervuert and Iberoamericana, 1997.

Kohut, Karl, and Sonia V. Rose, eds. *Pensamiento europeo y cultura colonial.* Frankfurt and Madrid: Vervuert and Iberoamericana, 1997.

Kramer, Roswitha. "' . . . ex ultimo angulo orbis': Atanasio Kircher y el Nuevo Mundo." In *Pensamiento europeo y cultura colonial,* edited by Karl Kohut and Sonia V. Rose, pp. 320–77. Frankfurt and Madrid: Vervuert and Iberoamericana, 1997.

Kubler, George. "Vico's Idea of America." In *Studies in Ancient American and European Art: The Collected Essays of George Kubler,* edited by Thomas F. Reese, pp. 296–300. New Haven, Conn.: Yale University Press, 1985.

Kubler, George, and Charles Gibson. *The Tovar Calendar: An Illustrated Mexican Manuscript, ca. 1585.* Memoirs of the Connecticut Academy of Arts and Sciences, vol. 11. New Haven, Conn.: Yale University Press, 1951.

Kupperman, Karen Ordall, ed. *America in European Consciousness, 1493–1750.* Chapel Hill: University of North Carolina Press, 1995.

La Condamine, Charles-Marie de. "Mémoire sur quelques anciens monuments du Pérou, du temps des Incas." In *Histoire de L'Académie royale des sciences et Mémoires de la Académie, année 1746,* pp. 435–56. Berlin, 1748.

———. *Relation abregée d'un voyage fait dans l'interieur de l'Amérique méridionale.*

Bibliography

Despuis la côte de la Mer du Sud, jusqu'aux côtes du Bresil & de la Guiane en descendant la rivière des Amazones. Paris: Veuve Pissot, 1745.

Ladd, Doris M. *The Mexican Nobility at Independence, 1780–1826*. Latin American monographs, no. 40. Austin: Institute of Latin American Studies, University of Texas, 1976.

Lafaye, Jacques. *Quetzalcóatl et Guadalupe: La formation de la conscience nationale au Mexique*. Paris: Gallimard, 1974.

Lafitau, Joseph. *La vie et les moeurs des sauvages américains comparée aux moeurs des premier tems [sic]*. 4 vols. Amsterdam: Frères Westeinos, 1724–32.

Lafuente, Antonio, and Antonio Mazuecos. *Los caballeros del punto fijo. Ciencia, política y aventura en la expedición geodésica hispanofrancesa al virreinato del Perú en el siglo XVIII*. Madrid: Ediciones Serbal y Consejo Superior de Investigaciones Científicas, 1987.

Lafuente, Antonio, and Manuel Selles. *El observatorio de Cádiz (1753–1831)*. Madrid: Ministerio de Defensa, Instituto de Historia y Cultura Naval, 1988.

Lambeck, Peter. *Commentariorum de Augustissima Bibliotheca Caesarea Vindobonensi*. 8 vols. Vienna: M. Cosmerovij, 1665–79.

Landa, Diego de. *Relación de las cosas de Yucatán*. Edited by Miguel de Rivera. Crónicas de América, 7. Madrid: Historia 16, 1985.

La Peyrère, Isaac de. *Praeadamitae, sive, Exercitatio super versibus duodecimo, decimotertio, & decimoquarto, capitis quinti Epistolae D. Pauli ad Romanos: quibus inducuntur primi homines ante Adamum conditi*. Amsterdam: Louis and Daniel Elzevier, 1655.

La Porte, Joseph de, abbé. *Le voyageur françois ou la connaissance de L'ancien et du Nouveau monde*. 42 vols. Paris: Cellot, 1768–95.

Laurencich Minelli, Laura. "Bologna el il Mondo Nuovo." In *Bologna e il Mondo Nuovo*, edited by Laura Laurencich Minelli, pp. 9–23. Bologna: Grafis Edizioni, 1992.

Laurencín, Marqués de. *Don Agustín de Montiano y Luyando, primer director de la Real Academia de Historia. Noticias y documentos*. Madrid: Revista de Archivos, Bibliotecas y Museos, 1926.

Lavallé, Bernard. *Le marquis et le marchand: Les luttes de pouvoir au Cuzco, 1700–1730*. Paris: Editions du Centre national de la recherche scientifique, 1987. Translated into Spanish as *El mercader y el marqués: Las luchas de poder en el Cusco (1700–1730)*. Lima: Fondo, Banco Central de Reserva del Perú, 1988.

Legati, Lorenzo. *Museo Cospiano anneso aquello del famoso Ulisse Aldrovandi e donato a la sua patria dall'ilustrisimo signor Ferdinando Cospi*. Bologna: Giacomo Monti, 1677.

León Pinelo, Antonio de. *Epítome de la bibliotheca oriental, y occidental, náutica, y geográfica*. 1629. Edited by Andrés González de Barcia. 3 vols. Madrid: Francisco Martínez Abad, 1737–38.

León y Gama, Antonio de. *Descripción histórica y cronológica de las dos piedras que con ocasión del nuevo empedrado que se esta formando en la plaza principal de México se hallaron en ella en el año de 1790*. Vol. 1, 1792. Edited by Carlos María de Bustamante. 2 vols. in 1. Mexico City: Imprenta de Alejandro Valdés, 1832.

———. *Disertación física sobre la materia y formación de las auroras boreales.* Mexico City: Felipe de Zúñiga y Ontiveros, 1790.

———. *Instrucción sobre el remedio de las lagartijas: Nuevamente descubierto para la curación del cancro y otras enfermedades.* Mexico City: Felipe de Zúñiga y Ontiveros, 1782.

———. *Respuesta satisfactoria a la carta apologética que escribieron el Lic. Manuel Antonio Moreno y el Br. Alejo Ramón Sánchez. Y defensa contra la censura que en ella se hace de algunas proposiciones contenidas en la "Instrucción sobre el remedio de las lagartijas."* Mexico City: Felipe de Zúñiga y Ontiveros, 1783.

León, Nicolas, ed. *Bibliografía mexicana del siglo XVIII.* Boletín del Instituto Bibliográfico Mexicano, nos. 1, 4, 5, 7, 8, 10. 5 vols. in 6. Mexico City: Imp. de la viuda de Francisco Díaz León, 1902–8.

Leonard, Irving. *Don Carlos de Sigüenza y Góngora: A Mexican Savant of the Seventeenth Century.* Berkeley: University of California Press, 1929.

León-Portilla, Miguel. "Estudio preliminar." In Lorenzo Benaduci Boturini, *Idea de una nueva historia general,* edited by Miguel León-Portilla, ix–lxii. Mexico City: Porrúa, 1986.

Lestringant, Frank. *André Thevet, cosmographe des derniers Valois.* Geneva: Librairie Droz, 1991.

Lévesque de Pouilly, Louis-Jean. "Dissertation sur l'incertitude de l'Histoire des quatre premiers siècles de Rome." *Mémoires de littérature tirés des registres de l'Académie royale des inscriptions et belles lettres* 6 (1729): 14–21.

Levine, Joseph M. *The Battle of the Books: History and Literature in the Augustan Age.* Ithaca, N.Y.: Cornell University Press, 1991.

———. *Dr. Woodward's Shield: History, Science, and Satire in Augustan England.* Ithaca, N.Y.: Cornell University Press, 1977.

Locke, John. *Essay Concerning Human Understanding.* 1690. Edited by A. C. Fraser. Oxford: Oxford University Press, 1984.

Lockhart, James. *The Nahuas After the Conquest: A Social and Cultural History of the Indians of Central Mexico, Seventeenth Through Eighteenth Centuries.* Stanford: Stanford University Press, 1992.

Lopez, François. *Juan Pablo Forner et la crise de la conscience espagnole au XVIIIᵉ siècle.* Bordeaux: Bibliothèque de l'Ecole des hautes études hispaniques, 1976.

López de Gómara, Francisco. *La historia de las Indias y conquista de México.* Zaragoza: n. p., 1552.

Lorenzana, Francisco Antonio de, archbishop. "Fragmentos de un mapa de tributos o cordillera de los pueblos." In Hernán Cortés, *Historia de Nueva-España escrita por su esclarecido conquistador,* 171–76. Mexico City: Joseph Antonio de Hogal, 1770. See also *Matrícula de tributos* below.

Lozoya, Xavier. *Plantas y luces en México.* Barcelona: Ediciones del Serbal, 1984.

Lucian of Samosata. "How to Write History." In *Versions of History from Antiquity to the Enlightenment,* edited by Donald R. Kelly, pp. 64–68. New Haven, Conn.: Yale University Press, 1991.

Lynch, John. *Bourbon Spain, 1700–1808.* Oxford: Blackwell, 1989.

MacCormack, Sabine. "Perceptions of Greco-Roman and Amerindian Paganism in

Early Modern Europe." In *America in European Consciousness*, edited by Karen Ordall Kupperman, pp. 79–129. Chapel Hill: University of North Carolina Press, 1995.

———. *Religion in the Andes: Vision and Imagination in Early Colonial Peru*. Princeton, N.J.: Princeton University Press, 1991.

Mackintosh, James. *A Discourse on the Study of the Law of Nature and Nations*. 1798. London: Edward Lumley, 1835.

MacLachlan, Colin M., and Jaime E. Rodríguez O. *The Forging of the Cosmic Race: A Reinterpretation of Colonial Mexico*. 1980. Expanded ed. Berkeley and Los Angeles: University of California Press, 1990.

Macri, Marta J. "Maya and Other Mesoamerican Scripts." In *The World's Writing Systems*, edited by Peter Daniels and William Bright, pp. 172–82. Oxford: Oxford University Press, 1996.

Malaspina, Alejandro. *Los axiomas políticos sobre América*. Ca. 1788. Estudio introductorio y edición por Manuel Lucena Giraldo y Juan Pimentel Igea. Aranjuez: Doce Calles, 1991.

Mallon, Florencia. *Peasant and Nation: The Making of Postcolonial Mexico and Peru*. Berkeley and Los Angeles: University of California Press, 1995.

Maltby, William S. *The Black Legend in England: The Development of Anti-Spanish Sentiment, 1558–1660*. Durham, N.C.: Duke University Press, 1971.

Manuel, Frank Edward. *The Eighteenth Century Confronts the Gods*. Cambridge, Mass.: Harvard University Press, 1959.

Manzano, Juan. "Un compilador indiano: Manuel José de Ayala." *Boletín del Instituto de Investigaciones Históricas* 18, nos. 61–63 (1934–35): 152–240.

Maravall, José Antonio. "El sentimiento de nación en el siglo XVIII: La obra de Forner." In *Estudios de la historia del pensamiento español (siglo XVIII)*, pp. 42–60. Madrid: Biblioteca Mondadori, 1991.

———. *La cultura del Barroco: Análisis de una estructura histórica*. 2d ed. Barcelona: Ariel, 1980.

Marcus, Joyce. *Mesoamerican Writing Systems: Propaganda, Myth, and History in Four Ancient Civilizations*. Princeton, N.J.: Princeton University Press, 1992.

Márquez, Pedro José. *Delle case di città degli antichi romani secondo la dottrina di Vitrubio*. Rome: Presso il Salmoni, 1795.

———. "Apendix." In Antonio León y Gama, *Saggio dell' astronomia cronologia e mitologia degli antichi Messicani*, translated by P. J. Márquez, pp. 169–82. Rome: Presso il Salomoni, 1804.

———. *Due antichi monumenti di architettura messicana*. Rome: Presso il Salomoni, 1804.

Martínez, Alfonso, ed. *Francisco Xavier Clavigero en la Ilustración mexicana, 1731–1787*. Mexico City: El Colegio de México, 1988.

Maza, Francisco de la. *El guadalupanismo mexicano*. 1953. Lecturas mexicanas, 37. 3d ed. Mexico City: Fondo de Cultura Económica, Secretaría de Educación Pública, 1984.

Masdeu, Juan Francisco. *Historia crítica de España y de la cultura española*. 20 vols. Madrid: Antonio de Sancha, 1783–1807.

Masson de Morvilliers, Nicolas. "Espagne." In *Encyclopédie méthodique [Géographie]*, 1: 556–66. Paris and Liège: Panckoucke & Plomteaux, 1783.

Matrícula de tributos (Códice de Moctezuma), Museo Nacional de Antropología, México (Cód. 35–52). Codices selecti phototypice impressi, 68. Edited by Frances F. Berdan and Jacqueline de Durand-Forest. Graz, Austria: Akademische Druck-u. Verlagsanstalt, 1980. See also Lorenzana, Francisco Antonio de, above.

Matute, Alvaro. *Lorenzo Boturini y el pensamiento histórico de Vico.* Mexico City: Universidad Nacional Autónoma de México, 1976.

Mayans y Siscar, Gregorio. "Carta a Felix Yañez de Lima, Duque de Sotomayor." In *Cartas Morales, militares, civiles, i literarias de various autores españoles,* 3: 388–400. Valencia: Salvador Pauli, 1773.

———. *Conversación sobre El Diario de los literatos de España.* Madrid: Juan de Zúñiga, 1737.

———. *Epistolario II: Mayans y Burriel.* Edited by Antonio Mestre. Valencia: Publicaciones del Ayuntamiento de Oliva, 1972.

———. *Epistolario VIII. Mayans a Martínez Pingarrón. Historia cultural de la Real Biblioteca.* Edited by Antonio Mestre. Valencia: Publicaciones del Ayuntamiento de Oliva, 1987.

———. "Juicio aprovando la 'Oración latina a la Divina Sabiduria, patrona de la Academia Valenciana', su autor, el cavallero Lorenzo Boturini Benaducci." 1750. In *Obras Completas de Gregorio Mayans y Siscar,* edited by Antonio Mestre, 5: 391–95. Valencia: Publicaciones del Ayuntamiento de Oliva, 1986.

———. "Nova literaria ex Hispania." *Acta eruditorum* (1731): 432–40.

McClelland, Ivy Lilian. *The Origins of the Romantic Movement in Spain.* Liverpool: Liverpool University Press, 1975.

McClintock, Anne. *Imperial Leather: Race, Gender and Sexuality in the Colonial Contest.* Routledge: New York, 1995.

Meek, Ronald. *Social Science and the Ignoble Savage.* Cambridge: Cambridge University Press, 1976.

Mémoires concernant l'histoire, les sciences, les arts, les moeurs, les usages, &c. des Chinois, par les missionnaires de Pékin. 17 vols. Paris: Nyon, 1776–1814.

Memorias de la Real Academia de Historia. Vol 1. Madrid: Imprenta de Sancha, 1796.

Méndez, Cecilia. "Incas Sí, Indios No: Notes on Peruvian Creole Nationalism and Its Contemporary Crisis." *Journal of Latin American Studies* 28 (1996): 197–225.

Mera, Juán León. "Carta al señor Antonio Rubió y Lluch." *Revista Ecuatoriana,* no. 48 (Dec. 1892).

Mercati, Michele. *De gli obelischi di Roma.* Rome: Domenico Basa, 1589. Edited by Gianfranco Cantelli. Bologna: Capelli Editore, 1981.

Mestre, Antonio. "La imagen de España en el siglo XVIII: Apologistas, críticos y detractores." *Arbor* 115 (1983): 49–73.

———. *Historia, fueros y actitudes políticas: Mayans y la historiografía del XVIII.* Valencia: Publicaciones del Ayuntamiento de Oliva, 1970.

Mier, Servando Teresa de. *Obras completas: El heterodoxo Guadalupano,* edited by Edmundo O'Gorman. 3 vols. Mexico City: Universidad Nacional Autónoma de México, 1981.

Bibliography

Mignolo, Walter D. *The Darker Side of the Renaissance: Literacy, Territoriality, and Colonization*. Ann Arbor: University of Michigan Press, 1995.

Millares Carlo, Agustín. *Cuatro estudios biobibliográficos mexicanos*. Mexico City: Fondo de Cultura Económica, 1986.

Mills, Kenneth, and William Taylor, eds. *Colonial Spanish America: A Documentary History*. Wilmington, Del.: Scholarly Resources, 1998.

Molina, Juan Ignacio. *The Geographical, Natural, and Civil History of Chili [sic]*. 2 vols. London: Longman, 1809. Originally published as *Saggio sulla storia naturale de Chili* (1782) and *Saggio sulla storia civile de Chili* (1787).

Montesquieu, Charles de Secondat, baron de. *The Spirit of the Laws*. 1748. 2 vols. New York: Hafner, 1949.

Moreno Bonett, Margarita. *Nacionalismo novohispano: Mariano Veytia: Historia antigua, fundación de Puebla, guadalupanismo*. Mexico City: Universidad Nacional Autónoma de México, Facultad de Filosofía y Letras, 1983.

Moreno de los Arcos, Roberto. "Un eclesiástico criollo frente al estado Borbón." In José Antonio de Alzate, *Memorias y ensayos*, edited by R. Moreno de los Arcos, pp. 1–29. Mexico City: Universidad Nacional Autónoma de México, 1985.

——. "Ensayo biobibliográfico de Antonio de León y Gama." *Boletín del Instituto de Investigaciones Bibliográficas* 3 (1970): 43–145.

——. "La *Historia antigua de México* de Antonio León y Gama." *Estudios de Historia Novohispana* 7 (1981): 67–78.

——. "Las notas de Alzate a la *Historia antigua* de Clavijero." *Estudios de Cultura Nahuatl* 10 (1972): 359–92.

——. "Las notas de Alzate a la *Historia antigua* de Clavijero (Addenda)." *Estudios de Cultura Nahuatl* 12 (1976): 85–120.

——, comp. *Linneo en México: Las controversias sobre el sistema binario sexual, 1788–1798*. Mexico City: Universidad Nacional Autónoma de México, 1989.

Moreno, Manuel Antonio, and Alejo Ramón Sánchez. *Carta apologética de las reflexiones sobre el uso de las lagartijas*. Mexico City: Joseph Antonio de Hogal, 1782.

——. *Observaciones crítico-apologéticas sobre la respuesta satisfactoria de Antonio de León y Gama. Y la instruccion sobre el remedio de las lagartijas del mismo autor*. Mexico City: Herederos de Joseph de Jaúregui, 1783.

Morner, Magnus, ed. *The Expulsion of the Jesuits from Latin America*. New York: Knopf, 1965.

Motolinía, Toribio de Benavente. *Memoriales; o, Libro de las cosas de la Nueva España y de los naturales de ella*. Ca. 1536–43. Edited by Edmundo O'Gorman. Serie de historiadores y cronistas de Indias, 2. 2d ed. Mexico City: Universidad Nacional Autónoma de México, Instituto de Investigaciones Históricas, 1971.

Moxó y de Francolí, Benito María de. *Cartas Mejicanas*. 1805. 2d ed. Genoa: Pellas, 1839.

——. *Entretenimientos de un prisionero en las provincias del Rio de La Plata*. 2 vols. Barcelona: J. Torner, 1828.

Mundy, Barbara. *The Mapping of New Spain: Indigenous Cartography and the Maps of the Relaciones Geográficas*. Chicago: University of Chicago Press, 1996.

Muñoz Pérez, José. "La Idea de América en Campomanes." *Anuarios de Estudios Americanos* 10 (1953): 209–65.

Muñoz, Juan Bautista. *Historia del Nuevo Mundo.* Madrid: Viuda de Ibarra, 1793.

——. *Juicio del tratado de la educación del M.R.P. D. Cesareo Pozzi.* Madrid: Joachim Ibarra, 1778.

——. "Memoria sobre las apariciones y el culto de Nuestra Señora de Guadalupe de México [1794]." In *Testimonios históricos guadalupanos,* edited by Ernesto de la Torre Villar and Ramiro Navarro de Anda, pp. 689–701. Mexico City: Fondo de Cultura Económica, 1982.

——. *Satisfacción a la carta crítica sobre las Historia del Nuevo Mundo.* Valencia: Joseph de Orga, 1798.

Murillo Velarde, Pedro. *Geographía histórica, donde describen los reynos, provincias, ciudades, fortalezas, mares, montes, ensenadas, cabos, ríos, y puertos, con la mayor individualidad, y exactitud. . . .* 10 vols. Madrid: Gabriel Ramírez and other imprints, 1752.

Nasarre y Ferriz, Blas Antonio. "Disertación o prólogo sobre las comedias de España." In *Comedias y entremeses de Cervantes.* Madrid: Antonio Marín, 1749.

Nava Rodríguez, María Teresa. "Reformismo ilustrado y americanismo: La Real Academia de la Historia, 1735–1792." Ph.D. diss., Universidad Complutense de Madrid, 1989.

Nuix, Juan. *Reflexiones imparciales sobre la humanidad de los españoles en las Indias contra los pretendidos filósofos y políticos. Para ilustrar las historias de MM. Raynal y Robertson.* Edited and translated by Pedro Varela y Ulloa. Madrid: Joachin Ibarrra, 1782.

——. *Riflessioni imparziali sopra l'umanitá degli Spagnuoli nell'Indie contro i pretesi filosofi e politici, per servire di lume alle storie de' Signori Raynal e Robertson.* Venice: [F. Pezzana], 1780.

O'Brien, Karen. "Between Enlightenment and Stadial History: William Robertson on the History of Europe." *British Journal for Eighteenth-Century Studies* 16 (1993): 53–63.

O'Gorman, Edmundo. "Estudio Introductorio." In Fernando de Alva Ixtlilxochitl, *Obras históricas,* 1: 1–257. Mexico City: Universidad Nacional Autónoma de México, 1975.

Onis, Carlos W. de, comp. *Las polémicas de Juan Bautista Muñoz.* Madrid: Ediciones José Porrúa Turanzas, 1984.

Ordóñez y Aguiar, Ramón. "Historia de la creación del cielo y la tierra conforme al sistema de la gentilidad americana. Theología de los Culebras figurada en ingeniosos gerolíphicos, symbolos, emblemas y metáphoras." 1794. In *Biblioteca mexicana del siglo XVIII,* edited by Nicolás León, sec. 1, pt. 4, pp. 1–265. *Boletín del Instituto Bibliográfico Mexicano,* 8. Mexico City: La viuda de Francisco Díaz León, 1907.

Osorio Romero, Ignacio. *La enseñanza del latin a los indios.* Mexico City: Universidad Nacional Autónoma de México, 1990.

——. *La luz imaginaria: Epistolario de Atanasio Kircher con los novohispanos.* Mexico City: Universidad Nacional Autónoma de México, 1993.

Outram, Dorinda. *The Enlightenment.* Cambridge: Cambridge University Press, 1995.

Pagden, Anthony. *European Encounters with the New World: From Renaissance to Romanticism.* New Haven, Conn.: Yale University Press, 1993.

——. *The Fall of Natural Man: The American Indian and the Origins of Comparative Ethnology*. Rev. ed. Cambridge: Cambridge University Press, 1986.

——. *Lords of All the World: Ideologies of Empire in Spain, Britain and France, c. 1500–c. 1800*. New Haven, Conn.: Yale University Press, 1995.

——. *Spanish Imperialism and the Political Imagination*. New Haven, Conn.: Yale University Press, 1990.

——. ed. *The Languages of Political Theory in Early-Modern Europe*. Cambridge: Cambridge University Press, 1987.

Pailles Hernández, María de la Cruz, and Rosalba Nieto Calleja. "Primeras expediciones a las ruinas de Palenque: Joseph Antonio Calderón y Antonio Bernasconi." *Arqueología: Revista de la Dirección de Arqueología del Instituto Nacional de Antropología e Historia*, 2d ser., 4 (1990), 103–5.

Paleotti, Gabriele. *Discorso intorno alle imagini sacre et profane*. Bologna: A. Benacci, 1582. Reprint, Bologna: Arnaldo Forni, 1990.

Pascual, Ricardo. *El botánico José Quer (1695–1764), primer apologista de la ciencia española*. Valencia: Cátedra e Instituto de Historia de la Medicina, 1970.

Patrizi, Francesco. *Della historia diece dialoghi ne' qvali si ragiona di tvtte le cose appartenenti all'historia, & allo scriuerla, & all'osseruarla: con gratia, & priuilegio per anni X*. Venice: Appresso A. Arrivabene, 1560.

Pauw, Cornelius de. "Amérique." In *Supplement à l'Encyclopédie*, 1: 344–54. Amsterdam: M. M. Rey, 1776–77.

——. *Oeuvres philosophiques de Pauw*. 7 vols. Paris: Jean-François Bastien, 1795.

——. *Philosophical Dissertations on the Egyptians and Chinese*. Translated by Capt. J. Thompson. 2 vols. London: T. Chapman, 1795. Originally published in French in 1794.

——. *Recherches philosophiques sur les américains, ou Mémoires intéressants pour servir à l'histoire de l'espèce humaine*. 1768–69. 2 vols. New edition in 3 vols. that includes *Une Dissertation critique par Dom Pernety & de la Défense de l'auteur des Recherches contre cette dissertation*. Berlin: G. J. Decker, 1770.

——. *Recherches philosophiques sur les Grecs*. 2 vols. Berlin, 1787.

Paxman, David B. "Language and Difference: The Problem of Abstraction in Eighteenth-Century Language Study." *Journal of the History of Ideas* 54 (1993): 19–36.

Pazzi de Bonneville, Zacharie de. *De l'Amérique et des américains, ou Observations curieuses de philosophe La Douceur, qui a parcouru cet hemisphere pendant la dernière guerre, en faisant le noble métier de tuer des hommes sans les manger*. Berlin: Samuel Pitra, 1771.

Pernety, Antoine-Joseph. *Dissertation sur l'Amérique et les américains, contre les Recherches philosophiques de Mr. de P*. Berlin, G. J. Decker, 1770. Reprinted in the 1770 edition of Pauw's *Recherches*.

——. *Examen des "Recherches philosophiques sur l'Amérique et les américains" et de la "Défense" de cet ouvrage*. 2 vols. Berlin: G. J. Decker, 1771.

Peset, José Luis. *Ciencia y libertad*. Madrid: CSIC, 1987.

Peset, José Luis, and Antonio Lafuente, "Ciencia e historia de la ciencia en la España ilustrada." *Boletín de la Real Academia de la Historia* 173, no. 2 (1981): 267–300.

Picart, Bernard. *Cérémonies et coutumes religieuses des peuples idolâtres, représentées par des figures dessinées de la main, de Bernard Picard. Avec une explication historique et quelques dissertations curieuses.* 2 vols. Amsterdam: J. F. Bernard, 1723–28.

Pignoria, Lorenzo. "Seconda parte delle imagini de gli dei indiani." In Vicenzo Cartari, *Imagini de gli dei delli antichi*, pp. 545–89. Padua: Pietro Paolo Tozzi, 1626.

Pimentel, Juan. *Malaspina o la física de la monarquía: Ciencia y política en el pensamiento colonial de Alejandro Malaspina (1754–1810)*. Madrid: Doce Calles, 1998.

Pinkerton, John. *Modern Geography: A Description of the Empires, Kingdoms, States and Colonies, with the Oceans, Seas and Isles in All Parts of the World: Including the Most Recent Discoveries and Political Alterations.* 3d ed. rev. 2 vols. London: T. Cadell and W. Davies . . . and Longman, Hurst, Rees, and Orme and Brown, 1811.

Pino, Fermín del, ed., *Ciencia y contexto histórico en las expediciones ilustradas a América*. Madrid: Consejo Superior de Investigaciones Científicas, 1988.

Pino, Fermín del, and Angel Guirao. "Las expediciones ilustradas y el estado español." *Revista de Indias* 47 (1987): 380–83.

Pinot, Virgilie. *La Chine et la formation de l'esprit philosophique en France (1640–1740)*. Paris: Librairie Orientaliste Paul Geuthner, 1932.

Platt, Tristan. "The Alchemy of Modernity: Alonso Barba's Copper Cauldrons and the Independence of Bolivian Metallurgy (1790–1890)." *Journal of Latin American Studies* 32 (2000): 1–54.

Pluche, Noël-Antoine, abbé. *Histoire du ciel consideré selon les idées des poètes, des philosophes, et de Moïse. Histoire du ciel: ou l'on recherche l'origine de l'idolatrie, et les méprises de la philosophie, sur la formation des corps célestes, & de toute la nature.* Paris: Chez la veuve Estienne, 1742.

Pocock, J. G. A. *Virtue, Commerce, and History*. Cambridge: Cambridge University Press, 1985.

Poole, Stafford. *Our Lady of Guadalupe: The Origins and Sources of a Mexican National Symbol*. Tucson: University of Arizona Press, 1996.

Popkin, Richard H. *The History of Scepticism from Erasmus to Spinoza*. Revised and expanded edition. Berkeley and Los Angeles: University of California Press, 1979. Originally published as *The History of Scepticism from Erasmus to Descartes* (Assen, Neth.: Van Gorcum, 1960, 1964).

———. *Isaac la Peyrère (1596–1676): His Life, Works, and Influence*. Leiden: Brill, 1987.

Popol Vuh: The Definitive Edition of the Mayan Book of the Dawn of Life and the Glories of Gods and Kings. Translated by Dennis Tedlock. New York: Simon & Schuster, 1985.

Prakash, Gyan, ed. *After Colonialism: Imperial Histories and Postcolonial Displacements*. Princeton, N.J.: Princeton University Press, 1995.

Pratt, Mary Louise. *Imperial Eyes: Travel Writing and Transculturation*. London: Routledge, 1992.

Prévost, Antoine-François, abbé. *Histoire générale des voyages, ou, Nouvelle collection de toutes les relations de voyages par mer et par terre qui ont été publiées jusqu'à présent dans les différentes langues de toutes les nations connues.* 20 vols. Paris: Didot, 1746–89.

Purchas, Samuel. "A discourse of the diversity of letters used by the divers nations in the world; the antiquity, manifold use and variety thereof, with exemplary descriptions of above threescore several alphabets, with other strange writings." In Purchas, *Hakluytus Posthumus*, 1: 485–505.

——. *Hakluytus Posthumus, or Purchas His Pilgrimes: Contayning a history of the world in sea voyages and lande travells by Englishmen and others*. 1625. 20 vols. Glasgow: J. MacLehose & Sons, 1905–7.

——, comp. "The History of the Mexican Nation Described in Pictures [Codex Mendoza]." In Purchas, *Hakluytus Posthumus*, 15: 412–504.

Quiñonez Keber, Eloise. *Codex Telleriano-Remensis: Ritual, Divination, and History in a Pictorial Aztec Manuscript*. Austin: University of Texas Press, 1995.

Quiñonez Keber, Eloise, ed., with the assistance of Susan Schroeder and Frederic Hicks. *Chipping Away on Earth: Studies in Prehispanic and Colonial Mexico in Honor of Arthur J. O. Anderson and Charles E. Dibble*. Lancaster, Calif.: Labyrinthos, 1994.

Ramírez, Santiago. *Datos para la historia del Colegio de Minería*. Mexico City: Imprenta del Gobierno Federal, 1890.

Ramusio, Giovanni Battista. *Delle navigationi et viaggi . . .* 3 vols. Venice: Heredi di L. Givnti, 1550–65.

Raynal, Guillaume-Thomas. *Histoire philosophique et politique, des établissemens et du commerce des Européens dans les deux Indes*. 6 vols. Amsterdam: n.p., 1770.

——. *Histoire philosophique et politique, des établissemens et du commerce des Européens dans les deux Indes*. 7 vols. Maastricht: Jean-Edme Dufour, 1774.

——. *Histoire philosophique et politique, des établissemens et du commerce des Européens dans les deux Indes*. 10 vols. Geneva: Jean Leonard Pellet, 1781.

Restall, Mathew. *Maya Conquistador*. Boston: Beacon Press, 1998.

Reyes-Valerio, Constantino. *Arte indocristiano*. Mexico City: Secretaría de Educación Pública, 1978.

Ricard, Robert. *The Spiritual Conquest of Mexico*. Translated by Lesley Byrd Simpson. Berkeley and Los Angeles: University of California Press, 1966. Originally published as La *"conquête spirituelle" du Mexique: Essai sur l'apostolat et les méthodes missionaires des ordres mendiants en Nouvelle-Espagne de 1523–24 à 1572* (Paris: Institut d'ethnologie, 1933).

Río, Antonio del. *Description of the ruins of an ancient city, discovered near Palenque, in the kingdom of Guatemala . . . translated from the original manuscript report of Captain Don Antonio del Río. Teatro critico Americano; or, a critical investigation and research into the history of the Americas by Doctor Paul Felix Cabrera*. London: H. Berthoud, and Suttaby, Evance and Fox, 1822.

Rivosecchi, Valerio. *Esotismo in Roma Barocca: Studi sul Padre Kircher*. Rome: Bulzoni Editore, 1982.

Robertson, Donald. *Mexican Manuscript Painting of the Early Colonial Period: The Metropolitan School*. New Haven, Conn.: Yale University Press, 1956.

——. "The Sixteenth-Century Mexican Encyclopedia of Fray Bernardino de Sahagún." *Journal of World History* 9 (1966): 617–27.

Robertson, William. *The History of America*. 2 vols. London: W. Strahan, 1777.

———. *The Works of William Robertson.* Edited by Alex Stewart. 12 vols. Edinburgh: P. Hill, 1818.

Roger, Jacques. *Buffon: Un philosophe au Jardin du Roi.* Paris: Fayard, 1989.

Román y Zamora, Jerónimo. *Repúblicas de Indias: Idolatrías y gobierno en México y Perú antes de la conquista.* 1575. 2 vols. Madrid: Victoriano Suárez, 1897.

Ronan, Charles E. *Francisco Javier Clavigero, S.J. (1731–1787): Figure of the Mexican Enlightenment: His Life and Works.* Rome: Institutum Historicum S.I.; Chicago: Loyola University Press, 1977.

Rossi, Paolo. *The Dark Abyss of Time: The History of the Earth and the History of Nations from Hooke to Vico.* Translated by Lydia G. Cochrane. Chicago: University of Chicago Press, 1984.

Roubaud, Pierre-Joseph-André, abbé. *Histoire générale de l'Asie, de l'Afrique et de l'Amérique.* 15 vols. in 8. Paris: Desventes de la Doué, 1770–75.

Rousseau, Jean-Jacques. *Discourse on the Origins and Foundations of Inequality Among Men.* 1755. In *The Collected Writings of Rousseau,* edited by Roger D. Masters and Christopher Kelly, vol. 3. Hanover, N.H.: University Press of New England, 1992.

Rowe, J. H. "Probanza de los Incas." *Histórica* 9 (1985): 193–245.

———. "La constitución Inca del Cuzco." *Histórica* 9 (1985): 35–73.

Rubial García, Antonio. *Una monarquía criolla: La provincia agustina de México en el siglo XVII.* Mexico City: Universidad Nacional Autónoma de México, 1990.

Rycaut, Paul. "The translator to the reader." In Inca Garcilaso de la Vega, *The Royal Commentaries of Peru in Two Parts.* London: Jacob Tonson, 1688.

Said, Edward. *Orientalism.* New York: Random House, Vintage Books, 1979.

Sahagún, Bernardino de. *General History of the Things of New Spain: Florentine Codex.* Ca. 1579. Edited and translated by Charles Dibble and Arthur J. O. Anderson. 13 vols. in 12. Santa Fe, N.M.: School of American Research; Salt Lake City, Utah : University of Utah, 1950–82.

Sánchez, Miguel. "Imagen de la Virgen María Madre de Dios de Guadalupe [1648]." In *Testimonios históricos guadalupanos,* edited by Ernesto de la Torre Villar and Ramiro Navarro de Anda, pp. 152–281. Mexico City: Fondo de Cultura Económica, 1982.

Sánchez-Blanco Parody, Francisco. *Europa y el pensamiento español del siglo XVIII.* Madrid: Alianza, 1991.

Sangro, Raimondo di (Sansevero), *Lettera apologetica [della] difesa del libro lettere d'una Peruana per rispetto aall suppozionion de'quipu.* Naples: n.p., 1750.

———. *Supplica di San Severo alla santita di Benedetto XIV, in difesa e rischiaramento della sua Lettera apologetica sul proposito de' quipu de' peruani.* Naples: Salzano e Castaldo, 1753.

Sarmiento de Gamboa, Pedro. *Historia índica.* 1572. In *Obras completas de Garcilaso de la Vega,* vol. 4. Biblioteca de Autores Españoles, vol. 135. Madrid: Atlas, 1960.

Sarmiento, Martín. "Plano de un nuevo y facil método para recoger infinitos materiales y ciertas memorias que puedan servir de sólido fundamento; si en España se piensa en formar una general descripción geográfica completa de toda la peninsula y de toda la América, y qual no tiene asta ahora nación alguna propuesto." In *Escritos geográficos*. pp. 85–136. Santiago de Compostela: Xunta de Galicia, 1996.

Sarrailh, Jean-Louis. *L'Espagne éclairée de la seconde moitié du XVIIIᵉ siècle*. Paris: Impr. nationale, 1954.

——. "Voyageurs français au XVIIIᵉ siècle." *Bulletin hispanique* 36, no. 1 (1934): 29–78.

Saugnieux, Joël. *Les jansénistes et le renouveau de la prédication dans l'Espagne de la seconde moitié du XVIIIᵉ siècle*. Lyon: Presses universitaires de Lyon, 1976.

Schaffer, Simon. "Self Evidence." In *Questions of Evidence*, edited by James Chandler et al., pp. 56–91. Chicago: University of Chicago Press, 1994.

Schérer, Jean-Benoît. *Recherches historiques et géographiques sur le Nouveau-Monde*. Paris: Brunet, 1777.

Schreyer, Rüdiger. "'Pray what language did your wild couple speak, when first they met?' — Language as the Science of Man in the Scottish Enlightenment." In *The "Science of Man" in the Scottish Enlightenment: Hume, Reid and Their Contemporaries*, edited by Peter Jones, pp. 149–77. Edinburgh: Edinburgh University Press, 1989.

Schroeder, Susan. "Father José María Luis Mora, Liberalism, and the British and Foreign Bible Society in Nineteenth-Century Mexico." *The Americas* 50 (Jan. 1994): 377–97.

——. "Looking Back at the Conquest: Nahua Perceptions of Early Encounters from the Annals of Chimalpain." In *Chipping Away on Earth*, edited by Eloise Quiñonez Keber, pp. 81–94. Lancaster, Calif.: Labyrinthos, 1994.

Schwaller, John Frederick. "Don Bartolomé de Alva, Nahuatl Scholar of the Seventeenth Century." In *Chipping Away on Earth*, edited by Eloise Quiñonez Keber, pp. 95–103. Lancaster, Calif.: Labyrinthos, 1994.

Sepúlveda, Juan Ginés de. *Demócrates segundo, o, De las justas causas de la guerra contra los indios*. 1541. Edición crítica bilingüe, traducción castellana, introducción, notas e índices por Angel Losada. 2d ed. Madrid: Consejo Superior de Investigaciones Científicas, Instituto Francisco de Vitoria, 1984.

——. *Opera cum edita tum inedita*. 4 vols. Madrid: Typographia Regia Gazeta, 1780.

Serrera, Ramón María. "Manuel José de Ayala: Un colaborador decisivo en el proyecto historiográfico de Juan Bautista Muñoz." In *Documentación y archivos de la colonización española: La Rábida, 8–12 octubre de 1979*, 2: 253–63. Semana Internacional de Archivos, Universidad de la Rábida. Madrid: Ministerio de Cultura, Dirección General de Bellas Artes, Archivos y Bibliotecas, Subdirección General de Archivos, 1980.

Shaftesbury, Anthony Ashley Cooper, earl of. *Soliloquy: Or, Advice to an Author*. In id., *Characteristicks of Men, Manners, Opinions, Times*, vol. 1. London: J. Purser, 1737–38.

Shapin, Steven. *A Social History of Truth: Civility and Science in Seventeenth-Century England*. Chicago: University of Chicago Press, 1994.

Shapin, Steven, and Simon Schaffer. *Leviathan and the Air Pump: Hobbes, Boyle, and the Experimental Life*. Princeton, N.J.: Princeton University Press, 1985.

Sharp, L. W. "Charles Mackie, the First Professor of History at Edinburgh University." *Scottish Historical Review* 41 (1962): 23–45.

Sher, Richard B. *Church and University in the Scottish Enlightenment: The Moderate Literati of Edinburgh*. Princeton, N.J.: Princeton University Press, 1985.

Sierra Nava-Lasa, Luis. *El cardenal Lorenzana y la ilustración*. Madrid: Fundación Universitaria Española, 1975.

Sigüenza y Góngora, Carlos de. *Teatro de virtudes políticas que constituyen a un príncipe advertidas en los monarchas antiguos del mexicano imperio*. 1680. Facsimile ed. Mexico City: Miguel Angel Porrúa and Universidad Nacional Autónoma de México, 1986.

Simons, Bente Bittman. "Hieroglyphica Mexicana: A Manuscript in the Royal Library at Copenhagen." *Tlalocan* 4, no. 2 (1963): 169–72.

Singer, Thomas C. "Hieroglyphs, Real Characters, and the Idea of Natural Language in English Seventeenth-Century Thought." *Journal of the History of Ideas* 50, no. 1 (1989): 49–70.

Slaughter, Mary. *Universal Languages and Scientific Taxonomies*. Cambridge: Cambridge University Press, 1982.

Sloan, Phillip R. "The Idea of Racial Degeneracy in Buffon's *Histoire Naturelle*." *Studies in Eighteenth-Century Culture* 3 (1973): 243–321.

Smith, Adam. *The Wealth of Nations*. 1776. London: Penguin Books, 1986.

Smith, Anthony D. *Nationalism and Modernism: A Critical Survey of Recent Theories of Nations and Nationalism*. London: Routledge, 1998.

Smith, Bernard. *European Vision and the South Pacific*. 2d ed. New Haven, Conn.: Yale University Press, 1988.

Smitten, Jeffrey. "Impartiality in Robertson's History of America." *Eighteenth-Century Studies* 19 (1985): 56–77.

———. "The Shaping of Moderation: William Robertson and Arminianism." *Studies in Eighteenth-Century Culture* 22 (1992): 281–300.

Solano, Francisco de. "El Archivo de Indias y la promoción del americanismo científico." In *Carlos III y la ciencia de la Ilustración*, edited by Manuel Selles, Jose Luis Peset, and Antonio Lafuente, pp. 277–96. Madrid: Alianza Universidad, 1988.

Solórzano y Pereira, Juan de. *Política indiana*. Biblioteca de Autores Españoles, 252–56. 5 vols. Madrid: Atlas, 1972. Originally published under the title *Disputationem de indiarum iure*, 2 vols. (Madrid: Francisco Martínez, 1629–39); later enlarged, translated, and published as *Política indiana* (Madrid: Diego Díaz de la Carrera, 1648).

Sommer, Doris. *Foundational Fictions: The National Romances of Latin America*. Berkeley and Los Angeles: University of California Press, 1991.

Spence, Jonathan D. *The Memory Palace of Matteo Ricci*. New York: Viking Penguin, 1984. Reprint. Penguin Books, 1985.

———. "The Paris Years of Arcadio Huang." *Granta* 32 (1990): 122–32.

Steneck, Nicholas H. "Albert on the Psychology of Sense Perception." In *Albertus Magnus and the Sciences*, edited by James A. Weisheipl, O.P., pp. 263–90. Toronto: Pontifical Institute of Medieval Sciences, 1980.

———. *Science and Creation in the Middle Ages*. Notre Dame, Ind.: University of Notre Dame Press, 1976.

Stephens, John Lloyd. *Incidents of Travel in Central America, Chiapas and Yucatan*. 2 vols. London: J. Murray, 1841.

Stiffoni, Giovanni. *Verità della storia e ragioni del potere nella Spagna del primo '700*. Milan: Franco Angeli, 1989.

Stillingfleet, Edward. *Origines sacrae, or, A Rational Account of the Grounds of Christian Faith as to the Truth and Divine Authority of the Scriptures and the Matters Therein Contained*. 1662. 3d ed. London: Henry Mortlock, 1666.

Stoler, Ann Laura. *Race and the Education of Desire: Foucault's History of Sexuality and the Colonial Order of Things*. Durham, N.C.: Duke University Press, 1995.

Tanck de Estrada, Dorothy. "Justas florales de los botánicos ilustrados." *Díalogos* 18, no. 4 (1982): 19–31.

Taylor, René. *El arte de la memoria en el Nuevo Mundo*. Madrid: Swan, 1987.

Taylor, William B. "'. . . de corazón pequeño y ánimo apocado': Conceptos de los curas párrocos sobre los indios en la Nueva España del siglo XVII." *Relaciones*, no. 39 (1989): 5–67.

——. *Magistrates of the Sacred: Priests and Parishioners in Eighteenth-Century Mexico*. Stanford: Stanford University Press, 1998.

Tenorio-Trillo, Mauricio. *Mexico at the World's Fairs: Crafting a Modern Nation*. Berkeley and Los Angeles: University of California Press, 1996.

Thévenot, Melchisédec. *Relations de divers voyages curieux ou qui ont* [sic] *esté traduites d'Hacheyt, de Purchas et d'autres voyageurs. . . .* Paris, 1672.

——. *Relations de divers voyages curieux, qui n'ont point esté* [sic] *publiées et qu'on a traduit ou tiré des originaux des voyageurs françois, espagnols, allemands, portugais, anglois, hollandois, persans, arabes et autres orientaux. . . .* 2 vols. Paris: T. Moette, 1696.

Thompson, I. A. A. "Castile, Spain and the Monarchy: The Political Community from *patria natural* to *patria nacional*." In *Spain, Europe and the Atlantic World*, edited by Richard L. Kagan and Geoffrey Parker. Cambridge: Cambridge University Press, 1995.

Thurner, Mark. *From Two Republics to One Divided: Contradictions of Postcolonial Nationmaking in Andean Peru*. Durham, N.C.: Duke University Press, 1997.

Tietz, Manfred. "L'Espagne et *l'Histoire des deux Indes* de l'abbe Raynal." In *Lectures de Raynal: L'Histoire des deux Indes en Europe et en Amérique au XVIIIe siècle*, edited by Hans-Jurgen Lüsebrink and Manfred Tietz. Oxford: Voltaire Foundation, 1991.

Tonalamatl Aubin. *The Tonalamatl of the Aubin Collection: An Old Mexican Picture Manuscript in the Paris National Library (Manuscripts Mexicains No. 18–19)*. Edited by Eduard Seler. London: Hazell, Watson & Viney, 1900–1901.

Torquemada, Juan de. *De los veinte libros rituales y monarchia indiana con el origen y guerra de los Indios Occidentales. De sus poblaciones, descubrimiento, conquista, conversión y otras cosas maravillosas de la mesma tierra distribuidas en tres volúmenes*. Seville: Mathias Clavijo, 1615.

——. *Primera [segunda, tercera] parte de los veinte i un libros rituales i monarchíia indiana, con el origen y guerras, delos Indios Occidentales, de sus poblaciones descubrimiento, conquista, conversión, y otras cosas maravillosas de lamesma tierra*. Edited by Andrés González de Barcia. 3 vols. Madrid: N. Rodríguez Franco, 1723.

——. *Monarquía indiana*. 4th ed. Biblioteca Porrúa, 41–43. 3 vols. Mexico City: Porrúa, 1969.

Torre Revello, José. "Documentos relativos a D. Lorenzo Boturini." *Boletín del Archivo General de la Nación (México)* 7 (1936), 5–45, 224–55, 362–401, 565–95.

Torre Villar, Ernesto de la. "Defensa y elogio de la cultura mexicana." In *Juan José de Eguiara y Eguren y la cultura mexicana*, ed. id., pp. 133–49.

———, ed. *Juan José de Eguiara y Eguren y la cultura mexicana.* Mexico City: Universidad Nacional Autónoma de México, 1993.

Torre Villar, Ernesto de la, and Ramiro Navarro de Anda, eds. *Testimonios históricos guadalupanos.* Mexico City: Fondo de Cultura Económica, 1982.

Toulmin, Stephen. *Cosmopolis: The Hidden Agenda of Modernity.* Chicago: University of Chicago Press, 1990.

Tuck, Richard. *Hobbes.* Oxford: Oxford University Press, 1989.

Ulloa, Antonio de, and Jorge Juan y Santacilia. *Relación histórica del viaje a la América meridional hecho de orden de S. Mag. Para medir algunos grados de meridiano terrestre, y venir por ellos en conocimiento de la verdadera figura, y magnitud de la tierra, con otras varias observaciones astronómicas, y phísicas.* 5 vols. Madrid: A. Marin, 1748.

———. *Voyage to South America: Describing at large the Spanish cities, towns, provinces, etc. on that extensive continent. Interspersed throughout with reflections on the genius, customs, manners, and trade of the inhabitants; together with the natural history of the country and an account of their gold and silver mines.* 2 vols. London: L. Davis & C. Reymers, 1758.

Urton, Gary. *History of a Myth: Pacariqtambo and the Origin of the Inkas.* Austin: University of Texas Press, 1990.

Valadés, Diego. *Retórica cristiana.* Facsimile of the 1579 Latin text with Spanish translation. Edited by Esteban J. Palomera, Alfonso Castro Pallares, and Tarsicio Herrera Zapién. Translated by Tarsicio Herrera Zapién [et al.]. Mexico City: Universidad Nacional Autónoma de México, Fondo de Cultura Económica, 1989.

Vargas Alquicira, Silvia. *La singularidad novohispana en los jesuitas del siglo XVIII.* Mexico City: Universidad Nacional Autónoma de México, 1989.

Vargas Ugarte, Rubén. *Don Benito María de Moxó y de Francolí: Arzobispo de Charcas.* Buenos Aires: Imprenta de la Universidad, 1931.

Vega, Mariano Antonio de la. *La más verdadera copia del divino Hércules del cielo y sagrado Marte de la Iglesia, el glorioso archangel señor San Miguel a las sagradas plantas de María nuestra señora en su milagrosa aparecida imagen de Guadalupe para protección, y amparo de este nuevo mexicano mundo.* Mexico City: Imprenta del Nuevo Rezado, 1753.

Velasco, Juan de. *Historia del reino de Quito en la América meridional.* 1788–89. 3 vols. Quito: Casa de la Cultura Ecuatoriana, 1977.

Venturi, Franco. *Settecento riformatore.* Turin: G. Einaudi, 1969–98.

———. "Un Vichiano tra Messico e Spagna: Lorenzo Boturini Benaduci." *Revista storica italiana* 87 (1975): 770–84.

Vico, Giambattista. *Opere.* Edited by Fausto Nicolini. Milan: Riccardo Ricciardi, 1953.

Vienna Codex. *Codex Vindobonensis Mexicanus 1, Österreichische Nationalbibliothek Wien.* 2 vols. Graz, Austria: Akademische Druck- u. Verlagsanstalt, 1963.

———. *Codex Vindobonensis Mexicanus 1: Vollständige Faksimile-Ausgabe im Originalformat.* Codices selecti phototypice impressi, 5. Edited by Otto Adelhofer. Graz, Austria: Akademische Druck- u. Verlagsanstalt, 1974.

Villegas, Antonio Claudio de. *La piedra de la águila de México, el príncipe de los apóstoles y padre de la universal iglesia, Sr. San Pedro.* Mexico City: Imprenta del Nuevo Rezado, 1750.

Voltaire [François-Marie Arouet de]. *Essai sur les moeurs et l'esprit des nations.* 1757. Edited by René Pomeau. 2 vols. Paris: Editions Garnier Frères, 1963.

———. "Lettres Chinoises, Indiennes, et Tartares à M. Pauw." In *Oeuvres Complètes,* 8: 452–98. Paris: Gernier Frères, 1879.

———. *Oeuvres historiques.* Edited by René Pomeau. Paris: Gallimard, 1957.

Walker, Charles F. *Smoldering Ashes: Cuzco and the Creation of Republican Peru, 1780–1840.* Durham, N.C.: Duke University Press, 1999.

———. "The Patriotic Society: Discussions and Omissions About Indians in the Peruvian War of Independence." *The Americas* 55 (Oct. 1998): 275–98.

Warburton, William, bishop of Gloucester. *The Divine Legation of Moses Demonstrated: On the principles of a religious deist, from the omission of the doctrine of a future state of reward and punishment in the Jewish dispensation: in six books.* 2d ed., cor. and enl. 2 vols. in 3. London: Fletcher Gyles, 1738–42.

———. *Essai sur les hiéroglyphes des Egyptiens où l'on voit l'origine et les progrès du langage et de l'écriture, l'antiquité des sciences en Egypte, et l'origine du culte des animaux — avec des observations sur l'antiquité des hiéroglyphes scientifiques et des remarques sur la chronologie et sur la première écriture des Chinois.* 2 vols. Paris: J. L. Guerin 1744.

———. *The Works of the Right Reverend William Warburton.* 7 vols. London: John Nichols, 1788.

Widdifield, Stacie G. *The Embodiment of the National in Late Nineteenth-Century Mexican Painting.* Tucson: University of Arizona Press, 1996.

Wilkins, John. *An essay towards a real character, and a philosophical language: An alphabetical dictionary, wherein all English words according to their various significations, are either referred to their places in the philosophical tables, or explained by such words as are in those tables.* London: S. Gellibrand, 1668. Facsimile reprint, Menston, Yorkshire: Scholar Press, 1968.

Whitaker, Arthur P. "The Dual Role of Latin America in the Enlightenment." In *Latin America and the Enlightenment,* ed. id., pp. 3–21.

———, ed. *Latin America and the Enlightenment.* 1942. 2d ed. Ithaca, N.Y.: Great Seal Books, Cornell University Press, 1961.

Wood, P. B. "The Natural History of Man in the Scottish Enlightenment." *History of Science* 27 (1989): 89–123.

Wood, Stephanie G. "Pedro Villafranca and Juana Gertrudis Navarrate: Title Forger and His Widow (Eighteenth-Century New Spain)." In *Struggle and Survival in Colonial America,* edited by David G. Sweet and Gary B. Nash. Berkeley and Los Angeles: University of California Press, 1981.

Worm, Ole. *Museum Wormianum; seu, Historia rerum rariorum, tam naturalium, quam artificialium, tam domesticarum, quam exoticarum, quae Hafniae Danorum in aedibus authoribus servantur.* . . . Amsterdam: Ludovicum & Danielem Elzevirios, 1655.

Ximénez de Bonilla, Joachim Ignacio, Joseph Francisco de Ozaeta y Oro, and Joseph Francisco de Aguirre y Espinosa. *El segundo quinze de enero de la corte mexicana. Solemnes fiestas, que a la canonizacion del mystico doctor san Juan de la Cruz celebró la Provincia de san Alberto de carmelitas descalzos esta Nueva España.* Mexico City: Joseph Bernardo de Hogal, 1730.

Yates, Francis. *The Art of Memory.* Chicago: University of Chicago Press, 1966.

Young, Robert. *White Mythologies: Writing History and the West.* New York: Routledge, 1990.

Zamora, Margarita. *Language, Authority, and Indigenous History in the Comentarios Reales de los Incas.* Cambridge: Cambridge University Press, 1988.

Zárate, Agustín de. *Historia del descubrimiento y conquista del Perú, con las cosas naturales que señaladamente allí se hallan y los sucessos que ha avido.* Anvers: Martín Nucio, 1555.

Zuidema, R. T. "Bureaucracy and Systematic Knowledge in Andean Civilizations." In *The Inca and Aztec States, 1400–1800,* edited by G. Collier, R. Rosaldo, and J. Wirth, pp. 419–58. New York: Academic Press, 1982.

———. "Myth and History in Ancient Peru." In *The Logic of Culture,* edited by Ino Rossi, pp. 150–75. South Hadley, Mass: Bergin & Garvey, 1982.

Index

In this index an "f" after a number indicates a separate reference on the next page, and an "ff" indicates separate references on the next two pages. A continuous discussion over two or more pages is indicated by a span of page numbers, e.g., "57–59." *Passim* is used for a cluster of references in close but not consecutive sequence.

Index

Index

Index

Index

Index

Index